ANDRÉ I

Python

DEVELOPER'S HANDBOOK

SAMS 201 West 103rd Street, Indianapolis, Indiana 46290

Python Developer's Handbook

International Standard Book Number: 0-672-31994-2

Library of Congress Catalog Card Number: 00-105615

Printed in the United States of America

First Printing: November 2000

02 01 00   4 3 2 1

Trademarks

Warning and Disclaimer

Acquisitions Editor
Shelley Johnston

Development Editor
Scott D. Meyers

Managing Editor
Charlotte Clapp

Project Editor
Dawn Pearson

Copy Editor
Rhonda Tinch-Mize

Indexer
Cheryl Landes

Proofreaders
Katherin Bidwell
Bob LaRoche

Technical Editor
James Henstridge

Team Coordinator
Amy Patton

Media Developer
Dan Scherf

Interior Designer
Gary Adair

Cover Designer
Alan Clements

Contents at a Glance

Table of Contents

About the Author

My name is **André dos Santos Lessa**. I decided to follow an IT career when I was just 11 years old; that happened the day I first saw a real computer—well, actually it was just a TK85. On my next birthday after that fateful day, I got a TK90X. Then came the MSX, 386, 486, and so forth. This long-time background has opened many doors (and Windows!) to me. I got both my graduate and my post-graduate degrees in the computer field.

At this time, I am an IT consultant with little more than eight years of professional IT experience, ranging from database administration to Web design. Currently, I work for Emplifi Inc., where I use my best technical skills to support projects at Deloitte Consulting.

As I really like undertaking new technologies, mostly anything Web related, I've created and designed some interesting sites for the Web. www.lessaworld.com, www.bebemania.com.br, and www.alugueaqui.com.br are my little toys.

The most recent endeavour that I became part of is called iTraceYou.com, which is an international and well-grounded project that brings a new security philosophy to good old services that we are used to. It is scheduled to be released by October, 2000.

I was born in Rio de Janeiro, Brazil, but I moved to the United States in 1998 in a quest for new challenges for my career. When I am not working (just a few seconds per day), I try to spend some time with my wife Renata. Currently, we live in the city of Pittsburgh, and she is pregnant with our first child, who is called João Pedro.

If necessary, you can contact me by sending a note to my main email account, which is webmaster@lessaworld.com.

Dedication

I dedicate this book to my son, a little boy named João Pedro. Even though
we haven't met yet, he already has acquired a special place in my heart.
We love you JP!

Acknowledgments

I would like to render my acknowledgments to the ones who most shared my life during the last few months while I wrote this book, giving me support and inspiration to conclude this beautiful work.

God

My parents, Neuza & Josué   My wife, Renata

Thank you all!

In addition, I would like to express gratitude to my entire family and friends for being so friendly, and for supporting my wife and I in our decision to move to the United States.

... and of course, for sending Brazilian goodies and baby gifts to us by mail!

Beth, Bruno, Carol, Cleber, Dinda Teca, Djalminha, Gabriel Jorge, Gustavo, Jorge, Juliana, Lucas, Matheus, Ney, Patricia Beatriz, Penha, Rafael, and Victor. And if I forgot about you, consider yourself included in this list!

Thanks folks! (*Valeu galera!*)

Also, I would like to thank everyone at Macmillan for the patience and comprehension that they had every time I was late in my milestones.

A special *thank you* goes to my Technical Editor James Henstridge for providing outstanding suggestions and remarks about the contents of this book.

Rhonda, you were great correcting my English mistakes and reviewing my writings!

Thanks Katie, thanks Mandie. I do know I gave you a lot of work, didn't I?

Dawn, Amy, Scott, even though we didn't have much contact, I know that you were all there every time this book needed you. God bless you all!

And last, but not least, Shelley, thanks for discovering me! I still remember that day, March 14, when I got your email asking me if I had ever considered authoring. Well, this book says everything. Thank you very much for this opportunity.

Tell Us What You Think!

As the reader of this book, *you* are our most important critic and commentator. We value your opinion and want to know what we're doing right, what we could do better, what areas you'd like to see us publish in, and any other words of wisdom you're willing to pass our way.

You can email or write me directly to let me know what you did or didn't like about this book—as well as what we can do to make our books stronger.

Please note that I cannot help you with technical problems related to the topic of this book, and that due to the high volume of mail I receive, I might not be able to reply to every message.

When you write, please be sure to include this book's title and author as well as your name and phone or fax number. I will carefully review your comments and share them with the author and editors who worked on the book.

Email: `webdev_sams@mcp.com`
Mail: Mark Taber
           Associate Publisher
           Sams Publishing
           201 West 103rd Street
           Indianapolis, IN 46290 USA

INTRODUCTION

When I was a little kid, I had this dream where a snake would rule and dominate the entire world (actually, I guess that a penguin was also part of the dream...but never mind). I didn't pay much attention to the fact at that time because I thought the dream was caused by an overexposure to all those Japanese series that were popping up on the screens. Later, in my teenage years, there was this science project where I had to spend some time studying snakes to display at an exhibition. After analyzing Red Tail boas and coral snakes, I found this 3-year old giant of 10 feet, 40+ pounds. Instantly, I recognized that snake as being the same one that I had seen in my dream years before. Its name was Python, but at that time, I still couldn't figure out what was the relationship between that reptile and the world domination.

Fifteen years ago, I was trying to select a channel in my old TV set, when a special program caught my attention—A huge animated foot was dancing in the opening titles. After the program started, there were a group of funny guys who were playing jokes about parrots and lumberjacks. After watching tons of episodes and all their five films, I decided to write a book about them. I noticed that they were called Python too. Maybe that was the answer. That troupe would dominate the entire world. I wanted to let everyone know about it. Initially I had planned to write about the actors and their most famous sketches, but I had to abandon the idea when I realized that my editors wouldn't give me enough time to write a book of approximately 25,030 pages. That would be a nice bestseller, though.

Even though none of the previous facts has really happened, both have at least one thing in common—the name Python. Python is also a scripting language whose name's origin has much to do with the English troupe than with the legless reptile. This book will guide you step-by-step through the universe of Python, a fantastic programming language that can help you to implement solutions for almost all types of IT challenges that you might face. Almost all IT-related tasks, such as the manipulation of database systems, or the design of Web-driven applications can be managed using Python. Maybe that's the answer for my dream.

For the last couple of months, I've been trying to organize all the information about Python that I have available, arranging them in this book. I can't say that I have included every little thing in the book, but I do know that I have covered the most important aspects of the Python language. Note that along the 5-month development period of this book, Python had several version upgrades, which made things way more difficult to organize. So, I apologize if something important is missing.

This book is organized into 18 chapters and some additional appendixes, where each one covers a specific aspect of the language. Inside each chapter, you will find many hints about how to use Python to meet your needs. As you might agree with me, it is impossible to cover every single aspect of the language in such a complete and up-to-date way. That's why I choose to provide Web links to other sources of material that I think will be useful for your learning.

What this book covers?

A short answers is

The book starts with a very extensive review of the language and the modules that come as part of the Python distribution. It goes through Object-Oriented Programming, Networking, Web Development, Graphical Interfaces, and other important topics. The last chapter covers JPython, a version of Python that runs in Java systems.

A long answer is

Chapter 1 explains what Python is, why Python must be used, where to get support and how to go through each installation process.

Chapter 2 is a complete review of the Python programming language. By the end of this chapter, you will learn how to create Python applications.

Chapter 3 shows which main modules extensions are currently available and for what purposes they can be used. The focus here is to expand your knowledge about the Python libraries, showing the resources that you already have available in the Python programming language.

Chapter 4 demonstrates how to handle exception situations and how to avoid error messages.

Chapter 5 introduces the OO methodology in a very complete and direct way. You will be able to easily create and use objects and classes in your programs after reading this chapter.

Chapter 6 discusses extending and embedding Python. You will learn how to extend Python methods using other languages and how to call Python methods from within other applications.

Chapter 7 explains objects interfacing and distribution. The information provided in this chapter explains objects distribution and how to use them from within other systems.

Chapter 8 shows all the database options available within Python. For those that don't know anything about database yet, it explains how databases work and how to execute basic SQL statements.

Chapter 9 provides very useful information concerning the use and manipulation of some advanced topics, including images, sounds, threads, and scientific Python Modules.

Chapter 10 explains basic network concepts and invites you to play with these concepts using Python programs.

Chapter 11 provides information concerning how to use Python for Internet development. It also introduces you to some well-known Python third-party Web applications.

Chapter 12 provides information concerning how to use Python for scripting programming.

Chapter 13 provides information concerning how to use Python for data parsing and manipulation, such as XML parsing and mail processing.

Chapter 14 shows what the available GUI options for graphic designing in Python are.

Chapter 15 provides Tkinter information. For those that don't know yet, Tkinter is the standard Python GUI.

Chapter 16 shows some performance suggestions, and guides you through the process of writing clean code within style.

Chapter 17 introduces a handful programming tools. You will learn how to go through all the development stages without fear, including how to debug, compile, and distribute Python applications.

Chapter 18 demonstrates how easy it is to mix Java and Python using JPython.

Now that you know that you have a lot of interesting material to learn, I suggest you accept my hint:

The best way to read this book is by sitting on a comfortable beach chair, or laying on your bed, and relaxing. If for some reason, if you think the topic is getting boring, just turn the page and go to another chapter until you find something that you like. Later, you can return to where you originally left. This book can be read from the start, or you can go directly to the chapter that teaches a specific functionality. It's your choice!

So, what are you waiting for? Turn this page at once, and get ready to start dominating the world.

PART I
Basic Programming

CHAPTER

CHAPTER 1

Introduction

Nobody expects the Spanish Inquisition

This chapter explains to you why Python is considered to be a good language, why it should be used, what its main features are, where you can find support, and how to go through each installation process.

Introduction to Python

Python is an open source language that is getting a lot of attention from the market. It combines ease of use with the capability to run on multiple platforms because it is implemented focusing on every major operating system. Guido van Rossum created the language nearly 11 years ago and since then, Python has changed through the years, turning itself into one of the most powerful programming languages currently available.

Python is a good prototype language. In just a few minutes, you can develop prototypes that would take you several hours in other languages. It also embodies all object-oriented concepts as part of its core engine. Therefore, creating programming object-oriented applications in Python is much easier than it would be in other languages such as Java or C++.

As I just said, Python is an open source project. Consequently, it is truly free. No copylefts or copyrights are involved in its license agreement. You can change it, modify it, give it away, sell it, and even freely distribute it for commercial use. Its copyright only protects the author from legal problems that might occur if someone decides to sue the author for errors caused by using Python, or if someone else tries to claim ownership of the language.

Maybe you still don't know Python, but many companies are out there using it. The problem is these companies don't want to go public talking about it because they think that using Python without getting the attention of their competitors is a good strategy. Okay, I know that you are curious to know who in the world is using Python. Organizations like Industrial Light and Magic, Yahoo!, Red Hat, and NASA are some of companies that run Python applications.

> **Note**
> You can always check out the latest news about Python by visiting
> http://www.python.org/News.html.

Nowadays, many developers are contributing to Python's support. That means that, currently, a lot of people are testing and designing modules for the language. If you spend some time visiting Python's official Web site, you can get a list of several development groups that are working hard to give Python some support to new technologies, such as XML and image processing.

Both Perl and Java already have a large group of programmers who are very devoted to their programming languages, and, today, Python is starting to get there.

Notice that Python is a language extremely easy to code if you have ever programmed before. Guido claims to have fun every time he has to do something using Python. Learning Python through this book will be exciting too. Soon, you will have some practice and understand the reason I say that.

In this chapter, I give you a quick overview of Python's main features. The other chapters of this book cover in detail the topics that I mention next.

Python!? What Is It?

Let's define Python:

Python is an interpreted, high-level programming language, pure object-oriented, and powerful server-side scripting language for the Web. Like all scripting languages, Python code resembles pseudo code. Its syntax's rules and elegant design make it readable even among multiprogrammer development teams. The language doesn't provide a rich syntax, which is really helpful. The idea behind that is to keep you thinking about the business rules of your application and not to spend time trying to figure out what command you should use.

Quoting Guido van Rossum—"Rich syntax is more of a burden than a help."

It is also true (and later you will have a chance to check it out) that Python is interactive, portable, easy to learn, easy to use, and a serious language. Furthermore, it provides dynamic semantics and rapid prototyping capabilities.

Python is largely known as a glue language that connects existing components. It is embeddable in applications from other languages (C/C++, Java, and so on), and it is also possible to add new modules to Python, extending its core vocabulary.

Python is a very stable language because it has been in the market for the last 10 years and also because its interpreter and all standard libraries have their source code available along with the binaries. Distributing the sources for everyone is a good development strategy because it makes developers from all around the world work together. Anyone can submit suggestions and patches to the official development team, led by Python's creator—Guido van Rossum.

Guido is the coauthor of the second implementation of the scripting language ABC—a language that was used, mostly, for teaching purposes in the '80s by a small number of people. Python is directly derived from ABC.

Python was born in an educational environment, in the Christmas of 1989 at CWI in Amsterdam, Netherlands. Guido was a researcher at CWI at that time. Initially, it was just a project to keep him busy during the holidays. Later, it became part of the Amoeba Project at CWI. Its first public release was in February of 1991.

For a long time, Python's development occurred at CNRI in Reston, VA in the United States. In June of 2000, the Python development team moved to PythonLabs, a member organization of the BeOpen Network, which is maintained by the lead developers of the Python language, including Guido.

On October 27, 2000 the entire PythonLabs Team has left BeOpen.com because of some mutual disagreements concerning the future of Python. The Team is now working for Digital Creations (the makers of Zope - http://www.digicool.com/), and Guido has just announced the idea of creating a non-profit organization called Python Software Foundation (PSF)in order to take ownership of future Python developments.

By the way, Python was named after the British comedy troupe Monty Python. It had a comedy series called *Monty Python's Flying Circus* on the BBC in the '70s. Guido is a huge fan.

As many Monty Python quotes are throughout the chapters of this book as in any other Python book. That is something of a standard behavior among Python authors, and I won't be the one who will try to change it.

> **Note**
> "Nobody expects the Spanish Inquisition" is one of the most famous quotes that is always recited by Guido. Each chapter of this book is headed by a famous Monty Python quote.

Why Use Python?

Let's take a look at an interesting scenario:

Imagine that you don't have a team of programmers who are professionally trained. In addition to that, you are in a position to choose a programming language that would be the best solution for projects that require GUI implementations and the use of complex routines along with OOP technology. Unfortunately, and by chance, you don't have much money to spend in a big investment, well... If I were you, I would pick up Python as my choice.

But if you are simply a programmer who, for this moment, only wants to know what the significant advantages are that Python has to offer you, maybe you are asking yourself why you need this language if you already know many others.

The answer is quite simple. Although the original plan is not to turn Python into an all-purpose language, you can easily do almost anything if you know how. The next couple of paragraphs list and explain why Python is a cool programming language and what things make Python more flexible than other languages.

Readability

Python's syntax is clear and readable. The way Python's syntax is organized imposes some order to programmers. Experts and beginners can easily understand the code and everyone can become productive in Python very quickly. It is also important to mention that Python has fewer "dialects" than other languages, such as Perl. And because the block structures in Python are defined by indentations, you are much less likely to have bugs in your code caused by incorrect indentation.

It Is Simple to Get Support

The Python community always provides support to Python users. As we already know, Python code is freely available for everyone. Therefore, thousands of developers worldwide are working hard to find bugs and create patches to fix those bugs. Furthermore, many people are creating new enhancements to the language and sending them for approval.

Fast to Learn

The language is very easy to learn because its source code resembles pseudo code. It doesn't ask for long and strange lines of code. Therefore, less training is a direct result. Companies don't need to spend much time to have their programmers coding in Python. Once you start learning Python, you can do useful coding almost immediately. And after some practice, your productivity will suddenly increase.

You can design a high-level, object-oriented programming code in a friendly and interpreted Python environment. This feature works great for small tasks.

Fast to Code

Python provides fast feedback in several ways. First, the programmer can skip many tasks that other languages require him to take. Therefore, it reduces both the cost of program maintenance and the development time. If necessary, Python enables a fast adaptation of the code. You can change the high-level layer of your application without changing the business rules that are coded within your modules.

The interactive interpreter that comes with the Python distribution brings rapid development strategies to your project. In spite of traditional programming languages that require several distinct phases (such as compiling, testing, and running) and other scripting languages that require you to edit the code outside the execution environment, Python is a ready-to-run language. Every time you use Python's interactive interpreter, you just need to execute the code you have. A direct benefit of this feature over Perl is the way you can interactively test and play around with your code.

Python provides a bottom-up development style in which you can build your applications by importing and testing critical functions in the interpreter before you write the top-level code that calls the functions.

The interpreter is easily extensible. It enables you to embed your favorite C code as a compiled extension module.

Reusability

Python encourages program reusability by implementing modules and packages. A large set of modules has already been developed and is provided as The Standard Python Library, which is part of the Python distribution.

You can easily share functionality between your programs by breaking the programs into modules, and reusing the modules as components of other programs.

Portability

Besides running on multiple systems, Python has the same interface on multiple platforms. Its design isn't attached to a specific operational system because it is written in portable ANSI C. This means that you can write a Python program on a Mac, test it using a Linux environment, and upload it to a Windows NT server. Everything mentioned here is possible because Python supports most of its features everywhere. However, you must know that some modules were developed to implement specific mechanisms of some operational systems and, of course, programs that use those modules don't work in all environments.

But, wait a minute. This problem affects only some specific modules. Usually, you can make most of your applications run on multiple platforms without changing one line of code. How many other languages can claim this type of behavior?

Python is well integrated with both UNIX and Windows platforms. The Macintosh environment also supports Python applications, even though it doesn't provide a full set of solutions yet. But don't worry. Developers are currently working on that.

Object-Oriented Programming

Usually, scripting languages have object-orientation support included in the language as an add-on. However, everything in Python, as in Smalltalk, is designed to be object-oriented. You can start programming using non-OO structures, but it doesn't take too long for you to find out that it is much simpler if you use its OO features. Some of the implemented OO functionality in Python is inheritance and polymorphism.

Overall Conclusion

The overall conclusion is that Python is a fantastic language that provides all these features for free. I assure you that if you want all these features in any other language, you will have to buy costly third-part libraries. Every detail in Python's project is part of a huge plan to have the most used and necessary features of other languages in a unique environment.

If someone asks which are the cases that Python doesn't provide the best solution, I would have just one answer: applications that require huge amounts of low-level data processing. That is said because, as you already know, Python is an interpreted language; and for that reason, it is proven to be a little bit slower than compiled languages. However, even in cases such as this, Python makes it easy to replace bottlenecks with C implementations, which speeds things up without sacrificing Python's features.

If you have already decided that Python is exactly what you need, be sure to go through all the following chapters. It will be fun.

Main Technical Features

Now that you already know many reasons why you should use Python, let's focus on some of its main technical features.

Automatic Memory Management

Python objects are collected whenever they become unreachable. Python identifies the "garbage," taking the responsibility from you.

Exception Handling

The exception handling support helps you to catch errors without adding a lot of error checking statements to the code. By the way, it is said that Python programs never crash; they always return a `traceback` message.

Rich Core Library

Many extension modules were already developed and became part of *The Standard Python Library* of tools, which can be used by programmers in any Python application. Besides those generic modules, we have others that are specific for particular platforms or environments. *The Standard Python Library* makes the tasks that are simple in theory also simple in practice.

In a short time, programmers can make their Python programs speak to HTTP, FTP, SMTP, Telnet, POP, and many other services because Python modules perform all the common daily tasks. You can download a Web page, parse HTML files, show windows on the screen, and even use—as part of your programs—built-in interfaces that were created to handle many operational system services.

Web Scripting Support and Data Handling

Python enables you to write CGI programs that work fine in several environments. Have you ever imagined switching platforms without changing the code? All right, it's possible if Python is the choice. There is even more: You can parse XML, HTML, SGML, and every other kind of text by using Python built-in classes and regular expression methods.

Built-In Elements

Python provides a huge list of useful built-in elements (the language's basic data structure) along with many special operations that are required to correctly process them. This list is as follows:

- Data types—such as strings, tuples, lists, hash tables, and so on

- Operations—like searching routine statements (in and not in), sorting, and so on

Development Flow

Even though it doesn't have any compilation or linking process, Python supports byte compilation. The compiled code is saved in an intermediate language called bytecode that can be accessed by any system that has a Python virtual machine. This feature offers a kind of portability similar to the one that Java also offers. Applications can be used in several different systems without the need for compilation. Furthermore, you can create a standalone executable and securely distribute your applications.

Clear Syntax and a Diversity of Useful Lexical Elements

The way Python is organized seems to encourage object-oriented programming because everything is an object. In addition to that, it has various helpful lexical elements, such as the following:

- Operator overloading—The same operator has different meanings according to the elements that are being referenced.

- Dynamic typing—You don't need to assign types in your code. After you assign a value to an object, it instantly knows what type it should assume. You can even assign different types to the same variable within the same program.

- Name resolution—Each structure (module, class, and so on) defines its own scope of names.

- Indentation—There are no line-end markers as in Java and C++, where programmers need to use semicolons. Python defines indentations by using block structures.

Embeddable and Extendable

Python can be embedded in applications written in many other programming and scripting languages. Whenever you need to have a programmable interface for your applications, give Python a chance. Python is well known for easily gluing everything.

Python also enables you to add low-level modules to the interpreter. Those built-in modules are easily written in C and C++. Extension modules are easily created and maintained using Python. For tasks like this, you can develop components in C and run them through Python subclasses.

Objects Distribution

Python can be used to implement routines that need to talk to objects in other applications. For example, Python is a great tool to glue Windows COM components. Besides that, Python also has a few CORBA implementations that enable you to use cross-platform distributed objects, as well.

Databases

Python has interfaces to all major commercial databases, provides several facilities to handle flat-file databases, and implements object-persistence systems that can save entire objects to files. But the greatest database feature is that Python defines a standard database API, which makes it easy to port applications to different databases.

GUI Application

You can create applications that implement graphical user interfaces (GUIs), which are portable to many system calls, libraries, and windowing systems such as Windows MFC, Macintosh, Motif, and UNIX's X Window System. This is possible because many GUI bindings were developed for Python. The Python distribution is bundled with Tkinter, a standard object-oriented interface to the Tk GUI API that has become the official GUI development platform for Python.

Introspection

You can develop programs in Python to help in the creation of other programs in Python. The most important examples are the Debugger and the Profiler. And there is even more: Python has an Integrated Development Environment (IDLE) developed using Python for use with Python.

Third-Party Projects Integration

The Python Extension *NumPy (Numerical Extensions to Python)* along with the Python Library *PIL (Python Imaging Library)* prove that everyone who contributes to the language can make his projects almost a required complement to the standard Python distribution.

Python Distribution

At the time of this writing, the last official version of Python is version 2.0, released on October 16, 2000. Prior to that, we had version 1.6 final released on September 5, 2000, and version 1.5.2 released on April 13, 1999.

After release 2.0, Guido plans to work on two more 2.*x* releases that might be available by the end of 2000 or January 2001. After that, all his attention will be dedicated to a total Python redesign, a future project called Python 3000. Despite many rumors that have been spread in the Python community, Guido affirms that this mythical version is "not as incompatible as people fear."

This book was planned to be a Python 1.5.2 book. But it turned out to cover the migration from 1.5.2 to 2.0. That's why you will see much of the text focusing on release 1.5.2, and special notes about release 2.0.

The latest Python source codes for your UNIX, Windows, or Mac system are maintained under the CVS revision control system. *CVS (Concurrent Version System)* is a version control system that stores and manages the code that is in process of development. Remember! The source code available through CVS might be slightly different from the one released along with the last official release.

If you want to download the source code from CVS, go to `http://www.python.org/download/cvs.html` and check out the instructions that show how to get the appropriate CVS client for your system. The Python CVS tree is currently hosted by SourceForge at `http://sourceforge.net/projects/python/`.

It is normal to have more than one Python installation in your system. You can install the official version in one location and build the CVS source code in some other location.

Guido van Rossum, the creator of Python, maintains high-quality Python documentation at Python's official Web site. You can download Python's documents from `http://www.python.org/doc/`. There are versions in HTML, PostScript, and PDF. Part of this documentation is included in the distribution packages.

The 1.5.2 distribution comes with five tutorials that you should wisely go through:

- The Python Tutorial
- The Library Reference
- The Language Reference
- Extending and Embedding Python
- The Python/C API

The new release 2.0 also contains the following manuals:

- Distributing Python Modules
- Installing Python Modules
- Documenting Python

The first two manuals above cover how to setup the the Python Distribution Utilities ("Distutils") in order to create source and built distributions. The former uses the module developer's point-of-view, and the latter uses the end-user's point-of-view.

The last manual shows how to follow some standard guidelines for documenting Python.

Python's current documentation is also available for download at `http://www.python.org/doc/current/download.html`.

More information about Python 2.0 documentation and downloading can be found at `http://www.PythonLabs.com`.

System Requirements

Python runs on many platforms. Its portability enables it to run on several brands of UNIX, Macintosh, Windows, VMS, Amiga, OS/2, Be-OS, and many others. Most all platforms, which have a C compiler, support Python. You can try to compile Python yourself in any architecture you want because the source code is distributed along with the binaries.

You should also have a text editor because sometimes it is easier to use an application like `emacs`, `pico`, `notepad`, or other similar one, instead of using the interpreter or the graphical development environment. If you are using `emacs`, make sure that python-mode is installed because it makes it a lot easier to develop Python code. See Chapter 17, "Development Tools," for details.

After downloading the source code at `http://www.python.org/download/` `download_source.html`, you can carefully play around with it and if you want to go one step further, port it to another platform.

If you are using UNIX, it's going to be necessary to have `tar` and the GNU `gzip` programs in-hand in order to unpack the downloaded files.

If you are using Windows, you must have WinZip available for the task.

GNU `gzip` is available at `http://www.gnu.org/software/gzip/gzip.html` and WinZip is available at `http://www.winzip.com`.

Depending on the system that you are using, you might need to get a C compiler in case you have need to download the source code instead of the binary distribution.

Right now it is okay to use the binary distributions (whenever they are available), but when you become more confident with the language, you might want to build a Python version that uses your own extensions. So, you will need to have a C compiler.

Remember that you are free to use Python's source code any way you want. The full C source code is freely available for download.

Installing and Configuring Python

Setting up Python in your system is a very easy process because all versions are freely available and highly documented. Check the following instructions that show how to download the files from the binary repository. Each distribution includes reference manuals that demonstrate in detail how to install and configure Python for that specific environment. See Chapter 17 for details about how to build Python from source code.

Python's Web site—`http://www.python.org/download`—has a section that gives you access to all distributions that are available for download (see Figure 1.1).

Up-to-date versions for the most popular distributions are always available.

Keep this URL because we will go to the site later to download other Python items that we might need.

UNIX Environment

The UNIX distribution is, in my opinion, the best distribution. It comes with POSIX bindings, and it supports environment variables, files, sockets, and so on. It is perfect for all flavors of UNIX.

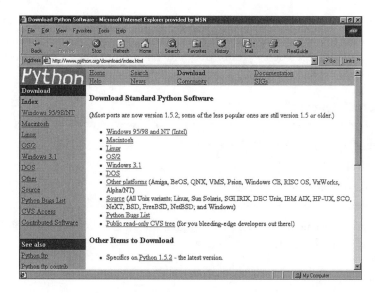

Figure 1.1
Python's download Web page is the place where you can get the latest Python releases.

Linux Installation

These days, all the major Linux distributions include Python, which makes your life simple because you don't have to download the files. Sometimes, Python is even automatically installed for you. Just make sure that you have the latest version.

If you already have Python installed in your machine, and you've got a new Python RPM package, you must execute the following command in order to update the RPM: (Note that this filename reflects the 1.5.2 version.)

```
rpm -Uhv python-1.5.2-2.i386.rpm
```

Otherwise, run the following command in your Linux prompt to install the RPM package.

```
rpm -ihv python-1.5.2-2.i386.rpm
```

When the installation process is over, check to see whether everything went fine by typing **python** at the prompt. You should get access to the Python interpreter, and when you are satisfied, press Ctrl+D to leave it.

Perfect! Now you are ready to start coding in Python.

In case you are using a Linux system that doesn't offer RPM support, you need to download the source code and compile it in your machine. Or, check whether your Linux distribution included Python. Instructions for compiling Python are provided in Chapter 17.

Other UNIX Systems

If you are running a UNIX system other than Linux, you need to download the source code and compile it in your own machine.

Download the file `py152.tgz` from `http://www.python.org/download/download_source.html`. Note that this file corresponds to version 1.5.2. You might need to change the filename for the latest version.

Following the instructions listed in the `README` file of the distribution will show you how to build and install the source code.

Macintosh Environment

MacPython is a Python version available for the Macintosh. Jack Jansen maintains it, and you can have full access to the entire documentation at his Web site. Currently, version 1.5.2 is available for download at `http://www.cwi.nl/~jack/macpython.html`. Beta versions from version 1.6 are also available.

You can also download this distribution at Python's official Web site at `http://www.python.org/download/download_mac.html`. The full distribution is available in one unique file that also contains Tkinter and an interactive development environment.

Windows Environment

The Win32 and COM extensions by Mark Hammond are the result of an excellent work that is successfully reducing the distance between the overall performance of Python for UNIX and Python for Windows platforms. The following instructions show how to install the Python version for Windows systems. Note that to install the Win32 extensions, you need to install a separate package called `Win32all-xxx.exe`. You should replace the *xxx* with the number of the latest available release.

The installation process is very straightforward within Win32 systems (Windows 95/98/2000 and NT). Go to the Python for Windows download page at `http://www.python.org/download/download_windows.html` and choose a location. If the location you selected isn't available at the moment, choose a mirror site.

Let's download the py152.exe file (Python's version 1.5.2). Now that you have downloaded the file, save it to a location on your local hard disk.

Double-clicking the file will launch an Installation Wizard as shown in Figure 1.2.

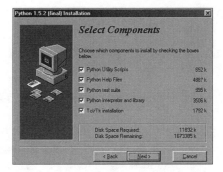

Figure 1.2
PythonWin's Installation Wizard guides you through a very simple installation process.

Select everything and confirm the selections. The installation process will start and after Python is installed, you will be asked if you also want to install Tcl/Tk (see Figure 1.3). I strongly suggest that you install it too because later you will learn how to create GUI interfaces using Tkinter. After you confirm it, the Wizard will guide you through Tcl's 8.0.5 for Windows installation. Choose the full installation, confirm it, and that's it. Your Windows system is fully configured to use both PythonWin and IDLE.

Figure 1.3
Installing Tcl/Tk now enables you to create GUI applications later.

I suggest that you spend some time going through all the documentation that was installed in your machine.

Right now you might have everything already set up in your environment.

If you decide later to download and build the source code, download the same source code that is provided for UNIX systems at

`http://www.python.org/download/download_source.html`.

Get the file `py152.tgz` and follow the instructions listed in the README file. It clearly explains how you could use Microsoft Visual C++ 5.0 to build the source code. See Chapter 17 for more details.

If you are interested in downloading Python 2.0, the following link takes you directly to its download page.

`http://www.pythonlabs.com/products/python2.0/download_python2.0.html`

At PythonLabs, you have the source tarball available to build Python from the source in the platform of your choice. Note that if you are running Windows, you can download and run the Windows installer as well.

The following links cover the 2.0 distribution.

News about Python 2.0

`http://www.pythonlabs.com/products/python2.0/news.html`

Python 2.0 Manuals

`http://www.pythonlabs.com/doc/manuals/python2.0/`

Python 2.0 - The new license

`http://www.pythonlabs.com/products/python2.0/license.html`

> **Note**
> A special note is necessary here to let you know that Python 2.0 doesn't run a separate Tcl/Tk installer anymore. It installs all the files it needs under the Python directory. This was made to avoid conflicting problems with other Tcl/Tk installations that you might have on your system.

Python and Other Languages

Scripting languages, as everyone knows, are slower than compiled languages. Python uses its interpreter to manage most of the things you need to worry about when using compiled languages. The consequence is that you have a productive application in a short period. However, the application doesn't run as fast as a compiled version. Okay; it is slower, but who cares? Nowadays, the development time is a great differential between companies. It doesn't matter whether an application runs slower or faster in

Python than in other languages. The fact is that you have saved a considerable amount of time. And by the way, it's not as slow as many people say.

Python incorporates the best of scripting languages (Perl, Tcl, Awk) and systems languages (Java, C, C++). If you work in large projects, the use of Python will give you fast and reliable results.

However, Python doesn't beat other languages all the time. C and C++ are good for performance-critical modules of an application because they are system languages that talk almost directly to the processor. For that reason, many programmers create Python extensions using these languages when time is crucial for the project.

Python Versus C/C++

The following is a list of differences between Python and C/C++:

- Python's array constructs don't have the same number of problems that arrays written in C have.

- Most of the memory allocation and reference errors that we easily get when coding C/C++ programs are eliminated as Python performs automatic memory management.

- Python checks array references for boundary violations.

- In many cases, developing an application in Python requires much less code than an equivalent application in C.

In general, Python is a great tool to test C/C++ applications. Python adds some contribution to C/C++ projects by gluing components and handling interfaces to test them.

In addition to C/C++, Python is often compared to Perl, Java, and Tcl.

Python Versus Perl

Python is easier to learn than Perl, and it presents a more readable code. Perl is an excellent language too. Perl is great for work that requires text manipulation and data extraction, and it is also a great language for system administrators. The Windows distribution of Perl is apparently pretty good, so it can be used productively under Windows. However, Perl is much more productive when used in a UNIX environment. Python's productivity is platform-independent. Another important difference is that Python was designed to be fully object-oriented and Perl had object-orientation implemented later as an add-on to the language. One problem with Perl is that because "there's more than one way to do it," different programmers in large projects might know different subsets of the language and will not be able to read each other's code.

Python Versus Tcl

Python's syntax is much clearer than Tcl's. Besides, it is the fastest one, and it needs less C extensions than those Tcl requires when doing the same job. Similar to Tcl, Python uses Tk as its standard GUI. Also, Python has more data types than just strings.

Python Versus Smalltalk

The following list shows some differences between Python and Smalltalk:

- Python has scalability because it can handle small routines and large applications equally well.

- Python is much easier to learn than Smalltalk.

- Python enables the use of C and C++ code in programs that require a good performance because it is extensible.

- As most of Smalltalk's users come from the scientific society, the Numeric Python Extension becomes helpful by covering many mathematical aspects and making them easily written in Python.

Python Versus Java

Python offers dynamic typing and a rapid development environment that requires less code and no compilation phase. Although Python runs slower than Java, it is the more portable one.

JPython

It's a new Python implementation that is 100% written in Java. You can use all the features of Python languages along with the entire universe of Java classes. The integration between JPython and Java is better than the integration between Python and C++ because JPython can use Java classes without needing a wrapper generator. Several other reasons why you should consider giving JPython a try are as follows:

- JPython is interactive, as is CPython.

- JPython applications can import Java classes directly and, whenever required, integrate Java classes with their own JPython classes.

- JPython compiles directly to Java bytecode, generating Java `.class` files, which can be used to create applets.

By the way, JPython programmers also refer to Non-Java Python as CPython in order to distinguish Python's Java Implementation from Python's C implementation.

Conclusion

Now, just imagine projects that require several layers of application design. Do you think that these projects' leaders have some kind of problem to scale up their applications? If you've been in a situation like that, have you ever thought about using the same language for all your needs? Are you going to have a programmer coding in JavaScript? (That language doesn't support exception handling.)

Say that you need to create some Java routines, using Servlets, for the back end. What if this programmer doesn't know Java? Are you going to explain Java to him, or are you going to hire a Java programmer?

Nowadays, technology and projects are moving too fast. You don't have time to teach new technologies to the people who are coding your applications. This is one more reason to stick with Python. You have the flexibility to play in all bases and do almost everything using the same language.

I am sure you are satisfied now that you know the reasons why Python is a fantastic language. What are you waiting for? I strongly encourage you to use Python now.

For more information about Python versus other languages, check out the following URL:

`http://www.python.org/doc/Comparisons.html.`

Patches and Bugs List

In case you notice something bizarre happening while you are coding, you can check it out in order to find out whether it is a bug or not.

A query tool is provided by Python's official Web site to enable searches in the bug's list. Go to `http://www.python.org/search/search_bugs.html` and perform your search. You will be able to identify which bugs are opened, resolved, and so on.

If you think that you might have caught a new bug, you can fill out a form to let the developer's team know about it. Remember to ALWAYS check the Python Bugs List before reporting a bug. It is also good to take a look at the current CVS tree before reporting any bugs.

If you have fixed a bug and want to submit your patch to the PSA team, follow the standard Patch Submission Guidelines at `http://www.python.org/patches/`.

PSA and the Python Consortium

The Python Software Activity (PSA) was established by CNRI Inc. to be the home of Python and to guide its development according to the common interests of the Python development community. A large number of contributions are submitted periodically. The PSA Web site stores the official documentation and download area of Python distributions. PSA's creation has taken some of the responsibility that Guido had. As a result, a group is working to develop Python, instead of just one man. This fact helps propagate the maturity of Python's development strategy.

You can obtain more information about the PSA by visiting its official home page at `http://www.python.org` (see Figure 1.4). That is the place where all the information about Python gets officially organized and published. Note that with the move of Guido and his team to PythonLabs, the future of PSA is uncertain. The information currently available says that CNRI, which manages the existing PSA, will determine its future at the end of the current membership term, on October 1, 2000.

Figure 1.4

The Python Software Activity (PSA) official home page.

Several *Special Interest Groups (SIGs)*, hosted by PSA, are currently studying and developing special topics of Python, such as XML Processing, String Processing, Python in Education, Distributed Objects, and many other important topics. To find out what newest groups are being formed and to participate in the discussions that are conducted in their mailing lists, take a look at `http://www.python.org/sigs/`. Much of Python's real work takes place on Special Interest Group mailing lists.

Behind the PSA, a group of companies and individuals helps to propagate the Python voice. They work together, creating conferences and keeping their Web site up-to-date. If you want to be part of the PSA, get more details at `http://www.python.org/psa/`.

After you become a member of the PSA, you are eligible to have an account on the Web site `http://starship.python.net`.

Today, this site is filled with information provided by many Python developers from all around the world.

On Oct 25, 1999, the Python Consortium was publicly announced and officially began its mission "to ensure Python's continued support and development."

The membership fees that are received by the Consortium members support the development of Python and JPython. Many organizations have already registered as part of the Consortium (for more information, see `http://www.python.org/consortium/`).

The *Corporation for National Research Initiatives (CNRI)* is a nonprofit organization that hosts the Python Consortium. Check out its Web site at `http://www.cnri.reston.va.us/`.

Even with his transition to PythonLabs, Guido van Rossum remains the Technical Director of the Python Consortium, and BeOpen.com continues to be just a member.

Support and Help

Python has a Usenet newsgroup called `comp.lang.python`. This newsgroup is an excellent source of Python information and support. The guys who really know the language always hang out there.

One of the best ways to keep yourself up-to-date to the Python world is to sign up for the Python general mailing lists and to always check the newsgroup for some information that might be helpful for you.

Go to `http://www.python.org/psa/MailingLists.html` and look for the list that provides the level of information that you need. At this time, there are four main mailing lists:

Tutor is a list for beginners who have basic knowledge and need simple and straight answers.

JPython is a list that openly discusses the Python implementation for Java.

Announcements is a list that doesn't have huge traffic. The objective of this list is just to publish important notices to the Python community.

An open discussion mailing list generates an average of 100 daily messages and covers everything related to general Python discussion topics.

Python Conferences and Workshops

The Python community has organized many workshops and conferences to discuss Python hot topics. You can have access to the materials that were used for the presentations, and you can also download many technical documents provided by the people who have participated in the conferences and workshops.

For more details about the latest events and upcoming ones, check out the Web page at `http://www.python.org/workshops/`.

Summary

Python is an interpreted, high-level programming language, pure object-oriented and powerful server-side scripting language for the Web. It is an open source project that doesn't have any copylefts or copyrights involved in its license agreement.

You should consider moving to Python because it is simple to get support from the Python community; it is fast to learn and code it; it offers object-oriented programming support; and it provides a readable, reusable, and portable coding language.

The main technical features that distinguish Python from the other languages are as follows:

- Automatic memory management
- Exception handling management

- Rich core library

- Web scripting support and data handling

- Rich built-in elements

- Clear syntax and useful lexical elements

- Embeddable and Extendable language

- Objects Distribution support

- Databases support

- GUI applications support

- Introspection

- Easily integrated to third-party projects.

Python runs on many platforms, such as Microsoft Windows, Linux, and Macintosh. The source code and the documentation are freely downloadable. It is also available for downloading the binaries for some systems.

Python is always compared against other languages and, usually, it wins.

Python has an implementation in Java called JPython.

Two institutions have guided the Python community along the last few years: the Python Software Activity (PSA) and The Python Consortium. The PSA took the responsibility of creating Python conferences and workshops and keeping the Python official Web site up and running, whereas The Python Consortium supported the development of Python and JPython. Today, the future of these two institutions is a little uncertain because Guido and his whole development team have moved to BeOpen.com to support PythonLabs.com.

The Python community has been doing a great job by providing help to new Python aficionados. Most of this help is provided through the mailing lists, newsgroups, bug lists, and other available forms of support.

By the way, Python has nothing to do with those legless reptiles. It was named after the British comedy troupe Monty Python.

CHAPTER 2
Language Review

Spam spam spam spam spam spam spam and spam!

This chapter offers a complete review of the Python programming language. After you finish reading it, you will understand and master the concepts of this language. Furthermore, you will learn everything that is necessary to write useful Python programs.

Language Review

Some people say that Python is a magic language because it enables you to do almost everything with a minimum amount of code. The coding speed depends only on your effort to acquire the required knowledge to decide which commands you should use. Different from other languages, Python doesn't sell the idea of being able to code one task in many ways. The reason for that is because there is only one dialect of Python. Therefore, the core language doesn't provide a huge number of grammar styles and definitions. Consequently, you can keep the entire vocabulary in your mind without too much effort.

After spending some time studying Python, you can easily master the whole set of instructions that shapes the core language. As Python doesn't have any hard-to-remember commands, the language is very comfortable and simple. Most of the work that you have to do is identify the right module for your needs. By the way, Python's standard library of modules is very complete and well documented.

This chapter will guide you across the lines of code that are required to reach the stardom. Among other things, handling control statements and performing files management will become easy tasks for you.

Later, in the following chapters, you will learn how to go through each important Python module and understand what it does and how useful it can be for you.

Now, let's roll up our sleeves and start working.

The Shell Environment

The Python language is wrapped within a shell development environment. The main component of this shell is a *command line interpreter*, which is perfect for practicing, learning, and testing your programs.

Command Line Interpreter

The command line interpreter is the heart of Python's shell environment. To access the command line interpreter, you need to switch to the prompt of your operating system. The following examples presume that the python directory is in your system's `path` environment variable.

On a UNIX system, you must type

```
$ python
```

If you are running MS Windows, just say

```
c:\> python
```

Note that in both cases, you just need to type the word `python`; the rest is part of the shell prompt.

The Python for Windows installation also provides access to the command line interpreter by clicking its icon on the Start menu (see Figure 2.1).

After the command line interpreter is loaded (see Figure 2.2), you can start coding your own programs.

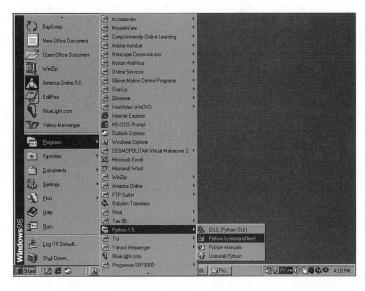

Figure 2.1

By clicking on the Python (command line) icon, you gain access to the shell environment.

Figure 2.2

Python's command line interface is now ready to use.

Instead of using the command line interpreter, you can also use a graphical user interface called IDLE (see Figure 2.3).

Note
See Chapter 16, "Development Environment," for details about using IDLE.

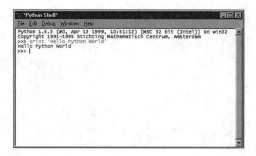

Figure 2.3
IDLE *is Python's GUI interpreter.*

As you can see by looking at the coding area in both Figures 2.2 and 2.3, the interpreter's primary prompt is a >>>.

Let's start interacting with Python by running a variation of the standard "hello world" program.

```
>>> print "Hello Python World"
Hello Python World
```

The previous example demonstrates that the screen is the standard output device for commands that are typed in the interpreter's prompt. Next, another example is demonstrated. Note that the first command doesn't print anything because it is just an assignment operation. The result of the operation is passed to and stored at the informed variable. On the other hand, the second command has its output redirected to the standard output, which enables you to see the result of the operation.

```
>>> alfa = 3 + 2
>>> alfa * 4
20
```

Python's syntax automatically indicates when a statement requires a subblock. The interpreter's secondary prompt ... means that the next line is a continuation from the current line and not a new line. In some cases, when you finish entering a multiline statement, you need to type ENTER at the beginning of the first line located after the end of the code block. By doing so, you will return to the primary prompt.

Four basic situations that use a secondary prompt are as follows:

- When you explicitly add a line continuation with a backslash \ literal:

```
>>> print "I am a lumberjack " + \
... "and I am OK."
```
```
I am a lumberjack and I am OK.
```

- When parenthetical expressions are incomplete:

```
>>> print ("I am a lumberjack " + \
... "and I am OK.")
```
```
I am a lumberjack and I am OK.
```

```
>>> a = {
... 'song': 'lumberjack'
... }
```

- Multiline statements ending with a :

```
>>> if 1==2:
...     print "This line will never be printed"
...
>>>
```

- When you comment a line:

```
>>> # The next function statement returns 2 plus 2.
... 2+2
```
```
4
```

Tip
If you need to quit the interpreter while working on UNIX or MS Windows systems, press CTRL+D or CTRL+Z, respectively.

Programs

Until now, all the examples were written directly in the interpreter environment. However, most Python programs are executed as external scripts, being loaded from files.

You can write your own Python scripts by using any text editor of your choice. Remember to always save your files using the `.py` extension.

As with any other UNIX scripting language, Python scripts (for UNIX) need a special handling.

First, you need to put a "shebang" in the first line of the script. This line declares the location of Python's interpreter in your system. For example

```
#!/usr/local/bin/python
```

Note that this example works only if Python was installed under the given mounting point. Most Linux systems have Python installed under /usr by default, so the preceding example will not work. Today, the following line of code seems to be more common, and does not depend on where Python is installed:

```
#!/usr/bin/env python
```

If you are running your scripts on an MS Windows environment, you can keep this line of code for portability purposes because the literal # is only used to identify comment lines that are ignored by the interpreter, so it will cause no harm to your programs.

> **Tip**
> The "shebang" line is only meaningful when you work on a UNIX system.

If you don't know where Python is located on your UNIX system, use the following command:

```
$ whereis python
```

Also, remember to set the permissions on your script to 755 in order to let every user be able to execute it.

```
$ chmod +x scriptname.py
```

or

```
$ chmod 755 scriptname.py
```

As you cannot directly execute Python scripts in the MS Windows systems through the command line, you have two options: Either double-click the file using Windows Explorer or call the interpreter, passing the filename as an argument. For example,

```
c:\>python scriptname.py
```

Another way to call the interpreter on Windows systems is by typing `start scriptname.py` at the shell prompt. This command will find and execute the program associated with the extension `.py`.

If you want to open the interpreter after executing a program, use the `-i` argument when calling the script. The interpreter will run your script, and after it executes all the commands, it will open its command-line interface for you. Here's how to call the script with a command-line option:

```
c:\python -i scriptname.py
```

Otherwise, after the script finishes its execution, it will automatically close the interpreter.

After spending some time creating Python programs, you might find some `.pyc` files in the same directory in which you are saving your `.py` scripts. See Chapter 17, "Development Tools," to know more about this other file extension.

Indentation

Python delimits code blocks by using indentation. There is no concept of `{}`s or `Begin/Ends` as in other languages. When you indent a block of code, you define the way the statements are grouped. It also reduces errors due to bad indentation. For instance, the following C or Perl code looks like a single `if` statement, but the second statement is always executed:

```
if (expression)
    statement1;
    statement2;
```

Python doesn't suffer from this problem because indentation defines block structure.

Another great aspect of this implementation is that you can reduce the size of your code while using indentation instead of conventional block delimiters.

> **Tip**
> Keep in mind that tabs are internally converted to spaces (`1 tab = 8 spaces`), and blank lines are ignored when part of scripts.

I suggest you write one statement per line, using a `newline` (ENTER) to terminate each line. If you decide to have more than one statement in the same line, you need to separate them by using semicolons, as shown in the following:

```
>>> print "When AH "; print "were young..."
```

Remember that you must put a backslash \ at the end of lines that need to be broken into two lines:

```
>>> t = "Nobody expects " + \
... "the Spanish inquisition"
```

Lexical Analysis

It is unnecessary to declare the type of a variable in Python programs. The same variable name might have different types at different occasions because it is re-initialized every time a value gets assigned to it, as illustrated in the following:

```
>>> x = "Albatross!!"
>>> print x
Albatross!!
>>> x = 123
>>> print x
123
```

You can assign any object type to a variable (for example, functions, classes, and modules). The following example shows how you can create a variable that references the round() function object:

```
>>> x = round
>>> print x(27.234523, 2)
27.23
```

You don't have to worry about deallocating variables in Python. Python objects are collected whenever they become unreachable because Python does reference counting. This means that as long as there is a reference to an object, the object isn't collected. When you delete a reference to an object, its reference counting goes down by one, and when the count has dropped to 0, it is eligible for garbage collection. Note that under CPython, objects are deallocated as soon as the reference count reaches 0.

The problem with reference counting is that you can create circular references, such as the following:

```
>>> a = [1, 2, 3]
>>> b = [4, 5, 6]
>>> a.append(b)
>>> a
[1, 2, 3, [4, 5, 6]]
```

```
>>> b.append(a)
>>> a
[1, 2, 3, [4, 5, 6, [...]]]
>>> b
[4, 5, 6, [1, 2, 3, [...]]]
>>> del a
>>> del b
```

Now, you can never refer to variables a and b, nor to their contents again, and because each one of them is still referenced by the other list, they cannot be collected, either. Note that recursion is indicated by the [...] element. I know that it is fairly easy to fall into this trap, and although some work is being done to cure this problem, I strongly suggest that you avoid recursive constructs. As you might notice, del removes the reference to the object, which could cause it to be deallocated if its reference count reaches 0.

You can monitor the reference counting of an object by using the sys.getrefcount() function:

```
>>> import sys
>>> sys.getrefcount(b)
3
```

Note that you can break the circular reference if you insert the following lines between the appends and dels:

```
>>> del a[-1]
>>> del b[-1]
```

Actually, we are just breaking the references by removing the [...] entries from the lists. Note that the release 2.0 of Python makes sure that deleting objects is safe even for deeply nested data structures. The Python interpreter is now using a new mechanism to collect unused objects. From time to time, this mechanism performs a cycle detection algorithm that searches for inaccessible cycles and deletes the participating objects. This process has been named *Garbage Collection of Cycles*.

There are a couple of parameters of the garbage collection that you can manipulate. The module gc provides functions that helps you out with that. Of course, you always have the option to disable this feature. To do so, simply specify the argument "*-without-cycle-gc*" when running the Python configure script.

Reserved Words

Python has reserved a group of words for its own use. Those words have specific meanings that cannot be changed. You cannot use these words as identifiers in your code.

```
"and, assert, break, class, continue, def, del, elif, else, except,
 exec, finally, for, from, global, if, import, in, is, lambda, not,
 or, pass, print, raise, return, try, while"
```

Identifiers

Python identifiers are any objects created by programmers (such as variables, classes, and so on). Identifiers can be named using any of the following characters: A-Z, a-z, 0-9, and _. However, they can't start with a digit.

You must write your code carefully because Python identifiers are case sensitive.

The special characters: $, %, and @, aren't allowed to be part of an identifier's name. Besides that, $ and @ can be used only in a program, inside quoted strings. The % character may be used in a program because it is the mod operator.

Built-In Data Types

Built-in data types are types that are already built into the interpreter. They are divided into two groups:

Immutable Data Types

These objects cannot have their values altered (for example, strings, numbers, and tuples).

Mutable Data Types

These objects can have their values manipulated (for example, lists and dictionaries).

Sometimes, it becomes necessary to assign a null value to a variable using the special data type known as None:

```
>>> x = 1
>>> x
1
>>> print x
1
```

```
>>> x = None
>>> x
>>>
```

As you could see, nothing was returned. However, if you try to print this value, the `print` method of the object will specially handle the `None` value by returning a `None` result. This is shown in the following:

```
>>> print x
None
```

Numbers

Python provides the following numeric data types: integer, floating-point, hexadecimal (base 16), and octal (base 8). Some examples of these data types are `43`, `1.5`, `0xB3`, and `045`, respectively.

> **Tip**
> Hexadecimal numbers must always be preceded by `0x`, and octal numbers must be preceded by `0`.

Python can do a lot of things with numbers:

It can write equations:

```
>>> 3*(3.0/34)
0.264705882353
```

It can use functions:

```
>>> round(12.32,1)
12.3
```

It can make comparisons:

```
>>> x = 2
>>> 0<x<5
1
```

It can make binary operations, such as `shifting` and `masking`:

```
>>> 16<<2
64
>>> 40&0xab
40
>>> 2|1
```

```
3
>>> ~2
-3
>>> 3^4
7
```

A very important detail is the fact that Python truncates `integer` divisions:

```
>>> 3/2
1
```

If you really want the decimals, you have two options. Either you pass a converted number to the division function, or you put a decimal point in your number, as illustrated here:

```
>>> x = 3
>>> float(x)/2
1.5
>>> x
3
>>> 3.0/2
1.5
```

Python supports long integers—with unlimited size. To let Python know that it should handle an integer as a long integer, you need to put an `L` at the end of the number:

```
>>> 2L**100
1267650600228229401496703205376L
```

Otherwise you get an error message:

```
>>> 2**100
Traceback (innermost last):
  File "<stdin>", line 1, in ?
OverflowError: integer pow()
```

Chapter 4, "Exception Handling," teaches you how to interpret this exception message.

Python also handles complex numbers in the format (`real part + imaginary part`):

```
>>> 2j**2
(-4+0j)
```

Strings

Python considers a string as a sequence of characters. Therefore, every time you use, for example, the string `"Parrot"`, internally Python handles it as the sequence `["P",` `"a"`, `"r"`, `"r"`, `"o"`, `"t"]`. The first indexer value is always the number zero. Hence, to have access to the letter `P`, you need to say `"Parrot"[0]` and to access the letter `a`, you need to say `"Parrot"[1]`. Using the same concept, we can get access to all the other elements.

The following is an example of string operators:

```
>>> "dead parrot " + "sketch"  # concatenation
"dead parrot sketch"
>>> "parrot " * 2              # repetition
"parrot parrot"
>>> "parrot"[1]               # indexing
"a"
>>> "parrot"[-1]              # indexing backward
"t"
>>> "parrot"[1:3]            # slicing (*)
"ar"
```

When slicing, it isn't necessary to include both first and last elements. Whenever you omit one of the elements, it is assumed that you want everything in that direction. Note that the second argument is always a positional reference.

```
>>> "parrot"[1:]
"arrot"
>>> "parrot"[:3]
"par"
```

Always remember that assigning `z = x` doesn't make a copy of the object `x`. Instead, it creates a new reference for that object (as you already saw in the earlier round example). If you have to create a copy of a sequence named `x`, you need to type:

```
>>> z = x[:]
```

The variable `z` will identify the middle of the variable `x`, and it will be initialized with everything from the left direction plus everything from the right direction. Note that since Python 1.5, `id(s) == id(s[:])` for strings because of string interning.

Strings cannot be modified after creation. It isn't possible to assign a value to a substring because strings are immutable. See the error message in the next example:

```
>>> t = "pxrrot"
>>> t[1:2] = "a"
Traceback (innermost last):
  File "<stdin>", line 1, in ?
TypeError: object doesn't support slice assignment
```

In cases like this, the usual solution is a little trick:

```
s = s[:left_element] + new_substring + s[right_element:]
```

For example

```
>>> t = "pxrrot"
>>> t = t[:1] + "a" + t[2:]
>>> t
"parrot"
```

Let me show you other useful operations that you can do with strings:

```
>>> len("parrot")          # Get its length
6
>>> "parrot" < "sketch"    # Compare one string against another.
1
>>> "t" in "parrot"        # This logical test needs a char left operand
1
>>> "\n, \0, \x"           # Use escape codes
"\012, \000, \\x"
```

Table 2.1 lists the escape codes supported by Python strings.

Table 2.1   *Escape Codes Supported by Python Strings*

Escape Code	Description
\\	backslash
\'	single quote
\"	double quote
\b	backspace
\e	escape
\0	null
\n	linefeed, also known as \012
\v	vertical tab
\t	horizontal tab

Table 2.1   *Escape Codes Supported by Python Strings*

Escape Code	Description
\r	carriage return
\f	form feed
\0nn	octal value, the nn domain is: 0..7
\xnn	hexa value, the nn domain is: 0..9, A..F, a..f

Next is an example of escape code:

```
>>> print "I am a lumberjack\nand I am OK"
I am a lumberjack
and I am OK
```

You can use either single quotes or double quotes. They are both interpreted the same way.

Both strings `'Spam'` and `"Spam"` are basically the same thing.

Python also accepts triple quotes for remarks that span across several lines:

```
>>> t = """I am a lumberjack
... and I am OK"""
>>> print t
I am a lumberjack
and I am OK
>>> t
"I am a lumberjack\012and I am OK"
```

Note that the escape code `\012` becomes part of the string.

If you need to create strings with the / (slash literal), you must use raw strings. Raw strings are identified by the letter r right before the first quote, as shown in the following:

```
>>> print r"\n, \f, \x"
\n, \f, \x
```

There is one more thing that I think you should know about strings. The enclosing backticks `` tell the interpreter to understand that the enclosed object is of string data type:

```
>>> n = 123
>>> print `n` + " Parrot"
123 Parrot
```

> **Note**
> Python doesn't treat the contents of back quotes as commands to execute, as do
> Perl and sh.

Prior to version 2.0, you had to rely on the string module to manipulate your string
objects because the string-manipulation functionality was in the string module. With
this new release, the methods were pushed to the string type. Note that old string
module was not removed from the distribution because it is still necessary for
backwards compatibility.

The following example shows how to call a method from a string object.

```
>>> 'Python '.join('World')
Python World
```

Note that 'Python '.join('World') is equivalent to the old string module:
string.join("World", "Python ")

Besides the methods that were inherited from the string module, two new methods
were added: startswith() and endswith().

s.startswith(t) is equivalent to s[:len(t)] == t

and

s.endswith(t) is equivalent to s[-len(t):] == t.

Unicode Support

Unicode is a new immutable string data type supported by Python 2.0. Basically, it can
represent characters using 16-bit numbers, instead of the 8-bit numbers used by the
ASCII standard, which means that Unicode strings can support up to 65,536 distinct
characters. Note that when combining an 8-bit string and an Unicode string, the
resulting string is an Unicode string.

In order to write a Unicode string in Python, you need to use the notation u"string".
If you need to write arbitrary Unicode characters, you can use the new escape
sequence, \uHHHH, where HHHH is a 4-digit hexadecimal number from 0000 to FFFF.
Note that you can also use the existing \xHHHH escape sequence. Another option is to
use octal escapes whenever you need to write characters up to U+01FF (represented by
\777).

True and False Logical Values

Falsity is represented by zeros, empty structures, or the value None (for example, 0, [ ], {}, ( ), None).

Logical Truth is represented by results different from zero and non-empty structures (for example, 1, [2], (1,2,3), "abc"). The following if statement checks whether the variable t has any value; in this case, the statement returns true, allowing the block contents to be executed:

```
>>> t = "Parrot"
>>>     if t:
...          print "Parrot"
...
Parrot
```

Operators

Next, I list the available Python operators in their precedence order. I also provide some specific details about some of them.

1. (), [], {}

2. `object`

3. object[i], object[l:r], object.attribute, function()

   The . (dot) operator is used to access attributes and methods of a variable (object). In the following example, the dot enables the object t to access its method append.

   ```
   >>> t = ["p","a","r","r","o"]
   >>> t.append("t")
   >>> t
   ["p","a","r","r","o","t"]
   ```

4. +x, -x, ~x

   These are bitwise operators.

5. x**y

6. x*y, x/y, x%y

   The % (modulo) operator lets you know whether a number is divisible by another number. For example, if a % b == 0, a is divisible by b.

7. x+y, x-y

8. x<<y, x>>y

   These operators provide shifting operations. The << operator ensures left shifting (at bit level), and the >> operator ensures right shifting (at bit level).

   ```
   >>> x = 2          # the binary representation is 0010
   >>> x << 1         # the binary representation will be 0100
   ```
   ```
   4
   ```

9. x & y

   The bitwise AND operator

10. x ^ y

    The bitwise XOR (exclusive OR) operator

11. x | y

    The bitwise OR operator

12. <, <=, >, >=, ==, !=, <>, is, is not, in, not in

    The operators in and not in work only with lists. Another aspect of this group is that there's an important difference between the == operator and the = assigning symbol.

    is checks whether two variables refer to the same object. On the other hand, is not checks whether two variables don't refer to the same object.

    The == operator ensures equality testing, whereas = assigns a value to a variable.

    Tip
    Keep in mind that x = y doesn't create a new copy of y. Instead, it makes a reference to it. However, if later you define x=x+1, a new reference for x is created, and then they become different because the operator has created a new object.

    Note that x.append(5) doesn't create a new reference to x because x changes itself without using a = operator.

13. not

14. and

15. or, lambda args:expr

As a good programmer, you need to know that logical operations can also be emulated by using if statements. Note that the return values are not limited to zeros and ones.

The operation a and b can be written as the following:

```
>>> def newand(a,b):
...      if not a:         #If a is false
...          return a
...      else:
...          return b
...
```

The operation a or b can be written as the following:

```
>>> def newor(a,b):
...      if a:             #If a is true
...          return a
...      else:
...          return b
...
```

The operation not a can be written as the following:

```
>>> def newnot(a):
...      if not a:     #If a is false
...          return 0
...      else:
...          return 1
...
```

Augmented Assignment

Starting with Python 2.0, the language also implements a full set of augmented assignment operators. That includes: +=, -=, *=, /=, %=, **=, &=, |=, ^=, »=, and «=

For example, instead of saying x = x+1, you can choose to say x += 1

Expressions

Python operators support a wide range of expressions, such as

```
>>> x,y,z = z-x, y*z, x+y # Parallel assignment: example 1
>>> x,y,z = 5,4,3            # Parallel assignment: example 2
```

```
>>> a,b = b,a            # Switching assignments
>>> a = b = c = 10       # Multiple assignments
>>> string.atof(s)       # Functions support
>>> 20 < x < 40          # Multiple range testing
```

The last example is equivalent to

```
>>> 20 < x and x < 40
```

Built-In Functions

The following functions are always available when you load the Python interpreter. You don't need to import them because they are already part of the __builtin__ module, which is always imported when you launch Python.

apply()

It executes a given *function*, passing the arguments provided.

basic syntax: apply(function, (tuple of positional arguments) [, dictionary of keywords arguments])

```
>>> apply (raise_salary, (6000), {'employee':'John', 'id':13})
```

Note that starting at Python 1.6, the functionality of apply is now available with normal function calling, such as

```
>>> args = (6000,)
>>> kwargs = { 'employee':'John', 'id':13}
>>> raise_salary(*args, **kwargs)
```

coerce()

coerce is used to try to convert the two given arguments x and y to the same type, returning them as a tuple.

basic syntax: coerce(x, y)

```
>>> coerce(42,5.4)
(42.0, 5.4)
```

filter()

It creates a new list by taking each element of *list* for which *function* evaluates to true.

basic syntax: filter(function, list)

```
>>> a = range (4)
>>> b = filter(lambda x: x < 3, a)
>>> print b
[0,1,2]
```

globals()
It returns the global namespace dictionary.

basic syntax: `globals()`

input()
It provides an input interface for the user. Only numbers are accepted.

basic syntax: `input([prompt])`

```
a = input("Please, type a number greater than 5: ")
if a<5:
    print "a is not greater than 5"
```

locals()
It returns the local namespace dictionary

basic syntax: `locals()`

map()
It applies a *function* to each element of *list*, producing another list. If *function* is set to None and multiple lists are provided, a tuple matrix is generated in the format of a list.

basic syntax: `map(function, list)`

```
>>> lst = map(None, [1,2,3,4], [1,2,3,4,5,6])
>>> lst
[(1, 1), (2, 2), (3, 3), (4, 4), (None, 5), (None, 6)]
```

open()
It opens a file. (See the section "File Handling" for details.)

basic syntax: `open(filename [,mode [,bufsize]])`

pow()
It returns x**y or (x**y) % z, depending on the number of arguments that are transported.

basic syntax: `pow(x, y [,z])`

`raw_input()`

It reads from standard input (`sys.stdin`), returning the read data as a string. *prompt* is an optional text that can be displayed in the screen.

basic syntax: `raw_input(`*[prompt]*`)`

`reduce()`

It applies a *function* cumulatively to the items in *sequence* (implied loop), returning a single value. *initializer* is an optional starting value.

basic syntax: `reduce(`*function, sequence [,initializer]*`)`

```
>>> import operator
>>> a = [1,2,3]
>>> print reduce(operator.add, a)
6
```

The equivalent Python code for this function is something like

```
def reduce(func, list):
    ret = list[0]
    for x in list[1:]:
        ret = func(ret, x)
    return ret
```

`__import__()`

This is a function invoked by the import statement. To import a module, you just need to inform the *module name*.

basic syntax: `__import__(`*module_name [,globals() [, locals() [,from list]]]*`)`

```
>>> modname = "string"
>>> string = __import__(modname)
>>> string
```

`reload()`

It reloads an already imported *module*. Internally, it calls the __import__ function.

basic syntax: `reload(`*module*`)`

Sequence Functions

The next set is built-in functions that deal with sequences.

```
range()
```
It returns a list of numbers according to the transported information.

basic syntax: `variable = range([initial_value,] final_value-1 [, step])`

```
>>> lst = range(1,5)
>>> lst
[1, 2, 3, 4]
```

See the section "Data Structures" for details.

```
xrange()
```
It is similar to `range()`, but it doesn't assign the returned list to a variable, Therefore, it doesn't use as much memory, so you won't run out of memory by typing `xrange(2000000000)`, for instance.

basic syntax: `xrange([initial_value,] final_value-1 [, step])`

See the section "Data Structures" for details.

```
len()
```
It returns the length/number of elements of *string*.

basic syntax: `len(variablename)`

```
max()
```
It returns the maximum/largest element of *sequence*.

basic syntax: `max(sequence)`

```
>>> max(1, 2, 3)
3
>>> max("MY BRAIN HURTS")
"Y"
```

```
min()
```
It returns the minimum/smallest element of *sequence*.

basic syntax: `min(sequence)`

```
>>> min("MY BRAIN HURTS")
" "
```

```
zip()
```
It returns a list of tuples where each tuple contains the i-th element from each of the given sequences. This function generates a resulting list whose length is exactly the same as of the shortest given sequence. Note that, on the other hand, the function `map(None, sequence1, sequence2, ...)` pads the resulting list with `None` when the sequences don't have the same length.

basic syntax: `zip(sequence1, sequence 2, sequence3, ...)`

Object Manipulation

The next set is built-in functions that deal with object handling.

```
setattr()
```
It sets a new *value* for *object.name*

basic syntax: `setattr(object, name, value)`

```
getattr()
```
It returns the *attribute* from *object*. This command is equivalent to `object.attribute`.

basic syntax: `getattr(object, attribute)`

```
hasattr()
```
It returns `1` if *object* has *attribute*, `0` if it doesn't.

basic syntax: `hasattr(object, attribute)`

```
delattr()
```
It deletes the *attribute* from *object*. This command is equivalent to `del object.attribute`.

basic syntax: `delattr(object, attribute)`

```
type()
```
It returns the type of *object*.

basic syntax: `type(object)`

```
>>> type("andre")
<type "string">
```

`dir()`
It returns a list of attribute names from the active namespace. *object* can be anything (a variable, a module, a class, and so on).

basic syntax: `dir([object])`

`callable()`
It returns 1 if *object* is callable. Otherwise, it returns 0.

basic syntax: `callable(object)`

`hash()`
It returns a hash value for *object*.

basic syntax: `hash(object)`

`id()`
It returns the system unique identifier of *object*.

basic syntax: `id(object)`

`vars()`
It returns the symbol table of *object* or a dictionary from the local namespace.

basic syntax: `vars([object])`

Mathematical/Logical Functions

The next set is built-in functions that deal with mathematical and logical operations.

`abs()`
It returns the absolute value of *number*.

basic syntax: `abs(number)`
```
>>> abs(-12), abs(34), abs(+20.23), abs(-10.82)
(12, 34, 20.23, 10.82)
```

`cmp()`
It returns -1 when x<y; 0 when x==y, 1 when x>y

basic syntax: `cmp(x,y)`
```
>>> cmp(10,20), cmp(25,25), cmp(30,25)
(-1, 0, 1)
```

round()

It rounds *number* to the given number of *decimals*. Note that the provided number is rounded to an integer by default.

basic syntax: round(*number [,decimals]*)

divmod()

It returns a tuple (quotient, remainder), resulting in the expression *dividend/divisor*.

basic syntax: divmod(*dividend, divisor*)

```
>>> divmod(25/3)
(8, 1)
```

Code Functions

The next set is built-in functions that deal with Python bytecode manipulation.

eval()

It evaluates the compiled code *string* object as if it were Python code, and returns the result. *globals* and *locals* define the namespaces for the operation. Note that eval can evaluate expressions only—not arbitrary statements. Therefore, eval('import string') won't work.

basic syntax: eval(*string [,globals [,locals]]*)

```
>>> a = eval('2 * y + (20 / x)')
```

exec()

exec is a statement that executes a *string* containing Python code. *globals* and *locals* define the namespaces for the operation.

basic syntax: exec *string [in globals [,locals]]*

```
>>> a='for b in range(4):\n print b,\n'
>>> exec a
0 1 2 3
```

execfile()

It executes the statements included in the *file* provided. *globals* and *locals* define the namespaces for the operation.

basic syntax: execfile(*file [,globals[,locals]]*)

```
>>> execfile("c:\\python\program2.py")
```

You can redefine the global and the local namespaces for these functions by creating dictionaries, just like the next example shows. If you omit the values, the current environment namespace is always used.

```
>>> globalsvar = {'x': 7}
>>> execfile("c:\\python\\program2.py", globalsvar)
```

compile()

It compiles a code object (*string*) that optionally might be located in a *file*. The *type* value depends on the following: if *string* is a sequence of statements, *type* is "exec"; if *string* is a single expression, *type* is "eval"; and if *string* is an executable statement, *type* is "single".

basic syntax: compile(*string, file, type*)

```
>>> a = "for i in range(0,10): print i,"
>>> b = compile(a, "", "exec")
>>> exec b
0 1 2 3 4 5 6 7 8 9
>>> a = "123 * 2"
>>> c = compile(a, "", "eval")
>>> d = eval(c)
>>> d
246
```

> **Tip**
> If you need to evaluate or execute the same code many times in your application, the application will get more optimized if you compile all the source code first.

Type Conversion

The next set is built-in functions that deal with data type conversion.

int()

It converts *object* to an integer number.

basic syntax: int(*object*)

long()

It converts *object* to a long integer.

basic syntax: long(*object*)

As of Python 2.0, the functions `int()` and `long()` have an optional *base* argument, which can be used when the first argument is a string. Note that if you try to use this second argument with a value that is not a string, you get a `TypeError` exception message. The following examples demonstrate what happens when we use this argument: `int('450', 10)` returns 450, and `int('25', 16)` returns 37.

float()
It converts *object* to a floating-point number.

basic syntax: `float(object)`

complex()
It creates a complex number in the format (*real* number + *imaginary* number)

basic syntax: `complex(real [,imaginary])`

str()
It returns the printable representation of *object*. It returns the same value that a "`print object`" statement does.

basic syntax: `str(object)`

repr()
It is equivalent to the enclosing backticks ` `` `. It returns an expression that can be evaluated.

basic syntax: `repr(object)`

You can use either `repr()` or ` `` ` to get the representation of an escape character.

```
>>> repr('spam\n')
"'spam\\012'"
```

tuple()
It creates a tuple based on *sequence*.

basic syntax: `tuple(sequence)`

list()
It creates a list based on *sequence*.

basic syntax: `list(sequence)`

chr()
It converts an *integer* into one character.

basic syntax: chr(*integer*)

ord()
It returns the ASCII value of *string*.

basic syntax: ord(*string*)

hex()
It converts an *object* into a hexadecimal value.

basic syntax: hex(*object*)

oct()
It converts an *object* into an octal value.

basic syntax: oct(*object*)

unicode()
This function takes an 8-bit string and creates a Unicode string.

basic syntax: unicode(*string [, encoding] [, errors]*)

encoding and errors are some additional arguments that you can also provide to the function. The first one is a string that names the *encoding* to use. errors defines what to do when an invalid character is used for the current encoding. You have three options for values here: strict causes an exception to be raised on any encoding error, ignore simply ignores any errors, and replace replaces the invalid character with the official replacement character U+FFFD whenever it finds any problem.

unichr()
This function returns a 1-length Unicode string containing the given character.

basic syntax: unichr(*character*)

Control Statements

Python implements all the necessary types of control statements that your program might require. The syntax provided by Python's if, for, and while statements should be enough for your needs.

> **Tip**
> Remember to type a colon at the end of each line where you enter a statement declaration.

if/elif/else

The general syntax for the `if/elif/else` statement is as follows:

```
1: if <condition>:
2:      <statements>
3: [elif <condition>:
4:      <statements>]
5: [elif <condition>:
6:      pass]
7: ...
8: [else:
9:      <statements>]
```

Note that both `elif` and `else` clauses are optional. As you can see in lines 3 through 7, it is only necessary to use `elif` when you need to handle multiple cases. That is exactly how you implement the `switch/case` statements from other languages.

Line 6 introduces you to an empty clause that does nothing. It is called `pass`.

for

The `for` statement implements loops within a *sequence* (list). Each element in the *sequence* assigns its value to *variable* on its turn. The general syntax is as follows:

```
for <variable> in <sequence>:
    <statements>
[else:
    <statements>]
```

The `else` clause is only executed when the `for` statement isn't executed at all, or after the last loop has been executed. In other words, the `else` statement is always executed unless the `break` statement is executed inside the loop.

Let's see some examples:

```
>>> for n in [1,2,3,4,5]:
...     print n,
...
1, 2, 3, 4, 5
```

```
>>> t = [(1,2),(2,4),(3,6)]
>>> for t1, t2 in t:
...     print t1, t2
...
1 2
2 4
3 6
```

while

The `while` statement implements a loop that executes the *statements* while the *condition* returns true.

```
while <condition>:
    <statements>
[else:
    <statements>
```

The `else` clause is only executed when the `while` statement isn't executed at all, or after the last loop has been executed. In other words, the `else` statement is always executed unless the `break` statement is executed inside the loop.

The following example demonstrates the use of the `while` statement:

```
>>> x = 5
>>> while x > 0:
...     print x,
...     x = x-1
...
5 4 3 2 1
```

The next example implements an infinite loop because the `pass` statement does nothing and the condition will always be `true`.

```
>>> while 1:
...     pass
```

break/continue

Next are two commands that can be used inside `for` and `while` types of loop.

break

The `break` clause exits a loop statement without executing the `else` clause.

```
>>> for n in [1, 2, 3]:
...      print n,
...      if n == 2:
...          break
... else:
...      print "done"
...
1 2
```

continue

The continue clause skips the rest of the loop block, jumping all the way back to the loop top.

```
>>> x = 5
>>> while x > 0:
...      x = x - 1
...      if x == 3:
...          continue
...      print x,
...
4 2 1 0
```

Data Structures

Python implements a variety of data structures, such as lists, tuples, ranges, and dictionaries (also known as hash tables).

Lists

Lists are mutable sequences of objects indexed by natural numbers that can be changed after they are created.

Lists are very flexible and easy to create. They are always enclosed in brackets:

```
>>> lst = [1,2,3,4]   # this is simple list
```

A list can have elements of different data types:

```
>>> lst = [1, "ni!", 2]
```

Lists can also include other lists:

```
>>> lst = [1, "ni!", [1,2,"Albatross!!"]]
```

A list uses the same operators that `strings` use. For example, you need to use slice notation to grab a range of elements from a list.

```
>>> lst = [1, "ni!", [1, 2, 3, 4, "Albatross!!", 3]]
>>> lst[1]
"ni!"
```

To grab elements from lists that are located inside other lists, you need to use a pair of brackets to represent each list. Check out the next couple of examples.

```
>>> lst = [1, "ni!", [1, 2, 3, 4, "Albatross!!", 3]]
>>> lst[2][4]
"Albatross!!"
>>> lst[2][4][5]
"r"
```

Let's see some examples of operations that can be applied to a list.

Identifying an Entry
```
>>> lst = ["p", "a", "r", "r", "o", "t"]
>>> lst.index("o")
4
```

Assigning Values to a List
```
>>> lst = ["p", "a", "r", "r", "o", "t"]
>>> lst[1] = "aaaaaaaaaaaaa"
>>> lst
["p", "aaaaaaaaaaaaa", "r", "r", "o", "t"]
```

Assigning Values to a Slice
```
>>> lst = ["p", "a", "r", "r", "o", "t"]
>>> lst[1:4] = ["aaaaaaaaaaaaa", "rrr", "rrrr"]
>>> lst
["p", "aaaaaaaaaaaaa", "rrr", "rrrr", "o", "t"]
```

Inserting Values
The following example starts inserting values at index number 6.
```
>>> lst = ["p", "a", "r", "r", "o", "t"]
>>> lst[6:] = [" ", "s", "k", "e", "t", "c", "h"]
['p', 'a', 'r', 'r', 'o', 't', ' ', 's', 'k', 'e', 't', 'c', 'h']
```

If the list was longer than 6 elements, the statement would overwrite a portion of the list. Note that you can also insert a value in this list with

```
>>> lst.insert(6, val)
```

Deleting a Value

```
>>> lst = ["p", "a", "r", "r", "o", "t"]
>>> del lst[-1]
>>> lst
["p", "a", "r", "r", "o"]
>>> del lst[0:2]
["r", "r", "o"]
```

The following example converts objects to their string representation:

```
>>> lst = [10,20,30,"inquisition","lumberjack"]
>>> text = ""
>>> for element in lst:
...     text = text + `element`
...     # enables the concatenation of any object
...     print text
...
10
1020
102030
102030'inquisition'
102030'inquisition''lumberjack'
```

List Comprehension

Starting with release 2.0, there is a new notation to create lists whose elements are computed from another list (or lists). The method is called List Comprehension, and it adopts the following format:

```
[ expression for expression1 in sequence1
            [for expression2 in sequence2]
            [... for expressionN in sequenceN]
            [if condition] ]
```

All for...in clauses are evaluated and iterated from left to right. That means that the resulting list is a cartesian product of the given sequences. For example, if you have three lists of length 5, the output list has 125 elements. The if clause is optional, but when present, it can limit the number of pairs that will become part of the resulting list by adding pairs to the resulting list only when the result condition of the `if` statement evaluates to true. Check the following example:

```
letters = 'py'
numbers = (1.52, 1.6, 2.0)
>>> [ (l,n) for l in letters for n in numbers]
[('p', 1.52), ('p', 1.6), ('p', 2.0), ('y', 1.52), ('y', 1.6),
('y', 2.0)]
```

This new concept is more efficient than a `for` loop with an `if` statement along with a `list.append()` function call.

Built-In Methods

To list all the `built-in` methods of a list, go to the interpreter and type **dir([])**.

Let's practice the methods that you have found, and see what happens to our list `lst`.

```
>>> lst = [0, 1, 2]
>>> lst.append(5)        # appends the element 5 to the list
>>> lst
[0, 1, 2, 5]
>>> lst.append((5, 6))   # appends the tuple (5, 6)
>>> lst
[0, 1, 2, 5, (5, 6)]
>>> lst.pop()            # removes the last element of the list
(5, 6)
>>> lst
[0, 1, 2, 5]
>>> lst.insert(2,7)      # inserts the element 7 at index number 2
>>> lst
[0, 1, 7, 2, 5]
>>> lst.pop(2)           # removes the element at index number 2
7
>>> lst
[0, 1, 2, 5]
>>> lst.reverse()        # reverse the list order
>>> lst
[5, 2, 1, 0]
>>> lst.sort()           # sorts the list elements
>>> lst
[0, 1, 2, 5]
>>> lst.extend([3, 4, 5]) # adds this list to our original list
>>> lst
```

```
[0, 1, 2, 5, 3, 4, 5]
>>> lst.count(5) # counts the number of elements number 5 that exist.
2
>>> lst.index(3) # returns the associated index of element 3.
4
>>> lst.remove(2) # removes the element number 2 (not the index!!!)
>>> lst
[0, 1, 5, 3, 4, 5]
```

Note that up to release 1.5.2, whenever you used `lst.append (1,2)`, a tuple `(1,2)`
would be appended to the list `lst`. Now, with release 2.0, when you do that, you get an
`TypeError` exception followed by a message like "`append requires exactly 1
argument; 2 given`". Don't panic! To fix that, you just need to add an extra pair of
parenthesis, like this: `lst.append ((1,2))`.

Ranges

A range is an actual list of integers. The `built-in` function `range()` provides this data
structure.

```
>>> r = range(2,5)
>>> print r
[2,3,4]
```

When the first argument is left out, it is assumed to be zero.

```
>>> r = range(3)
>>> print r
[0,1,2]
```

When you provide a third argument to the `range()` function, you specify the interval
that you want to exist between the list elements.

```
>>> r = range(2,10,2)
>>> print r
[2, 4, 6, 8]
```

Let's see an example of stepping backward:

```
>>> r = range(5,1,-1)
>>> print r
[5, 4, 3, 2]
```

The xrange() function computes the values only when they are accessed. This function returns an XrangeType object, instead of storing a large list of numbers in a variable.

```
>>> for n in xrange(10):
...         print n,
...
0, 1, 2, 3, 4, 5, 6, 7, 8, 9
```

The previous example also works with the range() function, although it will store the whole list in memory.

It is possible to assign a reference to the return value of the xrange() function to a variable, as you will see next. Note that we are *not* storing the values, only a reference to the function.

```
>>> lst = xrange(10)
>>> lst
(0, 1, 2, 3, 4, 5, 6, 7, 8, 9)
```

However, you can convert this reference later into a real list by using the tolist() method.

```
>>> lst.tolist()
[0, 1, 2, 3, 4, 5, 6, 7, 8, 9]
```

Tuples

A tuple is a sequence of immutable Python objects.

The general syntax of a tuple is as follows:

```
variable = (element1, element2, ...)
```

It looks like a list without the brackets. Note in the following examples that parentheses are optional.

```
>>> t = (1,)
>>> print t
(1,)
>>> t = 1,
>>> print t
(1,)
>>> t = ()          # this is an empty tuple.
>>> print t
```

```
()
>>> t = (1,2,3)
>>> print t
(1,2,3)
>>> t = 1,2,3
>>> print t
(1,2,3)
```

Note that in the previous example, it is necessary to use the comma when defining a length-1 tuple. Otherwise, the variable being created wouldn't be defined as of type tuple. Instead, the interpreter would think that you wanted to assign a numeric value to the variable.

A tuple really looks like a list. The difference between tuples and lists is that tuples are immutable.

You can bypass this rule if you bind a new structure to the old tuple variable.

```
>>> t = 10,15,20
>>> t = t[0],t[2]
>>> t
(10,20)
```

Other Interesting Facts About Tuples

• They support indexing.

```
>>> t = 10,20,30,40
>>> print t[1]
20
```

• You will see, later in this chapter, that you need to use tuples whenever you need to return more than one value from a function.

```
>>> Def tuplefunction():
...            return 10, 20, 30
...
>>> x, y, z = tuplefunction()
>>> print x, y, z
10 20 30
```

Dictionaries (hash tables)

Dictionaries illustrate the only mapping type of Python. They represent finite sets of objects indexed by nearly arbitrary values. I say *nearly* because dictionary keys cannot be variables of mutable type, which are compared by value rather than by object identity.

Python dictionaries are also known as associative arrays or hash tables. The general syntax of a dictionary is as follows:

```
variable = {"key1":"value1", "key2":"value2", ...}
```

Dictionaries are always enclosed in braces. They associate key elements with value elements—keys and values are displayed separated by a colon.

The values of a dictionary can be of any type, but the keys must be of an immutable data type (such as strings, numbers, or tuples). Dictionary keys have no natural order and are always listed in arbitrary order because it uses a hash technique to implement a fast lookup.

Let's focus now on the operations that we can implement with dictionaries. First, let's create a simple dictionary.

```
>>> dic = {"bird":"parrot", "fish":"tuna", "dino":"t-rex"}
```

Now, let's apply some operations to it:

```
>>> dic["fish"]        # value lookup
"tuna"
>>> dic["animal"]      # raises a KeyError exception
Traceback (innermost last):
  File "<stdin>", line 1, in ?
KeyError: animal
>>> del dic["fish"]  # deletes the key fish
>>> print dic
{'bird': 'parrot', 'dino': 't-rex'}
>>> dic["dino"] = "brontosaur"  # updates an entry
>>> dic["parrot age"] = 58         # adds an entry
>>> dic
{"bird": "parrot", "dino": "brontosaur", "parrot age": 58}
>>> len(dic)           # provides the number of keys
3
```

Built-In Methods

The following sequence of commands shows the built-in methods that are implemented for dictionaries.

```
>>> dic = {"a":1, "b":2, "c":3}
>>> dic.keys()    # creates a list of keys. Very used in for statements.
["a","b","c"]
>>> dic.values()      # creates a list of values
["1","2","3"]
>>> dic.items()       # creates a tuple with the dictionary elements
[("a","1"),("b","2"),("c","3")]
>>> dic.has_key("a") # returns 1 if key exists. Otherwise it returns 0.
1

# dic.get(value, default)
# If key exists, returns its value. Otherwise it returns the second arg.
>>> dic.get("b", None)
2

# dic.update(dictionary)
# adds the dictionary in the argument to the original dictionary.
>>> dic.update({"d":4})

>>> newdic = dic.copy()          # creates a copy of the dictionary
>>> keys = dic.keys()
>>> keys.sort()                  # sorts the dictionary keys
>>> dic.clear()          # removes all the items from the dictionary.
```

Python 2.0 contains a brand-new method for dictionaries, which is called
setdefault(). This method returns the value for the given key (exactly as the get()
method would do). However, if the given key is not found, it returns the given default
value, and at the same time, it initializes the given key with the default value, as
demonstrated in the following code.

```
if dict.has_key( key ):
    return dict[key]
else:
    dict[key] = ["default value"]
    return dict[key]
```

is the same of saying

```
return dict.setdefault(key, "default value")
```

Functions and Procedures

Functions and procedures are blocks of code that you can access from several different parts of your code. As you already know, Python gives you some `built-in` functions, but you can also create your own functions. Yours are called `user-defined functions`. Functions and procedures provide better modularity for your application and a high degree of code reusing.

Procedures are functions that don't return a value. The only difference between a function and a procedure is that a procedure has either a `return` command without arguments (that returns `None`), or it doesn't have any return statement. From now on, I will use only the word `function`.

While functions are being executed, they create their own `namespace`.

Every time you invoke a function, such as `function(a,b,c)`

- Python does a search within its `namespaces` looking for `function` to identify whether this is a python object.

- Python creates a tuple of the *arguments* that were passed. Following our example, we have *arguments*=(a,b,c).

- Python invokes the function internally like this: `apply(function,arguments)`.

As you can see, tuples are an unavoidable concept inside the language.

Python, by nature, allows introspection to an unprecedented degree. You can separate a function name from its parameters, store them in some place, play around with them, and later use the `apply` `built-in` function to execute the function.

Functions

Functions always start with the abbreviation `def`. Their end is defined by the last line of the indented block of code that goes underneath.

The general format of a function is as follows:

```
def functionname(arg1, arg2, ...):  # tuple of arguments
    "documentation string"          # optional
    <statements>
```

Let's see a real example now:

```
>>> def addnumbers(x,y):
...       "This function returns arg1 + arg2"
...       return x + y
...
>>> addnumbers(3,4)
9
```

Remember that to call a function without arguments, it's necessary to use empty parentheses.

```
>>> variable = name()      # instead of variable = name
```

As a matter of fact, remember that you can assign functions to variables.

```
>>> x = abs
>>> print x(-2)          # it's the same as saying print abs(-2)
-2
```

`x = abs` returns the own function, and assigns its value to `x`.

Python uses *dynamic namespaces*. In order to show that, the next example uses the value of `n`, available at the time of calling the function, because `n` isn't defined inside the function nor is it part of its list of arguments. `n` is part of the global namespace of the function.

```
>>> def add_to_n(arg):
...       return n + arg
...
```

Variables that have values assigned to them inside a function always belong to the function `namespace`. Study the next example to learn how to change a global variable inside a function by using the keyword `global`.

```
>>> x = 10
>>> def nudge():
...       global x
...       x = 20
...       return x
...
```

Python implements procedural abstraction. Although this topic has a scary name, it is something very easy and simple. Python offers this feature by providing anonymous functions implemented with the keyword `lambda`. This type of abstraction can be used

when the function is just an expression. In other words, lambda is just another way of
writing def, except that it doesn't have to be named, and you can only put an
expression in it. (The return is implicit.) It is intended to be just a shorthand to write
small functions easier as shown in the following:

```
>>> f = lambda x: x * 2
>>> f(20)
40
```

The previous case can also be written as follows:

```
>>> def f(x):
...          return x * 2
>>> f(30)
60
```

Here's another example:

```
>>> def compose(func1,func2,y):
...       f = lambda x, f1=func1, f2=func2: f1(f2(x))
...       return f(y)
...
>>> compose(chr,abs,-65)
'A'
```

Note that in this last example, it is necessary to pass the default arguments to the
lambda function because Python has only local and global namespaces.

lambda is very useful for functions—such as map, filter, and reduce—that need a
function as an argument.

```
>>> def listtostring(list):
...       return reduce(lambda string, item: string + chr(item), list, "")
...
>>> listtostring([1,2,3,4,5])
"\001\002\003\004\005"
```

Parameters

All parameters (arguments) in the Python language are passed by reference. Modules,
classes, instances, and other functions can be used as arguments to functions and
examined dynamically. Keep in mind that you don't need to specify the object type of
an argument. By default, arguments have a positional behavior, and you need to
inform them in the same order that they were defined.

```
>>> def powerdivision(x,y):
...          return x/y
...
>>> print powerdivision(4,2)
2
```

Whenever mutable objects (dictionaries and lists)—that are transported to a function as arguments—change within the function, their external values also change.

```
>>> a = [1]
>>> def changelist(argument):
...       argument.append(4)
...
... changelist(a)
>>> a
[1,4]
```

Python also offers you *named* arguments. This type is different from *positional* arguments because it enables you to call a function and pass argument names and values in an arbitrary way—the order isn't important at all.

Both function calls

```
>>> connect(port=80, name="www.bebemania.com.br")
```

and

```
>>> connect(name="www.bebemania.com.br", port=80)
```

are executed perfectly well and in the same way (when the function is implemented, of course).

Default arguments are also allowed by the syntax. If the argument isn't provided, the default value takes place. The default value is optional. Even though its absence doesn't break your program, its presence cuts many lines from your code, as shown in the following:

```
>>> def connect(port=80):
```

The following example demonstrates namespace handling along with default arguments:

```
>>> a = 5
>>> def test(b = a):
...       print b
...
```

```
>>> test()
5
>>> test(2)
2
>>> a = 10
>>> test()          # Note that the b wasn't reassigned
5
```

This effect is because the value of a was collected when the function was created.

In some cases, you cannot pre-identify the number of arguments that you might need. For this kind of situation, you can use the special symbols * and ** next to a generic argument name.

*args gets a tuple of values in the received order; **args gets a dictionary mapping argumentname:value.

```
>>> def showargs(*args):
...        # defines a list of an undefined number of arguments.
...        print args
...
>>> showargs(10,20,30)
(10, 20, 30)

>>> def add(*args):
...        sum=0
...        for arg in args:
...            sum=sum+arg
...        return sum
...
>>> add(1,2,3,4)
10
>>> add(1,2,3,4,5,6,7)
28
```

Returning Values

The return expression halts the execution of a function, but when it's followed by an expression, it returns the expression.

```
>>> def returnargument(x):
...        return x
...
>>> 5
5
```

A function can return multiple values by using tuples.

```
>>> def returntuple(s,p):
...     return (s,p)
...
>>> x = 10
>>> y = 20
>>> a, b = returntuple(x,y) # or (a, b) = returntuple(x,y)
>>> print a, b
10, 20
```

It is also possible for a function to have no `return` at all. When that happens, the value `None` is returned.

Built-In Methods

When you have a function `f`, the following `built-in` methods can be accessed:

```
>>> f.__doc__ or f.func_doc          # "documentation string"
>>> f.__name__ or f.func_name        # "function name"
>>> f.func_code                      # byte-compile code
>>> f.func_defaults      # tuple containing the default arguments
>>> f.func_globals      # dictionary defining the global namespace
```

Let's get the `documentation string` of the `join` function, which is part of the `string` module.

```
>>> import string
>>> print string.join.__doc__
join(list [,sep]) -> string
joinfields(list [,sep]) -> string
Return a string composed of the words in list, with intervening
occurences of sep.  Sep defaults to a single space.
(join and joinfields are synonymous)
```

Dynamic Namespace

Maybe you haven't noticed yet, but Python uses dynamic namespace concepts. Each function, module, and class defines its own namespace when it is created.

When you inform an instruction, command, or statement to Python, it searches first inside the local namespace and afterwards inside the global namespace.

Python has the following namespaces:

Built-in names—int, string, def, print, and so on

Global names—Declared as global and assigned at the top-level of a module

Local names—Assigned inside a function

When you are writing your code, you have two forms of writing an object name. You can use qualified names and unqualified names. Qualified names use object namespaces as references, for example:

```
>>> print objectnamespace.objectname
```

Unqualified names deal with scopes, provided the object is in your namespace. For example

```
>>> print objectname
```

Modules and Packages

A *module* is a collection of classes, functions, and variables saved in a text file.

When referencing a module within your Python application, you don't need to specify the file suffix—your program text files must carry a .py extension. Modules can be written in Python or in C. No matter what option you use, you call both types of modules using the same syntax. The following syntax imports and creates the global namespace for a module:

```
import <module>
```

A module filename called yourmodule.py should be mentioned in your import clause as follows:

```
>>> import yourmodule
```

It is also possible to have multiple modules imported at the same time, using just one import statement as follows:

```
>>> import m1, m2, m3
```

> **Tip**
> An interesting fact you should know is that all the code is executed when it is imported for the first time.

Some modules are always available in Python. Others (including yours) are files and need to be imported (in most cases, those files have .py or .pyc suffixes). To be imported, a file must have been saved in one of the directories listed in the sys.path variable.

If you need your module to be runnable and importable at the same time, you need to put something like the following line of code at the end of the file:

```
If __name__ == "__main__": your_function()
```

> **Tip**
> Remember that in UNIX, you need to change the permission of a file to make it executable.

You can find out the contents of a module by typing:

```
dir(<module>)
```

For example,

```
>>> dir(math)
```

Now we will talk about packages.

A *package* is a collection of modules in the same directory. Package names must be subdirectories of one of the directories listed in the sys.path variable.

A package directory must have, at least, an empty __init__.py file, and it might contain subpackages (subdirectories). Each subdirectory also needs, at least, an empty __init__.py file.

In the statement

```
>>> import a.b
```

the module named a.b designates a submodule named b inside a package called a.

When you import a package, its subpackages aren't imported all together. You need to explicitly say that in the __init__.py file.

It would be similar to saving the following line in the __init__.py file of your package:

```
import subpackage1, subpackage2, subpackage3
```

Remember that to locate modules and packages, Python uses the paths that are stored at sys.path. This variable is a simple list, like any other, and you can add any directory to this list that you want. Type **sys.path** at the prompt of your interpreter to know the current contents of this variable.

A new feature incorporated to release 2.0 is the possibility to rename modules when importing them. The syntax for that can be either

```
import module as newname
```

or

```
from module import name as newname
```

This feature is equivalent to the code

```
import module
newmodule = module
del module
```

Built-In Methods

All these built-in functions are part of the __builtin__ module, and you can use them after you have a module or package named m.

```
>>> m.__dict__              # lists the module dictionary
>>> m.x = m.__dict__["x"]    # provides access to a specific attribute
>>> m.__doc__             # returns the documentation string
>>> m.__name__            # returns the name of the module
>>> m.__file__            # returns the file name
>>> m.__path__            # returns the fully qualified package name
```

from **in Contrast to** import

The import and from statements allow one module to refer to objects from another module's namespace. They help eliminate problems with different modules that have some internal names equal. The next examples discuss the possible ways to use these statements.

```
>>> import string
>>> print string.join(list)
```

The previous example imports the string module as a local reference to an external module, allowing fully qualified references to any other objects in the string namespace.

The next example adds the join() function to the namespace of the current module. This method allows you to control exactly which names you import into your local namespace from a module.

```
>>> from string import join
>>> print join(list)
```

Now, take a look at the next line:

```
>>> from string import *
```

The problem with this syntax is that if the string module defines its own dosomething() function, you lose the dosomething() that might exist in your current namespace.

If you instead do a simple import string, you will keep your current dosomething() function. However, the dosomething() function from the string module will now be accessed by string.dosomething().

> **Tip**
> The main reason that you don't want to do from <module> import * is to avoid namespace clashing.

Also, let me tell you that identifiers beginning with _ (one underscore), such as _salary, aren't imported by a from <module> import * clause.

```
>>> import package1.string
>>> print package1.string.join(list)
```

The previous example loads the module string from the package package1.

```
>>> from package1 import string
>>> print string.join(list)
```

In order to access the string module, you need to reference its objects by typing string.<object>. This is the recommended notation to import a module from a package.

```
>>> from package1.string import join
>>> print join(list)
```

In the syntax form <package.module> import <object>, the <object> can be a subpackage of the package, a function, a class, a variable, and so on.

```
>>> from package1 import *
```

If you just say from package import *, it isn't guaranteed that all modules will be import unless you insert the following piece of code in the __init__.py file of the package.

```
__all__ = ["module1","module2","module3"]
```

This is a list containing the names of the package modules that should be imported:

```
>>> from package.subpackage.module import *
```

Whenever you use a structure like package.subpackage.module, Python ensures that the package's __init__.py is loaded first. Afterwards, the subpackage's __init__.py is loaded, and only after they have been imported will the module finally be imported. After a package is loaded, there is no difference between a package and a module. Module objects represent both of them.

Releasing and Reloading Modules

After you have imported a module, you can release it from the system memory at anytime you want. The following example is to give you an idea of what I am talking about:

```
import string, sys
    lst = ["a","b","c","d"]
    print string.join(lst,"-")
del string
del sys.modules["string"]
```

Note that you also need to delete the module's reference, which exists in the sys.module variable.

The command reload <module> reloads and re-executes a module. Note that objects created before the reloading will use the previous version until they are re-created. Try to avoid using this command.

You can easily find out what the imported modules are by typing

```
>>> sys.modules.key()
['os.path', 'operator', 'os', 'exceptions', '__main__', 'ntpath',
'strop', 'nt', 'sys', '__builtin__', 'site', 'signal', UserDict',
'string', 'stat', 'cmath']
```

Input and Output

Python, as any other language, provides means to get input from the user and also to display information to him.

Let's see how we can handle it.

```
>>> x = input ("type anything: ")
>>> print "You have typed ", x
```

Note that the input prompt can be anything, even an empty one.

If the user types 5, x is properly treated as a number. To make x become a string, the user must explicitly type the quotes.

To avoid this problem, you can use the raw_input function:

```
>>> x = raw_input ("type anything: ")
>>> print "You have typed ", x
```

Now, it doesn't matter whether the user types the quotes.

Note that the print command requires objects to be separated by commas:

```
>>> print "parrot", "sketch"
parrot sketch
```

Displaying Information

Let's delve a little bit deeper into this topic.

Python has three standard file objects, which are available from the sys module. The interpreter uses them to provide input and output facilities. (Refer to Chapter 3, "Python Libraries," for details and examples—the sys module.)

They are known as sys.stdin, sys.stdout, sys.stderr

print statements are mapped to the sys.stdout. Hence, they send the textual representation of objects to the standard output stream:

```
>>>import sys
>>>sys.stdout.write("Nudge-nudge\n")
Nudge-nudge
```

Did you know that it is possible to re-map the standard output device?

Yes, that is possible.

You can run the following code to write to a file:

```
>>> sys.stdout = open("outputtest.txt", "w")
>>> print "hello"
>>> sys.stdout.close

>>> sys.stdout = sys.__stdout__
>>> sys.exit()
```

Note that sys.__stdout__ stores the original stdout.

The last line restores the sys.__stdout__ original value to such an extent that new print statements will display onscreen, instead of being sent to a file.

As additional information, this program uses sys.exit() to quit its execution (refer to Chapter 3 for details).

Starting with release 2.0, the print statement can have its output directed to a file-like object, as it is demonstrated in the following example.

```
print >> sys.stderr, "Sorry, you cannot do that!"
```

Formatting Operations

Python provides formatting operations similar to the printf() function from the C language.

Take a look at the following example:

```
>>> print "Mr. Lumberjack! do not sing!"
```

What if you don't want to hard-code the name inside the string? Compare the previous line of code against the following one:

```
>>> print "Mr. %s, do not sing!" % someone
```

Flexible, don't you think? And by the way, the order of the elements doesn't affect the final result.

Therefore, saying

```
>>> print "Mr. %s" % someone
```

is the same as saying

```
>>> print someone % "Mr. %s"
```

As a matter of fact, the following example shows how Python handles multiple format arguments. Note that you need to provide a tuple of values to fill the position indicated by the formatting operators (see Table 2.2).

```
>>> print "The %s has %i wings" % ("parrot", 2)
```

Table 2.2   *Formatting Operators Table*

Formatting Operator	Description
%d	decimal integer
%i	decimal integer
%u	unsigned integer
%o	octal integer
%x	hexadecimal integer
%X	hexadecimal integer (uppercase letters)
%f	floating point as [-]m.dddddd
%e	floating point as [-]m.dddddde±xx
%E	floating point as [-]m.dddddE±xx
%g, %G	floating point where the exponent is less than -4 or greater than the precision
%s	any printable object (such as strings)
%c	a single character
%%	the literal %

The following code is another simple example:

```
>>> value = 14
>>> print "The value is %d" % value
The value is 14
```

Next, you will see some special ways to format operations by putting special characters between the % literal and the formatting operator. Before going through the examples, we need to initialize some variables.

```
>>> intg = 42
>>> fltn = 13.142783
>>> strg = "hello"
>>> dict = {"xx":13, "yy":1.54321, "zz":"parrot"}
```

- You can use dictionary key names in parentheses.

```
>>> print "%(zz)s" % dict
parrot
```

- By using the - literal, you can left align the string block.

```
>>> print "%-8dend" % fltn
"13      end"
```

- By using the + literal, you can show positive and negative numerical signs.

```
>>> print "%+d" % intg
+42
```

- If you insert a zero, you will get a zero-filling.

```
>>> print "%08d " % intg
"0000042"
```

- Maximum field width (strings)

```
>>> print "%0.2s" % strg
"he"
```

- Period (.) + precision (floating-point numbers)

```
>>> print "%0.2f" % fltn
13.14
```

- Minimum number of digits (integer)

```
>>> print "%0.10f" % intg
0000000042
```

Tip
A * can be used in the place of any number. It uses the next value that matches that format in a tuple.

```
>>> print "%*.*f" % (5,3,2.45)
2.450
```

> **Note**
> Python 2.0 contains a new format string called %r, which prints the `repr()` value of
> the given argument. You can clearly see the difference between %r and %s by
> looking at the following example.
>
> `'%r %s' % ('Python', 'Python')`
>
> returns the string
>
> `'Python' Python`

File Handling

Python's core language supports all the basic functions that are necessary to
manipulate files. It isn't necessary to import any modules to use them. Whenever you
use the open function to get access to a file, Python creates a file object that supports
all the built-in methods that apply to this new object.

Opening a File

basic syntax: `file = open (filename[, mode[, buffersize]])`

The mode can be r, w, or a (read, write, and append, respectively). If none of them are
mentioned, read mode is assumed.

If you are working with a binary file, add the letter b to the mode indicator (for
example, rb or wb). The b stands for binary mode (text translation mode).

You can also place a + sign to the mode letter to indicate a read/write open (for
example, r+ or w+)—it is useful when you need to perform both operations (read and
write) in the file. Remember that if you use w+, it will first truncate the file length to
zero.

The last argument in the open syntax is the buffersize clause, which means

- `0 = unbuffered`
- `1 = line buffered`
- If buffersize is greater than 1, its value is equal to the buffer size, in bytes.
- If negative, the buffer size is the system default(default behavior).

Here's an example: *V2.2 use file instead of open*

```
file = open("foo.txt", "r")
line = file.readline()
```

NB on windows use backslash for path
forward slash
i.e c:/mydir/tem/fi6.txt.

```
line = line[:-1]          #chop off the newline character
while line:
    print line
    line = file.readline()
    line = line[:-1]
file.close()
```

Supported Methods

The following methods are supported by all file objects.

`read()`
It reads up to n bytes. But, if you don't provide any argument, read() reads all available data from the file.

basic syntax: `file.read([nbytes])`

```
>>> file = open("foo.txt").read()
```

If you say `file = open("foo.txt").read(100)`, Python will read the file up to its first 100 bytes.

`readline()`
It reads only one line at a time (until, and including, the newline character).

basic syntax: `file.readline()`

```
>>> file=open("test.txt","r")
>>> while 1:
...      line = file.readline()
...      if not line:
...          break
...
```

Both read() and readline() functions return an empty string for EOF.

`readlines()`
It reads the entire file into a list of strings.

basic syntax: `file.readlines()`

```
>>> file=open("test.txt","r")
>>> for line in file.readlines():
...      print line
...
```

`write()`
It writes a string to a file.

basic syntax: `file.write(string)`

```
>>> file.write('Spam')
```

`writelines()`
It writes a list of strings to a file.

basic syntax: `file.writelines(list)`

```
>>> file.writelines(["We are the knights who say ...","ni!"])
```

`seek()`
It goes to a new file `position`. If `how=0`, it starts from the beginning of the file; if `how=1`, the position is relative to the current position; if `how=2`, the position is relative to the end of the file. The default value for `how` is 0.

basic syntax: `file.seek(position[, how])`

`tell()`
It returns the current file pointer.

basic syntax: `file.tell()`

`Fileno()`
It returns an integer file descriptor.

basic syntax: `file.fileno()`

`flush()`
It flushes the internal buffer.

basic syntax: `file.flush()`

`close()`
It closes the file.

basic syntax: `file.close()`

```
truncate()
```
It truncates the file.

basic syntax: `file.truncate([size])`

Now, let's mix two distinct concepts. The next line of code takes the filename and the file extension from two variables, and combines them to create the name of a file that should be opened.

```
>>> file=open ("%s.%s" % (file_name, file_extension)).read()
```

Remember that you need to escape your backslashes to prevent them from being interpreted as beginning a character code. See the next example.

```
>>> file=open('C:\Autoexec.bat')        # wrong way
>>> file=open('C:\\Autoexec.bat')       # right way
```

The functions that you saw in this chapter are perfect for handling strings. Chapter 8, "Working with Databases," explains how to use other file handling functions to save entire objects into a file.

File Object Attributes

Some special attributes for files are as follows:

```
>>> file.closed # returns 0 if the file is closed; 1 otherwise
>>> file.mode   # returns the I/O mode for the file
>>> file.name   # returns the name of the file
```

Summary

Python is a language that doesn't ask too much from programmers while they are learning it. A programmer can code almost anything using a minimum amount of code. Python provides a command-line interpreter, which is the interface to its shell environment.

Python programs can be typed and executed directly in the interpreter or stored and called from files. No matter where the programmer is entering the code, indentation is vital. It is extremely critical that all code blocks follow the indentation rules defined by the language.

Python does object reference counting in order to keep you away from the job of deallocating variables by doing its own memory management.

The language has two groups of built-in data types that already exist in the interpreter: the immutable data types (for example, strings, numbers, and tuples) and the mutable data types (for example, lists and dictionaries).

Python also provides a number of built-in functions that are always available when you load the interpreter. Besides that, it enables you to define and use your own group of functions, which are called user-defined functions. Apart from that, Python also implements procedural abstraction using the function `lambda`.

The basics control statements `if`, `for`, and `while` are provided by Python too. They all have predictable behavior. However, the statements `for` and `while` also implement the `else` structure.

Python defines three types of dynamic namespace: built-in names, global names, and local names. This feature allows you to encapsulate your objects within distinct scopes.

You can use modules and packages (collections of modules) to store your programs. Both are well supported by Python.

All the regular features that provide input and output operations are currently supported by Python. Along with that, Python's core language supports all the basic functions necessary to manipulate files.

Code Example

This is a very simple benchmark application that offers you a general overview of Python programming. Note that this version doesn't provide any type or error handling and the interface is still very rough.

Before going through the code, you must first understand what the program does. Figure 2.4 shows an interaction with the program.

The program consists of two questions that should be answered by an *n* number of companies. These questions cover the number of IT employees and the total IT cost of a company. The benchmark uses the `total cost / employee` value to calculate the statistics.

Figure 2.4
This example covers many aspects of basic Python concepts.

After checking the results, you have the option to save them in a file, and later when opening the application again, you get the option to visualize them again.

Listing 2.1 *Benchmark Tool (File benchmark.py)*

```
 1: ###
 2: # Program: Benchmark tool
 3: # Author: Andre S Lessa
 4: ###
 5:
 6: ### import modules
 7:
 8: import sys
 9: import string
10: import operator
11:
12: ### create dictionary of questions
13:
14: def definequiz():
15:     questions = {}
16:     questions["1"] = "What is the number of IT employees of this
        company?"
```

Listing 2.1   *(continued)*

```
17:     questions["2"] = "What is the total IT cost of this company?"
18:
19:     return questions
20:
21: ### Loop to collect companies data
22:
23: def collectresults():
24:     company = getcompanyname()
25:     while company:
26:         if company == "":
27:             break
28:
29:         quizkeys = quiz.keys()
30:         quizkeys.sort()
31:         for question in quizkeys:
32:             showquestion(lo_question=question, lo_company=company)
33:
34:         company = getcompanyname()
35:
36:     if len(answers) > 0:
37:         generateresults()
38:         showresults(gl_companies, gl_avg, gl_max, gl_min)
39:
40:         userinput = raw_input ("Do you want to save your results ? ")
41:         if string.upper(userinput[0]) == "Y":
42:             saveresults(gl_companies, gl_avg, gl_max, gl_min)
43:
44:     return
45:
46: ### Generate benchmark results
47:
48: def generateresults():
49:     global gl_companies, gl_avg, gl_max, gl_min
50:
51:     gl_companies = string.join(answers.keys(), ",")
52:
53:     company_count = len(answers.keys())
54:
55:     lo_avg = []
56:
57:     for company in answers.keys():
58:         lo_employees = answers[company][0][1]
```

Listing 2.1 *(continued)*

```
59:            lo_cost = answers[company][1][1]
60:            average = (float(lo_cost) / int(lo_employees))
61:            lo_avg = lo_avg + [average]
62:
63:        gl_max = max(lo_avg)
64:        gl_min = min(lo_avg)
65:        gl_avg = reduce(operator.add, lo_avg) / company_count
66:
67:        return
68:
69: ### Interface to enter company name
70:
71: def getcompanyname():
72:        print "Please enter the company name, " \
73:        "or press ENTER when you are done."
74:        userinput = raw_input()
75:        return userinput
76:
77: ### Displays questions and collect results
78:
79: def showquestion(lo_question, lo_company):
80:        print quiz[lo_question]
81:        if answers.has_key(lo_company):
82:            answers[lo_company] = answers[lo_company] + \
83:            [coerce(lo_question, raw_input())]
84:        else:
85:            answers[lo_company] = [coerce(lo_question, raw_input())]
86:        return
87:
88: ### Save results in a file
89:
90: def saveresults(*arguments):
91:        file = open(filename, "w")
92:        for value in arguments:
93:            file.write(repr(value)+"\n")
94:        file.close
95:        showresults(gl_companies, gl_avg, gl_max, gl_min)
96:        print "The results were saved."
97:        print
98:
```

Listing 2.1   *(continued)*

```
 99: ### Load results from a file
100:
101: def loadresults():
102:     count = 0
103:     file = open(filename, "r")
104:     line = file.readline()
105:     line = line[:-1]
106:     while line:
107:         if count == 0:
108:             lo_companies = line
109:         if count == 1:
110:             lo_avg = float(line)
111:         elif count == 2:
112:             lo_max = float(line)
113:         elif count == 3:
114:             lo_min = float(line)
115:         line = file.readline()
116:         line = line[:-1]
117:         count = count + 1
118:     file.close()
119:     return(lo_companies, lo_avg, lo_max, lo_min)
120:
121: ### Show results in the screen
122:
123: def showresults(lo_companies, lo_avg, lo_max, lo_min):
124:     print "Companies : "
125:     print lo_companies
126:     print "-----------------------------------------"
127:     print "%0.2f is the average cost/employees" % lo_avg
128:     print "%0.2f is the maximum cost/employees" % lo_max
129:     print "%0.2f is the minimum cost/employees" % lo_min
130:     print
131:     return
132:
133: ### Main action block
134:
135: def main():
136:     print
137:     print "Welcome to the benchmark tool!"
138:     print
139:
```

Listing 2.1   *(continued)*

```
140:      userinput = raw_input("Do you want to load the saved results ? ")
141:
142:      if userinput == "":
143:          collectresults()
144:      elif string.upper(userinput[0]) == "Y":
145:          gl_companies, gl_avg, gl_max, gl_min = loadresults()
146:          showresults(gl_companies, gl_avg, gl_max, gl_min)
147:      else:
148:          collectresults()
149:
150:      print
151:      sys.exit()
152:
153: ### Global Variables
154:
155: quiz = definequiz()
156: answers = {}
157: filename = "results.txt"
158: gl_companies = ""
159: gl_avg = 0
160: gl_max = 0
161: gl_min = 0
162:
163: main()
```

Note that the program effectively starts at line 155, when the global variables are declared, and soon after that, the main() function is executed.

The following list shows some of the important concepts that are provided by this simple example.

Lines 8-10—Loads the required modules.

Lines 15-17, 53, 81—Dictionary manipulation.

The answers dictionary has the following structure:

{company1: [(question1,answer1), (question2,answer2), company2: [(question1,answer1), (question2,answer2), ...}

Note that the dictionary values are lists of tuples.

Line 27—break statement that exits the while loop.

Lines 29,30—Sorts dictionary keys.

Line 32—Named arguments.

Line 40—User input.

Lines 41, 51—Uses functions from imported modules.

Line 41—String manipulation.

Lines 53, 63-65—Uses built-in functions.

Line 90—Function with undefined number of arguments.

Lines 81-85—Creates and inserts a tuple in the dictionary.

Line 93—Adds a newline character to the value.

Line 104—Reads a line (delimited by the newline character).

Line 105—Removes the newline character.

Line 127—Formats the numbers to display only two decimals.

Line 151—Exits the application.

Line 163—Calls to the function that initializes the program.

CHAPTER 3
Python Libraries

All right, it's a fair cop, but society is to blame.

This chapter shows what main module services and extensions are currently available for the Python programming language. The focus here is to expand your knowledge by introducing the most used modules and listing some examples for you.

Python Libraries

The first chapter has given you a good introduction about the Python core language. Everything you have successfully learned will be applied from now on. All the topics covered in the previous chapters are the building blocks for your Python mastering.

Now we will concentrate on this chapter. Python's standard distribution is shipped with a rich set of libraries. These libraries intend to offer flexibility to the programmers.

The libraries (also known as modules) cover many topics, such as the following:

Python core services—A group of modules, such as sys and os, that enable you to interact with what is behind the interpreter.

Network and Internet services—Python has modules for almost everything that is Internet related. You have many network client protocol implementations that handle the most used Internet services, such as HTTP and FTP. Python also provides support for parsing mark-up languages, like XML and HTML.

Regular expressions—The `re` module is a very comprehensive choice for text manipulation because it provides Perl 5 style patterns and matching rules.

These are just some of the features implemented by the modules that are reviewed by this chapter.

The Library Reference

The robustness of Python's library is something amazing. Many users have contributed to the development of these modules during the last few years.

Some modules were written in C and are built into the interpreter. Others are written in Python and can be loaded by using the `import` command.

Keep in mind that some of the interfaces may change slightly (for instance, bug fixes) with the next release. Therefore, I suggest that you visit Python's Web site once in a while, and keep yourself up-to-date. You can always browse the latest version of the Python Library Reference at

```
http://www.python.org/doc/lib
```

I encourage you to use this chapter in order to get a quick overview about the existing Python libraries. After you have exhausted all the material provided by this book, check out the online Python Library Reference to see the minor details about each one of these Python module interfaces.

This chapter introduces you to the practical side of several modules' utilization. The next pages show what main functions each module exposes, and, whenever possible, some examples are listed.

Some of the modules—such as `debugger(pdb)`, `profiler`, `Tkinter` (the standard Python GUI API) and `re`—aren't deeply studied here because they are presented in detail in other chapters of this book. Whenever this happens, the chapter number is mentioned next to the module name.

The Standard Library of Modules

This book covers the latest version of the Standard Library of Modules that is available at the time of this writing. The modules are presented in the same order as they are shown in Python's official documentation. This was done to make the work of cross-referencing easier for you.

The following topics are the group names that organize the modules you will find.

Python Services

String

Miscellaneous

Generic Operational System

Optional Operational System

Debugger

Profiler

Internet Protocol and Support

Internet Data Handling

Restricted Execution

Multimedia

Cryptographic

UNIX Specific

SGI IRIX Specific

Sun OS Specific

MS Windows Specific

Macintosh Specific

Undocumented Modules

Python Services

This first group of modules is known as Python Services. These modules provide access to services related to the interpreter and to Python's environment.

sys

The sys module handles system-specific parameters, variables, and functions related to the interpreter.

```
sys.argv
```
This object contains the list of arguments that were passed to a program.

If you pass arguments to your program, for example, by saying,

```
c:\python program.py -a -h -c
```

you are able to access those arguments by retrieving the value of `sys.argv`:

```
>>> import sys
>>> sys.argv
["program.py", "-a", "-h", "-c"]
```

You can use this list to check whether certain parameters are transported to the interpreter.

```
>>> If "-h" in sys.argv:
>>>     print "Sorry. There is no help available."
```

```
sys.exit()
```
This is a *function* used to exit a program. Optionally, it can have a `return code`. It works by raising the `SystemExit` exception. If the exception remains uncaught while going up the call stack, the interpreter shuts down.

basic syntax: `sys.exit([return_code])`

```
>>> import sys
>>> sys.exit(0)
```

The `return_code` argument indicates the return code that should be passed back to the caller application.

The `sys` module also contains three file objects that take care of the standard input and output devices (see Chapter 1, "Introduction," for more details about these objects).

  `sys.stdin`—File object that is used to read data from the standard input device. Usually it is mapped to the user keyboard.

  `sys.stdout`—File object that is used by every `print` statement. The default behavior is to output to the screen.

  `sys.stderr`—It stands for standard error output. Usually, it is also mapped to the same object of `sys.stdout`.

Example:

```
>>> import sys
>>> data = sys.stdin.readlines()
>>> str = "Counted %d lines." % len(data)
>>> sys.stdout.write (str)
```

Now, save the previous example in a file named countlines.py, and test it by typing the following instructions on your prompt:

```
On Unix: cat coutlines.py | python countlines.py
On DOS and Windows: type countlines.py | python countlines.py
```

sys.modules
It is a *dictionary* that contains the modules that were loaded by the current session.

sys.platforms
This is a *string* that shows the current platform (for example, "win32", "mac", "linux-i386").

You can test which platform is running a program by doing something like this:

```
if sys.platforms == "win32"
    <do something>
elif sys.platform == "mac"
    <do something else>
```

sys.path
This is the *list* of directories that are searched to find the location of a module at the time of importing it.

```
>>> import.sys
>>> sys.path
['', 'C:\\Program Files\\Python\\Lib\\plat-win',
'C:\\Program Files\\Python\\Lib', 'C:\\Program Files\\Python\\DLLs',
'C:\\Program Files\\Python\\Lib\\lib-tk','C:\\PROGRAM FILES\\PYTHON\\DLLs',
'C:\\PROGRAM FILES\\PYTHON\\lib',
'C:\\PROGRAM FILES\\PYTHON\\lib\\plat-win',
'C:\\PROGRAM FILES\\PYTHON\\lib\\lib-tk',
'C:\\PROGRAM FILES\\PYTHON']
```

You can easily update this list to include your own directories.

```
sys.builtin_module_names
```
This is the list of modules that are not imported as files.

```
>>> import sys
>>> sys.builtin_module_names
('__builtin__', '__main__', '_locale', '_socket', 'array', 'audioop',
'binascii', 'cPickle', 'cStringIO', 'cmath', 'errno', 'imageop', 'imp',
'marshal', 'math', 'md5', 'msvcrt', 'new', 'nt', 'operator', 'pcre',
'regex', 'rgbimg', 'rotor', 'select', 'sha', 'signal', 'soundex', 'strop',
'struct', 'sys', 'thread', 'time', 'winsound')
```

For all the next sys objects, see Chapter 4, "Exception Handling," for details.

```
sys.exc_info()
```
Provides information about the current exception being handled.

```
sys.exc_type, sys.exc_value, sys.exc_traceback
```
It is another way to get the information about the current exception being handled.

```
sys.last_type, sys.last_value and sys.last_traceback
```
Provides information about the last uncaught exception.

Python 2.0 contains a mode detailed version information function called
`sys.version_info`. This function returns a tuple in the format *(major, minor, micro, level, serial)*. For example, suppose the version number of your Python system is
`3.0.4alpha1`, the function `sys.version_info()` returns `(3, 0, 4, 'alpha', 1)`. Note
that the level can be one of the following values: *alpha*, *beta*, or *final*.

Another set of functions added to Python 2.0 are: `sys.getrecursionlimit()` and
`sys.setrecursionlimit()`. These functions are responsible for reading and modifing
the maximum recursion depth for the routines in the system. The default value is
1000, and you can run the new script `Misc/find_recursionlimit.py` in order to know
the maximum value suggested for your platform.

types

The `types` module stores the constant names of the built-in object types.

`FunctionType`, `DictType`, `ListType`, and `StringType` are examples of the built-in type
names.

You can use these constants to find out the type of an object.

```
>>> import types
```

```
>>> if type("Parrot") == types.StringType:
...     print "This is a string!"
...
This is a string
```

The complete list of built-in object types, that are stored at the `types` module, can be found in Chapter 5, "Object-Oriented Programming."

UserDict

The `UserDict` module is a class wrapper that allows you to overwrite or add new methods to dictionary objects.

UserList

The `UserList` module is a class wrapper that allows you to overwrite or add new methods to list objects.

operator

The `operator` module stores functions that access the built-in standard operators. The main reason for the `operator` module is that `operator.add`, for instance, is much faster than `lambda a,b: a+b`.

For example, the line

```
>>> import operator
>>> operator.div(6,2)
3
```

provides the same result that the next line does.

```
>>> 6 / 2
3
```

This module is mostly used when it becomes necessary to pass an operator as the argument of a function. For example

```
1: import sys, glob, operator
2: sys.argv = reduce(operator.add, map(glob.glob, sys.argv))
3: print sys.argv
```

To run the previous example, save the code in a file and execute it by switching to your OS prompt and typing:

```
python yourfilename.py *.*
```

The heart of this example is Line 2. Let's interpret it:

The `glob.glob()` function is applied for each element of the original `sys.argv` list object (by using the `map()` function). The result is concatenated and reduced into a single variable `sys.argv`. The concatenation operation is performed by the `operator.add()` function.

traceback

The `traceback` module supports `print` and `retrieve` operations of the *traceback stack*. This module is mostly used for debugging and error handling because it enables you to examine the *call stack* after exceptions have been raised.

See Chapter 4 for more details about this module.

linecache

The `linecache` module allows you to randomly access any line of a text file.

For example, the next lines of code belong to the file `c:\temp\interface.py`.

```
import time, sys
name = raw_input("Enter your name: ")
print "Hi %s, how are you?" % name
feedback = raw_input("What do you want to do now? ")
print "I do not want to do that. Good bye!"
time.sleep(3)
sys.exit()
```

Check the result that is retrieved when the function `linecache.getline(file,linenumber)` is called.

```
>>> import linecache
>>> print linecache.getline("c:\\temp\interface.py",4)
feedback = raw_input("What do you want to do now? ")
```

pickle

The `pickle` module handles object serialization by converting Python objects to/from portable strings (`byte-streams`).

See Chapter 8, "Working with Databases," for details.

cPickle

The `cPickle` module is a faster implementation of the `pickle` module.

See Chapter 8 for details.

copy_reg

The `copy_reg` module extends the capabilities of the `pickle` and `cpickle` modules by registering support functions.

See Chapter 8 for details.

shelve

The `shelve` module offers persistent object storage capability to Python by using *dictionary* objects. The *keys* of these dictionaries must be `strings` and the *values* can be any object that the `pickle` module can handle.

See Chapter 8 for more details.

copy

The `copy` module provides shallow and deep object copying operations for lists, tuples, dictionaries, and class instances.

`copy.copy()`
This function creates a shallow copy of the x object.

```
>>> import copy
>>> x = [1, 2, 3, [4, 5, 6]]
>>> y = copy.copy(x)
>>> print y
[1, 2, 3, [4, 5, 6]]
>>> id(y) == id(x)
0
```

As you can see at the end of the previous example, the new list is not the old one.

As you can see, this function provides the same result that y=x[:] does. It creates a new object that references the old one. If the original object is a mutable object and has its value changed, the new object will change too.

`copy.deepcopy()`
It recursively copies the entire object. It really creates a new object without any link to the original structure.

basic syntax: variable = copy.deepcopy(*object*)

```
>>> import copy
>>> listone = [{"name":"Andre"}, 3, 2]
>>> listtwo = copy.copy(listone)
```

```
>>> listthree = copy.deepcopy(listone)
>>> listone[0]["name"] = "Renata"
>>> listone.append("Python")
>>> print listone, listtwo, listthree
[{"name":"Renata"}, 3, 2, "Python"]
[{"name":"Renata"}, 3, 2]
[{"name":"Andre}, 3, 2]
```

marshal

The `marshal` module is an alternate method to implement Python object serialization. It allows you to read/write information in a binary format, and convert data to/from character strings. Basically, it is just another way to do byte stream conversions by using serialized Python objects. It is also worth mentioning that `marshal` is used to serialize code objects for the .pyc files.

This module should be used for simple objects only. Use the `pickle` module to implement persistent objects in general.

See Chapter 8 for details.

imp

The `imp` module provides mechanisms to access the internal `import` statement implementation. You might want to use this module to overload the Python `import` semantics. Note that the `ihooks` module provides an easy-to-use interface for this task.

imp.find_module()
This function identifies the physical location of a given *module name*.

basic syntax: `file, path, desc = imp.find_module(modulename)`

imp.load_module()
This one loads and returns a *module object* based on the information provided.

basic syntax: `obj = imp.load_module(modulename,file,path,desc)`

```
>>> import imp
>>> def newimport(modulename):
...      file, path, desc = imp.find_module(modulename)
...      moduleobj = imp.load_module(modulename,file,path,desc)
...      return moduleobj
...
... math = newimport(math)
```

```
... math.e
2.71828182846
```

imp.getsuffixes()
It lists the precedence order in which files are imported when using the `import` statement.

Typing the following commands in my environment accomplishes this:

```
>>> import imp
>>> imp.get_suffixes()
[('.pyd', 'rb', 3), ('.dll', 'rb', 3), ('.py', 'r', 1), ('.pyc', 'rb', 2)]
```

Note that if I have a module stored in a file called `mymodule.pyc`, and I enter the command `import mymodule` at the interpreter, the system initially searches for a file called `mymodule.pyd`, and then for one called `mymodule.dll`, one called `mymodule.py`, and finally it searches for a file called `mymodule.pyc`.

> **Tip**
> When importing packages, this concept is ignored because directories precede all entries in this list.

parser

The `parser` module offers you an interface to access Python's internal `parser trees` and code compiler.

symbol

The `symbol` module includes constants that represent the numeric values of internal nodes of Python's parse trees. This module is mostly used along with the parser module.

token

The `token` module is another module that is used along with the `parser` module. It stores a list of all constants (`tokens`) that are used by the standard Python tokenizer. These constants represent the numeric values of leaf nodes of the parse trees.

keyword

The `keyword` module tests whether a string is a Python keyword. Note that the keyword-checking mechanism is not tied to the specific version of Python being used.

`keyword.kwlist`
This is a list of all Python keywords.

```
>>> import keyword
>>> keyword.kwlist
['and', 'assert', 'break', 'class', 'continue', 'def', 'del', 'elif',
 'else', 'except', 'exec', 'finally', 'for', 'from', 'global', 'if',
 'import', 'in', 'is', 'lambda', 'not', 'or', 'pass', 'print', 'raise',
 'return', 'try', 'while']
```

`keyword.iskeyword()`
This function tests whether a string is a Python keyword:

```
>>> import keyword
>>> str = "import"
>>> keyword.iskeyword(str)
1
```

tokenize

The `tokenize` module is an analysis tool that provides a lexical scanner for Python source code.

pyclbr

The `pyclbr` module offers class browser support in order to provide information about classes and methods of a module.

See Chapter 5 for details.

code

The `code` module interprets base classes, supporting operations that pertain to Python code objects. In other words, it can simulate the standard interpreter's interactive mode.

The next code opens a new interpreter within your interpreter:

```
>>> import code
>>> interpreter = code.InteractiveConsole()
>>> interpreter.interact()
```

codeop

The `codeop` module offers a function to compile Python code. This module is accessed by the `code` module and shouldn't be used directly.

pprint

The pprint (*pretty printer*) module prints Python objects so that the interpreter can use them as input for other operations.

```
>>> import pprint
>>> var = [(1,2,3),"Parrot"]
>>> pprint.pprint(var)
[(1,2,3),"Parrot"]
```

repr

The repr module is an alternate repr() function implementation that produces object representations that limit the size of resulting strings.

```
>>> import repr
>>> var = ["Spam" * 10]
>>> print var
['SpamSpamSpamSpamSpamSpamSpamSpamSpamSpam']
>>> print repr.repr(var)
['SpamSpamSpam...mSpamSpamSpam']
```

py_compile

The py_compile module is a single function that compiles Python source files, generating a byte-code file.

```
>>> import py_compile
>>> py_compile.compile("testprogram.py")
```

compileall

The compileall module compiles all Python source files that are stored in a specific directory tree. Note that compileall uses py_compile.

compileall.compile_dir()

This function byte-compiles all source files stored in the provided directory tree.

basic syntax: compile.compile_dir(*directory*)

```
>>> import compileall
>>> compileall.compile_dir("c:\\temp")
Listing c:\temp ...
Compiling c:\temp\program3.py ...
Compiling c:\temp\program4.py ...
Compiling c:\temp\program5.py ...
1
```

dis

>   The `dis` module is a Python `byte-code` dissassembler. This module enables you to
>   analyze Python `byte-code`.

new

>   The `new` module implements a runtime interface that allows you to create various
>   types of objects such as class objects, function objects, instance objects, and so on.

site

>   The `site` module performs site-specific packages' initialization. This module is
>   automatically imported during initialization.

user

>   The `user` module is a user-specific mechanism that allows one user to have a standard
>   and customized configuration file.

__builtin__

>   The `__builtin__` module is a set of `built-in` functions that gives access to all
>   `built-in` Python identifiers. You don't have to import this module because Python
>   automatically imports it.
>
>   Most of the content of this module is listed and explained in the section "Built-In
>   Functions" of Chapter 2, "Language Review."

__main__

>   The `__main__` module is the top-level script environment object in which the
>   interpreter's main program executes. This is how the `if __name__ == '__main__'`
>   code fragment works.

The String Group

This group is responsible for many kinds of string services available. These modules
provide access to several types of string manipulation operations.

Note that since release 2.0, all these functions are tied directly to *string* objects, as
methods. The `string` module is still around only for backward compatibility.

string

The `string` module supports common string operations by providing several functions and constants that manipulate Python strings.

`string.split()`
This function splits a `string` into a list. If the `delimiter` is omitted, white-spaces are used.

basic syntax: `string.split(string [,delimiter])`

```
>>> print string,split("a b c")
["a","b","c"]
```

`string.atof()`
It converts a `string` to a floating number.

basic syntax: `string.atof(string)`

`string.atoi()`
It converts a `string` to an integer. `atoi` takes an optional second argument: `base`. If omitted, the start of the string (for instance, `0x` for hexadecimal) is used to determine the base.

basic syntax: `string.atoi(string[, base])`

`string.atol()`
It converts a `string` to a long integer. `atol` takes an optional second argument: `base`. If omitted, the start of the string (for instance, `0x` for hexadecimal) is used to determine the basic syntax: `string.atol(string[, base])`

`string.upper()`
It converts a `string` to uppercase.

basic syntax: `string.upper(string)`

`string.find()`
It returns the index position of the `substring` within `string`. Optionally, you can specify the string's range that should be used in the search.

basic syntax: `string.find(string, substring[, start [,end]])`

`string.join()`
This function joins the *string* elements of a *list* using separator to separate them.

basic syntax: `string.join(`*list, separator*`)`

`string.capitalize()`
It capitalizes the first character of *string*.

basic syntax: `string.capitalize(`*string*`)`

`string.capwords()`
This function capitalizes the first letter of each word in `string` and removes repeated, leading, and trailing whitespace.

basic syntax: `string.capwords(`*string*`)`

`string.lower()`
It converts all characters in *string* to lowercase.

basic syntax: `string.lower(`*string*`)`

`string.lstrip()`,`string.rstrip()` **and** `string.strip()`
These functions remove leading and/or trailing whitespace from *string*.

basic syntaxes:

```
string.lstrip(string)
string.rstrip(string)
string.strip(string)
```

`string.ljust()`,`string.rjust()` **and** `string.center()`
These functions define the alignment of *string* within a variable of *width* characters.

basic syntaxes:

```
string.ljust(string, width)
string.rjust(string, width)
string.center(string, width)
```

`string.replace()`
It replaces a *maximum* number of occurrences of *oldtext* with *newtext* in *string*. If *maximum* is omitted, all occurrences are replaced.

basic syntax: `string.replace(`*string, oldtext, newtext [,maximum]*`)`

`string.zfill()`
It inserts zeros on the left side of a `string` that has `width` characters.

basic syntax: `string.zfill(`*`string, width`*`)`

Next, I list a few constants that can be used to test whether a certain variable is part of a specific domain:

```
>>> import string
>>> string.digits
"0123456789"
>>> string.octdigits
"01234567"
>>> string.uppercase
"ABCDEFGHIJKLMNOPQRSTUVWXY"
>>> string.hexdigits
"0123456789abcdefABCDEF"
>>> string.lowercase
"abcdefghijklmnopqrstuvwxy"
```

Let's write an example that uses `string.uppercase`:

```
>>> text = "F"
>>> if text in string.uppercase:
...     print "%s is in uppercase format" % text
...
"F is in uppercase format"
```

`string.maketrans()`
Returns a translation table that maps each character in the *from* string into the character at the same position in the *to* string. Then this table is passed to the translate function. Note that both *from* and *to* must have the same length.

basic syntax: `string.maketrans(`*`from, to`*`)`

`string.translate()`
Based on the given table, it replaces all the informed characters, according to the table created by the `string.maketrans` function. Optionally, it deletes from the given string all characters that are presented in `charstodelete`.

basic syntax: `string.translate(`*`string, table[, charstodelete]`*`)`

re

The `re` module performs Perl-style regular expression operations in strings, such as matching and replacement.

> **Tip**
> As a suggestion, always use `raw string` syntax when working with regular expression because it makes the work of handling special characters simpler.

```
>>> import re
>>> data = r"Andre Lessa"
>>> data = re.sub("Lessa", "L.", data)
>>> print data
Andre L.
```

See Chapter 9, "Other Advanced Topics," for more details about creating regular expression patterns.

> **Note**
> It is expected that in version 1.6, the `re` module will be changed to a front end to the new `sre` module.

regex

The `regex` module is an obsolete module since Python version 1.5. This module used to support regular expression search and match operations.

If necessary, you can use the `regex-to-re` HOWTO to learn how to migrate from the `regex` module to the `re` module. Check out the address `http://www.python.org/doc/howto/regex-to-re/`.

regsub

The `regsub` module is another obsolete module. It also handles string operations (such as substitution and splitting) by using regular expressions. The functions in this module are not thread-safe, so be careful.

struct

The `struct` module interprets strings as packed binary data. It processes binary files using the functions `pack()`,`unpack()`, and `calcsize()`. This module allows users to write platform-independent, binary-file manipulation code when using the big-endian or little-endian format characters. Using the native formats does not guarantee platform independence.

`fpformat`

The `fpformat` module provides functions that deal with floating point numbers and conversions.

`StringIO`

The `StringIO` module creates a string object that behaves like a file, but actually, it reads and writes data from string buffers. The `StringIO` class, which is exposed by the `StringIO` module supports all the standard file methods.

```
>>> import StringIO
>>> str = StringIO.StringIO("Line 1\nLine 2\nLine 3")
>>> str.readlines()
['Line1\012', 'Line2\012', 'Line3']
```

An additional method provided by this class is `StringIO.getvalue()`

It returns and closes the `string object`.

basic syntax: `variable = stringobject.getvalue()`

```
>>> import StringIO
>>> text = "Line 1\nLine 2\nLine 3"
>>> str = StringIO.StringIO()
>>> str.write(text)
>>> result = str.getvalue()
"Line 1\012Line 2\012Line 3"
```

`cStringIO`

The `cStringIO` is a faster version of the `StringIO` module. The difference is that you cannot subclass this module. It is necessary to use `StringIO` instead.

Miscellaneous

This group handles many functions that are available for all Python versions.

`math`

The `math` module provides standard mathematical functions and constants. It doesn't accept complex numbers, only integers and floats. Check out the following example:

```
import math
>>> math.cos(180)
```

```
-0.598460069058
>>> math.sin(90)
0.893996663601
>>> math.sqrt(64)
8.0
>>> math.log(10)
2.30258509299
>>> math.pi       # The mathematical constant pi
3.14159265359
>>> math.e        # The mathematical constant e
2.71828182846
```

cmath

The cmath module also provides standard mathematical functions and constants. However, its implementation enables it to accept complex numbers as arguments. All the returned values are expressed as complex numbers.

random

The random module generates pseudo-random numbers. This module implements all the randomizing functions provided by the whrandom module plus several pseudo-random real number generators. These random modules aren't very secure for encryption purposes.

random.choice()
It randomly picks one element from list.

basic syntax: random.choice(*list*)

```
>>> lst = ["A","l","b","a","t","r","o","s","s","!","!"]
>>> while lst:
...     element = random.choice(lst)
...     lst.remove(element)
...     print element,            # inserts a linefeed
...
b l o A s r ! ! t s a
```

random.random()
It returns a random floating-point number between 0.0 and 1.0.

basic syntax: random.random()

```
random.randint()
```
It returns a random integer n, where x <= N <= y.

basic syntax: `random.randint(x,y)`

whrandom

The `whrandom` module provides a Wichmann-Hill floating-point pseudo-random number generator. This module is mostly useful when you need to use multiple independent number generators.

```
whrandom.whrandom()
```
This function initializes multiple random generators using the same seed.

```
>>> import whrandom
>>> rga = whrandom.whrandom(2,1,3)
>>> rgb = whrandom.whrandom(2,1,3)
>>> rga.random()
0.0337928613026
>>> rgb.random()
0.0337928613026
```

bisect

The `bisect` module has an array bisection algorithm that provides support for keeping lists in sorted order without the need for sorting them out all the time.

array

The `array` module is a high efficiency array implementation that handles large lists of objects. The array type is defined at the time of creation.

By using this module, you can create an `ArrayType` object that behaves exactly like any other list, except that it isn't recommended for storing elements of different types.

```
>>> import array
>>> s = "This is a string"
>>> a = array.array("c", s)
>>> a[5:7] = array.array("c", "was")
>>> print a.tostring()
This was a string
```

Note that `NumPy` provides a superior array implementation, which can be used for more than just numeric algorithms.

Note that Python 2.0 has improved the `array` module, and new methods were added to its array objects, including: `count()`, `extend()`, `index()`, `pop()`, and `remove()`.

ConfigParser

The `ConfigParser` module is a basic configuration file parser that handles structures similar to those found in the Microsoft Windows INI file.

> **Note**
> Note that as of Release 2.0, the `ConfigParser` module is also able to write config files as well as read them.

fileinput

The `fileinput` module helps you by writing a loop that reads the contents of a file, line by line.

```
>>> import fileinput
>>> for line in fileinput.input("readme.txt"):
...         if line.isfirstline:
...             print "<< This is the first line >>"
...             print "filename = %s" % line.filename
...             print " -------------------------"
...         else:
...             print "<< This is the line number %d>>" % line.lineno
...         print line
...
```

calendar

The `calendar` module provides general calendar-related functions that emulate the UNIX `cal` program, allowing you to output calendars, among other things.

cmd

The `cmd` module is a simple interface used as a framework for building command line interpreters and shells. You just need to subclass its `cmd.Cmd` class in order to create your own customized environment.

shlex

The `shlex` module helps you write simple lexical analyzers (tokenizers) for syntaxes that are similar to the UNIX shell.

Generic Operational System

This group of services provides interfaces to operating system features that you can use in almost every platform. Most of Python's operating system modules are based on the Posix interface.

os

The os module is a portable OS API that searches for Operating-System–dependent built-in modules (mac, posix, nt), and exports their functionality using the same interface. Certain tools are available only on platforms that support them. However, it is highly recommended that you use this module instead of the platform-specific modules, which are really an implementation detail of os. By using the os module, you make your program more portable.

os.environ
This is a *dictionary* that contains all the environment variables.

You can search for a specific variable:

```
>>> import os
>>> path = os.environ["PATH"]     #USER, EDITOR, etc...
```

or list all of them:

```
>>> for key in os.environ.keys():
...         print key, " = " , os.environ[key]
...
```

os.name
It returns the name of the current system.

```
>>> name = os.name        # "posix","dos","mac","nt"
nt
```

os.getcwd()
This function returns the current working directory.

```
>>> os.getcwd()
'C:\\Program Files\\Python'
```

os.curdir

This is a simple constant that returns the OS-specific string used to identify the current directory.

```
>>> os.curdir
'.'
```

os.listdir()

If `directory` is omitted, it lists the filenames of the current directory. Otherwise, it lists the filenames of `directory`.

basic syntax: os.listdir(*[directory]*)

```
>>> files = os.listdir(os.curdir)
```

os.rename()

It renames a file.

basic syntax: os.rename(*oldfile, newfile*)

os.chmod()

It changes the `file` mode. This is a UNIX command.

basic syntax: os.chmod(*file, mode*)

os.system()

It opens an Operating System subshell and executes the command.

basic syntax: os.system(*command*)

```
>>> os.system("rm -rf " + filename)
```

os.popen()

This is a UNIX function that returns a file-like object. It allows you to execute a `shell` command and read the standard output of external pipes (by setting `mode` to r) or write to their standard input (by setting `mode` to w). The default mode is r. Note that even though popen is a UNIX function, it is also implemented on the other Python ports.

basic syntax: os.popen(*shell command, mode*)

```
>>> file = os.popen('sed \'s/yes/no/g' > output','w')
>>> file.write("yes\n")
>>>
>>> file = os.popen('cat manual.txt', 'r')
>>> f = file.read()
```

`os.remove()`
It deletes a `file`.

basic syntax: `os.remove(file)`

`os.mkdir()`
It creates a new `directory`.

basic syntax: `os.mkdir(directory)`

`os.rmdir()`
It removes an existing `directory`.

basic syntax: `os.rmdir(directory)`

`os.removedirs()`
It is a wrapper for `rmdir` that deletes everything under the `directory`.

basic syntax: `os.removedirs(directory)`

`os.path`

The `os.path` is a module imported by the `os` module that exposes useful common functions to manipulate pathnames. Remember that you don't have to explicitly import `os.path`. You get it for free when you import `os`.

`os.path.exists()`
It returns `true` if `path` really exists.

basic syntax: `os.path.exists(path)`

`os.path.isfile()`
It returns `true` if the specified `path` is a file.

basic syntax: `os.path.isfile(path)`

`os.path.isdir()`
It returns `true` if the specified `path` is a directory.

basic syntax: `os.path.isdir(path)`

`os.path.split()`

It splits `filename`, returning a tuple that contains the directory structure and filename, which together combine the original `filename` argument.

basic syntax: `os.path.split(filename)`

dircache

The `dircache` module reads directory listings using a cache. Note that this module will be replaced by the new module `filecmp` in Python 1.6.

stat

The `stat` module works along with the `os` module by interpreting information about existing files that is extracted by the `os.stat()` function and stored on a tuple structure. This tuple contains the `file size`, the `file owner group`, the file `owner name`, the `last accessed` and `last modified` dates, and its `mode`.

statcache

The `statcache` module is a simple optimization of the `os.stat()` function.

statvfs

The `statvfs` module stores constants that are used to interpret the results of a call to the `os.statvfs()` function. By the way, the `os.statvfs` provides information about your file system.

```
>>> import statvfs, os
>>> stat = os.statvfs(".")
>>> maxfnl = stat[statvfs.F_NAMEMAX]
>>> print "%d is the maximum file name length" % maxfnl
>>> print "that is allowed on your file system."
255
```

cmp

The `cmp` module is used to compare files. Note that this module will be replaced by the new module `filecmp` in Python 1.6.

cmpcache

The `cmpcache` module is a more efficient version of the `cmp` module for file comparisons. Note that this module will be replaced by the new module `filecmp` in Python 1.6.

time

The time module exposes functions for time access and conversion. It is important to remember that there are no Year 2000 issues in the Python language.

time.time()
It returns the current timestamp in seconds since the UNIX epoch began (start of 1970, UTC - Universal Time Coordinated).

basic syntax: time.time()

time.localtime()
It converts a time expressed in seconds into a time tuple. This tuple has the following format: (4digitsyear, month, day, hour, minute, second, day of week, day of year, daylight savings flag).

basic syntax: time.locatime(*seconds*)

time.asctime()
It converts a time tuple into a 24-character string.

basic syntax: time.asctime(*tuple*)

```
>>> import time
>>> time.time()
957044415.14
>>> time.localtime(time.time())
(2000, 4, 29, 17, 42, 14, 5, 120, 1)
>>> time.asctime(time.localtime(time.time()))
'Sat Apr 29 17:42:59 2000'
```

time.sleep()
It suspends the execution of a program for a specific number of seconds.

basic syntax: time.sleep(*seconds*)

```
>>> import time
>>> time.sleep(10)      # waits for 10 seconds
```

sched

The sched module implements a general-purpose event scheduler.

getpass

The `getpass` module implements a portable function that enables the user to type a password without echoing the entry in the screen.

basic syntax: `getpass.getpass([prompt])`

This module also provides a function to collect information about the user's login.

basic syntax: `getpass.getuser()`

```
import getpass
defaultpwd = "Ahhhhh"
user = getpass.getuser()
print "Hello %s," % user
pass = getpass.getpass("Please, type the password. ")
if pass == defaultpwd:
     print "Welcome back to the system!!
else:
     print r"You've just activated the detonation process.Sorry"
```

curses

The `curses` module is a terminal independent I/O interface to the curses UNIX library.

For more details, check out the `curses` HOWTO at
`http://www.python.org/doc/howto/curses/curses.html`.

getopt

The `getopt` module is a parser for command-line options and arguments (`sys.argv`). This module provides the standard C `getopt` functionality.

```
1: >>> import getopt
2: >>> args = ['-h','-r','origin.txt','—file','work.txt','755','777']
3: >>> opts, pargs = getopt.getopt(args, 'hr:', ['file='])
4: >>> opts
5: [('-h', ''), ('-r','origin.txt') , ('—file','work.txt')]
6: >>> pargs
7: ['755','777']
```

Before transporting arguments to this function, line 2 shows you that single options must be preceded by a single hyphen and long options must be preceded by double hyphens.

In line 3, note that single options that require an argument must end with a colon. On the other hand, long options that require an argument must end with an equal sign.

The getopt.getopt() returns two values: A tuple that contains pairs of (option, argument) values (line 5), and a list of standalone arguments that aren't associated with any options (line 7).

tempfile

The tempfile module generates unique temporary filenames based on templates defined by the variables tempfile.tempdir and tempfile.template.

tempfile.mktemp()
This function returns a temporary filename. It doesn't physically create or remove files.

basic syntax: filename = tempfile.mktemp()

```
>>> import tempfile, os
>>> temp = tempfile.mktemp()
>>> open(temp, 'w')
>>> os.close(file)
>>> os.remove(file)
```

tempfile.TemporaryFile()
This function returns a file object that is saved in your temporary local folder (/tmp or c:/temp, for example). The system removes this file after it gets closed.

basic syntax: fileobject = tempfile.TemporaryFile()

errno

The errno module makes available the standard errno system symbols, such as EACCES, EADDRINUSE, and EDEADLOCK.

Each symbol is associated to a constant error code value.

```
>>> import errno
>>> errno.ELOOP
10062
```

More information about this module and its symbols is provided in Chapter 4.

glob

The `glob` module finds and returns pathnames matching a specific `pattern`, just like the `UNIX shell` does.

basic syntax: glob.glob(*pattern*)

```
>>> import glob
>>> lst = glob.glob("c:\\*.txt")
>>> print lst
['c:\\FRUNLOG.TXT', 'c:\\DETLOG.TXT', 'c:\\BOOTLOG.TXT', 'c:\\SETUPLOG.TXT',
 'c:\\NETLOG.TXT', 'c:\\RESETLOG.TXT']
```

fnmatch

The `fnmatch` module uses wildcards to provide support for UNIX shell-style filename pattern matching. These wildcards are different from those normally used by the `re` module.

fnmatch.fnmatch()
This function returns 1 (`true`) if the provided filename matches the pattern defined.

basic syntax: fnmatch.fnmatch(*filename, pattern*)

```
>>> import fnmatch
>>> fnmatch.fnmatch("foo.gif", "*.gif")
1
```

fnmatch.translate()
This function converts a `fnmatch-style` pattern into a regular expression.

basic syntax: variable = fnmatch.translate(*pattern*)

```
>>> import fnmatch
>>> regexpr = fnmatch.translate("*.txt")
>>> print regexpr
.*\.txt$
```

shutil

The `shutil` module provides high-level file operations. Essentially, it offers many file-copying functions and one directory removal function.

```
shutil.copyfile()
```
It makes a straight binary copy of the source file, calling it `newcopy`.

basic syntax: `shutil.copyfile(source, newcopy)`

```
shutil.rmtree()
```
It deletes the `path` directory, including all of its subdirectories, recursively. If `ignore_errors` is set to `0`, errors are ignored. Otherwise, the `onerror` function argument is called to handle the error. If the clause `onerror` is set to `None`, an exception is raised when an error occurs.

basic syntax: `shutil.rmtree(path, ignore_errors=0, onerror=None)`

locale

The `locale` module provides access to the `POSIX` locale mechanism, enabling internationalization services. This module defines a set of parameters that describe the representation of strings, time, numbers, and currency.

The good thing about using this module is that programmers don't have to worry about the specifics of each country where their applications are executed.

mutex

The `mutex` module defines a `mutex` class that allows mutual-exclusion support via acquiring and releasing locks.

Optional Operational System

The next set of modules implements interfaces to optional operational system features. Keep in mind that these features are not available for all platforms.

signal

The `signal` module provides mechanisms to access `POSIX` signals in order to let the programmer set her own signal handlers for asynchronous events.

A good example is the case when it is necessary to monitor the users, checking whether they press CTRL+C to stop the execution of a program. Although Python provides default handlers, you can overwrite them by creating your own.

```python
import signal, sys
def signal_handler(signal, frame):
    print "You have pressed CTRL+C"
```

```
        signal.signal(signal.SIGINT, signal.SIG_IGN)
        print "Now, you can\'t stop the script with CTRL+C " \
        "for the next 10 seconds!"
        signal.signal(signal.SIGALRM, alarm_handler)
        signal.alarm(10)
        while 1:
            print "I am looping"

def alarm_handler(signal, frame):
    print "Now you can leave the program"
    sys.exit(0)


signal.signal(signal.SIGINT, signal_handler)
print "Press CTRL+C"
while 1:
    continue
```

Some of the available signals you can use are as follows:

SIGALRM	Alarm
SIGCONT	Continue
SIGING	Terminal interrupt character
SIGQUIT	Terminal Quit character
SIGTERM	Termination
SIG_IGN	Signal handler that ignores a signal

socket

The `socket` module provides access to a low-level BSD socket-style network interface.

See Chapter 10, "Basic Network Background," for details.

select

The `select` module is used to implement polling and to multiplex processing across multiple I/O streams without using threads or subprocesses. It provides access to the BSD `select()` function interface, available in most operating systems.

On windows it only works for `sockets`. On UNIX, it is used for `pipes`, `sockets`, `files`, and so on.

See Chapter 10 for details.

thread

The thread module supports lightweight process threads. It offers a low-level interface for working with multiple threads.

See Chapter 9 for details.

threading

The threading module provides high-level threading interfaces on top of the thread module.

See Chapter 9 for details.

Queue

The Queue module is a synchronized *queue class* that is used in thread programming to move Python objects between multiple threads.

See Chapter 9 for details.

anydbm

The anydbm module is a generic dbm-style interface to access variants of the dbm database.

See Chapter 8 for details.

dumbdbm

The dumbdbm module is a simple, portable, and slow database implemented entirely in Python.

See Chapter 8 for details.

dbhash

The dbhash module provides a function that offers a dbm-style interface to access the BSD database library.

See Chapter 8 for details.

whichdb

The whichdb module provides a function that guesses which dbm module (dbm, gdbm, or dbhash) should be used to open a specific database.

See Chapter 8 for details.

bsddb

The `bsddb` module provides an interface to access routines from the Berkeley `db` library.

See Chapter 8 for details.

zlib

The `zlib` module provides functions that allow compression and decompression using the `zlib` library. The compression that is provided by this module is compatible with `gzip`.

For more details check out the `zlib` library home page at
`http://www.cdrom.com/pub/infozip/lib`.

gzip

The `gzip` module offers support for `gzip` files. This module provides functions that allow compression and decompression using the GNU compression program `gzip`.

This module has a class named `GzipFile` that can be used to read and write files compatible with the GNU `gzip` program. The objects that are generated by this class behave just like file objects. The only exception is that the `seek` and `tell` methods aren't part of the standard implementation.

```
>>> import gzip
>>> gzipfile = gzip.GzipFile("backup.gz")
>>> contents = gzipfile.read()
>>> print contents
```

rlcompleter

The `rlcompleter` module provides a *completion function* for the `readline` module.

The `readline` module is a UNIX module that is automatically imported by `rlcompleter`. It uses a compatible GNU readline library to activate input editing on UNIX.

Debugger

The `pdb` module defines an interactive source code debugger for Python programs. You can use this tool to verify and modify variables and to set and examine breakpoints. It allows inspection of stack frames, single stepping of source lines, and code evaluation. This module is based on the module bdb, which implements a generic Python debugger base class.

See Chapter 17,"Development Tools," for details.

Profiler

The profiler module is a code execution profiler. This tool can be used to analyze statistics about the runtime performance of a program. It helps you to identify what parts of your program are running slower than the expected and what can be done to optimize it. The pstats module works along with the profiler module in order to analyze the collected data.

See Chapter 17 for details.

Internet Protocol and Support

These are the modules that implement internet protocols and support for related technology.

For examples and details about the following modules, refer to Chapters 10–12.

cgi

The cgi module is used to implement CGI (common gateway interface) scripts and process form handling in Web applications that are invoked by an HTTP server.

See Chapter 12, "Scripting Programming," for details.

urllib

The urllib module is a high-level interface to retrieve data across the World Wide Web. It opens any URL using sockets.

See Chapters 10 and 12 for details.

httplib

The httplib module implements the client side of the HTTP (Hypertext Transfer Protocol) protocol.

> **Tip**
> HTTP is a simple text-based protocol used for World Wide Web applications.

See Chapters 10 and 12 for details.

ftplib

The `ftplib` module implements the client side of the FTP protocol. You can use it for mirroring FTP sites. Usually the `urllib` module is used as an outer interface to `ftplib`.

See Chapters 10 and 12 for details.

gopherlib

The `gopherlib` module is a minimal client-side implementation of the `Gopher` protocol.

poplib

The `poplib` module provides a low-level, client-side interface for connecting to a POP3 server using a client protocol, as defined in the Internet standard RFC 1725.

See Chapter 10 for details.

imaplib

The `impalib` module provides a low-level, client-side interface for connecting to an IMAP4 mail server using the `IMAP4rev1` client protocol, as defined in the Internet standard RFC 2060.

See Chapter 10 for details.

nntplib

The `nntplib` module implements a low-level interface to the client side of the NNTP (Network News Transfer Protocol) protocol—a service mostly known for implementing newsgroups.

See Chapter 10 for details.

smtplib

The `smtplib` module provides a low-level client interface to the SMTP protocol that can be used to send email to any machine in the Internet that has an SMTP or ESMTP listener daemon.

See Chapter 10 for details.

telnetlib

The `telnetlib` module implements a client for the telnet protocol.

urlparse

The `urlparse` module manipulates a URL string, parsing it into tuples. It breaks a URL up into components, combines them back, and converts relative addresses to absolute addresses.

See Chapters 10 and 12 for details.

SocketServer

The `SocketServer` module exposes a framework that simplifies the task of writing network servers. Rather than having to implement servers using the low-level socket module, this module provides four classes that implement interfaces to the mostly used protocols: `TCPServer`, `UDPServer`, `UnixStreamServer`, and `UnixDatagramServer`. All these classes process requests synchronously.

See Chapter 10 for details.

BaseHTTPServer

The `BaseHTTPServer` module defines two base classes for implementing basic HTTP servers (also known as Web servers).

See Chapter 10 for details.

SimpleHTTPServer

The `SimpleHTTPServer` module provides a simple HTTP server request-handler class. It has an interface compatible with the `BaseHTTPServer` module that enables it to serve files from a base directory.

See Chapter 10 for details.

CGIHTTPServer

The `CGIHTTPServer` module defines a simple HTTP server request-handler class. It has an interface compatible with `BaseHTTPServer` that enables it to serve files from a base directory, but it can also run CGI scripts.

See Chapters 10 and 12 for details.

asyncore

The `asyncore` module provides the basic infrastructure for writing and handling asyncronous socket service clients and servers that are the result of a series of events dispatched by an event loop.

See Chapter 10 for details.

Internet Data Handling

This group covers modules that support encoding and decoding of data handling formats and that are largely used in Internet applications.

For more details and examples about using these modules, see Chapter 13, "Data Manipulation."

sgmllib

The `sgmllib` module is an SGML (Standard Generalized Markup Language) parser subset. Although it has a simple implementation, it is powerful enough to build the HTML parser.

htmllib

The `htmllib` module defines a parser for text files formatted in HTML (Hypertext Markup Language).

htmlentitydefs

The `htmlentitydefs` module is a dictionary that contains all the definitions for the general entities defined by HTML 2.0.

xmllib

The `xmllib` module defines a parser for text files formatted in XML (Extensible Markup Language).

formatter

The formatter module is used for generic output formatting by the HTMLParser class of the htmllib module.

rfc822

The rfc822 module parses mail headers that are defined by the Internet standard RFC 822. The headers of this form are used in a number of contexts including mail handling and in the HTTP protocol.

mimetools

The mimetools module provides utility tools for parsing and manipulation of MIME multipart and encoded messages.

> **Tip**
> MIME (multipurpose Internet mail extensions) is a standard for sending multipart multimedia data through Internet mail.

MimeWrite

The MimeWrite module implements a generic file-writing class that is used to create MIME-encoded multipart files.

multifile

The multifile module enables you to treat distinct parts of a text file as file-like input objects. Usually, this module uses text files that are found in MIME encoded messages.

binhex

The binhex module encodes and decodes files in binhex4 format. This format is commonly used to represent files on Macintosh systems.

uu

The uu module encodes and decodes files in uuencode format. This module does its job by transferring binary data over an ASCII-only connection.

binascii

The binascii module implements methods to convert data between binary and various ASCII-encoded binary representations.

base64

The `base64` module performs base64 encoding and decoding of arbitrary binary strings into text strings that can be safely emailed or posted. This module is commonly used to encode binary data in mail attachments.

xdrlib

The `xdrlib` module is used extensively in applications involving Remote Procedure Calls (RPC). Similarly, it is often used as a portable way to encode binary data for use in networked applications. This module is able to encode and decode XDR data because it supports the external data representation (XDR) Standard.

mailcap

The `mailcap` module is used to read `mailcap` files and to configure how MIME-aware applications react to files with different MIME types.

> **Note**
> `mailcap` files are used to inform mail readers and Web browsers how to process files with different MIME types.

mimetypes

The `mimetypes` module supports conversions between a filename or URL and the MIME type associated with the filename extension.

Essentially, it is used to guess the MIME type associated with a file, based on its extension, as shown in Table 3.1.

Table 3.1   *Some MIME Type Examples*

Filename Extension	MIME Type Associated
`.html`	text/html
`.rdf`	application/xml
`.gif`	image/gif

quopri

The `quopri` module performs encoding and decoding of MIME quoted printable data. This format is primarily used to encode text files.

mailbox

The mailbox module implements classes that allow easy and uniform access to read various mailbox formats in a UNIX system.

mhlib

The mhlib module provides a Python interface to access MH folders and their contents.

mimify

The mimify module has functions to convert and process simple and multipart mail messages to/from the MIME format.

netrc

The netrc module parses, processes, and encapsulates the .netrc configuration file format used by the UNIX FTP program and other FTP clients.

Restricted Execution

Restricted Execution is the basic framework in Python that allows the segregation of trusted and untrusted code. The next modules prevent access to critical operations mostly because a program running in trusted mode can create an execution environment in which untrusted code can be executed with limited privileges.

rexec

The rexec module implements a basic restricted execution framework by encapsulating, in a class, the attributes that specify the capabilities for the code to execute. Code executed in this restricted environment will only have access to modules and functions that are believed to be safe.

Bastion

The Bastion module provides restricted access to objects. This module is able to provide a way to forbid access to certain attributes of an object.

Multimedia

The next several modules implement algorithms and interfaces that are mainly useful for multimedia applications.

audioop

The `audioop` module manipulates raw audio data, such as samples and fragments.

imageop

The `imageop` module manipulates raw image data by operating on images consisting of 8- or 32-bit pixels stored in Python strings.

aifc

The `aifc` module is devoted to audio file access for `AIFF` and `AIFC` formats. This module offers support for reading and writing files in those formats.

sunau

The `sunau` module provides an interface to read and write files in the `Sun AU` sound format.

wave

The `wave` module provides an interface to read and write files in the `WAV` sound format. It doesn't support compression/decompression, but it supports mono/stereo channels.

chunk

The `chunk` module provides an interface for reading files that use `EA IFF 85` data chunks. This format is used in the `AIFF`/`AIFF-C`, `RMFF`, and `TIFF` formats.

colorsys

The `colorsys` module defines bidirectional conversions of color values between colors expressed in `RGB` and three other coordinate systems: `YIQ`, `HLS`, and `HSV`.

rgbimg

The `rgbimg` module allows Python programs to read and write SGI `imglib .rgb` files—without requiring an SGI environment.

imghdr

The `imghdr` module determines the type of an image contained in a file or byte stream.

sndhdr

The `sndhdr` module implements functions that try to identify the type of sound contained in a file.

Cryptographic

The following modules implement various algorithms of cryptographic nature.

For more information about this topic, you can also check out the following Web site:

`http://starship.python.net/crew/amk/python/crypto.html`

It contains cryptographic modules written by Andrew Kuchling for reading and decrypting PGP files.

md5

The md5 module is a cryptographically secure hashing algorithm that implements an interface to RSA's MD5 message digest algorithm. Based on a given string, it calculates a 128-bit message signature.

sha

The sha module is a message digest algorithm that implements an interface to NIST's secure hash algorithm, known as sha. This module takes a sequence of input text and generates a 160-bit hash value.

mpz

The mpz module implements the interface to part of the GNU multiple precision integer libraries.

rotor

The rotor module implements a permutation-based encryption and decryption engine. (The design is derived from the Enigma device, a machine used by the Germans to encrypt messages during WWII.)

```
>>> import rotor
>>> message = raw_input("Enter the message")
>>> key = raw_input("Enter the key")
>>> newr = rotor.newrotor(key)
>>> enc = newr.encrypt(message)
>>> print "The encoded message is: ", repr(enc)
>>> dec = newr.decrypt(enc)
>>> print "The decoded message is: ", repr(dec)
```

UNIX Specific

This group of modules exposes interfaces to features that are specific to the UNIX environment.

posix

The `posix` module provides access to the most common POSIX system calls. Do not import this module directly; instead, I suggest that you import the `os` module.

```
>>> uid = posix.getuid()        # returns the user id
```

pwd

The `pwd` module provides access to the UNIX `passwd` (password database) file routines.

pwd.getpwnam()

Returns the password of a given user.

basic syntax: `password = getpwnam(username)[1]`

```
>>> import pwd, getpass
>>> pw = pwd.getpwnam(getpass.getuser())[1]
```

grp

The `grp` module provides access to the UNIX group database.

crypt

The `crypt` module offers an interface to the UNIX `crypt` routine. This module has a hash function based on a modified DES algorithm that is used to check UNIX passwords.

To encrypt:

```
newpwd = crypt.crypt(passwordstring, salt)
```

`salt` consists of a two-random character seed used to initialize the algorithm.

To verify:

```
If newpwd == crypt.crypt(passwordstring, newpwd[:2])
import getpass
```

```
import pwd
import crypt

uname = getpass.getuser()        # get username from environment
pw = getpass.getpass()           # get entered password

realpw = pwd.getpwnam(uname)[1]  # get real password
entrpw = crypt.crypt(pw, realpw[:2])    # returns an encrypted password
if realpw == entrpw:             # compare passwords
    print "Password Accepted"
else:
    print "Get lost."
```

dlmodule

The `dlmodule` module exposes an interface to call C functions in shared objects that handle dynamically linked libraries. Note that this module is not needed for dynamic loading of Python modules. The documentation says that it is a highly experimental and dangerous device for calling arbitrary C functions in arbitrary shared libraries.

dbm

The `dbm` module is a database interface that implements a simple UNIX `(n)dbm` library access method. `dbm` objects behave like dictionaries in which keys and values must contain string objects. This module allows strings, which might encode any python objects, to be archived in indexed files.

See Chapter 8 for details.

gdbm

The `gdbm` module is similar to the `dbm` module. However, their files are incompatible. This module provides a reinterpretation of the GNU `dbm` library.

See Chapter 8 for details.

termios

The `termios` module provides an interface to the POSIX calls for managing the behavior of the POSIX tty.

TERMIOS

The `TERMIOS` module stores constants required while using the `termios` module.

tty

The `tty` module implements terminal controlling functions for switching the `tty` into `cbreak` and `raw` modes.

pty

The `pty` module offers utilities to handle the pseudo-terminal concept.

fcntl

The `fcntl` module performs file and I/O control on UNIX file descriptors. This module implements The `fcntl()` and `ioctl()` system calls, which can be used for file locking.

pipes

The `pipes` module offers an interface to UNIX shell pipelines. By abstracting the pipeline concept, it enables you to create and use your own pipelines.

posixfile

The `posixfile` module provides file-like objects with support for locking. It seems that this module will become obsolete soon.

resource

The `resource` module offers mechanisms for measuring and controlling system resources used by a program.

nis

The `nis` module is a thin wrapper around Sun's NIS library.

syslog

The `syslog` module implements an interface to the UNIX `syslog` library routines. This module allows you to trace the activity of your programs in a way similar to many daemons running on a typical GNU/Linux system.

```
import syslog
syslog.syslog('This script was activated' )
print "I am a lumberjack, and I am OK!"
syslog.syslog('Shutting down script' )
```

Use the command `tail -f /var/log/messages` to read what your script is writing to the log.

popen2

The `popen2` module allows you to create processes by running external commands and to connect their accessible streams (`stdin`, `stdout`, and `stderr`) using pipes.

```
import os,popen2
str1 = os.popen('ls','r').read()
print str1
out1,in1 = popen2.popen2('cat')
in1.write(str1)
in1.close()
str2 = out1.read()
out1.close()
print str2
```

> **Note**
> Note that as of release 2.0, functions popen2, popen3, popen4 are supported on the Windows Platform.

commands

The `commands` module provides functions that execute external commands under UNIX by implementing wrapping functions for the `os.popen()` function. Those functions get a system command as a `string` argument and return any output generated by that command.

SGI IRIX Specific

The following features are specific to SGI's IRIX Operating System.

al

The `al` module implements access to the audio functions of the SGI Indy and Indigo workstations.

AL

The `AL` module stores constants that are used with the `al` module.

cd

The `cd` module provides an interface to the Silicon Graphics CD-ROM Library.

fl

The `fl` module provides an interface to the FORMS Library (by Mark Overmars) for GUI applications.

FL

The `FL` module stores constants that are used with the `fl` module.

flp

The `flp` module defines functions that can load stored form designs created by the form designer (`fdesign`) program that comes with the FORMS library (the `fl` module).

fm

The `fm` module implements an interface that provides access to the IRIS font manager library.

gl

The `gl` module implements an interface that provides access to the Silicon Graphics graphic library. Note that this is different for OpenGL. There is a wrapper for OpenGL called PyOpenGL. More details can be found at Chapter 14, "Python and GUIs."

DEVICE

The `DEVICE` module defines the constants that are used with the `gl` module.

GL

The `GL` module stores the constants that are used with the `gl` module.

imgfile

The `imgfile` module implements support to access SGI's `imglib` image files.

jpeg

The `jpeg` module provides image file access (read and write) to the JPEG compressor and decompressor format written by the Independent JPEG Group (IJG).

Sun OS Specific

These modules implement interfaces that are specific to the Sun OS Operating System.

sunaudiodev

The sunaudiodev module implements an interface that gives you access to the Sun audio hardware.

SUNAUDIODEV

The SUNAUDIODEV module stores the constants that are used with the sunaudiodev module.

MS Windows Specific

The next modules define interfaces that are specific to the Microsoft Windows Operating System.

msvcrt

The msvcrt module implements many functions that provide access to useful routines from the Microsoft Visual C++ runtime library.

winsound

The winsound module implements an interface that provides access to the sound-playing environment provided by Windows Platforms.

Macintosh Specific

The following modules implement specific interfaces to the Macintosh Operating System.

For more information about Macintosh module, take a look at the online Macintosh Library Reference at http://www.python.org/doc/mac.

`findertools`

The `findertools` module provides access to some of the functionality presented in the Macintosh `finder`. It launches, prints, copies, and moves files; it also restarts and shuts down the machine.

`macfs`

The `macfs` module is used to manipulate files and aliases on the Macintosh OS.

`macostools`

The `macostools` module implements functions for file manipulation on the Macintosh OS.

Undocumented Modules

Currently, the modules listed in this section don't have any official documentation. However, you might find some information about them in this book, by browsing an updated version of the online library reference, or by checking some other Web site.

Frameworks

The next modules represent some Python frameworks that don't have any official documentation yet.

> `Tkinter`—This module allows you to create GUIs (graphical user interfaces) because it implements an interface to the Tcl/Tk windowing libraries (see Chapter 15, "Tkinter," for details).

> `Tkdnd`—This module provides drag-and-drop support for `Tkinter`.

> `test`—This package is responsible for the regression-testing framework.

Miscellaneous Useful Utilities

At this time this book went to press, the following modules didn't have any official documentation.

`dircmp`
This module defines a class on which to build directory comparison tools.

tzparse
This module is an unfinished work to parse a time zone specification.

ihooks
The ihooks module is a framework that manages the co-existence of different import routines.

Platform Specific Modules

These are implementation details of the os module.

dospath, macpath, posixpath, ntpath

These modules are for their platforms what the os.path module is for the UNIX platform. They can all be used by any platform in order to handle pathnames of different platforms.

Multimedia

At the time this book went to press, the following modules didn't have any official documentation.

audiodev, sunaudio, toaiff

Obsolete

The following modules became obsolete as of release 1.6:

stdwin, soundex, cml, cmpcache, dircache, dump, find, grep, packmail, poly, zmod, strop, util, and whatsound.

Note that release 2.0 hasn't made any module obsolete. All modules that were replaced were moved to the lib-old subdirectory of the distribution. That list, includes: cmp, cmpcache, dircmp, dump, find, grep, packmail, poly, util, whatsound, zmod.

ni
Before version 1.5a4, the ni module was used to support import package statements.

dump
The dump module prints the definition of a variable. Note that this module can be substituted for the pickle module.

```
>>> import dump
>>> var = (10, 20, 30, 40)
>>> dump.dumpvar("newvar", var)
newvar = (10, 20, 30, 40)
```

Extension Modules

The following modules are obsolete tools to support GUI implementations.

stdwin—This module provides an interface to the obsolete STDWIN. STDWIN is an unsupported platform-independent GUI interface that was replaced by Tkinter.

stdwinevents—Interacts with the stdwin module by providing piping services.

New Modules on Python 2.0

Next, you a have a list of new modules that were introduced to Python recently. As always, I suggest you take a look at the 2.0 documentation for details about any given module.

atexit—Registers functions to be called when Python exits. If you already use the function sys.exitfunc(), you should change your code to import atexit, and call the function atexit.register(), passing as an argument the function that you want to call on exit.

codecs—Provides support (base classes) for Unicode encoders and decoders, and provides access to Python's codec registry. You can use the functions provided by this module to search for existing encodings, or to register new ones. Most frequently, you will adhere to the function codecs.lookup(encoding), which returns a 4-function tuple: (encoder, decoder, stream_reader, stream_writer). This module along with the unicodedata module was added as part of the new Unicode support to Python 2.0. The condec class defines the interface for stateless encoders and decoders. The following functions and classes are also available in this module.

codec.encode()—Takes a Unicode string, and returns a 2-tuple (8-bit-string, length). The length part of the tuple shows how much of the Unicode string was converted.

codec.decode()—Takes an 8-bit string, and returns a 2-tuple (ustring, length). The length part of the tuple shows how much of the 8-bit string was consumed.

codecs.stream_reader(file_object)—This is a class that supports decoding input from a stream. Objects created with this class carry the read(), readline(), and readlines() methods, which allow you to take the given encoding of the object, and read as a Unicode string.

codecs.stream_writer(file_object)—This is a class that supports encoding output to a stream. Objects created with this class carry the write() and writelines() methods, which allow you to pass Unicode string to the object, and let the object translate them to the given encoding on output.

unicodedata—This module provides access to the Unicode 3.0 database of character properties. The following functions are available:

`unicodedata.category(u'P')` returns the 2-character string 'Lu', the 'L' denoting it's a letter, and 'u' meaning that it's uppercase.

`unicodedata.bidirectional(u'\x0660')` returns 'AN', meaning that U+0660 is an Arabic number.

encodings—This is a package that supplies a wide collection of standard codecs. Currently, only the new Unicode support is provided.

distutils—Package of tools for distributing Python modules.

filecmp—This module comes into place of both the `cmp.py`, the `cmpcache.py` and `dircmp.py` modules.

gettext—Provides an interface to the GNU gettext message catalog library in order to supply internationalization (I18N) and localization (L10N) support for Python programs.

imputil—This module is an alternative API for writing customized import hooks in a simpler way. It is similar to the existing ihooks module.

linuxaudiodev—Provides audio for any platform that supports the Open Sound System (OSS). Most often, it is used to support the `/dev/audio` device on Linux boxes. This module is identical to the already existing `sunaudiodev` module.

mmap—This module works on both Windows and Unix to treat a file as a memory buffer, making it possible to map a file directly into memory, and make it behave like a mutable string.

pyexpat—This module is an interface to the Expat XML parser.

robotparser—Initially at `Tools/webchecker/`, this module parses a `robots.txt` file, which is used for writing web spiders.

sre—This module is a new implementation for handling regular expressions. Although it is still very raw, its features include: faster mechanism, and support to unicode. The idea of the development team is to reimplement the re module using sre (without making changes to the re API).

tabnanny—Originally at `Tools/scripts/`, this module checks Python sources for tab-width dependance (ambiguous indentation).

urllib2—This module is an experimental version of urllib, which will bring new and enhanced features, but will be incompatible with the current version.

UserString—This module exposes a base class for deriving objects from the string type.

xml—This package covers the whole-new XML support and it is organized in three subpackages: xml.dom, xml.sax, and xml.parsers.

webbrowser—A module that provides a platform independent API to launch a web browser on a specific URL.

_winreg—This module works as an interface to the Windows registry. It contains an enhanced set of functions that has been part of PythonWin since 1995.

zipfile—This module reads and writes zip-format archives (the format produced by PKZIP and zip applications. Not the one produced by the gzip program!).

Summary

Python's standard distribution is shipped with a rich set of libraries (also known as modules). This chapter introduces you to the practical side of several modules' utilization.

The following items are groups that organize all the modules that are mentioned in this chapter.

Python Services

The modules from this group provide access to services related to the interpreter and to Python's environment.

The String Group

This group is responsible for many kinds of string services available. Its modules provide access to several types of string manipulation operations.

Miscellaneous

This group handles many functions that are available for all Python versions, such as mathematical operations and randomizing functions.

Generic Operational System

This group of services provides interfaces to operating system features that you can use in almost every platform.

Optional Operational System

This set of modules implements interfaces to optional operational system features.

Debugger

The pdb module defines an interactive source code debugger for Python programs.

Profiler

The profiler module is a code execution profiler.

Internet Protocol and Support

These are the modules that implement internet protocols and support for related technology.

Internet Data Handling

This group covers modules that support encoding and decoding of data handling formats and that are largely used in Internet applications.

Restricted Execution

These modules prevent access to critical operations.

Multimedia

This group of modules implements algorithms and interfaces that are mainly useful for multimedia applications.

Cryptographic

These modules implement various algorithms of cryptographic nature.

OS Specific (UNIX, SGI IRIX, SUN OS, MS Windows, and Macintosh)

These groups of modules expose interfaces to features that are specific to the OS environment of each one of them.

Undocumented Modules

This group contains the modules that currently don't have any official documentation.

New Modules in Python 2.0

These are the new modules that will be part of the next release of Python.

CHAPTER 4

Exception Handling

Oh my God, he's fallen off the edge of the cartoon.

This chapter's aim is to teach you how to handle exception situations and how to manage error messages. Certainly the next couple of pages will guide you through a fantastic "catch-all-errors" kind of programming experience.

Exception Handling

Exceptions are mostly used for error handling and event notification. They work by breaking the regular flow of a program and jumping to a special set of statements that handle the exception case. Python has many standard exceptions, which are exceptions already built into the language. Python also supports user-defined exceptions, which are exceptions created by users. The provided exceptions are almost no different from user-defined exceptions—the only difference is that they are defined in one of the files in the standard library (`exceptions.py`).

Any unexpected program behavior drives the interpreter to raise an exception. Many scenarios can help an exception to be raised, such as dividing a number by zero or reading from a nonexistent file. Note that the programmer can also manually raise exceptions with the `raise` statement.

The default behavior of Python, when it encounters unhandled exceptions, is to terminate the program and to display a traceback message that describes the error condition. My goal in this chapter is to show you how to handle those exceptions.

If you don't handle exceptions in your program, Python's interpreter returns a traceback message that shows the error message, the exception type, the function that contains the error, and the line of code that has caused the error. Hence, a complete history of what has caused the error is provided.

So that you can start learning how Python raises and handles exceptions, I will define the following example:

```
>>> a = {"a":1,"b":2}
>>> def returnelement(element):
...     print a[element]
...
```

Now, we will call this function:

```
>>> print returnelement("c")
```

Note that "c" is not part of the *a* dictionary. Therefore, Python raises an exception that displays the following traceback message.

```
Traceback (innermost last):
  File "<stdin>", line 1, in ?
  File "<stdin>", line 2, in returnelement
KeyError: c
```

The last line of the traceback message tells us what exception was raised and what element has caused the exception to be triggered. If we run the previous code in the interpreter, the File clause is set to "*<stdin>*" by default because the code lines come from the keyboard and not from a file. However, if we run the code from an external file, the filename becomes part of the File clause. It is also worth mentioning that the line numbers are relative to the statement where the error occurred when the code was entered interactively. So, we get line 2 in the traceback because the exception occurred on the second line of the function, which was treated as a single statement. The outermost part of the trace says line 1 because the call to returnelement was treated as a one-line statement.

Next to the filename, we have a line number, which is the line in which the error has been triggered. Next to the line number is the name of the function that caused the error.

Tip
By handling exceptions, you can save a lot of time while testing your code.

Exceptions can be handled by using either `try`/`except` or `try`/`finally` statements. The difference between them is that an `except` clause is only executed when an exception is raised, and a `finally` clause is always executed; it doesn't matter whether an exception is raised or not. Also, the `try`/`finally` block doesn't catch the exception like `try`/`except` can.

Next is the standard structure for a `try`/`except` statement:

```
try:
    <statements>
except [<exception_name> [, <instance_variable>]]:
    <exception handling statements>
[else:
    <statements executed only when no exception is raised>]
```

The `else` block must be inserted after the last exception block, and it is only executed when the `try` block doesn't raise any errors.

In order to handle multiple exceptions, you can use multiple `except` clauses for the same `try` block.

The next example raises an error message whenever it can't find a given element.

```
>>> name = ["Andre","Renata","Joao","Rebecca"]
>>> def getname(order):
...     try:
...         if order < 10:
...             data = name[order]
...         else:
...             file = open("names.txt")
...             data = file.readline()
...             file.close()
...         return data
...     except IndexError:
...         print "This name is not in the list."
...     except IOError:
...         print "The file names.txt does not exist."
...
>>> getname(0)
"Andre"
>>> getname(8)
"This name is not in the list."
>>> getname(20)
"The file names.txt does not exist."
```

Python syntax also enables you to use a single except clause that handles all exceptions. The general syntax for the except clause for handling all exceptions is to not specify any exception types at all, such as

```
try:
    <statements>
except:
    <exception handling statements>
```

Next, you have the syntax and an example for handling multiple exception types.

```
except (exception1, exception 2, exception 3)[, variable]:
```

```
>>> name = ["Andre","Renata","Joao","Rebecca"]
>>> def getname(order):
...     try:
...         if order < 10:
...             data = name[order]
...         else:
...             file = open("names.txt")
...             data = file.readline()
...             file.close()
...         return data
...     except (IndexError, IOError):
...         print "Data not available."
...
>>> getname(8)
"Data not available."
>>> getname(20)
"Data not available."
```

You can also use try/except statements to ignore exceptions. The next structure uses a pass statement to ignore an exception whenever it gets raised. However, note that if an exception is raised, all the remaining statements in the try block will not be executed.

```
try:
    <statements>
except <exception_name>:
    pass
```

In the next example, we use exceptions not to catch and handle an unexpected error, but to ignore errors that we know might happen when the code is running. As you can see, an exception is raised every time you try to convert a *text string* into a *float* number in line 6. However the `pass` statement in line 8 simply ignores the problem.

```
 1: >>> import string
 2: >>> list = ["1","3","Monkey","Parrot","10"]
 3: >>> total = 0
 4: >>> for z in list:
 5: >>>     try:
 6: >>>             total = total + string.atof(z)
 7: >>>     except:
 8: >>>             pass
 9: >>> print total
10: 14
```

Standard Exceptions (Getting Help from Other Modules)

Apart from the `exception` module, other Python modules offer you some advanced functionality to handle exceptions. We will talk about the `sys` and the `traceback` modules.

You can use the `sys.exc_info()` thread-safe function to get information about the current exception being handled. This function returns a tuple of values that is equivalent to the values provided by three other *sys module* objects:

sys.exc_type—Returns the exception type

sys.exc_value—Returns the exception value

sys.exc_traceback—Returns a traceback object

```
Note that these objects only work when called from within an except clause.>>>
import sys
>>> try:
...     1/0
... except:
...     print sys.exc_type, ":", sys.exc_value
exceptions.ZeroDivisionError : integer division or modulo
```

The last example can also be implemented as

```
>>> import sys
>>> try:
...     1/0
... except:
```

```
...      info = sys.exc_info()
...      exc_type = info[0]
...      exc_value = info[1]
...      exc_traceback = info[2]
...      print exc_type, ":", exc_value
...
exceptions.ZeroDivisionError : integer division or modulo
```

A more compact way to assign the values to the variables is by using sequence unpacking, as is demonstrated by the following:

```
exc_type, exc_value, exc_traceback = self.exc_info()
```

The Python module called `traceback`, which is part of the standard Python library, helps you to debug the `call stack` after an exception has been raised.

```
 1: >>> import traceback
 2: >>> try:
 3: ...      1/0
 4: ... except:
 5: ...      print "The next lines show the traceback message"
 6: ...      print "----------------------------------------"
 7: ...      traceback.print_exc()
 8: ...      print "----------------------------------------"
 9: ...
10: The next lines show the traceback message
11: ----------------------------------------
12: Traceback (innermost last):
13:    File "<stdin>", line 2, in ?
14: ZeroDivisionError: integer division or modulo
15: ----------------------------------------
```

The previous program chooses the right time to display the traceback message by using the `traceback.print_exc()` function (line 7).

You can also extract the traceback information by parsing the results of `sys.exc_traceback`.

```
>>> import sys, traceback
>>> try:
...          result = 1/0
... except:
...          trace = traceback.extract_tb(sys.exc_traceback)
...          for filename, lineno,function,message in trace:
...              print "File name: ", filename
```

```
...                print "Error message: ", message
...                print "Line: ", lineno
...                print "Function: ", function
...
```

By using the objects sys.last_type, sys.last_value, and sys.last_traceback, you can get the details about the last *uncaught* exception. When I say that, I mean the last exception that had a traceback message displayed.

```
>>> import sys
>>> x = 0
>>> 1 / x
Traceback (innermost last):
  File "<stdin>", line 1, in ?
ZeroDivisionError: integer division or modulo
>>> 1.0 / 10
0.1
>>> print sys.last_type
exceptions.ZeroDivisionError
>>> print sys.last_value
integer division or modulo
```

Raising Exceptions

There are several ways to raise exceptions. You can either raise your own exceptions or Python standard exceptions by using any of the four techniques listed as follows:

- raise *class*
- raise *exception*, *argument*
- raise *exception*, *(argument1, argument2, ...)*
- raise *exception (argument1, argument2, ...)*

Note that the second and third forms of raising exceptions use the old form of passing arguments with the exception. I recommended using only the first and fourth forms.

Passing None, as the second argument, to the raise statement is equivalent to omitting it.

raise class, None is equivalent to raise class()

Check the following cases.

```
raise IndexError()
raise IndexError
raise IndexError("x is out of range")
raise IndexError, "x is out of range"
```

In the previous lines, the examples use a standard exception called `IndexError`. However, you can raise any one of the supported *built-in* exceptions.

Look at another example that uses a different exception:

```
op = raw_input("Enter an operator: ")
op1 - input("Enter first operand: ")
op2 = input("Enter second operand: ")
if op == "+":
      print op1 + op2
else:
      raise RuntimeError("I don't know this command")
```

In the next chapter, after learning how you can handle classes, you will be able to easily understand this next example. For the present time, take a deep breath and just have some fun.

This example raises an exception that blocks your access to nonexistent members of the c class.

```
1: >>> class c:
2: ...      def __init__(self, name):
3: ...              self.name = name
4: ...      def __getattr__(self, attr):
5: ...              if attr <> "name":
6: ...                      raise AttributeError
7: ...
8: >>> a = c("Andre")
9: >>> a.name
10: 'Andre'
11: >>> a.age
```

The following traceback message is generated after running the command located at line 11.

```
Traceback (innermost last):
  File "<stdin>", line 1, in ?
  File "<stdin>", line 6, in __getattr__
AttributeError
```

As you can see, line 5 checks the name of the attribute that is being passed to the method. That makes the exception in line 6 to always be raised when the attribute name is not "name".

However, note that if you assign something to a.age, as demonstrated next, getting the value of a.age will no longer cause the error. To handle that, you would need to write a code to deal with the __setattr__ method, but that would be another example.

```
>>> a.age = 32
>>> print a.age
32
```

Raising an Exception to Leave the Interpreter

Raising the SystemExit exception is a generic way to leave the Python interpreter.

```
C:\Program Files\Python>python
Python 1.5.2 (#0, Apr 13 1999, 10:51:12) [MSC 32 bit (Intel)] on win32
Copyright 1991-1995 Stichting Mathematisch Centrum, Amsterdam
>>> raise SystemExit
C:\Program Files\Python>
```

The next example demonstrates how you can trap the SystemExit exception.

```
>>> try:
...     raise SystemExit
... except SystemExit:
...     print "Sorry. You can not leave."
...
Sorry. You can not leave.
```

The sys.exit() function raises an exception SystemExit that, if not caught, causes the thread to exit silently.

```
>>> import sys
>>> try:
...     sys.exit()
... except SystemExit:
...     print "I have already told you. You can not leave."
...
I have already told you. You can not leave.
```

Raising an Exception to Leave Nested Loops

Sometimes you are so deeply involved in your data structures that you only want to get out of all your nested loops quickly. Normally, you would have to use break for each level of interaction. The next example demonstrates how to handle this situation by using exceptions.

```
>>> ExitLoop = "ExitLoop"
>>> try:
...     i=1
...     while i < 10:
...             for j in xrange(1,5):
...                     print i,j
...                     if (i==2) and (j==3):
...                             raise ExitLoop
...             i = i + 1
... except ExitLoop:
...     print "i=2 and j=3 is a special case."
...
1 1
1 2
1 3
1 4
2 1
2 2
2 3
i=2 and j=3 is a special case.
```

Raising String Exceptions

Older versions used to support only strings for both Python standard exceptions and user-defined exceptions.

```
>>> NetworkError = "NetworkError"
>>> raise NetworkError, "Bad hostname"
```

Nowadays, Python supports both strings and exception classes. There are costs to using class exceptions because they must be instantiated to be caught. Note that most people don't use exceptions to control the flow of their program, so they don't occur much.

However, classes give you much more flexibility to generalize the type of error that you want to catch.

> **Tip**
> Try to define your own exceptions as classes instead of strings.

Instancing an Exception Class

Every time an exception is raised, an instance of the exception class is created. The next syntax demonstrates how to catch a class instance in your program.

```
try:
    <statements>
except exception, instance:
    <statements>
```

The `instance` variable is an instance of the raised exception. Therefore, it inherits attributes from the exception class.

Each instance has an attribute called `args` that returns the error string in a tuple format.

```
>>> try:
...     a = [1,2]
...     print a[4]
... except IndexError, b:
...     print b.args
...
('list index out of range',)
```

Particularly, the `EnvironmentError` exception has a *2-tuple* or *3-tuple* structure that can be translated as (*error number*, *string error message*, and an optional *filename*).

```
>>> try:
...     file = open("Parrot")
... except EnvironmentError, b:
...     print b.args
...
(2, 'No such file or directory')
```

When the instance belongs to a `SyntaxError` class exception, four special attributes are also returned: *filename*, *lineno*, *offset*, and *text*.

```
>>> try:
...     a = "x===10"
...     exec a
... except SyntaxError, b:
...     print b.args
...
('invalid syntax', (None, 1, 4, 'x===10'))
```

> **Note**
> Modules are parsed before being run, so syntax errors in a file can't be caught by
> `try`/`except` blocks that surround the error. You can catch it from the bit of code that
> imported the module, however.

Debugging Your Code

Exceptions are very good for helping to debug your code. You can use the `assert`
command to raise a debugging exception that transports a message to your exception
handling code.

The syntax is `assert <TestStatement> [, argument]`

This command raises an `AssertionError` exception whenever `<TestStatement>`
evaluates to `false`.

For example

```
>>> def divide (a,b):
...     assert b != 0, "Can't divide by zero"
...     return a/b
>>>
>>> divide(10,0)
Traceback (innermost last):
  File "<stdin>", line 1, in ?
  File "<stdin>", line 2, in divide
AssertionError: Can't divide by zero
```

The assert command is equivalent to

```
>>> if __debug__:c
>>>     if not (<TestStatement>):
>>>         raise AssertionError [, argument]
```

`__debug__` is a *built-in* name and has its value set to `true` by default. To set `__debug__`
to `false`, it is necessary to change the interpreter to run in *optimized mode*.

> **Tip**
> Calling the interpreter with the `-O` option activates the *optimized mode*.
>
> `c:\>python -O`

> Currently, Python's command-line option `-X` turns all standard exceptions into
> strings. Version 1.6 is expected to have this option removed, and make all standard
> exceptions into classes. User code that deals with string exceptions will still be
> supported, but not encouraged.

See Chapter 17, "Development Tools," for more details about other command-line options that you can transport as configuration parameters to the interpreter.

Catching Exceptions

Look at an example that shows how to catch a specific exception message.

```
 1: >>> def zerodivision(x):
 2: ...       return 1/x
 3: ...
 4: >>> def test(x):
 5: ...       try:
 6: ...             print zerodivision(x)
 7: ...       except ZeroDivisionError:
 8: ...             print "You can not divide this number by Zero"
 9: ...
10: test(0)
```

In line 7, we are specifying the exact exception type that we want to catch.

You can also replace lines 7 and 8 from the previous example with the text from the next snippet. The difference is that this new scenario also shows the error message provided by the interpreter.

```
except ZeroDivisionError, error_message:
    print "You can't divide this number by Zero - ", error_message
```

Besides catching Python standard exceptions, it is also possible to catch user-defined, *non-Error* exceptions.

```
>>> found = "Item found"
>>> def searcher(arg):
...       if arg == 1:
...             print "executing the routine."
...       else:
...             raise found
...
>>> try:
...       searcher()
>>> except found:
...       print "The routine has failed."
... else:
...       print "The routine was successfully concluded"
```

The next example re-raises an exception because the `win32pipe` module is not present in the system.

```
>>> try:
...     import win32pipe
... except:
...     raise ImportError, "The module is not available"
Traceback (innermost last):
  File "<stdin>", line 4, in ?
ImportError: The module is not available
```

The next example actually shows how to raise the same exception (provided the exception is a class exception). This type of implementation doesn't require you to know the name of the exception being raised.

```
>>> import sys
>>> try:
...     import win32pipe
... except:
...     raise sys.exc_value
Traceback (innermost last):
  File "<stdin>", line 4, in ?
ImportError: No module named win32pipe
```

The following code catches an `IOError` exception and raises a `SystemExit` exception by using the `sys.exit()` function.

```
>>> import sys
>>> try:
...     file = open("file.txt")
... except IOError:
...     print "Error opening file for reading"
...     sys.exit(0)
```

Catching Standard Errors

The `errno` module makes available the standard `errno` system symbols, which can be used to check the meaning of an error.

```
>>> import errno
>>> try:
>>>     file = open("test.py")
>>> except IOError, (errcode, errmsg):
>>>     if errcode == errno.ENOENT:
>>>         print "File does not exist!"
>>>
```

You can check the entire list of error symbols by typing,

```
>>> import errno
>>> dir(errno)
['E2BIG', 'EACCES', 'EADDRINUSE', 'EADDRNOTAVAIL', EAFNOSUPPORT', 'EAGAIN',
 'EALREADY', 'EBADF', 'EBUSY', 'ECHILD', 'ECONNABORTED', 'ECONNREFUSED',
 'ECONNRESET', 'EDEADLK', 'EDEADLOCK', 'EDESTADDRREQ', 'EDOM', 'EDQUOT',
 'EEXIST', 'EFAULT', 'EFBIG', 'EHOSTDOWN', 'EHOSTUNREACH', 'EILSEQ',
 'EINPROGRESS', 'EINTR', 'EINVAL', 'EIO', 'EISCONN', 'EISDIR', 'ELOOP',
 'EMFILE', 'EMLINK', 'EMSGSIZE', 'ENAMETOOLONG', 'ENETDOWN', 'ENETRESET',
 'ENETUNREACH', 'ENFILE', 'ENOBUFS', 'ENODEV', 'ENOENT', 'ENOEXEC', 'ENOLCK',
 'ENOMEM', 'ENOPROTOOPT', 'ENOSPC', 'ENOSYS', 'ENOTCONN', 'ENOTDIR',
 'ENOTEMPTY', 'ENOTSOCK', 'ENOTTY', 'ENXIO', 'EOPNOTSUPP', 'EPERM',
 'EPFNOSUPPORT', 'EPIPE', 'EPROTONOSUPPORT', 'EPROTOTYPE', 'ERANGE',
 'EREMOTE', 'EROFS', 'ESHUTDOWN', 'ESOCKTNOSUPPORT', 'ESPIPE', 'ESRCH',
 'ESTALE', 'ETIMEDOUT', 'ETOOMANYREFS', 'EUSERS', 'EWOULDBLOCK', 'EXDEV',
 'WSABASEERR', 'WSAEACCES', 'WSAEADDRINUSE', 'WSAEADDRNOTAVAIL',
 'WSAEAFNOSUPPORT', 'WSAEALREADY', 'WSAEBADF', 'WSAECONNABORTED',
 'WSAECONNREFUSED', 'WSAECONNRESET', 'WSAEDESTADDRREQ', 'WSAEDISCON',
 'WSAEDQUOT', 'WSAEFAULT', 'WSAEHOSTDOWN', 'WSAEHOSTUNREACH',
 'WSAEINPROGRESS', 'WSAEINTR', 'WSAEINVAL', 'WSAEISCONN', 'WSAELOOP',
 'WSAEMFILE', 'WSAEMSGSIZE', 'WSAENAMETOOLONG', 'WSAENETDOWN',
 'WSAENETRESET', 'WSAENETUNREACH', 'WSAENOBUFS', 'WSAENOPROTOOPT',
 'WSAENOTCONN', 'WSAENOTEMPTY', 'WSAENOTSOCK', 'WSAEOPNOTSUPP',
 'WSAEPFNOSUPPORT', 'WSAEPROCLIM', 'WSAEPROTONOSUPPORT', 'WSAEPROTOTYPE',
 'WSAEREMOTE', 'WSAESHUTDOWN', 'WSAESOCKTNOSUPPORT', 'WSAESTALE',
 'WSAETIMEDOUT', 'WSAETOOMANYREFS', 'WSAEUSERS', 'WSAEWOULDBLOCK',
 'WSANOTINITIALISED', 'WSASYSNOTREADY', 'WSAVERNOTSUPPORTED', '__doc__',
 '__name__', 'errorcode']
```

Use the `os.strerror()` function to \retrieve the system message associated to a specific error symbol.

```
>>> import os, errno
>>> os.strerror(errno.EPERM)
"Operation not permitted"
```

try/finally

The `try/finally` statement is good for clean-up actions. The code in the `finally` block is always executed, no matter whether the `try` block fails or not.

```
1: try:
2:     f = open("c:\\autoexec.bat")
3:     lines = f.readlines()
4: finally:
5:     f.close()                # it is always executed
6: print "It is done"          # it is executed on success only
```

The previous piece of code opens a file and tries to read its lines. It is not necessary to check whether the process raises an error in order to close the file because the `close` function in line 5 is always executed, no matter what. Now, take a look at line 6. The `print` statement is only executed when the `finally` block is bypassed because when an error is raised, the `finally` block is executed and the program is terminated immediately afterwards if the exception is not handled, leaving the exception unhandled.

Tip
`finally` and `except` clauses cannot be used together along with a unique `try` clause.

Creating User-defined Exceptions

Python allows you to create your own exceptions by subclassing any standard Python exception.

Note
Take a look at Chapter 5, "Object-Oriented Programming," for more details about working with classes.

```
>>> import exceptions
>>> class ConfigError (exceptions.Exception):
...     def __init__(self, arg=None):
...         self.args = arg
...
>>> try:
...     raise ConfigError("Bad hostname")
... except ConfigError, e:
...     print e.args
...
Bad hostname
```

The `import` statement from the previous example isn't really necessary because the `exceptions` module contents are automatically imported by the interpreter. Remember that you can't use the prefix `"exceptions"` because the `exceptions` module is not available in the __main__ namespace until you import it.

The next example uses the class created in the previous example as a base class to create a new class.

```
>>> class TimeoutError(ConfigError):

...     def printargs(self):
...         print self.args
...
>>> try:
...     raise TimeoutError, "Timeout"
... except TimeoutError, e:

...     e.printargs()
...
Timeout
```

As you could see, just by overriding the __init__ method, you are able to create your own exception classes.

You can also change the output of a traceback message by overwriting the __str__ method.

```
>>> class ConfigError(Exception):
...     def __init__(self, args=None):
...         self.args = args

...     def __str__(self):
...         return "\nError in the module configuration\n" + \
...                 `self.args` + "\n"...
>>> raise ConfigError, "bad hostname"
Traceback (innermost last):
  File "<stdin>", line 1, in ?
__main__.ConfigError
Error in the module configuration
bad hostname
```

The Standard Exception Hierarchy

Python comes filled with many built-in exceptions. All these exceptions are part of the exceptions module, which is always loaded prior to any program execution.

The following structure identifies the standard exception hierarchy, and, immediately afterwards, it is given the description of each exception type.

This structure, which resembles a tree, shows you that all exceptions are derived from a base class named Exception. If we highlight, for example, the ImportError exception, we note that it is a subclass of the StandardError class. In addition to that, the StandardError class is a subclass of the Exception class. Table 4.1 shows the structure.

Table 4.1 *The Exception Class Hierarchy*

```
Exception
    SystemExit
    StandardError
            KeyboardInterrupt
            ImportError
            EnvironmentError
                    IOError
                    OSError
            EOFError
            RuntimeError
                    NotImplementedError
            NameError
                    UnboundLocalError
            AttributeError
            SyntaxError
            TypeError
            AssertionError
            LookupError
                    IndexError
                    KeyError
            ArithmeticError
                    OverflowError
                    ZeroDivisionError
                    FloatingPointError
            ValueError
            SystemError
            MemoryError
```

Exception—This is the root class. All exception classes are subclasses of this base class. Every user exception class should be derived from this class too.

SystemExit—This is an *exception* because it isn't really an error message. Instead, it can be used to exit a program. The important thing is that this exception doesn't return any traceback message.

StandardError—It is the base class for all errors (except for SystemExit, of course).

KeyboardInterrupt—It is raised when an interrupt key, such as CTRL+C, is pressed.

ImportError—It is raised when Python cannot find a module to import.

EnvironmentError—This is the base class for errors that occur outside the Python environment. The IOError and OSError classes subclass it.

IOError—It is raised by I/O operation errors.

OSError—This one is raised by operating system errors, usually generated by the os module.

EOFError—Exception raised when an End-of-File (EOF) error occurs.

RuntimeError—This is a special type of exception raised by errors that aren't covered by any of the other exceptions.

NotImplementedError—Methods or functions that aren't implemented should raise this exception.

```
>>> def updateregistry():
>>>      raise NotImplementedError
```

NameError—It is raised when the interpreter finds a name that is neither in the local nor in the global namespace.

UnboundLocalError—This is a new exception that was created for version 1.6. It subclasses the NameError exception, raising an error when a local variable is undefined.

AttributeError—It is raised by attribute reference and attribute assignment kinds of errors. Note that starting with version 1.6, this exception will have a more friendly error message, which is expected to break some code that assumes the message to be exactly equivalent to the attribute name.

SyntaxError—It is raised by syntax errors.

TypeError—This exception is raised when you try to apply a function operation to an object of inappropriate type.

AssertionError—This kind of exception is raised when an `assert` statement fails by evaluating to false.

LookupError—This is the base class for `indexing` and `key` errors. The `IndexError` and `KeyError` classes subclass it.

IndexError—It is raised by "sequence out of range" errors.

KeyError—It is raised when a *key* is not found in a dictionary.

ArithmeticError—This is the base class for arithmetic errors. The classes `OverflowError`, `ZeroDivisionError`, and `FloatingPointError` subclass it.

OverflowError—This exception is raised when the result is so large that it makes the operation overflow.

ZeroDivisionError—It is raised when an operation that tries to divide a number by zero is performed.

FloatingPointError—This exception is raised by `floating-point` operation errors. Note that on Linux systems, you are required to enable the `SIGFPE` handling with the `fpectl` module to use this exception.

ValueError—This one is raised when you try to perform an action using the right type but the wrong value.

SystemError—It is raised if a Python's interpreter internal error takes place.

MemoryError—This exception is raised by a recoverable out-of-memory error.

As exception classes are grouped within other exception classes (known as base classes), it becomes much easier to catch several different types of errors/exceptions by using just one `except` clause.

Base classes are never raised, but can be used to catch up errors.

The next scenario shows how to cover multiple exceptions by declaring only the base class exception.

```
>>> dict = {1:"First Element",2:"Second Element"}
>>> list = [13,14,15,16]
```

Based on these structures, we get the following error messages when we try any *out-of-range* type of operations.

```
>>> dict[3]
Traceback (innermost last):
  File "<stdin>", line 1, in ?
```

```
KeyError: 3
>>> list[8]
Traceback (innermost last):
  File "<stdin>", line 1, in ?
IndexError: list index out of range
```

The following example is able to catch both IndexError and KeyError exceptions.

```
>>> def getelement(element):
>>>     try:
>>>         if element < 10:
>>>             print dict[element]
>>>         else:
>>>             print list[element]
>>>     except LookupError:
>>>         print "Sorry. This element does not exist"
>>> getelement(1)
First Element
>>> getelement(20)
Sorry. This element does not exist
```

Now, let's talk about release 2.0. Check the next code.

```
def showcounter():
    print "counter=", counter
    counter = counter + 1
showcounter()
```

The previous code raises an exception on the print statement in both 1.5.2 and 2.0 release. However, in 1.5.2 a NameError exception is raised, while in 2.0 a new exception is raised. This new exception is called UnboundLocalError, which is a subclass of the NameError exception.

Talking about new exceptions, the Python 2.0 release comes with two more brand-new exceptions. They are called TabError and IndentationError, and they are subclasses of the SyntaxError exception.

Summary

Python exceptions are mostly used for error handling and event notification. If you don't handle exceptions in your program, Python's interpreter returns traceback messages.

Python comes filled with many built-in exceptions. All these exceptions are part of the `exceptions` module, which is always loaded prior to any program execution.

Exceptions can be handled by using either `try`/`except` or `try`/`finally` statements. The difference between them is that an `except` clause is only executed when an exception is raised, and a `finally` clause is always executed, no matter whether an exception is raised or not. The `try`/`finally` statement is good for clean-up actions, but remember that it doesn't actually catch the exceptions.

Python supports both strings and exception classes. As exception classes are grouped within other exception classes (known as base classes), it becomes much easier to catch several different types of errors/exceptions by using just one `except` clause. Base classes are never raised, but can be used to catch up errors.

You can either raise your own exceptions or use Python standard exceptions. Python allows you to create your own exceptions by subclassing any standard Python exception.

Exceptions can be raised for several purposes (for example, exit the interpreter, leaving nested loops, and so on). Every time an exception is raised, an instance of the exception class is created.

The `assert` command helps debug your code by raising a debugging exception.

Besides the `exceptions` module, the `sys`, the `errno`, and the `traceback` modules also offer you some advanced functionality to handle exceptions.

Code Examples

This first example returns the square root of a given input value. If the input value is negative or if it is a character, two traceback messages are displayed.

Listing 4.1   *Square root (File squareroot.py)*

```
1: ###
2: # Program: Square root
3: # Author: Andre S Lessa
4: ###
5:
6: ### import modules
7:
8: import sys, traceback, math
9:
```

Listing 4.1 *(continued)*

```
10: try:
11:     n = float(raw_input("Please, enter a number: "))
12:     print "The sqrt of %f is %f" % (n, math.sqrt(n))
13:
14: except (ValueError, TypeError, OverflowError):
15:     print "-----------------------------------------"
16:     print "This is the standard traceback message:"
17:     print ""
18:     traceback.print_exc()
19:
20:     print "-----------------------------------------"
21:     print "This is the customized traceback message:"
22:     print ""
23:     info = sys.exc_info()
24:     exc_type = info[0]
25:     exc_value = info[1]
26:     exc_traceback = info[2]
27:
28:     trace = traceback.extract_tb(sys.exc_traceback)
29:     print "Exception Type:  ", exc_type
30:     print "Error Message:   ", exc_value
31:     print "File name:       ", trace[0][0]
32:     print "Error message:   ", trace[0][1]
33:     print "Line:            ", trace[0][2]
34:     print "Function:        ", trace[0][3]
35: else:
36:     print "Everything went just fine."
```

The except clause in line 14 covers ValueError, OverflowError, and TypeError exceptions.

The else clause in line 35 is only executed when no exception is raised.

The next lines show the two traceback messages that are displayed by this program: Python standard traceback message and a customized version.

```
C:\python> s:\python\squareroot.py
Please, enter a number: i
-----------------------------------------
This is the standard traceback message:

Traceback (innermost last):
  File "s:\python\squareroot.py", line 11, in ?
```

```
      n = float(raw_input("Please, enter a number: "))
ValueError: invalid literal for float(): i
- - - - - - - - - - - - - - - - - - - - - - - - - - - - - - - - - - - - - -
This is the customized traceback message:


Exception Type:    exceptions.ValueError
Error Message:      invalid literal for float(): i
File name:          s:\python\squareroot.py
Error message:      11
Line:                ?
Function:           n = float(raw_input("Please, enter a number: "))
```

This example uses multiple except clauses (lines 17 and 20). It also takes advantage of the assert command to raise a debug exception (line 15).

Listing 4.2   *Internet country codes (File countrycode.py)*

```
 1: ###
 2: # Program: Country code
 3: # Author: Andre S Lessa
 4: ###
 5:
 6: ### import modules
 7:
 8: import sys, string
 9:
10: matrix = {"brazil":"br","france":"fr","argentina":"ar","usa":"us"}
11:
12: def getcode(country):
13:     try:
14:         data = matrix[string.lower(country)]
15:         assert data != "br", "You cannot select this country " + \
                                 "for this action!"
16:         return data
17:     except KeyError:
18:         print sys.exc_type, ":", "%s is not in the list." % \
                sys.exc_value
19:         print
20:     except AssertionError, b:
21:         print b
22:         print
23:
24: while 1:
```

Listing 4.2   *(continued)*

```
25:     country = raw_input("Enter the country name or press x to exit: ")
26:     if country == "x":
27:         break
28:     code = getcode(country)
29:     if code != None:
30:         print "%s's country code is %s" % (country, code)
31:         print
```

The following *screen dump* shows the execution of this program. Note that the program doesn't end after an exception has been raised.

```
C:\>python s:\python\countrycode.py
Enter the country name or press x to exit: Mexico
exceptions.KeyError : mexico is not in the list.

Enter the country name or press x to exit: USA
USA's country code is us

Enter the country name or press x to exit: Brazil
You cannot select this country for this action!

Enter the country name or press x to exit: Argentina
Argentina's country code is ar

Enter the country name or press x to exit: x

C:\Python>
```

See more *exception handling* cases in the final section of the next chapter.

CHAPTER 5

Object-Oriented Programming

Is it a bird? No! Is it a plane? No! It's bicycle repair man!

This chapter introduces object-oriented methodology in a very complete and straightforward way. You will be able to easily create and use objects and classes in your programs after going through the next pages of material.

Object-Oriented Programming

Python uses the traditional class architecture for object-oriented programming (OOP).

The object-oriented model adopted by Python

- Promotes modular design
- Promotes and facilitates Python software reusability
- Uses notions of real-world objects to develop programs
- Results in better quality software (but, of course, you can write bad code with any paradigm)

Object-oriented programming promotes data abstraction, information hiding, encapsulation, and modular programming.

Saying that OOP promotes data abstraction means that we define the functions that operate on the data. The ideal scenario provides encapsulated data that can be accessible only through the class methods. However, in Python, we cannot totally block the programmer from accessing the information that is stored inside a class.

Encapsulation, Inheritance, and Polymorphism are the most important thoughts provided by OOP. Python doesn't strictly follow the standard concepts, but you will see how far it goes.

Encapsulation—Data can only be accessed or manipulated by means of a set of interface functions. Encapsulation of data enables information hiding. Python provides encapsulation through conventions rather than strictly enforcing it, which can be preferable.

Inheritance—With inheritance, the derived class (also known as subclass, descendant, or child class) inherits the data members and class methods of its base (parent) class.

Polymorphism—It enables a function to have several different kinds of interfaces. Depending on the parameters used by the caller, the class knows which interface should be used. Python achieves this through its dynamic typing and late binding.

An Introduction to Python OOP

A *class* defines a category of objects in terms of the data it encapsulates and the operations on the data that are allowed by the interface functions. Essentially, a class is a template from which objects can be created.

Each object created from a class is an *instance* of a class. They all look alike and exhibit a similar behavior.

A class stores object *attributes* (also known as data members) and the behavior of objects (mostly known as *methods*). This behavior can be inherited from other (*base*) classes. The non-method attributes of the class are usually referred to as *class members* or *class attributes* so that they are not confused with instance attributes.

Each class has its own namespace in which all the assignments and function definitions occur.

Class Instances

A class instance is a Python object, and similar to every Python object, it has the following properties: *identity*, *object type*, *attributes*, *methods*, and *value*.

I will use the following class definition as the basis for the next explanations. First, let's declare the c class, and then we will create an instance of this class called obj.

```
>>> class c:
...     def __init__(self, value=None):
...         self.name = value
...
>>> obj = c()
>>> obj.name = "Andre"
```

The *identity* is the memory location allocated for the object. It can be identified by using the id() function.

```
>>> id(obj)
6623988
```

The *object type* is the object's internal representation. It defines the supported methods and operation for each object. You can use the type() function in order to find out the type of a specific object.

```
>>> type(obj)
<type 'instance'>

>>> type(obj.name)
<type 'string'>
```

While we're talking about object types, let's take a quick break from the whole class issue and examine the types for Python objects defined in extension modules, which do not necessarily act like classes.

Table 5.1 lists all Python built-in object types defined by the types module. Note that almost all the types shown in this table are unrelated to Python classes.

Table 5.1   *Built-In Object Types Defined by the* types *Module*

Built-In Object Type	Description
NoneType	the None (null) object
IntType	integer
LongType	arbitrary precision integer
FloatType	floating point
ComplexType	complex number
StringType	list of characters

Table 5.1   *(continued)*

Built-In Object Type	Description
ListType	list
TupleType	tuple
XrangeType	returned by xrange()
DictType	dictionary
BuiltinFunctionType	built-in functions
BuiltinMethodType	built-in methods
FuntionType	user-defined function
ClassType	class object/definition
InstanceType	class object instance/class instance
MethodType	bound class method
UnboundMethodType	unbound class method
ModuleType	module
FileType	file
CodeType*	raw byte-compiled code
FrameType*	represent execution frame
TracebackType*	stacks the traceback information of an exception
SliceType*	generated by extended slices
EllipsisType*	it is used in extended slices

*The checked types indicate internal Python objects that can be exposed to the user.

The *attributes* and *methods* of an object are bound properties that must be accessed by putting a dot (.) after the object name.

```
>>> obj.name
"Andre"
```

At last, the *value* of an object is better visualized by an example.

```
>>> obj.name = "Andre"
```

The string "Andre" is the value assigned to the name attribute of the object obj.

Python Classes and Instances

In Python, a class is a user-defined data type, and as in most other languages, you define Python classes using the keyword `class`.

```
class <class name>:
    <class statements>
```

The *class statements* section contains any valid Python statement that defines class constants or class methods. Note that the contents of the variable namespace formed by executing the commands in the class statement make up the class dictionary.

Two ways to create classes are

- You can define it from scratch.

```
class <class name>:
    ["documentation text"]
    <class statements>
```

- You can create a new class that inherits properties of other classes. This is called *subclassing*, and you will learn more about it later in this chapter.

```
class <class name> [(baseclass1, baseclass2, ...)]:
    ["documentation text"]
    <statements>
```

A class definition starts at the keyword `class` and ends at the last line of the indented block of code that goes underneath.

Methods and class constants define a class namespace. Usually, a class has several methods, and they must all start with the keyword `def`.

> **Tip**
> Methods are how to call functions in a class.

All methods have the additional argument `self` as the first argument in the method header—The convention is to call it `self` because it could be any other name. Python's `self` argument is similar to the `this` keyword in *C*++. Its function is to transport a reference of the object in a way that when a method is called, it knows which object should be used.

```
>>> class a:
...     def __init__(self):
...         print self
...
```

```
>>> b = a()
>>> b
<__main__.a instance at 795420>
```

In order to reference an attribute within a class, you need to use either
`self.attribute` or `classname.attribute`. Note that the `self.attribute` syntax is to
remove ambiguities between instance variables and function local variables. Also,
`self.attribute` and `classname.attribute` are different. The second sets class
attributes, which will affect all instances of the class.

```
>>> class c:
...     def __init__(self, value=None):
...         self.name = value
...
```

To reference an attribute while using a class instance, you have to use
`instancename.attribute`.

```
>>> obj.name
```

A class can also contain class variable assignments. These variables are shared by all
the class instances. Class variables are useful when the assignment of default values to
instances is required. Class variables do *not* have the `self.` prefix.

For example

```
>>> class Student:
...     default_age = 20                   # class variable
...     def __init__ (self):
...         self.age = Student.default_age    # instance variable
```

Note that in the previous example, we had to use `Student.default_age` instead of
using only `default_age` because the global namespace for a method is the module in
which it was defined—not the class namespace.

The next example creates an instance variable that has the same name of the class
variable.

```
>>> class Student:
...     default_age = 20                  # class variable
...     def __init__ (self, age):
...         self.default_age = age        # instance variable
```

Suppose that you have the following code stored in a file called
`c:\python\studentfile.py`. This code defines three different variables named
`default_age` (at lines 2, 4, and 9).

```
1: class Student:
2:     default_age = 20                # base class variable
3:     def __init__(self, age):
4:         self.default_age = age      # base class instance variable
5:
6: class Newstudent(Student):
7:     "New student class"
8:     def __init__(self, age=20):
9:         self.default_age = age      # instance variable
```

The following code imports the previous module. Which variable is being used by the
instance call at line 5?

```
1: >>> import sys
2: >>> sys.path = sys.path + ['c:\\python']
3: >>> import studentfile
4: >>> Joao = studentfile.Newstudent(15)
5: >>> Joao.default_age
6: 15
```

Tip
In order for Python to find your modules, the directory where you save them must be
an entry of the `sys.path` list.

The answer is the instance variable of the newstudent class (line 9 from the first
listing). In cases like this, the search order is defined as

1. instance variables

2. class variables

3. base classes variables—note that the search order for base classes makes the
   deepest-level classes used first

   ```
   >>> Renata = studentfile.newstudent()
   >>> print Renata.default_age
   20
   ```

The following variation is slightly different than the previous code. This example
shows what you need to do to make the class `Newstudent` call the superclass's `__init__`
method.

```
6: class Newstudent(Student):
7:     "New student class"
8:     def __init__(self):
9:          Student.__init__(self, Student.default_age)
```

Note that we are calling the __init__ method of the Student class (the superclass). The class constant Student.default_age is also used in this example. It is important to say that when calling unbound methods (methods that are not tied to an instance) like this one, you must explicitly say that the first argument is self.

```
1: >>> Joao = studentfile.Newstudent()
2: >>> Joao.default_age
3: 20
```

Attributes of a Class

Next, I list the attributes that classes expose to programmers.

classname.__dict__—This attribute contains the class namespace dictionary.

```
>>> studentfile.newstudent.__dict__
{'__init__': <function __init__ at 799e90>, '__doc__': 'New student
class', '__module__': 'studentfile'}
```

classname.__doc__—This one returns the documentation string of the class.

```
>>> studentfile.newstudent.__doc__
'New student class'
```

classname.__name__—This attribute returns the class name.

```
>>> studentfile.newstudent.__name__
'newstudent'
```

classname.__module__—This one provides the module name that contains the class.

```
>>> studentfile.newstudent.__module__
'studentfile'
```

classname.__bases__—This is a tuple containing the names of the base classes.

```
>>> studentfile.newstudent.__bases__
(<class studentfile.student at 799e00>,)
```

The Python Class Browser

The pyclbr module offers you the possibility of browsing all the information about classes that is stored in a specific module.

readmodule()

This function reads the module and returns a dictionary in the format {classname:classinfo}, where classinfo is an instance object of the class.

basic syntax: variable = pyclbr.readmodule(*module*)

```
>>> import pyclbr
>>> moduletobrowse = pyclbr.readmodule("profile")
>>> for classname, classinfo in moduletobrowse.items():
...     print "Class name: %s" % classname
...
Class name: HotProfile
Class name: OldProfile
Class name: Profile
```

or, if you use our student example

```
>>> import pyclbr
>>> moduletobrowse = pyclbr.readmodule("studentfile")
>>> for classname, classinfo in moduletobrowse.items():
...     print "Class name: %s" % classname
...
Class name: student
Class name: newstudent
```

If you need to go deeper than that, you can look at the classinfo object.

Python Instances

Each instance defines its own namespace of data, and it inherits behavior from the class (and possible base classes) that have originated it.

In order to create a new instance of a class, you just need to say

```
newinstance = classname()
```

Suppose that you have a Person class like this

```
class Person:
    def __init__(self, name):
        self.name = name
        self.family = []
```

```
        def addmember(self, member):
            self.family.append(member)
```

For example, if you want to create a new instance of the chef class, you must type:

```
>>> anthony =  Person()
```

You can also pass arguments to the __init__ function of the class. These arguments can be used to set the initial values of an object. Let's see how it works.

```
>>> anthony = Person("anthony")
```

To call the methods of a class, you have to use the dot notation:

```
>>> anthony.addmember("son")
```

You also need to use the dot notation to have access to variables (attributes) of each instance.

```
>>> anthony.family
["son"]
```

An interesting detail about Python object attributes is that they don't need to be declared inside the class before they get used because they can be created dynamically.

```
>>> class DummyClass:
...     pass
...
>>> colors = DummyClass()
>>> color.alarm = "red"
```

The next example dynamically creates multiple attributes for the colors instance.

```
>>> class record:
...     def __init__(self, **args):
...         self.__dict__.update(args)
...
>>> colors = record(alarm="red", normal="green")
>>> colors.normal
'green'
```

isinstance() **and** issubclass()

The built-in functions isinstance() and issubclass() are always available without the need for importing any module because they are part of the __builtin__ module.

```
isinstance()
```
This function tests whether an object is an instance of a class. It returns 1 if the object is an instance. Otherwise, it returns 0. Note that this function handles subclass relationships as well—for instance, `isinstance(subclassinstance, superclass)` returns `true`.

basic syntax: `isinstance(instance_object, class_object)`

```
>>> class a:
...     pass
...
>>> inst = a()
>>> isinstance(inst,a)
1
```

As you can see next, you can also use this function to identify the object's type. Note however, that this is behavior that works for non–instance objects. Floats and ints act quite differently from Python class instances (for instance, there is no way to subclass `types.IntType`).

```
>>> import types
>>> isinstance(3, types.IntType)
1
>>> isinstance(3, types.FloatType)
0
```

```
issubclass()
```
This function returns 1 if the class object `classobj1` is a subclass (derived class) of the class object `classobj2`.

basic syntax: `issubclass(classobj1, classobj2)`

```
>>> class a:
...     pass
...
>>> class b(a):
...     pass
...
>>> issubclass(a,b)
1
```

Instance Attributes

`obj.__dict__`—This is the dictionary that contains all the attributes defined for the obj instance.

```
>>> colors.__dict__
{'alert': 'yellow', 'alarm': 'red', 'norma': 'green'}
```

obj.__class__—It shows the class that has created the obj instance.

```
>>> colors.__class__
<class __main__.record at 7883a0>
```

To get just the name of the class, use

```
>>> colors.__class__.__name__
'record'
```

obj.__methods__—This attribute is a list of all supported methods of the obj instance. Note that this attribute is available for lists and dictionaries, which are not class instances.

```
>>> a=[1,2]
>>> a.__methods__
['append', 'count', 'extend', 'index', 'insert', 'pop', 'remove','reverse',
'sort']

>>> b={1:''}
>>> b.__methods__
['clear', 'copy', 'get', 'has_key', 'items', 'keys', 'update', 'values']
```

Methods Handling

Whenever you have to write methods in your classes, always keep in mind that the namespace searching order for attributes and methods is instance, class, and base classes; and don't forget that self is always the first or only argument to be used in method headers.

Accessing Unbounded Methods

The next example shows what you should do in order to unbind a class method and use it outside the class definition.

```
1: obj = classname()
2: umethod = classname.methodname()
3: umethod(obj, args)
```

Line 1: Creates a class instance object.

Line 2: Creates an object that references the class method. The method is still unattached to the object at this stage.

Line 3: Executes the class method by transporting the instance reference (obj) and the list of arguments (args).

Note that the first argument to an unbound method must be an instance of the correct class, or an exception will be thrown.

Handling Global Class Variables

The next example defines a function that prints a class variable. Every time a new instance is created, Globalcount increases.

```
>>> def printGlobalcount():
...     print Globalcount.n
...
>>> class Couting:
...     n = 0
...     def __init__(self):
...         Globalcount.n = Globalcount.n + 1
...
>>> inc = Couting()
>>> inc = Couting()
>>> printGlobalcount()
2
```

The next code overwrites the class variable *x* when subclassing the baseclass class.

```
>>> class baseclass:
...     x = 5
...     def multiply(self, a):
...         return a * (self.__class__.x)
...
>>> class inherited(baseclass):
...     x = 9
...
>>> x = inherited()
>>> x.multiply(2)
18
```

After a method is defined, it uses the variable values that are associated to the current namespace.

```
>>> class A:
...       n = 1
...       def printn(self):
...             print self.n
...
>>> class B(A):
...       n = 2
...
>>> class C(B):
...       n = 3
...
>>> obj1 = C()
>>> obj1.printn()
3

>>> obj2 = B()
>>> obj2.printn()
2
```

Calling Methods from Other Methods

The next code exposes how simple it is to create a method to call another method.

```
>>> class c:
...       def funcx(self):
...             self.funcy()
...       def funcy(self):
...             print "Ni!"
...
>>> obj = c()
>>> obj.funcx()
Ni!
```

Special Methods

Python exposes some special methods that are easily highlighted in the code because they start and end with __ (double underscores). These methods override (inherit) built-in functions of the same name that are provided by Python itself. The next list shows some of the most used special methods.

__init__(self)—This is the constructor method, which is called during creation of instances. Usually, this is the place where the instance variables are initialized, among other things.

__str__(self)—This method is called when str() is called on instances of this type. It specifies how the object must be displayed when it is used as a string (for example, when a print command is applied to an object).

__repr__(self)—This method is called when repr() is called on instances of this type. This method provides a readable representation of the object. Usually, it is possible to re-create an object by using this method. Although not guaranteed, and the standard repr of an instance can't be executed to re-create the instance.

__getattr__(self, name)—Implement this method to trap or modify the access to nonexisting members, for example, returning the attribute self.name.

__setattr__(self, name, value)—This method allows you to control setting of attributes in the instance. It assigns the given value to the self.name instance's attribute. Note that you can also use "self.__dict__['attr'] = ..." to set attributes from within __setattr__ (if you do it the normal way, you will get infinite recursion).

__delattr__(self,name)—Implement this method to delete a specific attribute of an object. It's like saying del self.name.

__del__(self)—The __del__ method covers the deletion of the object. Be careful because sometimes it isn't immediately used when an object is destroyed (JPython behavior). CPython's garbage collector destructs objects as soon as their reference count reaches zero.

__cmp__(self,other)—Implement this method to compare and return a negative, zero, or positive number.

__hash__(self)—Implement this method to generate a 32-bit hash index.

__nonzero__(self)—Implement this method to return 0 or 1 for truth-value testing.

__call__(self)—Classes that implement the __call__ method are callable, and their instances can be invoked like a function. This is the concept used by the built-in functions. The syntax obj(*args) is equivalent to obj.__call__(*args).

__getitem__(self, index)—This method supports list indexing, returning self[index].

```
>>> class Seq:
...     def __getitem__(self, i):
...         if i < 5:
...             return i
...         else:
...             raise IndexError
```

```
...
>>> s = Seq()
>>> for i in s:
>>>     print i,
0, 1, 2, 3, 4
>>> print s[2]
2
>>> print s[6]
Traceback (innermost last):
  File "<stdin>", line 1, in ?
  File "<stdin>", line 6, in __getitem__

IndexError
```

Next, you have some more special methods that deal with sequence and number-related methods.

__len__(self)—This method is called to return the length of the instance when len() is called on an instance of this type.

__add__ (self, other)—Implement this method to return self + other.

__sub__ (self, other)—Implement this method to return self − other.

__mul__ (self, other)—Implement this method to return self * other.

__div__ (self, other)—Implement this method to return self / other.

__mod__ (self, other)—Implement this method to return self % other.

__neg__ (self)—Implement this method to return self negated.

__pos__ (self)—Implement this method to return self positive.

__abs__ (self)—This method is called to return the absolute value of self when abs() is called on instances of this type.

__inv__ (self)—Implement this method to return the inverse of self.

__lshift__ (self, other)—Implement this method to return self shifted left by other.

__rshift__ (self, other)—Implement this method to return self shifted right by other.

__and__ (self, other)—Implement this method to return the bitwise and value of self and other.

__or__ (self, other)—Implement this method to return the bitwise or value of self and other.

__xor__ (self, other)—Implement this method to return the bitwise exclusive or value of self and other.

__not__ (self)—Implement this method to return the outcome of not self. (Note that there is no __not__() discipline for object instances; only the interpreter core defines this operation.)

__setitem__ (a, b, c)—Implement this method to set the value of a at index b to c.

__delitem__ (a, b)—Implement this method to remove the value of a at index b.

__getslice__ (a, b, c)—Implement this method to return the slice of a from index b to index c−1.

__setslice__ (a, b, c, v)—Implement this method to set the slice of a from index b to index c−1 to the sequence v.

__delslice__ (a, b, c)—Implement this method to delete the slice of a from index b to index c−1.

The next example has a class definition that overrides some methods. Note that every instance of this class is callable.

```
>>> class Author:
...     def __init__(self, argname):
...         self.name = argname
...     def __str__(self):
...         return self.name
...     def __repr__(self):
...         return `self.name`
...     def __call__(self, other):
...         return self.name + other
...
>>> obj = Author("Andre")
>>> print obj
Andre
>>> obj
'Andre'
>>> obj(" Lessa")
'Andre Lessa'
```

Python 2.0 has added a special set of operators to the language, which are called *augmented assignment operators*. These operators can be overriden by inserting an '*i*' in front of the name, for example, __isub__ implements in-place __sub__ (in other words, the -= operator).

Also in this new release, you have access to the built-in method __contains__, which gives you access to customize the in operator.

Method Attributes

A method implements some special attributes that can be accessed from within the class that implements it.

Suppose that you have a method called *method*:

method.__doc__—Returns the documentation string of *method*.

method.__name__—Returns the *method* name.

method.im_class—Returns the class that has defined *method*.

method.im_self—Returns the instance associated with *method*.

The next example retrieves and prints the __init__ method's documentation string.

```
>>> class c:
...     def __init__(self):
...             "This is a method "
...             print self.__init__.__doc__
...
>>> obj = c()
This is a method
```

Overloading Operators

Python operators are implemented for a class by implementing the equivalent special methods. This feature is called *operator overloading*.

Extensive support exists for operators overloading via the double-underscored special methods such as __add__ and __init__.

Note that the following expressions are equivalent:

```
a * b = __mul__(a, b)
```

```
len(a) = __len__(a)
```

```
a + b = __add__(a,b)
```

The following example overrides the __add__ method and returns a tuple of results.

```
>>> class c:
...         def __init__(self, x, y):
...              self.x = x
...              self.y = y
...         def __add__(self, other):
...              return (self.x + other.x, self.y + other.y)
...
>>> obj1 = c(5,2)
>>> obj2 = c(10,4)
>>> print obj1 + obj2
(15, 6)
```

Of course, in real life, you would be more likely to want to return an instance of the class c, rather than just a tuple.

Some others built-in methods you can use or overwrite are as follows:

```
__sub__(self, other)
```

```
__div__(self, other)
```

```
__abs__(self)
```

```
__hex__(self)
```

```
__int__(self)
```

Another small example

```
>>> class C:
...         def __init__(self, value):
...              self.value = value
...         def __sub__(self, other):
...              return self.value - other.value
...
```

```
>>> vara = C(5)
>>> varb = C(3)
>>> varc = vara - varb
>>> print varc
```
2

Inheritance

A subclass is a class that inherits attribute names and methods from another class—the operation is called *subclassing*.

A base class (superclass) is defined as a class that another class inherits attributes from. Base classes are listed in parentheses in a subclass header. You have to separate base classes by putting commas between them, within the parentheses.

When you create a subclass, you can add or overwrite any methods of its base classes.

Python classes can be created:

- From scratch

  ```
  >>> class A:
  ...     pass
  ...
  ```

- By using single inheritance

  ```
  >>> class B(A):
  ...     pass
  ...
  ```

- By using multiple inheritance

  ```
  >>> class D(B,C):
  ...     pass
  ...
  ```

For a conceptual standpoint, take a look at the following example

Where,

Base class = `writing tools`

subclass = `pen`

subclass = `chalk`

Both subclasses pen and chalk inherit characteristics of the base class writing tools.

The subsequent class defines a complex class called Employee.

```
class Employee:
    def __init__(self,name,salary=0):
        self.name = name
        self.salary = salary
        self.family = []
    def raisesalary(self, percent):
        self.salary = self.salary + (self.salary * percent)
    def work (self):
        print self.name, "writes computer code."
    def hasfamily(self):
        return len(self.family) == 0        # returns a boolean result
    def addmember(self, x):
        self.family.append(x)
    def removemember(self, x):
        if len(self.family) > 0:
            x = self.family[-1]
            del self.family[-1]
            return x
```

The next class is a subclass of the Employee class.

```
class Person(Employee):
    "this is the class Person"
    def __init__ (self, name):
        Employee.__init__ (self, name, 50000)
    def work (self):
        print self.name, "works like any other employee."
```

Inherited methods of base classes aren't automatically called. It is necessary to call them explicitly. That's why, in the previous example, the Person.__init__ method had to call the Employee.__init__ method.

It is always necessary to pass the self argument because base classes don't know what instance is being used. The previous example passes three parameters to the base class's __init__ method (the self reference, an argument, and a default value for the other argument).

Multiple inheritance is defined by entering multiple classes in the header of a new class. The order used for informing the base classes really does matter. The precedence order, for a search in the base classes, starts at the classes located at the left side.

```
class A:
    pass
class B(A):
    pass
class C:
    pass
class D(B,C):
    pass
```

The precedence order for class D inheritance is: B, A, C.

> **Tip**
> You always have to use fully qualified names when calling a superclass's method (if it has been overridden) because if the class has multiple base classes containing the same symbol, the first one found is used.

```
>>> class A:
...     def __init__(self, name):
...         self.name = name
...     def printname(self):
...         print 'The name %s belongs to class A!' % self.name
...
>>> class B(A):
...     __baseclass=A
...     def __init__(self, name):
...         self.__baseclass.__init__(self,name)
...     def printname(self):
...         print 'The name %s belongs to class B!' % self.name
...         self.__baseclass.printname(self)
...
>>> class C(B):
...     __baseclass=B
...     def __init__(self, name):
...         self.__baseclass.__init__(self,name)
...     def printname(self):
...         print 'The name %s belongs to class C!' % self.name
...         self.__baseclass.printname(self)
...
```

```
>>> A("monkey").printname()
The name monkey belongs to class A!
>>> B("parrot").printname()
The name parrot belongs to class B!
The name parrot belongs to class A!
>>> C("ant").printname()
The name ant belongs to class C!
The name ant belongs to class B!
The name ant belongs to class A!
```

Polymorphism

The concept of polymorphism doesn't really apply to Python objects because Python doesn't offer type declaration. This concept (having a function or method work for multiple argument types) is something you get for free with Python because of the dynamic typing. It does exist, but you don't usually explicitly code for it. When handling an obj.method expression, the meaning of method depends on the type, or *class*, of the object obj.

Python doesn't know what type of object implements an interface until the program is running. This feature is called *runtime binding*.

Python variables are typed, just not explicitly so. They are typed implicitly as the program uses them. For instance, if a program invokes abs(x), it doesn't make sense for x to be any object but a number. Therefore, the variable x is informally typed.

The capability of dealing with objects at different levels of abstraction is one of the most important features of object-oriented programming and a very important part of Python.

The next example shows how you can use just one function to implement polymorphism in Python. C++ refers to this variety of polymorphism as *method overloading*.

```
>>> class polymorph:
...     def handle_int(self, argint):
...         print '%d is an int' % argint
...     def handle_str(self, argStr):
...         print '%s is a string' % argStr
...     def handle(self, arg):
...         if type(arg) == type(1):
...             self.handle_int(arg)
```

```
...               elif type(arg) == type(''):
...                   self.handle_str(arg)
...               else:
...                   print "%s is not a string nor an integer" % arg
...
>>> p = polymorph()
>>> p.handle(10)
10 is an integer

>>> p.handle("Albatross!!")
Albatross!! is a string
```

The following code implements a class that *does not work* because the program tries to apply the general concept of polymorphism. This is a very common mistake that always catches programmers who don't know this concept doesn't exist in Python.

Note that we try to define two different implementations of the same method (see lines 3 and 6). Right below this sample of code, you can see a traceback message that is provided by the interpreter when we try to run it.

```
1:>>> ## Beginning of a Python class THAT DOES NOT WORK...
2:...
3:>>> class Polimorpherror:
4:...      def __init__(self):
5:...          print 'No arguments!'
6:...      def __init__(self, args):
7:...          print 'One argument!'
8:...          self.args = args
9:...
10:>>> ## End of a python class THAT DOES NOT WORK
11:...
12:>>> x = Polimorpherror()
>>> x = Polimorpherror()
Traceback (innermost last):
   File "<stdin>", line 1, in ?
TypeError: not enough arguments; expected 2, got 1
```

You cannot do method overloading as shown in the previous example. The next example presents a suggestion for the correct way to implement a solution for this problem.

```
>>> class Polimorpherror:
...     def __init__(self, args=None):
...         if args == None:
...             print 'No arguments!'
...         if args == 1:
...             print 'One argument!'
...             self.args = args
...
```

The behavior of overloaded functions and methods is better implemented in Python using default arguments or by explicitly looking at the types of the arguments passed into the function.

If you have a class for which you need to specify both a default constructor and a constructor that takes initial values of state as arguments, I suggest that you do so by transporting default arguments to the __init__ method.

```
>>> class Animal:
...     def __init__(self, name = "Parrot"):
...         self.name = name
...     def printAnimal(self):
...         print self.name
...
>>> p = Animal()
>>> p.printAnimal()
Parrot
>>> p = Animal("Monkey")
>>> p.printAnimal()
Monkey
```

If you want to initialize a variable but you don't want to enforce an object type, you can use the None type.

```
>>> class Animal:
...     def __init__(self, name = None):
...         self.name = name
...     def printAnimal(self):
...         print self.name
...
```

Encapsulation

All Python attributes (variables and methods) are public. Even though you cannot have private attributes in Python, you can use the following two agreements:

- By convention, attributes preceded with a single underscore (for example, _n) are to be viewed as internal variables, not to be used externally.

- Attributes starting with double underscores (for example, __n) aren't explicitly exported. They are renamed to _Class__Variablename when byte compiled. Because the name of a class is used as part of the variable name, the attribute __n (when inside a subclass) isn't the same __n variable defined at a base class. This is probably the closest to private that you will get. But, it isn't really a private implementation because when you know the name of the class, you can access the attribute. C++ programmers probably know this as *name mangling*.

We cannot say that Python supports private attributes because it is still possible to have access to the attributes if you know the class and attributes names. For example, in a class called C, the attribute self.__attr becomes self._C__attr, when exported from the class. Hence, you can access this attribute by referencing it as _C__attr.

```
>>> class Number:
...     def __init__(self, value):
...         self._n = value
...         self.__n = value
...     def __repr__(self):
...         return '%s(%s)' % (self.__class__.__name__, self._n)
...     def add(self, value):
...         self._n = self._n + value
...     def incr(self):
...         self._n = self._n + 1
...
```

Based on the previous class, we will have some interactive examples next.

```
>>> a = Number(20)
>>> a
Number(20)
>>> a.add(4)
>>> a
Number(24)
>>> a.incr()
>>> a
Number(25)
```

```
>>> a._n
25
>>> a._n = 30
>>> a
Number(30)
>>> a._Number__n
20
```

The important thing to remember is that nothing in Python is *private* (unless it is hidden within a C extension type).

To demonstrate that you can use default arguments to help storing the environment variables in a variable from the *class namespace*, the next example initializes the value of the variable n by using a default argument. The value of n is assigned at the time of defining the function and is stored at the class *namespace*.

```
>>> v = 10
>>> class C:
...     def storen(self, n=v):
...         return n
...
>>> objA = C()
>>> objA.storen()
10
>>> v = 20
>>> objB = C()
>>> objB.storen()
10
>>> n = 30
>>> objC = C()
>>> objC.storen()
10
```

Note that the value of n remains constant for all instances of the class c.

The following example shows that it is possible to manipulate the internal attributes of an object by directly accessing the members of a class.

```
>>> class fun:
...     def __init__(self):
...         self.total = None
...
>>> a = fun()
>>> b = fun()
```

```
>>> a.total = 2
>>> b.total = 3
>>> print a, b
2 3
```

In this next example, we hide the a() method definition by preceding it with two underscores. Note that if you later need to access this method (and you don't want to rename it), you must create a reference to the method, as shown in the following example.

```
>>> class C:
...       def __a(self):
...            print "ni!"
...       b = __a
...
>>> a = C()
>>> a.b()
ni!
```

Metaclasses

A *metaclass* is just a class that is used as a template to create class-like entities.

Normally, you create instances based on classes. The goal here is to create classes (*metainstances*) based on other classes (*metaclasses*). The resulting metainstances are used as base classes for your own classes.

The whole idea is to offer you the possibility of operating Python's internal class-handling engine. Everything that usually happens behind the scenes while manipulating your classes and objects now can be accessed and changed. The meta-instance makes it easier for you to handle the task of modifying the attribute lookup behavior of objects.

Prior to Python, version 1.5, it was necessary to use C extensions in order to define metaclasses.

The subsequent code defines a simple metaclass and its supporting classes. Note that this structure doesn't cover the whole model.

```
1: >>> import types
2: >>> class METACLASS:
3: ...      def __init__(self, name, bases, namespace):
4: ...            self.__name__ = name
```

```
 5: ...          self.__bases__ = bases
 6: ...          self.__namespace__ = namespace
 7: ...      def __call__(self):
 8: ...          return METAINSTANCE(self)
 9: ...
10: >>> class METAINSTANCE:
11: ...      def __init__(self, metaclass):
12: ...          self.__metaclass__ = metaclass
13: ...      def __getattr__(self, name):
14: ...          try:
15: ...              value = self.__metaclass__.__namespace__[name]
16: ...          except KeyError:
17: ...              raise AttributeError, name
18: ...          if type(value) is not types.FunctionType:
19: ...              return value
20: ...          return METHODWRAPPER(value, self)
21: ...
22: >>> class METHODWRAPPER:
23: ...      def __init__(self, function, metainstance):
24: ...          self.function = function
25: ...          self.instance = metainstance
26: ...          self.__name__ = self.function.__name__
27: ...      def __call__(self, *args):
28: ...          return apply(self.function, (self.instance,) + args)
29: ...
```

Line 2 : Defines the metaclass METACLASS.

Lines 3-6 : Creates a new metaclass. The __init__ method expects three arguments: The metainstance name, a tuple of base classes, and a dictionary of the metainstance namespace.

Lines 7-8 : Invokes METAINSTANCE.__init__ when METACLASS is called, returning a metainstance.

Line 10 : Defines the metainstance METAINSTANCE.

Line 13 : Handles the access to attributes of the user instance by checking whether it is part of the user class namespace (lines 14-17). If the attribute is a value, it returns the value. Otherwise, if the attribute is a function, it returns an instance of the METHODWRAPPER class, which is actually the result of the function call.

Line 22 : Defines the METHODWRAPPER class, which handles all the accesses to the method attributes of the user class.

Now that we are ready to call metaclasses, you can use metainstances as base classes of your own classes, trapping the access to your class objects. The next line of code creates an instance of a metainstance.

```
>>> BASECLASS = METACLASS('BASECLASS', (), {})
```

Let me explain to you what is really happening here:

We are creating a class called BASECLASS whose behavior is inherited from the METACLASS constructor class. The METACLASS.__init__ method is invoked at this stage.

From now on, every class that you create—which uses BASECLASS as the base class—will inherit the whole behavior that you have specified in the METACLASS definition.

The following code exemplifies a user class that has our BASECLASS as the base class.

```
>>> class CEO(BASECLASS):
...     def push(self, name):
...         self.name = [name]
...     def pop(self):
...         if len(self.name) > 0:
...             item = self.name[-1]
...             del self.name[-1]
...             print item
...
```

Now it's time to illustrate the use of this whole concept.

```
>>> ITCEO = CEO()
>>> ITCEO.push("Andre")
>>> ITCEO.pop()
['Andre']
>>> ITCEO.name
[]
```

Note that ITCEO = CEO() invokes METACLASS.__call__, which creates a METAINSTANCE instance, whereas all the other calls invoke METAINSTANCE.__getattr__.

More details about metaclasses can be found at the following addresses:

http://www.python.org/doc/essays/metaclasses/

and Mess—The Meta-Extension System Set (old stuff) at
http://starship.python.net/crew/da/mess/doc/Tutorial.

Mess is a set of extensions that allows the creation of new types, among other things. It's not certain whether it will ever be integrated into Python, but its documentation can provide a lot of help in understanding metaclass concepts.

Maybe you will like to take a look at the `ExtensionClass` extension by Digital Creations that uses metaclasses to allow creation of class-like objects in C (and is a lot easier to use than Mess). This extension illustrates how the Python class mechanism can be extended, and provides a lightweight mechanism developed for making Python extension types more class-like. Classes can be developed in an extension language, such as C or C++, and treated like other Python classes.

`http://www.digicool.com/releases/ExtensionClass/`

Summary

Python is a language that implements object-oriented programming (OOP) by supporting classes and class instances.

A class is a template from which objects can be created. It has its own namespace and stores object attributes and methods, which can be inherited from other base classes— a process called *subclassing*.

A class can also contain class variable assignments. These variables are shared by all the class instances, and they are part of the class namespace. All class attributes (variables and methods) are public.

In order to identify the right variable that is used when you get multiple variables with the same name within your code, the following search order is followed: instance variables, class variables, and base class variables.

Python has a module called `pyclbr` (Python Class Browser) that offers you the possibility of browsing all the information about classes that is stored in some other specific module. Note that most of this information can also be deduced through introspection. `pyclbr` gives you another benefit in that you don't need to import the module.

Each object created from a class is an *instance* of a class, which has some specific properties: identity, object type, attributes, methods, and value.

Classes and instances have built-in attributes that provide access to their internal definitions (namespace, name, and so on).

The built-in functions `isinstance()` and `issubclass()` are provided to help determine the inheritance properties of instance and class objects.

Each instance defines its own namespace of data, and it inherits behavior from the class (and possible base classes) that have originated it.

Python object attributes don't need to be declared inside the class before they get used because they can be created dynamically.

Class methods can be unbound and used outside a class definition. They also carry some special attributes that can be called from within the class that implements them. These attributes enable the access to the method's name, the method's documentation string, and so on.

All method definitions must carry the argument `self`, whose function is to transport a reference of the object in a way so that when a method is called, it knows which object should be affected.

Python exposes some special methods, such as __init__(), __str__(), and so on. These methods inherit built-in functions of the same name that are provided by Python itself.

Python operators can be re-created by remapping their built-in functions and methods. This feature is called *operator overloading*. Extensive support exists for operators overloading via the double-underscored special methods such as __add__() and __div__().

Python classes can be created from scratch by using single inheritance and multiple inheritance.

A *subclass* is a class that inherits attribute names from another class, whereas a *base class* is defined as a class that another class inherits attributes from. When you create a subclass, you can add or overwrite any method from its base classes. However, inherited methods of base classes aren't automatically called. It is necessary to call them explicitly.

The order used to inform the base classes in a class header is really important. The precedence order for attribute searches in the base classes starts at the class located at the left side.

Python doesn't offer type declaration because it doesn't know what type of object implements an interface until the program is running. This feature is called *runtime binding*.

A single underscore preceding the attribute name is used to point out internal attributes that shouldn't be used externally. Attributes starting with double underscores aren't explicitly exported.

Python also offers you the possibility of operating its internal class handling engine by using metaclasses and metainstances. A metaclass is just a class used as a template to create class-like entities, and the use of metainstance makes it easier for you to handle the task of modifying the attribute lookup behavior of objects.

Code Examples

This application subclasses an exception class and executes the commands stored in a file. The filename is asked by the application.

Listing 5.1   *Configuration File (File configfile.py)*

```
 1: ###
 2: # Program: Configuration File
 3: # Author:   Andre S Lessa
 4: ###
 5:
 6: ### import modules
 7:
 8: import exceptions, sys
 9:
10: configfile = raw_input("Configuration File: ")
11:
12: class ConfigError (exceptions.Exception):
13:     def __init__(self, arg=None):
14:         self.args = arg
15:
16: try:
17:     try:
18:         file = open(configfile)
19:         lines = file.readlines()
20:     finally:
21:         file.close()
22: except:
23:     print "Error. Invalid file name."
24:     sys.exit()
25:
```

Listing 5.1   *(continued)*

```
26: lines[0] = lines[0][:-1]
27:
28: if lines[0] != "CFG2000":
29:     raise ConfigError, "Invalid header."
30:
31: lines = lines[1:]
32:
33: for line in lines:
34:     try:
35:         exec line
36:     except LookupError, b:
37:         if b.args[0] == "list index out of range":
38:             print "Error. Invalid index entry"
39:         else:
40:             print "Error. Generic LookupError entry"
41:     except SystemExit:
42:         print "Error. sys.exit() cannot be used."
```

Lines 12-14: The class `ConfigError` is created. It inherits all the attributes from the `exceptions.Exception` class.

Line 29: Raises our new exception class.

In order to test this program, we have to create a file called *config.txt* that contains the following lines:

```
CFG2000
print
print "Configuration File"
print "-----------------"
server = "SRV001"
port = 80
print "Server: ", server
print "Port:   ", port
```

The next interaction shows how to call the program. It also shows the results provided by the program when no exception is raised.

```
C:\ Python>python configfile.py
Configuration File: config.txt


Configuration File
-----------------
```

```
Server:   SRV001
Port:      80
```

```
C:\Program Files\Python>
```

This simple program creates a class structure that stores and prints a list of groceries.

Listing 5.2 *Groceries List (File groceries.py)*

```
 1: ###
 2: # Program: Groceries List
 3: # Author:   Andre S Lessa
 4: ###
 5:
 6: ### import modules
 7:
 8:
 9: class grocery:
10:     "Items that you need to buy at the grocery store."
11:     def __init__(self, name, quantity=1):
12:         self.name = name
13:         self.quantity = quantity
14:
15: items = {}
16: print "Type ENTER when you are done."
17: while 1:
18:     name = raw_input("Grocery name: ")
19:     if name == "":
20:         break
21:     quantity = raw_input("%s quantity: " % (name))
22:     if quantity == "":
23:         items[name] = grocery(name)
24:     else:
25:         items[name] = grocery(name,quantity)
26:
27: print "----------------------\nList of groceries to buy"
28: print "----------------------"
29:
30: for item in items.keys():
31:     print "Grocery : ", items[item].name,
32:     print "\tQuantity: ", items[item].quantity
33:
34: print "---------"
```

Line 9: Declares the grocery class.

Line 10: The class's documentation text.

Line 11: A default value is defined for the `quantity` argument.

Lines 22-25: Uses a different interface to initialize the object, depending on the information provided.

Lines 31-32: Provides access to the object attributes.

The next interaction shows how the program works.

```
C:\Python>python groceries.py
Type ENTER when you are done.
Grocery name: bananas
bananas quantity: 12
Grocery name: apples
apples quantity: 6
Grocery name: pears
pears quantity: 8
Grocery name: pineapple
pineapple quantity:
Grocery name:
. . . . . . . . . . . . . . . . . . . . . . .
List of groceries to buy
. . . . . . . . . . . . . . . . . . . . . . .
Grocery :   pineapple     Quantity:   1
Grocery :   pears         Quantity:   8
Grocery :   apples        Quantity:   6
Grocery :   bananas       Quantity:   12
. . . . . . . . . .

C:\Python>
```

This file introduces two classes and one function that extensively manipulate class methods and attributes.

Listing 5.3   *Company employees (File company.py)*

```
1: ###
2: # Program: Company employees
3: # Author:  Andre S Lessa
4: ###
5:
```

Listing 5.3 *(continued)*

```
 6: ### import modules
 7:
 8: import types
 9:
10: class Employee:
11:     "Generic class for all company employees"
12:
13:     __employees = 0
14:
15:     def __init__(self,name,salary=500.00):
16:         self.name = name
17:         self.salary = salary
18:         self.family = []
19:         Employee.__employees = Employee.__employees + 1
20:
21:     def __str__(self):
22:         return "employee: %s" % self.name
23:
24:     def raisesalary(self, percent):
25:         self.salary = self.salary + (self.salary * (1.0/percent))
26:
27:     def job(self):
28:         print self.name, "writes Python code."
29:
30:     def hasfamily(self):
31:         return len(self.family) > 0
32:
33:     def addmember(self, name):
34:         self.family.append(name)
35:
36:     def removemember(self, arg):
37:         if len(self.family) > 0:
38:             if type(arg) == type(1):
39:                 self.removemember_int(arg)
40:             elif isinstance(arg, types.StringType):
41:                 self.removemember_str(arg)
42:
43:     def removemember_int(self, index):
44:         member = self.family[index]
45:         del self.family[index]
46:         return member
47:
```

Listing 5.3   *(continued)*

```
48:      def removemember_str(self, name):
49:          for member in self.family:
50:              if member == name:
51:                  del self.family[self.family.index(member)]
52:                  return member
53:
54:      def __getitem__(self, index):
55:          member = self.family[index]
56:          return member
57:
58: class Leader(Employee):
59:     "Company's Leader of the employees"
60:     def __init__ (self, name):
61:         Employee.__init__ (self, name, 1500.00)
62:     def job(self):
63:         print self.name, "supervises who writes Python code."
64:
65: def totalemployee():
66:     return  Employee._employee_employees
```

Line 10: Defines the Employee class.

Line 13: Class variable __employees.

Line 19: Increments the number of employees.

Line 31: Returns a logical value (0 or 1).

Lines 36-41: Implements polymorphism by enabling the user to enter both string and integer values.

Lines 43-52: Helper methods for the polymorphism implementation.

Line 54: Enables the slicing of employees instances.

Line 58: Defines a subclass Leader that inherits attributes from the Employee class.

Lines 60-63: The __init__() and the job() methods are overwritten.

Line 65: Provides a function that returns the total number of employees who are currently part of the class.

The following interaction shows how the classes must be used.

```
>>> import company
>>> andre = company.employee("Andre") # Creates an employee instance
```

```
>>> print andre
employee: Andre
>>> print andre.salary
500
>>> andre.raisesalary(10) # Raises his salary in 10 percent
>>> andre.salary
550.0
>>> andre.job()                           # Shows his job description
Andre writes Python code.
>>> andre.hasfamily()
0
>>> andre.addmember("Renata")             # Add a member to his family
>>> andre.addmember("Joao Pedro")         # Add a member to his family
>>> andre.addmember("Rebecca")            # Add a member to his family
>>> andre.hasfamily()                     # Returns 1 or 0
1
>>> andre.family
['Renata', 'Joao Pedro', 'Rebecca']
>>> andre.removemember("Joao Pedro")   # Remove string member from list
>>> andre.family
['Renata', 'Rebecca']
>>> andre.removemember("Renata
>>> andre.family
['Rebecca']
>>> andre.removemember(0) # Remove index member from list
>>> andre.family
[]
>>> andre.addmember("Joao Pedro")
>>> andre.addmember("Renata")
>>> andre.addmember("Rebecca")
>>> andre[0]
'Joao Pedro'
>>> andre[1
'Renata'
>>> andre[2]
'Rebecca'
>>> company.totalemployee()# Shows the total number of employees
1
>>> renata = company.employee("Renata")
>>> company.totalemployee()
2
>>> Joao = company.Leader("Joao Pedro")   # Creates a leader instance
```

```
>>> Joao.salary
1500.0
>>> Joao.job()
Joao Pedro makes food
>>> company.totalemployee()
3
>>>
```

PART II

Advanced Programming

CHAPTER

CHAPTER 6

Extending and Embedding Python

What is your name? ... What is your quest? ... What is your favorite color?

The information provided in this chapter is a big step for those who want to be highly specialized in Python programming. It demonstrates how you can create Python extension modules in C and C++, and how you can embed Python objects in other non-Python applications.

Extending and Embedding Python

Python has the capability to glue applications together. No doubt this is one of Python's most important and well-known features. The reason for that is mostly because Python provides a two-way communication channel to C by supporting both embedding and extending functionality. Whenever you use Python code to call C code, you are extending Python. On the other hand, if you use C code to call Python code, you are embedding Python. Even though these features can bring great results to your application, most programmers never need to use these Python capabilities. Well, most programmers will have to use the results of someone else extending Python.

We already know that Python can be used to write simple code in a shorter time. However, we can also use C/C++ code to provide efficient and fast data processing, such as create built-in modules containing functions, variables, exceptions; define new built-in object types in C; and call C library functions and system calls.

Python has a good relationship with C because Python's interpreter is written in C, and since the beginning, the interpreter has been ready to work with extension modules. Furthermore, the fact that C is supported on almost all platforms makes Python a good choice between cross-platform languages. By writing extension modules in Python, you can generate tight C/C++ interfaces that can be used both in production environments and in efficient prototype testing wrappers.

Currently, many Python-contributed modules (implemented as C extensions) provide interfaces to many different system components. Those extension modules allow Python to talk to already existing subroutine libraries, to native application programmer interfaces, and to special-purpose devices. They are imported and handled the same as any other Python module written in Python.

The extension modules are used mostly to add new functionality to Python when there is no other way to interface Python with a particular system or hardware. Sometimes, when Python code is inefficient, extension modules are also used to boost performance.

If you need to call Python routines from inside your application, you can use the embedding functionality to have them called by your application.

In order to write Python extensions, you must have the source code for the Python interpreter and access to a C or C++ compiler. If you are running Windows, your compiler choice should be *Microsoft Visual C++ version 5* or later. Note that most Linux distributions have a package that contains all the necessary files needed for compiling extensions, so you don't need a full source distribution in this case. On Red Hat like systems, this package is called `python-devel`.

The Python official documentation and the links that are listed throughout this chapter are a good source of information about this topic.

Embedding and Extending the Python Interpreter:

```
http://www.python.org/doc/current/ext/ext.html
```

Some people using Win32 claim to have successfully used the Free Borland Compiler to compile Python extension modules.

Free Borland Compiler:

```
http://www.borland.com/bcppbuilder/freecompiler/
```

Some people also successfully used GNU gcc with the mingw32 runtime. There is some info at `http://starship.python.net/crew/kernr/mingw32/Notes.html`

The Python/C API

Python provides an intuitive and clean C Application Programmers Interface (API) that exposes the interface to the Python runtime system. This API provides a great number of functions to manipulate Python objects and built-in types from C and C++. Most of the functions work in much the same way as they would when called from the interpreter.

To include this API in your C/C++ program, you just need to add the header `"<Python.h>"` to your source code.

Internally, this header file includes both Python and *C* header files, including: `<stdio.h>`, `<string.h>`, `<errno.h>`, and `<stdlib.h>`. Therefore, you don't need to include these again once you include `"<Python.h>"`.

> Python/C API Reference Manual (This link takes you to the official and latest documentation about the Python/C API.):
>
> `http://www.python.org/doc/current/api/api.html`

Check Appendix A, "Python/C API" of this book for more details and for a complete list of the interface functions provided by the Python/C API.

Extending

Because Python cannot access C/C++ functions in a straightforward way, it is necessary to handle the conversion between Python and C/C++ data types when putting them to work together. That is when we use the Python extension modules. These extensions work like a thin wrapper of functions written in C/C++ that are necessary to bring the C/C++ functionality to the developer.

It is widely known that interpreted languages execute intensive applications slower than compiled languages. As a result, it is a good choice to implement as extension modules the application routines that need to run fast, such as network access, database manipulation, and routines that intensively use the graphical interface.

Keep in mind that you always have to think about whether it is really necessary to implement routines as extension modules. Are you sure that the processing speed will get better by calling C functions instead of just using plain Python?

Before starting to implement anything in C, I suggest that you analyze and test your Python code. Check to see whether it can be optimized. Profile it, and only if you find some big problem, create C extensions. As an example, if you have the execution time of a function that only accounts for 1% of the program execution time, you have only reduced total execution time by 0.5%.

And remember, before you implement some surreal extension, to first check the Python distribution and the contributed modules. What you need might already be there.

Some good links to where you can check for existing modules are

The Python contributed modules page at

```
http://www.python.org/download/Contributed.html
```

The Vaults of Parnassus collection of Python resources at

```
http://www.vex.net/~x/parnassus/
```

The extension modules should be used to write specific operations, and not complete applications. By doing this, you will spend less time developing the wrapping interfaces.

The next two links provide a good source of information about writing an extension module:

"How to Write a Python Extension," by Michael P. Reilly:

```
http://starship.python.net/crew/arcege/extwriting/pyext.html
```

"Extension Classes, Python Extension Types Become Classes," by Jim Fulton:

```
http://www.digicool.com/releases/ExtensionClass/
```

Creating New Extensions

I presume that if you came this far, you are sure that you want to use extension modules. So, let's start developing something.

First, in many places, you will see the naming convention for extension module files defined as *modulename*module.c. Second, all extension modules must include the Python/C API "<Python.h>" system header file.

The next example is an extension module called helloworldmodule.c that is used to demonstrate how easy it is to create a Python extension.

```
/* File: helloworldmodule.c */

#include "<Python.h>"

/* external function*/
static PyObject *sayhello(PyObject *self)
{
  return Py_BuildValue("s","Hello Python World!");
}


/* name binding table */
static PyMethodDef hellomethods[] = {
  {"say", sayhello, METH_VARARGS },
  {NULL, NULL}                   /* sentinel */
};


/* initialization function*/
DL_EXPORT(void) inithello()
{
    Py_InitModule("hello", hellomethods);
}
```

After linking this module to your interpreter, it becomes promptly accessible for your use (see Figure 6.1).

It is important to stick to the naming convention because when the module is first imported, the init*modulename*() function is called.

Every time you implement a C function that Python will call, you have to define two arguments. The first one is called self, and it is a pointer to the called object. The argument self is used when implementing built-in methods to point to the bound object. When a function is implemented, self is set to NULL.

The other argument is usually called args, which is a pointer to a tuple object that contains the arguments of the function.

Figure 6.1
As you can see, there is no difference between the way you use an extension module and the other modules.

Check out another example. This one passes arguments between Python and C.

```
/* File: systemmodule.c*/

#include "<Python.h>"

static PyObject *system_command(PyObject *self, PyObject *args)


{
    int   return_status;
    char *program;
    char *argument;
    static char statement[255];

    if (!PyArg_ParseTuple(args, "ss", &program, &argument))
        return NULL;

    sprintf(statement, "%s %s", program, argument);

    return_status = system(statement);
    return Py_BuildValue("i", return_status);
}

static PyMethodDef systemmethods[] = {
    {"command", system_command, METH_VARARGS},
```

```
   {NULL, NULL}
};


DL_EXPORT(void) initsystem() {
   Py_InitModule("system", systemmethods);
}
```

The next set of instructions calls the command() function that is part of the system module, which is stored in the systemmodule.c file.

```
>>> import system
>>> system.command("dir","|more")
```

All interface items are Python objects. Thus, function arguments and return values are pointers to PyObject structures. PyObjects are C representations of real Python objects. All PyObjects have a reference count.

You shouldn't declare a variable of type PyObject. Instead, you have to declare PyObject * pointers to the actual storage of the object. Because all Python objects have a similar behavior, they can be represented by a single C type (PyObject *). Note that a variable of type PyObject can be defined, but it won't be of much use.

In order to implement basic extensions, you essentially use the following commands:

PyArg_ParseTuple(args, format, arg1 [, arg2 [,...]])—Checks the argument types and converts them to C values. It returns a true value when the checking and the conversion doesn't return any errors.

PyArg_ParseTuple—Used to parse the PyObject that contains the function arguments (args). The *second argument* is a format string that lists the object types that you expect to collect, and all the other arguments are pointers to be filled with values from the parsing operation. Note that you can add the function name to the format string to make error messages a bit more informative.

Py_BuildValue(format, Cvar1 [, Cvar2 [,...]])—Converts C objects into Python Objects based on the formatting string. Py_BuildValue is mostly used when it is necessary to return values to the Python interpreter.

> **Tip**
> C functions that return a void argument must return the Python type called None.
>
> ```
> Py_INCREF(Py_None);
> return Py_None;
> ```

For this other example, let's create a function that takes two Python objects and returns a pointer to a Python object.

```c
/* File: divisionmodule.c*/

#include "<Python.h>"

static PyObject *division_function(PyObject *self, PyObject *args)

  { PyObject *result = NULL;
    long a, b;

    if (PyArg_ParseTuple(args, "ii", &a, &b)) {
      result = Py_BuildValue("i", a / b);
    }

    return result;
  }

static PyMethodDef divisionmethods[] = {
  {"divide", division_function, METH_VARARGS},
  {NULL, NULL},
};


DL_EXPORT(void) initdivision()
  {
    Py_InitModule("division", divisionmethods);
  }
```

Importing an Extension Module

As you could see in the previous example, in order to allow Python to import your module, a few steps are required.

1. Create a method array. Each element of this array is a structure that contains: the function's name to be exported to the Python interface, the C function's name and a indicator that shows how arguments must be passed. Each function of the

module to be exported to Python must be an element in this array. Note that the last element of the array works as a sentinel, and it must contain NULLs.

```
static PyMethodDef systemmethods[] = {
    {"command", system_command, METH_VARARGS},
    {NULL, NULL}
};
```

The third argument of each array entry can be

METH_VARARGS means that the arguments are in a tuple format.

METH_VARARGS | METH_KEYWORDS indicates that keyword arguments are also allowed. It will just pass a NULL for the extra argument if no keyword arguments are given.

The *modulename*methods[] array has a fourth optional element, which is a *documentation string*.

2. Create the initialization function of the module. This function should be declared as non-static. All the others should be defined as static in order to avoid name conflicts with other modules.

The init*modulename*() function is automatically called by the interpreter. The DL_EXPORT() definition is used to expose the module entry point. Note that the DL_EXPORT macro only does something on the Win32 platform.

```
DL_EXPORT(void) initsystem() {
    Py_InitModule("system", systemmethods);
```

In this example, the Py_InitModule creates a "system" module object based on the array systemmethods.

You can verify that by checking the sys.modules dictionary after importing the extension module.

Formatting Strings

Whenever you use the PyArg_ParseTuple() or the Py_BuildValue() function, you must follow a mechanism that is based on some formatting tables, which are mentioned next, in order to make the correct conversion between Python types and C types.

Both functions check the arguments type by looking at a formatting string. All the elements of the formatting string must match in type and number with the variables that are also part of the function's list of arguments.

Sometimes, it isn't strictly necessary to have both sides (C and Python) matching in type. The reality is that the receiving field only has to be big enough to fit the received value; hence, the Python type called `float` is easily stored by a C `double` variable. Of course, using a C type that doesn't match the format character will cause problems that might only affect some platforms.

The literals |, :, and ; have special meanings when placed inside a formatting string.

|—The remaining arguments in the formatting string are optional. The C variables will keep their original values in case they aren't assigned to any arguments. You should make sure that the variables are initialized for optional arguments.

:—The string after the colon is the function name to be called in case of error messages.

;—The string after the semicolon is the user error message that must substitute for the original error message.

> **Tip**
> A given formatting string must contain only one | with : or ; because : and ; are
> mutually exclusive.

Table 6.1 covers all the elements that can be part of a `PyArg_ParseTuple`'s formatting string. Just to remind you, `PyArg_ParseTuple()` is used to convert Python objects into C objects.

Table 6.1   *A* `PyArg_ParseTuple`'s *Formatting String Elements*

Element	Python Type	C Type	Notes
s	string	char *	The C string is NULL terminated;
			The Python string cannot be None and it cannot contain embedded NULLs, otherwise, a TypeError exception is raised.
s#	string	char *, int	Pointer to the character string and its length. Note that s# allows embedded NULLs in the string.
z	string or None	char *	Python string can be None. If that happens, the C pointer is set to NULL.
z#	string or None	char *, int	Similar to s#.
b	integer	char	Stores a tiny int (8-bit integer) in a char.

Table 6.1   *(continued)*

Element	Python Type	C Type	Notes
h	integer	`short int`	
i	integer	`int`	
l	integer	`long int`	
c	string of length 1	`char`	
f	float	`float`	
d	float	`double`	
D	complex	`Py_complex`	
O	object	`PyObject *`	The C variable (of type `PyObject *`) stores an s pointer to the address of the Python `object`. The object reference count isn't increased.
O!	object	`typeobject,` `PyObject *`	Similar to O, but it also looks at the address of the Python-type object that specifies the required type. If the Python object doesn't match the required type, a *TypeError* exception is raised.
O&	object	function, variable	Converts a Python object into a C variable of arbitrary type (`void *`), using a function. It is equivalent to: `status = function(object, variable)`. The returned status should be 1 for success and 0 for failure.
s	string	`PyStringObject *`	Similar to O, but it expects a `string` object. It raises a `TypeError` exception otherwise.

Note
Using anything other than the given types could very easily cause problems on some architectures.

If the Python object is a tuple, the number of matching variables passed to the C function must be equal to the number of formatting elements informed. A tuple is indicated in the formatting string by placing the formatting elements between parenthesis.

The `Py_BuildValue` function is used to return values to the Python program that has called the extension module. Its functionality is similar to `PyArg_ParseTuple`.

This function doesn't create a tuple of one element automatically, unless you enclose the single formatting element in parentheses.

Table 6.2 covers the `Py_BuildValue` function and all the elements that can be part of its formatting string. Just to remind you, this function is used to convert C objects into Python objects.

Table 6.2   *A* `Py_BuildValue`'s *Formatting String Elements*

Element	C type	Python type	Notes
s	char *	string	If the C string pointer is NULL, None is returned.
s#	char *, int	string	Converts the C pointer to a character string and its length into a Python string object. If the C pointer is NULL, None is returned.
z	char *	string or None	Similar to s.
z#	char *, int	string or None	Similar to s#.
b	char	integer	
h	short int	integer	
i	int	integer	
l	long int	integer	
c	char	string of length 1	
f	float	float	
d	double	float	
O	PyObject *	object	It increments the reference count of the transported object.
O!	typeobject, PyObject *	object	
O&	function, variable	object	It returns a Python object, or NULL if an error occurs.
S	PyObject *	object	Same as O.
N	PyObject *	object	Similar to O, except that the reference count isn't incremented.

The following list complements the previous table by showing how Python tuples, lists, and dictionaries are generated.

- Matching items between parenthesis are converted into a Python tuple.

- Matching items between square brackets are converted into a Python list.

- Matching items between curly braces are converted into a Python dictionary. Each consecutive pair of values forms a dictionary entry in the format (key, value).

Exporting Constants

In addition to methods, you can also export *constants* back to Python. You just need to bind the constant name to the module namespace dictionary.

```
/* File: pimodule.c*/

#include "<Python.h>"

static PyMethodDef pimethods[] = {
    {NULL, NULL}
};

DL_EXPORT(void)
initpi()
  { PyObject *module, *dictionary;
    PyObject *pivalue;

    module = Py_InitModule("pi", pimethods);
    dictionary = PyModule_GetDict(module);

    pivalue = PyFloat_FromDouble(3.1415926);
    PyDict_SetItemString(dictionary, "pi", pivalue);
    Py_DECREF(pivalue);
  }
```

Error Checking

You must indicate errors in your extension module by returning NULL to the interpreter because functions signal errors by returning NULL. If your function has no return at all, you need to return the None object.

```
return Py_BuildValue("");
```

or

```
Py_INCREF(Py_None);
return Py_None;
```

In case you need to raise an exception, you can do that prior to the `return NULL` statement. Note that returning `NULL` without raising an exception is bad.

Handling Exceptions

Exceptions work as functions in the Python/C API. For example, to raise an `IndexError` exception, you just need to call `PyExc_SetString()` prior to the `return NULL` statement.

Extension modules also support the creation of new exception types.

```
/* File: testexceptionmodule.c*/

#include "<Python.h>"

static PyObject *exception = NULL;

static PyMethodDef testexceptionmethods[] = {
    {NULL, NULL}
};

DL_EXPORT(void)
inittestexception()
  { PyObject *module, *dictionary;
    module = Py_InitModule("testexception", testexceptionmethods);
    dictionary = PyModule_GetDict(module);

    exception = PyErr_NewException("testexception.error", NULL, NULL);
    PyDict_SetItemString(dictionary, "error", exception);
  }
```

If you need to raise your just-created exception, just call it:

```
PyErr_SetString(exception, "I could not do that");
```

Check Appendix A for more information about the Python/C API exception functions, including how to handle threads in your extensions.

Reference Counting

We all know that programmers are responsible for dynamic memory allocation and deallocation in C and C++.

However, Python extensions don't benefit from all the security provided by the Python runtime system. There are a lot of things that you have to be worried about. The main thing is reference counting.

The core Python counts references to every Python object that is created, which enables it to deallocate an object when it doesn't have any more references.

If an object's reference count reaches 0, this object is marked for deallocation. If this same object references other objects, their references are decremented too. The code for deallocating referenced objects occurs in the object destructor.

The counter is incremented when a reference to the object is created, and it is decremented when the reference is deleted. If the reference count becomes zero, the object is released. That's how Python works.

However, Python extensions don't have this functionality built in. You have to increment (Py_INCREF) and decrement (Py_DECREF) the references by yourself.

You can be sure that your reference counting is wrong if your system crashes when you either return a value from the extension module or when you exit the application.

Too few Py_INCREFs can cause the application to freeze at an unspecific time, whereas too few Py_DECREFs cause memory leaks that drive the application to use more and more memory for the process.

An object reference count is defined as the number of owned references to it. The owner of a reference is responsible for calling Py_DECREF(). It is also possible to borrow a reference to an object. The borrower should neither call Py_DECREF() nor use the reference after the reference owner has disposed of it. If you are borrowing a reference, make sure that you are absolutely certain the owner will not release the reference while you are using it.

To make a borrowed reference to become an owned reference, you just need to call Py_INCREF() for the mentioned object.

Take a look at following lines of code:

```
PyObject *O;
    if (! PyArg_ParseTuple(args, "O", &O)) return NULL;
```

You don't need to call Py_DECREF() before leaving the module that implements this kind of code because PyArg_ParseTuple() returns borrowed references, and releasing references that you don't own can cause you severe problems. `Py_INCREF` and `Py_DECREF` are implemented as macros, so only pass a variable as the argument because the argument is evaluated twice after macro expansion.

Python Official Documentation—Reference Counts

```
http://www.python.org/doc/current/api/refcounts.html
```

"Debugging Reference Count Problems," by Guido van Rossum

```
http://www.python.org/doc/essays/refcnt.html
```

Building Extensions in C++

Python has a C-based interpreter, and it becomes a bit harder to adjust code to compile it as C++ because Python has some restrictions when it comes to creating extension modules using C++. However, there are some things that you can do in order to reduce your problems. The next hints will help you to link Python to a C++ compiler.

The problems depend on the C++ compiler that you are using. However the most common ones are discussed in the following paragraphs.

If the Python interpreter is compiled and liked by a C compiler, you cannot use global or static C++ objects with constructors. Unless you use a C++ compiler. But, you can initialize the globals in the module's init function instead.

You need to place `extern "C" { ... }` around the Python include files. You need to define the Python API as a C segment to the C++ compiler as well.

```
extern "C"{
#include "<Python.h>"
}
```

If the header files for Python on your machine already include the `extern "C" { ... }` stuff, adding an extra `extern "C"` block will cause an error on most compilers (as the `extern "C"` syntax is not valid C).

Functions that are going to be called by the interpreter (in particular, module initialization functions) have to be declared using `extern "C"`.

```
extern "C" {
    DL_EXPORT(void)
    initmodulename()
    {
        Py_InitModule("modulename", modulename_methods);
```

```
    }
}
```

This same declaration could also be written as

```
extern "C" DL_EXPORT(void)
    initmodulename()
    {
        Py_InitModule("modulename", modulename_methods);
```

You have these same concerns when building a dynamic module. In fact, there are more concerns (for instance, the DL_EXPORT stuff isn't required if the module is statically linked to the interpreter).

You can use Python to access many C++ class libraries. You just need to have the right wrapper that provides the necessary access to the libraries.

> **Tip**
>
> When embedding Python in your C++ code, it isn't necessary to recompile Python itself using C++. However, if you want to use C++ extension modules, the Python interpreter might have to be compiled with a C++ compiler though recent Linux distributions should work fine without a recompile.
>
> For more information, check out
>
> "Binding Python to C++," by Guido van Rossum
>
> `http://www.python.org/workshops/1994-11/C++Python.txt`

Compiling and Linking Extension Modules

Two options are available for building Python extension modules. The first one compiles and links the module into the interpreter. This option makes the module always available to the interpreter.

The second option doesn't require that you recompile the interpreter because it dynamically links the modules to the system.

Linking Static Extensions to the Interpreter

Before starting, make sure that you have already compiled the interpreter's source code (refer to Chapter 17, "Development Tools," for more details). Building and installing Python before adding new modules is essential to have the libraries and other files in the right places.

Static Extensions on UNIX

On UNIX, Python modules written in C are easily identified by looking at the `/usr/lib/Python1.5` directory. Most of the time, they are the shared library files with the `.so` extension. Although, if you are using HPUX, the extension is `.sl`, and on some others it is just `.o`.

The next few steps show how to create static extensions on UNIX.

1. You need to copy your module to the `Modules` directory.

2. You have to add the following entry to the end of the `/modules/Setup.in` configuration file, which is located in the Python source tree. This file has the list of all the external libraries needed by the interpreter.

```
*static*
modulename filename
```

For example,

```
hello /mnt/hda/python/helloworldmodule.c
```

If your extension module requires additional libraries, add the argument `-llibraryname` at the end of the line.

For example,

```
hello /mnt/hda/python/helloworldmodule.c -l/mnt/hda/python/auxmodule.c
```

The `*static*` flag builds the modules as static modules. The other option is to use the `*shared*` flag, which means that they have to be built as shared modules (known as DLLs on Windows).

The last step is to recompile Python as normal to include the extra module by typing `./`**configure** and **make** in the top of the Python Source tree. The Python interpreter is rebuilt after that.

To execute the new interpreter and test your new extension module, just call it like this:

```
./python
```

Static Extensions on Windows

The following instructions are based on the use of Microsoft Visual C++ version 5.

First, you need to inform Python's `include path`. To do that, go to Tools, Options, Directories (see Figure 6.2).

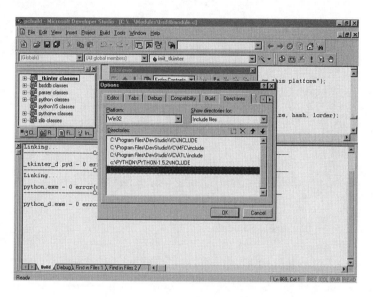

Figure 6.2

You need to inform the include path.

It is also necessary to inform the library's location (see Figure 6.3). You need to add the `python15.lib` directory to your Tools, Options, Directories, Library files.

Now, the rest is easy.

1. Using a text editor, open the `\PC\config.c` file.

2. Look for the first comment. You need to add an external reference to the `init` function of your module.

   ```
   /* -- ADDMODULE MARKER 1 -- */
   extern void initmodulename();
   ```

3. Locate the next comment. You need to add the module name and the init function.

   ```
   /* -- ADDMODULE MARKER 2 -- */
   {"modulename", initmodulename},
   ```

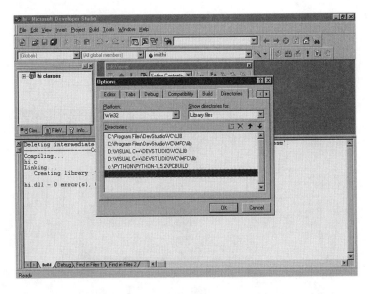

Figure 6.3
You need to inform the python15.lib path.

4. Using a text editor, open the `/PCbuild/python15.dsp` file.

5. Go to the end of the file. Locate the entry that references the `yuvconvert.c` source file. You need to add the location of your module's source file just before that entry.

```
SOURCE=..\Modules\yourmodulenamemodule.c
# End Source File
# Begin Source File

SOURCE=..\Modules\yuvconvert.c
# End Source File
# End Target

# End Project
```

6. Using Microsoft Visual C++, open the `/PCbuild/pcbuild.dsw` workspace.

7. Select the `Batch Build` option and say `Rebuild All`.

By default, the EXE file and the DLLs will be saved in your `/Pcbuild/` directory.

Linking Dynamic Extensions to the Interpreter

Now look at what you should do in order to create dynamic extension modules.

Dynamic Extensions on UNIX

The next few steps show how to build Dynamic extensions on UNIX.

1. Put the reference to your module in the `Setup.in` file. If your module references other source files, you should include them too. You might want to create a new `Setup.in` file in the directory containing your module.

   ```
   *shared*
   spam helloworldmodule.c
   ```

2. Copy the `Makefile.pre.in` file to the directory where your module is located.

3. Type

   ```
   make -f Makefile.pre.in boot
   make
   ```

This process creates a `helloworldmodule.so` file.

You could also try

```
gcc -c -I/usr/local/include/python1.5 helloworldmodule.c
gcc -shared helloworldmodule.o -o helloworldmodule.so
```

Dynamic Extension on Windows

Next, how you can build a Dynamic Extension on Windows is illustrated.

1. Create a directory in the Python top-level directory. Give it the name of your module.

   For example, `c:\python\Python-1.5.2\pimodule`

2. Copy your *modulename*`module.c` file to this directory.

3. Copy the files `example.def`, `example.dsp`, `example.dsw`, and `example.mak`, which are located at the `/PC/example_nt` directory of the standard distribution to your new directory. Don't forget to rename the prefix of these files in order to match the name of your module.

4. On each file, replace the occurrences of `example` with your module name.

5. Choose the `Build` Menu option in order to generate your *modulename*`.dll`.

A subdirectory was created underneath your working directory. This subdirectory, called `Release`, contains your `modulename.dll`.

A tool created by David Ascher is very useful to create Python extension modules. It uses a UNIX `Setup.in` file to generate and build a Microsoft Visual C++ project. This tool is called `compile.py`.

To use it, you just need to put your C module and the `compile.py` file in the same directory, and execute the tool. When fired, the program creates a MS Visual C++ project (`.dsp` extension) and the workspace (`.dsw` extension).

Along with those files, it also creates a subdirectory called `/pyds` in which it stores the python extension module (`.pyd` extension).

In order to use this extension in your application, the interpreter needs to be able to locate the `.pyd` file by looking at the `sys.path`'s variable.

`compile.py` is available at

`http://starship.python.net:9673/crew/da/Code/compile`

Installing and Using Dynamic Modules

You have four simple choices:

- Place your `module.so` or `module.dll` in a directory that is defined by your PYTHONPATH environment variable. The `site-packages` directory under the `lib` directory is a good place to put your extension modules.

- At runtime, you can add the extension module's path to `sys.path`.

- On Windows, you can place the extension module in the same directory of the `python.exe` file.

- Put the extension in the current directory when you start Python.

You won't find any difference while running dynamic modules. They act exactly the same way as the static modules that are linked to the interpreter.

Accessing Generic DLLs

Sam Rushing has created an extension module called `calldll` that enables Python to call any function that is part of a Windows DLL. It doesn't matter whether the DLL is a Python extension.

The problem to remember is that errors caused by non-Python extension DLLs don't return exception codes but error messages.

With this module you can call any function in any `DLL`. This means that you can do just about anything on Win32. This module includes a library that gives access to lots of the system GUI features, and a 'callback' generator for `i386`, which lets external functions call back into Python as if it were C. (Much of the Win32 API uses callbacks.)

Along with that, you can access ODBC by directly calling functions in `odbc32.dll` using a wrapper module called `odbc.py`. The ODBC module is implemented using `calldll`, and it has a few extra practical pieces; code for managing data sources, installing ODBC itself, and creating and maintaining Jet (Microsoft Access) databases. It has also been tested with ODBC drivers from Oracle and Objectivity. Of course, using `calldll` destroys any platform or architecture independence your program may have had.

You can see more details at `http://www.nightmare.com/software.html`.

SWIG—The Simple Wrapper Interface Generator

SWIG (Simple Wrapper and Interface Generator) is an automated tool create by David Beazley used to write interfaces between Python and existing C libraries. These interfaces can contain several single functions.

The programmer doesn't have to write any special wrapping functions to provide the glue between the Python scripting language and the C functions.

SWIG works by reading an interface file that contains function and method prototypes. It automatically does the necessary type conversion, checks the code for error, produces a C file, compiles the file, and builds it into a shared object file.

It works by taking the declarations commonly found in C/C++ header files and using them to generate the glue code (wrappers) that scripting languages need to access the underlying C/C++ code.

SWIG is better suited as a mechanism for controlling a variety of C programs because it enables someone to combine bits and pieces of completely different software packages without waiting for someone else to write a special purpose module.

The handling of datatypes when using SWIG for prototyping and control application is very easy because whenever SWIG finds an unknown datatype, it simply assumes that it is some kind of complex datatype. Consequently, wrapping a complex C program doesn't imply too much work.

SWIG provides a convenient way of building Python interfaces to libraries.

You just need to write simple interface definitions, which SWIG uses to generate the C program that conforms to the Python/C extension guidelines.

SWIG makes it even easier to use scripting languages by automating the process of connecting scripting languages to C/C++ code.

Many reasons you should try SWIG are as follows:

You can easily replace the `main()` function of a C program with Python's interpreter.

C/C++ code is easily tested because you can call C functions and libraries directly from your scripting environment.

Debugging your C code also becomes easier once you use Python's interpreter. Remember that you don't need to change your C code in order to use SWIG.

SWIG can integrate different C/C++ programs together by turning them into extension modules. After the extensions are created, Python can combine and use them to generate new applications.

SWIG understands and parses ANSI C/C++ syntax.

The output of SWIG is a fully functional scripting language module.

As SWIG is designed to work with existing C/C++ code, it will be rarely necessary to change your existing programs.

Your C/C++ code remains separate from your Python code.

SWIG output can be freely extended and customized.

Now, the most interesting thing is that you don't need to master all the details about the Python/C API in order to use the basics of SWIG to create your Python extension modules. SWIG automates the process of generating a Python extension based on the header of the functions that you want to export.

Take a look at the following example and see how simple it is to generate a wrapper file. We will first create an input file, and call it `helloworld.i`.

```
// file: helloworld.i

%module helloworld
%{
#include "helloworld.h"
%}

char *say();
```

Now, we will use SWIG to generate the wrapper file. We need to pass an argument to SWIG informing that the wrapper must be created for the Python language. That's because SWIG works with many different languages.

```
% swig -python helloworld.i
Generating wrappers for Python...
%
```

As you can see, a wrapper file called `helloworld_wrap.c` was created for you.

More information about SWIG can be found at the following Web pages:

SWIG official Web site:

```
http://www.swig.org
```

SWIG Users Guide—Chapter 9, "SWIG and Python":

```
http://www.swig.org/Doc1.1/PDF/Python.pdf
```

"Using SWIG to Control, Prototype, and Debug C Programs with Python":

```
http://www.swig.org/papers/Py96/python96.html
```

"Feeding a Large-scale Physics Application to Python":

```
http://www.swig.org/papers/Py97/beazley.html
```

"Interfacing C/C++ and Python with SWIG":

```
http://www.swig.org/papers/PyTutorial97/PyTutorial97.pdf
```

"The Benefits of Scripting Languages," by John Ousterhout:

```
http://www.scriptics.com/people/john.ousterhout/scripting.html
```

Other Wrappers

Besides SWIG, there are other very interesting wrapper projects, such as SIP, which is specifically designed for integrating C++ class libraries with Python by generating compilable C++ code from a set of specification files that are similar to C++ header files.

"SIP—Python Bindings for Qt and KDE," by Phil Thompson:

```
http://www.river-bank.demon.co.uk/software/
```

"Python + KDE Tutorial," by Boudewijn Rempt:

`http://www.xs4all.nl/~bsarempt/python/tutorial.html`

"SCXX (Simplified CXX) is a lightweight C++ wrapper for dealing with PyObjects," by Gordon McMillan:

`http://starship.python.net/crew/gmcm/scxx.html`

"CXX—A facility for creating Python extensions in C++," by Paul F. Dubois:

`http://www.foretec.com/python/workshops/1998-`
`11/proceedings/papers/dubois/dubois.html`

Note that this last document is very instructive because it shows how to create new object types in Python by using CXX.

Embedding

We will now talk about how to embed Python inside other programs. Python offers a clean interface that allows embedding to occur.

You might be asking yourself why would you want to do it. Well, the answer is quite simple; as a scripting language, Python can wire its interpreter into other programs to enable you to make calls to specific Python functions and execute particular Python statements from them.

Those programs will have the capability to load Python scripts and execute Python services that belong to specific Python modules. You can also call Python functions directly from your C code and access the Python objects that are returned by them.

In order to embed Python inside a program, you just need to use the Python API—the Python EXE is not necessary.

Implementing Callback Functions

Embedding Python allows you to access and use the Python interpreter from inside your application. But what happens if you need to call back your application functions from inside Python?

For this reason, it is a good practice to provide a module written in C that exposes an API related to the application. Therefore, when embedding Python within your routines, you can make your application communicate both ways with your Python program by accessing the Python extension modules.

Embedding the Python Interpreter

The next example adds Python functionality to a C program.

```
// File: embedding.c

#include <stdio.h>
#include <Python.h>
int main(int argc, char **argv)
{
  Py_Initialize();
  PyRun_SimpleString("print 'Hello Python World'");
  printf("You are my visitor number %i", args);
  Py_Finalize();
  return(0);
}
```

Python provides a set of function calls that provide an interface to the Python interpreter. The most important ones are

- `Py_Initialize`—Initializes and allocates the internal resources of the interpreter in order to start using the API.

- `PyRun_SimpleString`—Executes Python code strings in the context of the __main__ module. Each string must be a complete Python command. This high-level function reads from a character buffer and returns 0 for success and -1 when exceptions occur. Another function called `PyRun_String` provides more control of the code execution. The source code of this function is available in your installation in the `Python/pythonrun.c` file.

   Tip
   Remember that you need to inform the new line character at the end of each command line to make sure that the interpreter validates the command.

- `Py_Finalize`—Releases the internal resources and shuts down the interpreter. You should always call this function before leaving the program.

- `PyRun_SimpleFile`—Executes Python commands that are stored in a file. This function reads from a FILE pointer.

Check out this other example:

```
// File: embedding2.c

#include "Python.h"
main(int argc, char **argv)
```

```
{
    Py_Initialize();
    PySys_SetArgv(int argc, char **argv);
    PyRun_SimpleString("print 'Hello Python World'\n");
    PyRun_SimpleString("print sys.argv\n");
    PyFinalize();
    Py_Exit(0);
}
```

- `PySys_SetArgv`—This function sets the values for the `sys.argv` list.

You can access a module written in Python from C by getting a pointer to the module object as follows:

```
module = PyImport_ImportModule("<modulename>");
```

If the module hasn't been imported yet (that is, it isn't yet present in sys.modules), this function initializes the module; otherwise it simply returns the value of `sys.modules["<modulename>"]`.

It doesn't enter the module into any namespace—it only ensures that it has been initialized and it is stored in `sys.modules`.

You can then access the module's attributes (that is, any name defined in the module) using `PyObject_GetAttrString()` as follows:

```
attr = PyObject_GetAttrString(module, "<attrname>");
```

It is also possible to assign values to variables in the module using the `PyObject_SetAttrString()` function.

There is a very straightforward example of embedding Python in a C program in the file `/Demo/embed/demo.c`, which is part of your Python distribution source code.

Embedding on UNIX

On UNIX, you must link your C application against the Python interpreter library, which is called `libpython1.5a`.

When compiling the `yourprogram.c` into a object file (`yourprogram.o`), you need to specify the directory of the Python distribution.

For example,

```
gcc -g -c yourprogram.c
```

Note

You need to make sure that the header files required by your program are correctly installed on your system.

When compiling the object file into an executable file, you need to include the libraries and references for any extension modules embedded into the Python interpreter itself.

Check the `Makefile` file of the Python interpreter to know the files that must be mentioned.

```
Listing 6.1  File: Makefile...
VERSION= 1.5

LIBPYTHON= $(blddir)/libpython$(VERSION).a

LIBS= -lreadline -ltermcap -lcurses -lgdbm -ltk8.0 -ltcl8.0 -lX11 -ldl
SYSLIBS= -lm
MODLIBS= -L/usr/X11R6/lib -I/usr/local/pgsql/include
-L/usr/local/pgsql/lib -lcrypt
ALLLIBS= $(LIBPYTHON) $(MODLIBS) $(LIBS) $(SYSLIBS)
...
```

All the libraries found in the `Makefile` file are used as arguments to the function that compiles the object file, as you can see next.

```
gcc yourprogram.o /usr/local/contrib/Python-1.5.2/libpython1.5.a
-L/usr/X11R6/lib -I/usr/local/pgsql/include -L/usr/local/pgsql/lib
-lcrypt -lreadline -ltermcap -lcurses -lgdbm -ltk8.0 -ltcl8.0 -lX11
-ldl -lm -o yourprogram
```

The last step is to type **make** to build the application.

Note

In order to compile an extension module for use with the embedded python interpreter, you just need to compile the module into the executable and make sure that you call the `init` function for the module after initializing the interpreter.

Embedding Python in C++

You don't have to recompile your interpreter. You just need to write your main program in C++ and use a C++ compiler to compile and link your program.

Embedding Python in Other Applications

On Windows, Python itself is implemented in a `DLL` called `Python15.dll`. Note that the file `Python.exe` is a small program that calls all the routines stored in the `DLL`. This is a good example showing that it must be easy to embed Python because it already embeds itself.

Besides all this talk about embedding Python in C and C++ applications, Python can also be embedded in other applications, such as Delphi. However, note that implicitly, the embedding process is at the C level too.

Dr. Dietmar Budelsky and Morgan Martinet merged their two separate projects and created The Python for Delphi project. The purpose of this project is to provide an interface to the Python language in Delphi.

This project consists of a set of components that wrap the `Python15.dll` into Delphi. These components let you easily execute Python scripts, create new Python modules and new Python types. You can create Python extensions as DLLs and much more. Currently, it supports Delphi versions 3, 4, and 5.

The Python for Delphi project:

`http://www.multimania.com/marat/delphi/python.htm`

NSAPI/NSAPY

A real-life example of how Python can be used by other applications is in the case of embedding Python under Netscape HTTP Servers that support the NSAPI module protocol.

This marriage brings several add-ons to the Netscape Server mostly because of the general scripting capabilities acquired from the Python language.

In order to do this embedding, it is necessary to use the `Nsapy`, which is an extension that works by embedding the interpreter within Netscape HTTP Servers that use NSAPI.

NSAPI—The Netscape Server API:

`http://oradb1.jinr.ru/netscape/NSAPI/`

"Nsapy," by Gregory Trubetskoy:

`http://www.ispol.com/home/grisha/nsapy/nsapy.html`

Example of embedding Python under a Netscape Commerce server:

`http://starship.python.net/crew/aaron_watters/embed/`

Summary

This chapter exposes the extending and embedding functionality that gives Python the credit of possessing the capability to glue applications together.

Whenever you use Python code to call C code, you are extending Python. On the other hand, if you use C code to call Python code, you are embedding Python.

Python has a good relationship with C because Python's interpreter is written in C, and since its beginning, the interpreter has been ready to work with extension modules.

The extension modules are mostly used to add new functionality to Python when there is no other way to interface Python with a particular system or hardware. Sometimes, when Python code is inefficient, extension modules are also used to boost performance.

If you need to call Python routines from inside your application, you can use the embedding functionality to have them called by your compiled language.

Python provides an intuitive and clean C Application Programmers Interface (API) that exposes the interface to the Python runtime system. This API provides a great number of functions to manipulate Python objects and built-in types from C and C++.

In order to use your new extension modules, you can't forget to create the initialization function of the module and the method array that assigns the internal function names with the function names that are exposed in the module's interface.

The most important functions of an extension module are `PyArg_ParseTuple` and `Py_BuildValue`. They handle all the interfacing between C and Python. Both functions check the argument's type by looking at a formatting string. Tables 6.1 and 6.2 (one for each function) list all the possible formatting strings.

In addition to methods, you can also export *constants* back to Python. You just need to bind the constant name to the module namespace dictionary.

You must indicate errors in your extension module by returning `NULL` to the interpreter because functions signal errors by returning `NULL`. You can also use exception functions defined by the Python/C API. New exceptions can be created and stored at extension module as well.

Python extensions don't benefit from all the safety provided by the Python runtime system. There are a lot of things that you have to be worried about. The main thing is reference counting, which is handled by the `Py_INCREF` and `Py_DECREF` functions.

It becomes harder to adjust and compile code as C++ because Python has a C-based interpreter that has some restrictions when it comes to creating extension modules using C++.

Two options are available for building Python extension modules. The first one compiles and links the module into the interpreter. This option makes the module always available to the interpreter.

The second option doesn't require that you recompile the interpreter because it dynamically links the modules to the system.

SWIG is an automated tool create by David Beazley that is used to write interfaces between Python and existing C libraries. These interfaces can contain several single functions. The programmer doesn't have to write any special wrapping functions to provide the glue between the Python scripting language and the C functions. Besides SWIG, other applications (such as SIP and SCXX) are suitable for helping programmers wrap their C code.

While embedding Python in your programs, you will have the ability to load Python scripts and execute Python services that belong to specific Python modules. You can also call Python functions directly from your C code and access the Python objects that are returned by them. In order to embed Python inside a program, you just need to use the Python API—the Python EXE isn't necessary. When embedding Python in your C++ code, it isn't necessary to recompile Python itself using C++.

In order to start the Python API service in your program, it is necessary to call the Py_Initialize function. To shutdown the Python interpreter, it is necessary to call the Py_Finalize function.

Python can be easily embedded in various languages and applications, such as C++, Delphi and Netscape Servers.

Code Examples

Listing 6.1   *Benchmark Extension (File benchmarkmodule.c)*

```
1: #include "<Python.h>"
2:
3: static PyObject *
4: benchmark_generate(PyObject *self, PyObject *args);
5: {
6:   int index, number_of_arguments;
7:   PyObject *numberslist = NULL;
```

Listing 6.1   *(continued)*

```
 8:    PyObject *check_value = NULL;
 9:    PyFloatObject *aux_float = NULL;
10:    double element_value;
11:    double minimum_value = 100;
12:    double maximum_value = 0;
13:    char *exist_check;
14:
15:    if (!PyArg_ParseTuple (args, "OO", &numberslist, &check_value))
16:       return NULL;
17:
18:    if (!PyList_Check(numberslist))
19:    {
20:      PyErr_SetString(PyExc_TypeError, "Invalid list of values !");
21:      return NULL;
22:    }
23:
24:    if (!PyFloat_Check(check_value))
25:    {
26:      PyErr_SetString(PyExc_TypeError, "Invalid checking value !");
27:      return NULL;
28:    }
29:
30:    number_of_arguments = PyList_Size(numberslist);
31:    exist_check = "No";
32:
33:    for (index=0; index<number_of_arguments; index++)
34:    {
35:       aux_float = (PyFloatObject *) PyList_GetItem(numberslist, index);
36:       if (!PyFloat_Check(aux_float))
37:       {
38:          PyErr_SetString(PyExc_TypeError, "Invalid list value !");
39:          return NULL;
40:       }
41:       element_value = PyFloat_AsDouble(aux_float);
42:       if (element_value < 0 )
43:       {
44:          PyErr_SetString(PyExc_TypeError, "The values cannot be less than 0
              !");
45:          return NULL;
46:       }
47:
48:       if (element_value > 100 )
```

Listing 6.1   *(continued)*

```
49:        {
50:            PyErr_SetString(PyExc_TypeError,
                    "The values cannot be greater than 100 !");
51:            return NULL;
52:        }
53:
54:        if (element_value < minimum_value)
55:            minimum_value = element_value;
56:
57:        if (element_value > maximum_value)
58:            maximum_value = element_value;
59:
60:        if (element_value == PyFloat_AsDouble(check_value))
61:            exist_check = "Yes";
62:    }
63:    return Py_BuildValue("(ffs)", minimum_value, maximum_value,
                    exist_check );
64: }
65:
66: static PyMethodDef benchmark_methods[] = {
67:        {"generate", benchmark_generate, METH_VARARGS, "Minimum Value,
                Maximum Value"},
68:        {NULL, NULL}
69: };
70:
71: DL_EXPORT(void) initbenchmark()
72: {
73:    Py_InitModule("benchmark", benchmark_methods);
74: }
```

Line 9: `PyFloatObject` is a subtype of `PyObject`.

Line 18: Checks whether the first argument is a list.

Line 24: Checks whether the type of the second argument is a float.

Line 26: Raises a `TypeError` exception.

Line 30: Returns the list's length.

Line 60: `PyFloat_AsDouble` converts a Python Float into a C double.

Next, you can see a small interaction with this program. To execute it, we have to pass two arguments: The first one is a list of numbers, and the second one is a float number. This program returns the minimum and maximum values from the list, along with a logical test that informs whether the float number is part of the list.

```
Python 1.5.2 (#0, May 30 2000, 00:16:14) [MSC 32 bit (Intel)] on win32
Copyright 1991-1995 Stichting Mathematisch Centrum, Amsterdam
>>> import benchmark
>>> benchmark.generate([1.1],1.1)
(1.1, 1.1, 'Yes')
>>> benchmark.generate([1,2,3],4.5)
(1.0, 3.0, 'No')
>>>
```

Wrapping C Functions

By wrapping functions, you can use C code files, without changing them. Every time you feel the need to include a C source code file in your Python project, it is necessary to create a special module that wraps its functions, and to include a reference to the file in the python15.dsp.

The next example wraps the functions stored in the cfunctions.c file.

Listing 6.2   *File:* cfunctions.c

```c
#include <stdio.h>

void display_info(char *user, char *domain, char *country) {

    if (country == "USA")
        printf("%s@%s\n", user, domain);
    else
        printf("%s@%s.%s\n", user, domain, country);
}

int calc_year (int f_year, int m_year, int l_year) {
    int result;
    result = ((l_year + m_year + f_year) / 3);
    return result;
}
```

Listing 6.3 *File:* wrappermodule.c

```c
1: #include "Python.h"
2:
3: extern void display_info(char *, char *, char *);
4: extern int calc_year(int, int, int);
5:
6: static PyObject *wrapper_display_info(PyObject *self, PyObject *args,
                                              PyObject *kwargs)
7: {
8:     char *user = "None";
9:     char *domain = "None";
10:    char *country = "None";
11:    static char *keywords[] = {"user","domain","country",NULL};
12:
13:    if (!PyArg_ParseTupleAndKeywords(args, kwargs, "|sss", keywords,
            &user, &domain, &country)){
14:        return NULL;
15:    }
16:
17:    display_info(user, domain, country);
18:    return Py_BuildValue("");
19: }
20:
21: static PyObject *wrapper_calc_year(PyObject *self, PyObject *args) {
22:    int f_year, m_year, l_year, result;
23:    if (!PyArg_ParseTuple(args, "iii", &f_year, &m_year, &l_year)) {
24:        return NULL;
25:    }
26:    result = calc_year(f_year, m_year, l_year);
27:    return Py_BuildValue("i", result);
28: }
29:
30: static PyMethodDef wrappermethods[] = {
31:    {"display_info", wrapper_display_info, METH_VARARGS|METH_KEYWORDS},
32:    {"calc_year", wrapper_calc_year, METH_VARARGS},
33:    {NULL, NULL}
34: };
35:
36: void initwrapper() {
37:    Py_InitModule("wrapper", wrappermethods);
38: }
```

Lines 3 and 4: Identify which functions are external to this file.

Line 11: Creates a dictionary of keywords to be accepted by the function.

Line 13: `PyArg_ParseTupleAndKeywords()` parses the Python-level parameters by accepting a third `"PyObject *"` parameter.

Line 31: The `METH_VARARGS|METH_KEYWORDS` clause makes it clear that keyword elements are expected.

Next, you can see a small interaction with this program. The first function builds an email address based on the information provided. The other one calculates the average age of a family of three people based on the number of years that are passed to the function.

```
Python 1.5.2 (#0, May 30 2000, 00:56:46) [MSC 32 bit (Intel)] on win32
Copyright 1991-1995 Stichting Mathematisch Centrum, Amsterdam
>>> import wrapper
>>> wrapper.display_info("andre2530","aol.com","br")
andre2530@aol.com.br
>>> wrapper.calc_year(10, 30, 35)
25
>>>
```

CHAPTER 7

Objects Interfacing and Distribution

This is an EX parrot!

This chapter provides information that explains how to interface objects from different applications using Python. First, it demonstrates the techniques to control both external objects from Python and Python objects from external programs. Later, it lists the Python projects currently being developed in this area of study.

Object Interfacing and Distribution

Python has very comprehensive support for object interfacing and distributing technologies. It is particularly well integrated with the Windows platform; its programs can interact with COM and DCOM services.

The `win32com` Python extensions developed by Mark Hammond can be used to interface Python to Microsoft's COM and ActiveX architectures. This package, which is part of the PythonWin distribution, enables Python to be used in Active Server Pages, or as a COM controller that can exchange information with other COM-aware applications, such as Microsoft Word and Visual Basic.

Object-oriented design and programming is specifically beneficial in distributed environments where the encapsulation and subsequent independence of objects enable distribution of an application over a network.

The possibilities of heterogeneous machine architectures, physically distant locations, and independent component failures make it difficult to program distributed object systems.

A number of distributed-processing environments, such as OMG's CORBA and Microsoft's DCOM, have been developed to attempt to hide these problems from programmers, reducing the complexity of their task. Besides the most famous object models, an international standard known as the Reference Model for Open Distributed Processing (RM-ODP) is currently being developed.

Python is one of the languages supported by *Xerox PARC*'s ILU (Inter-Language Unification), which is a free CORBA-compatible distributed object system. To this date, many distributed applications systems have been developed in Python using this technology.

The Hector project at the University of Queensland, Australia, also uses Python.

Interfacing Objects

Currently, one of the biggest problems with both COM and DCOM architectures is that they are supported only by Windows systems. However, most operating systems have their own native way of connecting systems together at a remote procedure call level. At the time of this writing, there are some unconfirmed rumors that Microsoft is planning to create an interface to the Windows operating system using the XML-RPC protocol. This development would bring a whole new world to the Windows applications by increasing their connectivity with all the other platforms. Note that Microsoft has already produced a similar protocol called *SOAP*.

The COM-based technologies are the focus of Microsoft's development plans for Windows, ranging from operating systems and languages to messaging and databases. Nowadays, new COM-based technologies are found in a lot of places inside your Windows system, such as the ActiveX controls and VBScript processing. OLEDB, for example, is the successor to ODBC. ODBC gives access to relational databases, whereas OLEDB provides a more versatile level of access, so that the same API can be used to retrieve data from all kinds of sources, ranging from flat text files, through Excel spreadsheets, up to ODBC databases.

Introduction to COM Objects

Let's learn a little about what is behind the Microsoft Common Object Model (COM) technology before seeing how you can use it along with Python.

COM is the most widely used component software model in the world. It provides a rich set of integrated services, a wide choice of easy-to-use tools, and a large set of available applications. COM underlies a large majority of the new code developed for Windows and Windows NT operating systems, whether created by Microsoft or by others.

COM consists of a well-defined, mature, stable, and freely available specification, as well as a reference implementation, which has been widely tested and adopted worldwide. It provides the richest set of existing services for applications today, as well as the largest set of development tools available for any component or object model on the market. Of course, Windows is the only Operating System in which you can be assured of finding COM, which makes us think that COM doesn't appear to be a standard because it doesn't provide cross-platform solutions.

The COM Specification

COM is a specification and a set of services that enables you to create modular, object-oriented, customizable and upgradable, distributed applications using a number of languages. You can even use components that you already have written in other languages.

The COM specification describes the standards that you need to follow in order to create interoperable COM components. This standard describes what COM objects should look like and how they should behave. The specification is backed up by a set of services, or APIs. The COM library provides these services, which are part of the operating system for Win32 platforms, and available as a separate package for other operating systems.

COM components can be packaged as EXE or DLL files—COM provides the communication mechanism to enable components in different modules to talk to each other. They are true objects in the usual sense—they have identity, state, and behavior. COM components that implement a common interface can be treated polymorphically, enabling easy customization and upgrades of your applications.

COM components link with each other dynamically, and COM defines standard ways of locating components and identifying their functionality, so individual components are swappable without having to recompile the entire application.

COM provides a communication mechanism that enables components to interact across a network. More importantly, COM provides location transparency to applications (if desired) that enables them to be written without regard to the location of their components. The components can be moved without requiring any changes to the application.

COM is a binary standard. Any language that can cope with the binary standard can create or use COM objects. The number of languages and tools that support COM increases every day. C, C++, Java, JScript, Visual Basic, VBScript, Delphi, and PowerBuilder form just part of that growing list, which means that any one of these languages can easily interoperate with Python. Keep in mind that COM is a standard for interaction between programs—an Object Request Broker service.

COM is the object model that underlies most of the Microsoft technologies; here are a few of those COM applications:

- ActiveX uses COM to provide controls.

- OLE uses COM to combine documents.

- OLEDB and ADO use COM for data access.

- DirectX uses COM for graphics.

Any COM-aware program is able to interact with other COM-aware programs. One program can even execute commands of the other. The program that executes the method call is called the *COM server*, and the program that calls the object method is called the *COM client*. Because COM is a Microsoft product, most applications for Windows can act as COM servers or clients.

Python's support for the COM technology is included in the Python for Windows (PythonWin) extensions.

COM Interfaces

The COM technology is very broad and complex. Basically, it enables objects to be shared among many applications, without applications knowing the implementation details of the objects. Objects that implement the COM technology can communicate with each other without the need for knowing the others' details.

COM components do business with interfaces. An interface defines functionality, but not implementation. Objects must handle the implementation. COM objects are small pieces of self-contained software that interact with other applications by exposing well-defined, language-independent interfaces.

COM is an object model that relies heavily on interfaces. These interfaces are entirely separate from their implementations. Although COM defines the interfaces, its model doesn't provide the interface's implementation. Each object's class has the task of defining the implementations. The interfaces can be standard ones that other objects also expose, or they can be special ones that are particular to that object. A unique ID, called an IID (Interface ID), identifies each interface. IIDs use *Universally Unique Identifiers* (*UUID*). UUID is a format used for many COM IDs to allocate a unique identification string for objects. Many tools can generate unique UUIDs. As you will see later in this chapter, Python's pythoncom module has a function called `CreateGuid()` that generates UUID strings.

In order to create an object, COM locates the required class and creates an instance of it. The concept of COM classes is identical to the other Python classes. Additionally, each COM class needs to implement two identifiers: Class ID (`_reg_clsid_`), which is another UUID, and Program ID (`_reg_progid_`), which is a identification string that must be easier to remember than the Class ID. This string is not guaranteed to be unique. In order to create an object, the programmer must specify either the *progid*, or the *clsid*.

All interfaces are derived from the IUnknown interface. Therefore, they support its methods. The IUnknown interface is the base of all COM interfaces. This interface contains only three methods:

- `AddRef()` and `Release()` are used for managing COM lifetimes, which are based on reference counts.

- `QueryInterface()` is used for obtaining a reference to one of the other interfaces that the object exposes. In other words, interfaces are obtained by using the `IUnknown::QueryInterface()` method.

IStream, IStorage, and IPropertyPage are examples of standard interfaces defined by COM. They define file-like operations, file system-like semantics, and how a control exposes a property page, respectively. Besides the standard interfaces, COM also enables you to define your own custom interfaces by using an Interface Definition Language (IDL).

The IDispatch interface enables any COM objects to be used from a scripting environment. This interface was designed explicitly for languages that cannot use normal COM interfaces. The objects that implement this interface are known as *automation objects* because they expose a programmable interface that can be manipulated by another program. This interface exposes dynamic object models whose methods and properties can be determined at runtime. Basically, this interface is used whenever you are handling an object whose interface is not known at compile time, or if there is no compile time at all.

> **Note**
> Note for CORBA programmers: IDispatch is equivalent to the interface repository and dynamic invocation interface that are standard parts of CORBA.

To access a method or a property of an object, you can use either late or early binding. All the examples that you see in this book use late bindings because the Python interpreter doesn't know what the object interfaces look like. It doesn't know which are the methods and properties that compound the object. It just makes the calls dynamically, according to the function names that you provide.

Late bindings use the IDispatch interface to determine the object model at runtime. Python function win32com.client.Dispatch() provides this runtime facility. Most examples in this chapter use the IDispatch interface. However, the win32com.client.Dispatch() function hides many implementation details from us. Internally, Python converts the names into IDs using the internal function GetIDsOfNames(). Then, this ID is passed as an argument to the Invoke() function.

You can try to improve the performance of your program by calling the Invoke() function directly. Usually, the performance gets better when names are not resolved at runtime. Just be careful to provide the right ID. If you implement this way, an early binding operation is executed.

For the early bindings, we have the concept of *Type Libraries*, wherein the object model is exposed at compile time. In this kind of implementation, you don't call the methods and properties directly. The GetIDsOfNames() method gets an ID for the method or property that you want to use, and the Invoke() method makes the call.

For example, a function call would be invoked as

```
id = GetIDsOfNames("YourMethodCall")
Invoke(id, DISPATCH_METHOD)
```

And a property would be collected as

```
id = GetIDsOfNames("ObjectProperty")
Invoke(id, DISPATCH_PROP_GET)
```

Usually, you don't have to worry about this kind of implementation. You just say

```
YourObject.YourMethodCall()
```

and

```
YourObject.ObjectProperty
```

In order to implicitly call the `Invoke()` method without causing data type problems, the `IDispatch` interface assumes the data type `VARIANT` for all variables. That's because late bindings do not know the specific types of the parameters, whereas early bindings do.

Late bindings do not know about parameters passed by reference, so no parameters are passed by reference. However, early bindings accept parameters passed by reference, and return them as tuples.

COM objects can be implemented as `InProc` objects, which are implemented as `DLLs`. These objects are loaded into the calling process providing that best performance because no marshalling is required. Of course, for most objects, some marshaling will be needed to marshal Python parameters into a form that can be passed to the COM object.

The other option is to implement COM objects as *LocalServer/RemoteServer* objects. This kind of object is implemented as a standalone `EXE`, which is safer than the first option because of process isolation.

COM can also be used to decide which implementation should be used. If both types of implementation are available, the caller interface is able to decide which option is the best one to choose.

The Windows Registry

All the information concerning a `COM` object, such as the mapping between its progid and clsid, is stored in the Windows Registry. The Windows Registry also stores the name of the DLL file of an `InProc` object, and the name of the EXE `LocalServer` object. Object security, threading models, and many other details are also stored there.

Check the following link for more details about the COM specification:

Microsoft—Common Object Model

```
http://www.microsoft.com/com/resources/specs.asp
```

ADO

ActiveX Data Objects (ADO) is an automation-based interface for accessing data. This technology uses the OLE DB interface to access an extensive range of data sources, including but not limited to data provided by the ODBC.

Microsoft Remote Data Service (RDS) is a component of ADO that provides fast and efficient data frameworks for applications hosted in Microsoft Internet Explorer. RDS uses data-aware ActiveX controls to provide data access programming to Web developers, who need to build distributed, data-intensive applications for use over networks. RDS is based on a client/server, distributed technology that works over HTTP, HTTPS (HTTP over Secure Sockets layer), and DCOM application protocols.

ActiveX

An *ActiveX control* is an OLE control that can live inside an HTML page; it can be simple Window objects, such as buttons, text boxes, or scrollbars. It also can be quite complicated, for example, a bar chart graph display can be an ActiveX control. An entire spreadsheet can also be a single control. Each ActiveX control has properties and reacts to external events. Its properties can be modified to change its appearance. For example, its containing program can set color and fonts. External events such as a mouse click or keyboard input can cause a control's event handler to execute. Note that the ActiveX technology is another Windows only thing, and not really any use in a cross platform environment.

Microsoft's Web browser, Internet Explorer, is ActiveX-aware, meaning that Web application developers can package ActiveX components to create more dynamic content in their Web pages.

ActiveX controls use COM technologies to provide interoperability with other types of COM components and services. ActiveX controls provide a number of enhancements specifically designed to facilitate distribution of components over high-latency networks and to integrate controls into Web browsers. These enhancements include features such as incremental rendering and code signing, which enables users to identify the authors of controls before allowing them to execute.

Implementing COM Objects in Python

In order to implement COM objects in the Python version of Windows, you need a set of extensions developed by Mark Hammond and Greg Stein. Part of the `win32com` package, these extensions enable you to do everything that is COM-related, including writing COM clients and COM servers.

The following link takes you to the download page of these extensions:

`http://www.python.org/download/download_windows.html`

All the Win32 extensions (including the COM extensions) are part of the `win32all` installation package. This package also installs the `PythonWin` IDE in your machine.

The latest version of this whole package is located at the win32all home page. Search for the `win32all.exe` file:

`http://www.python.org/windows/win32all/`

You can also go directly to Mark Hammond's starship home page, which might have more recent beta releases of this package:

`http://starship.python.net/crew/mhammond/`

After installing the package in your machine, take a look at the `readme.htm` file, which is stored at the `win32com` directory.

COM support for Python is compounded of the core PythonCOM module, which supports the C++ code, and the other modules that implement helper code in Python. The whole package is known as `win32com`.

The `win32com` Package

The `win32com` support is standalone, as it does not require PythonWin. The `win32com` package itself does not provide any functionality. Some of the modules contained in this package are

win32com.pythoncom—Provides core C++ support for COM objects and exposes COM object methods, such as `QueryInterface()` and `Invoke()`, just as the C++ API does. Note that all the reference counting is automatically done for you. Programmers rarely access this module directly. Instead, they usually use the `win32com` wrapper classes and functions written in Python to provide a nice, programmable interface.

win32com.client—Provides support for COM clients (for example, using Python to start Microsoft Excel and create a spreadsheet). The COM client support enables Python to manipulate other COM objects via their exposed interfaces. All client-side `IUnknown`-derived objects, including `IDispatch`, are supported.

win32com.server—Provides support for COM servers (for example, creating and registering a COM server object in Python and using a language such as Visual

Basic or Delphi to access the Python objects). The COM server support enables Python to create COM servers, which can be manipulated by another COM client. All server-side IUnknown-derived objects are supported.

win32com.axscript—This is the ActiveX Scripting implementation for Python.

win32com.axdebug—This is the Active Debugging implementation for Python.

win32com.mapi—Provides utilities for working with MAPI and the Microsoft Exchange Server.

Talking to Windows Applications

The COM technology has been part of the Windows world for a long time. The COM genealogy can be traced back to DDE (Dynamic Data Exchange). DDE was the first device for transferring data between various applications in a multi-tasking computer. After some time, DDE was expanded to Object Linking and Embedding (OLE)—note that COM was invented as part of OLE. The creation of the Visual Basic Extensions (VBXs) enhanced the OLE technology for visual components, originating a new standard called OLE2, which was based on top of COM. Soon, the OLE2 technology became more integrated with COM, which is a general-purpose mechanism. Nowadays, COM is mostly known, in part, because of the ActiveX technology.

Professional applications such as Microsoft Office and the Netscape browser enable you to control their objects using COM. Therefore, programs written in Python can be easily used to control those applications.

COM passes string objects as Unicode characters. Before using these objects in Python, it's necessary to convert them to strings. The Python-2.0 Unicode string type is not the same as the string type, but it is easy to convert between the two.

PythonWin comes with a basic COM browser (Python Object browser). This program helps you to identify the current objects in your system that implement COM interfaces.

To run the browser, select it from the PythonWin Tools menu, or double-click on the file win32com\client\combrowse.py.

Note that there are other COM browsers available, such as the one that comes with the Microsoft Visual C++.

If you study the file \python\win32com\servers\interp.py, which is installed as part of your PythonWin distribution, you will learn how to implement a very simple COM server. This server exposes the Python interpreter by providing a COM object that handles both the `exec` and `eval` methods. Before using this object, register it by running the module from Python.exe. Then, from Visual Basic, use CreateObject('Python.Interpreter') to initialize the object, and you can start calling the methods.

Word and Excel

Let's quit talking and get to some practicing. Our objective here is to open and manipulate Microsoft applications from Python.

The first thing that you need to do is to import the COM client and dispatch the right object. In the next example, a variable is assigned a reference to an Excel application:

```
>>> import win32com.client
>>> xl = win32com.client.Dispatch("Excel.Application")
```

The following does the same thing, but this time the reference is to a Word application.

```
>>> wd = win32com.client.Dispatch("Word.Application")
```

`Excel.Application` and `Word.Application` are the Program IDs (progid), which are the names of the objects for which you want to create an instance. Internally, these objects have a Class ID (clsid) that uniquely registers them in the Windows Registry. The matching table between progids and clsids is stored in the Windows Registry and the matching is performed by the COM mechanism.

It is not an easy job to identify an application progid, or to find out object methods and attributes. You can use COM browsers to see what applications have COM interfaces in your system.

For the Microsoft Products, you can take a look at the documentation; it is a good source of information.

Not necessarily every COM object implements the same interface. However, there are similarities.

For example, if the previous assignments have just created the objects and you want to make them visible, you have to type

```
>>> xl.Visible = 1   # Sets the visible property for the Excel application
>>> wd.Visible = 1   # Sets the visible property for the Word application
```

To close both programs and release the memory, you need to say

```
>>> xl = None
>>> wd = None
```

or, you could use

```
>>> del xl, wd
```

These were simple examples of implementing COM clients in Python. Next, we will see how to implement a Python COM server by creating a Python interface that exposes an object. The next block of code registers the interface in the Windows Registry.

Note that every new COM object that you create must have a unique clsid, but you don't have to worry about it. The complex algorithm that works behind the scenes is ready to generate a unique identification, as shown here:

```
>>> import pythoncom
>>> print pythoncom.CreateGuid()
```

Your COM server is defined next. You have to execute the program in order to make the COM object available in the system. Store it on a file, and double-click on it.

```
 1: class TaxApplication:
 2:     _public_methods_ = ['PAtax']
 3:     _reg_progid_ = "Tax.Application"
 4:     _reg_clsid_ = "{D2DEB6E1-3C6D-11D4-804E-0050041A5111}"
 5:
 6:     def PAtax(self, amount, tax=0.07):
 7:         return amount + (amount * tax)
 8:
 9: if __name__=='__main__':
10:     print "Registering COM server"
11:     import win32com.server.register
12:     win32com.server.register.UseCommandLine(TaxApplication)
```

Line 2: Exposes the method to be exported.

Line 3: Defines the name that the COM client application must use to connect to the object.

Line 4: Defines the unique Class ID (clsid) used by the object.

Line 12: Registers the TaxApplication class.

In order to test the program, we need to have an external COM client. Let's use the Visual Basic for Applications Editor, which is present in both Excel and Word.

Open your Microsoft application, type **ALT+F8** in the Macro dialog box, and select the option that creates a macro. Now, you need to type the following block of code:

```
Sub Tax()

    Set TaxApplication = CreateObject("Tax.Application")
    newamount = TaxApplication.PAtax(100)
    MsgBox newamount
    Set TaxApplication = Nothing


End Sub
```

Now, if you press F5, Visual Basic should display a message box showing the result of our simple tax operation, which, in our case, is *107*.

To unregister your COM object you can either pass the argument --unregister when calling your script, or you can use the following line of code inside your Python program:

```
>>> win32com.server.register.UnregisterClasses(TaxApplication)
```

A very comprehensive example of using Microsoft Word and Excel is stored in the testMSOffice.py file, which is part of your PythonWin distribution. It's worth checking out!!!

Word

The following code implements a simple wrapper for the Microsoft Word Application. To test it you need to create a Word document and replace its path in the code. The program will open this file, replace the first occurrence of the string "#name#" within the file, add a small bit of text to the end of the line, and print the file.

```
import win32com.client
False = 0
True = -1
wdLine = 5

class WordApp:
    def __init__(self):
        self.app = win32com.client.Dispatch("Word.Application")
    def open(self, document_file):
        self.app.Documents.Open(document_file)
```

```
    def replace(self, source_selection, new_text):
        self.app.Selection.HomeKey(Unit=wdLine)
        self.app.Selection.Find.Text = source_selection
        self.app.Selection.Find.Execute()
        self.app.Selection.TypeText(Text=new_text)
    def addtext(self, new_text):
        self.app.Selection.EndKey(Unit=wdLine)
        self.app.Selection.TypeText(Text=new_text)
    def printdoc(self):
        self.app.Application.PrintOut()
    def close(self):
        self.app.ActiveDocument.Close(SaveChanges =False)

worddoc = WordApp()
worddoc.open(r"s:\template.doc")
worddoc.replace("#name#", "Andre Lessa")
worddoc.addtext(" What do you want to learn ?")
worddoc.printdoc()
worddoc.close
```

If you type in the name of the object's attribute that accesses the `Dispatch` method, you get as a result, the COM object name:

```
>>> worddoc.app
<COMObject Word.Application.>
```

This object is an example of a *dynamic dispatch* object. The provided name indicates that the object is a generic COM object, and affirms that Python doesn't know anything about it, except the name that you used to create it. All the information about this object is built dynamically.

Besides dynamic dispatches, you can also use *static dispatches*, which involve the generation of a `.py` file that contains support for the specific COM object. In CORBA speak, this is called stub generation, or IDL compilation.

In order to generate the Python files that support a specific COM object, you need to execute `win32com\client\makepy.py`. A list of Type Libraries will be displayed. Select one (for example, 'Microsoft Word 8.0 Object Library') and click OK. You can also call the makepy.py program directly from the command prompt by typing **makepy.py "Microsoft Word 8.0 Object Library"**.

Now, Python knows exactly how to handle the interfaces before invoking the COM object. Although, you can't see any differences, you can check that Python really knows something else now by querying the COM object:

```
>>> import win32com.client
>>> wd=win32com.client.Dispatch("Word.Application")
>>> wd
<win32com.gen_py.Microsoft Word 8.0 Object Library._Application>
```

Note that Python knows the explicit type of the object now.

All the compiled information is stored in a file in the win32com/gen_py directory. You probably won't understand the filename because it is encoded. Actually, you don't need to use this file at all. All the interface information is made available via win32com.client.Dispatch and win32com.client.constants.

If you really need to identify the name of the module that was generated, you can use the win32com.client.gencache module. This module has two functions: GetModuleForCLSID and GetModuleForProgID that return Python module objects you can use in your code.

makepy.py also automatically installs all generated constants from a library of types in an object called win32com.clients.constants. After creating the object, all the constants become available to you.

In the previous example, we had to initialize the constant wdLine, because the constants were not available. Now, after running makepy.py, you can replace the line

```
self.app.Selection.EndKey(Unit=wdLine)
```

with

```
self.app.Selection.EndKey(Unit=win32com.clients.constants.wdLine)
```

and remove the initialization line

```
wdLine = 5
```

The next example uses the wdWindowStateMaximize constant to maximize Microsoft Word:

```
>>> w.WindowState = win32com.client.constants.wdWindowStateMaximize
```

Excel

Next, we'll see how to create COM clients using Microsoft Excel. The principle is very simple. Actually, it is the same one used previously for wrapping Microsoft Word, as it is demonstrated in the following example.

```
>>> import win32com.client
>>> excelapp = win32com.client.Dispatch("Excel.Application")
>>> excelapp.Visible = 1
```

Note that we have to change the `Visible` property in order to see the Excel application. The default behavior is to hide the application window because it saves processor cycles. However, the object is available to any COM client that asks for it.

As you can see in the example, Excel's progid is `Excel.Application`.

After you create the Excel object, you are able to call its methods and set its properties. Keep in mind that the Excel Object Model has the following hierarchy: Application, WorkBook, Sheet, Range, and Cell.

Let's play a little with Excel. The following statements write to the workbook:

```
>>> excelapp.Range("A1:C1").Value = "Hello", "Python", "World"
>>> excelapp.Range("A2:A2").Value = 'SPAM! SPAM! SPAM!'
```

Note that you can also use tuples to transport values:

```
>>> excelapp.Range("A1:C1").Value = ('Hello', 'Python', 'World')
```

To print a selected area, you need to use the `PrintOut()` method:

```
>>> excelapp.Range("A1:C1").PrintOut()
```

What about entering date and time information? The following examples will show you how to set the Date/Time format for Excel cells.

First, call Excel's time function:

```
>>> excelapp.Cells(4,3).Value = "=Now()"
>>> excelapp.Columns("C").EntireColumn.AutoFit()
```

The `AutoFit()` function is required in order to display the information, instead of showing `"#######"`.

Now, use Python to set the time you want:

```
>>> import time, pythoncom
>>> excelapp.Cells(4,1).Value = pythoncom.MakeTime(time.time())
```

```
>>> excelapp.Range("A4:A4").NumberFormat = "d/mm/yy h:mm"
>>> excelapp.Columns("A:C").EntireColumn.AutoFit()
```

Note that the `Cells()` structure works like a numeric array. That means that instead of using Excel's notation of letters and numbers, you need to think of the spreadsheet as a numeric matrix.

Visual Basic

In order to implement a COM object using Python you need to implement a Python class that exposes the functionality to be exported. It is also necessary to assign two special attributes to this class, as required by the Python COM implementation.

The first attribute is the Class ID (`_reg_clsid_`). This attribute must contain a UUID, which can be generated by calling the `pythoncom.CreateGuid()` function. The other attribute is a friendly string that you will use to call the COM object (`_reg_progid_`), as follows:

```
class COMCalcServer:
    _reg_clsid_ = '{C76BEA61-3B39-11D4-8A7C-444553546170}'
    _reg_progid_ = 'COMCALCSERVER.VERSION1'
    _public_methods_ = ['mul','div','add','sub']
    ...
```

Other interesting attributes are

- `_public_methods`—A list of all method names that you want to publicly expose to remote COM clients.

- `_public_attrs`—A list of all attribute names to be exposed to remote COM clients.

- `_readonly_attrs`—A list of all attributes that can be accessed, but not set. This list should be a subset of the list exposed by `_public_attrs`.

After creating the class, you need to register your COM object. The general technique is to run the module that implements the COM object as a script, in order to register the object:

```
if __name__ == '__main__':
    import win32com.server.register
    win32com.server.register.UseCommandLine(COMCalcServer)
```

Notice that you need to inform the class object, and not a class instance. After the
UseCommandLine() function has been successfully executed, the following message is
returned by the Python interpreter:

```
Registered: COMCALCSERVER.VERSION1
```

When you have your COM object up and running, any automation-capable language,
such as Python, Visual Basic, Delphi, or Perl, can use it.

The following example is a complete program that implements a calculator. First, you
need to collect the unique IDs for your class:

```
Python 1.5.2 (#0, Apr 13 1999, 10:51:12) [MSC 32 bit (Intel)] on win32
Copyright 1991-1995 Stichting Mathematisch Centrum, Amsterdam
>>> import pythoncom
>>> print pythoncom.CreateGuid()
<iid:{C76BEA60-3B39-11D4-8A7C-444553546170}>
```

After informing the new clsid value to the _reg_clsid_ attribute, we have the
following program:

```
# File: comcalcserver.py

class COMCalcServer:
    _reg_clsid_ = '{C76BEA61-3B39-11D4-8A7C-444553546170}'
    _reg_progid_ = 'COMCALCSERVER.VERSION1'
    _public_methods_ = ['mul','div','add','sub']
    def mul(self, arg1, arg2):
        return arg1 * arg2
    def div(self, arg1, arg2):
        return arg1 / arg2
    def add(self, arg1, arg2):
        return arg1 + arg2
    def sub(self, arg1, arg2):
        return arg1 - arg2


if __name__ == '__main__':
    import win32com.server.register
    win32com.server.register.UseCommandLine(COMCalcServer)
```

Make sure that all methods are included in the _public_methods_. Otherwise, the
program will fail. Now, go to the DOS prompt and execute the program to register
the COM object:

```
C:\python>c:\progra~1\python\python comcalcserver.py
Registered: COMCALCSERVER.VERSION1
```

To create the Visual Basic COM client, you need to create a Visual Basic Form that contains all the implementation details (see Figure 7.1).

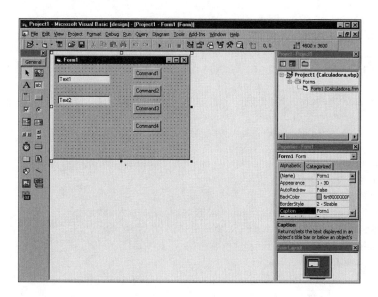

Figure 7.1
A design for creating the Visual Basic Form.

Most of the time, the initialization steps are stored in the Form_Load section in order to be executed when the application starts:

```
Dim COMCalcServer as Object
Set COMCalcServer = CreateObject("COMCALCSERVER.VERSION1")
```

Remember to always deallocate the objects before exiting the application. It's good practice to do it in the Form_Unload section:

```
Set COMCalcServer = Nothing

Public COMCalcServer As Object
Private Sub Form_Unload(Cancel As Integer)
    Set COMCalcServer = Nothing
End Sub

Sub InitCOMCalcServer()
    Set COMCalcServer = CreateObject("COMCALCSERVER.VERSION1")
```

```
    Exit Sub
End Sub

Private Sub Command1_Click()
    Dim result As Double
    result = COMCalcServer.Mul(Val(Text1), Val(Text2))
    MsgBox Text1 & "*" & Text2 & "=" & Str(result)
End Sub
Private Sub Command2_Click()
    Dim result As Double
    result = COMCalcServer.Div(Val(Text1), Val(Text2))
    MsgBox Text1 & "/" & Text2 & "=" & Str(result)
End Sub
Private Sub Command3_Click()
    Dim result As Double
    result = COMCalcServer.Add(Val(Text1), Val(Text2))
    MsgBox Text1 & "+" & Text2 & "=" & Str(result)
End Sub
Private Sub Command4_Click()
    Dim result As Double
    result = COMCalcServer.Sub(Val(Text1), Val(Text2))
    MsgBox Text1 & "-" & Text2 & "=" & Str(result)
End Sub

Private Sub Form_Load()
    Text1 = 0
    Text2 = 0
    Command1.Caption = "Mul"
    Command2.Caption = "Div"
    Command3.Caption = "Add"
    Command4.Caption = "Sub"
    InitCOMCalcServer
End Sub
```

While executing the application (see Figure 7.2), your Visual Basic application will be talking to the Python COM object behind the scenes.

The next example is based on the previous one. This one implements a callback function. The VB program calls a Python function that clearly manipulates the Visual Basic Form object.

You need to add or replace the following functions in the Visual Basic code:

```
Sub InitCOMCalcServer()
    Set COMCalcServer = CreateObject("COMCALCSERVER.VERSION2")
```

```
      Exit Sub
End Sub


Private Sub Form_Load()
    Text1 = 0
    Text2 = 0
    Command1.Caption = "Mul"
    Command2.Caption = "Div"
    Command3.Caption = "Add"
    Command4.Caption = "Sub"
    InitCOMCalcServer
    COMCalcServer.updatecaption Me
End Sub
```

Figure 7.2
A Visual Basic executable running.

The following new function must be created in the Python code, too. The *VB function call* uses the keyword Me to send a reference of the Form object to Python's updatecaption() method:

```
def updatecaption(self, object):
    Form = win32com.client.Dispatch(object)
    Form.Caption = "Python COM Routine is Active"
```

The following code is a full replacement to be used with this example. Remember to create a new _reg_clsid_ for this new example.

```
# File: comcalcserver2.py


class COMCalcServer:
    _reg_clsid_ = '{C76BEA64-3B39-11D4-8A7C-444553546170}'
    _reg_progid_ = 'COMCALCSERVER.VERSION2'
    _public_methods_ = ['mul','div','add','sub', 'updatecaption']
```

```python
    def mul(self, arg1, arg2):
        return arg1 * arg2
    def div(self, arg1, arg2):
        return arg1 / arg2
    def add(self, arg1, arg2):
        return arg1 + arg2
    def sub(self, arg1, arg2):
        return arg1 - arg2
    def updatecaption(self, object):
        import win32com.client
        Form = win32com.client.Dispatch(object)
        Form.Caption = "Python COM Routine is Active"

if __name__ == '__main__':
    import win32com.server.register
    win32com.server.register.UseCommandLine(COMCalcServer)
```

The result of running this example is shown in Figure 7.3.

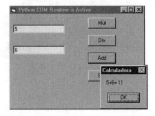

Figure 7.3
Python/Visual Basic callback implementation.

Every script that defines a COM class can be used to unregister the class, too. Python automatically knows that, when you pass the argument --unregister to the script, you want to remove all the references to this class from the Windows Registry.

```
C:\python>python comcalcserver2.py --unregister
Unregistered: COMCALCSERVER.VERSION2
```

Handling Numbers and Strings

Whenever you have a Python method as part of a COM server interface that returns a number or a string, as shown in the next few lines of code:

```
def GetNumber(self):
    return 25

def GetString(self, name):
    return 'Your name is %s' % name
```

The COM client written in Visual Basic must handle the methods as follows

```
Dim num as Variant
num = Server.GetNumber
Dim str as Variant
str = Server.GetString("Andre")
MsgBox str
```

Python and Unicode do not really work well together in the current version of Python. All strings that come from COM will actually be Unicode objects rather than string objects. In order to make the previous code work in a COM environment, the last line of the GetString() method must become

```
return 'Your name is %s' % str(name)
```

The conversion of the "name" to "str(name)" forces the Unicode object into a native Python string object. In Python-2.0, if the win32com stuff starts using native Python Unicode strings, the str() call will cause the Unicode string to be reencoded in UTF8.

Handling Lists and Tuples
When you have a Python method as part of a COM server interface that returns a list or a tuple, as illustrated in the next example:

```
def GetList(self):
    return [1,2,3,4]
```

The COM client written in Visual Basic must handle the method as follows:

```
Dim arry as Variant
arry = Server.GetList
Debug.Print UBound(arry)
For Each item in arry
Debug.Print item
Next
```

Delphi

Using Delphi to implement a COM client is very similar to using Visual Basic. First, you need to register the COM class. The following code is similar to the one used for the Visual Basic example.

```python
# File: comcalcserver.py

class COMCalcServer:
    _reg_clsid_ = '{C76BEA61-3B39-11D4-8A7C-444553546170}'
    _reg_progid_ = 'COMCALCSERVER.VERSION1'
    _public_methods_ = ['mul','div','add','sub']
    def mul(self, arg1, arg2):
        return arg1 * arg2
    def div(self, arg1, arg2):
        return arg1 / arg2
    def add(self, arg1, arg2):
        return arg1 + arg2
    def sub(self, arg1, arg2):
        return arg1 - arg2

if __name__ == '__main__':
    import win32com.server.register
    win32com.server.register.UseCommandLine(COMCalcServer)
```

Now, you need to create a Delphi form to support all the COM client activities (see Figure 7.4).

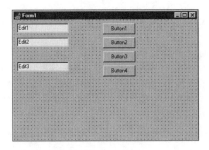

Figure 7.4

Delphi design: A form with three Edit boxes and four buttons.

```
unit Calcform;

interface

uses
  Windows, Messages, SysUtils, Classes, Graphics, Controls, Forms, Dialogs,
  StdCtrls, OLEAuto;

type
  TForm1 = class(TForm)
    Button1: TButton;
    Edit1: TEdit;
    Edit2: TEdit;
    Edit3: TEdit;
    Button2: TButton;
    Button3: TButton;
    Button4: TButton;
    procedure FormCreate(Sender: TObject);
    procedure Button1Click(Sender: TObject);
    procedure Button4Click(Sender: TObject);
    procedure Button3Click(Sender: TObject);
    procedure Button2Click(Sender: TObject);
  private
    { Private declarations }
  public
    { Public declarations }
  end;

var
  Form1: TForm1;
  COMCalcServer: Variant;
implementation

{$R *.DFM}

procedure TForm1.FormCreate(Sender: TObject);
begin
    try
        COMCalcServer := CreateOleObject('COMCALCSERVER.VERSION1');
        Form1.Caption := 'Python COM Routine is Active';
        Edit1.text := '';
        Edit2.text := '';
        Edit3.text := '';
```

```
        Button1.Name := 'mul';
        Button2.Name := 'div';
        Button3.Name := 'add';
        Button4.Name := 'sub';

    except
        MessageDlg('An error has happened!', mtError, [mbOk],0);
        Application.Terminate;
    end;
end;

procedure TForm1.Button1Click(Sender: TObject);
var tmp1float, tmp2float : Real;
    tmp3string : String;
begin
    tmp1float := StrToFloat(Edit1.text);
    tmp2float := StrToFloat(Edit2.text);
    tmp3string := FloatToStr(COMCalcServer.mul(tmp1float, tmp2float));
    Edit3.text := tmp3string;
end;

procedure TForm1.Button2Click(Sender: TObject);
var tmp1float, tmp2float : Real;
    tmp3string : String;
begin
    tmp1float := StrToFloat(Edit1.text);
    tmp2float := StrToFloat(Edit2.text);
    tmp3string := FloatToStr(COMCalcServer.div(tmp1float, tmp2float));
    Edit3.text := tmp3string;
end;

procedure TForm1.Button3Click(Sender: TObject);
var tmp1float, tmp2float : Real;
    tmp3string : String;
begin
    tmp1float := StrToFloat(Edit1.text);
    tmp2float := StrToFloat(Edit2.text);
    tmp3string := FloatToStr(COMCalcServer.add(tmp1float, tmp2float));
    Edit3.text := tmp3string;
end;

procedure TForm1.Button4Click(Sender: TObject);
var tmp1float, tmp2float : Real;
```

```
    tmp3string : String;
begin
    tmp1float := StrToFloat(Edit1.text);
    tmp2float := StrToFloat(Edit2.text);
    tmp3string := FloatToStr(COMCalcServer.sub(tmp1float, tmp2float));
    Edit3.text := tmp3string;
end;

end.
```

After compiling and running the application, you should see the interface shown in
Figure 7.5.

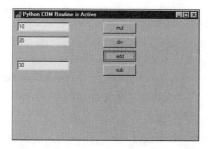

Figure 7.5
Delphi Calculator Application.

Distributing Objects with Python

There are some other packages that enable you to talk to other programs on platforms
without COM support. As for the object distribution models, Python has many projects
currently being developed.

The Inter-Language Unification system (ILU) is a free and stable multi-language
object interface system.

The Object Request Broker is the mechanism that lets objects transparently make
requests to—and receive from—other objects located locally or remotely. The ORB
component is also commonly referred to as *CORBA*, which stands for *Common Object
Request Broker Architecture*. omniORBpy is an almost complete implementation of the
current Python CORBA mapping.

Fnorb is an Object Request Broker (ORB) that is compliant with the CORBA 2.0 specification from the Object Management Group (OMG). Fnorb implements a single language mapping from OMG IDL to Python. This implementation is excellent for those who want to learn CORBA. Another project worth mentioning is the ORBit-python project, which a binding for ORBit, the CORBA orb used by GNOME and some other projects.

DCOM is the COM technology that distributes objects between different machines on the network. It defines a protocol that enables software components to communicate directly over a network in a reliable, secure, and efficient manner.

The Object Management Facility (OMF) is an object-oriented middleware environment for the process automation area. Even though it doesn't contain any Python code, it is heavily tested using Python scripts. The object model used by OMF is similar to other distributed object systems, such as OMG's CORBA and Xerox's ILU. OMF is implemented in C++, with APIs for other languages, including Python. It is said that the Python API was primarily created for writing test programs, but it has since been used to write various tools for application development and runtime management.

Hector is a distributed object system developed at the University of Queensland, Australia. It is written almost entirely in Python. Hector attempts to provide application objects with a consistent environment, regardless of their physical location, through a series of transparencies.

Inter-Language Unification (ILU)

The Inter-Language Unification system (ILU) is a free and stable multi-language object interface system, whose interfaces hide implementation distinctions between different languages, address spaces, and operating system types. ILU can be used to build multilingual, object-oriented class libraries with well-specified, language-independent interfaces. It can also be used to implement distributed systems and to define and document interfaces between the modules of nondistributed programs. ILU interfaces can be specified in either the OMG's CORBA Interface Definition Language (OMG IDL) or ILU's Interface Specification Language (ISL).

ILU is primarily about interfaces between modules of program structure. Each module encapsulates the part of a program that has high adhesion internally and low connection to other parts of the program. The main goal of ILU is to create object-oriented interfaces that can communicate with those modules. ILU does all the translating and communicating necessary to use all kinds of modules in a single program. Its mechanism optimizes calls across module interfaces to involve only what it is necessary for the calling and called modules to interact. The notion of a module should not be confused with the independent concept of a program instance, which is translated as a combination of code and data running in one memory image, such as the UNIX processes.

ILU standardizes many of the issues involved in providing proper inter-module independence, such as memory management and error detection and recovery strategies. ILU also includes an implementation of the Object Management Group's CORBA Internet Inter-Orb Protocol (IIOP), and can be used to write CORBA services or clients, as well. ILU provides a standard notation to write its interfaces—ISL, which stands for Interface Specification Language. ISL is a declarative language, which can be processed by computer programs that enables you to define exceptions, constants, object and non-object types. Next, you have a sample of what ISL looks like:

```
INTERFACE CalcMachine;
EXCEPTION DivideByZero;
TYPE Calculator = OBJECT
  METHODS
    SetValue (v : REAL),
    GetValue () : REAL,
    Divide (v : REAL) RAISES DivideByZero END
  END;
```

ILU provides a program, islscan, which can be used to check the syntax of an ISL specification, parse the specification, and summarize it to standard output.

After you've defined an interface, you then need to supply an implementation of your module, which can be done in any language supported by ILU.

The program python-stubber is used to read an ISL file, and generate all the Python code that is required to support the ISL interface. One of the files generated is 'Interface.py', which contains the definitions of all the Python types for that interface:

```
% python-stubber CalcMachine.isl
client stubs for interface "CalcMachine" to CalcMachine.py ...
server stubs for interface " CalcMachine " to CalcMachine__skel.py ...
%
```

To provide an implementation of your interface, subclass the generated Python class for the Calculator class:

```
# CalculatorImpl.py
import CalcMachine, CalcMachine__skel
class Calculator (CalcMachine__skel.Calculator):
```

```python
    def __init__ (self):
        self.value = 0.0
    def SetValue (self, value):
        self.value = value
    def GetValue (self):
        return self.value
    def Divide (self, value):
        try:
            self.value = self.value / value
        except ZeroDivisionError:
            raise CalcMachine.DivideByZero
```

Each instance of a `CalculatorImpl.Calculator` object inherits from `CalcMachine__skel.Calculator`, which in turn inherits from `CalcMachine.Calculator`. Each has an instance variable called value, which maintains a running total of the accumulator for that instance. We can create an instance of a `CalcMachine.Calculator` object by simply calling `CalculatorImpl.Calculator()`.

A very simple program to demonstrate the use of the `CalcMachine` module is listed next. To run this program, you have to type the command `python divide.py <NUMBER_TO_DIVIDE>`.

```python
# File: divide.py
import CalcMachine, CalculatorImpl, sys, string

def main (argv):
    calc = CalculatorImpl.Calculator()
    if not calc:
        error("Error creating the calculator")
    calc.SetValue (10.0)
    divisor = string.atof(argv[1])
    calc.Divide(divisor)
    print "the division result is", calc.GetValue()
    sys.exit(0)
main(sys.argv)
```

This program would be compiled and run as follows:

```
% python divide.py 5.0
the division result is 2.0
%
```

ILU also supports the use of the interface definition language OMG IDL, defined by the Object Management Group (OMG) for its Common Object Request Broker

Architecture (CORBA). That kind of support allows more programmers to easily use ILU because OMG's IDL uses a syntax similar to C++. However, because CORBA doesn't implement some of the concepts found in ILU, programmers can't implement all types of ILU interface using OMG IDL.

ILU is available for free at

`ftp://ftp.parc.xerox.com/pub/ilu/ilu.html`

Using ILU with Python: A Tutorial

`ftp://parcftp.parc.xerox.com/pub/ilu/misc/tutpython.html`

CORBA Binding and Implementation

The Object Request Broker (ORB) is the mechanism that lets objects transparently make requests to—and receive from—other objects located locally or remotely. The ORB is the middleware that establishes the client/server relationship between objects.

Using an ORB, a client object can transparently invoke a method on a server object, which can be on the same machine or across a network. The ORB intercepts the call and is responsible for finding an object that can implement the request, pass it the parameters, invoke its method, and return the results. The client does not have to be aware of where the object is located, its programming language, its operating system, or any other system aspects that are not part of an object's interface. The client is not aware of the mechanisms used to communicate with, activate, or store the server objects. The ORB serves as the foundation for building distributed object applications. Note that CORBA can short circuit requests to objects in the same address space, as ILU and COM can, if the implementation supports this.

The ORB component, or CORBA, is a set of specifications defining the ways software objects should work together in a distributed environment. The organization that drives the specifications, the Object Management Group (OMG), has hundreds of members representing a major portion of the software industry. The members work together to propose, review, and finally adopt a set of specifications to enable software objects to be developed independently and yet work together in a harmonic fashion.

The fundamental piece of CORBA is the ORB, or Object Request Broker. The ORB can be viewed like a channel carrying objects between the clients (those that consume the objects) and the servers (those that produce the objects). The consumers are provided with object interfaces, which are defined using a language called the Interface Definition Language. The detailed implementation of the objects by the producers is totally shielded from the consumers. The ORB is usually just a library that the program links to that marshals object requests. The promised benefits of making the software objects from different vendors publicly known made those vendors highly endorse OMG's specifications.

At the most basic level, CORBA is a standard for distributed objects. CORBA enables an application to request that an operation be performed by a distributed object and that the results of the operation be returned to the application making the request. The application communicates with the distributed object performing the operation. This is basic client/server functionality, in which a client issues a request to a server, and the server responds to the client. Data can pass from the client to the server and is associated with a particular operation on a particular object. Data is then returned to the client in the form of a response. Note that just like COM/DCOM, CORBA can be used to access objects that are local to the process, machine, or non-local.

DCOM is a Microsoft-specific distribution solution, whereas CORBA products are available from more than 20 different vendors, and they support Microsoft and non-Microsoft operating systems. CORBA is an excellent mechanism to bridge between Microsoft desktops and UNIX servers.

There is no explicit need to choose between DCOM and CORBA. Distributed applications can be developed using both CORBA and DCOM. For example, a client application might be developed to access a set of OLE automation objects, and OLE automation objects might in turn access CORBA Objects running on a non-Microsoft platform such a UNIX. The OMG has defined a COM/CORBA interworking specification that standardizes this sort of bridging.

> **Note**
> Python can be used to create wrappers between COM and CORBA systems.

CORBA is more mature than DCOM; it has existed since 1990, and commercial implementations have been available since 1992. DCOM wasn't available in beta form until 1996. Also, a large number of different companies have developed CORBA ORBs. This level of competition increases the robustness of CORBA solutions on the whole. It also ensures compatibility—a vendor's CORBA ORB is of much greater value if it can talk to a competitor's ORBs.

One of the advantages of DCOM over CORBA is the fact that DCOM is well suited to front-end application development. If entire distributed application runs under Microsoft platforms, DCOM might be a good choice. DCOM can also be used with CORBA. Of course, using DCOM will lock you into Win32 in the future, which might not be a good thing even if you are using Win32 at the moment.

The CORBA distributed object system is becoming an important standard in developing industrial-strength client/server and Web applications. It is also used as an

IPC layer between a number of components in both the Gnome and KDE desktop environments for UNIX.

In the current development phase of the CORBA binding for Python, the OMG board of directors has adopted the specification, and the finalization task force has completed its report. After approval, this report will become an available specification. omniORBpy is an almost complete implementation of the current Python/CORBA mapping. It is currently in beta, but is very stable.

More information about the omniOrbpy interface, which is provided by omniORB, can be found at

`http://www.uk.research.att.com/omniORB/omniORB.html`

Other interesting links for you include

CORBA IDL Parser—by Sam Rushing

`http://www.nightmare.com/software.html`

This parser uses Aaron Watters' kwParsing parser-generator package to construct a CORBA IDL parser in Python.

Object Management Group

Common Object Request Broker Architecture 2.0

OMG TC Document 96.03.04, July 1995

`http://www.omg.org/docs/ptc/96-03-04.ps`

Python Distributed Objects Special Interest Group

`http://www.python.org/sigs/do-sig/`

Fnorb

Fnorb is written in Python and its framework supports only Python. The implementation provided by this object-model helps you to learn more about CORBA systems.

Fnorb is an object request broker (ORB) compliant with the CORBA 2.0 specification from the Object Management Group (OMG). Fnorb implements a single language mapping from OMG IDL to Python. Because of the interpreted and interactive nature of Python, and the simplicity of the mapping (as compared to mappings with C++ and Java), Fnorb is ideally suited as a tool for the rapid prototyping, testing, and scripting of CORBA systems and architectures.

The pair Python/Fnorb is ideal for prototyping complex CORBA architectures, for using as a scripting tool, and for building test harnesses for all your CORBA development projects.

The combination of Python and Fnorb provides the existing CORBA community with a much needed tool for rapid prototyping and scripting, and gives those new to CORBA a great way to learn the fundamental concepts without being swamped by the intricacies of a "heavyweight" language mapping.

Like ILU from Xerox PARC, Fnorb gives the Python programmer access to the wonderful world of CORBA. It supports all CORBA 2.0 data types (including Any's) and provides a full implementation of IIOP. Unlike ILU, Fnorb is Python and CORBA/IDL-specific, which makes it simple, lightweight, and easy to install and use.

Using Fnorb, you no longer have to use other languages to write CORBA clients and servers—you can use Python now. This makes Fnorb ideal for prototyping complex CORBA architectures, for use as a scripting tool, and for building test harnesses for all your CORBA development projects.

The Python language mapping used by Fnorb is based on a specification document being prepared by members of the DO-SIG (Distributed Objects - Special Interest Group). One goal of Fnorb is to enable the Python community to experiment with the mapping before attempting to set it in stone via the OMG standardization process.

Fnorb is being developed at the CRC for Distributed Systems Technology based at the University of Queensland in Brisbane, Australia. Fnorb is released under a free for non-commercial use license. Another license must be acquired to use it commercially.

Official Fnorb home page

```
http://www.fnorb.org/
```

Jeff Rush's Fnorb Web page

```
http://starship.python.net/crew/jrush/Fnorb/
```

Provides Fnorb tips, techniques, and Linux RPMs for Fnorb.

DCOM

DCOM is Microsoft's way of distributing objects between different machines on the network. DCOM, or Distributed Common Object Model, defines the specifications that an object must obey to interoperate with other objects using Microsoft distributing architecture.

The core of DCOM is the Common Object Model, defined and refined from the earlier Object Link and Embedding implementation. Started naively as a way to enable documents to be embedded or linked into another document, OLE has completely reinvented itself.

The *Common Object Model (COM)* lays the foundation for objects to gain knowledge about, and to make use of, each other; thus they can engage in so-called component-based computing. DCOM extends the capability to include the constituent objects on other machines connected through the network.

The Distributed Common Object Model (DCOM) is a protocol that enables software components to communicate directly over a network in a reliable, secure, and efficient manner. Previously called Network OLE, DCOM is designed for use across multiple network transports, including Internet protocols such as HTTP. DCOM is based on the Open Software Foundation's DCE-RPC spec and will work with both Java applets and ActiveX components through its use of the (COM).

DCOM enables objects to be remote from their caller, and it handles all marshalling across machines and necessary security. Configuration tools enable an administrator to configure objects so that neither the object nor the caller needs any changes.

The following Microsoft article takes you to the download page of the DCOM configuration tool (`dcomcnfg.exe`), which was not included on the Windows 98 2nd Edition CD:

`http://support.microsoft.com/support/kb/articles/Q253/3/11.ASP`

Sometimes, code changes can be used to explicitly control the source of objects.

OMF

Object Management Facility (OMF) is an object-oriented middleware environment for the process automation area. It is used as the middleware foundation for several ABB [the ABB Industrial Systems AB (Sweden)] control system applications. Although it doesn't contain any Python code, it is heavily tested using Python scripts.

OMF includes the all-important features of an object request broker. A type definition language defines the interface and provides mappings to multiple programming languages. Objects can be distributed transparently on heterogeneous platforms. Furthermore, services for naming, type management, messaging, and persistence are available. OMF contains features particularly for real-time distributed control, such as high-speed communication, asynchronous messaging, message prioritization, and support for different bus protocols.

OMF is a distributed object system specifically designed for the process control industry. The object model is similar to other distributed object systems, such as OMG's CORBA and Xerox's ILU. What makes OMF different from these is its interaction model. The OMF interaction model specifies that, after finding a set of objects, OMF has to select what methods to call (for each object) and what attributes to get or set. It also has to choose when to perform the operation (at request, at event, periodically). After all this is done, OMF sends a single request for all objects.

OMF is implemented in C++, with APIs for other languages, including Python. Created for writing test programs, Python API has since then been used to write various tools (testing tools, development tools, and maintenance tools) to aid in application development and runtime management.

The OMF API for Python is implemented in two layers: The lower layer is written using a slightly modified version of Jack Jensen's modulator tool, whereas the higher layer is completely written in Python. On top of this API there are a few utility classes, such as the OMF agent, in which the agent lets the user treat OMF objects as local Python objects with attributes and methods, as follows:

```
from OMFagent import Agent
# Connect to an object in the network
ai = Agent('AI1.1')
# Get the Analog Input's value
# This will actually result in an RPC
value = ai.VALUE
```

The Agent code is surprisingly small, but results in a drastically higher abstraction layer than the bare OMF API. This is a rather simple class because of Python's dynamic typing.

Using Python in a Distributed Object System—by Daniel Larsson

```
http://www.python.org/workshops/1996-06/papers/d.larsson-dist-objs.html
```

Hector

Hector is a distributed object system written almost entirely in Python, taking advantage of the language's many features.

This specification provides a communication transparency layer enabling negotiation of communication protocol qualities, comprehensive support services for application objects, and novel interaction architecture. Its framework sits above other distributed environments, providing open negotiation and interoperability of communication protocols, high level description of component services and their requirements, a rich set of support services for objects and an interaction framework which enables the description of workflow-like interactions between autonomous objects.

Hector attempts to provide application objects with a consistent environment, regardless of their physical location, through a series of transparencies. Designed with the goal of supporting a dynamic, global system of distributed objects, it embraces diversity through extensibility. Specifically, it supports the following features while maintaining transparent usage of object services:

- Multiple parties in high-level interaction bindings

- Multiple object implementation languages

- Multiple interaction models

- Multiple transport protocols

Hector is structured as four layered components representing decreasing levels of abstraction. These layers are the Object, Language, Encapsulation (or Kernel), and Communication layers.

The initial language layer supports Python. Python Language Binding is available by default because the visible kernel classes are actually written in Python, making the wrapper classes very simple.

Hector: Distributed Objects in Python—by David Arnold, Andy Bond, Martin Chilvers, and Richard Taylor

`http://www.python.org/workshops/1996-06/papers/d.arnold/paper.html`

Elvin Has Left the Building: A Publish/Subscribe Notification Service with Quenching

`http://www.dstc.edu.au/Research/Research/Projects/Elvin/mirror/`
`www.dstc.edu.au/Elvin/papers/AUUG97/AUUG97.html`

Summary

This chapter explains how to use Python to interface objects from different applications on a single machine, and across networks through distributed systems. Python has very comprehensive support for object interfacing and distributing technologies.

COM is the most widely used component software model in the world when it comes to object interfacing. COM provides a rich set of integrated services, a wide choice of easy-to-use tools, and a large set of available applications.

The COM genealogy can be traced back to DDE (Dynamic Data Exchange). DDE was the first device for transferring data between various applications in Windows. After some time, DDE was expanded to Object Linking and Embedding (OLE). The creation of the Visual Basic Extensions (VBXs) enhanced the OLE technology for visual components, originating a new standard called OLE2. Soon, the OLE2 technology became COM, which is a general-purpose mechanism.

Many technologies, currently in the market, are COM-based. For example, we have ActiveX, OLE, OLEDB, ADO, and DirectX.

The entire set of information that belongs to a COM object is stored in the Windows Registry.

In order to implement COM interfaces with Python, you need to install the `win32com` Python extensions developed by Mark Hammond. These extensions are part of the PythonWin installation.

The COM support for Python is made of the `PythonCOM` module, which supports the C++ code, and other modules that implement helper code in Python. Known as `win32com"`, this package provides support for COM client and COM server interfaces. The access to objects' methods and properties can be either by late or early binding.

PythonWin also comes with a COM browser (Python Object browser). This program helps you identify the objects currently running on your system that offer COM interfaces.

Many kinds of software and languages, such as, Microsoft Word, Excel, Visual Basic, and Delphi provide ways to interoperate with COM objects. Therefore, as you can see in the examples of this chapter, it is very easy to "talk" to these objects.

In order to implement COM object using Python, you must design a Python class that exposes the functionality to be exported. This class must carry some special attributes that will uniquely identify the COM interface in your system. After elaborating the class, you need to register it. The operation is simple: It simply saves the class information in your Windows Registry. The option to unregister classes is also available.

Python can handle its many different types of objects across COM interfacing transactions perfectly well. Numbers, strings, core objects, lists, and tuples have implementations that handle their exposure to the interfaces.

Python has many projects currently being developed for object distribution models.

The Inter-Language Unification system (ILU) is a free and stable multi-language object interface system.

The Object Request Broker lets objects transparently make requests to—and receive from—other objects located locally or remotely. The ORB component is also commonly referred to as CORBA (Common Object Request Broker Architecture). omniORBpy is an almost complete implementation of the current Python/CORBA mapping.

Fnorb is an Object Request Broker (ORB) compliant with the CORBA 2.0 specification from the Object Management Group (OMG). Fnorb implements a single language mapping from OMG IDL to Python. This implementation is excellent for those who want to learn CORBA.

DCOM is the COM technology that distributes objects between different machines on the network. It defines a protocol that enables software components to communicate directly over a network in a reliable, secure, and efficient manner.

The Object Management Facility (OMF) is an object-oriented middleware environment for the process automation area. Even though it doesn't contain any Python code, it is heavily tested using Python scripts. The object model used by OMF is similar to other distributed object systems, such as OMG's CORBA and Xerox's ILU. OMF is implemented in C++, with APIs for other languages, including Python. Python API was originally designed for writing test programs, but has since been used to write various tools to aid in application development and runtime management.

Hector is a distributed object system developed at the University of Queensland, Australia. It is written almost entirely in Python. Hector attempts to provide application objects with a consistent environment, regardless of their physical location, through a series of transparencies.

Code Examples

Parking Lot (File parkinglot.py)

This example generates a Python COM server that exposes a parking lot object. The example uses a Visual Basic graphical interface to manipulate the vehicles of this parking lot. Each vehicle is a Python Object that is also defined as a Python COM Server object.

The first thing to do is to generate two clsids: one for each object.

```
>>> import pythoncom
>>> print pythoncom.CreateGuid()
BD2CB7C0-3BB9-11D4-804E-0050041A5111
>>> print pythoncom.CreateGuid()
BD2CB7C1-3BB9-11D4-804E-0050041A5111
```

Now, we take these ids and use them to create a module.

Listing 7.1   *parkinglot.py*

```
 1: # File: parkinglot.py
 2:
 3: from win32com.server.exception import Exception
 4: import win32com.server.util
 5:
 6: class ParkingServer:
 7:     _reg_clsid_ = '{BD2CB7C0-3BB9-11D4-804E-0050041A5111}'
 8:     _reg_progid_ = 'Python.ParkingServer'
 9:     _public_methods_ = ['ParkVehicle', 'UnparkVehicle',
10:                 'GetVehiclesCount', 'IdentifyVehicle',
11:                 'GetLocationList']
12:
13:     def __init__(self):
14:         self.Vehicles = [Vehicle()]
15:
16:     def ParkVehicle(self, floor=1, model="", license="", color=""):
17:         VehicleToPark = Vehicle()
18:         VehicleToPark.floor = floor
19:         VehicleToPark.model = str(model)
20:         VehicleToPark.license = str(license)
21:         VehicleToPark.color = str(color)
22:         self.Vehicles.append(VehicleToPark)
23:
24:     def UnparkVehicle(self,index):
25:         del self.Vehicles[index]
26:
27:     def IdentifyVehicle(self, index):
28:         return win32com.server.util.wrap(self.Vehicles[index])
29:
30:     def GetLocationList(self):
31:         return map(lambda x:x.GetLocation(), self.Vehicles)
32:
```

Listing 7.1 *(continued)*

```
33:     def GetVehiclesCount(self):
34:         return len(self.Vehicles)
35:
36: class Vehicle:
37:     _reg_clsid_ = '{BD2CB7C1-3BB9-11D4-804E-0050041A5111}'
38:     _reg_progid_ = 'Python.Vehicle'
39:     _public_methods_ = ['GetLocation']
40:     _public_attrs_ = ['floor','model','license','color']
41:
42:     def __init__(self, floor=1, model = 'Dodge Neon',
                        license = 'LKS-92020', color = 'Red'):
43:         self.floor = floor
44:         self.model = model
45:         self.license = license
46:         self.color = color
47:
48:     def GetLocation(self):
49:         return 'The %s %s license %s is on the %d floor' % \
50:                   (self.color, self.model, self.license, self.floor)
51:
52: def RegisterClasses():
53:     print "Registering COM servers..."
54:     import win32com.server.register
55:
56:     win32com.server.register.UseCommandLine(ParkingServer)
57:     print "ParkingServer Class registered."
58:
59:     win32com.server.register.UseCommandLine(Vehicle)
60:     print "Vehicle Class registered."
61:
62: def UnRegisterClasses():
63:     print "Unregistering COM server..."
64:     import win32com.server.register
65:
66:     win32com.server.register.UnregisterClasses(ParkingServer)
67:     print "ParkingServer Class unregistered."
68:
69:     win32com.server.register.UnregisterClasses(Vehicle)
70:     print "Vehicle Class unregistered."
71:
72: if __name__=='__main__':
73:     import sys
```

Listing 7.1   *(continued)*

```
74:     if "-unregister" in sys.argv:
75:             UnRegisterClasses()
76:     else:
77:             RegisterClasses()
```

Lines 9–11: List of methods to be exported to the COM interface.

Line 13: Initializes parking with one vehicle [object].

Lines 20–21: As COM interfaces use Unicode objects, it is necessary to convert the objects to string.

Line 28: Wraps the Python Object before sending it to the COM client.

Line 31: Calls the appropriate GetLocation() method f or each Vehicle object in the Python List. Then, it returns a whole new list of strings.

Line 33: Counts the number of vehicles in the parking lot.

Line 52: Registers both COM servers.

Line 62: Unregisters both servers. (Unregistering them is necessary to clean up the Windows Registry.)

Line 72: Automatically registers the classes when the module is executed as a script.

Line 74: If the user calls the script at the command prompt passing the -unregister argument, the UnRegisterClasses() methods are executed.

When you have the module stored in the file, you can double-click on the file to execute it, or you can go to a DOS prompt and manually call it to register the server:

```
C:\python parkinglot.py
Registering COM server...
ParkingServer Class registered.
Vehicle Class registered.
```

Listing 7.2 implements the Visual Basic 5 project that provides the client interface for our Python COM server. It is the code for the main form.

Listing 7.2   *frmMain.frm*

```
1: Option Explicit
2: Public ParkingServer As Object
3: Public newVehicle As Object
4: Private Sub cmdPark_Click()
```

Listing 7.2   *(continued)*

```
 5:     Set newVehicle = CreateObject("Python.Vehicle")
 6:     newVehicle.floor = 1
 7:     newVehicle.model = ""
 8:     newVehicle.license = ""
 9:     newVehicle.Color = ""
10:     If frmVehicle.ModifyInfo(newVehicle) Then
11:         ParkingServer.ParkVehicle newVehicle.floor, newVehicle.model,
                newVehicle.license, newVehicle.Color
12:         RefreshVehiclesList
13:     End If
14:     Set newVehicle = Nothing
15: End Sub
16:
17: Private Sub CmdUnpark_Click()
18:     Dim CarSpot As Integer
19:     Dim Vehicle As Object
20:     If Vehicles.ListIndex = -1 Then
21:         Exit Sub
22:     Else
23:         CarSpot = Vehicles.ListIndex
24:         ParkingServer.UnparkVehicle CarSpot
25:         RefreshVehiclesList
26:     End If
27: End Sub
28:
29: Private Sub cmdUpdate_Click()
30:     Dim CarSpot As Integer, Vehicle As Object
31:     If Vehicles.ListIndex = -1 Then
32:         Exit Sub
33:     Else
34:         CarSpot = Vehicles.ListIndex
35:         Set Vehicle = ParkingServer.IdentifyVehicle(CarSpot)
36:         If frmVehicle.ModifyInfo(Vehicle) Then RefreshVehiclesList
37:     End If
38: End Sub
39:
40: Private Sub cmdInitializeServer_Click()
41:      If ParkingServer Is Nothing Then
42:         On Error GoTo cmdInitializeServer_Click_CreationError
43:         Set ParkingServer = CreateObject("Python.ParkingServer")
44:         On Error GoTo 0
45:         lblStatus.Caption = "The ParkingServer is up and running..."
```

Listing 7.2   *(continued)*

```
46:          cmdInitializeServer.Caption = "&Stop Server"
47:          Vehicles.Visible = True
48:          cmdPark.Visible = True
49:          CmdUpdate.Visible = True
50:          CmdUnpark.Visible = True
51:          Label2.Visible = True
52:          lbvehicles_number.Visible = True
53:          RefreshVehiclesList
54:          Vehicles.ListIndex = 0
55:          Vehicles.SetFocus
56:          Exit Sub
57:      Else
58:          Vehicles.Visible = False
59:          cmdPark.Visible = False
60:          CmdUpdate.Visible = False
61:          CmdUnpark.Visible = False
62:          lbvehicles_number.Visible = False
63:          Label2.Visible = False
64:          Set ParkingServer = Nothing
65:          cmdInitializeServer.Caption = "&Start Server"
66:          lblStatus.Caption = "The ParkingServer is not running."
67:          Exit Sub
68:      End If
69: cmdInitializeServer_Click_CreationError:
70:      MsgBox "An error has happened while initializing the ParkingServer."
71: End Sub
72:
73: Public Sub RefreshVehiclesList()
74:      Dim VehiclesList As Variant, VehiclesInList As Variant,
             highlighted As Integer
75:      lbvehicles_number.Caption = ParkingServer.GetVehiclesCount
76:      highlighted = Vehicles.ListIndex
77:      Vehicles.Clear
78:      VehiclesList = ParkingServer.GetLocationList
79:      For Each VehiclesInList In VehiclesList
80:          Vehicles.AddItem VehiclesInList
81:      Next VehiclesInList
82:      If highlighted < Vehicles.ListCount Then Vehicles.ListIndex =
             highlighted
83:      Vehicles.SetFocus
84: End Sub
85:
```

Listing 7.2   *(continued)*

```
86: Private Sub Form_Load()
87:     Vehicles.Visible = False
88:     cmdPark.Visible = False
89:     CmdUpdate.Visible = False
90:     CmdUnpark.Visible = False
91:     Label2.Visible = False
92:     lblStatus.Caption = "The ParkingServer is not running."
93: End Sub
```

Lines 2–3: The Python COM Objects are declared as `Objects` at the Form level.

Line 14: Releases the `Vehicle` object from the memory.

Line 20: Check whether the list is empty.

Line 35: Calls the Python `IdentifyVehicle()` method, which returns a Vehicle Object according to the indexing position (spot) provided as the function argument.

Line 76: Stores the index associated to the selected vehicle.

Line 78: Python sends a list of strings that becomes an array-type Variant.

Lines 82–83: Returns the focus to the last selected list item.

Listing 7.3 is used by the project's form, which enables you to type each vehicle's data.

Listing 7.3   *frmVehicle.frm*

```
 1: Public Function ModifyInfo(VehicleToModify As Object) As Boolean
 2:     txt_floor.Text = Str(VehicleToModify.floor)
 3:     txt_model.Text = VehicleToModify.model
 4:     txt_license.Text = VehicleToModify.license
 5:     txt_color.Text = VehicleToModify.Color
 6:     Show 1
 7:     VehicleToModify.floor = Val(txt_floor.Text)
 8:     VehicleToModify.model = txt_model.Text
 9:     VehicleToModify.license = txt_license.Text
10:     VehicleToModify.Color = txt_color.Text
11:     ModifyInfo = True
12: End Function
13:
14: Private Sub FormExit_Click()
15:     Me.Visible = False
16: End Sub
```

Lines 2–5: The public attributes of the Vehicle Object, *_public_attrs_*, are transported to the form objects.

Lines 14–16: If you close the window, the values are not transported back to the form. You must click on the OK button, which hides the form and brings the control back to the ModifyInfo() function.

When you execute this project, you have an easy-to-use interface that connects to the COM servers and accesses all the public methods that are implemented (see Figure 7.6).

Figure 7.6
Parking lot demonstration.

If you have problems trying to connect to the server, check whether you have registered the class from the Python console.

CHAPTER 8
Working with Databases

Nudge, nudge. Wink, wink. Say no more!

Sometimes, the machine's memory is not enough, and we need to store data somewhere else. That is what this chapter talks about—it shows all the database options that Python has available. For those who still don't know anything about databases, this chapter briefly explains how they work, and it also lists and explains the basic SQL statements that you need to know.

Working with Databases

For simplicity, let's say that databases are summarized as the place where you store and update data. Python is able to connect to a wide variety of databases.

The simplest solution to handle databases in Python is to use plain text files. A tiny variation of this method is to store the information in binary format.

The next possible solution is to use the indexing mechanism provided by the dbm-like modules. This mechanism provides better performance than our first option because it automatically organizes the data. It works by implementing dictionary structures that are used to store information. This option enables you to encode Python objects, and efficiently archive them in indexed files without having to go through the details of parsing and unparsing the information.

For this reason, object serialization and persistence storing are also present in this chapter. Both concepts are very helpful when it comes to storing information. Their roles are to translate Python objects to strings before archiving them to the file system or before transferring them to another process.

The last solution is to use "real" databases' systems by importing third-party database extension modules, such as the native Python interfaces to MySQL, Oracle, and Sybase database systems.

If your database doesn't have a native interface to Python, don't worry. Python also offers ODBC extensions that will enable you to connect to any database that supports ODBC, and as you know, almost all database servers have ODBC drivers available nowadays.

In the worst-case scenario, many client/server database systems provide C libraries that connect to their databases. If you are a dedicated hacker, you can create extension modules that talk to these C libraries connecting to the database.

For more information about using databases versus Python, check Python's Web site at the following URL:

```
http://www.python.org/topics/database/
```

Flat Databases

The simplest way to store any kind of information in Python is using flat files. You just need to use the open function that we already studied in Chapter 2, "Language Review." Two options are available: You can either store the information as simple text or as binary data.

Text Data

The next example is a straightforward case of using flat files to store and to retrieve information. First we try to read from the file. If the file doesn't exist, it is created, and the information provided by the user is saved on it.

```
filename = "myflatfile.txt"
try:
    file = open(filename, "r")
    data = file.read()
    file.close()
```

```
        print data
except IOError:
    data = raw_input("Enter data to save:")
    file = open(filename,"w")
    file.write(data)
    file.close()
```

Binary Data—The `struct` Module

The `struct` module is largely used to manipulate code of platform-independent binary files. It is a good choice for handling small files. For large files, you should consider using the `array` module.

Binary data files are much less likely to be platform independent. Also, it is easier to extend a text file format without breaking compatibility.

The `struct` module works by converting data between Python and binary data structures, which normally interact using functions written in C.

This module implements only three functions: `pack`, `unpack`, and `calcsize`.

- `pack`—Takes the list of values and returns a binary object based on the `formatstring` provided.

  `binobject = pack (formatstring, value1, value2, value3, ...)`

- `unpack`—Returns a Python tuple containing the original values. It uses the `formatstring` to translate the `string`.

  `pythontuple = unpack (formatstring, string)`

- `calcsize`—Provides the size in bytes of the structure matching the format string.

  `no_of_bytes = calcsize(formatstring)`

The next example packs the values (1, 2, 3) into binary format based on the format string `"ihb"`, and later converts them back to the original values.

```
>>> import struct
>>> buffer = struct.pack("ihb", 1,2,3)
>>> print repr(buffer)
'\001\000\000\000\002\000\003'
>>> print struct.unpack('ihb', buffer)
(1,2,3)
```

Note that the binary data is represented as a Python string.

The next example is based on a binary file that stores three different objects. The first one is the author's initial, the second one is the number of bytes used by an article written by the author, and the last object is the article itself.

```
>>> import struct
>>> data = open('mybinaryfile.dat').read()
>>> start, stop = 0, struct.calcsize('cl')
>>> author, num_bytes = struct.unpack('cl', data[start:stop])
>>> start, stop = stop, start + struct.calcsize('B'*num_bytes)
>>> bytes = struct.unpack('B'*num_bytes, data[start:stop])
```

The next table shows the list of formatting units that can be used by this module.

Table 8.1   *Formatting Units Used by the* struct *Module*

Format	C Type	Python Type
b	signed char	Integer
B	unsigned char	Integer
c	char	String of length 1
d	double	Float
f	float	Float
h	short	Integer
H	unsigned short	Integer
i	int	Integer
I	unsigned int	Integer
l	long	Integer
L	unsigned long	Integer
p	char[]	String
P	void *	Integer
s	char[]	String
x	pad byte	No value

Are you looking for more information about handling binary data? Check out the file npstruct-980726.zip at the following address:

http://www.nightmare.com/software.html

Sam Rushing has created an extension module useful for parsing and unparsing binary data structures. It is similar to the standard struct module, but with a few extra features (bit-fields, user-function-fields, byte order specification, and so on), and a different API that is more convenient for streamed and context-sensitive formats like network protocol packets, image, and sound files.

DBM (Database Managers) Databases

Now, let's look at this other mechanism for storing data. The next modules store data in dbm-style format. This format specifies a simple disk-based storage facility that handles data in a way equivalent to dictionaries. The objects are manipulated by using unique key strings. Each of these modules is an interface to a specific library.

dbm, gdbm, and dbhash are database modules that are part of the standard Python distribution.

Also included with the standard Python distribution is the anydbm module, which is a generic interface to all the dbm-like modules. It uses the modules that are installed.

The dbhash module provides a function that offers a dbm-style interface to access the BSD database library.

All these modules have some behavior in common. For example, to open the files, the following syntax is used by all of them.

```
dbhandle = open(filename [, flag [,mode]])
```

Where, *filename* is the database filename; *flag* can have one of the following values: r (read-only access), w (read/write access), c (create the database), n (force the creation of a new database); and *mode* specifies the file access mode (specific for UNIX systems).

The following operations are supported:

```
dbhandle[key] = value        # Set the value of a given key entry
value = dbhandle[key]        # Get the value of a given key entry
dbhandle.has_key(key)        # Test whether a key exists
dbhandle.keys()               # Returns a list of the current keys available
del dbhandle[key]            # Delete a key
dbhandle.close()             # Close the file
```

For all these dbm-like modules, the keys and the values to be stored must be of type *string*. Later, you will see a module called shelve with a behavior similar to these dbm-like modules. However, it stores persistent objects.

Each module provides its own exception, which is called *modulename*.error.

```
>>> import anydbm
>>> try:
```

```
...        dbhandle = anydbm.open("datafile","r")
... except anydbm.error:
...        print "Error while opening file"
...
Error while opening file
>>>
```

This is a simplified database system based on key/value pairs. Depending on the module and the system, it uses one or two files to store the data (for example, both gdbm and bsddb use a single file).

The disadvantage of this kind of implementation is that it is not portable. The storage format is specific to a particular hardware platform and operating system. Also, it is not designed for large volumes of data. The smaller the file, the better the performance. This is caused by the original specification, which wanted information to be accessed in a single system call. After some interactions, the data file gets very fragmented, full of data holes, which drives the performance to very low indexes. Of course, they are very efficient when you do lots of reads and almost no writes.

If you have a data file but you don't know which database you used to create it, take a look at the whichdb module.

The whichdb module provides a function that guesses which dbm module (dbm, gdbm, or dbhash) should be used to open a specific database. However, using the anydbm module should take care of guessing the format for you.

Another important fact you must know is concerning the storage size limitation of each key/value pair, which is also known as *bucket size*. The dbm module accepts between 1K and 2K of data. However, both gdbm and bsddb don't have any limitation at all.

dbm **Module**

The dbm module is a database interface that implements a simple UNIX dbm library access method. dbm objects behave similar to dictionaries in which keys and values must contain string objects. This module allows strings, which can encode any Python object, to be archived in indexed files. dbm is the original implementation of the DBM toolkit. The main function of this module opens a dbm database and returns a dbm object that behaves similar to a dictionary.

```
>>> import dbm
>>> dbhandle = dbm.open("datafile", "c")
>>> dbhandle["animal"] = "parrot"
>>> dbhandle["country"] = "Spain"
>>> dbhandle.close()
```

```
>>>
>>> dbhandle = dbm.open("datafile ", "r")
>>> for key in dbhandle.keys():
        print dbhandle[key]
parrot
Spain
>>> db.close()
```

gdbm **Module**

The gdbm module is similar to the dbm module. However, their files are incompatible. This module provides a GNU/FSF reinterpretation of the GNU dbm library. This module supports multi-user application, it is faster than the dbm module (the performance gets better when the number of records increases), and it was already ported to a larger number of platforms.

Check out the GNU Web site for more details:

```
http://www.gnu.org/software/gdbm/gdbm.html
```

```
>>> import gdbm
>>> key = raw_input("key: ")
>>> data = raw_input("value: ")
>>> dbhandle = gdbm.open("DATABASE","w")
>>> while not(dbhandle.has_key(key)):
...     dbhandle[key]=value
...     key = raw_input("key: ")
...     data = raw_input("value: ")
...
>>> dbhandle.close()
```

The gdbm module implements the following additional methods:

```
dbhandle.firstkey()
```

Returns the first key in the database.

```
dbhandle.nextkey(key)
```

Returns the next key located after the provided key.

```
dbhandle.reorganize()
```

Reorganizes the database by eliminating unused disk space that is created when deletions occur.

```
dbhandle.sync()
```

Synchronizes the database file by writing unsaved data to the disk.

If you append "*f*" to the `flag` clause in the `open` statement, Python opens the database in fast mode. This means that data is not automatically saved to disk. You must call the `sync` method in order to save all the unwritten information to disk. This is done to improve performance.

bsddb **Module**

The `bsddb` module is part of the standard Python distribution. In addition to the dictionary-like behavior, this module also supports B-trees (which allows traversing the keys in sorted order), extended linear hashing, and fixed- and variable-length records. Although this module has the more complex implementation, this is the fastest dbm-like module.

The `bsddb` module provides an interface to access routines from the Berkeley `db` library, a C library of database access methods copyrighted by Sleepycat Software. This library provides full transactional support, database recovery, online backups, and separate access to locking, logging, and shared-memory caching subsystems.

More information about the `Berkeley DB package` can be found at `http://www.sleepycat.com`.

The `bsddb` module implements the following `open` interfaces:

```
dbhandle = hashopen(filename [, flag [,mode]])
```

Handles hash format files.

```
dbhandle = btopen(filename [, flag [,mode]])
```

Handles btree format files.

```
dbhandle = rnopen(filename [, flag [,mode]])
```

Handles record-based files.

Along with the previous interfaces, this module also provides the following additional methods—these methods are used to move a cursor across the database.

```
cursor = dbhandle.set_location(key)
```

Moves the cursor to the location indicated by the `key` and assigns the location's value to the `cursor` variable.

```
cursor = dbhandle.first()
```

Moves the cursor to the first element and assigns its value to the `cursor` variable.

```
cursor = dbhandle.next()
```

Moves the cursor to the next element and assigns its value to the `cursor` variable.

```
cursor = dbhandle.previous()
```

Sets the cursor to the previous element and assigns its value to the cursor variable.

```
cursor = dbhandle.last()
```

Moves the cursor to the last element and assigns its value to the cursor variable.

```
dbhandle.sync()
```

Synchronizes the database file by writing unsaved data to the disk.

These methods are not supported by the `hash` format databases.

Although the standard Python distribution installs the `bsddb` module on Windows machines, there is another interesting Win32 port of the `bsddb` module, which was created by Sam Rushing. For more information, check out `http://www.nightmare.com/software.html`.

dbhash **Module**

The `dbhash` module provides a "clean" open interface to the Berkeley DB hash database. Note that the `bsddb` module must be installed before trying to call `dbhash` because the `bsddb` module is used to open the databases.

The syntax to open the hash database is the same as the one used by the other dbm-like modules.

```
dbhandle = open(filename [, flag [,mode]])
```

This module provides the following additional methods:

```
dbhandle.first()
```

Returns the first element.

```
dbhandle.last()
```

Returns the last element.

```
dbhandle.next(key)
```

Returns the next element after the key element.

```
dbhandle.previous(key)
```

Returns the previous element before the key element.

```
dbhandle.sync()
```

Synchronizes the database file by writing unsaved data to the disk.

Let's look at an example:

```
>>> import dbhash
>>> key = raw_input("key: ")
>>> data = raw_input("value: ")
>>> dbhandle = dbhash.open("DATABASE","w")
>>> while not(dbhandle.has_key(key)):
...     dbhandle[key]=value
...     key = raw_input("key: ")
...     data = raw_input("value: ")
...
>>> dbhandle.close()
```

anydbm **Module**

The anydbm module opens (or creates) a database using the best implementation available. It searches within the available databases using the following order: Berkeley bsddb, gdbm, and dbm. It only loads the dumbdbm module when none of the others are available. Actually, the module doesn't know what database packages are installed and available—it just tries to use them.

```
>>> import anydbm
>>> def opendatabase(filename, flag):
...     try:
...         dbhandle = anydbm.open(filename, flag)
...     except:
...         raise "Error opening file " + anydbm.error
...     return dbhandle
...
>>> dbhandle = opendatabase("mydata","c")
```

dumbdbm **Module**

The dumbdbm module is a simple, portable, and slow dbm-style database implemented entirely in pure Python. It shouldn't be used for development because it is slow, inefficient, and inconsistent. The only case acceptable for using this module is when no other module is available.

whichdb **Module**

The whichdb module tries to identify which database was used to create a given file. This module implements a function of the same name. The syntax is

```
dbtype = whichdb(filename)
```

This function returns the module name (for example, gdbm) when the format is identified.

The function returns an empty string if the format is not identified. Note that databases created using the dumbdbm module were not supported by this module prior to Python 2.0.

The function returns None if the file doesn't exist or if it can't be opened.

```
import whichdb
dbtype = whichdb.whichdb("filename")

if dbtype:
    handler = __import__(result)
    dbhandle = handler.open("filename","r")
    print dbhandle.keys()
if dbtype = "":
    print "I cannot recognize this file "
if dbtype = None:
    print "An error happened while reading this file"
```

> **Note**
> You shouldn't need to use this module. anydbm uses whichdb to work out what module to use to open a database.

Object Serialization and Persistent Storage

These other modules provide persistent storage of arbitrary Python objects. Whenever you need to save objects whose value is not a simple string (such as None, integer, `long integer`, `float`, `complex`, `tuple`, `list`, `dictionary`, `code object`, and so on), you need to serialize the object before sending it to a file.

Both `pickle` and `shelve` modules save serializable objects to a file.

By using these persistent storage modules, Python objects can be stored in relational database systems. These modules abstract and hide the underlying database interfaces, such as the Sybase module and the Python Database API.

Included in the standard Python distribution, the `pickle` module can convert Python objects to and from a string representation.

The `cPickle` module is a faster implementation of the `pickle` module.

The `copy_reg` module extends the capabilities of the `pickle` and `cpickle` modules by registering support functions.

The `marshal` module is an alternate method to implement Python object serialization. It allows you to read/write information in a platform independent binary format and convert data to/from character strings (the module only supports the simple built-in types). Basically, it is just another way to do `byte stream` conversions by using serialized Python objects. This module is used to serialize the compiled bytecode for Python modules.

This module should be used for simple objects only. Use the `pickle` module to implement persistent objects in general.

Persistent Storage of Python Objects in Relational Databases is a paper by Joel Shprentz presented at the Sixth Python Conference. For more information, check out `http://www.python.org/workshops/1997-10/proceedings/shprentz.html`.

pickle **Module**

The `pickle` module serializes the contents of an object into a stream of bytes. Optionally, it can save the serialized object into a file object. It is slower than the `marshal` module.

```
>>> import pickle
>>> listobj = [1,2,3,4]
>>> filehandle = open(filename, 'w')
>>> pickle.dump(filehandle, listobj)
>>> filehandle = open(filename, 'r')
>>> listobj = pickle.load(filehandle)
```

The next functions are the ones implemented by the pickle module.

```
pickle.dump(object, filename [,bin])
```

This function serializes and saves an object into a file. The `bin` argument specifies that the information must be saved as *binary* data. This function is the same as the following:

```
p = pickle.Pickler(filename)
p.dump(object)
```

If an unsupported object type is serialized, a `PicklingException` is raised.

```
pickle.dumps(object [,bin])
```

This function has the same behavior of `dump`. The difference is that this one returns the serialized object.

```
pickle.load(file)
```

Restores a serialized object from a file. This function is the same as the following:

```
object = pickle.Unpickler(file).load()
```

The next example serializes the information and converts it back again.

```
>>> import pickle
>>> value = ("parrot", (1,2,3))
>>> data = pickle.dumps(value)
>>> print pickle.loads(data)
("parrot", (1,2,3))
```

`cPickle` **Module**

This module implements the same functions that the `pickle` module does. The difference is that `cPickle` is much faster because it doesn't support subclassing of the `Pickler` and `Unpickler` objects. See the next example code. It uses the fastest pickle module available on the system.

```
try:
    import cPickle
    pickle = cPickle
except ImportError:
    import pickle
```

`copy_reg` **Module**

This module registers new types to be used with the `pickle` module. It extends the capabilities of the `pickle` and `cPickle` modules by supporting the serialization of new object types defined in C extension modules.

The next example corrects the fact that the standard `pickle` implementation cannot handle Python code objects. It registers a code object handler by using two functions:

- dumpdata—Takes the code object and returns a tuple that can only contain simple data types.

- loaddata—Processes the tuple.

```
import copy_reg, pickle, marshal, types

def loaddata(data):
    return marshal.loads(data)

def dumpdata(code):
    return loaddata, (marshal.dumps(code),)

copy_reg.pickle(types.CodeType, dumpdata, loaddata)

script = """
x = 1
while x < 10:
    print x
    x = x - 1
"""

code = compile(script, "<string>", "exec")
codeobj = pickle.dumps(code)

exec pickle.loads(codeobj)
```

> **Note**
>
> Note that starting at Python 2.0, the `copy-reg` module can't be used to register pickle support for classes anymore. It can only be used to register pickle support for extension types. You will get a `TypeError` exception from the `pickle()` function whenever you try to pass a class to the function.

marshal **Module**

This module is only used to serialize simple data objects because class instances and recursive references in lists, tuples, and dictionaries are not supported. It works similar to `pickle` and `shelve`.

This module implements the following functions:

```
marshal.dump(value, filename)
```

Writes the value in the opened filename.

```
marshal.load(filename)
```

Returns the next readable value from file.

```
marshal.dumps(value)
```

Only returns the string.

```
marshal.loads(string)
```

Returns the next readable value from string.

Errors in the value manipulation will raise a ValueError exception.

```
>>> import marshal
>>> value = ("spam", [1,2,3,4])
>>> data = marshal.dumps(value)
>>> print repr(data)
'(\002\000\000\000s\004\000\000\000spam[\004\000\000\000i\001\000\000\000i\002\0
00\000\000i\003\000\000\000i\004\000\000\000'
>>> print marshal.loads(data)
("spam", [1,2,3,4])
```

The next example handles code objects by storing precompiled Python code.

```
import marshal
script = """
x = 1
while x < 10:
    print x
    x = x - 1
"""

code = compile(script, "<script>", "exec")
codeobj = marshal.dumps(code)

exec marshal.loads(codeobj)
```

shelve **Module**

The shelve module is also part of the standard Python distribution. Built on top of the pickle and anydbm modules, it behaves similar to a persistent dictionary whose values can be arbitrary Python objects.

The shelve module offers persistent object storage capability to Python by using *dictionary* objects. Both keys and values can use any data type, as long as the pickle module can handle it.

```
import shelve
key = raw_input("key: ")
data = raw_input("value: ")
dbhandle = shelve.open("DATABASE","w")
while not(dbhandle.has_key(key)):
    dbhandle[key]=data
    key = raw_input("key: ")
    data = raw_input("value: ")
dbhandle.close()
```

The shelve module implements a shelf object which supports persistent objects that must be serializable using the pickle module. In other words, a shelf is a dbm (or gdbm) file that stores pickled Python objects. It stores dictionary structures (pickled objects) on disks. For that purpose, it uses dbm-like databases, such as dbm or gdbm. The file it produces is, consequently, a BINARY file. Therefore, the file's format is specific to the database manager used in the process.

To open a shelve file, the following function is available:

```
shelve.open(filename)
```

The file is created when the filename does not exist. The following methods and operations are also supported:

```
dbhandle[key] = value      # Set the value of a given key entry
value = dbhandle[key]      # Get the value of a given key entry
dbhandle.has_key(key)      # Test whether a key exists
dbhandle.keys()            # Returns a list of the current keys available
del dbhandle[key]          # Delete a key
dbhandle.close()           # Close the file
```

Next, I present a simple example of the shelve module using the following:

```
>>> import shelve
>>> dbhandle = shelve.open("datafile", "c")
>>> dbhandle["animal"] = "parrot"
>>> dbhandle["country"] = "Spain"
>>> dbhandle["weekdays"] = 5
>>> dbhandle.close()
>>>
```

```
>>> dbhandle = shelve.open("datafile ", "r")
>>> for key in dbhandle.keys():
        print dbhandle[key]
parrot
Spain
5
>>> db.close()
```

Locking

As a matter of fact, even though modules such as gdbm and bsddb perform locking, shelves don't implement locking facilities. This means that many users can read the files at the same time. However, only one user can update the file at a given moment. An easy way to handle the situation is by locking the file while writing to it. A routine like this must be implemented because it is not part of the standard distribution.

More Sources of Information

PyVersant

PyVersant is a simple Python wrapper for the Versant commercial OODBMS. By using PyVersant in the Python command prompt, you can interactively find objects, look at their values, change those values, and write the object back to the database, among other things. More information is provided at the following site:

```
http://starship.python.net/crew/jmenzel/
```

Details about Versant OODBMS are shown at the following site:

```
http://www.versant.com/
```

ZODB

The *Zope Object Database* is a persistent-object system that provides transparent transactional object persistence to Python applications. For more information, check out the following site:

```
http://www.zope.org/Members/michel/HowTos/ZODB-How-To
```

ZODB is a powerful object database system that can be used with or without Zope. As a database, it offers many features. Note that ZODB uses other database libraries for the actual storage.

More information about Zope can be found in Chapter 11, "Web Development."

The ODBC Module

ODBC (Open Database Connectivity) is a standard interface created by Microsoft; hence, it is fully supported by the Windows platform. It provides access to almost every database. Currently, the ODBC implements the ANSI standard SQL3.

To configure the ODBC settings for a database in your Windows system, you must use the ODBC Data Source Administrator, which is located at the Windows Control Panel.

The two major advantages of choosing to code an application to the ODBC API are as follows:

- Portable Data Access Code—The ODBC API is available on all major databases.

- Dynamic Data Binding—This allows the user or the system administrator to easily configure an application to use any ODBC compliant data source. This is perhaps the single biggest advantage of coding an application to the ODBC API. Dynamic binding allows the end user to pick a data source—that is, an SQL Server—and use it for all data applications without having to worry about recompiling the application. The ODBC module implements the Python DB API, so you can get this level of abstraction at the DB API level. Also, you don't explicitly recompile Python code.

EShop kindly donated the ODBC module to the public domain. This module is included in the PythonWin distribution. For more details, check out the site at `http://www.python.org/windows/win32/odbc.html`.

The next example shows how you can open a ODBC connection using Python.

```
import dbi, odbc
try:
        connection = odbc.odbc('DSN=mydatabase;UID=mylogin;
        PASSWORD=mypassword')
        cursor = connection.cursor()
        cursor.execute('select name, email from USERS')
        while 1:
                record = cursor.fetchone()
                if not record: break
                print record
        connection.close()
except NameError,e:
        print 'NameError: ', e
```

Three ways (at least) to access ODBC from Python on the Windows platform are as follows:

- DB API—Python Database API
- calldll—Sam Rushing's calldll module
- DAO—Microsoft Data Access Objects

ODBC Example for Windows Platforms

The first thing you need is to create a DSN for your database in the ODBC Data Source Administrator.

The PythonWin distribution comes with an odbc module, which by the way is very stable. However, it is no longer going to be improved. This odbc module works along with the dbi module. Both files conform to the Version 1.0 of the Python Database API, providing a minimum implementation.

The whole ODBC functionality is made up of two extension files:

- odbc.pyd—The odbc module itself
- dbi.pyd—The database independence utilities module

The dbi module must be imported before you import the odbc module.

```
import dbi, odbc, pprint
connection = odbc.odbc('DSN=mydatabase;UID=myuser;PWD=mypassword')
cursor = connection.cursor()
cursor.execute('SELECT name, email FROM USERS')
data = mycursor.fetchall()
cursor.close()
connection.close()
pprint.pprint(data)
[('andre','andre@bebemania.com.br'), ('renata', None)]
```

Let's see some of the functions and attributes exposed by the odbc connection and cursor objects.

```
fetchall()            # fetches all the rows
fetchone()            # fetches only one row
fetchmany(n)          # fetches n number of rows
mycursor.arraysize    # number of rows fetched.
mycursor.description  # structure of the cursor
```

`mycursor.execute()` supports DML and DDL. However, it doesn't support prepared statements.

The `dbi` module handles both date and time formats. All date results are returned as `dbi` date objects.

```
>>> pprint.pprint(data)
[('col1', <DbiDate object at 12e4b34>)]
>>> dateobj = data[0][1]
>>> dateobj
<DbiDate object at 12e4b34>
>>> int(dateobj)
984046200
>>> str(dateobj)
'Fri Jun 02 00:00:00 2000'
```

The next command shows the preferred way to pass *date* values back to the ODBC driver because this is the standard ODBC syntax for embedding dates in SQL strings.

```
mycursor.execute("UPDATE tablename SET columnname={d '1999-04-15'}")
```

mxODBC

mxODBC is an extension package created by Marc-André Lemburg that exposes interfaces to ODBC 2.0 database drivers. This package implements the standard Database API. Among other things, it supports more than one database per process and it has preconfigured scripts for MySQL, Oracle, Informix, and more. This package exposes an `odbc` module for both Windows and UNIX. One of the most important differences between this module and the one that comes in the PythonWin distribution might be that this one supports prepared statements, hence, you can separate the SQL structure from the actual values. The engine parses a statement once, creates a handle for it. After that, you just need to pass the correct parameters that should be used for each interaction.

This package also possess an enhanced set of date and time types for moving data between both Windows and UNIX systems. You can blame the `mxDateTime` package for that. The `mxDateTime` package might become part of the `mxODBC` package in the near future. Check it out at

```
http://starship.python.net/crew/lemburg/mxODBC.html
```

calldll

You can also use the `calldll` package, developed by Sam Rushing, to call the functions that are part of the Microsoft ODBC DLL. One problem with using this DLL is that it doesn't have any similarity to the Python DB API. Another problem is that if you call the ODBC functions with the wrong arguments, your program might fail. The function calls have a low-level interface that doesn't handle exceptions as nicely as Python does. For more information, check out

`http://www.nightmare.com/software.html`.

> **Caution**
> This is one of the most dangerous ways to access databases. `calldll` removes almost all the safety Python gives you.

unixODBC

`unixODBC` is a complete, free/open, ODBC solution for UNIX/Linux. The `unixODBC` Project goals are to develop and promote `unixODBC` to be the definitive standard for ODBC on the Linux platform. This is to include GUI support for KDE. For more information, check out `http://www.unixODBC.org`.

Other Interesting ODBC Web Pages

The next few links introduce some interesting material that you can use to understand and use ODBC techniques.

ODBC Hints—by John Dell'Aquila

`http://www.python.org/windows/OdbcHints.html`

Full ODBC manual

`http://www.solidtech.com/developer/documentation.html`

ADO (ActiveX Data Objects)

ActiveX Data Objects (ADO) is an Automation-based interface technology for accessing data. ADO uses the OLE DB interface to access a broad range of data sources, including but not limited to data provided via ODBC.

Although ODBC seems to be the standard in the market, ADO offers significant benefits. ADO is a rich and fully featured object model (see Chapter 7, "Objects Interfacing and Distribution," for details). The library name in which ADO lives is called ADODB. The ADO object model gives you fantastic flexibility.

Users of *RDO (Remote Data Objects)* and DAO should have no problem moving to ADO because the overall design of ADO comes from Microsoft's experience in developing those interfaces.

Microsoft's *Remote Data Service (RDS)* is a component of ADO that provides fast and efficient data connectivity and the data-publishing framework for applications hosted in Microsoft Internet Explorer. It is based on a client/server distributed technology that works over HTTP, HTTPS (HTTP over Secure Sockets layer), and DCOM application protocols. Using data-aware ActiveX controls, RDS provides data access programming in the style of Microsoft Visual Basic to Web developers who need to build distributed, data-intensive applications for use over corporate intranets and the Internet. The use of ADO ties your application to Win32, whereas using the Python DB API does not.

After you have created the Connection object, you need to open a database connection by assigning a string value to the Open method. This string can be the name of a *DSN (Data Source Name)* or a complete connection string.

```
>>> import win32com.client
>>> adoConn = win32com.client.Dispatch('ADODB.Connection')
>>> adoConn.Open('data source=mySQLServer;')
>>> adoRS = adoConn.Execute ('truncate table tmp_table')
>>> args = "34,25"
>>> del adoRS
>>> adoRS = adoConn.Execute ('insert into tmp_table values ('+args+')')
>>> args = "11,12"
>>> del adoRS
>>> adoRS = adoConn.Execute ('insert into tmp_table values ('+args+')')
>>> del adoRS
>>> (adoRS, success) = adoConn.Execute ('Select c1, c2 from tmp_table')
>>> while not adoRS.EOF:
...     vl_a = adoRS.Fields('c1').Value
...     vl_b = adoRS.Fields('c2').Value
...     print vl_a, vl_b
...     adoRS.MoveNext()
...
34 25
11 12
>>> adoRS.MoveFirst()
>>> (adoRS, success) = adoConn.Execute ('Select c1, c2 from tmp_table')
>>> print vl_a, vl_b
34 25
```

Using SQL

SQL stands for *Structured Query Language*. It was developed in the mid-1970s by IBM Research to serve as an English interface query language to the System R relational database prototype.

SQL consists of a list of powerful and flexible commands that are used to manipulate information collected in tables, by operating and controlling sets of records at a time.

- SQL is an interactive query language for *ad hoc* database queries.
- SQL is a database programming language.
- SQL is a data definition and data administration language.
- SQL is the language of networked database servers.
- SQL helps protect the data in a multi-user networked environment.

Nowadays, SQL servers are the dominant model for creating client/server applications. The most important tendency among database servers of any size is the revelation of SQL as the choice for the manipulation, definition, and control of data.

SQL has been an ISO standard for a long time. It is a powerful language for databases that adhered to the relational model.

The relational model clearly separates the physical aspects of data from their logical implementation. It frees you from being concerned with the details of how data is stored and makes the access to data purely logical.

By using SQL statements, you just need to specify the tables, columns, and row qualifiers to get to any data item.

SQL Mini-Tutorial

The idea behind this mini-tutorial is to teach you how to change and query the database. Of course, this book does not cover everything. It should give you a brief understanding of the concepts and basic usage of SQL statements. If it becomes necessary to delve deeper in this topic, the last heading of this section contains a list of Web sites that have some beneficial and complete SQL tutorials.

Selecting the Information

In a relational database, data is stored in tables. In our example, we have the USERS Table. ID, NAME, EMAIL, and AGE are the columns of this table.

Table 8.2   USERS

ID	NAME	EMAIL	AGE
1	Andre	alessa@bebemania.com.br	25
2	Renata	rtaveira@bebemania.com.br	30
3	Cleber	clessa@bebemania.com.br	45
4	Beth	beth@alugueaqui.com.br	40

Now, say that you want to know the EMAIL and the AGE of each user. You have to use the SELECT statement as follows:

```
SELECT EMAIL, AGE
FROM USERS
```

The following list is the result of your query:

EMAIL	AGE
alessa@bebemania.com.br	25
rtaveira@bebemania.com.br	30
clessa@bebemania.com.br	45
beth@alugueaqui.com.br	40

Let me explain to you what you have done: you asked to see all the rows from the USERS table, filtering only the EMAIL and AGE columns. Note that column names and table names do not have spaces—they must be entered as just one word. The general syntax for a SELECT statement (when selecting all the rows from a table) is

```
SELECT Column1Name, Column2Name, ...
FROM TableName
```

> **Note**
> This basic syntax doesn't filter which rows are selected or do anything else interesting.

You can use the asterisk symbol in order to retrieve all the columns from a table without typing every column name:

```
SELECT * FROM TableName;
```

Relational Operators

Six important relational operators exist in SQL, and after introducing them, we'll see how they're used:

=	Equal
<>	Not Equal
<	Less Than
>	Greater Than
<=	Less Than or Equal To
>=	Greater Than or Equal To

The WHERE clause of a SELECT statement specifies which rows of a table must be selected. For example, let's determine which users are 25 years old.

```
SELECT NAME
FROM USERS
WHERE AGE = 25;
```

The resultset is as follows:

```
NAME
Andre
```

Joins

Good database design suggests that each table in a database must contain data of only one single entity. Detailed information can be acquired by joining tables according to their primary and foreign keys. For example, we will create Table 8.3.

Table 8.3   NATIONALITY

ID	ORIGIN
1	Greek
2	Spain
6	USA
8	Brazil

Let's discuss the concept of keys. A primary key is a column or set of columns that uniquely identifies the rest of the data in any given row. For example, in the USERS table, the ID column uniquely identifies each row.

A foreign key is a column in a table that is a primary key of another table. It means that any data in a foreign key column must exist in the other table where that column is the primary key. For example, in the NATIONALITY table, the column ID is a foreign key to the primary key of the USERS table, which is the ID column.

The purpose of these keys is to associate data across tables, eliminating data redundancy in the tables—this is the power of relational databases.

To find the names of the user whose name comes from Spain, use the following query:

```
SELECT USERS.NAME
FROM USERS, NATIONALITY
WHERE USERS.ID = NATIONALITY.ID
AND NATIONALITY.ORIGIN = "Spain"
```

The resultset is as follows:

```
NAME
Renata
```

Using Aggregate Functions

I will present five important aggregation functions: SUM, AVG, MAX, MIN, and COUNT. They are called aggregation functions because they summarize the results of a query, rather than listing all the rows.

- SUM()—Returns the total value of a given column, based on the selected rows.

- AVG()—Returns the average value of the given column.

- MAX()—Returns the highest value in the given column.

- MIN()—Returns the lowest value in the given column.

- COUNT(*)—Returns the number of rows that satisfy the WHERE clause.

Let's look at some examples:

```
SELECT     SUM(AGE), AVG(AGE)
FROM       USERS
```

The resultset is as follows:

```
SUM      AVG
135      33.75
```

```
SELECT      COUNT(*)
FROM        USERS
WHERE       AGE > 30
```

The resultset is as follows:

```
COUNT(*)
2
```

Sometimes, when you are working with aggregation functions, the group by clause might be required. For instance, let's say that you need to list the average age by username from your USERS table. The following SELECT statement can be used to group the resultset of your query.

```
SELECT      NAME, AVG(AGE)
FROM        USERS
GROUP BY    NAME
```

Adding Data

To insert rows in a table, use the following syntax:

```
INSERT INTO <TABLE NAME> [(<COLUMN1 NAME>, <COLUMN2 NAME>, ...)]
 VALUES (<VALUE1>, <VALUE2>, ...);
```

> **Note**
> In order to *not* use the column name part of your statement (because it's optional), in most cases, you need to provide values for all the columns of your table.

For example

```
INSERT INTO USERS (ID, NAME, EMAIL, AGE) VALUES (5, "Bruno",
 "bruno@alugueaqui.com.br", 17)
```

Deleting Data

Let's delete a row from a table.

```
DELETE FROM USERS
WHERE NAME = "Cleber"
```

If more than one row exists in which NAME = "Cleber", the other row will be deleted too. Using the primary key is a good way to uniquely identify a row for deletion.

To delete all the rows from the table, type the following:

```
DELETE FROM USERS
```

Updating Data

Let's update the age of one user.

```
UPDATE USERS
SET AGE = 18
WHERE NAME = "Bruno"
```

This statement sets Bruno's age to 18. If we had more than one *Bruno* in our database, we would have to include more conditions in the WHERE clause. It is also possible to update multiple columns at the same time—you just need to separate the attribution statements with commas.

```
UPDATE USERS
SET AGE = 18, EMAIL = "bruno@bebemania.com.br"
WHERE NAME = "Bruno" AND ID = 5
```

Cool SQL Language Web Pages

The Introduction to Structured Query Language site can be found at http://w3.one.net/~jhoffman/sqltut.htm.

Several links to SQL material can be found at http://www.lessaworld.com/links_basics_sql.html.

PostgreSQL Databases

PostgreSQL is a free (open-source) SQL database. It is a sophisticated Object-Relational database system derived from Postgres4.2. It conforms to (most of) ANSI SQL and offers many interesting capabilities, including subselects, transactions, and user-defined types and functions. It is the most advanced open-source database available anywhere.

Commercial Support is also available. For details, check out its Web site at http://www.postgresql.org.

pg Module

The pg module was written by D'Arcy J.M. Cain in order to provide an interface to the PostgreSQL database system. It embeds the PostgreSQL query library allowing easy use of its powerful features from a Python script. This module is available for download at http://www.druid.net/pygresql.

The `pg` module exposes its own DB API interface specification, as you can see next.

```
>>> import pg
>>> for rs in pg.DB('dbname').query('SELECT * FROM USERS').dictresult():
...     print rs
...
```

> **Note**
> At the time of this chapter was written, it was announced that the latest version of `pygresql` began supporting the Python DB API 2.0.

MySQL **Modules**

`MySQL` is a true multiuser, multithreaded SQL database server. It is a client/server implementation that consists of a server daemon `mysqld` and many different client programs and libraries. `MySQL` is very fast for performing queries, but can slow down if lots of updates are being performed. Also, it doesn't have transaction support. For more information, check out `http://www.mysql.com`.

MySQLdb **Module**

You need to get and build the `MySQLdb` module before using it. Check out `http://dustman.net/andy/python/MySQLdb`.

```
>>> import MySQLdb
>>> connection = MySQLdb.connect(host="spam", db="client", port=3316, \
...                              user="alessa", passwd="1020erw")
...
>>> con = connection.cursor()
>>> sql_statement = "SELECT * FROM USERS WHERE AGE > 21"
>>> con.execute(sql_statement)
>>> result_set = con.fetchall()
>>> connection.close()
```

Python Interface for MySQL

This interface was designed by Joseph Skinner and modified by Joerg Senekowitsch. For more information, check out `http://www.mysql.com/Contrib/MySQLmodule-1.4.tar.gz`.

The GadFly **SQL Module**

The `GadFly` SQL module is a SQL database engine written entirely in Python by Aaron Watters in compliance with the Python Database API. It uses fewer system resources than `PostgreSQL`, and its speed is comparable to Microsoft Access. However, it doesn't have the performance of commercial software (such as Oracle). This module is easily used by client/server applications because it includes TCP/IP support.

This module entirely fits in a small file, so it doesn't leave huge footprints.

Because it only supports a small subset of the SQL language, it offers excellent code for those who want to learn more about SQL parsing engines and client/server communications. For more information, check out http://www.chordate.com/gadfly.html.

MetaKit **Database Engine**

MetaKit is a C++ library for storage, transport, and manipulation of structured objects and collections. The next examples show how the MetaKit database engine does on-the-fly restructuring:

Example 1

```
>>> import Mk4py
>>> dbhandle = Mk4py.Storage('datafile.mk',1)
>>> workspace = dbhandle.getas('users[name:S,email:S]')
>>> workspace.append(name='Andre',email='alessa@bebemania.com.br')
>>> workspace.append(name='Renata',email='rtaveira@bebemania.com.br')
>>> dbhandle.commit()
```

Example 2

```
>>> import Mk4py
>>> dbhandle = Mk4py.Storage('datafile.mk',1)
>>> workspace = dbhandle.getas('users[name:S,email:S,age:I]')
>>> for user in workspace:
...     print user.name
...     user.age = input('age: ')
...
>>> dbhandle.commit()
>>> for user in workspace.sort():
>>>     print user.name, user.email, user.age
```

If you run these two examples in order, you'll have restructured on-the-fly. It will be instant, regardless of the number of rows. If for any reason the transaction is not completed, neither will the restructure be. For more information, check out their Web site at http://www.equi4.com/metakit/python.html.

Python DB API

The quest to provide a standard way to interface to database systems drove a group of people to develop Python Database API. The Python DB API is maintained by the Database Special Interest Group (DB-SIG). For more information, check out their Web site at `http://www.python.org/sigs/db-sig/`.

The following list shows all the database modules that currently implement the Python DB API specification proposed by the DB-SIG. This means that after you understand the API, you will be able to handle, in a similar way, all the databases that are manipulated by the following modules:

- GadFly—A simple relational database system implemented in Python based on the SQL Structured Query Language, including a DB-API compliant interface. Maintained by Aaron Watters.

  `http://www.chordate.com/gadfly.html`

- Informix—Currently maintained by Stephen J. Turner.

  `http://starship.python.net/crew/sturner/informixdb.html`

- Informix (Kinfxdb)—A completely new Informix module, called `Kinfxdb`. Maintained by Alexander Kuznetsov.

  `http://thor.prohosting.com/~alexan/`

- Interbase (Kinterbasdb)—An interface for Interbase 4.0 and 5.0. Maintained by Alexander Kuznetsov.

  `http://thor.prohosting.com/~alexan/Kinterbasdb/`

- MySQL—A `MySQL` module that is thread-safe and aims for compatibility with the 2.0 DB-API. It requires a newer version of MySQL, version 3.22.19 or higher.

  `http://dustman.net/andy/python/MySQLdb/`

- mxODBC—The `mxODBC` package provides a nearly 100% Python DB API compliant interface to databases that are accessible via the ODBC API. Many databases include ODBC libraries, so this might be the only module you need. Maintained by M. A. Lemburg.

  `http://starship.python.net/crew/lemburg/mxODBC.html`

- ODBC—This module is currently available in the PythonWin distribution. It's public domain code, but unfortunately has no designated support person(s). The best option for support is to ask questions on comp.lang.python newsgroups, where other PythonWin users can answer them.

  `http://www.python.org/windows/win32/odbc.html`

- DCOracle—An open source interface to Oracle from Digital Creations.

  `http://www.zope.org/Products/DCOracle/`

- Sybase—Maintained by Peter Godman.

  `http://starship.python.net/crew/pgodman/`

This is the information available at the time this book was written. For an updated list of modules, check out `http://www.python.org/topics/database/modules.html`.

DB-API Specification v2.0

The following specification is available online at `http://www.python.org/topics/database/DatabaseAPI-2.0.html`.

Comments and questions about this specification can be directed to the SIG for Database Interfacing with Python at the email address `db-sig@python.org`.

For more information on database interfacing with Python and available packages, see the Database Topics Guide at `http://www.python.org`.

This document describes the Python Database API Specification 2.0. The previous version 1.0 is still available online at the Python Web site as a reference. Package writers are encouraged to use this version of the specification as the basis for new interfaces.

This API has been defined to encourage similarity between the Python modules that are used to access databases. By doing this, we hope to achieve a consistency leading to more easily understood modules, code that is generally more portable across databases, and a broader reach of database connectivity from Python.

The interface specification consists of several sections:

- Module Interface
- Connection Objects
- Cursor Objects

- Type Objects and Constructors

- Implementation Hints

- Major Changes from 1.0 to 2.0

Module Interface

Access to the database is made available through connection objects. The module must provide the following constructor for these:

connect(parameters...)—This is a constructor for creating a connection to the database. Returns a *Connection Object*. It takes a number of parameters that are database dependent.[1]

These module globals must be defined:

apilevel—This string constant states the supported DB API level. Currently only the strings '1.0' and '2.0' are allowed.

If not given, a Database API 1.0 level interface should be assumed.

threadsafety—This integer constant states the level of thread safety that the interface supports. Possible values are

0—Threads cannot share the module.

1—Threads can share the module, but not connections.

2—Threads can share the module and connections.

3—Threads can share the module, connections, and cursors.

Sharing in the previous context means that two threads can use a resource without wrapping it using a mutex semaphore to implement resource locking. Note that you cannot always make external resources thread safe by managing access using a mutex: The resource might rely on global variables or other external sources that are beyond your control.

paramstyle—This string constant states the type of parameter marker formatting expected by the interface. Possible values are as follows:[2]

```
'qmark'    = Question mark style, e.g. '...WHERE name=?'
'numeric'  = Numeric, positional style, e.g. '...WHERE name=:1'
'named'    = Named style, e.g. '...WHERE name=:name'
'format'   = ANSI C printf format codes, e.g. '...WHERE name=%s'
'pyformat' = Python extended format codes, e.g. '...WHERE name=%(name)s'
```

The module should make all error information available through these exceptions or subclasses thereof:

Warning—This exception is raised for important warnings such as data truncations while inserting, and so on. It must be a subclass of the Python StandardError (defined in the module exceptions).

Error—This exception is the base class of all other error exceptions. You can use this to catch all errors with one single 'except' statement. Warnings are not considered errors and thus should not use this class as base. It must be a subclass of the Python StandardError (defined in the module exceptions).

InterfaceError—This exception is raised for errors that are related to the database interface rather than the database itself. It must be a subclass of Error.

DatabaseError—This exception is raised for errors that are related to the database. It must be a subclass of Error.

DataError—This exception is raised for errors that are because of problems with the processed data such as division by zero, numeric value out of range, and so on. It must be a subclass of DatabaseError.

OperationalError—This exception is raised for errors that are related to the database's operation and not necessarily under the control of the programmer; for example, an unexpected disconnect occurs, the data source name is not found, a transaction could not be processed, a memory allocation error occurred during processing, and so on. It must be a subclass of DatabaseError.

IntegrityError—This exception is raised when the relational integrity of the database is affected; for example, a foreign key check fails. It must be a subclass of DatabaseError.

InternalError—This exception is raised when the database encounters an internal error; for example, the cursor is not valid anymore, the transaction is out of sync, and so on. It must be a subclass of DatabaseError.

ProgrammingError—This exception is raised for programming errors; for example, table not found or already exists, syntax error in the SQL statement, wrong number of parameters specified, and so on. It must be a subclass of DatabaseError.

NotSupportedError—This exception is raised in case a method or database API was used that is not supported by the database; for example, requesting a .rollback() on a connection that does not support transaction or has transactions turned off. It must be a subclass of DatabaseError.

This is the exception inheritance layout:

```
StandardError
|__Warning
|__Error
    |__InterfaceError
    |__DatabaseError
        |__DataError
        |__OperationalError
        |__IntegrityError
        |__InternalError
        |__ProgrammingError
        |__NotSupportedError
```

Note
The values of these exceptions are not defined. They should give the user a good
idea of what went wrong though.

Connection Objects

Connections Objects should respond to the following methods:

close()—It closes the connection now (rather than whenever __del__ is called).
The connection will be unusable from this point forward; an Error (or subclass)
exception will be raised if any operation is attempted with the connection. The
same applies to all cursor objects trying to use the connection.

commit()—It commits any pending transaction to the database. If the database
supports an autocommit feature, this must be initially off. An interface method
might be provided to turn it back on.

Database modules that do not support transactions should implement this method
with void functionality.

rollback()—This method is optional because not all databases provide transaction
support.[3]

In case a database does provide transactions, this method causes the database to roll
back to the start of any pending transaction. Closing a connection without
committing the changes first will cause an implicit rollback to be performed.

cursor()—It returns a new *Cursor Object* using the connection. If the database does
not provide a direct cursor concept, the module will have to emulate cursors using
other means to the extent needed by this specification. [4]

Cursor Objects

These objects represent a database cursor, which is used to manage the context of a fetch operation. They should respond to the following methods and attributes:

description—This read-only attribute is a set of seven-item sequences. Each of these sequences contains information describing one result column: (name, type_code, display_size, internal_size, precision, scale, null_ok). This attribute will be None for operations that do not return rows or if the cursor has not had an operation invoked via the executeXXX() method yet.

The type_code can be interpreted by comparing it to the Type Objects specified in the following section.

rowcount—This read-only attribute specifies the number of rows that the last executeXXX() produced (for DQL statements such as select) or affected (for DML statements such as update or insert).

The attribute is -1 in case no executeXXX() has been performed on the cursor, or the rowcount of the last operation is not determinable by the interface.[7]

callproc(procname[,parameters])—This method is optional because not all databases provide stored procedures.[3]

It calls a stored database procedure with the given name. The sequence of parameters must contain one entry for each argument that the procedure expects. The result of the call is returned as modified copy of the input sequence. Input parameters are left untouched, and output and input/output parameters are replaced with possibly new values.

The procedure can also provide a resultset as output. This must then be made available through the standard fetchXXX() methods.

close()—It closes the cursor now (rather than whenever __del__ is called). The cursor will be unusable from this point forward; an Error (or subclass) exception will be raised if any operation is attempted with the cursor.

execute(operation[,parameters])—It prepares and executes a database operation (query or command). Parameters can be provided as sequence or mapping and will be bound to variables in the operation. Variables are specified in a database-specific notation (see the module's paramstyle attribute for details).[5]

A reference to the operation will be retained by the cursor. If the same operation object is passed in again, the cursor can optimize its behavior. This is most effective for algorithms in which the same operation is used, but different parameters are bound to it (many times).

For maximum efficiency when reusing an operation, it is best to use the `setinputsizes()` method to specify the parameter types and sizes ahead of time. It is legal for a parameter to not match the predefined information; the implementation should compensate, possibly with a loss of efficiency.

The parameters can also be specified as list of tuples to insert multiple rows in a single operation, but this kind of usage is depreciated: `executemany()` should be used instead.

Return values are not defined.

`executemany(operation,seq_of_parameters`
It prepares a database operation (query or command) and then executes it against all parameter sequences or mappings found in the sequence seq_of_parameters.

Modules are free to implement this method using multiple calls to the `execute()` method or by using array operations to have the database process the sequence as a whole in one call.

The same comments for `execute()` also apply accordingly to this method.

Return values are not defined.

`fetchone()`
It fetches the next row of a query resultset, returning a single sequence, or None when no more data is available.[6]

An Error (or subclass) exception is raised if the previous call to executeXXX() did not produce any resultset or no call was issued yet.

`fetchmany([size=cursor.arraysize])`
It fetches the next set of rows of a query result, returning a sequence of sequences (for example, a list of tuples). An empty sequence is returned when no more rows are available.

The number of rows to fetch per call is specified by the parameter. If it is not given, the cursor's arraysize determines the number of rows to be fetched. The method should try to fetch as many rows as indicated by the size parameter. If this is not possible because of the specified number of rows not being available, fewer rows can be returned.

An `Error` (or subclass) exception is raised if the previous call to `executeXXX()` did not produce any resultset or no call was issued yet.

Performance considerations are involved with the size parameter. For optimal performance, it is usually best to use the `arraysize` attribute. If the size parameter is used, it is best for it to retain the same value from one `fetchmany()` call to the next.

fetchall()

It fetches all (remaining) rows of a query result, returning them as a set of sequences (for example, a list of tuples). Note that the cursor's `arraysize` attribute can affect the performance of this operation.

An `Error` (or subclass) exception is raised if the previous call to `executeXXX()` did not produce any resultset or no call was issued yet.

nextset()

This method is optional because not all databases support multiple resultsets.[3]

This method will make the cursor skip to the next available set, discarding any remaining rows from the current set.

If there are no more sets, the method returns `None`. Otherwise, it returns a true value and subsequent calls to the fetch methods will return rows from the next resultset.

An `Error` (or subclass) exception is raised if the previous call to `executeXXX()` did not produce any resultset or no call was issued yet.

arraysize

This read/write attribute specifies the number of rows to fetch at a time with `fetchmany()`. It defaults to 1, which means to fetch a single row at a time.

Implementations must observe this value with respect to the `fetchmany()` method, but are free to interact with the database a single row at a time. It can also be used in the implementation of `executemany()`.

setinputsizes(*sizes*)

This can be used before a call to `executeXXX()` to predefine memory areas for the operation's parameters.

`sizes` is specified as a sequence—one item for each input parameter. The item should be a Type Object that corresponds to the input that will be used, or it should be an integer specifying the maximum length of a string parameter. If the item is `None`, no predefined memory area will be reserved for that column. (This is useful to avoid predefined areas for large inputs.)

This method would be used before the `executeXXX()` method is invoked. Implementations are free to have this method do nothing, and users are free to not use it.

`setoutputsize(size[,column])`
It sets a column buffer size for fetches of large columns (for example, LONGs, BLOBs, and so on). The column is specified as an index into the result sequence. Not specifying the column will set the default size for all large columns in the cursor.

This method would be used before the `executeXXX()` method is invoked.

Implementations are free to have this method do nothing, and users are free to not use it.

Type Objects and Constructors

Many databases need to have the input in a particular format for binding to an operation's input parameters. For example, if an input is destined for a DATE column, it must be bound to the database in a particular string format. Similar problems exist for Row ID columns or large binary items (for example, BLOBs or RAW columns). This presents problems for Python because the parameters to the `executeXXX()` method are not typed. When the database module sees a Python string object, it doesn't know if it should be bound as a simple CHAR column, as a raw BINARY item, or as a DATE.

To overcome this problem, a module must provide the constructors defined later to create objects that can hold special values. When passed to the cursor methods, the module can then detect the proper type of the input parameter and bind it accordingly.

A Cursor Object's `description` attribute returns information about each of the result columns of a query. The `type_code` must be *equal* to one of Type Objects defined in the following. Type Objects can be equal to more than one type code. (For example, DATETIME could be equal to the type codes for date, time, and timestamp columns; see "Implementation Hints" for details.)

The module exports the following constructors and singletons:

Date(year, month, day)—This function constructs an object holding a date value.

Time(hour, minute, second)—This function constructs an object holding a time value.

Timestamp(year, month, day, hour, minute, second)—This function constructs an object holding a timestamp value.

DateFromTicks(ticks)—This function constructs an object holding a date value from the given ticks value (number of seconds since the epoch; see the documentation of the standard Python `time` module for details).

TimeFromTicks(ticks)—This function constructs an object holding a time value from the given ticks value (number of seconds since the epoch; see the documentation of the standard Python `time` module for details).

TimestampFromTicks(ticks)—This function constructs an object holding a time stamp value from the given ticks value (number of seconds since the epoch; see the documentation of the standard Python `time` module for details).

Binary(string)—This function constructs an object capable of holding a binary (long) string value.

STRING—This type object is used to describe columns in a database that are string based (for example, `CHAR`).

BINARY—This type object is used to describe (long) binary columns in a database (for example, `LONG`, `RAW`, `BLOB`s).

NUMBER—This type object is used to describe numeric columns in a database.

DATETIME—This type object is used to describe date/time columns in a database.

ROWID—This type object is used to describe the Row ID column in a database.

SQL `NULL` values are represented by the Python `None` singleton on input and output.

> **Note**
> Usage of UNIX ticks for database interfacing can cause troubles because of the limited date range they cover.

Implementation Hints
The next list provides some suggestions about using this API.

- The preferred object types for the date/time objects are those defined in the mxDateTime package (`http://starship.python.net/~lemburg/mxDateTime.html`). It provides all necessary constructors and methods both at Python and C level.

- The preferred object type for Binary objects are the buffer types available in standard Python starting with version 1.5.2. See the Python documentation for details. For information about the C interface, take a look at `Include/bufferobject.h` and `Objects/bufferobject.c` in the Python source distribution.

- Here is a sample implementation of the UNIX ticks based constructors for date/time delegating work to the generic constructors:

```
import time
def DateFromTicks(ticks):
    return apply(Date,time.localtime(ticks)[:3])
def TimeFromTicks(ticks):
    return apply(Time,time.localtime(ticks)[3:6])
def TimestampFromTicks(ticks):
    return apply(Timestamp,time.localtime(ticks)[:6])
```

- This Python class allows implementing the previous type objects even though the description type code field yields multiple values for one type object:

```
class DBAPITypeObject:
    def __init__(self,*values):
        self.values = values
    def __cmp__(self,other):
        if other in self.values:
            return 0
        if other < self.values:
            return 1
        else:
            return -1
```

Note

The resulting type object compares equal to all values passed to the constructor.

- Here is a snippet of Python code that implements the exception hierarchy defined previously:

```
import exceptions
class Error(exceptions.StandardError):
    pass
class Warning(exceptions.StandardError):
    pass
class InterfaceError(Error):
    pass
class DatabaseError(Error):
    pass
class InternalError(DatabaseError):
    pass
class OperationalError(DatabaseError):
    pass
```

```
class ProgrammingError(DatabaseError):
    pass
class IntegrityError(DatabaseError):
    pass
class DataError(DatabaseError):
    pass
class NotSupportedError(DatabaseError):
    pass
```

Note
In C you can use the `PyErr_NewException(fullname, base, NULL)` API to create the exception objects.

Major Changes from Version 1.0 to Version 2.0

The Python Database API 2.0 introduces a few major changes compared to the 1.0 version. Because some of these changes will cause existing DB API 1.0 based scripts to break, the major version number was adjusted to reflect this change.

These are the most important changes from 1.0 to 2.0:

- The need for a separate `dbi` module was dropped and the functionality merged into the module interface itself.

- New constructors and Type Objects were added for date/time values, the RAW Type Object was renamed to BINARY. The resulting set should cover all basic data types commonly found in modern SQL databases.

- New constants (`apilevel`, `threadlevel`, `paramstyle`) and methods (`executemany`, `nextset`) were added to provide better database bindings.

- The semantics of `.callproc()` needed to call stored procedures are now clearly defined.

- The definition of the `.execute()` return value changed. Previously, the return value was based on the SQL statement type (which was difficult to implement correctly)—it is undefined now; use the more flexible `.rowcount` attribute instead. Modules are free to return the old style return values, but these are no longer mandated by the specification and should be considered database interface dependent.

- Class-based exceptions were incorporated into the specification. Module implementers are free to extend the exception layout defined in this specification by subclassing the defined exception classes.

Open Issues

Although the version 2.0 specification clarifies a lot of questions that were left open in the 1.0 version, there are still some remaining issues:

- Define a useful return value for `.nextset()` for the case in which a new resultset is available.

- Create a fixed point numeric type for use as loss-less monetary and decimal interchange format.

Footnotes

1. As a guideline, the connection constructor parameters should be implemented as keyword parameters for more intuitive use and follow this order of parameters:

```
dsn       = Data source name as string
user      = User name as string          (optional)
password  = Password as string           (optional)
host      = Hostname                      (optional)
database  = Database name                 (optional)
```

For example, a connect could look like this:

```
connect(dsn='myhost:MYDB',user='guido',password='234$')
```

2. Module implementers should prefer *numeric*, *named*, or *pyformat* over the other formats because these offer more clarity and flexibility.

3. If the database does not support the functionality required by the method, the interface should throw an exception in case the method is used.

   The preferred approach is to not implement the method and thus have Python generate an `AttributeError` in case the method is requested. This allows the programmer to check for database capabilities using the standard `hasattr()` function.

   For some dynamically configured interfaces, it might not be appropriate to require that the method be made available dynamically. These interfaces should then raise a `NotSupportedError` to indicate the inability to perform the rollback when the method is invoked.

4. A database interface can choose to support named cursors by allowing a string argument to the method. This feature is not part of the specification because it complicates semantics of the `.fetchXXX()` methods.

5. The module will use the __getitem__ method of the parameters object to map either positions (integers) or names (strings) to parameter values. This allows for both sequences and mappings to be used as input.

   The term *bound* refers to the process of binding an input value to a database execution buffer. In practical terms, this means that the input value is directly used as a value in the operation. The client should not be required to "escape" the value so that it can be used—the value should be equal to the actual database value.

6. The interface can implement row fetching using arrays and other optimizations. It is not guaranteed that a call to this method will only move the associated cursor forward by one row.

7. The rowcount attribute might be coded in a way that updates its value dynamically. This can be useful for databases that return useable rowcount values only after the first call to a .fetchXXX() method.

Summary

This chapter shows all the database options that Python has available. The simplest solution to handle databases in Python is to use plain text files. A tiny variation of this method is to store the information in binary format.

The next solution is to use the indexing mechanism provided by the dbm-like modules (such as dbm, gdbm, and dbhash). DBM stands for Database Manager, and it has its own storing implementation. This format specifies a simple, disk-based storage facility that handles data in a way equivalent to dictionaries. The objects are manipulated by using unique key strings.

These are database modules that are part of the standard Python distribution, and each one of them is an interface to a specific library.

Also included in the standard Python distribution is the anydbm module, which is a generic interface to all the dbm-like modules. It uses whichever modules are installed.

The dbhash module provides a function that offers a dbm-style interface to access the BSD database library.

The `whichdb` module provides a function that guesses which `dbm` module (`dbm`, `gdbm`, or `dbhash`) should be used to open a specific database.

The `dumbdbm` module is a simple, portable, and slow dbm-style database implemented entirely in pure Python.

Also, a group of other modules provide persistent storage of arbitrary Python objects. Whenever you need to save objects whose value is not a simple `string` (such as `None`, `integer`, `long integer`, `float`, `complex`, `tuple`, `list`, `dictionary`, `code object`, and so on), you need to serialize the object before sending it to a file.

Included in the standard Python distribution, the `pickle` module can convert Python objects to and from a string representation.

The `cPickle` module is a faster implementation of the `pickle` module.

The `copy_reg` module extends the capabilities of the `pickle` and `cpickle` modules by registering support functions.

The `marshal` module is an alternate method to implement Python object serialization.

The `shelve` module offers persistent object storage capability to Python by using `dictionary` objects. Both keys and values can use any data type, as long as the `pickle` module can handle it.

ODBC is a standard interface, created by Microsoft, that provides access to almost every database. Python's official ODBC module is included in the `PythonWin` distribution, which is very stable, by the way. However, it is no longer going to be improved. This `odbc` module works along with the `dbi` module.

Besides this `odbc` module, we have other technologies (such as `mxODBC`, `calldll`, and `unixODBC`) that make the task of opening ODBC connections easier. Although ODBC seems to be the standard in the market, ADO offers significant benefits. ADO is a rich and fully featured object model.

In order to correctly manipulate data, the use of SQL is essential. SQL consists of a list of powerful and flexible commands that are used to manipulate information collected in tables, by operating and controlling sets of records at a time. The main SQL commands are: `SELECT`, `INSERT`, `DELETE`, and `UPDATE`.

`PostgreSQL`, `MySQL`, `GadFly`, and `Metakit` are some of the SQL database mechanisms that run on Python.

Many third-party database extension modules are available for Python, such as the native Python interfaces to MySQL, Oracle, and Sybase database systems.

The quest to provide a standard way to interface to database systems drove a group of people to develop a Python Database API. The Python DB API is maintained by the Database Special Interest Group (DB-SIG). GadFly, mxODBC, MySQL, odbc, and many other modules have already adopted this API. This API has been defined to encourage similarity between the Python Modules that are used to access databases.

CHAPTER 9
Other Advanced Topics

I'd like to have an argument please.

This chapter provides very useful information concerning the use and manipulation of images, sounds, threads, and other specific Python Modules.

Other Advanced Topics

After spending some time learning the basics of Python, you will soon face the need for implementing more advanced programs; programs that need to perform very specific tasks, such as converting image file formats or handling regular expressions. This chapter provides a general overview of some important advanced Python topics that you might need to use.

- Image manipulation
- Sounds
- Restricted environment
- Numeric Python
- Regular expressions
- Threads

Each one of these items is discussed, and a brief explanation is provided along with syntax formats and examples.

As you already know, this book presents many links to resources that have proven to be of great help in allowing users to use Python in their day-to-day work.

Manipulating Images

Python has comprehensive support for handling image files. The foundation of this structure is based on the Python Imaging Library (commonly known as PIL).

PIL is a set of Python modules that compound an extensive framework written by Fredrik Lundh, from Secret Labs AB. PIL is able to convert and manipulate image files of several different formats (such as GIF, JPEG, and PNG), and provides powerful graphics capabilities. Its framework is cross-platform, which allows it to perform image manipulation and processing in different systems using the same code. PIL also supports some Windows-specific extensions that enable it to display images using the Windows API.

Some of the main features of PIL are summarized in the following:

- PIL can load image objects from a variety of formats.

- It enables the Python interpreter to handle image objects.

- PIL enables a rich set of image operations to be applied to those objects.

- It saves images files to disk.

- It uses graphical interfaces, such as Tkinter and PythonWin in order to show the resulting images.

- It allows you to create thumbnails automatically from a collection of images.

- You can create, read, and write different images formats, including JPEG, GIF, and TIFF.

- It provides supports to some animation formats, such as FLI and MPEG.

- It automatically identifies file formats.

- PIL can be used to make file conversions between graphic files of different formats.

- PIL also handles changes in the image file's color table (for example, it can change the color table of a file from RGB to grayscale).

These are just some of things you can do with PIL. You are invited to create an image object in the interpreter using PIL, and play around for a while.

PIL's home page and download center is located at the following site:

```
http://www.pythonware.com/products/pil/index.htm
```

Similar to Python itself, PIL is copyrighted but can be used without fee.

Python Imaging Library

The `Image` class is the most important class of PIL. To use it, you need to import the `Image` module, and launch the `open` method. This method is very fast because it doesn't decode the whole image. It just reads the image header in order to start working with the file.

```
>>> import Image
>>> im = Image.open("c:\\logo.gif")
```

As you can see in the next example, you can also load an image (GIF or JPEG) straight from a URL without saving it to a file first. Note that `filelocation` is any file handle like python object.

```
>>> filename = "http://www.lessaworld.com/images/brazil.gif "
>>> filelocation = urllib.urlopen(filename)
>>> im = Image.open(filelocation)
```

Every image object that is created by the `open` function exposes three attributes: `format`, `size`, and `mode`.

> `im.format`—Identifies the source format of the image.

> `im.size`—It is a 2-tuple variable that contains the image's width and height.

> `im.mode`—Provides the image mode, such as grayscale (`L`), `CMYK`, or `RGB` mode. The attribute called `Image.MODES` lists all the modes supported by the library.

```
>>> print im.format, im.size, im.mode
GIF (200, 130) L
```

If you want to generate a thumbnail image, you need to call the `thumbnail` method and provide the size of the new image. Note that a new object isn't created because the change is applied to the old object. Therefore, the image must be copied if you need both the original and thumbnail images.

```
>>> im.thumbnail((50, 32))
```

After you have done everything that you need, you can think about saving the new file. Notice that the first argument in the save method is the name of the output file, and the second argument is the format to be saved. If the format argument is omitted, the format is deduced from the file extension.

```
>>> outfile = "a:\\out.jpg"
>>> im.save(outfile, "JPEG")
```

Many other methods can be applied on the image. For cutting, pasting, and merging images, you can use im.crop(), im.paste(), and im.transpose(). For resizing and rotating an image, im.resize() and im.rotate() are available.

For a complete tutorial about using PIL, check out the *Python Imaging Library Handbook* at the following site:

```
http://www.pythonware.com/library/pil/handbook/index.htm
```

Other Modules

Besides PIL, some other modules can help you manipulate graphic and image files.

imghdr Module

This module recognizes image files based on their headers' first few bytes. The imghdr module is part of the standard distribution. This module implements the what() function, which returns the file type.

```
>>> import imghdr
>>> imgfile = imghdr.what("d:\\logo.gif")
>>> print imgfile
gif
```

The file types currently supported are: SGI image library, GIF ('87 and '89 variants), PBM (portable bitmap), PGM (portable graymap), PPM (portable pixmap), TIFF (can be in Motorola or Intel byte order), Sun raster file, X bitmap (X10 or X11), JPEG data in JFIF format, BMP, and PNG.

GD Module

The GD module is an interface to the GD GIF library that allows your code to quickly draw images complete with lines, arcs, text, multiple colors, cut and paste from other images, and flood fills, and to write out the result as a .GIF file. This module is currently no longer maintained. Newer gd libraries generate png images rather than gifs. Also, GD is not Free Software as it has commercial use restrictions. For more information, check out the following site:

```
http://starship.beopen.com/crew/richard/gdmodule/
```

WBMP **Module**

WBMP is a wireless bitmap format, the graphic format used by WAP mobile phones. A WBMP module for PIL is available for download at http://www.rcp.co.uk/distributed/Downloads

The filename is wbmpconvsrc.zip. The download includes a script for converting between WBMP and any other PIL supported bitmap format.

PyOpenGL **Module**

OpenGL, created by Silicon Graphics, is a portable library for rendering. It is a complex API with superior performance that became an industry standard for 2D and 3D graphics.

The Open GL home page is located at http://www.opengl.org.

PyOpenGL is a wrapper class for the OpenGL library that is maintained by David Ascher. It can be found at http://starship.python.net/crew/da/PyOpenGL.

Working with Sounds

Python has many modules that can provide audio support for your programs by allowing you to listen to your favorite audio CDs and read/write audio files (such as .wav, .aifc, and so on). Next, I present some of the most important modules. However, keep in mind that other modules exist that are not mentioned here.

winsound **Module**

The winsound module implements an interface that grants access to the sound-playing environment provided by Windows Platforms. This module is able to play wave sound files (.wav).

This module implements the function PlaySound, which has the following syntax: PlaySound(sound, flags).

```
>>> import winsound
>>> winsound.PlaySound(r'C:\WINNT\Media\tada.wav', winsound.SND_FILENAME)
```

The following flag constants, which are also defined by this module, can be used as bitwise arguments to the PlaySound function:

SND_FILENAME—The sound is a wave filename.

SND_ALIAS—The sound is a control panel sound association name.

SND_LOOP—This plays the sound repeatedly; must also specify SND_ASYNC.

SND_MEMORY—The sound is a memory image of a wave file.

SND_PURGE—This stops all instances of the specified sound.

SND_ASYNC—The PlaySound returns immediately.

SND_NODEFAULT—This does not play a default beep if the sound cannot be found.

SND_NOSTOP—This does not interrupt any sounds currently playing.

SND_NOWAIT—This returns immediately if the sound driver is busy.

> **Tip**
>
> Before going further in this topic, let me present a small introduction about audio concepts that is applicable for the understanding of the next couple of modules.
>
> Audio files have a number of parameters that describe the audio data. The sampling rate or frame rate is the number of times per second the sound is sampled. The number of channels indicate whether the audio is mono, stereo, or quadro. Each frame consists of one sample per channel. The sample size is the size in bytes of each sample. Thus a frame consists of nchannels*samplesize bytes, and a second's worth of audio consists of nchannels*samplesize*framerate bytes.
>
> For example, CD quality audio has a sample size of two bytes (16 bits), uses two channels (stereo), and has a frame rate of 44,100 frames/second. This gives a frame size of 4 bytes (2*2), and a second's worth occupies 2*2*44100 bytes, that is, 176,400 bytes.

sndhdr **Module**

The sndhdr module is a collection of routines that help recognize sound files.

```
>>> import sndhdr
>>> audioinfo = sndhdr.what("c:\windows\media\start.wav")
('wav', 22050, 2, -1, 4)
```

The function sndhdr.whathdr() recognizes various types of sound file headers as it understands almost all headers that SOX can decode. The function sndhdr.what() calls sndhdr.whathdr(), and the return tuple contains the following items, in this order:

- file type (as SOX understands it)

- sampling rate (0 if unknown or hard to decode)

- number of channels (0 if unknown or hard to decode)

- number of frames in the file (-1 if unknown or hard to decode)
- number of bits/sample; 'U' for U-LAW, or 'A' for A-LAW

If the file doesn't have a recognizable type, it returns None; and if the file can't be opened, IOError is raised.

To compute the total time, divide the number of frames by the sampling rate (a frame contains a sample for each channel).

wave **Module**

This module enables you to read, parse, and create wave (.wav) files where file is either the name of a file or an open file pointer. The open file pointer must have methods read(), seek(), and close(). When the setpos() and rewind() methods are not used, the seek() method is not necessary. This function returns an instance of a class with the following public methods:

Table 9.1   *Public Methods Exposed by the* wave *Module for an Instance of a Class That Can Read from a File*

Public Method	Description
getnchannels()	Returns the number of audio channels (1 for mono, 2 for stereo).
getsampwidth()	Returns sample width in bytes.
getframerate()	Returns sampling frequency.
getnframes()	Returns number of audio frames.
getcomptype()	Returns compression type ('NONE' for linear samples).
getcompname()	Returns human-readable version of compression type ('not compressed' linear samples)
getparams()	Returns a tuple consisting of all the previous in the order shown.
getmarkers()	Returns None (for compatibility with the aifc module).
getmark(id)	Raises an error because the mark does not exist (for compatibility with the aifc module).
readframes(n)	Returns at most n frames of audio.
rewind()	Rewinds to the beginning of the audio stream.
setpos(pos)	Seeks to the specified position.
tell()	Returns the current position.
close()	Closes the instance (makes it unusable).

The position returned by `tell()` and the position given to `setpos()` are compatible and have nothing to do with the actual position in the file. The `close()` method is called automatically when the class instance is destroyed.

The syntax for writing wave files is `f = wave.open(file, 'w')` where `file` is either the name of a file or an open file pointer. The open file pointer must have methods `write()`, `tell()`, `seek()`, and `close()`. This function returns an instance of a class with the following public methods:

Table 9.2   *Public Methods Exposed by the* `wave` *Module for an Instance of a Class That Can Write to a File*

Public Method	Description
setnchannels(n)	Sets the number of channels.
setsampwidth(n)	Sets the sample width.
setframerate(n)	Sets the frame rate.
setnframes(n)	Sets the number of frames.
setcomptype(type, name)	Sets the compression type and the human-readable compression type.
setparams(tuple)	Sets all parameters at once.
tell()	Returns current position in output file.
writeframesraw(data)	Writes audio frames without patching up the file header.
writeframes(data)	Writes audio frames and patches up the file header.
close()	Patches up the file header and closes the output file.

You should set the parameters before the first `writeframesraw` or `writeframes`. The total number of frames does not need to be set, but when it is set to the correct value, the header does not have to be patched up. It is best to first set all parameters, perhaps possibly the compression type, and then write audio frames using `writeframesraw`. When all frames have been written, either call `writeframes('')` or `close()` to patch up the sizes in the header. The `close()` method is called automatically when the class instance is destroyed.

```
>>> import wave
>>> audio = wave.open('c:\\windows\\media\\tada.wav', 'r')
>>> audio.getnchannels()
2
>>> audio.getsampwidth()
2
>>> audio.getframerate()
```

```
22050
>>> audio.getnframes()
42752
```

aifc Module

The aifc module, which stands for *Audio Interchange File Format*, is devoted to audio file access (reading/writing) in the AIFF and AIFC formats. This module has some functionality that only works on IRIX systems, but it partially works fine on Windows systems, as well.

```
>>> dev = aifc.open("test.aifc", "w")
>>> dev.setframerate(22050)
>>> dev.setsampwidth(2)
>>> dev.setnchannels(2)
>>> dev.writeframes('123456787654321'*20000)
>>> dev.close()
```

Note that, the method aifc.writeframes() is equivalent to the audiodev.Audiodev.writeframesraw. Both methods write data to the output file, and they can only be called after the audio file parameters have been set.

You can hear the file that is generated by using the QuickTime Player on Macintosh systems, or the MediaPlayer on Windows systems.

audiodev Module

The audiodev module provides a generic interface for audio output, which is used by Macintoshes, the SGI UNIX(IRIX) and SunOS/Solaris platforms. Note that there is a module called linuxaudiodev specific for Linux systems.

```
>>> import audiodev, aifc
>>> afile = aifc.open("test.aifc", "r")
>>> dev = audiodev.AudioDev()
>>> dev.setoutrate(afile.getframerate())
>>> dev.setsampwidth(afile.getsampwidth())
>>> dev.setnchannels(afile.getnchannels())
>>> data = afile.getsampwidth()*afile.getnchannels()*afile.getframerate()
>>> while 1:
...     frames = afile.readframes(data)
...     if not data:
...         break
...     dev.writeframes(frames)
...
>>>
```

The `setoutrate()` method defines the frequency rate of the sound wave; in this case, it is set to 22.05Khz.

The `setsampwidth()` method defines the sample width in number of bytes.

The `setnchannels()` method establishes the number of channels that we want to use. The previous example defines that we want to hear the sound in stereo.

The previous modules are all part of the standard distribution. Now, I will talk about some third-party modules.

The *PythonWare Sound Toolkit (PST)* reads sound files in different formats, and plays them on a variety of hardware platforms. Similar to Python itself, the PythonWare Sound Toolkit is copyrighted but can be used without a fee. This also applies to commercial applications. The current release reads AU, VOC, and WAV files, and plays them on Windows and Sun boxes.

For more information and download, visit the Web page:

`http://www.pythonware.com/products/pst/index.htm`

The following link is an interesting resource that provides a Python package that plays audio CDs on your Linux system:

`ftp://starship.python.net/pub/crew/amk/unmaintained/linux-cd.tgz`

If you are really interested in playing around with audio CDs, you'd better check the CDDB module. `CDDB.py` provides an easy way for Python programs to fetch track and disc information on audio CDs. This information is acquired from CDDB, a very large online database of track listings and other information on audio CDs. Included is a C extension module to enable Python to read track listings from audio CDs under Linux, FreeBSD, Solaris, and Win32. The interface to this extension module is portable and is intended to be ported to other operational systems easily.

You can check it out at `http://csl.cse.ucsc.edu/~ben/python/`.

Restricted Execution Mode

Restricted Execution is the basic framework in Python that allows the segregation of trusted and untrusted code. These modules prevent access to critical operations mostly because a program running in trusted mode can create an execution environment in which untrusted code can be executed with limited privileges.

Two modules implement Python support to restricted execution: `rexec` and `Bastion`.

The rexec module implements a basic restricted execution framework by encapsulating, in a class (which is called RExec), the attributes that specify the capabilities for the code to execute. Code executed in this restricted environment will only have access to modules and functions that are believed to be safe.

The idea is to use a program that runs in trusted mode to create an execution environment in which you can define limits to be applied on the execution of the untrusted code.

The rexec.RExec() creates an instance of the RExec class. By doing so, you implement a restricted environment. You can also subclass the RExec class, and change any one of the *class variables* that define the environment by modifying the __init__() method of the class.

RExec.ok_builtin_modules—Tuple of module names that can be imported.

RExec.nok_builtin_names—Tuple of built-in functions not available to the class.

RExec.ok_path—List of directories to be searched when importing modules.

RExec.ok_sys_names—Tuple of available function names from the sys module.

RExec.ok_posix_names—Tuple of available function names from the os module.

The following methods are called while inside a restricted environment:

r_import(modulename [,globals [,locals]])—Loads a module and is similar to the built-in import function.

r_open(filename [, mode [, buffersize]])—Opens a file and is similar to the built-in open function.

r_unload(modulename)—Unloads a given module.

r_reload(modulename)—Reloads a module and is similar to the built-in reload function.

The methods s_import(), s_unload(), and s_reload() have functionality similar to the previous methods, except that they also allow the use of sys.stdin, sys.stdout, and sys.stderr.

When you create an instance of the RExec class, the instance has the following methods available:

r_exec(code)—Same as the exec statement.

r_eval(code)—Same as the eval statement.

r_execfile(filename)—Same as the execfile statement.

The methods s_eval(), s_exec(), and s_execfile() have functionality similar to the previous methods, except that they also allow the use of sys.stdin, sys.stdout, and sys.stderr.

Protecting the Application Environment

The next example shows how you can use the rexec module to protect your processing environment. We subclass the rexec.RExec class, and we redefine the r_import method in order to block the access to the import implementation.

```
import rexec
class ExecEnv(rexec.RExec):
    def r_import(*args):
        raise SystemError, "The import function is not enabled."
myEnv = ExecEnv()
myEnv.s_exec("import sys")
```

Bastion is the other module used to provide restricted access to objects. This module is able to deny access to certain attributes of an object.

The basic syntax is Bastion.Bastion(object, filter).

```
import Bastion
>>> class parrot:
...     def __init__(self):
...         self.color = "blue"
...     def setcolor(self, color):
...         self.color = color
...     def getcolor(self):
...         return self.color
...
>>> myparrot = parrot()
>>> my = Bastion.Bastion(myparrot, lambda x:x in ['setcolor','getcolor'])
>>> my.getcolor()
'blue'
>>> my.setcolor("green")
>>> my.getcolor()
'green'
>>> my.color
Traceback (innermost last):
  File "<stdin>", line 1, in ?
  File "C:\Program Files\Python\Lib\Bastion.py", line 78, in __getattr__
    attribute = self._get_(name)
  File "C:\Program Files\Python\Lib\Bastion.py", line 121, in get2
    return get1(name)
```

```
 File "C:\Program Files\Python\Lib\Bastion.py", line 117, in get1
    raise AttributeError, name
AttributeError: color
>>>
```

As you could see, we prohibited the user to access the `color` attribute directly. It is necessary to use either the `getcolor()` method or the `setcolor()` method in order to manipulate it. The first argument of the `Bastion` function is the original object that carries all the attributes, and the second argument is a function that must return `true` for the attributes that can be accessed by the new object.

Scientific Computing

Python is extensively used for scientific computing because it enables a rapid prototyping and execution of a number of functions. Scientists and engineers often have needs for high-performance computation tools that are also easy to use and modify. Many also want to be able to use a general-purpose language instead of a specialized tool, allowing them to integrate networking, GUI's, and so on in their high-performance work. Several modules have been developed to address these needs around the Python language.

In this section, I cover the Numeric Python extensions (`NumPy`), which provide efficient operations on large multidimensional arrays, and it has proven to be the right choice when talking about scientific computing with Python.

Besides `NumPy`, many other scientific tools are available. The Python community has created several extensions for manipulating data and functions, interfaces to data plotting libraries, storage solutions for scientific data, and much more. If you want to deeply discuss scientific computing with Python, you can look for the plot-sig (the Plotting Special Interest Group).

If you spend some time browsing around scientific Web pages, you will be surprised about the number of people who are really using Python for their projects.

For more information, visit the following Web sites:

Scientific computing topic at Python's Web site:

`http://www.python.org/topics/scicomp/`

Simple Numerical Recipes in Python was written by William Park to describe few elementary numerical routines in Python:

`http://www.python.org/topics/scicomp/recipes_in_python.html`

Python for Science—An Introduction to Python for Scientists:

```
http://starship.python.net/crew/hinsen/
```

Numerical Extensions

The most powerful way to face scientific computing in Python systems is to use Python Numerical Extensions (commonly known as *NumPy*). The Numerical Python extensions were originally written by Jim Hugunin (JPython's author), but the responsibility to continue the project now belongs to a group of python users from the Lawrence Livermore National Laboratory. The languages that were used to guide the development of NumPy include Basis, MATLAB, FORTRAN, S and S+, and others.

The NumPy package adds a fast, compact multidimensional array language facility to Python. *One-dimensional arrays* are similar to standard Python sequences and *two-dimensional arrays* are similar to matrices from linear algebra. This package also includes tools for working with linear algebra, *Fast Fourier Transforms (FFTs)*, random numbers, and so forth.

In addition, NumPy adds two new types to Python: A sequence type (to implement multidimensional arrays), and a new type of function called a universal function (ufunc). Numeric Python consists of a set of modules:

Numeric.py (and Its Helper Modules multiarray, umath, and fast_umath)

This module defines two new object types and a set of functions that manipulate these objects, as well as converting them and other Python types. The objects are the new array object (technically called multiarray objects), and universal functions (technically ufunc objects). The array objects are generally homogeneous collections of potentially large numbers of numbers. Universal functions (ufuncs) are functions that operate on arrays and other sequences.

The Numeric module provides, in addition to the functions needed to create the previous objects, a set of powerful functions to manipulate arrays, select subsets of arrays based on the contents of other arrays, and other array-processing operations. Note that only Numeric need be imported.

RandomArray.py (and Its Helper Module ranlib)

This module provides a high-level interface to a random-number generator (ranlib), which supplies a uniform distribution generator of pseudo-random numbers, as well as some convenience functions:

For more information, check out *Additions to RandomArray Module*, by Lee A.
Barford:

```
http://numpy.sourceforge.net/RandomArray-additions.html
```

FFT.py **(and Its Helper Module** fftpack**)**

This module provides a high-level interface to the fast Fourier transform routines
implemented in the FFT-PACK library if it is available, or to the compatible but less
optimized fftpack library that ships with Numeric Python.

The FFT module provides a high-level interface to the fast Fourier transform
routines, which are implemented in the FFTPACK library. It performs one- and two-
dimensional FFT's, forward and backwards (inverse FFTs), and includes efficient
routines for FFTs of real-valued arrays. It is most efficient for arrays whose size is a
power of two.

LinearAlgebra.py **(and Its Helper Module** lapack_litemodule**)**

This module provides a high-level interface to the linear algebra routines implemented
in the LAPACK library if it is available, or to the compatible but less optimized
lapack_lite library that ships with Numeric Python. It includes functions to solve
systems of linear equations and linear least squares problems, invert matrices, compute
eigenvalues and eigenvectors, generalized inverses, determinants, as well as perform
singular value decomposition.

People such as scientists and engineers—who need to manipulate large arrays of
numbers quickly, efficiently, and stylishly—find in these extensions a great tool, whose
power is compared against other numeric languages such as MATLAB and IDL.

A good point is that everything you can do using Numerical Python is also possible to
be written using core Python data structures, such as lists and tuples. The problem is
that the program will run much too slow. However, if you have a couple of huge
Numerical Python arrays, the speed of adding them up is close to the speed of doing it
in C. Therefore, processing sophisticated numeric operations using NumPy provides
similar results as running the same process using a compiled language, but without the
compile time overhead or having to worry about bugs in the low-level array
operations.

The following links are great sources of information about the Numeric Python
extensions:

Numerical Python

```
http://numpy.sourceforge.net
```

Numerical Python—Documentation

You should consider taking a look at the official documentation for NumPy. The tutorial walks you through a set of numeric manipulations.

```
http://numpy.sourceforge.net/numpy.pdf
```

Numerical Python Project

The Numerical Python Project Page has releases, links to the FTP site, a bug tracking system, and a browser for the source repository plus instructions on how to use CVS anonymously.

```
http://numpy.sourceforge.net
```

and

```
http://sourceforge.net/project/?group_id=1369
```

Numerical Python arrays in C extension modules

```
http://starship.python.net/crew/hinsen/NumPyExtensions.html
```

Writing C Extensions using Numerical Python

```
http://oliphant.netpedia.net/packages/Numerical_Extensions.pdf.gz
```

Installing NumPy

Note that before building Numerical Python, you need to obtain and install the `Distutils` package.

> **Tip**
> The `Distutils` package will be distributed with Python beginning with the 1.6 release. Its purpose is to define a standard for installing Python modules. For details, check out `http://www.python.org/sigs/distutils-sig/`

Currently, NumPy has two distribution options available.

On Win32 platforms, such as Microsoft Windows 95, 98, and NT, a binary installer is available at

```
ftp://ftp-icf.llnl.gov/pub/python/NumPy.exe
```

This installer is simple to use (simply double-click on the `NumPy.exe` file and answer questions on each screen in turn). Running this installer will perform all the needed modifications to your Python installation so that NumPy works.

For both UNIX and other platforms, NumPy must be compiled from the source. The source distribution for NumPy is part of the `LLNLPython` distribution, which is available at

`ftp://ftp-icf.llnl.gov/pub/python/Numeric-xx.y.tgz`

There is also RPMs for Linux available from the `numpy` Web site at
`http://sourceforge.net/project/filelist.php?group_id=1369`.

The file is a gzipped tarfile that should be uncompressed using the `gunzip` program and un-tarred with the `tar` program:

```
csh> gunzip Numeric-xx.y.tgz
csh> tar xf Numeric-xx.y.tar
```

Follow the instructions found in the top-level directory for compilation and installation procedures.

The standard Python installer for the Macintosh (available at `http://www.python.org/download/download_mac.html`) optionally installs the NumPy extensions, although these are typically not the most up-to-date files.

Other Scientific Extensions

Next, you have access to some extra Python extension modules that deal with scientific computation.

ScientificPython

`ScientificPython` is a collection of Python modules that are useful for scientific computing. In this collection, you will find modules that cover basic geometry (vectors, tensors, transformations, vector, and tensor fields), quaternions, automatic derivatives, (linear) interpolation, polynomials, elementary statistics, nonlinear least-squares fits, unit calculations, Fortran-compatible text formatting, 3D visualization via VRML, and two Tk widgets for simple line plots and 3D wireframe models. For more information, check out the following site:

`http://starship.python.net/crew/hinsen/scientific.html`

Pyfort **(The Python/Fortran Connection Tool)**

`Pyfort` allows you to wrap your own Fortran routines in Python. For more information, check out

`http://pyfortran.sourceforge.net`

RNG

RNG is a random number package from LLNL. For more information, check out

```
ftp://numpy.sourceforge.net/pub/numpy/RNG-2.0.tgz
```

pyclimate

This package contains some tools used for climate variability analysis. It makes extensive use of Numerical Python. For more information, check out

```
http://lcdx00.wm.lc.ehu.es/~jsaenz/pyclimate/index.html
```

GmatH

GmatH is a Gnome interface to the Numerical Python extensions. For more information, check out

```
http://gmath.sourceforge.net/index.html
```

Real

real.py is a library that introduces a new class, called Real, of arbitrarily precise numbers, allowing computations with "infinite" precision. This package handles a floating point number with a large number of decimal places (more than double by far). For more information, check out

```
ftp://ftp.python.org/pub/python/contrib-09-Dec-1999/DataStructures/
real-accurate.pyar
```

Computer Programming for Everybody

Some great efforts are being made in bringing Python to classrooms in order to prepare young people for our new computer reality.

Bringing a computer language to the class is not a new idea. Many schools already teach some kind of programming language. However, Python is a very high-level language, a human-readable language, not just computer-readable, it has a more up-to-date design, and what you learn from Python can be adapted to other languages.

Everyone needs to know a little about computers these days, no matter what profession is chosen. It is said that some day in the near future, everyone will have to know how to code a computer program. Python is a great language that possesses all the features required for teaching computer logic to tomorrow's scientists.

For more information, see the following:

Computer Programming for Everybody, by Guido van Rossum

```
http://www.python.org/doc/essays/cp4e.html
```

EDU-SIG: Python in Education

`http://www.python.org/sigs/edu-sig/`

Check out the following four-part essay entitled *Numeracy + Computer Literacy* series by Kirby Urner, who uses Python to teach various math concepts in the *Oregon Curriculum Network*. This material will give you a clear idea of how Python can be approached for education.

`http://www.inetarena.com/~pdx4d/ocn/cp4e.html`

Regular Expressions

We already know that the `string` module is used to apply basic manipulation operations on strings; meanwhile, at the time of developing advanced routines, you might need to enhance Python's string-processing capabilities. That's when you should consider using the `re` module (`re` stands for *regular expression*).

Regular expressions are strings, which contain a mix of text and special characters, that let you define complicated pattern matching and replacement rules for other strings.

Some of the special characters that compound regular expressions must be preceded by backslashes in order to be matched. Consequently, regular expressions are usually written as raw strings because they tend to use a lot of backslashes. That means that instead of writing `"\\b(usa)\\d"`, it is much easier to say `r"\b(usa)\d"`.

Older versions of Python used to support the following regular expression obsolete modules are: `regexp`, `regex`, and `regsub`.

Table 9.3 *Special Characters Recognized by the* `re` *Module*

Special Character	What It Matches
.	Any character (except newline by default).
^	The start of the string, or of a line (in case of multiline re's).
$	The end of the string, or of a line (in case of multiline re's).
*	Any number of occurrences of the preceding expression.
+	1 or n number of occurrences of the preceding expression.

Table 9.3 *(continued)*

Special Character	What It Matches
|	Either the preceding re or the following re, whichever is true.
?	1 or 0 number of occurrences of the preceding expression.
*?	Similar to *, but it matches as few occurrences as possible.
+?	Similar to +, but it matches as few occurrences as possible.
??	Similar to ?, but it matches as few occurrences as possible.
{m, n}	From m to n occurrences of the preceding expression. It matches as many occurrences as possible.
{m, n}?	From m to n occurrences of the preceding expression. It matches as few occurrences as possible.
[list]	A set of characters, such as r"[A-Z]".
[^list]	Characters that are not in the list.
(re)	Matches the regular expression as a group. It specifies logical groups of operations and saves the matched substring.
Anystring	The string anystring.
\w	Any alphanumeric character.
\W	Any non-alphanumeric character.
\d	Any decimal digit.
\D	Any non-decimal digit.
\b	Empty strings at the starting or ending of words.
\B	Empty strings that are not at the starting or ending of words.
\s	Matches a whitespace character.
\S	Matches any non-whitespace character.
\number	Text already matched by the group *number*.
\A	Only at the start of the string.
\Z	Only at the end of the string.
\\	The literal backslash.
(?:str)	Matches str, but the group can't be retrieved when matched.
(?!str)	If not followed by str (for example, only matches r"Andre (?!Lessa)" if it doesn't find "Andre Lessa").
(?=str)	If followed by str.

Table 9.3   *(continued)*

Special Character	What It Matches
`(?=.*str)`	If followed at some point by `str` (for example, only matches r"Andre `(?=.*Lessa)`" if it finds something similar to "Andre S Lessa"). This syntax doesn't consume any of the string, so in this example, the `re` only matches the "Andre " portion of the string.
`(?#str)`	This is just to insert a comment in the middle of the regular expression string.
`(?P<name>...)`	Matches the regular expression that follows the name and creates a group name.
`(?P=name)`	Matches the same things that the group name has matched.
`.*`	Any number of characters.

In case you need to know a full definition of the syntax, visit the following link:

`http://www.python.org/doc/current/lib/re-syntax.html`

Next, you have the regular expression flags. These flags are used as `bitwise-or` operators in the `re` functions.

re.`DOTALL` (also used as re.`S`)—Allows the dot character to match all characters, including newlines.

re.`IGNORE` (also used as re.`I`)—Allows non case sensitive matching.

re.`LOCALE` (also used as re.`L`)—Enables locale settings for \w, \W, \b, and \B.

re.`MULTILINE` (also used as re.`M`)—Applies ^ and $ for each line, and not for each string.

re.`VERBOSE` (also used as re.`X`)—Ignores unescaped whitespace and comments.

Let's look at our first example of regular expressions. Suppose that you have the following conversation text:

```
oldtext = """
    That terrible dead PARROT sketch must end!
    Oh, Come on! It is a terrific parrot joke.
    I agree, but I don't like to see dead parrot.
    Ok. I will suggest a new terrific parrot sketch."""
```

Okay. Now our challenge is to create an expression that is able to identify all the words "parrot" that

1. Are preceded by either `"terrible"` or `"terrific"` (such as `"terrible parrot"`, `"terrific parrot"`).

2. Are not immediately preceded by the word `"dead"`.

3. Are separated from the previous word by a whitespace (`"terribleparrot"` does not work).

4. Are not followed by the word `"joke"`, hence, `"parrot joke"` is an invalid string.

5. Are followed by a whitespace, and right after, by the word `"sketch"` (neither `"parrotsketch"` nor `"parrot old sketch"` are valid).

6. The matching must not be case sensitive.

The word `"parrot"` that gets identified must be replaced with the word `"spam"`.

The following code is a possible solution for this problem:

```
 1: import re
 2: restring = re.compile(
 3:      r"""\b(terrible|terrific)
 4:         (?!dead)
 5:         (\s+
 6:          parrot
 7:         (?!joke)
 8:         \s+sketch)""",
 9:      re.DOTALL | re.IGNORECASE | re.VERBOSE)
10: newline = restring.sub(r'\1 spam', oldtext)
```

We are calling the `compile` function (line 2), which generates a compiled regular expression object called `restring`. Then, we call the class method `sub` (line 10) to substitute the matches found in the text variable that we have already defined (`oldtext`). The `sub()` method replaces the entire matched section of the string. Note that the `r'\1 spam'` argument uses `\1` to make sure that the result collected in the first group of parenthesis (`"Terrible"` and `"Terrific"`) is placed right before the word `"spam"`.

Regular Expression Functions and Object Methods

The `re` module implements just one exception—the `error` exception, which is raised only when a regular expression string is not valid.

Next, you have the list of available `re` functions.

```
re.compile()
```
Compiles a regular expression pattern string and generates a regular expression object.

```
RegExpObject = compile(string [, flags])
```

For details about the `flags` argument, check out the previous list of available flags.

Every regular expression object exposes the following attributes and methods:

```
RegExpObject.search()
```
Searches for the compiled pattern in the string.

```
MatchObject = RegExpObject.search(string [,startpos] [,endpos])
```

It uses the `startpos` and `endpos` arguments to delimit the range of the search.

All functions that are supposed to return a `MatchObject` when the function succeeds, return `None` when a fail occurs.

```
RegExpObject.match()
```
Checks whether the initial characters of `string` match the compiled pattern.

```
MatchObject = RegExpObject.match(string [,startpos] [,endpos])
```

It uses the `startpos` and `endpos` arguments to delimit the scope of the matching.

```
RegExpObject.findall()
```
Finds nonoverlapping matches of the compiled pattern in `string`.

```
MatchList = RegExpObject.findall(string)
```

```
RegExpObject.split()
```
Splits the `string` by the occurrences of the compiled pattern.

```
StringList = RegExpObject.split(string [, maxsplit])
```

```
RegExpObject.sub()
```
Substitutes the matches of pattern in `string` with `newtext`.

```
RegExpObject.sub(newtext, string [, count])
```

The replacements are done `count` number of times, starting from the left side of string. When you leave out the `count` argument, you are not really saying don't perform the substitution at all, but apply it as many times as necessary.

`RegExpObject.subn()`
It is similar to sub. However, it returns a tuple that contains the new `string` and the number of substitutions executed. When you leave out the count argument, you are not really saying don't perform the substitution at all, but apply it as many times as necessary.

`RegExpObject.subn(`*`newtext,`* *`string`* `[,` *`count`*`])`

`re.search()`
Searches for the `pattern` in the `string`.

`MatchObject = search(`*`pattern,`* *`string`* `[,`*`flags`*`])`

`re.match()`
Sees whether the initial characters of `string` match the `pattern`.

`MatchObject = match(`*`pattern,`* *`string`* `[,`*`flags`*`])`

`re.findall()`
Finds nonoverlapping matches of `pattern` in `string`.

`MatchList = findall(`*`pattern,`* *`string`*`)`

`re.split()`
Splits the `string` by the occurrences of `pattern`.

`StringList = split(`*`pattern,`* *`string`* `[,` *`maxsplit`*`])`

`re.sub()`
Substitutes the matches of `pattern` in `string` with `newtext`.

`sub(`*`pattern,`* *`newtext,`* *`string`* `[,` *`count`*`])`

The replacements are done count number of times, starting from the left side of string.

`re.subn()`
It is similar to sub(). However, it returns a tuple that contains the new string and the number of substitutions executed.

`subn(`*`pattern,`* *`newtext,`* *`string`* `[,` `count = `*`0`*`])`

`re.escape()`
Backslashes all the nonalphanumeric characters of `string`.

```
newstring = escape(string)
```

Each `RegExpObject` also implements the following methods and attributes:

> `RegExpObject.flags`—Returns the flag arguments used at the compilation time of the regular expression object.

> `RegExpObject.groupindex`—Returns a dictionary that maps symbolic group names to group numbers.

> `RegExpObject.pattern`—Returns the object's original pattern string.

Each `MatchObject` implements the following methods and attributes:

> `MatchObject.group([groupid,...])`—Once you provide a list of group names or numbers, Python returns a tuple containing the text matched by each of the groups.

> `MatchObject.groupdict()`—Returns a dictionary that contains all the named subgroups of the match.

> `MatchObject.groups()`—Returns a tuple that contains all the text matched by all groups.

> `MatchObject.start([group])` and `MatchObject.end([group])`—Returns the first and last positions of the substring matched by the group.

> `MatchObject.span([group])`—Returns a tuple that contains both the `MatchObject.start` and the `MatchObject.end` values.

> `MatchObject.pos` and `MatchObject.endpos`—Returns the `pos` and `endpos` values, which were passed to the function when creating it.

> `MatchObject.string`—Returns the `string` value, which was passed to the function when creating it.

> `MatchObject.re`—Return the `RegExpObject` that was used to generate the `MatchObject` instance.

> **Special Note for Python 2.0 Users**
> All the internals of the `re` module were changed in Python 2.0. Now, the regular expression engine is located in a new module called SRE written by *Fredrik Lundh of Secret Labs AB*. The reason for that was to allow Unicode strings to be used in regular expressions along with 8-bit strings. Pay attention to the `re` module as it continues to be the front-end module, which internally calls the SRE module.

Threads

Let's start by quickly defining a thread. Many people still have some kind of confusion when it comes to clarifying the difference between threads and processes.

When you run any program in your computer, the CPU creates a process for that program. This process is defined as a group of elements that compound a single program. These elements are the memory area reserved for the program, a program counter, a list of files opened by the program, and a call stack where all the variables are stored. A program with a single call stack and program counter is a single threaded program.

Now, suppose you have different tasks inside your program that you need to execute several times simultaneously. What do you do? Maybe you are thinking about calling the whole program several times. Wrong answer! Think about all the resources that you are consuming without actually using them!

The solution to implement this multithreaded program is to create a function that implements the code which needs to be executed several times concurrently, and then, create a thread that uses only this function.

A *thread* is a program unit that processes multiple time-consuming actions as parallel tasks in the background of your main application process. Sometimes threads are difficult to debug because the circumstances in which they occur are hard to simulate.

Python Threads

Python threads can be implemented on every operational system that supports the POSIX threads library. But actually, the Python threading support doesn't always use POSIX threads. In the python-2.0 source tree, there are beos, cthread, lwp, nt, os2, pth, pthread, sgi, solaris, and wince thread implementations. In certain environments that support multithreading, Python allows the interpreter to run many threads at once.

Python has two threading interfaces: The `thread` module and the `threading` module. The use of these Python's native threading built-in modules enables the code to be portable across all platforms that support Python.

The `thread` module supports lightweight process threads. It offers a low-level interface for working with multiple threads.

On the other hand, the `threading` module provides high-level threading interfaces on top of the `thread` module.

Besides these two modules, Python also implements the `Queue` module. This is a synchronized *queue class* used in thread programming to move Python objects between multiple threads in a safe way.

Threads have limitations on some platforms. For instance, Linux thread switching is quite fast, sometimes faster than NT thread switching.

Programs—such as Tkinter, CORBA, and ILU—that rely on a main loop to dispatch events can complicate the design of threads. Definitively, they do not have a good relationship with threaded programs. Main loops are usually used by Graphical User Interfaces not to allow the main thread to exit.

MacPython is currently not built with thread support. That is because no posix-compatible thread implementation was available, making Python integration hard. However, this has changed with GUSI2 (a *posix* I/O emulation library), and the upcoming MacPython 1.6a1 is planned to have threads.

The Windows Operation System adds many additional features to Python's implementation of threads. The win32 package provides as additional features for Python's thread support:

- The `win32process` module—An interface to the win32 Process and Thread API's.

- The `win32event` module—A module that provides an interface to the win32 event/wait API.

The threading model provided by the COM technology allows objects not designed to work as threads to be used by other objects that are thread-aware.

Python's interpreter cannot handle more than one thread at the same time. The global interpreter lock is the internal mechanism which guarantees that the Python interpreter executes only one thread simultaneously. Although this is not a problem for single-threaded programs, or programs on single-processor machines, it can become trouble on performance-critical applications that run on multiprocessor computers. If your threads are doing IO work, other threads can execute during reads and writes.

Check out Appendix A, "Python/C API," for information about handling threads using the Python/C API. You can also see the latest documentation about it at

`http://www.python.org/doc/current/api/threads.html`

You might also want to look at the `thread` and `threading` modules in the library reference, which are documented at

`http://www.python.org/doc/current/lib/module-thread.html`

and

`http://www.python.org/doc/current/lib/module-threading.html`

Anton Ertl has a Web page that exposes very interesting material about the differences between the various threading techniques:

```
http://www.complang.tuwien.ac.at/forth/threaded-code.html
```

Python Thread Modules

Python includes two threading modules, assuming that your Python was configured for threads when it was built. One provides the primitives, and the other provides higher-level access. In general, Python relies on operating system threads unless you specifically compile it by activating the thread directive. This should offer adequate performance for all but the most demanding applications.

Thread Module

The following four functions are available in this module:

- `thread.allocate_lock()`—Creates and returns a lock object. This object has the following three methods:

  `lckobj.acquire([flag])`—It is used to acquire a lock. If the flag is omitted, the function returns `None` when it acquires the lock. If flag is set to `0`, the lock is only acquired when it can be immediately acquired. Anything different from `0` blocks the methods until the lock is released. This process cannot be interrupted. This function returns `1` if the lock is acquired, and `0` if not.

  `lckobj.release()`—Releases the lock.

  `lckobj.locked()`—Returns `1` if the object has a successful lock. Otherwise, it returns `0`.

- `thread.exit()`—Raises a `SystemExit` exception that ends the thread. It is equivalent to `sys.exit()` function.

- `thread.get_ident()`—Gets the identifier of the current thread.

- `thread.start_new_thread(func, args [,kwargs])`—Starts a new thread. Internally, it uses the `apply` function to call `func` using the provided arguments. This method requires the second argument (`args`) to be a tuple.

As there isn't any main loop in the next program, the `time.sleep` function (line 30) doesn't allow the child threads be killed because it doesn't allow the main thread exit. If this function weren't there, the other threads would be killed immediately when the main thread exited. You can test this by commenting the last line.

```
1: import thread, time
2: class VCR:
```

```
 3:     def __init__(self):
 4:         self._channel = {}
 5:         self._channel['1'] = self.channel_KDSF
 6:         self._channel['2'] = self.channel_FOKS
 7:         self._channel['3'] = self.channel_CBA
 8:         self._channel['4'] = self.channel_ESTN
 9:     def channel(self, selection, seconds):
10:         self._channel[selection] (seconds)
11:     def channel_KDSF(self, seconds_arg):
12:         thread.start_new_thread(self.record, (seconds_arg,'1. KDSF'))
13:     def channel_FOKS(self, seconds_arg):
14:         thread.start_new_thread(self.record, (seconds_arg,'2. FOKS'))
15:     def channel_CBA(self, seconds_arg):
16:         thread.start_new_thread(self.record, (seconds_arg,'3. CBA'))
17:     def channel_ESTN(self, seconds_arg):
18:         thread.start_new_thread(self.record, (seconds_arg,'4. ESTN'))
19:     def record(self, seconds, channel):
20:         for i in range(seconds):
21:             time.sleep(0.0001)
22:         print "%s is recorded" % (channel)
23:
24: myVCR = VCR()
25:
26: myVCR.channel('1', 700)
27: myVCR.channel('2', 700)
28: myVCR.channel('3', 500)
29: myVCR.channel('4', 300)
30: time.sleep(5.0)
```

The time.sleep() function in line 21 is necessary to allow other threads to run. If you don't use this function, there will be no timing gap between commands to be used by the other threads.

Threading Module
Besides exposing all the functions from the thread module, this module also provides the following additional functions:

Threading.activeCount()—This function returns the number of active thread objects.

Threading.currentThread()—This function returns the thread object in current control.

Threading.enumerate()—This function returns a list of all active thread objects.

Each `Threading.Thread` class object implements many methods, including

`threadobj.start()`—This method invokes the run method.

`threadobj.run()`—This method is called by the start method. You can redefine this one.

`threadobj.join([timeout])`—This one waits for the threads to complete. The optional timeout argument must be provided in seconds.

`threadobj.isAlive()`—Returns 1 if the run method of the thread object has concluded. If not, it returns 0.

In the next example, you want to subclass the `Thread` class, and define a new run method for the subclass. In order to activate the thread, you need to call the `start()` method, not the `run()` method. The `start` method creates the new thread that executes the `run` method.

```
import Threading
import time, random
class NewThread(Threading.Thread):
    def run(self):
        init = 0
        max = random.randint(1,10)
        while init < max:
            init = init + 1
            time.sleep(0.0001)
        print max

threads = []
for i in range(20):
    threadobj = NewThread()
    threadobj.start()
    threads.append(threadobj)

for thread in threads:
    thread.join()

print "---- THE END ----"
```

Just as a suggestion, try commenting the `for` loop near the end of the program. The reason for using it is to guarantee that all the threads are executed.

As final notes about this topic, I would like to highlight that

- The processing time of a thread in a multithreaded program is equal to the CPU time of the program, divided by the number of threads that have been created. Well, that is an estimate because some threads might take a lot more CPU time than others.

- Multithreaded programs have their data shared among all the threads, so it might cause *race conditions* (a state of inconsistent in a program). You have to be very careful when updating data used by multiple threads. Usually, the solution for this kind of problem is to lock the code before changing the data in order to keep all the threads synchronized.

For more information about threading, check out *Python and Indirect Threading*, by Vladimir Marangozov:

```
http://starship.python.net/crew/vlad/archive/threaded_code/
```

Microthreads

If you are really thinking about diving into multitasking applications, another option that you should consider is called *microthreads*. It implements threading by tweaking the execution order of Python's virtual machine, rather than by interrupting the processor. The microthread approach is much newer and much less deeply tested, but it might be more straightforward for your application.

Simulations and high-volume mission critical applications typically prefer large numbers of lightweight threads. There is a Stackless Python implementation that implements lightweight microthreads (see `http://www.stackless.com` for more information).

With microthreads, all your simulation threads run within a single operating system thread. They are useful when you want to program many behaviors happening simultaneously. Simulations and games often want to model the simultaneous and independent behavior of many people, many businesses, many monsters, many physical objects, many spaceships, and so forth. With microthreads, you can code these behaviors as Python functions. Additionally, the microthread library includes a rich set of objects for interthread communication, synchronization, and execution control.

> **Tip**
> Keep in mind that you need to have the Stackless Python in order to use the microthread library.

Microthreads switch faster and use much less memory than OS threads. The restrictions on microthreads (not shared by OS threads) are that they will only provide context-switching within Python code, not within C or Fortran extensions, and they won't help you take advantage of multiple processors. Also, microthreads will not take advantage of multiple CPUs in a box.

You can run thousands of microthreads at the same time. However, microthreads can hang on some blocking I/O operations; they are so new that there isn't yet a lot of practical experience with which operations (input or output) are troublesome.

For details, check out *Python Microthreads*, by Christian Tismer and Will Ware:

```
http://world.std.com/~wware/uthread.html
```

Summary

This chapter provides a general overview of some important advanced Python topics that you might need to use on a regular basis. They are image manipulation, sounds, restricted environment, Numeric Python, regular expressions, and threads.

Python has comprehensive support for handling image files. The foundation of this structure is based on the Python Imaging Library (commonly known as PIL). Its framework is cross-platform, which allows it to perform image manipulation and processing in different systems using the same code. Besides PIL, some other modules (such as `imghdr`, GD, WBMP, and PyOpenGL) can help you manipulate graphic and image files.

`winsound`, `wave`, `sndhdr`, `aifc`, and `Audiodev` are some of the Python modules that provide audio support for your programs by allowing you to listen to your favorite audio CDs and read/write audio files (such as `.wav`, `.aifc`, and so on). All these modules are part of the standard distribution. However, there are some great third-party Python audio modules too. The PythonWare Sound Toolkit (PST) reads sound files in different formats, and plays them on a variety of hardware platforms. It is really cool!

Restricted execution is the basic framework in Python that allows the segregation of trusted and untrusted code. Two modules implement Python support to restricted execution: `rexec` and `Bastion`. These modules prevent access to critical operations mostly because a program running in trusted mode can create an execution environment in which untrusted code can be executed with limited privileges. The idea is to use a program that runs in trusted mode to create an execution environment in which you can define limits to be applied on the execution of the untrusted code.

Python is also extensively used for scientific computing because it enables a rapid prototyping and execution of a number of functions. The Python Numerical Extensions (commonly known as `NumPy`) provides efficient operations on large multi-dimensional arrays because it adds a fast and compact multidimensional array language facility to Python. `NumPy` has also proven to be the correct powerful choice when talking about scientific computing with Python. Other scientific extensions, such as `ScientificPython`, `Pyfort`, `RNG`, `pyclimate`, `GmatH`, and `Real` are also part of the constant work of many Python developers who want to turn Python into a more complete scientific language.

While I'm talking about scientific and school projects, there is a very important project that recommends the idea of teaching Python to young people at schools. The project is titled "Computer Programming for Everybody," and it was created by Guido van Rossum.

Regular expressions are strings—containing a mix of text and special characters—that let you define complicated pattern matching and replacement rules for other strings. You can, for example, search for a specific pattern of data in a whole text file, and substitute it for other text.

Python has two threading interfaces: the `thread` module and the `threading` module. The use of these native threading built-in modules enables the code to be portable across all platforms that support Python. The `thread` module supports lightweight process threads. It offers a low-level interface for working with multiple threads. On the other hand, the `threading` module provides high-level threading interfaces on top of the `thread` module. Besides these two modules, Python also implements the `Queue` module, which is a synchronized *queue class* that is used in thread programming to move Python objects between multiple threads in a safe way. Besides these two implementations, Python developers can use `microthreads` too. This technology implements threading by tweaking the execution order of Python's virtual machine, rather than by interrupting the processor.

Code Examples

Next, you have some code examples that demonstrate the concepts illustrated by this chapter.

HTML Parsing Tool (File: `parsing.py`)

We are going to use the `exchange.html` as the source of information for this program. The idea is to read the file, replace all the occurrences of the domain name "lessaworld" for "bebemania", and add hyperlinks for all email and Web pages references that exist there.

Listing 9.1   *File:* exchange.html

```
<HTML>
<HEAD>
<TITLE>Exchange Rates Home Page</TITLE>
</HEAD>
<BODY>
<p align=justify>
<b>List of current files that we have available at this site:</b></p>
<br>
http://www.lessaworld.com/exchange/real.txt <br>
http://www.lessaworld.com/exchange/pound.txt <br>
http://www.lessaworld.com/exchange/dollar.txt <br><br>

Many people are currently working to keep these exchange rates updated.<br>
Andre (andre@bebemania.com.br) handles all the Brazilian Real operations,
 meanwhile,Joao Pedro (jp@bebemania.com.br) takes care of pounds and
 dollars.<br><br>

</BODY>
</HTML>
```

The following code implements the parsing program.

Listing 9.2   *File:* parsing.py

```
 1:
 2: import re, sys
 3:
 4: TextOriginal = open("exchange.html").read()
 5:
 6: TextIn = re.sub("lessaworld", "bebemania", TextOriginal)
 7:
 8: operation_result = re.search(r'<title>(.*?)</title>', TextIn
    ,re.IGNORECASE)
 9: if operation_result:
10:     HTML_TITLE = operation_result.group(1)
11:
12: link_pattern = re.compile(r'((ftp|http)://[\w-]+(?:\.[\w-]+)*(?:/[\w-]*)*
                             (?:\.[\w-]*)*)')
13: links = re.findall(link_pattern, TextIn)
```

Listing 9.2   *(continued)*

```
14: TextIn = re.sub(link_pattern, r"<a href=\1>\1</a>", TextIn)
15:
16: email_pattern = re.compile(r'([a-zA-Z][\w-]*@[\w-]+(?:\.[\w-]+)*)')
17: emails = re.findall(email_pattern, TextIn)
18: TextIn = re.sub(email_pattern, r"<a href=mailto:\1>\1</a>", TextIn)
19:
20: FileOut = open("newexchange.html", "w")
21: FileOut.write(TextIn)
22: FileOut.close()
23:
24: print '"%s" is done.' % (HTML_TITLE)
```

Line 4: Opens and reads the original file.

Line 6: Replaces occurrences of `"lessaworld"` with `"bebemania"`.

Lines 8–10: Locates the Web page title.

Line 10: The first group is the element between parenthesis in the regular expression of line 8.

Line 12: Creates a regular expression that locates all the Web addresses in the text.

Line 13: Creates a list of all the elements (links) that were found by the matching.

Line 14: Adds the hyperlinks for all the Web links that were found.

Line 16: Creates a regular expression that locates all the email addresses in the text.

Line 17: Creates a list of all the elements (emails) that were found by the matching.

Line 18: Adds the hyperlinks for all the email addresses that were found.

Lines 20–22: Creates a new file with the new content.

In order to execute the routine, you just need to call it from the OS prompt, and then check the resulting file in your browser.

```
S:\python> python parsing.py
"Exchange Rates Home Page" is done.
S:\python>
```

TV Network Audiences (File: `audience.py`)

The next example demonstrates the use of the `Queue` module. The idea is to have several threads running and sharing information at the same time. The program starts several threads that execute some time-consuming operations, while the main thread is generating numbers that are used by all the other threads.

Listing 9.3   *File:* audience.py

```
 1:
 2: import threading, time
 3: import Queue, random
 4:
 5: class VCR(threading.Thread):
 6:     channels = ["KDSF", "FOKS", "CBA", "ESTN"]
 7:
 8:     def __init__(self, queue, channel, seconds):
 9:         self.__queue = queue
10:         self.seconds = seconds
11:         self.network = VCR.channels[channel-1]
12:         threading.Thread.__init__(self)
13:     def run(self):
14:         for i in range(self.seconds):
15:             time.sleep(0.0001)
16:             self.public = self.__queue.get()
17:             print "After %d seconds, %d people were watching %s" % \
18:                 (self.seconds, self.public, self.network)
19:
20: queue = Queue.Queue(0)
21:
22: VCR(queue, 1, 60).start()
23: VCR(queue, 2, 40).start()
24: VCR(queue, 3, 35).start()
25: VCR(queue, 4, 75).start()
26:
27: audience = 0
28: while audience < random.randint(200,300):
29:     queue.put(audience)
30:     audience = audience + 1
31:     print "The audience now has %d people." % (audience)
32:     time.sleep(0.001)
33:
34: time.sleep(10)
```

Line 5: Defines a subclass of the Thread class.

Line 6: Creates a class variable.

Line 13: Implements the functionality that is executed when the thread is started.

Line 15: Pauses the execution, in order to let other threads run simultaneously.

Line 16: Gets the current value in the Queue.

Line 20: Initializes the Queue object that is shared by all threads.

Lines 22–25: Starts all the threads.

Lines 28–32: Implements a routine that keeps generating numbers to be passed to the thread.

Line 29: Sends a value to the queue in order to be collected by the threads.

Line 34: Pauses the main thread so that the other threads can end normally.

PART III
Network Programming

CHAPTER 10

Basic Network Background

Albatross! Albatross! Albatross!

This chapter exposes basic and advanced network concepts, and invites you to learn a little more about them by using Python routines.

Networking

Networking...This is the word behind all new technology that arrives in the market these days.

It doesn't matter if you are transferring a file via FTP or browsing your favorite Web site, the network infrastructure is right behind you. To support all these functionalities, Python has a number of complex protocol implementations available over the top of a low-level access to the Internet. This low-level access is totally based on the concept of *sockets*.

High-level implementations make light work of many types of network interaction that we want to implement most often (for example, browse the Web, send an email, and so on). Of particular note are the Web-based protocols and the support for manipulating the data that might be retrieved using them.

Now that the Internet seems to be not only part of our present, but also of our future, networking has definitively become part of our lives. Therefore, it is good for you to know a little about it.

Networking Concepts

Networking systems are well-defined by the *OSI/ISO* (*Open Systems Interconnection/ International Standards Organization*) seven-layer model, which suggests the following levels of the networking process: physical, data link, network, transport, session, presentation, and application. However, keep in mind that, in practice, protocols span multiple layers, and you shouldn't worry if your application doesn't fit in this model. Most of today's networking stacks (including TCP/IP) use less layers that are not quite as well separated as in the OSI model. Consequently, if you try to map a TCP/IP session onto the OSI model, you will get a bit confused because some layers are merged, and some others are removed.

Physical layer—Defines the information necessary to transport data over physical components, such as cables.

Data link layer—Defines how data is passed to and from the physical components. Point-to-point error correction is usually performed at this layer.

Network layer—Organizes the network by assigning distinct addresses for its elements, so the information in traffic can be routed to the right computers. The IP protocol works at this layer.

Transport layer—Packs the data and makes sure that the data transfer between the machines is error-free. TCP and UDP are protocols that implement these responsibilities.

Session layer—Handles each individual connection (session) made by the machines.

Presentation layer—Used to overcome differences such as different formats for integers on different platforms. TCP/IP makes this the application's responsibility, and Python has some modules to help with this (for instance, the `struct` module).

Application layer—Implements your final product, your application. FTP clients, SMTP/POP3 mail handlers, and HTTP browsers are examples of complete applications that run over your network.

Network connections can be of two types: connection-oriented or connectionless (packet-oriented).

Let's talk about the pair TCP/IP, which is a packet-oriented implementation. Nowadays, I can't imagine a unique machine that doesn't support it. TCP/IP is the most widely used networking protocol possibly because it is robust and untied to any particular physical medium, and maybe also because the specifications are freely available.

TCP/IP was originally created by the United States Department of Defense, and soon, this protocol combination became the network of choice for the U.S. government, the Internet, and the universities. This tuple runs on virtually every operating system platform, which makes it strong when internetworking between different LAN environments is required. Today, a great number of commercial and public networks are built on top of this implementation. Although the Internet grew out of the TCP/IP work done at universities and the U.S. Department of Defense, it didn't adopt TCP/IP until part of the way through.

The network layer of the TCP/IP stack is provided by the Internet Protocol (commonly known as IP). This protocol provides the basic mechanism for routing packets in the Internet because it sends packets of data back and forth without building an end-to-end connection.

IP doesn't understand the relationships between packets, and doesn't perform retransmission. (It is not a reliable communication protocol!) Therefore, it requires higher-level protocols such as TCP and UDP to provide a reliable class of service. It does ensure that the IP header is not corrupted though.

TCP stands for *Transmission Control Protocol*, and it is the main form of communication over the Internet because it provides a reliable, session-based service for the delivery of sequenced packets.

This connection-oriented protocol provides a reliable two-way connection service over a session. Each packet of information exchanged over a session is given a sequence number through which it gets tracked and individually acknowledged. Duplicate packages are detected and discarded by the session services. Sequence numbers are not globally unique or even necessarily unique to the session. Although in a small enough time window, they would be unique to the session.

The TCP/IP protocol doesn't provide an application interface layer—the application provides the application layer. However, sockets have emerged as TCP/IP's premier peer-to-peer API, providing a way of writing portable networking applications.

UDP, which stands for *User Datagram Protocol*, is another protocol that provides transport services. This protocol provides an unreliable but fast datagram service. They are unreliable in the sense that they are not acknowledged or tracked through a sequence number. After transmitting the diagram, you have to hope that it gets received. We don't know if the recipient is there, or even if he is expecting a diagram. Some statistics say that about 5% of the diagrams don't make it. That's depressing, isn't it?

> **Note**
> UDP is useful for streaming media, where a packet that is late is useless, so retransmission is not desirable.

UDP is a connectionless transport protocol that doesn't guarantee delivery or packet sequence. As an example, UDP is used by the `ping` command in order to check whether a host is reachable in the network.

No doubt the UDP protocol is faster than the TCP protocol. The reason is because the TCP protocol spends more time switching information between the machines in order to guarantee that the information gets transferred. That doesn't happen when using UDP, which makes it considerably faster than TCP. Another fact is that while transferring data packets, the TCP protocol waits until all the packets arrive, and organizes them in sequence for the client program. However, the UDP protocol doesn't do that. It allows the client program to decide how the packets should be interpreted because packets aren't received in any specific ordering format. The problem is that this kind of implementation is completely unreliable because there is no way to confirm whether the information has reached its destiny. If you need a stream-oriented protocol, TCP is about as fast as you will get it. If it was such a bad protocol, it would have been replaced by now.

Protocols

The most commonly used application protocols are built on top of TCP/IP infrastructures. Actually, they don't have to know any details about TCP nor about IP because a thin layer called `sockets` exists between TCP/IP and them.

Python has modules that handle and support the access to all the following protocols. These protocols use the services provided by the sockets in order to transport packets on the network and to make connections to other hosts.

- HTTP processes Web pages.

- FTP transfers files between different machines.

- Gopher browses Gopher servers.

- Telnet provides access to another machine.

- POP3 reads mail files on POP3 servers.

- IMAP reads mail files on IMAP servers.

- NNTP provides access to the Usenet news.

- SMTP sends mail to standard mail servers.

Addresses

A socket address, on the TCP/IP internet structure, consists of two parts: an Internet address (commonly known as an IP address) and a port number.

The IP address defines the addressing and routing of information around the network, uniquely identifying a network interface.

An IP address is a 32-bit number (a sequence of four bytes), usually represented by four decimal numbers ranging from 0 to 255, separated by dots. A IP address looks something similar to `128.85.15.53`.

Each IP number must be unique for each TCP/IP network interface card within an administered domain, which in most cases means that each machine connected to the Internet has a unique IP address. Actually, a networked machine can have more Internet addresses than network interfaces. This is quite common in virtual hosting situations.

A port is an entry point to an application/service that resides on a server. It is a number represented by a 16-bit integer. This number can range between 0 and 65535, but you can't freely use all of them inside your programs. Always choose a port number greater than 1024 because the range 0–1023 is reserved by the operation system for some network protocols. Specific ports are shown in Table 10.1.

Note
Ports `0-1023` are called privileged ports and on most systems only the super user can run applications that use them. If you do not specify a port for one of the end points of your connection, one from the `1024-65535` range will be chosen.

Table 10.1   *Many Server Programs Have Their Own Famous Ports*

Port	Protocol
20	FTP (data)
21	FTP (control)
23	Telnet
25	SMTP
80	HTTP
119	NNTP

A larger list of ports can be found in the /etc/services file on UNIX machines or c:\windows\services on Win95/Win98 machines.

Most of the time, you don't need to worry about knowing the IP addresses offhand. DNS services provide a translation between IP addresses and hostnames because it is much easier to remind a name than a sequence of numbers. You should know that extra mappings between IP addresses and hostnames can be added in the /etc/hosts or c:\windows\hosts file.

The conclusion is that if you need to connect your client program to an application running on a server, you just need to know the server's IP address or hostname, and the port number in which the application is listening.

Together TCP and IP provide the basic network services for the Internet.

Sockets

Sockets are objects that provide the current portable standard for network application providers on certain suites of network protocols (such as TCP/IP, ICMP/IP, UDP/IP, and so forth). They allow programs to accept and make connections, such as to send and receive data. It is important that each end of a network communication have a socket object in order to establish the communication channel.

Sockets were first introduced in 1981 as the UNIX BSD 4.2 generic interface that would provide UNIX-to-UNIX communications over networks. Since that occasion, sockets have become part of the BSD UNIX system kernel, and they have also been adopted on a lot of other UNIX-like Operating Systems, including Linux.

Support for sockets is also provided, in the form of libraries, on a multiplicity of non-BSD UNIX systems, including MS-DOS, Windows, OS/2, Mac OS, and most mainframe environments. The *Windows socket API*, known colloquially as *WinSock*, is a multivendor specification that has standardized the use of *TCP/IP* under Windows.

This library is based on the Berkeley sockets interface as well. Of course, WinSock is not as convenient as a real sockets interface because the socket descriptors can't be passed to the select function as file descriptors can.

The reason for all this multi-environment possibility is because sockets are implemented using a standard *C-level* interface, which makes it easier to implement in other operating systems.

Each socket has a type that defines the protocol which implements the environment where the socket is used. These types are specified at creation time. The three most popular socket types are: stream, datagram, and raw. stream and datagram sockets can interface directly to the TCP protocol, whereas the raw sockets interface to the IP protocol. Note, however, that sockets are not limited to TCP/IP. Stream over a *PF_INET* connection will give TCP, and datagram over *PF_INET* will give UDP.

The socket Module

The socket module is a very simple object-based interface that provides access to a low-level BSD socket-style network. Both client and server sockets can be implemented using this module.

This module provides an exception called error, which is raised every time a socket- or address-related error happens.

Now we will look at the methods that are implemented by this module.

socket(*family, type* [, *protocol*])—This method creates and returns a new socket object, which is an instance of the SocketType class.

The family value can be either AF_UNIX (for UNIX domain protocols) or AF_INET (for IPv4 protocols such as TCP and UDP). Note that Python currently doesn't support IPv6, IPX, and other protocols used also.

The socket *type* defines whether the socket is a stream socket (SOCK_STREAM, for the TCP protocol), a datagram socket (SOCK_DGRAM, for the UDP protocol), a raw socket (SOCK_RAW), or a *Sequenced connection-mode* (SOCK_SEQPACKET).

The third and optional argument (protocol) is only used along with raw sockets, which are used only with AF_INET families. This argument is a constant value that identifies the protocol to be used. The default value is 0 for all socket types, and the list of possible values is: IPPROTO_TCP, IPPROTO_UDP, IPPROTO_RAW, IPPROTO_IP, and IPPROTO_ICMP. Note that these constant values are returned by the getprotobyname() function.

gethostname()—Returns the hostname of the local machine.

gethostbyname(*hostname*)—Converts a hostname to an IP address.

gethostbyname_ex(*hostname*)—Returns a tuple (hostname, hostname_alias_list, host_ip_list).

gethostbyaddr(*ipaddress*)—Returns a tuple (hostname, hostname_alias_list, host_ip_list).

getprotobyname(*protocol*)—Returns a constant value that is equivalent to the protocol name.

getservbyname(*service, protocol*)—Returns the port number associate to the pair service+protocol. The protocol argument must be either 'tcp' or 'udp'.

Each socket object has the following methods:

accept()—Accepts a new connection and returns two values: a new socket object to be used while transferring data back and forth, and the address of the socket that this object is talking to.

bind(*hostname, port*)—Binds the socket to a port address.

close()—Closes the socket.

connect(*hostname, port*)—Connects to another socket, which can be an external socket or a local socket. The hostname for local sockets is localhost.

getpeername()—Returns the IP address and the port to which the socket is connected.

getsocketname()—Returns the IP address and the port of it's own socket.

listen(*max_connections*)—Starts listening to the port, waiting for other sockets to connect. Before it starts refusing connections, the OS queues the maximum number of connections that you inform.

makefile(*[mode [, buffersize]]*)—Creates a file object that you can use read() and write() on, which is useful for stream-oriented protocols. The arguments mode and buffersize have the same meaning as the built-in open() function.

The next two functions are normally used for receiving packets on a datagram oriented protocol such as UDP. recv(*buffersize*)—Returns the data string received from the socket. buffersize limits the maximum amount of data to be received.

recvfrom(*buffersize*)—Returns the data string received from the socket and the IP address that has originated from the socket. buffersize limits the maximum amount of data to be received.

The next two functions are usually used for sending packets on a datagram oriented protocol such as UDP.

send(*string*)—Sends the data string to the socket.

sendto(*string*, (*hostname*, *port*))—Sends the data string to the socket hosted by hostname at the provided port.

setblocking(*flag*)—Blocks all read and write operations until they can proceed if the flag is set to 1, the default value. If you change the value to 0, an error exception is raised when those operations cannot proceed.

shutdown(*flag*)—Shuts down the client sockets if the flag is set to 0. If the flag is set to 1, the server sockets are shut down. If the flag is set to 2, both types of sockets are shut down.

For those that already have Python 2.0 installed, you should know that as a result of some changes in the Python design, you are encouraged to use an extra pair of parenthesis when passing tuples as arguments to some functions of the socket module. Note that some funtions still accept the old interface, but you are encouraged to start using the new model right away, for example, socket.connect(('hostname', 80)). Among the functions that still accept the old interface, we have: socket.connect(), socket.connect_ex(), and socket.bind().

Starting with Python 2.0, it's available *OpenSSL* support for the socket module. That means that from now on you can encrypt the data you send over a socket using this implementation of the *Secure Socket Layer*. In order to have it properly installed you need to edit the Modules/Setup file to include *SSL* support before compiling Python. Doing so will add the socket.ssl() function to your socket module.

socket.ssl()

This function takes a socket object and returns an SSL socket.

basic syntax: socket.ssl(*socket*, *keyfile*, *certfile*)

Making Connections

Because we already know that sockets are mostly used for TCP and UDP connections, let's see how to implement those interfaces using Python. Initially, we will check the necessary steps to start a TCP connection.

The server application needs to

1. Create a socket.

2. Bind the socket to an available port.

3. Tell the system to start listening to that port.

4. Query the port for new connections.

After these steps are performed, the TCP client application just needs to

1. Create a socket.

2. Open a connection to the server.

When the server receives the client request to establish a connection, it processes the request and sends the response back to the client.

```
 1: # TCP server example
 2: import socket
 3: svrsocket = socket.socket(socket.AF_INET, socket.SOCK_STREAM)
 4: svrsocket.bind("", 8888)
 5: svrsocket.listen(5)
 6: while 1:
 7:     data_to_send = "This string could be anything"
 8:     clisocket, address = svrsocket.accept()
 9:     print "I got a connection from ", address
10:     clisocket.send(data_to_send)
11:     clisocket.close()
```

The first argument in line 3 is the family address protocol. Currently, Python supports only two values: AF_UNIX (for UNIX domain sockets) and AF_INET (for Internet sockets). If you are using a non-UNIX system, you must use the AF_INET protocol.

The second argument in line 3 defines the type of connection that must be open. The common choices are SOCK_STREAM for stream-based connections (TCP) and SOCK_DGRAM for datagram-based connection (UDP). Depending on your system, you might also have other options: SOCK_SEQPACKET, SOCK_RAW, SOCK_RDM, SOCK_PACKET (Obsolete).

After creating a server socket, you need to bind the socket to a port on the local machine (line 4). The socket will listen to this port and process all the requests that come to this port.

In this example, we are connecting to port 8888. Remember that you should not use port numbers up to 1024 because they are reserved for system services. The 20,000–30,000 range is also prohibited because it is reserved for the *Remote Procedure Call (RPC)* services. Of course you should use these port numbers if you are implementing one of those services.

Tip

On UNIX systems, you need to have root privileges to implement services on ports lower than 1024. NT systems implement the same concept where ports lower than 1024 can only be used by system (or root) processes or by programs executed by privileged users.

The listen() method (line 5) tells the server to start "listening" to the port, waiting for connections.

After a client connects to this server, the accept() method (line 8) is invoked, and a new socket is created. Note that two sockets are involved in the whole process: one to establish the connection, and the other one to manage all the transactions between the client and the server.

The following example implements the client version of our program:

```
1: # TCP client example
2: import socket
3: clisocket = socket.socket(socket.AD_INET, SOCK_STREAM)
4: clisocket.connect("lessaworld.com", 8888)
5: data = clisocket.recv(512)
6: clisocket.close()
7: print "The data received is ", data
```

The socket() method (line 3) creates a TCP socket that tries to connect to the server/port specified as arguments of the connect() method (line 4).

After the connection is set up, the recv() method (line 5) is used to read the data. In this example, we are limiting the maximum number of 512 bytes to be read.

The next task is to implement the same client/server architecture using the UPD protocol. The steps necessary to start a UDP connection are as follows:

1. Create a socket.

2. Bind the socket to an available port.

3. Query the port for new connections.

After these steps are performed, the UDP client application just needs to

1. Create a socket.

2. Send a request to the server.

When the server receives the client request to establish a connection, it sends the response back to the client. And that's it. As you know, there is no concept of connection here. The following code example demonstrates an example of how to handle an UDP server.

```
1: # UDP server example
2: import socket
3: svrsocket = socket.socket(socket.AF_INET, socket.SOCK_DGRAM)
4: svrsocket.bind("", 8000)
5: while 1:
6:     data, address = svrsocket.recvfrom(256)
7:     print address[0], "said : ", data
```

The recvfrom() method (line 6) is used to read datagrams that are sent to the port, which is informed in line 4. The recvfrom() method returns two arguments: the actual data and the address of the host that has sent the data.

The following code example demonstrates an example of how to handle an UDP client.

```
 1: # UDP client example
 2: import socket
 3: clisocket = socket.socket(socket.AF_INET, socket.SOCK_DGRAM)
 4: while 1:
 5:     data = raw_input("Type something: ")
 6:     if data:
 7:         clisocket.sendto(data, ("lessaworld.com", 8000))
 8:     else:
 9:         break
10: s.close()
```

To send data to the server implementation, you need to use the sendto() method (line 7). The first argument is the data you want to send, and the second one is a tuple containing both the hostname and the port number waiting for your connection.

The UDP implementation doesn't try to set up a connection before starting to send diagrams. When you transmit data using UDP, it's hard to know whether the other machine has received the datagram.

For more information about sockets, you should consider viewing Gordon McMillan's HOWTO on socket programming at

```
http://www.python.org/doc/howto/sockets/
```

Darrell Gallion's Web site also has some examples that might help you get started with sockets:

`http://www.dorb.com/darrell/sockets`

Asynchronous Sockets

The asyncore module provides the basic infrastructure for writing and handling asynchronous socket service clients and servers that are the result of a series of events dispatched by an event loop. This module is used to check what is happening with sockets in the system, and it implements routines to handle each situation. The core of this module is the `dispatcher` class.

`dispatcher ([socket])`

This is supposed to be the constructor of the `asyncore.dispatcher` class. To use this class, you need to subclass it, and override the method that you want to handle. This class is just a wrapper on top of a `socket` object. If the socket argument is omitted, you need to call the `create_socket()` method as shown in the following example:

```python
import asyncore
import socket
class Dispatcher(asyncore.dispatcher):
    def handle_write(self):
        self.send("data")
        self.close()

class DataServer(asyncore.dispatcher):
    def __init__(self, port=8888):
        self.port = port
        self.create_socket(socket.AF_INET, socket.SOCK_STREAM)
        self.bind(("", port))
        self.listen(5)
    def handle_accept(self):
        link, address = self.accept()
        Dispatcher(link)
dataserverobj = DataServer(8888)
asyncore.loop
```

This example overrides two methods from the `dispatcher` class: `handle_write()` and `handle_accept()`. The first one is called when the socket receives an attempt to be written, and the other one is called when the listening socket receives a connection request.

The other methods available in this class are as follows:

handle_connect()—Called when a connection is set up with success.

handle_expt()—Called when a connection fails.

handle_read()—Called when the socket has data available to be read.

handle_close()—Called when the connection to the socket is closed or reset.

handle_error(error_type, error_value, traceback)—Called whenever one of the other handlers causes a Python error.

readable()—Returns 1 if the object has data to be read, 0 if not.

writable()—Returns 1 if the object wants to write data, 0 if not.

The dispatcher class also provides methods that have a implementation similar to those available in the socket module. Here is the list: create_socket (equivalent to socket), connect, bind, listen, send, recv, accept, and close.

This module also reveals two functions:

asyncore.poll([timeout=0 [, exceptions=0]])—Pools for events, calling the proper handler functions. If you set the exceptions flag to 1, every exception generated in event handlers will be raised.

asyncore.loop([timeout=30])—Repeatedly calls asyncore.poll().

You can also check out the *Asynchronous Sockets Library*, by Sam Rushing, which is used for building asynchronous socket clients and servers:

http://www.nightmare.com/software.html

This is a single program that can simultaneously communicate with many other clients and servers, using and implementing multiple protocols running within a single address space on a single thread. Included in the library are sample clients, servers, and demonstrations for several Internet protocols, including HTTP, finger, DNS, POP3, and FTP.

The select Module

The select module is used to implement polling and to multiplex processing across multiple I/O streams without using threads or subprocesses. It provides access to the BSD select() function interface, available in most operating systems. On Windows, this function only works for sockets. On UNIX, it is used for pipes, sockets, files, or any other stream-compatible objects. Also note that the that `asyncore` module is built on top of the `select` module.

The `select` function accepts socket lists as arguments. The following example implements a loop that will keep checking the sockets in order to identify the exact moment when they become readable, writable, or signal an error. (An error is assigned whenever a socket tries to open a connection, and the connection fails. A few other conditions will trigger one of the sockets, not just connect errors.)

A socket becomes readable when it successfully gets a connection after calling the `listener`, or when it receives data. On the other hand, if a connection is set up after a non-blocking call to the `connect` method, the socket becomes writable.

```
import select
import socket
App_Socket = socket.socket(socket.AF_INET, socket.SOCK_STREAM)
App_Socket.bind("", 8888)
App_Socket.listen(5)
while 1:
    readable_sockets = [App_Socket]
    writable_sockets = []
    r, w, err = select.select(readable_sockets, writable_sockets, [], 0)
    if r:
        client, address = service.accept()
        client.send("data")
        client.close()
```

HTTP

HTTP (Hypertext Transfer Protocol) is a simple text-based protocol used for World Wide Web Applications. Both Web servers and Web browsers implement this protocol.

The HTTP protocol works by having a client that opens a connection, and sends a request header to a Web server. This request is a simple text-based form that contains the request method (GET, POST, PUT, ...), the name of the file that should be opened, and so forth.

The server interprets the request and returns a response to the client. This response contains the HTTP protocol version number, as well as a lot of information—such as cookies, document type and size, and so on—about the returned document.

For details about the HTTP specification, you'd better check:

```
http://www.w3.org/Protocols
```

Next, I list some Python projects that somehow use HTTP techniques.

M2Crypto, by Ng Pheng Siong's

M2Crypto makes the following features available to the Python programmer: RSA, DH, DSA, HMACs, message digests, symmetric ciphers, SSL functionality to implement clients and servers, and S/MIME v2.

```
http://mars.post1.com/home/ngps/m2/
```

> **Note**
> With Python-2.0, the socket module can be compiled with support for the OpenSSL
> library, so it can handle SSL without trouble.

CTC (Cut The Crap), by Constantinos Kotsokalis

This is a http proxy software written in Python, which cuts advertisement banners from your Web browser display.

```
http://softlab.ntua.gr/~ckotso/CTC/
```

Alfajor, by Andrew Cooke

Alfajor is an HTTP cookie filter, written in Python with an optional GUI. It acts as an HTTP proxy (you must configure your browser to use it) and can either contact sites directly or work with a second proxy (for example, a cache). Note that Alfajor does not fully conform to any HTTP version. However, in practice, it works with the vast majority of sites.

```
http://www.andrewcooke.free-online.co.uk/jara/alfajor/
```

Building Web Servers

In order to build Internet servers using Python, you can use the following modules:

SocketServer—It is a generic socket-based IP server.

BaseHTTPServer—It provides the infrastructed required by the next two modules.

SimpleHTTPServer—It allows you to have a simple Web server.

CGIHTTPServer—It enables the implementation of a CGI-compliant HTTP server.

The SocketServer **Module**

The SocketServer module exposes a framework that simplifies the task of writing network servers. Rather than having to implement servers using the low-level socket module, this module provides four basic server classes that implement interfaces to the protocols used most often: TCPServer, UDPServer, StreamRequestHandler, and DatagramRequestHandler. All these classes process requests synchronously. Each request must be completed before the next request can be started.

This kind of behavior is not appropriate if each request takes a long time to complete because it requires a lot of computation and the client might be slow to process all data. In order to handle the requests as separate threads, you can use the following classes: ThreadingTCPServer, ThreadingUDPServer, ForkingUDPServer, and ForkingTCPServer.

Both the StreamRequestHandler and DatagramRequestHandler classes provide two file attributes that can be used to read and write data from and to the client program. These attributes are self.rfile and self.wfile.

The following code demonstrates the usage of the StreamRequestHandler class, which is exposed by the SocketServer module.

```
import SocketServer
port = 8000
class myRequestHandler(SocketServer.StreamRequestHandler):
    def handle(self):
        print "connection from ", self.client_address
        self.wfile.write("data")

srvsocket = SocketServer.TCPServer(("", port), myRequestHandler)
print "The socket is listening to port", port
srvsocket.serve_forever()
```

> **Tip**
> Always remember that you need to use user-accessible ports numbers.

Next, you have the classes provided by this module:

TCPServer((hostname, port), request_handler)—Implements a server that supports the TCP protocol.

UDPServer((hostname, port), request_handler)—Implements a server that supports the UDP protocol.

`UnixStreamServer((hostname, port), request_handler)`—Implements a server that supports a stream-oriented protocol using UNIX domain sockets.

`UnixDatagramServer((hostname, port), request_handler)`—Implements a server that supports a datagram-oriented protocol using UNIX domain sockets.

In all four classes, the `request_handler` must be an instance of the `BaseRequestHandler` class, and usually, `hostname` is left blank.

Each one of these classes has its own instances of class variables.

`request_queue_size` stores the size of the request queue that is passed to the socket's `listen()` method.

`socket_type` returns the socket type used by the server. The possible values are `socket.SOCK_STREAM` and `socket.SOCK_DGRAM`.

The class instances implement the following methods and attributes:

`fileno()`—Returns the server socket's integer file descriptor.

`handle_request()`—Processes a single request, by creating an instance of the handler class and invoking its `handle()` method.

`serve_forever()`—Implements a loop to handle infinite requests.

`address_family`—Returns either `socket.AF_INET` or `socket.AF_UNIX`.

`RequestHandlerClass`—Holds the request handler class, which was provided by the user.

`server_address`—Returns the IP address and the port number being used by the server for listening.

`socket`—Returns the `socket` object used for approaching requests.

The `BaseHTTPServer` **Module**

The `BaseHTTPServer` module defines two base classes for implementing basic HTTP servers (also known as *Web servers*). This module is built on top of the `SocketServer` module. Note that this module is rarely used directly. Instead, you should consider using the modules `CGIHTTPServer` and `SimpleHTTPServer`.

The following code demonstrates the usage of the `BaseHTTPRequestHandler` class, which is exposed by the `BaseHTTPServer` module, to implement a simple HTTP Server.

```
import BaseHTTPServer
htmlpage = """
<html><head><title>Web Page</title></head>
<body>Hello Python World</body>
</html>"""
notfound = "File not found"
class WelcomeHandler(BaseHTTPServer.BaseHTTPRequestHandler):
    def do_GET(self):
        if self.path = "/":
            self.send_response(200)
            self.send_header("Content-type","text/html")
            self.end_headers()
            self.wfile.write(htmlpage)
        else:
            self.send_error(404, notfound)
httpserver = BaseHTTPServer.HTTPServer(("",80), WelcomeHandler)
httpserver.serve_forever()
```

The `HTTPServer((hostname, port), request_handler_class)` base class is derived from the `SocketServer.TCPServer`, hence, it implements the same methods. This class creates a `HTTPServer` object that listens to the `hostname+port`, and uses the `request_handler_class` to handle requests.

The second base class is called `BaseHTTPRequestHandler(request, client_address, server)`. You need to create a subclass of this class in order to handle HTTP requests. If you need to handle `GET` requests, you must redefine the `do_GET()` method. On the other hand, if you need to handle `POST` requests, you must redefine the `do_POST()` method.

This class also implements some class variables:

- `BaseHTTPRequestHandler.server_version`

- `BaseHTTPRequestHandler.sys_version`

- `BaseHTTPRequestHandler.protocol_version`

- `BaseHTTPRequestHandler.error_message_format`

This string should contain the code for a complete Web page that must be sent to the client in case an error message must be displayed. Within the string, you can reference some error attributes because this string is dynamically linked to the contents of an error dictionary.

```
"""<head><title></title></head><body>
Error code = %(code)d<br>
Error message = %(message)s<br>
Error explanation = %(explain)s<br></body>"""
```

Each instance of the `BaseHTTPRequestHandler` class implements some methods and attributes:

`handle()`—Implements a request dispatcher. It calls the methods that start with "do_", such as `do_GET()` and `do_POST()`.

`send_error(error_code [, error_message])`—Sends an error signal to the client.

`send_response(response_code [, response_message])`—Sends a response header according to the Table 10.2.

Table 10.2   *List of Response Codes and Messages Returned by the Web Server*

Code	Code Description
200	OK
201	Created
202	Accepted
204	No content available
300	Multiple choices
301	Moved permanently
302	Moved temporarily
303	Not modified
400	Bad request
401	Unauthorized
403	Forbidden
500	Internal server error
501	Not implemented
502	Bad gateway
503	Service unavailable

send_header(keyword, value)—Writes a MIME header, which contains the header keyword and its value, to the output stream.

end_header()—Identifies the end of the MIME headers.

The following object attributes are also exposed:

client_address—Returns a 2-tuple (hostname, port) that compounds the client address.

command—Identifies the request type, which can be POST, GET, and so on.

path—Returns the request path.

request_version—Returns the HTTP version string from the request.

headers—Returns the HTTP headers.

rfile—Exposes the input stream.

wfile—Exposes the output stream.

The SimpleHTTPServer **Module**

The SimpleHTTPServer module provides a simple HTTP server request-handler class. It has an interface compatible with the BaseHTTPServer module that enables it to serve files from a base directory. This module implements both standard GET and HEAD request handlers, as shown in this example:

```
import SimpleHTTPServer
import SocketServer
ServerHandler = SimpleHTTPServer.SimpleHTTPRequestHandler
httpserver = BaseHTTPServer.HTTPServer(("", 80), ServerHandler)
httpserver.serve_forever()
```

The current directory used to start up the server is used as the relative reference for all files requested by the client. This module implements the SimpleHTTPRequestHandler(request, (hostname, port), server) class. This class exposes the following two attributes:

- SimpleHTTPRequestHandler.server_version

- SimpleHTTPRequestHandler.extensions_map—A dictionary that maps file suffixes and MIME types

The CGIHTTPServer **Module**

The CGIHTTPServer module defines another simple HTTP server request-handler class. This module has an interface compatible with BaseHTTPServer, which enables it to server files from a base directory (the current directory and its subdirectories), and also allow clients to run CGI (Common Gateway Interface) scripts.

Requests are handled using the do_GET and do_POST methods. You can override them in order to meet your needs. Note that the CGI scripts are executed as the user nobody. The next example demonstrates the implementation of a simple HTTP Server that accepts CGI requests.

```
import CGIHTTPServer
import BaseHTTPServer
class ServerHandler(CGIHTTPServer.CGIHTTPRequestHandler):
    cgi_directories = ['/cgi-bin']
httpserver = BaseHTTPServer.HTTPServer(("", 80), Handler)
httpserver.serve_forever()
```

The CGIHTTPRequestHandler(request, (hostname, port), server) class is provided by this module. This handler class supports both GET and POST requests. It also implements the CGIHTTPRequestHandler.cgi_directories attribute, which contains a list of directories that can store CGI scripts.

Setting Up the Client Side of the HTTP Protocol

The httplib module implements the client side of the *HTTP (Hypertext Transfer Protocol)* protocol, and is illustrated as follows:

```
import httplib
url = "www.lessaworld.com"
urlpath = "/default.html"
host = httplib.HTTP(url)
host.putrequest("GET", urlpath)
host.putheader("Accept", "text/html")
host.endheaders()

errcode, errmsg, headers host.getreply()
if errcode != 200:
    raise RuntimeError
htmlfile = host.getfile()
htmlpage = htmlfile.read()
htmlfile.close()
return htmlpage
```

The previous example doesn't allow you to handle multiple requests in parallel because the `getreply()` method blocks the application while waiting for the server to respond. You should consider using the `asyncore` module for a more efficient and asynchronous solution.

This module exposes the HTTP class. The `HTTP([hostname [,port]])` class creates and returns a connection object. If no `port` is informed, `port` `80` is used; and if no arguments are informed at all, you need to use the `connect()` method to make the connection yourself. This class exposes the following methods:

`connect(hostname [,port])`—Establishes a connection.

`send(data)`—Sends data to the server after the `endheaders()` method is called.

`putrequest(request, selector)`—Writes the first line in the client request header. The `request` option can be one of the following most common request methods: `GET`, `POST`, `PUT`, or `HEAD`. `selector` is the name of the document to be opened.

`putheader(header, argument1 [, ...])`—Writes a header line in the client request header. Each line consists of the header, a colon and a space, and the list of arguments.

`endheaders()`—Indicates the end of the headers in the client request header by writing a blank line to the server.

`getreply()`—Returns a tuple (`requestcode`, `requestmsg`, `headers`) that is read after closing the client side of the connection. This tuple comes from the server's reply to the client message. The pair `requestcode` and `requestmsg` is something like (`500`, `"Internal server error"`). `headers` is an instance of the `mimetools.Message` class, which contains the HTTP headers that were received from the server.

`getfile()`—Wraps the data returned by the server as a file object in order to make reading it easy.

> **Note**
> Note that the `httplib` module packed with Python 2.0 has been rewritten by Greg Stein, in order to provide new interfaces and support for *HTTP/1.1* features, such as pipelining. Backward compatibility with the 1.5 version of httplib is provided, but you should consider taking a look at the documentation strings of the module for details.
>
> Also note that Python 2.0's version of the `httplib` module has support to "`https://`" URLs over SSL.

Accessing URLs

URL stands for *uniform resource locator*. URLs are those strings, such as
`http://www.lessaworld.com/`, that you have to type in your Web browser in order to
jump to a Web page.

Python provides the `urllib` and `urlparse` modules as great tools to process URLs.

> **Tip**
> Many applications today that have to parse Web pages always suffer with changes in
> the page design. However, these problems will go away when more structural formats
> (such as XML) start getting used to producing the pages.

The `urllib` Module

The `urllib` module is a high-level interface to retrieve data across the World Wide
Web, supporting any HTTP, FTP, and gopher connections by using sockets. This
module defines functions for writing programs that must be active users of the Web. It
is normally used as an outer interface to other modules, such as `httplib`, `ftplib`,
`gopherlib`, and so on.

To retrieve a Web page, use the `urllib.urlopen(url [,data])` function. This
function returns a `stream` object that can be manipulated as easily as any other regular
`file` object, and is illustrated as follows:

```
>>> import urllib
>>> page = urllib.urlopen("http://www.bog.frb.fed.us")
>>> page.readline()
```

This stream object has two additional attributes: `url` and `headers`. The first one is the
URL that you are opening, and the other is a dictionary that contains the page
headers, as illustrated in the next example.

```
>>> page.url
'http://www.bog.frb.fed.us'
>>> for key, value in page.headers.items():
...      print key, " = ", value
...
server  =  Microsoft-IIS/4.0
content-type  =  text/html
content-length  =  461
date  =  Thu, 15 Jun 2000 15:31:32 GMT
```

Next, you have a couple of other functions that are made available by the `urllib` module.

`urllib.urlretrieve(url [,filename] [,hook])`—Copies a network object to a local file.

```
>>> urllib.urlretrieve('http://www.lessaworld.com', 'copy.html')
```

`urllib.urlcleanup()`—Cleans up the cache used by `urllib.urlretrieve`.

`urllib.quote(string [,safe])`—Replaces special characters in string using `%xx` escape codes. The optional `safe` parameter specifies additional characters that should be quoted.

```
>>> urllib.quote('This & that @ home')
'this%20%26%20that%20%40%20home'
```

`urllib.quote_plus(string [,safe])`—Works just like `quote()`, but it replaces spaces by using plus signs.

`urllib.unquote(string)`—Returns the original value that was passed to `urllib.quote`.

```
>>> urllib.unquote('this%20%26%20that%20%40%20home')
'This & that @ home'
```

`urllib.urlencode(dict)`—Converts a dictionary into a URL-encoded string.

```
>>> dict = {'sex':'female', 'name':'renata lessa'}
>>> urllib.urlencode(dict)
'sex=female&name=renata+lessa'
```

Note
For those that have Python 2.0 installed, keep in mind that the new `urllib` module is able to scan environment variables for proxy configuration.

Also note that Python 2.0's version of the `urllib` module has support to "`https://`" URLs over SSL.

The `urlparse` **Module**

The `urlparse` module manipulates an URL string, parsing it into tuples. It is able to break an URL up into components, combines them back, and converts relative addresses to absolute addresses. Basically, it rips URLs apart, being able to put them together again.

Let's take a look at the functions that are provided by this module:

```
urlparse.urlparse()
syntax: urlparse.urlparse(urlstring [,default_scheme [,allow_fragments]])
```

Parses an URL into six elements—addressing scheme, network location, path, parameters, query, fragment identifier—returning the following tuple:

```
>>> urlparse('http://www.python.org/FAQ.html')
('http', 'www.python.org','FAQ.html','','','')
```

`urlparse.urlunparse(tuple)`—Constructs a URL string from a tuple as returned by `urlparse()`.

`urlparse.urljoin(base, url [,allow_fragments])`—Combines an absolute URL with a relative URL.

```
>>>urljoin('http://www.python.org', 'doc/lib')
'http://www.python.org/doc/lib'
```

The next example copies a Web page into a local file:

```
import urllib
pagehandler = urllib.urlopen("http://www.lessaworld.com")
outputfile = open("sitecopy.html", "wb")
while 1:
    data = pagehandler.read(512)
    if not data:
        break
    outputfile.write(data)
outputfile.close()
pagehandler.close()
```

If you are behind a firewall, here's a little trick you can do in order to use proxy servers to handle your connections:

```
1: import urllib
2: proxies = {'http' : 'http://proxy:80'}
3: urlopener = urllib.FancyURLopener(proxies)
4: htmlpage = urlopener.open('http://www.bog.frb.fed.us')
5: data = htmlpage.readlines()
6: print data
```

Line 2: Creates a dictionary that identifies the proxy location. Note that `proxy:80` corresponds to the name of the proxy server along with the port where it is listening to.

Line 3: Creates a new function that masks the proxy connection.

FTP

FTP is a popular way to transfer files from machine to machine across a network. It is convenient because there are FTP clients and FTP servers written for all the popular platforms.

FTP servers can work with both private users and anonymous users. The difference is that a private FTP server allows only system users to be able to connect via FTP, whereas an anonymous FTP server allows anyone on the network to connect to it and transfer files without having an account. Keep in mind that configuring an anonymous FTP server always exposes the security of your system.

The `ftplib` module implements the client side of the FTP protocol. You can use it for mirroring FTP sites. Usually the `urllib` module is used as an outer interface to `ftplib`. For uploads you probably want to use `ftplib`.

The FTP implementation provides one *control* port and one *data* port, which means that the actual transmission of data between client and server machines operates over a separate socket on a completely separate port in order to avoid deadlock problems.

Check out the Python Documentation for more information:

```
http://www.python.org/doc/lib/module-ftplib.html
```

Transferring Data

The following example shows how to read data from a FTP site:

```
1: #!/usr/local/bin/python
2: import ftplib
3: ftp = ftplib.FTP('ftp.lessaworld.com')
4: ftp.login()
5: ftp.cwd('downloads/programs')
6: ftp.retrlines('LIST')
7: file = open('filename.txt', 'w')
8: ftp.retrbinary('RETR filename.txt', file.write, 1024)
9: ftp.quit()
```

Line 2: Imports the `ftplib` module.

Line 3: Creates the FTP object and connects to a host server.

Line 4: Establishes an anonymous login.

Line 5: Uses the `cwd()` method to change the directory.

Line 6: Retrieves the resulting lines of the provided command. In our case, it lists the content of the directory.

Line 7: Creates a file on your local server.

Line 8: Retrieves the binary information passed to the FTP server, storing it into the mentioned file object.

> **Tip**
> Note that the interface uses FTP commands—such as LIST, STOR, and RETR—that you need to know. These commands are part of the FTP specification and have nothing to do with Python.

The next example uploads a file to the FTP server:

```
1: import ftplib
2: ftp = ftblib.FTP("ftp.lessaworld.com")
3: ftp.login("username", "password")
4: filename = "index.html"
5: ftp.storlines("STOR " + filename, open(filename))
6: filename = "app.exe "
7: ftp.storbinary("STOR " + filename, open(filename, "rb"), 1024)
```

Line 3: Provides a username and password to the FTP server in order to establish a connection.

Line 5: Uploads a TEXT file to the server.

Line 7: Uploads a binary file to the server.

SMTP/POP3/IMAP

SMTP and POP3 are the protocols used most in the Internet because they provide the necessary services to handle electronic mails (*emails*).

The *Simple Mail Transfer Protocol (SMTP)* is the official way to transfer mail over the Internet. This protocol is an Internet standard, specified in RFC-821. It defines how programs exchange email on the Internet.

The SMTP protocol is responsible for putting the email in mailboxes, and when it comes to removing the messages from there, it is necessary to use the POP3 protocol. The *Post Office Protocol (POP)* is used by mail readers that work on network clients and are connected to designated mail servers to send and receive mail. The purpose of this protocol is to allow remote access to a mailbox that is hosted by an external server. For your information, SMTP is also used to send the messages across the Internet.

Anyone who writes a POP client can communicate with a POP server because this protocol abstracts the details of the email to a system-independent level. This protocol was designed so that users could access their mail from machines that weren't configured for receiving mail. Also, all systems on the Internet mail system agree to use SMTP to handle mail. Storage of mail can vary on different systems, although this is not an OS issue, but an application issue.

IMAP (Internet Message Access Protocol) is another protocol that is being used for mail reading. It is a method of accessing electronic mail or bulletin board messages that are kept on a (possibly shared) mail server. In other words, it permits a client email program to access remote message stores as if they were local.

Handling Email Services

The `smtplib` module provides a low-level client interface to the SMTP protocol that can be used to send emails to any machine in the Internet that has an SMTP or ESMTP listener `daemon`. An example of this is as follows:

```
import smtplib
import string
host = "localhost"
fromclause = "alessa@bebemania.com.br"
toclause = "rtaveira@bebemania.com.br, jp@alugueaqui.com.br"
toclause = string.splitfields(toclause, ",")
msgbody = """
This email brings good news for you!!
Best Regards
"""
SMTPServer = smtplib.SMTP(host)
SMTPServer.sendmail(fromclause, toclause, msgbody)
SMTPServer.quit()
```

The `poplib` module provides a low-level `POP3` client-side interface for connecting to a `POP3` server using a client protocol, as defined in `RFC 1725`. This module is shown in the following:

```
import poplib, string
PopServerName = "mail.lessaworld.com"
PopServer = poplib.POP3(PopServerName)
print PopServer.getwelcome()
PopServer.user('AndreLessa')
PopServer.pass_('qwerty0987')
r, items, octets = PopServer.list()
msgid, size = string.split(items[-1])
r, msg, octets = PopServer.retr(msgid)
msg = string.join(msg, "\n")
print msg
```

See Chapter 13, "Data Manipulation," for details about using the module `rfc822` to parse the header lines and the modules `mimetools` and `mimify` to process the data attached to the message.

The `imaplib` module provides a low-level IMAP client-side interface for connecting to an `IMAP4` mail server using the `IMAP4rev1` client protocol, as defined in `RFC 2060`. This module is shown in the following:

```
 1: import imaplib, getpass, string
 2: host = "imap.lessaworld.com"
 3: user = "AndreLessa"
 4: pwd = getpass.getpass()
 5: msgserver = imaplib.IMAP4(host)
 6: msgserver.login(user, pwd)
 7: msgserver.select()
 8: msgtyp, msgitems = msgserver.search(None, "ALL")
 9: for idx in string.split(msgitems[0]):
10:     msgtyp, msgitems = msgserver.fetch(idx, "(RFC822)")
11:     print "Message %s\n" % num
12:     print "---------------\n"
13:     print "Content: %s" % msgitems[0][1]
14: msgserver.logout()
```

The `search` method (line 8) lists all the message items available at the IMAP server.

For more details about IMAP, check out the IMAP Connection Web site:

```
http://www.imap.org/
```

If you want to have more control over your emails, and you are willing to have it filtered, take a look at *SpamWall*, by Sam Rushing.

This program is a simple, powerful framework for building custom SPAM filters. SpamWall is a filtering proxy daemon that sits between your site's SMTP server and the outside world. It is modular and extensible. Included are two sample filters—a regular-expression based filter (like procmail) and a blacklist filter. For more information, check out

```
http://www.nightmare.com/software.html
```

Newsgroups—Telnet and Gopher

The `nntplib` module implements a low-level interface to the client side of the *NNTP (Network News Transfer Protocol)* protocol—a service mostly known for providing *newsgroups*.

This protocol is text-based because all the communication between the client and the server uses ASCII text. This protocol is also used to exchange Usenet news articles between servers.

Newsgroups are organized hierarchically, according to their levels, which are separated by *dots*. In `comp.lang.python` for example, `comp` defines computer-related newsgroups and `lang` defines that it refers to computer languages. It is shown as follows:

```
 1: import nntplib
 2: import string
 3: ServerAlias = "news.lessaworld.com"
 4: NewsGroup = "comp.lang.opensource"
 5: Keyword = raw_input("Enter keyword to search: ")
 6: NewsServer = nntplib.NNTP(ServerAlias)
 7: r, count, firstmsg, lastmsg, name = NewsServer.group(NewsGroup)
 8: r, messages = NewsServer.xover(first, last)
 9: for id, subject, author, date, msgid, refer, size, lines in messages:
10:     if string.find(subject, Keyword) >= 0:
11:         r, id, msgid, msgbody = NewsServer.article(id)
12:         print "Author: %s - Subject: %s - Date: %s\n" % \
13:               (author, subject, date)
14:         print "<-Begin Message->\n"
15:         print msgbody
16:         print "<-End Message->\n"
```

Line 6: Creates the NNTP object and connects to a NewsServer.

Line 7: Selects the newsgroup that you want to read.

Check out Python's documentation for more details about this module at the following URLs:

```
http://www.python.org/doc/lib/nntp-objects.html
```

and

```
http://www.python.org/doc/lib/module-nntplib.html
```

The `telnetlib` module implements a client for the telnet protocol. This protocol is used to connect to remote computers, usually via the port (23). After you have established your telnet connection, you can execute commands remotely on that computer through your telnet interface. The commands you use are UNIX commands, such as `ls`, `cd`, `pine`, `elm`, `talk`, `rm` provided that the telnet server is running on a UNIX box. If you have a windows telnet server, you would probably have an MS-DOS style command prompt.

The protocol is shown in the following:

```
import telnetlib
hostserver = "http://www.lessaworld.com"
newline = "\n"
username = "user02" + newline
password = "qwerty0987" + newline
telnet = telnetlib.Telnet(hostserver)
telnet.read_until("login: ")
telnet.write(username)
telnet.read_until("Password: ")
telnet.write(password)
while 1:
    command = raw_input("[shell]: ")
    telnet.write(command)
    if command == "exit":
        break
    telnet.read_all()
```

For implementation details, you can check out the official documentation at

```
http://www.python.org/doc/lib/module-telnetlib.html
```

and

```
http://www.python.org/doc/lib/telnet-objects.html
```

Gopher provides a distributed information delivery system around which a world *campus-wide information system (CWIS)* can readily be constructed. While providing a delivery vehicle for local information, Gopher facilitates access to other Gopher and information servers throughout the world.

The `gopherlib` module is a minimal client side implementation of the `Gopher` protocol. Although Gopher is an old protocol, it is still used by many universities. Gopher provides an hierarchical interface for both texts and binaries. This module is used by the `urllib` module to handle URLs that use the Gopher protocol. The `gopherlib` module is shown as follows:

```
import gopherlib
GopherServer = "gopher.lessaworld.com"
directory = gopherlib.send_selector("1/", GopherServer)
for topic in gopherlib.get_directory(directory):
    print topic
```

Check out the official documentation for more details:

```
http://www.python.org/doc/lib/module-gopherlib.html
```

Summary

Networking is the word behind all new technology that arrives in the market these days. Networking systems are well defined by the *OSI/ISO (Open Systems Interconnection/International Standards Organization)* seven-layer model, which suggests the following levels of networking process: Physical, Data Link, Network, Transport, Session, Presentation, and Application.

Network connections can be of two types: connection-oriented (such as TCP) or packet-oriented (such as UDP).

The network layer of the TCP/IP stack is provided by the Internet Protocol (commonly known as IP). The IP address defines the addressing and routing of information around the network, uniquely identifying a network interface.

The transport layer is provided by the TCP, which is the main form of communication over the Internet because it provides a reliable, session-based service for the delivery of sequenced packets.

UDP is a connectionless transport protocol that does not guarantee delivery or packet sequence. This protocol provides an unreliable but fast datagram service.

The most commonly used application protocols (such as HTTP, FTP, Gopher, Telnet, POP3, IMAP, SMTP, and NNTP) are built on top of TCP/IP infrastructures. Actually, they don't have to know any details about TCP nor about IP because there is a thin layer called "sockets" between TCP/IP and them.

A port is an entry point to an application/service that resides on a server.

Sockets are objects that allow programs to accept and make connections, such as to send and receive data. They are mostly used for TCP and UDP connections. The socket module is a very simple object-based interface that provides access to a low-level BSD socket-style network.

The asyncore module provides the basic infrastructure for writing and handling asynchronous socket service clients and servers that are result of a series of events dispatched by an event loop.

The select module is used to implement polling and to multiplex processing across multiple I/O streams without using threads or subprocesses.

In order to build Internet servers using Python, HTTP modules that you can use are as follows:

- SocketServer—It is a generic socket-based IP server.

- BaseHTTPServer—It provides the infrastructure required by the next two modules.

- SimpleHTTPServer—It allows you to have a simple Web server.

- CGIHTTPServer—It enables the implementation of a CGI-compliant HTTP server.

The httplib module implements the client side of the *HTTP (Hypertext Transfer Protocol)* protocol.

The urllib and urlparse modules are useful tools provided by Python to process URLs. The urllib module is a high-level interface to fetch data across the World Wide Web. It is normally used as an outer interface to other modules, such as httplib, ftplib, gopherlib, and so on. On the other hand, the urlparse module manipulates a URL string, parsing it into tuples.

The ftplib module implements the client side of the FTP protocol.

The smtplib module provides a low-level client interface to the SMTP protocol that can be used to send emails in the Internet.

The `poplib` module provides a low-level POP3 client-side interface for connecting to a POP3 server using a client protocol.

The `imaplib` module provides a low-level IMAP client-side interface for connecting to an IMAP4 mail server using the IMAP4rev1 client protocol.

The `nntplib` module implements a low-level interface to the client side of the *NNTP (Network News Transfer Protocol)* protocol—a service mostly known for providing *newsgroups*. This protocol is also used to exchange Usenet news articles between servers.

The `telnetlib` module implements a client for the telnet protocol. This protocol is used to connect to remote computers. After you have established your telnet connection, you can execute UNIX commands remotely on that computer through your telnet interface.

The `gopherlib` module is a minimal client-side implementation of the Gopher protocol.

CHAPTER 11

Web Development

We are the knights who say...ni!

This chapter provides information concerning how to use Python for Internet development support. It also introduces you to many Web applications and scripts developed using Python.

Web Development

This chapter exposes the reality between Python and the Internet by introducing some complete Web applications that have emerged from the Python community.

No doubt the most popular application area at this time is the Internet. Consequently, Python is acquiring a strong presence on the Web because its library of modules that interface to the main Internet protocols reach full maturity.

Python is a dynamic language absolutely useful for the Internet, mostly because it easily allows the establishment of interfaces with external systems.

Nowadays, some of the most important applications in the Internet are based on the HTTP protocol. Python's support to HTTP, which is the basic communication protocol underlying the Web, allows it to implement HTTP Servers (Web Servers) and clients (Web browsers). Python has been successfully used to implement an HTTP client called Grail, which is a Web browser full of features. On the other hand, Python has many options for HTTP Servers, also known as Web Servers. Python's standard library of modules comes with some basic HTTP Server implementations, such as `BaseHTTPServer` and `SimpleHTTPServer`. The advantage of using Python as a Web Server is that you have total control about what is going on in your application.

Besides the HTTP Servers that are part of Python's distribution, a number of other third-party Internet publishing tools are available for Python. Most of them are free for both commercial and noncommercial use, such as Medusa and Zope.

This chapter also points you to the most used Python scripts and technologies used for Web development. For more information, check out the Web Programming Topic Guide site:

```
http://www.python.org/topics/web/
```

This area in the Python's Web site covers Web-related programming with Python. It possesses links to several distinct Web topics, such as HTML, HTTP, Zope, and so on.

Configuring Web Servers for Python/CGI Scripts

The next topics show you how to configure the most used Web servers in the market. Mostly you will see how to handle Python CGI scripts within Apache and Microsoft IIS Web servers.

Python in Apache

First, let's see how Apache handles requests.

When a file is called, Apache executes an action, which internally is known as *handler*. These handlers are usually implicitly related to the files, based on the file type. However, new Apache releases are able to assign handles to filename extensions or file locations, instead of only work with the file type.

Python script files are handled in exactly the same way as other CGI scripts. Once a request is received, Apache calls the Python interpreter asking it to run the specific script. Depending on the Apache configuration, there are several actions to be performed when receiving a request (for instance, user authentication and file transfer).

Apache comes with a predefined set of handlers for basic routine tasks. However, there are several third-party handler applications that can be very useful as well, such as the mod_python and mod_pyapache modules. Using these modules is not strictly necessary, but it reduces the overhead of your server and increases the speed of your application. Both of these reasons occur because the Python interpreter is not called for every single connection anymore. You can create Apache Handlers by building them into the Web Server, adding them to the Action directive, or implementing a module.

The Apache official Web site is as follows:

http://www.apache.org/

Configuring Apache for Python

The following guidelines will help you configure your Apache installation to run Python in both Windows and UNIX systems. Steps 1–8 are specific for Win32 configurations.

1. Installing Python in the C:\Python directory is a more convenient way to handle environment paths.

2. It is convenient if you have your CGI files in the same drive as the WINNT system files.

3. Verify if you have a system variable called PATH that contains the Python interpreter's (python.exe) directory (if necessary, create it).

4. Create a system variable called PYTHONPATH. It must contain the list of directories to be used when searching for Python files.

5. Use ASSOC to setup a file extension for Python.

   ASSOC .py=PythonScript

6. Use FTYPE to associate the previous setting to the Python executable.

   FTYPE PythonScript=python.exe %1 %*

7. Add the extension .py to the system environment variable PATHEXT. This variable stores the list of executable extensions (for example, PATHEXT=.EXE;.COM;.BAT;.CMD;.py).

8. Install Apache on your system's root drive, that is, "c:\Apache". Installing Apache in this directory helps you during the whole configuration process.

9. Edit your C:\WINNT\system32\drivers\etc\hosts file, adding the IP address of your machine. This file is the NT equivalent to UNIX /etc/hosts table file.

The following steps tell you how to configure the Apache Web Server. Note that nowadays, the whole Apache configuration can be set using one unique file: `httpd.conf`.

10. In the `access.conf` file, make the following changes:

    ```
    <Directory /apache/htdocs>
    Options Indexes ExecCGI
    ```

11. In the `httpd.conf` file, make the following changes:

    ```
    ServerRoot /apache
    ```

12. In the `srm.conf` file, make the following changes. You also have the option to set PYTHONPATH here using the command `SetEnv`, instead of defining it as a system environment variable. Note that there are two `AddHandler` settings. The former identifies the extension to be associated with CGI scripts, and the latter allows you to use the `.cgi` extension in your files, in order to hide from crackers, the language used to implement your site. Of utmost importance is to make certain that you're using Python in unbuffered mode (SetEnv PYTHONUNBUFFERED 1) and to set (or pass) PYTHONPATH as a system environment variable. Forgetting to set either of these parameters is the most common reason for "premature end of header" errors.

    ```
    DocumentRoot /apache/htdocs
    ScriptAlias /cgi-bin/ /apache/cgi-bin/
    PassEnv PYTHONPATH
    SetEnv PYTHONUNBUFFERED 1
    AddHandler cgi-script .py
    AddHandler cgi-script .cgi
    ```

13. Place your scripts in your `cgi-bin` directory.

14. If you are using an UNIX system, make sure that the first line of your script contain a *shebang* to identify the location of the Python interpreter.

15. Optionally, you can configure the server to run scripts *only* from the `cgi-bin` directory by replacing the following line in the `access.conf` file:

    ```
    <Directory /path/to/your/httpd/cgi-bin> Options Indexes FollowSymLinks
      </Directory>
    ```

    with

    ```
    <Directory /path/to/your/httpd/cgi-bin> Options FollowSymLinks ExecCGI
      </Directory>
    ```

If you want to run your scripts from any directory, comment the previous setting and add the following one:

```
<Directory /path/to/your/httpd/htdocs> Options All </Directory>
```

16. Set the read and execute permissions of your script. If you are using an UNIX system, you should type `chmod 755 yourscript.py`.

At this time, you should be ready to launch your Web browser and to access your CGI script by typing its URL.

For UNIX, if Apache and Python are set up correctly, all you need to do is place the Python scripts in the `cgi-bin` directory and set their permissions correctly.

More information about this topic can be found at the newsgroup for discussions about running Apache under Windows at `comp.infosystems.www.servers.ms-windows`.

mod_python

`mod_python` is a module created by Gregory Trubetskoy that embeds the Python language interpreter within the Apache server, allowing Apache handlers to be written in Python. It provides nearly every possible handler to Apache.

`mod_python` brings a considerable boost in performance over the traditional CGI approach, and adds flexibility in designing Web-based applications. In order to run it, you must have at least `Python 1.5.2` and `Apache 1.3`.

`mod_python` handlers by default do not perform any function, unless specifically told so by a configuration directive. These directives begin with Python, end with Handler (for example, `PythonAuthenHandler`), and associate a handler with a Python function. Therefore, the main function of `mod_python` is to act as a dispatcher between Apache handlers and python functions written by developers.

The most commonly used one is `PythonHandler`. It is for a handler that has no specialized purpose, such as authentication. The default Apache action for this handler would be to read the file and send it to the client. Most applications you write will use this one handler. For more information, check out these sites:

mod_python Web site

`http://www.modpython.org/`

mod_python installation procedures

`http://www.modpython.org/live/mod_python-2.4/doc/installation.html`

`mod_pyapache`

This module will speed up the execution of your CGI scripts written in the Python Language. It handles CGI scripts faster than other normal CGI scripts because the server embeds the Python Interpreter. Therefore, the performance penalty of executing an external one is eliminated.

This module has the advantage of being CGI compatible—it works well when CGI scripts are simple and trusted and it provides total CGI control to your Python application. However, this module currently has some limitations, including the fact that it doesn't avoid database connections delay. Check out the following Web site for more information:

`http://www.msg.com.mx/pyapache/`

You will find the latest version of the module in the `ftp://www.bel-epa.com/pub/misc/` directory, where you will see a gzipped tar file named something like `PyApache-x.yy.tar.gz`.

AOLserver Web Server

This is a Web Server created and used by AOL. Note that anyone using AOLserver would be better off learning TCL. For details, see

`http://www.aolserver.com`

The project that embeds Python in the AOLServer Web Server, is now semi-stable for simple CGI-style operations, and provides a 4-5x speedup over the straight CGI.

Check it out at `http://pywx.sourceforge.net`.

Microsoft IIS and PWS

You can set up both Microsoft IIS Server and Personal Web Server (PWS) to call the Python interpreter to handle Python CGI scripts.

> **Tip**
> PWS is Microsoft's free basic Web server for the Windows 95 platform.

You need to pay close attention when using the PWS server because a version of PWS is part of the Front Page Personal Web Server, which doesn't run files from executable directories. Instead, it returns an error message. If you slide your mouse over the PWS icon in the taskbar, and it says `Personal Web Server`, you have the proper version.

Now, let's demonstrate how to configure IIS and PWS for Python/CGI scripting. I assume that you have already installed Python on your system.

On the Microsoft IIS server or on the Win95 MS Personal Web Server, you need to set up Python in the same way that you would set up any other scripting engine:

1. Run REGEDIT.EXE

2. Find the following key:

   ```
   HKEY_LOCAL_MACHINE\SYSTEM\CurrentControlSet\Services\W3SVC\Parameters\
   ScriptMap
   ```

3. Once there, select the menu selection EDIT, New, String Value, and enter the following line (using the correct path):

   ```
   .py :REG_SZ: c:\path\to\python.exe -u %s %s
   ```

Now, you are ready to call your scripts. Make sure that they are stored in an executable directory in the Web server.

The -u flag specifies unbuffered and binary mode for stdin, which is needed when working with binary data. This flag prevents cr-nl from being converted to newline combinations.

Most developers agree that exposing the language behind your script works similar to saying "Welcome" to crackers around the world. Therefore, it is suggested to hide these details by using another extension, for example, .cgi, for your CGI scripts. You don't need to change the extension of all your files, just the ones that will be exposed by your site's Web interface. The other modules can continue to have the .py extension. The line in the registry would resemble the following:

```
.cgi :REG_SZ: c:\path\to\python.exe -u %s %s
```

> **Note**
> Of course, this is no substitute for actually making sure that your scripts are secure.

After restarting your computer, everything gets set up, and every script (with the proper extension) located at an executable directory is sent to the Python interpreter.

Third-Party Internet Applications

Some completely developed Web applications, written in Python, are available for general use. You don't need to do any programming to use them. You just have to install, configure, and use them.

Grail Web Browser

Grail is a free Web browser written entirely in Python, using the Tkinter GUI (Tk, which is a free UI toolkit developed by John Ousterhout). Grail has the capability to manipulate SGML, HTML, URL's, images, and sound. Besides, it is easily extended to offer new functionality.

Being written in Python helps Grail to have a high adhesion to the Python language. Something similar happens to HotJava, which is a browser written entirely in Java.

For documentation and downloads, check out the following sites:

`http://grail.python.org` and `http://grail.cnri.reston.va.us/grail/`

Grail should run on any UNIX system to which Python and Tk have been ported— that is, almost all UNIX systems supporting X11. In particular, Grail is one of the few Web browsers that supports Solaris for Intel x86 processors. It now also runs on Windows and Macintosh because there are now stable ports of Tk to those platforms (you need a lot of RAM though). Grail supports the protocols and file formats commonly found on the World Wide Web, such as HTTP, FTP, and HTML. However, it is easily extended to support new protocols or file formats. Grail is distributed by CNRI in source form, free of charge (without warranties), and can be freely redistributed (within reason). Grail has not been worked on for a while, and doesn't support any of the latest standards you might expect in a browser.

Grail's design tries to provide a plug-in architecture, which allows the browser to easily support applets written in Python. Grail lets you download Python programs that execute inside Grail on your local machine. These little applications, which are called *applets* can do things such as display animations, interact with the user in new ways, even create additional menus that pop up dialogs if you like. Grail applets run in a restricted execution environment, so broken or malicious applets (*Trojan Horses*) can't erase your files or crash your computer.

Grail's Web site has an applet demo collection that you can explore.

Grail has many positive qualities, such as support to full HTML 2.0, including images, forms and image maps, as well as many HTML 3.2 features. It uses asynchronous document transfer and supports printing and saving documents, searching, bookmarks, history, and more. It also supports frames, file upload in forms, support for JPEG, TIFF, and XBM images, image printing, and tables (within the limitations of the Tk toolkit). It has preference panels, an I/O status display, a remote control interface, and many other nice features.

Apart from running applets, Grail is extensible in other areas, by writing so-called Grail plug-in modules. Grail plug-ins can be written for a number of new implementations, such as protocols (for example, CNRI's handle protocol), file formats (for example, for handling JPEG or sound directly), HTML tags (for example, tables), and preference panels. Check out the following site for more information:

Grail—The Browser For The Rest Of Us (DRAFT), by Guido van Rossum

`http://grail.cnri.reston.va.us/grail/info/papers/restofus.html`

Zope Web Application Server

The Z Object Publishing Environment, also known as Zope, is an open source object publishing system for the Web, developed by a company called Digital Creations. Zope is a complete dynamic Web site management Web platform used for building high-performance, dynamic Web sites. Essentially, it is a very complete framework for building Web applications, written in Python.

Check out the following sites for details:

`http://www.digicool.com` and `http://www.zope.org`

Zope is the leading Open Source Web-application server. Zope enables teams to collaborate in the creation and management of dynamic Web-based business applications such as intranets and portals. It also makes it easy to build features such as site search, news, personalization, and e-commerce into your Web applications.

Zope is a long running process, has a sophisticated authentication/authorization model, and has a useful SQL related product called *ZSQLMethod*, which provides an easy way to access a database from the Web application.

The following link is a technical introduction to object publishing with Zope. The document introduces Zope's object publishing facilities and shows you how to write and publish your own objects in Python. It has an excellent tutorial on integrating a Python module with the Zope ORB, Templates and Object Database.

`http://www.zope.org/Members/Amos/WhatIsObjectPublishing`

All requests made to the application server are mapped to Python objects. Therefore, whenever you make a call to a URL, as demonstrated in the following line of code

`http://host/path/to/object?name1=value1&name2=value2`

The server internally calls an object passing the pairs (name, value) as arguments.

Zope is not monolithic. Instead, it is composed of parts which can be deployed standalone with your own Python code support; for example, the Object Request Broker, HTML Templates (DTML) and the Object Database (ZOBD, Z Object Database, which stores Python objects) can all be abstracted from the mix.

Zope's templates are somehow similar to IIS ASP files. However, instead of being associated to Web pages, they are associated to Python objects.

You don't need to use Apache (PyApache/Httpdapy) in conjunction with Zope. In fact, Zope comes with a fast Web server of its own, which supports multiple protocols. On the other hand, it can also work with other Web servers as well. Most users do put Apache in front of Zope for reasons of flexibility. Because Zope is a long running process, they implement Persistent CGI, FastCGI, or ProxyPass.

If you need to find Web Hosting companies that support Zope, this might help: `http://www.zope.org/Resources/ZSP`.

Mailman—GNU Mailing List Manager

Mailman is a Web integrated mailing list manager that helps manage email discussion lists, much like Majordomo and Smartmail. Unlike most similar products, Mailman gives each mailing list a Web page, and allows users to subscribe, unsubscribe, and so on, over the Web. Even the list manager can administer his list entirely from the Web. Both users and system administrator can do almost everything through an Internet connection. Mailman also integrates most things people want to do with mailing lists, including archiving, mail-to-news gateways, and so on.

Mailing lists are great for meeting people and sharing common interests. Within Mailman, each mailing list has its own page that makes it much simpler to use. Each mailing list's Web page has an extensive Web-based user interface that is customizable on a per-list basis. This allows users to manage their own subscriptions, with support for temporarily disabling their accounts, selecting digest modes, hiding their email addresses from other members, and so on.

All Mailman actions—including subscription requests, list administration, and management reports—can be performed either through a Web interface or more traditional textual commands.

In order to use Mailman, you will need the following:

- A Web server that supports CGI scripts, such as Apache

- An SMTP daemon (also known as mail transfer agents, MTAs, or mail servers), such as Sendmail, Qmail, or Postfix

- Python 1.5 or newer

Mailman currently doesn't work on Windows. Instead, it runs on most UNIX-like systems. It is also compatible with most Web servers, browsers, and most SMTP servers. Actually, the only thing Mailman really requires of the mail server is the ability to setup aliases that execute commands.

Mailman is written primary in Python (in approximately 13,000 lines) with a few modules written in C (600 lines) for improved security (the C parts are the wrappers that handle securely changing to the correct permissions). Mailman exposes Python as an extension language that allows for customization of Mailman's interfaces.

In case you need to build Mailman from the source, it is necessary to have in hand: the GNU-make utility, an ANSI C Compiler, such as gcc, and Python 1.5 or higher.

Mailman is brought to you by the Mailman Cabal, which is currently composed of the following core developers: Barry Warsaw, Harald Meland, Ken Manheimer, Scott Cotton, and John Viega. Mailman was originally written by John Viega. Mailman is free software. It is distributed under the GNU General Public License.

The following lists some of the main features implemented by Mailman:

- Automatic Web-based, hypermail-style archiving, including provisions for private archives.

- Integrated gatewaying to and from Usenet.

- Smart bounce handling by using the Delivery Status Notification (DSN), which is described in RFC 1894. This feature enables automatic disposition (that is, configurable disabling, unsubscribing).

- Flexible and direct SMTP delivery of messages, including integrated fast bulk mailing.

- Smart spam protection.

- Multiple list owners and moderators are possible.

- Supports RFC934 and MIME digest delivery.

- Support for virtual domains.

- Mail-based administrative commands.

- A Web-based list administration interface for all administrative-type tasks, including list configuration, moderation (post approvals), selection of posting and subscribing rules, management of user accounts via the Web, and so on.

Among other responsibilities, Mailman keeps track of the mailing lists of all python.org activities, including the Python Special Interest Groups (Python SIGs).

As a practical matter, you'll need root access on your host to configure Mailman properly. Most open source products can be generated and initially tested by ordinary UNIX users. Some organizations have a policy that requires this. With Mailman, though, you'll at least need to create a new account and group (the default for both is "mailman") for Mailman's use.

Mailman, of course, powers the `Python-list`, which is a general discussion list for the Python programming language. You can see it working at

`http://www.python.org/mailman/listinfo/python-list`

Also check out the Mailman home page:

`http://www.gnu.org/software/mailman/mailman.html`

More information is also available at: `http://www.list.org`.

Christopher Kolar has made Mailman documentation available, primarily for list owners who aren't necessarily technical, but who own Mailman mailing lists. The GNU Mailman Documentation can be found at the following site:

`http://www.aurora.edu/~ckolar/mailman/`

Medusa Internet Server

Medusa is a Web server application that can be embeddable into a Python program, offering high-performance for HTTP, FTP, and other IP services. Medusa was written entirely in Python by Sam Rushing.

Medusa provides an Internet server framework for implementing asynchronous socket-based servers—TCP/IP, and on UNIX, UNIX domain sockets. The first release includes HTTP, FTP, and monitor servers. Medusa can simultaneously support several instances of either the same or different server types. For example, you could start up two HTTP servers, an FTP server, and a monitor server. Then you could connect to the monitor server to control and manipulate Medusa while it is running, entering and evaluating Python expressions (basically, a remote Python interpreter capability).

Out of the box, Medusa can run an unlimited number of HTTP and FTP servers within a single address space, without the use of threads. Capable of impressive hit rates, this server can solve your performance problems while handing you the most powerful server-side scripting language available.

Because Medusa is written entirely in Python, it is portable to any platform that implements the `socket` and `select` modules correctly. It has been tested on several UNIX platforms, Windows NT, and Windows 95.

Medusa is an elegant and efficient solution to a difficult programming problem. Medusa's core async-socket library is very stable because it has been in use virtually unchanged since 1995.

Medusa is an architecture for building long-running, very high-performance TCP/IP network servers (such as HTTP, FTP, and NNTP) in Python. Medusa is different from most other servers because it runs as a single process, multiplexing I/O with its various client and server connections within a single process/thread.

Medusa is in use now in several mission-critical applications, ranging from custom Web servers at extremely high-traffic sites to distributed data processing systems.

As Medusa is written in Python, it can be extended and modified at runtime, even by the end user. User scripts can be used to completely change the behavior of the server, and even add in completely new server types.

> **Note**
> According to `http://www.nightmare.com/medusa/license.html`, Medusa is now Free Software under the same license as Python, so you don't need a commercial use license.

For more details, check out the following site:

`http://www.nightmare.com/medusa/`

Other Applications

These other applications and scripts are utilities that might help you along your future development efforts.

BSCW

The BSCW group at GMD in Germany has implemented a shared workspace server for the Web as a collection of Python CGI scripts.

BSCW (Basic Support for Cooperative Work) is a "shared workspace" system, which enables collaboration over the Web and supports document upload, event notification, group management, and much more. To access a workspace, you only need a standard Web browser.

This group maintains a public BSCW server with which everyone is invited to use for creating their own shared workspaces. You only need an ordinary Web browser for registering with the public server and for accessing the server once you have created your login. If you want to upload documents, you might need an additional helper application. If you use their recommended Web browser (Netscape), this is not required.

For details, check out `http://bscw.gmd.de/` and `http://orgwis.gmd.de/`.

LDAP

The *Lightweight Directory Access Protocol (LDAP)* is a directory access protocol that runs directly over TCP/IP. It is documented in RFCs 1777 and 1778, and is a draft Internet standard. LDAP can be used to implement a native standalone LDAP directory service, or it can be used to access an X.500-based directory service.

Directory services such as LDAP are suitable for holding a lot of organizational information in a standardized database scheme. LDAP is a useful tool for providing centralized address books for the users of an organization—common mail client software such as Netscape Messenger or Outlook already uses directory services for retrieving personal data.

In some situations, there is a strong need for flexible LDAP client software that provides features such as the following:

- Add/modify LDAP entries

- Access to the directory without having LDAP capable client software (for example, via WWW)

- A secure LDAP client with clean login behavior

- Hiding the LDAP service behind a firewall

- Encryption for LDAP access over unsecured networks

In order to handle these issues, Michael Ströder developed web2ldap.py (formerly known as ldap-client-cgi.py), which is a full-featured, Web-based LDAP client written in Python. For more information, check out

`http://www.web2ldap.de`

There isn't any standard LDAP support module in Python at this time, but there is Python-LDAP. This project provides an LDAP client API for Python in the spirit of RFC1823. For more information, check out the following:

`http://python-ldap.sourceforge.net/`

This LDAP module provides access to the University of Michigan's Lightweight Directory Access Protocol library. It is more-or-less compliant with the interface described in RFC 1823, with the notable differences being that lists are manipulated via Python list operations, and errors appear as exceptions. It also works with OpenLDAP (http://www.openldap.org), which is a bit newer.

WebLog

WebLog is a group of Python modules containing several class definitions that are useful for parsing, manipulating, and postprocessing of common Web and Web proxy logfile formats.

The modules can be broken up into two types: parsing and postprocessing. The classes inside these modules are used by following the idea of first using a *parsing class* and then stacking *postprocessing classes* on top of it. These modules are reasonably fast, considering that they are written in a scripting language—especially the parsing modules, which are very well optimized.

Parsing Modules

The following modules contain class definitions that can help you to implement parsing routines.

common—Common (NCSA) Web log parser.

combined—Combined/extended Web log parser (adds referrer and agent).

squid—Squid Web Proxy Cache log parsers. This module contains two classes: AccessParser (for access.log), and StoreParser (for store.log). If you have full_mime_hdrs set in squid.conf, make sure to set the corresponding attribute in AccessParser. However, use of this will appreciably slow down analysis.

multiple—Combines log files of the same content from different servers.

Postprocessing Modules

The following modules contain class definitions that can help you to implement postprocessing routines.

url—Parses url and referer (if available) for components.

query—Parses queries into dictionaries.[1]

clean—Normalizes attributes of Web Log for more accurate analysis.[1]

resolve—Resolves client address to host and/or IP.

referer—Determines type of hit: local, offsite, manual, or file.[1]

limit—Limit output to certain domains, files, directories or times.[1]

---

[1]*Requires use of* url.Parse *first.*

For more details about WebLog, check out its Web site:

```
http://www.mnot.net/scripting/python/WebLog/
```

Site Management Tools

The following Python tools are used to manage Web sites. They implement several functions that simplify the daily tasks performed by webmasters, such as dead link checking, and object publishing.

WebDAV/PyDAV

WebDAV (World Wide Web Distributed Authoring and Versioning) is a set of extensions to the HTTP/1.1 protocol, which allows users to collaboratively edit, manage, and update files safely on remote Web servers. It was developed by the WebDAV working group of the Internet Engineering Task Force (IETF).

WebDAV provides a standard infrastructure for asynchronous collaborative authoring across the Internet in order to turn the Web into a collaborative environment.

WebDAV has the following core features: Metadata management, Name space management, Collections, Overwrite prevention, Version management, Access Control, and Locking (concurrency control).

For more information about WebDAV, check out its Web site at

```
http://www.webdav.org
```

PyDAV is a WebDAV (also known as DAV) server implemented in Python. Check out its Web site at the following address:

```
http://sandbox.xerox.com/webdav/
```

Zebra

Zebra is an XML-based preprocessing language that offers a compact syntax for expressing common Web design patterns. Similar to Zope, Zebra is a templating system that is able to preprocess Python code. Therefore, developers don't need to stick to the details of the language before starting a nice design. For more information, check out the following site:

```
http://zebra.sourceforge.net/
```

`httpd_log`

The HTTPD logfile reporting tool (`httpd_log`) is a graphical Web statistics tool that analyzes HTTP log files and generates a page of summary information, complete with statistical graphs. Richard Jones developed this tool.

You'd better check out the new release 4.0b1 because it uses the more accurate `PIL` module, instead of using the old `GD` graphic module. Although the release 3.0 is very stable, the graphing provided by the new release is more accurate.

Keep in mind that you need to install the PIL module (`PILGraph-0.1a7.tar.gz`) in order to use the release 4.0b1. For more information, check out

`http://starship.python.net/crew/richard/httpd_log/`

Linbot

Linbot is a site management tool that analyzes a site and allows the user to view a site map, check for broken internal and external links, missing images, and list other problems that were found. It downloads each page from the Web site, and parses its contents in order to collect all the site's information. Linbot is extensible, so new tests can be added by writing some Python code.

Some of the things that Webmasters can do periodically and without user intervention when using Linbot are listed as follows:

- View the structure of a Web site
- Track down broken links in Web pages
- Find potentially outdated Web pages
- List links pointing to external sites
- View portfolio of inline images
- Get a run down of problems sorted by author
- Locate pages that might be slow to download:

  `http://starship.python.net/crew/marduk/linbot/`

Python-Friendly Internet Solution Providers (ISPs)

The Web site "Python-friendly ISPs" lists Web site providers that support the execution of CGI scripts written in Python. These lists are separated into some specific categories:

- Python Installed System-Wide
- User May Install Python in Own Directories
- Providers with No Python Installed
- Other Providers (Python Support Unknown)

The address is `http://www.corrt.com/info/pyisp-list.html`

mxCGIPython

Instead of looking for an ISP that supports Python, you might be interested in the `mxCGIPython` tool, which helps you install Python on your ISP when your ISP either *won't* or *can't*. Marc-Andre Lemburg has put together a small Zip file, which contains all necessary `setup` and `config` files. For more information, check out the following:

`http://starship.python.net/~lemburg/mxCGIPython.html`

HTMLgen

If you need a module to help you generate HTML, you should check out `HTMLgen`, written by Robin Friedrich. It's a class library of objects corresponding to all the HTML 3.2 markup tags. It's used when you are writing in Python and want to synthesize HTML pages for generating a Web, for CGI forms, and so on. The following lines are some examples of using `HTMLgen`:

```
>>> print H(1, "Welcome to Python World")
<H1>Welcome to Python World</H1>
>>> print A("http://www.python.org/", "Python Web site")
<A HREF="http://www.python.org/">Python Web site</A>
```

HTMLgen is available for download at:

`http://starship.python.net/crew/friedrich/HTMLgen/html/main.html`

Document Template

When talking about generating HTML code, it might also be useful to consider `DocumentTemplate`, which offers clear separation between Python code and HTML code. `DocumentTemplate` is part of the Zope objects publishing system, but it can also be used independently. For more information, check out the following:

```
http:/www.digicool.com/
```

Persistent CGI

Persistent CGI architecture provides a reasonably high-performance, transparent method of publishing objects as long running processes via the World Wide Web (WWW). The current alternatives to CGI that allow the publishing of long-running processes, such as FastCGI and ILU, have some level of Web server and platform dependencies. Persistent CGI allows a long running process to be published via the WWW on any server that supports CGI, and requires no specific support in the published application.

> **Note**
> The latest version of Persistent CGI is bundled with the Zope software:
>
> ```
> http:/www.digicool.com/
> ```

Webchecker

Webchecker is not a CGI application but a Web client application. The `webchecker.py` script is located under the `tools/webchecker/` directory of your Python distribution. This tool enables you to check the validity of a site. In other words, given a Web page, it searches for bad links in it, and keeps a record of the links to other sites that exist in the page.

It requests all pages from the Web site via HTTP. After it loads a page, it parses the HTML code and collects the links. Pages are never requested more than once. The links found outside the original tree are treated as leaves, hence, they are checked, but their links won't be followed. Anyway, this script generates a report that contains all bad links and says which page(s) the links are referenced.

The `Linbot` system, as you will see later in this chapter, has a similar functionality, but its checks are more extensive than Web Checker's.

Check out thewebsucker module, which is also part of the `tools/webchecker` directory of the source. It mirrors a remote `url` locally.

LinkChecker

`Pylice`, a link checker written in Python, was renamed to `LinkChecker`. With `LinkChecker` you can check your HTML documents for broken links. The homepage for `LinkChecker` moved to the following:

`http://linkchecker.sourceforge.net`

You can find more information at

`http://fsinfo.cs.uni-sb.de/~calvin/software/`

FastCGI

FastCGI is a fast, open, and secure Web server interface that solves the performance problems inherent in CGI, without introducing the overhead and complexity of proprietary *APIs (Application Programming Interfaces)*.

The FastCGI application library that implements the FastCGI protocol (hiding the protocol details from the developer) is based on code from Open Market, and is in the public domain while being fully supported by Fast Engines. This library makes implementing FastCGI programs as easy as writing CGI applications.

The FastCGI interface combines the best aspects of CGI and vendor APIs. Like CGI, FastCGI applications run in separate, isolated processes. The main advantages of using FastCGI are

- Performance—FastCGI processes are persistent and do not create a new process for each request.

- Simplicity—It is easily migrated from CGI.

- Language independence—Like CGI, FastCGI applications can be written in any language.

- Process isolation—A buggy FastCGI application cannot crash or corrupt the core server or other applications.

- Non-proprietary—FastCGI was originally implemented in the Open Market Web server.

- Architecture independence—The FastCGI interface isn't tied to any particular server architecture.

- Support for distributed computing—FastCGI provides the ability to run applications remotely.

For details about the library, check out FASTCGI's official Web site at `http://www.fastcgi.org/`.

The following link forwards you to a white paper that explains the minor details of FASTCGI:

`http://www.fastcgi.org/whitepapers/fcgi-whitepaper.shtml`

The best place to go for Python FastCGI support is at
`http://www.digicool.com/releases/fcgi/`.

There is also an all Python (no extension module required) implementation of the
FastCGI application interface located at `http://starship.python.net/crew/robind/`.

Summary

This chapter exposes the reality between Python and the Internet by introducing some
complete Web applications that have emerged from the Python community.

Python's support to HTTP, which is the basic communication protocol underlying the
Web, allows it to implement HTTP servers (Web servers) and clients (Web browsers).
This chapter shows simple details about the configuration of Apache and Microsoft IIS
Server/Personal Web Server (PWS). Another Web server called AOLServer is also
introduced to you.

If you have Apache and you decide not to go through any CGI implementation, you
should consider embedding Python in this Web server.

`mod_python` is a module that embeds the Python language interpreter within the
Apache server, allowing Apache handlers to be written in Python. It brings a considerable boost in performance over the traditional CGI approach.

`mod_pyapache` is another module that embeds Python within the Apache server. This
module also handles CGI scripts faster than other normal CGI scripts.

Besides Web Servers and Web Clients, Python has some completely developed Web
applications, written in Python itself, which are available for general use.

Grail is a free Web browser written entirely in Python, using the Tkinter GUI. Grail
has the capability to manipulate SGML, HTML, URL's, images, and sound. Besides, it
is easily extended to offer new functionality. Grail's design tries to provide a plug-in
architecture, which allows the browser to easily support applets written in Python.
Apart from running applets, Grail is extensible in other areas by writing so-called
Grail plug-in modules.

The Z Object Publishing Environment (Zope) is an open source object publishing
system for the Web. Zope is a complete dynamic Website management Web platform
used for building high-performance, dynamic Web sites. It is composed of parts that
can be deployed standalone with your own Python code support: The Object Request
Broker, HTML Templates (DTML), and the Object Database (ZODB, or Z Object
Database, which stores Python objects) can all be abstracted from the mix.

Mailman is a Web integrated mailing list manager that helps managing email discussion lists. Unlike most similar products, Mailman gives each mailing list a Web page, and allows users to subscribe, unsubscribe, and so on, over the Web. All Mailman actions, including subscription requests, list administration, and management reports, can be performed either through a Web interface or more traditional textual commands.

Medusa is a Web server application that can be embedded into a Python program, offering high-performance for HTTP, FTP, and other IP services. Medusa was entirely written in Python too.

The following applications and scripts are utilities that might help you with future development efforts with Python.

BSCW is a shared Workspace Server for the Web, which is implemented as a collection of Python CGI scripts.

The web2ldap.py script (formerly known as ldap-client-cgi.py) is a full-featured, Web-based LDAP client written in Python.

WebLog is a group of Python modules containing several class definitions useful for parsing, manipulating, and postprocessing of common Web and Web proxy logfile formats.

The following Python tools are used to manage Web sites. They implement several functions that simplify the daily tasks performed by Webmasters, such as dead link checking, and object publishing.

WebDAV (World Wide Web Distributed Authoring and Versioning) is a set of extensions to the HTTP/1.1 protocol, which allows users to collaboratively edit, manage, and update files safely on remote Web servers.

Zebra is an XML-based preprocessing language that offers a compact syntax for expressing common Web design patterns. As Zope, Zebra is a templating system that is able to preprocess Python code.

The HTTPD logfile reporting tool (httpd_log) is a graphical Web statistics tool that analyzes HTTP log files and generates a page of summary information.

Linbot is a site management tool that analyzes a site and allows the user to view a site map, check for broken internal and external links, missing images, and list other problems that were found.

The Web site "Python-friendly ISPs" lists Web site providers that support the execution of CGI scripts written in Python. Another option that you have is to install Python on your ISP using the mxCGIPython tool.

HTMLgen is a module that helps you generate HTML. It contains a class library of objects corresponding to all the HTML 3.2 markup tags. When talking about generating HTML code, it might also be useful to consider DocumentTemplate, which offers clear separation between Python code and HTML code.

Webchecker is not a CGI application but a Web client application that enables you to check the validity of a site. LinkChecker is another tool that also allows you to check your HTML documents for broken links.

Persistent CGI architecture provides a reasonably high-performance, transparent method of publishing objects as long running processes via the World Wide Web.

FastCGI is a fast, open, and secure Web Server interface that solves the performance problems inherent in CGI, without introducing the overhead and complexity of proprietary APIs.

CHAPTER 12
Scripting Programming

strewth!

This chapter provides information about how to use Python as a CGI scripting language. You will learn how to put Python to work in your Web pages as a server-side component.

Web Programming

Python has a very extensive, well documented and portable module library that provides a large variety of useful modules. The Internet-related collection is particularly impressive, with modules that deal with everything from parsing and retrieving URLs to retrieving mail from POP servers, including CGI scripting.

Python is suitable for CGI programming on Windows, Mac, and UNIX platforms, allowing the creation of programs that provide services over the Internet. Its capability to create dynamic content makes the task of generating Web pages on-the-fly a very easy thing to do.

However, before starting to implement your Web pages using CGI scripts, you need to think about whether it is really necessary to build dynamic pages for your site. Keep in mind that if the information is not modified very often, static pages are the best solution because dynamic pages always slow down the server. You can decide whether to use it, but if you conclude that it would work for you, this chapter might help you a lot.

> **Note**
> It's also good to mention that if you need a way to periodically build auto-generated pages, you can implement solutions based on the use of cron on UNIX-like systems. For the Windows NT, you have both the at command, and the scheduled tasks extensions found in the newer copies of the Internet Explorer.

If your site becomes busy enough that the cost of starting a Python interpreter for each CGI request becomes significant, you can use Web Server modules (such as mod_python) to embed the Python interpreter in the server, hence, avoiding the startup time. Zope provides yet another way to have Python scripts without the interpreter startup time to worry about. Python code can also be invoked on top of Active Server Pages (ASP) under IIS.

An Introduction to CGI

CGI (Common Gateway Interface) is a standardized way for the Web Server to invoke an external program to handle the client request. It is possible for the external program to access databases, documents, and other programs as part of the request, as well, and present customized data to viewers via the Web. A CGI script can be written in any language, but here, of course, we are using only Python.

CGI enables you to handle from the low end of mail-forms and counter programs to the most complex database scripts that generate entire Web sites on-the-fly. CGI's job is to manage the communication between browsers and server-side scripts. Programs that implement CGI routines are called CGI programs or CGI scripts. These scripts are usually visualized, through the Web browser, in a directory called /cgi-bin, but their actual location in the file system varies.

You have two ways to pass the information from the browser to the CGI script: You can use either the POST or the GET method on your HTML Form. The POST method uses the *standard input* to transfer the information, whereas the GET method places the information into an environment variable.

The GET method has the limitation of the size of the environment variable and the advantage of making it possible to encapsulate an HTML Form within an URL. Another downside to the GET method is that it might leak information. If there is an external image (for instance, a banner ad) or an off site link the user clicks on the page generated by the CGI script, the form results will be passed to that third party through the referer header. Therefore, don't use banner ads or off-site links for the CGI script handling a GET form.

The POST method, in theory, has no limits to the amount of information that can be passed to the server. The disadvantage is that you can't send the information as part of the URL. You must have a form in your page.

Python uses the cgi module to implement CGI scripts and to process form handling in Web applications that are invoked by an HTTP server. The cgi module also hides the differences between GET and POST style forms.

Here is a very simple script to start you out with Python CGI processing:

```
1: #!/usr/bin/python
2: print "Content-Type: text/plain\n\n"
3: print "Hello Python World!"
```

Line 1: Path to the Python interpreter (UNIX only).

Line 2: Pass the MIME type to the browser in order to let it know how to render the information.

Line 3: Prints a string in the browser window.

In order to execute it, place it on a executable directory on your Web server and call it from your Web browser. If you are working on a UNIX-like OS, you need to run chmod a+x scriptname.

Sometimes, CGI implementations also cause slow response times in the system. Keep in mind that each CGI invocation creates a new process, starts a new instance of the Python interpreter, and imports all the necessary library modules. Okay, I suppose you got the picture.

The goal here is to let you know that sometimes the problem is not in the code, but in the infrastructure that surrounds it. Within your CGI script, you should consider avoiding using fork() as much as you can. But fork() is not the slow(est) part—it is the interpreter startup time and database connection setup. To get help with that, try using mod_pyapache or mod_python.

The following links take you to sites that demonstrate and clarify the use of CGI routines:

Python's Web Programming Topic Guide

`http://www.python.org/topics/web/`

vex.net's directory of Python Web page samples

`http://www.vex.net/py_examples/`

Aaron Watters's simple CGI examples

`http://starship.python.net/crew/aaron_watters/cgi/`

Fancy CGI Programming

`http://www.python.org/topics/web/fancy-cgi.html`

Python-CGI FAQ

`http://starship.python.net/crew/davem/cgifaq/`

The `cgi` Module

The `cgi` module accepts `sys.stdin` and environment variables set by the server as input sources. The output is sent directly to `sys.stdout`, carrying an HTTP header and the data itself.

A very simple header example would be

```
print "Content-type: text/html"
print
```

Note that it is necessary to have a new line at the end of the header information. In most cases, the previous line is all you will use in your scripts.

The `FieldStorage` class, which is implemented by this module, is able to read both the standard input (for POST calls) and the query string (for GET calls). In order to parse the contents of an HTML Form, you need to create an instance of this class.

This instance carries the following attributes:

- `fs.name`—This is the field's name.
- `fs.value`—This is the field's value.
- `fs.filename`—This client-side filename is used in uploads.

- fs.file—This is a file-like object from which data can be read.

- fs.type—This is the content type.

- fs.type_options—This dictionary of options is specified on the content-type line of the HTTP request.

- fs.disposition—This is the "content-disposition" field, None if not specified.

- fs.disposition_option—This is the dictionary of disposition options.

- fs.headers—This is a dictionary-like object containing all HTTP headers contents.

Each individual form field is defined as an instance of the MiniFieldStorage class, whereas on the contrary, multipart data (such as uploaded files) is defined as an instance of the FieldStorage class itself. Each instance is accessed as a dictionary whose keys are the Form's field names, and the values are their contents. These dictionaries also implement methods such as .keys() and .has_key(). If a specific form field has multiple values (for example, a selection list), a list of multiple MiniFieldStorage instances is generated and assigned to the appropriate key value in the dictionary. The use of MiniFieldStorage is pretty much transparent when using CGI, thus, you don't have to worry about these implementation details.

Note that uploaded files are read directly to the memory by accessing the value attribute of the class instance.

Also note that Python 2.0 provides a new method called getvalue() to the objects of the FieldStorage class, that implements the same functionality of a dictionary's get() method by returning the value attribute of the given object.

Functions

The following list shows some general functions exposed by the cgi module.

cgi.escape(string [,quote])—Translates "<", "&", ">" to "<", "&", ">". If you want to convert the double-quote character, you must set the quote flag to true.

cgi.parse_qs(string, keep_blank_values=0)—Parses a query string such as "country=USA&state=PA" to a dictionary-like format, for example, {"country": ["USA"], "state": ["PA"],...}

cgi.parse([file], ...)—Parses query strings from default file locations (such as, multiple file objects) from which data can be read, and generates a dictionary. The default behavior is to map the input to stdin.

For CGI debugging, the following functions are available:

`cgi.print_environ()`—Formats the shell environment in HTML.

`cgi.print_environ_usage()`—Prints a list of environment variables, used by CGI, in HTML.

`cgi.print_form(form)`—Formats a form in HTML.

`cgi.print_directory()`—Formats the current directory in HTML.

`cgi.test()`—Tests CGI script. It writes minimal HTTP headers and formats all information provided to the script in HTML form.

The following functions are not part of the CGI module, but they are very useful for CGI processing too.

`urllib.quote(string)`, `urllib.unquote(string)`—These functions do and undo convertions between literals (that are used in CGI applications) and their special translation codes, which are required when transporting the literals to URL format (for example, " " becomes "`%20`").

`urllib.urlencode(dictionary)`—Converts a dictionary `{"country":"USA",` `"state":"PA",...}` to query string format (for example, `"country=USA&state=PA"`). Note that this function has the opposite functionality of the `cgi.parse_qs()` function.

Creating, Installing, and Running Your Script

You are free to edit your Python scripts using your favorite text editor (such as, Notepad, IDLE, Editpad, pico, PythonWwin, vi, and so on). Of course, we can't forget about Emacs, which has one of the best Python editing modes available.

Remember to upload your scripts as text files to your Web server. In order to execute them, you need to make sure that they are in a "executable" directory, and that they have the right permissions.

As I said before, most often CGI scripts live in the server's special `cgi-bin` directory. You should consider verifying whether the files, that your script needs to read or write, are actually readable or writable, respectively, by other users. In UNIX, the command to set the permissions is `chmod`.

Creating, Installing, and Running Your Script

For example,

```
chmod 755 filename
```

The mode argument 755 defines that the file's owner can read, write, and execute the file, whereas the other users can only read and execute it.

The common UNIX mode values and their respective symbolic arguments are

- `chmod 755` for executable scripts, or `chmod a+rx`.
- `chmod 666` for writable files, or `chmod a+w`.
- `chmod 644` for readable files, or `chmod a+r`.

> **Tip**
> Keep in mind that commands and filenames are all case sensitive if the Web Server
> is on an OS with case-sensitive filenames.

For security reasons, the HTTP server executes your script as user "nobody", without any special privileges. Therefore, it can only read (write, execute) files that everybody can read (write, execute).

The current directory at execution time is usually the server's /cgi-bin directory, and the set of environment variables is different from what you get at login. In other words, don't count on the shell's search path variable for executables ($PATH) or the Python module search path variable ($PYTHONPATH) to be set to anything useful.

If you need to load modules from a directory that is not listed as part of the Python's default module search path, you can change the path variable in your script before trying to import them. In the following example, we add three more directory entries in the search path. Note that the last directory inserted, "/usr/python/testdict", is searched first.

```
import sys
sys.path.insert(0, "/usr/python/lib")
sys.path.insert(0, "/usr/tmp")
sys.path.insert(0, "/usr/python/testdict")
```

Instead of using "from cgi import *", you should use only "import cgi" because the cgi module defines many other names for backward compatibility that can interfere with your code.

It also might be useful for you to redirect the standard error (sys.stderr) to the standard output (sys.stdout). This will display all the error messages in the browser.

Sending Information to Python Scripts

Every time you use a URL to carry information to a CGI script, the data is transported as *name/value* pairs, separated by ampersands (&), and each pair is separated by an equal sign (=). Whitespaces between words are usually converted to the plus symbol (+).

For example,

```
http://www.lessaworld.com/cgi-script/app.py?animal=Parrot&type=Singer
```

Special characters are encoded to hexadecimal format (%HH) and preceded by the percent sign. Therefore, the string `"Parrot sketch"` is passed to the script as `"Parrot%20sketch"`.

As you can see, the previous example is implicitly using the GET method to pass the values to the CGI script. If you decide that the POST method is more suitable for your needs, you will need to use the urllib module in order to send the information. The following example demonstrates its use.

```
import urllib
request = urllib.urlencode({
    "animal": "Parrot", "type": "Singer"
})
page = urllib.urlopen("http://oemcomputer/cgi-script/app.py", request)
response = page.read()
```

Check the urllib documentation for details:

```
http://www.python.org/doc/current/lib/module-urllib.html
```

Table 12.1 contains a list of special characters and their encoded strings.

Table 12.1   *Encoded Strings Used to Represent Special Characters When Dealing with URLs*

Character	Encoded String
/	%2F
~	%7E
:	%3A
;	%3B
@	%40
&	%26

Table 12.1   *(continued)*

Character	Encoded String
space	%20
return	%0A
tab	%09

Working with Form Fields and Parsing the Information

The first thing that most beginners in the Web development area want to know is how to get information out of HTML forms and do something with it.

The following HTML code results in a Web page (see Figure 12.1) that queries the user about his login information. Note that we use the POST method in the form. Thus, the field values will not be displayed as part of the URL.

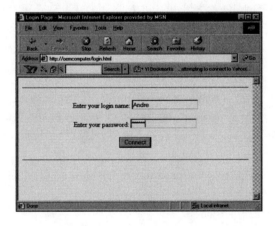

Figure 12.1
Login Form that calls a CGI script.

```
<HTML>
<HEAD><TITLE>Login Page</TITLE></HEAD>
<BODY>

<HR>
<CENTER>
<FORM method="POST" action="http://oemcomputer/cgi-bin/login.py">
<p> Enter your login name: <input type="text" name="login">
<p> Enter your password: <input type=password name="password">
```

```
<p> <input type="submit" value="Connect">
</FORM>
</CENTER>
<HR>

</form>
</BODY>
</HTML>
```

Also, pay attention to the way data fields are referenced in HTML forms. Each input element carries a `name` attribute that uniquely identifies the element within a form. For instance, the tag `<input type="text" name="login">` defines a data field called `"login"` that implements a text box.

Every CGI script must send a header (the `Content-type` tag) describing the contents of the document. The common values for this tag are `text/html`, `text/plain`, `image/gif`, and `image/jpeg`. A blank line is used to indicate the end of this header.

> **Tip**
> The `Content-type` tag is used by the client browser and does not appear in the generated page.

As you can see, a script is really executed, and not just displayed in the browser. Everything printed to `sys.stdout` by the script is sent to the client browser, whereas error messages go to an error log (`/usr/local/etc/httpd/logs/error_log in` Apache).

The following script is the CGI program called by the HTML form from the previous code.

```
 1: #!/usr/local/bin/python
 2: import cgi
 3:
 4: def header(title):
 5:     print "Content-type: text/html\n"
 6:     print "<HTML>\n<HEAD>\n<TITLE>%s</TITLE>\n</HEAD>\n<BODY>\n" \
 7:         % (title)
 8:
 9: def footer():
10:     print "</BODY></HTML>"
11:
```

```
12: form = cgi.FieldStorage()
13: password = "python"
14:
15: if not form:
16:     header("Login Response")
17: elif form.has_key("login") and form["login"].value != "" and \
18:      form.has_key("password") and form["password"].value == password:
19:     header("Connected ...")
20:     print "<center><hr><H3>Welcome back," , form["login"].value, \
21:         ".</H3><hr></center>"
22:     print r"""<form><input type="hidden" name="session" value="%s">
23:         </form>""" % (form["login"].value)
24:     print "<H3><a href=browse.html>Click here to start \
25:         browsing</a></H3>"
26: else:
27:     header("No success!")
28:     print "<H3>Please go back and enter a valid login.</H3>"
29:
30: footer()
```

This example first verifies if the form is a valid form (line 15). If it isn't, a blank screen is displayed. If the fields have a valid format, the form performs an action and processes the results (lines 17–25). The last case is when the validation rule is not followed, and an error message must be displayed. A full implementation should repeat the form, and point out the error to the user.

Next, we have a simple check list to use while developing CGI scripts. It shows the basic structure of CGI script creation.

1. Use `cgi.FieldStorage()` to parse the query.

2. Check the HTML form fields.

3. Take care of decoding, handling both GET and POST methods.

4. Perform the actions that are particular to your application.

5. Generate the proper HTTP/HTML data for output. The simplest way to write to the output is using `print` statements. Note that template solutions are also available, and for high-volume sites, it's almost a necessary implementation.

The following example is a small variation of the previous script. This one lists the values of all form fields.

```python
#!/usr/local/bin/python
import cgi

def header(title):
    print "Content-type: text/html\n"
    print "<HTML>\n<HEAD>\n<TITLE>%s</TITLE>\n</HEAD>\n<BODY>\n" % (title)

def footer():
    print "</BODY></HTML>"

form = cgi.FieldStorage()
formkeys = form.keys()
formkeys.sort()
header("Show form fields")

print '<UL>'
for k in formkeys:
    print '<LI>' + k + ':' + form[k].value + '</LI>'
print '</UL>'

footer()
```

The next example demonstrates that if you try to access a field that doesn't exist (line 15), an exception is generated. If you don't catch the exception with a `try`/`except` statement, this will stop your script, and the user will see a message like `"Internal Server Error"`. Also, note that the cgi dictionary of attribute/value pairs does not support the `values()` method (line 14).

```python
 1: #!/usr/local/bin/python
 2: import cgi
 3:
 4: def header(title):
 5:     print "Content-type: text/html\n"
 6:     print "<HTML>\n<HEAD>\n<TITLE>%s</TITLE>\n</HEAD>\n<BODY>\n" /
 7:     % (title)
 8:
 9: def footer():
10:     print "</BODY></HTML>"
11:
12: form = cgi.FieldStorage()
```

```
13: print form.keys()          # ['password', 'login']
14: # print form.values()      # Causes an error
15: # print form["hostname"].value   # Causes an error
16:
17: footer()
```

Security

You have to watch out when passing fields to the shell. Never pass any string received from the client directly to a shell command. Take a look at the following statement:

```
os.popen("dir %s" % form["filename"].value)
```

Now, imagine if the user types something like `*.* | del *.exe`.

In order to solve problems like this, you have a few different kinds of approaches. We will look some of them. First, you can choose to quote the variable:

```
filename = pipes.quote(form["filename"].value)
```

A second solution is to get rid of every character that is not part of the acceptable domain of values.

```
filename = re.sub(r"\W", "", form["filename"].value)
```

> **Note**
> You should test for acceptable input, rather than for unacceptable input. You don't want to get caught by surprise when someone thinks of some input string you didn't think of, or exploits a bug you don't know about.

The third, and most radical, solution is to test the form, and return an error message in case a valid condition is not established. For example,

```
if not re.match(r"^\w+$", filename):
    raise "Invalid file name."
```

If you invoke an external program (for example, via the `os.system()` or `os.popen()` functions), make very sure that you don't pass arbitrary strings received from the client to the shell. It is a bad idea to use form data provided by random people on the Web without validating it; especially if you're going to use that data to execute a system command or for acting on a database. Naively written CGI scripts, in any language, are favorite targets for malicious system crackers. This is a well-known security hole whereby clever hackers anywhere on the Web can exploit a naive CGI script to invoke arbitrary shell commands. Even parts of the URL or field names cannot be trusted because the request doesn't have to come from your form.

To be on the safe side, if you must pass a string that you have gotten from a form to a shell command, you should make sure that the string contains only alphanumeric characters, dashes, underscores, and periods.

Sessions

If you need to correlate requests from the same user, you must generate and assign a session key on the first contact of the user, and incorporate this session key in the next forms, or in the URLs.

If you implement the first solution, you need to use a hidden input field.

```
<input type="hidden" name="session" value="74ght2o5">
```

If you decide that the second option will work better for you, you need to add the information after the script's name (separating with a slash).

```
http://lessaworld.com/cgi-bin/dosomething.py/74ght2o5
```

The information is passed to the CGI script through the environment variables, as you can see next.

```
os.environment["PATH_INFO"] = "74ght2o5"
os.environment["PATH_TRANSLATED"] = "<rootdir>/74ght2o5"
```

Data Storage

The information manipulated by CGI scripts can come from any kind of data storage structure. The important thing to keep in mind is that your data must be capable of being managed and updated.

You have a number of options to use here. Plain files are the simplest way. Shelves can be used too—they are used to store whole Python objects, which avoids the parsing/unparsing of values. If you decide to go through dbm (or gdbm) files, you will find better performance as they use strings for key/value manipulations. If you really want to think about scalability or speed, you should consider choosing a real database. You can use the information that is provided in Chapter 8, "Working with Databases," to help you define which database would be the best solution for your case.

If you don't have a real database in hands, don't worry. A number of sites only use plain file databases, and they don't have anything to complain about.

Locking

Whenever you are not working with real solution database systems, locking problems can drive you nuts because you have to worry about every single detail. For example, shelves and dbm (or gdbm) database files have no protection against concurrent updates.

In order to implement a good and efficient locking solution in Python, the best approach is to write a routine that locks only when writing to the file. Python handles multiple readers well, and when it comes to a single writer, Python can support it too.

In order to study a complex implementation of a locking algorithm, you should consider seeing the Mailman source-code (precisely, the LockFile.py file). Although this routine does not run on Windows systems, it works well on UNIX machines, and besides, it supports NFS.

We all know how hard it is to implement a good locking solution. Occasionally your process dies, and you lose the pointer to the locked file; other times you see your program hanging because the process took longer than expected.

Cookies

A *cookie* is a piece of data that the Web Server asks the client to store on their system, which gets sent back to the server on subsequent visits. One use of cookies is to store customized information that belongs to the user who owns the browser.

Each time you visit a Web site that uses cookies, the server application is able to check for cookies in the client site by inspecting the HTTP header. If cookies are available, the client sends back all appropriate cookies for every request to the server.

The CGI script can update cookies at any time necessary, just before sending a Web page to the client browser. The format used to move cookies back and forth is the same one used for GET and POST requests.

In order to correlate sessions from the same user, you can also put cookies in the user's browser. This is very controversial, but useful. Keep in mind that many people turn off the use of cookies in their browsers. Thus, you cannot count on them in your applications. You should always have a solution ready in case the user's browser doesn't accept cookies.

> **Caution**
> If you have something to hide, it becomes very important to store the information in the cookies in a security format. You cannot let the user go to the cookies.txt file, which stores all the cookies information in the client machine, and change anything. In order to prevent that, you should consider storing the cookies using an encryption algorithm. Another important warning is that you shouldn't blindly trust the value of the cookie, the same as you shouldn't trust form variables.

In order to handle cookies in Python, Tim O'Malley has created a module called `Cookie.py` that is able to write `Set-Cookie` headers and parse the `HTTP_COOKIE` environment variable.

The following example demonstrates the use of cookies using the Cookie module.

The `Cookie.py` Module

Python has this module called `Cookie.py`, which basically handles everything that you might need to worry about for what concerns cookies.

```
Cookie.Cookie()
```
This class enables the creation of a cookie object.

```
>>> import Cookie
>>> mycookie = Cookie.Cookie()  # Create a new cookie
```

A cookie object generated by the `Cookie.py` module has a dictionary-like behavior. It exposes the following properties and methods, supporting all cookie attributes defined by RFC 2109.

```
mycookie['username'] = "Andre Lessa"  # Assign a value to a cookie
mycookie["books"] = 2                 # automatically pickles non-string
                             # objects (using cPickle or pickle)
mycookie["username"].value           # Returns the value associated with the
                                     # key.
"Andre Lessa"
print mycookie
Set-Cookie: books="I2\012.";
Set-Cookie: username="Andre Lessa";
```

Note that the `print` statement must be executed before the `content-type` header.

```
cookie.output()
```
This method outputs the contents of a cookie. You can also change the printable representation if you want.

```
mycookie.output()
'Set-Cookie: books="I2\\012.";\012Set-Cookie: username="Andre Lessa";'
mycookie.output("Cookie Attributes:")
'Cookie Attributes: books="I2\\012.";\012Cookie Attributes: username="Andre
Lessa";'
```

`cookie.load()`

This method is used to extract cookies from a given string. You won't have a problem using escaped quotation marks and nested semicolons in the string.

```
mycookie.load("userid=alessa;")
print mycookie
```
```
Set-Cookie: books="I2\012.";
Set-Cookie: username="Andre Lessa";
Set-Cookie: userid=alessa;
```
```
mycookie.load('username=\"JP Lessa\";books=4;cds=1')
print mycookie
```
```
Set-Cookie: cds=1;
Set-Cookie: userid=alessa;
Set-Cookie: books=4;
Set-Cookie: username="JP Lessa";
```
```
mycookie.load('dvds="I3\\012.";')       # automatically unpickles pickled
                                        # objects.
mycookie["dvds"].value        # returns the true value, instead of the
                              # encoded representation.
```
```
3
print mycookies
```
```
Set-Cookie: cds=1;
Set-Cookie: userid=alessa;
Set-Cookie: books=4;
Set-Cookie: dvds="I3\012.";
Set-Cookie: username="JP Lessa";
```

`Cookie.net_setfunc()` **and** `Cookie.user_setfunc()`

These two functions are defined in the Cookie module to help you encode and decode the contents of your cookies. `Cookie.net_setfunc()` takes in an encoded string and returns a value. On the other hand, `Cookie.user_setfunc()` takes in a value and returns the original encoded string.

Note that you are not obliged to use their implementations. You can override them at anytime, just by subclassing the `Cookie()` class, and redefining these methods. For more information, check out the following:

Cookie protocol—Netscape's documentation

```
http://devedge.netscape.com/library/documentation/communicator/jsguide4/
cookies.htm
```

Cookie.py—Python Module created by Tim O'Malley

```
ftp://ftp.bbn.com/pub/timo/python/Cookie.py
```

Creating Output for a Browser

You already know that straightforward print statements do a good job of sending information to the user's browser.

> **Tip**
> Check out Chapter 10, "Basic Network Background," for details about some third-party modules that automatically generate HTML code for you.

Now, what about redirecting people from one page to another? In the next example, as soon as a browser sees the `Location:` header, it will stop and try to retrieve the new page.

```
new_location = 'http://www.python.org/'
print 'Status: 302 Redirected'
print 'Location: %s\n' %  new_location
```

Maybe you are tired of just sending text to the user. What about sending images?

The next example demonstrates how you can output graphics, such as GIF files, using CGI scripts. As you can see, you just need to specify the correct `MIME-type` in order to tell the browser that you are sending an image.

```
import sys
gifimage = open('check.gif','rb').read()
# print HTTP headers
sys.stdout.write('Content-type: image/gif\n')
# print end-of-headers
sys.stdout.write('\n')
# print image
sys.stdout.write(gifimage)
```

> **Caution**
> Note that you cannot use `print image` because it would append a newline or a blank to the data, in case you use `print image,` (with the comma at the end), and the browser would not understand it.

The previous simple example takes an existing GIF image file and processes it. Keep in mind that it is also possible to produce dynamic graphics images through Python code, using the *Python Imaging Library*.

See `http://www.python.org/sigs/image-sig/Imaging.html` for details.

Using Templates

CGI programs usually contain many blocks of HTML code embedded within the scripts. This is a problem for many teams of HTML designers and developers. Imagine the case in which both kinds of professionals need to make changes in the same file, at the same time. This kind of situation can generate many accidental errors in the code.

The most common solution for this kind of trouble is to separate the Python code from the HTML code by using template files. In a later stage, the HTML template can be mixed with Python code using either formatting substitution or Python's regular-expression.

The basic idea is after you have finished reading the template file, replace all special placeholders, such as `<!-- # INSERT HERE # -->`, with the correct values.

Listing 12.1 defines a simple template that is going to be used by our Python script. Of course, real-production templates are more complex than this one.

Listing 12.1   *file: template1.html*

```
<html>
    <head>
        <title>My Application</title>
    </head>
    <body>
        <H1><center><!-- # INSERT HERE # --></center></H1>
    </body>
</html>
```

Note the customized tag tag>><!-- # INSERT HERE # -->. If you just open this template file, nothing will show up. However, after you run the script, the program will search for this tag and replace it with our new content before displaying to the users.

Next, you have the CGI script that makes everything possible. This script reads the entire template file, storing it in memory. Then, after applying a regular expression substitution, it swaps our special tag with the new content.

```
 1: import re
 2: filename = "template1.html"
 3: TemplateException = "Error while parsing HTML template"
 4: newContent = "Hello Python World"
 5: filehandle = open(filename, "r")
 6: data = filehandle.read()
 7: filehandle.close()
 8: matching = re.subn("<!-- # INSERT HERE # -->", newContent, data)
 9: if matching[1] == 0:
10:     raise TemplateException
11: print "Content-Type: text/html\n\n"
12: print matching[0]
```

Line 1: Makes the regular expression module available.

Line 2: Specifies the filename of the template file.

Line 3: Defines an exception that is raised when no replacements are made.

Line 4: Contains the string to replace.

Line 6: Reads the entire file as a string.

As I told you before, another possibility is to use formatting substitution. In this new scenario, we have to write the template file as shown in Listing 12.2.

Listing 12.2   *file: template2.html*

```
<html>
<head>
<title>My Application</title>
</head>
<body>
<b>Student:</b> %(student)s<br>
<b>Class:</b> %(class)s<br>
<hr>
Sorry, your application was <font color=red>refused</font>.<br>
If you have any questions, please call:<br>
<center>%(phone)s</center>
<hr>
</body>
</html>
```

The script necessary to handle this new format is correctly listed next. The main difference is that in this new script, you have to declare a dictionary that will be used to map the placeholders in the template file.

```
filename = "template2.html"
dictemplate = {'student': 'Andre', 'class': 'Math', 'phone': '555-5553'}
filehandle = open(filename, "r")
data = filehandle.read()
filehandle.close()
print "Content-Type: text/html\n\n"
print data % (dictemplate)
```

Uploading/Uploaded Files

Sometimes, it is necessary to receive files from users through the Web. This next example shows how to send a file across an HTTP connection using an HTML page, and how to later interpret it.

```
import cgi
form = cgi.FieldStorage()
if not form:
    print "Content-Type: text/html"
    print
    print """
    <form action = "/cgi-bin/uploadfiles.py" method="POST"
    enctype="multipart/form-data">
    <input type="file" name="filename">
    <input type="submit">
    </form>
    """
elif form.has_key("filename"):
    item = form["filename"]
    if item.file:
        data = item.file.read()
        print "Content-Type: text/html"
        print
        print cgi.escape(data)
```

When a certain form field represents an uploaded file, the value attribute of that field reads the entire file in memory as a string. Sometimes, this might not be what you really want. Another way to get the information is to test for an uploaded file by checking either the filename attribute or the file attribute. You can then read the data, at your convenience, from the file attribute.

> **Note**
> The `enctype="multipart/form-data"` part is very important because without it, only the filename is transmitted.

The next example is a slight variation of the previous example. This one assumes that you have a form with a field called `filename` that will transport a user file to the CGI script, and then it reads the uploaded file, line by line.

```python
import cgi
form = cgi.FieldStorage()
if not form:
    print "Content-Type: text/html\n\n"
    print """
    <form action = "/cgi-bin/uploadingfile.py" method="POST"
    enctype="multipart/form-data">
    <input type="file" name="filename">
    <input type="submit">
    </form>
    """
elif form.has_key("filename"):
    uploadedfile = form["filename"]
    if uploadedfile.file:
        print "Content-Type: text/html\n\n"
        linecounter = 0
        while 1:
            line = uploadedfile.file.readline()
            print line
            if not line:
                break
            linecounter = linecounter + 1
```

`cgiupload.py`

The `cgiupload` module is a simple attempt to upload files via HTTP. Although the mechanism is not as efficient as other protocols (for example, FTP), there are circumstances where using the http protocol has advantages such as when a user login/password is not required, or when using firewalls because most firewalls allow the HTTP protocol to pass through. Note that HTTP file upload is about as efficient as email attachments.

A short description with code about how to upload files via CGI is available at

`http://starship.python.net/crew/jbauer/cgiupload/index.html`

Note that Python's module `"ftplib"` provides better performance to transmit files over the network.

Zope also provides a mechanism to perform CGI file uploads. Check out the Web site at

`http://www.zope.org`

Environment Variables

Environment variables are one of the methods that Web servers use to pass information to a CGI script. They are created and assigned appropriate values within the environment that the server produces for the CGI script.

The next code generates a list of all environment variables that you have available at the moment, in your browser.

```
import os
print "Content-type: text/html\n"
print "<HTML><HEAD><TITLE>List of Environment Variables</TITLE></HEAD>"
print "<BODY>"
for k,v in os.environ.items():
        print "%s => %s<BR>" % (k,v)
print "</BODY></HTML>"
```

The following list is the output collected from my environment. Of course, yours might be different.

```
HTTP_ACCEPT_ENCODING => gzip, deflate
REMOTE_HOST => 10.15.108.33
SERVER_PORT_SECURE => 0
COMSPEC => C:\WINDOWS\COMMAND.COM
SERVER_PORT => 80
PATH_TRANSLATED => C:\Inetpub\wwwroot\cgi-bin\environment.py
REMOTE_ADDR => 10.15.108.33
WINBOOTDIR => C:\WINDOWS
INSTANCE_ID => 1
HTTP_ACCEPT_LANGUAGE => en-us
BLASTER => A220 I7 D1 T2
GATEWAY_INTERFACE => CGI/1.1
TEMP => C:\windows\TEMP
SNDSCAPE => C:\WINDOWS
HTTP_CONNECTION => Keep-Alive
HTTP_USER_AGENT => Mozilla/4.0 (compatible; MSIE 4.01; Windows 98)
WINDIR => C:\WINDOWS
```

```
CONTENT_LENGTH => 0
HTTP_HOST => www.lessaworld.com
PATH => C:\WINDOWS; C:\WINDOWS\COMMAND; M:\PVCS\WIN95; C:\MSSQL7\BINN;
SERVER_PROTOCOL => HTTP/1.1
HTTPS => off
PATH_INFO => /cgi-bin/environment.py
SERVER_NAME => www.lessaworld.com
REQUEST_METHOD => GET
LOCAL_ADDR => 10.15.108.33
SCRIPT_NAME => /cgi-bin/ environment.py
SERVER_SOFTWARE => Microsoft-IIS/4.0
CMDLINE => WIN
HTTP_ACCEPT => application/x-comet, application/vnd.ms-excel,
        application/msword, application/vnd.ms-powerpoint, */*
PROMPT => $p$g
TMP => c:\windows\TEMP
```

As an example, when checking the user environment variables, `os.environ['HTTP_USER_AGENT']` gives you the user's browser, and `os.environ['REMOTE_ADDR']` gives you the remote IP address. Note that the user might be running a browser that doesn't send a User-Agent HTTP header, so you might not be able to count on `os.environ['HTTP_USER_AGENT']`.

The following is a list of environment variables used by Web Servers:

AUTH_TYPE—This is the protocol-specific authentication method used to validate the user if the server supports user authentication, and the script is protected.

CONTENT_LENGTH—The length, in bytes, of the said content as given by the client through standard input (sys.stdin). This is needed when a script is processing input with the POST method, in order to read the correct number of bytes from the standard input. Some servers end the input string with EOF, but this is not guaranteed behavior.

CONTENT_TYPE—For queries that have attached information, such as HTTP POST and PUT, this is the content type of the query data.

DOCUMENT_ROOT—Sometimes it is useful to know the root directory over which all WWW document paths are resolved by the server, in order to compose absolute file paths for the files that your script handles. It is a good practice to have your script resolve paths in this way, both for security reasons and for portability. Another common use is to be able to figure out what the URL of a file will be if you only know the absolute path and the hostname.

GATEWAY_INTERFACE—The revision string of the CGI specification to which this server complies. The format is CGI/revision.

HTTP_ACCEPT—MIME types accepted by the client.

HTTP_COOKIE—Netscape persistent cookie value.

HTTP_FROM—Email address of client (often disabled).

HTTP_REFERER—The URL that referred (via a link or redirection) the Web client to the script. Typed URLs and bookmarks usually result in this variable being left blank. In many cases, a script might need to behave differently depending on the referrer. For example, you might want to restrict your counter script to operate only if it is called from one of your own pages. This will prevent someone from using it from another Web page without your permission. Or, the referrer might be the actual data that the script needs to process. By expanding on the previous example, you might also want to install your counter to many pages, and have the script figure out from the referrer which page generated the call and increment the appropriate count, keeping a separate count for each individual URL. Some proxies or Web browsers might strip off the HTTP_Referer header for privacy reasons.

HTTP_USER_AGENT—This is the name/version pair of the client browser issuing the request to the script. As with referrers, one might need to implement behaviors that vary with the client software used to call the script. A redirection script could make use of this information to point the client to a page optimized for a specific browser. Or, you might want it to block requests from specific clients, such as robots or clients that will not support appropriate features used by the normal script output.

PATH_INFO—The extra path information following the script's path in the URL. This is appended to the URL and marked by a leading slash. The server puts this information in the PATH_INFO variable, which can be used as a method to pass arguments to the script. The extra path information is given by the client. In other words, scripts can be accessed by their virtual pathname, followed by extra information at the end of this path. The extra information is sent as PATH_INFO. This information should be decoded by the server if it comes from a URL before it is passed to the CGI script.

PATH_TRANSLATED—Translated version of PATH_INFO, which maps it onto DOCUMENT_ROOT. Usually PATH_INFO is used to pass a path argument to the script. For example, a counter might be passed the path to the file where counts should be stored. The server also makes a mapping of the PATH_INFO variable onto the document root path and stores it in PATH_TRANSLATED, which can be used directly as an absolute path/file. You should use PATH_TRANSLATED rather than concatenating DOCUMENT_ROOT and PATH_INFO because the documents on the Web Server might be spread over more than just one directory (for instance, user directories under their home directories).

QUERY_STRING—QUERY_STRING is the equivalent of content passed through STDIN in POST, but for scripts called with the GET method. Query arguments are written in this variable in their URL-Encoded form, just as they appear on the calling URL. You can process this string to extract useful parameters for the script. The information following the ? in the URL that references a script is exactly what we call *query information*. It should not be decoded in any fashion. This variable should always be set when there is query information, regardless of command line decoding.

REMOTE_ADDR—This is the IP address from which the client is issuing the request. This can be useful either for logging accesses to the script (for example a voting script might want to log voters in a file by their IP in order to prevent them from voting more than once) or to block/behave differently for particular IP addresses. This might be a requirement in a script that has to be restricted to your local network, and maybe perform different tasks for each known host.

REMOTE_HOST—This variable contains the hostname from which the client is issuing the request (if the information is available via reverse lookup).

REMOTE_IDENT—If the HTTP server supports RFC 931 identification, this variable will be set to the remote username retrieved from the server. Otherwise, this variable should be left blank.

REMOTE_USER—If the server supports user authentication, and the script is protected, this is the username they have authenticated as.

REQUEST_METHOD—This is the method with which the request was made (usually GET, POST, or HEAD). It is wise to have your script check this variable before doing anything. You can determine where the input will be (STDIN for POST, QUERY_STRING for GET) or choose to permit operation only under one of the two methods. It is also useful to identify when the script is called from the command-line because, in that case, this variable will remain undefined. When using the cgi module, all this is taken care of for you.

SCRIPT_NAME—A virtual path to the script being executed, used for self-referencing URLs. This is very useful if your script will output HTML code that contains calls to itself. Having the script determine its virtual path, (and hence, along with

DOCUMENT_ROOT, its full URL) is more portable than hard coding it in a configuration variable. Also, if you prefer to keep a log of all script accesses in some file and want to have each script report its name along with the calling parameters or time, it is very portable to use SCRIPT_NAME to print the path of the script.

SERVER_NAME—The Web server's hostname, DNS alias, or IP address. This information can provide the capability to have different behaviors depending on the server that's calling the script.

SERVER_PORT—The Web server's listening port number to which the request was sent. This information complements SERVER_NAME, making your script portable. Keep in mind that not all servers run on the default port and thus need an explicit port reference in the server address part of the URL.

SERVER_PROTOCOL—The name and revision of the Server information protocol that the request came in with. It comes in the format: protocol/revision.

SERVER_SOFTWARE—This variable contains the name and version of the information server software answering the request. The format used by this variable is name/version.

Debugging and Testing Your Script

Before putting your CGI scripts online, you need to be sure that they are working fine. You have to test them carefully, especially in near bounds and out of bounds conditions. A script that crashes in the middle of its job can cause large problems, such as data inconsistency in a database application. This is why you would use a transaction when updating a database from a cgi script (if it was deemed important enough).

You should eliminate most of the problems by running your script from the command line. Only after performing this check should you test it from your http daemon.

You have to remember that Python is an interpreted language, which means that several syntax errors will only be discovered at runtime. You must be sure that your script has been tested in every segment of the control flow.

Python is good for debugging processes because if things go wrong, you get a traceback message that is beneficial. By default, tracebacks usually go to the server's error_log file.

Printing a traceback message to the standard output is complicated because the error could occur before the Content-type header is printed, in the middle of a HTML markup tag, or even worse: the error message could contain markup elements itself.

You also need to be sure that incorrect input does not lead to an incorrect behavior of your script. Don't expect that all parameters received by your script will be meaningful. They can be corrupted during communication, or some hacker could try to obtain more data than normally allowed.

The following code suggests a simple way to debug Python CGI scripts.

```
1: import cgi
2: print "Content-type: text/plain\n"
3: try:
4:     your_applicationcode()
5: except:
6:     print "<h1>You've got an error.</h1>"
7:     cgi.print_exception()
```

Line 4: Calls the function that implements your application.

Line 2: We are using a content type of text/plain so that you can see all the output of the script.

Line 7: Calls a CGI function that safely prints a traceback message.

Note that cookies handling affects this routine. Because cookies must be printed as part of HTTP headers, they need to be handled before the first newline (line 2). Therefore, the easiest solution is to move the \n into your application function, and into the exception handler clause.

```
import cgi
print "Content-type: text/html"
try:
    handle_cookies()
    print"\n"
    your_applicationcode()
except:
    print"\n"
    print "<h1>You've got an error.</h1>"
    cgi.print_exception()
```

When creating a debugging framework, it is desirable that the user should never see a server error. Instead, you must provide a fancy page that tells him what has happened, along with helper information.

As a suggestion, your framework could interpret every traceback message and email it to the support team. This is a very useful solution for warning about problems in a live Web site, and besides, logging errors can help the tracking of application problems.

If you are in the stage of doing quality-assurance testing procedures on your Web application, you should try to test it outside the live site first. Let's see how you can do it.

Check the script for syntax errors by doing something similar to python script.py. If you execute your script in this way, you are able to test the integrity and syntax of your code.

If you have your script written as a module, adding the following two lines to its end enables you to execute your library module from the command prompt.

```
if __name__ == "__main__":
    main()
```

A CGI script usually does not work from the command line. However, you should at least call it from the command line because if the Python interpreter finds a syntax error, a message will pop up on your screen. That's cool! At least you know if the syntax is all right. Otherwise, if you wait until you call your code through the Web, the HTTP server could send a very problematic error message to you.

Assuming that your script has no syntax errors, yet it does not work, you have no choice but to fake a form call to it.

If you are using UNIX csh or tcsh shells, and your script uses the cgi.FieldStorage class for form input, you can set the environment variables REQUEST_METHOD and QUERY_STRING.

```
setenv REQUEST_METHOD "GET"
setenv QUERY_STRING "animal=parrot"
```

For other shells, you use

```
REQUEST_METHOD="GET"
QUERY_STRING="animal=parrot"
export REQUEST_METHOD QUERY_STRING
```

Check if your script is located at an executable directory, and if so, try sending an URL request directly through the browser to the script. In other words, open your browser and call your script, without forgetting to send the attribute/value pairs. For instance,

```
http://yourhostname/cgi-bin/myapp.py?animal=parrot
```

If, for example, you receive an error number 404, it means that your server could not find the script in that directory. As you can see, this might help you test and debug your script through the Web.

Next, I list some considerations that you need to have in mind while debugging a Python CGI application. They are as follows:

- Import the traceback module as soon as possible. (It needs to be imported before the try/except statement.)

- Don't forget that you need to put a blank line \n just after the header's end.

- If you assign sys.stderr to sys.stdout, all error messages are sent to the standard output.

- Create a try/except statement, put all your application code inside it, and don't forget to call traceback.print_exc() in the except clause.

The following example exposes all the previous considerations:

```
import sys
import cgi
import traceback
print "Content-type: text/html"
print
sys.stderr = sys.stdout
try:
    n = 10
    while n>0:
        print "<hr>"
        print 10/(n-1) # This will cause an error when n=1
        n = n - 1
except:
    print "\n\n<PRE>"
    traceback.print_exc()
```

Note that the assignment to sys.stdout is necessary because the traceback object prints to the standard error output (stderr). The print "\n\n<PRE>" statement is being used to disable the word wrapping in HTML.

If your script calls external programs, make sure that Python's $PATH variable is set to the right directories because when it is inside a CGI environment, this variable does not carry useful values.

Python Active Scripting

Active Scripting is a technology developed by Microsoft that allows scripting languages to be embedded inside Web browsers. Currently, Microsoft Internet Explorer 4 and above supports client-side scripting, whereas Internet Information Server (IIS) supports server-side scripting, using a component called *Active Server Pages (ASP)*. In both cases, the scripting code is embedded inside the HTML code. There is a limitation to using Python as a client-side solution for your Web applications: Each client machine must have Python installed. That's probably the greatest disadvantage that Python has among the other Active Scripting languages because Internet Explorer provides core support for VBScript and JScript. Other problems with using Python as a client-side scripting language include the fact that it is only supported in Internet Explorer, it only works on Windows, and it requires that the Python Active Scripting component be installed. It is probably okay in controlled environments, but on the Internet, hardly anyone meets this criteria, so you can't rely on it.

In order to implement security procedures, not all Python commands are available. Commands that execute some critical operations—such as open files, create sockets, and so on—are hidden behind a "sandbox", in a concept similar to the one used by Java. For more information, check out

Python and Microsoft ActiveX Scripting

http://www.python.org/windows/win32com/ActiveXScripting.html

Active Scripting

http://msdn.microsoft.com/scripting

The Python for Windows extensions come with more details about the use of Active Scripting along with Internet Explorer. For now, let's take a look at the following code:

```
<script language=python>
msg = "Hello Python World! I am counting down!<br>"
document.write(msg)
counter = 10
while counter > 0:
    document.write(counter)
    document.write("<br>")
    counter = counter - 1
document.write("Booooom!")
</script>
```

This code must be inserted in a HTML file in order to be executed. Next, you have a slightly modified code. This one uses the alert() function to put a message box in the user's screen. As you already know, each application exposes its own object model, and for example, the alert() function is part of the object model exposed by the Internet Explorer, which is similar to the Dynamic HTML object model. Actually, everything here happens as COM transactions.

```
<script language=python>
msg = "Hello Python World! I am counting down!<br>"
document.write(msg)
counter = 10
while counter > 0:
    document.write(counter)
    document.write("<br>")
    counter = counter - 1
alert("Booooom!")
</script>
```

A script tag can be executed in two places: in the client machine (default behavior) or in the server. The next structure shows how to let the application know where it needs to execute the script.

```
<SCRIPT RunAt=Server Language=Python >
   #This code runs at the server
</SCRIPT>
<SCRIPT Language=Python >
   #This code runs at the client
</SCRIPT>
```

The next example demonstrates how you can cause your Python code to interact with standard HTML code. Note that you cannot use leading whitespaces in the Python block. In order to handle events such as the ones shown here, you need to have the notation `object_event` in mind. Also note that in Python, you have to inform the complete namespace of the object, including the *form name*. This is something that VBScript handles better by allowing you to use just the object name.

```
<FORM NAME = "myform">
  <INPUT TYPE="Text" NAME="txt1" SIZE=40><br>
  <INPUT TYPE="Text" NAME="txt2" SIZE=40><br>
  <INPUT NAME="B1" TYPE="BUTTON" VALUE="Click me">
  <SCRIPT LANGUAGE=Python>
def myform_onClick():
    myform.txt1.value = document.location
def txt1_onChange():
    myform.txt1.value = ""
    myform.txt2.value = ""
def txt2_onFocus():
    myform.txt2.value = myform.txt1.value
  </SCRIPT>
</FORM>
```

In order to have full exposition with the Active Scripting technology, you also need to take a look at *Windows Scripting Host (WSH)*. WSH is part of Windows 98 and 2000, but it can also be downloaded from http://msdn.microsoft.com/scripting for the other Windows environments (95 and NT). WSH runs Python files that have the extension .pys. These files are regular text files that can freely use the object model exposed by WSH. Note that .pys files are not correctly registered—you need to explicitly specify either cscript.exe or wscript.exe on the command line.

Now, that you are ready to write your programs, you might also need to debug your Active Scripts. You have two tools for the job, both provided by Microsoft:

- The first one is a free product called *The Windows Script Debugger*. This version can be downloaded from http://msdn.microsoft.com/scripting/.

- The other option is to use *Microsoft Visual Interdev* that comes as part of *Microsoft Visual C++*. This option is not free because it's attached to the commercial product.

Using COM Objects

Active Scripting is a COM-based technology that works by providing a specific language's object model to the user. In Chapter 7, "Objects Interfacing and Distribution," you learned that each application exposes a progID in order to interface with other systems. Therefore, when you say Language = Python inside a script tag, you are actually opening an interface to a progID called Python. As you might be wondering, VBScript, JScript, and Python are COM progIDs used to handle each one of these languages.

In our case, after you specify that the scripting language is Python, you acquire access to the interface exposed by the Python object model. As you can see in the next ASP example, within the COM scripting connection, you are still able to use other COM interfaces.

This example opens an ODBC connection to the database identified in the connection string. In order to test this example, make sure that your system has the informed DSN, and that the database has the necessary table. This code must be saved in a file using the .asp extension in order to let it run under Microsoft IIS.

After you execute it, it reads the selected columns from a database table and displays the columns and contents in a HTML table structure. Obviously you'll need this particular table in your database for it to work, but you should be able to adapt it. Note that this code is a straight conversion from VBScript, except for the fact that the Execute statement returns a tuple.

```
<%@ LANGUAGE = Python %>
<%
import win32com.client

oconn=win32com.client.Dispatch("ADODB.connection")
oconn.Open ("DSN=db_sql_server")
objRecords, thing = oconn.Execute (
  "SELECT currency_desc, symbol FROM tb_currency")

Response.Write("<TABLE border=1><TR>")

for objField in objRecords.Fields:
  Response.Write("<TH>"+objField.Name+"</TH>")

Response.Write("</TR>")

while not objRecords.EOF :
  Response.Write("<TR>")
```

```
    for objField in objRecords.Fields:
      Response.Write("<TD>"+objField.Value+"</TD>")
    objRecords.MoveNext()
    Response.Write("</TR>")

Response.Write("</TABLE>")

oconn.close
oconn=None
%>
```

ASP and Microsoft ActiveX Scripting

Active Server Pages, commonly referred to as ASP, is Microsoft's solution to server-side scripting applications. The difference between Active Server Pages and HTML pages is that with simple HTML pages, the client browser requests a Web page from a Web server. The server sends the file to the client, and the page is shown on the client's browser. On the other hand, with Active Server Pages, the server gets a chance to alter the file before sending it to the user. So, for every request for a file with an .asp extension, the server runs the file through a interpreter that parses the ASP commands. You can have your ASP code connect to any ODBC-compliant database, and dynamically insert the data into your HTML pages.

To use Active Server Pages, you must be running a Microsoft Web Server, specifically Internet Information Server (IIS) 3.0 or up—Microsoft's Internet Information Server is a Web Server that supports both CGI and ASP. If your Web site runs on a UNIX system, you can still use Active Server Pages, but you need to use third-party tools to translate the ASP before it is sent to the client. Of course, there are other (possibly better) options when not using IIS. ASP is not necessarily the best choice.

> **Tip**
> Note that for everything you can do with ASP, you can also do using straight CGI scripting.

ASP is not language dependent, and though most of the things you will find in the market are written in VBScript or JScript, you can actually configure ASP to use any other scripting language that supports the Microsoft ActiveX Scripting interface. This includes VBScript, JScript, PERLScript, PScript, and of course, Python.

The object model defined by ASP is different from the object model defined by Internet Explorer. The first thing you will notice is that ASP code has some special tags:

- The `<%@ language=Python %>` tag defines that all scripting tags after that will, by default, belong to Python.

- The `<% %>` tag is equivalent to `<script> </script>`.

- `<%= %>` allows you to replace part of the contents to be displayed with the value of a variable. For instance,

```
<%
name = "Andre" %>
Whassup <%= name %> !
```

There is no restriction on the commands that you can execute on a ASP page because all the execution takes place at the Server. Thus, in theory there would be no need for high security procedures. However, there is just as much need for security in ASP files as in CGI script when you are making use of untrusted input. The fact that there is no sandbox means you have to be especially careful not to compromise your system.

> **Note**
> ASP files are stored in files with the `.asp` extension.

One last detail about Python/ASP programs is that the print statement does not send the information to the screen. You need to use ASP's object model `Response.Write()` function to do it, as you can check in the following example.

```
<%@ language=Python %>
<%
text = "this text here does not use the print command" %>
A curious fact is that <%= text %>.
<br>
Note that we still need to pay attention to the indentation in this code.
<br>
The next code block lists all the server variables.
<br><br>
<%
for k in Request.ServerVariables:
    v = Request.ServerVariables(k)
    Response.Write("<b>%s</b>=" % (k))
    Response.Write("%s<br><br>" % (v))
%>
```

Of course, you could fix the print statement problem with the following code to make
print work again.

```
class ASPStdout:
    def write(self, bytes):
        Request.Write(bytes)
    def writelines(self, lines):
        for line in lines: self.write(line)
sys.stdout = ASPStdout()
```

In case you want to try something different, Microsoft Visual Interdev, which is a very
popular tool for ASP development, can be integrated with Python for Windows.
Although it doesn't have any specific knowledge about .py files, it doesn't expose any
problems when using them.

Using its working environment, you can test and debug Python's active scripts.
Another possible option that you have is to use a free debugger that can be found at
http://msdn.microsoft.com/scripting.

See http://starship.python.net/crew/pirx/asp/py_asp.html for more details about
using Python with ASP.

Python Server Pages

Python Server Pages is a server-side scripting engine designed along the lines of
Microsoft's Active Server Pages and Sun's Java Server Pages specification. The major
difference between ASP and PSP is that PSP is written in 100% Java and portable to a
wide variety of platforms, whereas Web applications written in ASP can be run only on
Microsoft platforms. Python Server Pages uses JPython as its scripting language,
which seems to be more appropriate for scripting Web sites than the Java language
itself in Java Server Pages.

A major benefit to using PSP is the huge number of add-on modules available for both
Python and JPython. You can access any module that is compatible with JPython from
within your PSP application's pages. Because JPython is itself written in Java, you can
access Java packages from your Python Server Pages application as well. For more
information, check out the following:

Python Server Pages

http://www.ciobriefings.com/psp

JRun

JRun is the Java Servlet engine recommended for use with PSP.

`http://www.allaire.com/products/jrun/index.cfm`

JPython

JPython is the scripting language used by PSP.

`http://www.jpython.org`

Summary

This chapter provides information about how to use Python as a CGI scripting language. Python is suitable for CGI programming on Windows, Mac, and UNIX platforms, allowing the creation of programs that provide services over the Internet.

Python uses the `cgi` module to implement CGI scripts and to process form handling in Web applications that are invoked by an HTTP server. This module accepts `sys.stdin` and environment variables set by the server as input sources. The output is sent directly to `sys.stdout` carrying an HTTP header and the data itself.

Every CGI script must send a header (the `Content-type` tag) describing the contents of the document. The common values for this tag are `text/html`, `text/plain`, `image/gif`, and `image/jpeg`. A blank line is used to indicate the end of this header.

You have to watch out when passing Form fields to the OS shell. Never pass any string received from the client direct to a shell command. Before putting your CGI scripts online, you need to be sure that they are working fine.

If you need to correlate requests from the same user, you must generate and assign a session key on the first contact of the user, and incorporate this session key in the next forms, or in the URLs.

In order to handle cookies in Python, you can use a module called `Cookie.py`, which is able to write `Set-Cookie` headers and parse the `HTTP_COOKIE` environment variable.

Python CGI scripts allow you to output not only text, but also graphics.

In order to separate Python code from HTML code, many developers have adopted the concept of template files. The HTML template can be mixed with Python code using either formatting substitution or Python's regular expression.

Sometimes, it is necessary to receive files from users through the Web. The properties provided by the cgi module offer means to send a file across an HTTP connection using an HTML page, and also to read files sent from a Web page.

Environmental variables are one of the methods that Web servers use to pass information to a CGI script. They are created and assigned appropriate values within the environment that the server produces for the CGI script.

Active Scripting is a COM-based technology developed by Microsoft that allows scripting languages to be embedded inside the HTML code. It works by providing a specific language's object model to the user. In our case, after you specify that the scripting language is Python, you acquire access to the interface exposed by the Python object model.

Active Server Pages, commonly referred to as ASP, is Microsoft's solution to server-side scripting applications.

Python Server Pages is a server-side scripting engine designed along the lines of Microsoft's Active Server Pages and Sun's Java Server Pages specification.

CHAPTER 13

Data Manipulation

I'm a lumberjack, and I'm okay! I sleep all night and I work all day.

This chapter provides information concerning how to use Python for data parsing and manipulation. You will learn how to interpret XML, SGML, and HTML documents and how to parse and manipulate email messages, among other things.

Parsing and Manipulating Data

As you might already know, Python can be used as an effective and productive tool to parse and manipulate information from the Web.

This chapter covers modules that support encoding and decoding of data handling formats, which are largely used in Internet applications. Here, I expose you to modules, such as xmllib, sgmllib, and htmllib, which are standard library modules for processing the main markup languages used in the Internet.

At the end of the chapter, you will be introduced to some other modules, such as mimetypes and mimetools, which are used for mail message manipulation, and data conversion.

XML Processing

The first standard that you will learn how to manipulate in Python is XML.

The Web already has a standard for defining markup languages like HTML, which is called SGML. HTML is actually defined in SGML. SGML could have been used as this new standard, and browsers could have been extended with SGML parsers. However, SGML is quite complex to implement and contains a lot of features that are very rarely used.

SGML is much more than a Web standard because it was around long before the Web. HTML is an application of SGML, and XML is a subset.

SGML also lacks character sets support, and it is difficult to interpret an SGML document without having the definition of the markup language (the DTD—Document Type Definition) available.

Consequently, it was decided to develop a simplified version of SGML, which was called XML. The main point of XML is that you, by defining your own markup language, can encode the information of your documents more precisely than is possible with HTML. This meas that programs processing these documents can "understand" them much better and therefore process the information in ways that are impossible with HTML (or ordinary text processor documents).

Introduction to XML

The *Extensible Markup Language (XML)* is a subset of SGML. Its goal is to enable generic SGML to be served, received, and processed on the Web in the way that is now possible with HTML. XML has been designed for ease of implementation and for interoperability with both SGML and HTML.

XML describes a class of data objects called XML documents and partially describes the behavior of computer programs that process them. XML is an application profile or restricted form of *SGML*, the *Standard Generalized Markup Language* (ISO 8879). By construction, XML documents are conforming SGML documents. An XML parser can check if an XML document is formal without the aid of a DTD.

XML documents are made up of storage units called *elements*, which contain either parsed or unparsed data, and are delimited by tags. Parsed data is made up of characters, some of which form character data, and some of which form markup elements. Markup encodes a description of the document's storage layout and logical structure. XML provides a mechanism to impose constraints on the storage layout and logical structure.

A software module called an XML parser is used to read XML documents and provide access to their content and structure. It is assumed that an XML parser is doing its work on behalf of another module, called the application. This specification describes the required behavior of an XML parser in terms of how it must read XML data and the information it must provide to the application. For more information, check out

Extensible Markup Language (XML) Recommendation

W3C Recommendation—Extensible Markup Language (XML) 1.0

```
http://www.w3.org/TR/REC-xml.html
```

Writing an XML File

As you can see next, it is simple to define your own markup language with XML. The next block of code is the content of a file called survey.xml. This code defines a specific markup language for a given survey.

```
<!DOCTYPE SURVEY SYSTEM "SURVEY.DTD">
<SURVEY>
  <CLIENT>
    <NAME>          Lessaworld Corp.          </NAME>
    <LOCATION>      Pittsburgh, PA            </LOCATION>
    <CONTACT>       Andre Lessa               </CONTACT>
    <EMAIL>         webmaster@lessaworld.com </EMAIL>
    <TELEPHONE>     (412)555-5555             </TELEPHONE>
  </CLIENT>
  <SECTION SECTION_ID="1">
  <QUESTION QUESTION_ID="1" QUESTION_LEVEL="1">
    <QUESTION_DESC>What is your favorite language?</QUESTION_DESC>
    <Op1>Python</Op1>
    <Op2>Perl</Op2>
  </QUESTION>
  <QUESTION QUESTION_ID="2" QUESTION_LEVEL="1">
    <QUESTION_DESC>Do you use this language at work?</QUESTION_DESC>
    <Op1>Yes</Op1>
    <Op2>No</Op2>
  </QUESTION>
  <QUESTION QUESTION_ID="3" QUESTION_LEVEL="1">
    <QUESTION_DESC>Did you expect the Spanish inquisition?</QUESTION_DESC>
    <Op1>No</Op1>
    <Op2>Of course not</Op2>
  </QUESTION>
```

```
    </SECTION>
</SURVEY>
```

In order to complement the XML markup language shown previously, we need a
Document Type Definition (DTD), just like the following one. The DTD can be part of
the XML file, or it can be stored as an independent file, as we are doing here. Note
the first line of the XML file, where we are passing the name of the DTD file
(survey.dtd). Also, it seems that XML is standardizing the use of XML Schemas
rather the DTDs.

```
<!ELEMENT SURVEY      (CLIENT, SECTION+)>


<!ELEMENT CLIENT (NAME, LOCATION, CONTACT?, EMAIL?, TELEPHONE?)>
<!ELEMENT NAME         (#PCDATA)>
<!ELEMENT LOCATION     (#PCDATA)>
<!ELEMENT CONTACT      (#PCDATA)>
<!ELEMENT EMAIL        (#PCDATA)>
<!ELEMENT TELEPHONE    (#PCDATA)>


<!ELEMENT SECTION      (QUESTION+)>
<!ELEMENT QUESTION     (QUESTION_DESC, Op1, Op2)>


<!ELEMENT QUESTION_DESC  (#PCDATA)>
<!ELEMENT Op1               (#PCDATA)>
<!ELEMENT Op2               (#PCDATA)>


<!ATTLIST SECTION      SECTION_ID     CDATA #IMPLIED>
<!ATTLIST QUESTION     QUESTION_ID    CDATA #IMPLIED
                       QUESTION_LEVEL CDATA #IMPLIED>
```

Now, let's understand how a DTD works. For a simple example, like this one, we need
two special tags called <!ELEMENT> and <!ATTLIST>.

The <!ELEMENT> definition tag is used to define the elements presented in the XML
file. The general syntax is

```
<!ELEMENT NAME CONTENTS>
```

The first argument (NAME) gives the name of the element, and the second one
(CONTENTS) lists the element names that are allowed to be underneath the element that
we are defining.

The ordering that we use to list the contents is important. When we say, for example,

```
<!ELEMENT SURVEY      (CLIENT, SECTION+)>
```

it means that we must have a CLIENT first, followed by a SECTION. Note that we have a special character (the plus sign) just after the second element in the content list. This character, as well as some others, has a special meaning:

- A + sign after an element means that it can be included one or more times.

- A ? sign indicates that the element can be skipped.

- A * sign indicates an entity that can be skipped or included one or more times.

> **Note**
> These characters have similar meanings to what they do in regular expressions. (Of course, not everything you use in an re can be used in a DTD.)

Note that #PCDATA is used to indicate an entity that carries the information.

<!ATTLIST>, the other definition tag in the example, defines the attributes of an element. In our DTD, we have three attributes, one for SECTION, and two for QUESTION.

An important difference between XML and SMGL is that elements in XML that do not have any contents (like <IMG> and <BR> of HTML) are written like this in XML:

```
<IMG SRC="stuff.gif"/>
```

or in an equivalent format, such as

```
<img src="stuff.gif"></img>
```

Note the slash before the final >. This means that a program can read the document without knowing the DTD (which is where it says that IMG does not have any contents) and still know that IMG does not have an end tag as well as what follows IMG is not inside the element.

For more information about XML and Python, check out the XML package. It comes with a Python XML-HOWTO in the doc directory, and very good examples:

```
http://www.python.org/sigs/xml-sig/status.html
```

Python XML Package

For those who want to play around with XML in Python, there will be a Python/XML package to serve several purposes at once. This package will contain everything required for basic XML applications, along with documentation and sample code— basically, something easy to compile and install.

A release candidate of the latest release of this package is now available as PyXML-0.5.5.tar.gz (GPG signature), dated June 5, 2000. This version contains SAX, the Pyexpat module, sgmlop, the prototype DOM code, and xmlproc, an XML parser written in Python.

The individual components contained in the Python/XML package include

- A Python implementation of SAX (Simple API for XML)

  A SAX implementation has been written by Lars Marius Garshol. Garshol has also written a draft specification of the Python version of SAX 1.0.

- An XML-HOWTO containing an overview of Python and XML processing. (This is still being actively revised.)

  Andrew Kuchling is working on this. A first draft of the XML-HOWTO is available, and introduces the SAX interface in tutorial form. A reference manual is available separately.

- A fairly stable Python interface to James Clark's Expat parser. A Pyexpat C extension has been written by Jack Jansen.

- Both Python and C implementations of the *DOM (Document Object Model)*.

  Stefane Fermigier's DOM package has been modified to match the final DOM W3C Recommendation.

- A module to marshal simple Python data types into XML. A module called xml.marshal is available. However, it might end up being superseded by Lotos, WDDX, or some other DTD.

The document called *Python/XML Reference Guide* is the reference manual for the Python/XML package, containing descriptions for several XML modules. For more information, check out the following sites:

Python/XML Reference Guide

http://www.python.org/doc/howto/xml-ref/

"SAX Implementation," by Lars Marius Garshol

http://www.stud.ifi.uio.no/~lmariusg/download/python/xml/saxlib.html

Draft specification of the Python version of SAX 1.0

http://www.stud.ifi.uio.no/~lmariusg/download/python/xml/sax-spec.html

XML-HOWTO

`http://www.python.org/doc/howto/xml/`

Pyexpat C extension written by Jack Jansen

`ftp://ftp.cwi.nl/pub/jack/python/pyexpat.tgz`

DOM Recommendation

`http://www.w3.org/TR/REC-DOM-Level-1/`

Stefane Fermigier's DOM package

`http://www.math.jussieu.fr/~fermigie/python/`

Python 2.0 was released with a lot of enhancements concerning the XML support, including a SAX2 interface and a re-designed DOM interface as part of the `xml` package. Note that the xml package that is shipped with Python 2.0 contains just a basic set of options for XML development. If you want (or need) to use the full XML package, you are suggested to install `PyXML`.

The `PyXML` distribution also uses the `xml` package. That's the reason why PyXML versions 0.6.0 or greater can be used to replace the `xml` package that is bundled with Python. By doing so, you will extend the set of XML functionalities that you can have available. That includes

- 4DOM, a full DOM implementation from FourThought, Inc

- The `xmlproc` validating parser, written by Lars Marius Garshol

- The `sgmlop` parser accelerator module, written by Fredrik Lundh

xmllib

The `xmllib` module defines a class `XMLParser`, which serves as the basis for parsing text files formatted in XML. Note that `xmllib` is not XML 1.0 compliant, and it doesn't provide any Unicode support. It provides simple XML support for ASCII only element and attribute names. Of course, it probably handles UTF8 character data without problems.

XMLParser()

The `XMLParser` class must be instantiated without arguments. This class provides the following interface methods and instance variables:

`attributes`—This is a mapping of element names to mappings. The latter mapping maps attribute names that are valid for the element to the default value of the attribute, or to None if there is no default. The default value is the empty dictionary. This variable is meant to be overridden and not extended because the default is shared by all instances of `XMLParser`.

`elements`—This is a mapping of element names to tuples. The tuples contain a function for handling the start and end tag, respectively, of the element, or None if the method `unknown_starttag()` or `unknown_endtag()` is to be called. The default value is the empty dictionary. This variable is meant to be overridden and not extended because the default is shared by all instances of `XMLParser`.

`entitydefs`—This is a mapping of entitynames to their values. The default value contains definitions for `lt`, `gt`, `amp`, `quot`, and `apos`.

`reset()`—Resets the instance. Loses all unprocessed data. This is called implicitly at the instantiation time.

`setnomoretags()`—Stops processing tags. Treats all following input as literal input (CDATA).

`setliteral()`—Enters literal mode (CDATA mode). This mode is automatically exited when the close tag matching the last unclosed open tag is encountered.

`feed(data)`—Feeds some text to the parser. It is processed insofar as it consists of complete tags; incomplete data is buffered until more data is fed or `close()` is called.

`close()`—Forces processing of all buffered data as if it were followed by an end-of-file mark. This method can be redefined by a derived class to define additional processing at the end of the input, but the redefined version should always call `close()`.

`translate_references(data)`—Translates all entity and character references in data and returns the translated string.

`handle_xml(encoding, standalone)`—This method is called when the <?xml ...?> tag is processed. The arguments are the values of the encoding and standalone attributes in the tag. Both encoding and standalone are optional. The values passed to `handle_xml()` default to None and the string no, respectively.

`handle_doctype(`*`tag, data`*`)`—This method is called when the `<!DOCTYPE...>` tag is processed. The arguments are the name of the root element and the uninterpreted contents of the tag, starting following the whitespace after the name of the root element.

`handle_starttag(`*`tag, method, attributes`*`)`—This method is called to handle `starttags` for which a start tag handler is defined in the instance variable elements. The tag argument is the name of the tag, and the method argument is the function (method) that should be used to support semantic interpretation of the start tag. The attributes argument is a dictionary of attributes; the key being the name and the value being the value of the attribute found inside the tag's `<>` brackets. Character and entity references in the value have been interpreted. For instance, for the start tag `<A HREF="http://www.python.org/">`, this method would be called as `handle_starttag('A', self.elements['A'][0], {'HREF':` `'http://www.python.org/'})`. The base implementation simply calls a method with attributes as the only argument.

`handle_endtag(`*`tag, method`*`)`—This method is called to handle `endtags` for which an end tag handler is defined in the instance variable elements. The tag argument is the name of the tag, and the method argument is the function (method) that should be used to support semantic interpretation of the end tag. For instance, for the endtag `</A>`, this method would be called as `handle_endtag('A',` `self.elements['A'][1])`. The base implementation simply calls method.

`handle_data(`*`data`*`)`—This method is called to process arbitrary data. It is intended to be overridden by a derived class; the base class implementation does nothing.

`handle_charref(`*`ref`*`)`—This method is called to process a character reference of the form `&#ref;`. `ref` can either be a decimal number, or a hexadecimal number when preceded by an `x`. In the base implementation, `ref` must be a number in the range 0-255. It translates the character to ASCII and calls the method `handle_data()` with the character as argument. If `ref` is invalid or out of range, the method `unknown_charref(ref)` is called to handle the error. A subclass must override this method to provide support for character references outside the ASCII range.

`handle_entityref(`*`ref`*`)`—This method is called to process a general entity reference of the form `&ref;` where `ref` is an general entity reference. It looks for ref in the instance (or class) variable entitydefs that should be mapping from entity names to corresponding translations. If a translation is found, it calls the method `handle_data()` with the translation; otherwise, it calls the method `unknown_entityref(ref)`. The default entitydefs defines translations for `&amp;`, `&apos;`, `&gt;`, `&lt;`, and `&quot;`.

`handle_comment(`*`comment`*`)`—This method is called when a comment is encountered. The comment argument is a string containing the text between the `<!`- and `->` delimiters, but not the delimiters themselves. For example, the comment `<!`-`text`-> will cause this method to be called with the argument `text`. The default method does nothing.

`handle_cdata(`*`data`*`)`—This method is called when a CDATA element is encountered. The data argument is a string containing the text between the `<![CDATA["` and `"]]>` delimiters, but not the delimiters themselves. For example, the entity `<![CDATA[text]]>` will cause this method to be called with the argument `text`. The default method does nothing, and is intended to be overridden.

`handle_proc(`*`name,  data`*`)`—This method is called when a processing instruction (PI) is encountered. The name is the PI target, and the data argument is a string containing the text between the PI target and the closing delimiter, but not the delimiter itself. For example, the instruction `<?XML text?>` will cause this method to be called with the arguments `XML` and `text`. The default method does nothing. Note that if a document starts with `<?xml ..?>`, `handle_xml()` is called to handle it.

`handle_special(`*`data`*`)`—This method is called when a declaration is encountered. The data argument is a string containing the text between the `<!` and `>` delimiters, but not the delimiters themselves. For example, the entity `<!ENTITY text>` will cause this method to be called with the argument `ENTITY text`. The default method does nothing. Note that `<!DOCTYPE ...>` is handled separately if it is located at the start of the document.

`syntax_error(`*`message`*`)`—This method is called when a syntax error is encountered. The message is a description of what was wrong. The default method raises a RuntimeError exception. If this method is overridden, it is permissible for it to return. This method is only called when the error can be recovered from. Unrecoverable errors raise a RuntimeError without first calling `syntax_error()`.

`unknown_starttag(`*`tag,  attributes`*`)`—This method is called to process an unknown start tag. It is intended to be overridden by a derived class; the base class implementation does nothing.

`unknown_endtag(`*`tag`*`)`—This method is called to process an unknown end tag. It is intended to be overridden by a derived class; the base class implementation does nothing.

unknown_charref(*ref*)—This method is called to process unresolvable numeric character references. It is intended to be overridden by a derived class; the base class implementation does nothing.

unknown_entityref(*ref*)—This method is called to process an unknown entity reference. It is intended to be overridden by a derived class; the base class implementation does nothing.

XML Namespaces

The xmllib module has support for XML namespaces as defined in the XML namespaces proposed recommendation.

Tag and attribute names that are defined in an XML namespace are handled as if the name of the tag or element consisted of the namespace (that is, the URL that defines the namespace) followed by a space and the name of the tag or attribute. For instance, the tag <html xmlns:html="http://www.w3.org/TR/REC-html40"> is treated as if the tag name was "http://www.w3.org/TR/REC-html40 html", and the tag <html:a href="http://frob.com"> inside the previous element is treated as if the tag name were "http://www.w3.org/TR/REC-html40 a" and the attribute name as if it were "http://www.w3.org/TR/REC-html40 src".

An older draft of the XML namespaces proposal is also recognized, but triggers warn about it.

XML Examples

The next example uses xmllib to parse a XML file. The file being used is the same survey.xml that you saw in the beginning of this chapter. Our proposal is to read the file, parse it, and convert it to a structure such as the following:

```
Survey of section number   1

1- What is your favorite language?
     Python
     Perl

2- Do you use this language at work?
     Yes
     No

3- Did you expect the Spanish inquisition?
     No
     Of course not
```

The following code implements a solution for our problem. Remember that XML tags are case sensitive, thus the code must be properly balanced. In this code, note that attributes are passed to the tag handlers in a dictionary, not in a tuple.

```python
import xmllib, string
class myparser(xmllib.XMLParser):
    def __init__(self):
        xmllib.XMLParser.__init__(self)
        self.currentquestiondesc = ''
        self.currentOp1 = ''
        self.currentOp2 = ''
        self.currentquestion = ''
        self.currentdata = []

    def handle_data(self, data):
        self.currentdata.append(data)

    def start_SURVEY(self, attrs):
        print "Survey of section number ",

    def end_SURVEY(self):
        pass

    def start_SECTION(self, attrs):
        print attrs['SECTION_ID']

    def end_SECTION(self):
        pass

    def start_QUESTION(self, attrs):
        self.currentquestion = attrs['QUESTION_ID']

    def end_QUESTION(self):
        print """
%(currentquestion)s- %(currentquestiondesc)s
    %(currentOp1)s
    %(currentOp2)s
""" % self.__dict__

    def start_QUESTION_DESC(self, attrs):
        self.currentdata = []
```

```
    def end_QUESTION_DESC(self):
        self.currentquestiondesc = string.join(self.currentdata,'')

    def start_Op1(self, attrs):
        self.currentdata = []

    def end_Op1(self):
        self.currentOp1 = string.join(self.currentdata,'')

    def start_Op2(self, attrs):
        self.currentdata = []

    def end_Op2(self):
        self.currentOp2 = string.join(self.currentdata,'')


if __name__ == "__main__":
    filehandle = open("survey.xml")
    data = filehandle.read()
    filehandle.close()

    parser=myparser()
    parser.feed(data)
    parser.close()
```

Let's see another example. The next one opens our survey.xml file and lists all the
questions available. It also tries to find question #4, but as we don't have it, it raises a
message to the user.

```
import xmllib

class QuestionNotFound:
    pass

class Parser(xmllib.XMLParser):

    def __init__(self, filename=None):
        self.found = 0
        xmllib.XMLParser.__init__(self)
        if filename:
            self.load(filename)

    def load(self, filename):
        while 1:
```

```
                xmldata=filename.read(1024)
                if not xmldata:
                    break
                self.feed(xmldata)
            self.close()

    def start_QUESTION(self, attrs):
        question_id = attrs.get("QUESTION_ID")
        print "I found Question #" + question_id
        if question_id == "4":
            self.found = 1

    def end_SECTION(self):
        if not self.found:
            raise QuestionNotFound
try:
    MyParser = Parser()
    MyParser.load(open("survey.xml"))
except QuestionNotFound(Exception):
    print "I couldn't find Question #4 !!!"
```

The SAX API

SAX is a common event-based interface for object-oriented XML parsers. The Simple API for XML isn't a standard in the formal sense, but an informal specification designed by David Megginson, with input from many people on the XML-DEV mailing list. SAX defines an event-driven interface for parsing XML. To use SAX, you must create Python class instances that implement a specified interface, and the parser will then call various methods of those objects.

SAX is most suitable for purposes in which you want to read through an entire XML document from beginning to end, and perform some computation, such as building a data structure representing a document, or summarizing information in a document (computing an average value of a certain element, for example). It isn't very useful if you want to modify the document structure in some complicated way that involves changing how elements are nested, though it could be used if you simply want to change element contents or attributes. For example, you would not want to re-order chapters in a book using SAX, but you might want to change the contents of any name elements with the attribute lang equal to greek into Greek letters. Of course, if this is an XML file, we would use the standard attribute xml:lang rather than just lang to store the language.

One advantage of SAX is speed and simplicity. There is no need to expend effort examining elements that are irrelevant to your application. You can therefore write a class instance that ignores all elements that aren't what you need. Another advantage is that you don't have the whole document resident in memory at any one time, which matters if you are processing huge documents.

SAX defines four basic interfaces; a SAX-compliant XML parser can be passed any objects that support these interfaces, and will call various methods as data is processed. Your task, therefore, is to implement those interfaces relevant to your application.

The SAX interfaces are as follows:

DocumentHandler—Called for general document events. This interface is the heart of SAX; its methods are called for the start of the document, the start and end of elements, and for the characters of data contained inside elements.

DTDHandler—Called to handle DTD events required for basic parsing. This means notation declarations (XML spec section 4.7) and unparsed entity declarations (XML spec section 4).

EntityResolver—Called to resolve references to external entities. If your documents will have no external entity references, you won't need to implement this interface.

ErrorHandler—Called for error handling. The parser will call methods from this interface to report all warnings and errors.

Because Python doesn't support the concept of interfaces, the previous interfaces are implemented as Python classes. The default method implementations are defined to do nothing—the method body is just a Python pass statement—so usually you can simply ignore methods that aren't relevant to your application. The one big exception is the ErrorHandler interface; if you don't provide methods that print a message or otherwise take some action, errors in the XML data will be silently ignored. This is almost certainly not what you want your application to do, so always implement at least the error() and fatalError() methods. xml.sax.saxutils provides an ErrorPrinter class that sends error messages to standard error, and an ErrorRaiser class that raises an exception for any warnings or errors.

Pseudo-code for using SAX looks similar to the following:

```
# Define your specialized handler classes
from xml.sax import saxlib
class docHandler(saxlib.DocumentHandler):
    ...
```

```
# Create an instance of the handler classes
dh = docHandler()
# Create an XML parser
parser = ...
# Tell the parser to use your handler instance
parser.setDocumentHandler(dh)
# Parse the file; your handler's method will get called
parser.parseFile(sys.stdin)
# Close the parser
parser.close()
```

For more information, check out the following sites:

SAX: The Simple API for XML

http://www.python.org/doc/howto/xml/SAX.html

David Megginson's SAX page

Megginson was the primary force behind SAX's development, and implemented the Java version of SAX.

http://www.megginson.com/SAX/

What is an Event-Based Interface?

This page explains what an event-based interface is, and contrasts the event-based SAX with the tree-based Document Object Model (DOM).

http://www.megginson.com/SAX/event.html

Writing an application for a SAX-compliant XML parser

Simon Pepping gives a short overview of the Simple API for XML (SAX). He describes how a SAX-compliant parser and a SAX application interact, and how one should proceed to write a SAX application. The description focuses on the Python implementation of SAX. The examples are written in Python.

http://www.hobby.nl/~scaprea/XML/

DOM: The Document Object Model

The *Document Object Model (DOM)* is a standard interface for manipulating XML and HTML documents developed by the *World Wide Web Consortium (W3C)*.

4DOM is a Python library developed by *FourThought LLC* for XML and HTML processing and manipulation using the W3C's Document Object Model for interface.

4DOM supports all of DOM level 1 (core and HTML), as well as core, HTML and Document Traversal from level 2. 4DOM also adds some helper components for DOM Tree creation and printing, python integration, whitespace manipulation, and so on.

4DOM is designed to allow developers to rapidly design applications that read, write, or manipulate HTML and XML. Check out

```
http://www.fourthought.com/4Suite/4DOM/
```

XSL Transformations (XSLT)

This W3C specification defines the syntax and semantics of XSLT, which is a language for transforming XML documents into other XML documents.

XSLT is designed for use as part of XSL, which is a stylesheet language for XML. In addition to XSLT, XSL includes an XML vocabulary for specifying formatting. XSL specifies the styling of an XML document by using XSLT to describe how the document is transformed into another XML document that uses the formatting vocabulary.

XSLT is also designed to be used independently of XSL. However, XSLT is not intended as a completely general-purpose XML transformation language. Rather, it is designed primarily for the kinds of transformations that are needed when XSLT is used as part of XSL. XSLT is also good for transforming some custom XML format into XHTML that can be displayed by a browser, for instance. For more information, check out

```
http://www.w3.org/TR/xslt
```

4XSLT is an XML transformation processor based on the W3C's specification, and written by FourThought LLC, for the XSLT transform language. Currently, 4XSLT supports a subset of the final recommendation of XSLT. For more information, check out the site:

```
http://www.fourthought.com/4Suite/4XSLT/
```

XBEL—XML Bookmark Exchange Language

The XML Bookmark Exchange Language, or XBEL, is an Internet bookmarks interchange format. It was designed by the Python XML Special Interest Group on the group's mailing list. It grew out of an idea for a demonstration of using Python for XML processing. Mark Hammond contributed the original idea, and other members of the SIG chimed in to add support for their favorite browser features. After debate that deviated from the original idea, compromises were reached that allow XBEL to be a useful language for describing bookmark data for a range of browsers, including the major browsers and a number of less widely used browsers.

At this time, the formal DTD was finalized and documentation was written. The formal DTD and the documentation are available online at the following sites:

```
http://www.python.org/topics/xml/xbel/
```

```
http://www.python.org/topics/xml/xbel/docs/html/xbel.html
```

Supporting software is provided as part of the Python XML package. This software is located in the `demo/xbel/` directory of the distribution. This includes command-line processes for converting XBEL instances to other common formats, including the Navigator and Internet Explorer formats. Note that the current release of the Grail Internet browser from CNRI supports XBEL as a native bookmarks format.

The script, created by Jürgen Hermann, on the following site, checks the URLs in an XBEL document:

```
http://cscene.org/%7ejh/xml/bookmarks/checkurls.py
```

RPC—What Is It?

A *Remote Procedure Call (RPC)* uses the ordinary procedure call mechanism that is familiar to every user in order to hide the intricacies of the network.

A client process calls a function on a remote server and suspends itself until it gets back the results. Parameters are passed the same as in any ordinary procedure. The RPC, similar to an ordinary procedure, is synchronous; clients and servers must run concurrently. Servers must keep up with clients. The process (or thread) that issues the call waits until it gets the results. Behind the scenes, the RPC runtime software collects values for the parameters, forms a message, and sends it to the remote server. (Note that servers must first come up before clients can talk to them.) The server receives the request, unpacks the parameters, calls the procedure, and sends the reply back to the client.

Asynchronous processing is limited because it requires threads and tricky code for managing threads. A procedure call is the name of a procedure, its parameters, and the result it returns.

Procedure calls are very important for the existence of computers. Every program is just a single procedure called *main*; every operating system has a main procedure called a *kernel*. There's a top level to every program that sits in a loop waiting for something to happen and then distributes control to a hierarchy of procedures that respond. This is at the heart of interactivity and networking, it's at the heart of software.

RPC is a very simple extension to the procedure call idea; it says, "let's create connections between procedures that are running in different applications or on different machines."

Conceptually, there's no difference between a local procedure call and a remote one, but they are implemented differently, perform differently (RPC is much slower), and therefore are used for different things.

Remote calls are marshaled into a format that can be understood on the other side of the connection. As long as two machines agree on a format, they can talk to each other. That's why Windows machines can be networked with other Windows machines, Macs can talk to Macs, and so on. The value in a standardized cross-platform format for RPC is that it allows UNIX machines to talk to Windows machines and vice versa.

A number of formats are possible. One possible format is XML. XML-RPC uses XML as the marshaling format. It allows Macs to easily make procedure calls to software running on Windows machines and BeOS machines, as well as all flavors of UNIX and Java, IBM mainframes, PDAs, and so on.

With XML it's easy to see what it's doing, and it's also relatively easy to marshal the internal procedure call format into a remote format.

Simple Object Access Protocol (SOAP)

SOAP is an XML/HTTP-based protocol for accessing services, objects, and servers in a platform-independent manner. For more information, check out

```
http://www.develop.com/soap
```

A minimal Python SOAP implementation is located at

```
http://casbah.org/Scarab/
```

This module is derived in part from Andrew Kuchling's `xml.marshal` code. It implements the SOAP "section 8" serialization using the same API as `pickle.py` (dump/load).

Scarab is an *Open Source Communications* library implementing protocols, formats, and interfaces for writing distributed applications, with an emphasis on low-end and lightweight implementations. Users can combine Scarab module implementations to build a messaging system to fit their needs, scaling from very simple messaging or data transfer all the way up to where CORBA can take over. Scarab implementations include support for such areas as distributed objects, remote procedure calls, XML messages, TCP transport, and HTTP transport.

PythonPoint

The `ReportLab` package contains a demo called `PythonPoint`, which has a simple XML for doing presentation slides and can convert them to PDF documents, along with imaginative presentation effects. The demo script that is provided in the Web site illustrates how easily complex XML can be translated into useful PDF. The demo output, pythonpoint.pdf, demonstrates some of the more exotic PDF capabilities:

```
http://www.reportlab.com/demos/demos.html
```

Pyxie

Pyxie is an Open Source XML processing library for Python developed by Sean McGrath. He has also written a book called *XML Processing with Python* for Prentice Hall. The book contains a description of the Pyxie library and many sample programs.

Pyxie is heavily based on a line-oriented notation for parsed XML known as PYX. Pyxie includes utilities, known as `xmln` and `xmlv`, that generate PYX.

PYX is independent of Python and a number of programs processing PYX have appeared in Java, Perl, and JavaScript:

```
http://www.digitome.com/pyxie.html
```

XML-RPC

XML-RPC is a specification and a set of implementations that allow software running on different operating systems and different environments to make procedure calls over the Internet. As a simple RPC protocol, it converts simple data types into an XML-based format, and then ships them over the network using HTTP-POST requests as the transport and XML as the encoding. The procedure executes on the server and the value it returns is also formatted in XML. Procedure parameters can be scalars, numbers, strings, dates, and so on; they can also be complex record and list structures.

XML-RPC is designed to be as simple as possible, while allowing complex data structures to be transmitted, processed, and returned. This re-use of high-level ideas such as XML and HTTP makes it inefficient in comparison to a binary format, but it also makes it easy to implement; implementations already exist for Java, Python, Perl, and Tcl, and Zope 2.0.

The XML-RPC library is copyrighted, but can be used without fee. This also applies to commercial applications. For more information, check out

XML-RPC

```
http://www.xmlrpc.com/
```

The XML-RPC specification documents the XML-RPC protocol implemented in Frontier 5.1.

```
http://www.xml-rpc.com/spec/
```

```
http://www.scripting.com/frontier5/xml/code/rpc.html
```

XML-RPC for Newbies, by Dave Winer

```
http://davenet.userland.com/1998/07/14/xmlRpcForNewbies
```

The Python Implementation

PythonWare's Fredrik Lundhs `xmlrpc` package provides everything you need to build clients and servers in Python:

```
http://www.pythonware.com/products/xmlrpc/
```

Secret Labs' `xmlrpclib` module is a client-side implementation of the XML-RPC protocol. This implementation is tightly integrated with Python, which makes it very easy to call remote methods. For example, here's the Python code needed to call one of Userland's sample servers:

```
betty = Server("http://betty.userland.com")
print betty.examples.getStateName(41)
```

This results in a remote call to the `examples.getStateName` method published by the `betty server`, with the integer 41 as the single argument. The result from this call is a string with the value `"South Dakota"`.

The marshalling and parsing classes provided by this module can also be used in XML-RPC server implementations. Sample code for Medusa and Python's SocketServer module is also included in the current release.

Working with Zope

Amos Latteier at Digital Creations has written an *XML-RPC How To for Zope Users*. Among other things, it contains code to handle authentication issues and access control.

The idea of using Zope to handle XML-RPC is based on the fact that every Zope object can respond to HTTP requests.

The *How To* covers the use of Zope as an XML-RPC server, and as an XML-RPC client. The document also shows how to extend Fredrik Lundh's XML-RPC Python module to support sending requests with basic authentication. It can be found at

```
http://www.zope.org/Members/Amos/XML-RPC
```

XDR Data Exchange Format

XDR is best described as a standard for data description and encoding. It uses a implicit typing language to describe intricate data formats in a concise manner—note that this language is not a programming language. Protocols such as Sun RPC (Remote Procedure Call) and the NFS (Network File System, which was initially built on top of RPC) use XDR to describe the format of their data because XDR is useful for transferring data between different computer architectures. XDR has been used to communicate with data between such diverse machines as the SUN WORKSTATION, VAX, IBM-PC, and Cray. It is a very portable implementation. For more information, check out

Internet standards—RFC 1014, External Data Representation

```
http://info.internet.isi.edu/in-notes/rfc/files/rfc1014.txt
```

xdrlib

The xdrlib module almost entirely supports the *External Data Representation Standard (XDR)* as described in RFC 1014, written by Sun Microsystems, Inc. on June 1987. Therefore, it is used extensively in networked applications, mainly the ones that need to handle RPC.

This module defines two exceptions, and two classes—one for packing variables into XDR representation, and another for unpacking from XDR representation:

Packer()—Packer is the class for packing data into XDR representation. The Packer class is instantiated with no arguments.

Unpacker(data)—Unpacker is the complementary class, which unpacks XDR data values from a string buffer. The input buffer is given as data.

Packer Objects

Packer instances have the following methods:

get_buffer()—Returns the current pack buffer as a string.

reset()—Resets the pack buffer to the empty string.

In general, you can pack any of the most common XDR data types by calling the appropriate pack_type() method. Each method takes a single argument, the value to pack. The following simple data type packing methods are supported: pack_uint(), pack_int(), pack_enum(), pack_bool(), pack_uhyper(), and pack_hyper(). The following methods support floating point number packing.

pack_float(value)—Packs the single-precision floating point number value.

pack_double(value)—Packs the double-precision floating point number value.

The following methods support packing strings, bytes, and opaque data:

pack_fstring(n, s)—Packs a fixed length string, s. n is the length of the string, but it is not packed into the data buffer. The string is padded with null bytes if necessary to guarantee 4 byte alignment.

pack_fopaque(n, data)—Packs a fixed length opaque data stream, similar to pack_fstring().

pack_string(s)—Packs a variable length string, s. The length of the string is first packed as an unsigned integer, and then the string data is packed with pack_fstring().

pack_opaque(data)—Packs a variable length opaque data string, similar to pack_string().

pack_bytes(bytes)—Packs a variable length byte stream, similar to pack_string().

The following methods support packing arrays and lists:

pack_list(list, pack_item)—Packs a list of homogeneous items. This method is useful for lists with an indeterminate size; that is, the size is not available until the entire list has been walked. For each item in the list, an unsigned integer 1 is packed first, followed by the data value from the list. pack_item is the function called to pack the individual item. At the end of the list, an unsigned integer 0 is packed.

pack_farray(n, array, pack_item)—Packs a fixed length list (array) of homogeneous items. n is the length of the list; it is not packed into the buffer, but a ValueError exception is raised if len(array) is not equal to n. As stated previously, pack_item is the function used to pack each element.

pack_array(list, pack_item)—Packs a variable length list of homogeneous items. First, the length of the list is packed as an unsigned integer, and then each element is packed as in pack_farray() stated previously.

Unpacker Objects
The Unpacker class offers the following methods:

reset(data)—Resets the string buffer with the given data.

get_position()—Returns the current unpack position in the data buffer.

set_position(position)—Sets the data buffer unpack position to position. You should be careful about using get_position() and set_position().

get_buffer()—Returns the current unpack data buffer as a string.

done()—Indicates unpack completion. Raises an error exception if all the data has not been unpacked.

In addition, every data type that can be packed with a Packer, can be unpacked with an Unpacker. Unpacking methods are of the form unpack_type(), and take no arguments. They return the unpacked object.

unpack_float()—Unpacks a single-precision floating point number.

unpack_double()—Unpacks a double-precision floating point number, similar to unpack_float().

In addition, the following methods unpack strings, bytes, and opaque data:

unpack_fstring(n)—Unpacks and returns a fixed length string. n is the number of characters expected. Padding with null bytes to guaranteed 4 byte alignment is assumed.

unpack_fopaque(n)—Unpacks and returns a fixed length opaque data stream, similar to unpack_fstring().

unpack_string()—Unpacks and returns a variable length string. The length of the string is first unpacked as an unsigned integer, and then the string data is unpacked with unpack_fstring().

unpack_opaque()—Unpacks and returns a variable length opaque data string, similar to unpack_string().

unpack_bytes()—Unpacks and returns a variable length byte stream, similar to unpack_string().

The following methods support unpacking arrays and lists:

unpack_list(*unpack_item*)—Unpacks and returns a list of homogeneous items. The list is unpacked one element at a time by first unpacking an unsigned integer flag. If the flag is 1, the item is unpacked and appended to the list. A flag of 0 indicates the end of the list. unpack_item is the function called to unpack the items.

unpack_farray(*n, unpack_item*)—Unpacks and returns (as a list) a fixed length array of homogeneous items. n is the number of list elements to expect in the buffer. As stated previously, unpack_item is the function used to unpack each element.

unpack_array(*unpack_item*)—Unpacks and returns a variable length list of homogeneous items. First, the length of the list is unpacked as an unsigned integer, and then each element is unpacked as in unpack_farray() previously.

In the following example, we pack a group of variables, unpacking them later.

```
import xdrlib

def f_packer(name, author, month, year):
    data = xdrlib.Packer()
    data.pack_string(name)
    data.pack_string(author)
    data.pack_uint(month)
```

```
        data.pack_uint(year)
        packed = data.get_buffer()
        return packed

def f_unpacker(packer):
        data = xdrlib.Unpacker(packer)
        return data

print "The original values are: 'Andre', 'Author', 10, 2000"
print

packed = f_packer('Andre', 'Author', 10, 2000)
print "The packed data is now defined by:", repr(packed)
print
print "And now, the original data again. (After unpacking it!)"
unpacked = f_unpacker(packed)
print repr(unpacked.unpack_string()), ", ", \
        repr(unpacked.unpack_string()), ", ", \
        unpacked.unpack_uint(), ", ",              \
        unpacked.unpack_uint()
unpacked.done()
```

```
The original values are: 'Andre', 'Author', 10, 2000

The packed data is now defined by:
'\000\000\000\005Andre\000\000\000\000\000\000\006Author\000\000\000\000\
000\012\000\000\007\320'

And now, the original data again. (After unpacking it!)
'Andre' , 'Author' , 10 , 2000
```

Note
If you are only handling simple data types and only with Python, it is probably easier to just use the marshal module.

Exceptions
Exceptions in this module are coded as class instances:

Error—This is the base exception class. Error has a single public data member msg containing the description of the error.

ConversionError—This class is derived from Error. Contains no additional instance variables.

Here is a simple example of how you would catch one of these exceptions:

```
>>> import xdrlib
>>> data = xdrlib.Packer()
>>> try:
...     data.pack_double("8.01")
... except xdrlib.ConversionError, ErrorObj:
...     print 'Error while packing the data:', ErrorObj.msg
...
Error while packing the data: required argument is not a float
>>>
```

Handling Other Markup Languages

The initial part of this chapter covers XML, which is, undoubtedly, a future promise for the Internet.

The next pages of this section describe additional modules that support other data format standards commonly used on the internet, SGML and HTML.

sgmllib

The `sgmllib` module is an SGML parser subset. Although it has a simple implementation, it is powerful enough to build the HTML parser.

This module implements the `SGMLParser()` class.

SGMLParser()

The `SGMLParser` class is instantiated without arguments. The parser is hardcoded to recognize the following constructs:

    a. Opening and closing tags of the form `<tag attr="value ...>` and `</tag>`, respectively.

    b. Numeric character references of the form `&#name;`.

    c. Entity references of the form `&name;`.

    d. SGML comments of the form `<!--text-->`. Note that spaces, tabs, and newlines are allowed between the trailing > and the immediately preceding -.

`SGMLParser` instances have the following interface methods (note that the interface is similar to the xmllib one):

`reset()`—Resets the instance. Loses all unprocessed data. This is called implicitly at instantiation time.

`setnomoretags()`—Stops processing tags. Treat all following input as literal input (CDATA). (This is only provided so that the HTML tag `<PLAINTEXT>` can be implemented.)

`setliteral()`—Enters literal mode (CDATA mode).

`feed(data)`—Feeds some text to the parser. It is processed insofar as it consists of complete elements; incomplete data is buffered until more data is fed or `close()` is called.

`close()`—Force processing of all buffered data as if it were followed by an end-of-file mark. This method can be redefined by a derived class to define additional processing at the end of the input, but the redefined version should always call `close()`.

`handle_starttag(tag, method, attributes)`—This method is called to handle start tags for which either a `start_tag()` or `do_tag()` method has been defined. The tag argument is the name of the tag converted to lowercase, and the method argument is the bound method that should be used to support semantic interpretation of the start tag. The attributes argument is a list of (name, value) pairs containing the attributes found inside the tag's <> brackets. The name has been translated to lowercase, and double quotes and backslashes in the value have been interpreted. For instance, for the tag `<A HREF="http://www.cwi.nl/">`, this method would be called as `unknown_starttag('a', [('href', 'http://www.cwi.nl/')])`. The base implementation simply calls a method with attributes as the only argument.

`handle_endtag(tag, method)`—This method is called to handle endtags for which an `end_tag()` method has been defined. The tag argument is the name of the tag converted to lowercase, and the method argument is the bound method that should be used to support semantic interpretation of the end tag. If no `end_tag()` method is defined for the closing element, this handler is not called. The base implementation simply calls method.

`handle_data(data)`—This method is called to process arbitrary data. It is intended to be overridden by a derived class; the base class implementation does nothing.

`handle_charref(`*ref*`)`—This method is called to process a character reference of the form &#ref;. In the base implementation, `ref` must be a decimal number in the range 0–255. It translates the character to ASCII and calls the method `handle_data()` with the character as argument. If `ref` is invalid or out of range, the method `unknown_charref(`*ref*`)` is called to handle the error. A subclass must override this method to provide support for named character entities.

`handle_entityref(`*ref*`)`—This method is called to process a general entity reference of the form &ref;, where `ref` is an general entity reference. It looks for `ref` in the instance (or class) variable entitydefs that should be a mapping from entity names to corresponding translations. If a translation is found, it calls the method `handle_data()` with the translation; otherwise, it calls the method `unknown_entityref(`*ref*`)`. The default entitydefs defines translations for &, &apos, >, <, and ".

`handle_comment(`*comment*`)`—This method is called when a comment is encountered. The comment argument is a string containing the text between the <!- and -> delimiters, but not the delimiters themselves. For example, the comment <!-text-> will cause this method to be called with the argument `text`. The default method does nothing.

`report_unbalanced(`*tag*`)`—This method is called when an end tag is found that does not correspond to any open element.

> **Tip**
> In order to handle all tags in your code, you need to overload the following two methods: `unknown_starttag` and `unknown_endtag`.

`unknown_starttag(`*tag, attributes*`)`—This method is called to process an unknown start tag. It is intended to be overridden by a derived class; the base class implementation does nothing.

`unknown_endtag(`*tag*`)`—This method is called to process an unknown end tag. It is intended to be overridden by a derived class; the base class implementation does nothing.

`unknown_charref(`*ref*`)`—This method is called to process unresolvable numeric character references. Refer to `handle_charref()` to determine what is handled by default. It is intended to be overridden by a derived class; the base class implementation does nothing.

`unknown_entityref(`*ref*`)`—This method is called to process an unknown entity reference. It is intended to be overridden by a derived class; the base class implementation does nothing.

Apart from overriding or extending the methods listed previously, derived classes can also define methods of the following form to define processing of specific tags. Tag names in the input stream are case independent; the tag occurring in method names must be in lowercase:

start_tag(*attributes*)—This method is called to process an opening tag. It has precedence over do_tag(). The attributes argument has the same meaning as described for handle_starttag() previously.

do_tag(*attributes*)—This method is called to process an opening tag that does not come with a matching closing tag. The attributes argument has the same meaning as described for handle_starttag() previously.

end_tag()—This method is called to process a closing tag.

Note that the parser maintains a stack of open elements for which no end tag has been found yet. Only tags processed by start_tag() are pushed on this stack. Definition of an end_tag() method is optional for these tags. For tags processed by do_tag() or by unknown_tag(), no end_tag() method must be defined; if defined, it will not be used. If both start_tag() and do_tag() methods exist for a tag, the start_tag() method takes precedence.

The following example opens an SGML file and collects the information regarding the page title.

```
import sgmllib
import string

filename = "index.html"
class CleanExit(Exception):
    pass

class Titlefinder(sgmllib.SGMLParser):
    def __init__(self, verbose=0):
        sgmllib.SGMLParser.__init__(self, verbose)
        self.title = self.data = None
    def start_title(self, attributes):
        self.data = []
    def end_title(self):
        self.title = string.join(self.data, "")
        raise CleanExit
    def handle_data(self, data):
```

```
            if self.data is not None:
                self.data.append(data)

    def get_title(filehandle):
        Parser = Titlefinder()
        try:
            while 1:
                sgmldata = filehandle.read(1024)
                if not sgmldata:
                    break
                Parser.feed(sgmldata)
            Parser.close()
        except CleanExit:
            return Parser.title
        return None

    filehandle = open(filename)
    title = get_title(filehandle)

    print "The page's title is: %s" % (title)
```

htmllib

This module defines a parser class that can serve as a base for parsing text files
formatted in the *Hypertext Markup Language (HTML)*. The class is not directly
concerned with I/O—it must be provided with input in string form via a method, and
makes calls to methods of a formatter object in order to produce output. The
HTMLParser class is designed to be used as a base class for other classes in order to add
functionality, and allows most of its methods to be extended or overridden. In turn,
this class is derived from and extends the SGMLParser class defined in module sgmllib.
The HTMLParser implementation supports the HTML 2.0 language as described in
RFC 1866. Two implementations of formatter objects are provided in the formatter
module.

The following is a summary of the interface defined by sgmllib.SGMLParser:

a. The interface to feed data to an instance is through the feed() method, which
takes a string argument. This can be called with as little or as much text at a time
as desired; "p.feed(a); p.feed(b)" has the same effect as "p.feed(a+b)". When
the data contains complete HTML tags, these are processed immediately;
incomplete elements are saved in a buffer. To force processing of all unprocessed
data, call the close() method.

For example, to parse the entire contents of a file, use

```
parser.feed(open('myfile.html').read())
parser.close()
```

b. The interface to define semantics for HTML tags is very simple: derive a class
    and define methods called `start_tag()`, `end_tag()`, or `do_tag()`. The parser will
    call these at appropriate moments: `start_tag` or `do_tag()` is called when an
    opening tag of the form `<tag ...>` is encountered; `end_tag()` is called when a
    closing tag of the form `<tag>` is encountered. If an opening tag requires a
    corresponding closing tag, such as `<H1>... </H1>`, the class should define the
    `start_tag()` method; if a tag requires no closing tag, such as `<P>`, the class
    should define the `do_tag()` method.

This module defines a single class: `HTMLParser(formatter)`. This is the basic HTML
parser class. It supports all entity names required by the HTML 2.0 specification
(RFC 1866). It also defines handlers for all HTML 2.0 and many HTML 3.0 and 3.2
elements. In addition to tag methods, the `HTMLParser` class provides some additional
methods and instance variables for use within tag methods. They are as follows:

`formatter`—This is the formatter instance associated with the parser.

`nofill`—This Boolean flag should be true when whitespace should not be
collapsed, or false when it should be. In general, this should only be true when
character data is to be treated as "preformatted" text, as within a `<PRE>` element.
The default value is false. This affects the operation of `handle_data()` and
`save_end()`.

`anchor_bgn(href, name, type)`—This method is called at the start of an anchor
region. The arguments correspond to the attributes of the `<A>` tag with the same
names. The default implementation maintains a list of hyperlinks (defined by the
`href` attribute) within the document. The list of hyperlinks is available as the data
attribute `anchorlist`.

`anchor_end()`—This method is called at the end of an anchor region. The default
implementation adds a textual footnote marker using an index into the list of
hyperlinks created by `anchor_bgn()`.

`handle_image(source, alt[, ismap[, align[, width[, height]]]])`—This
method is called to handle images. The default implementation simply passes the alt
value to the `handle_data()` method.

`save_bgn()`—Begins saving character data in a buffer instead of sending it to the formatter object. Retrieve the stored data via `save_end()`. Use of the `save_bgn()`/`save_end()` pair cannot be nested.

`save_end()`—Ends buffering character data and returns all data saved since the preceding call to `save_bgn()`. If the nofill flag is false, whitespace is collapsed to single spaces. A call to this method without a preceding call to `save_bgn()` will raise a `TypeError` exception.

The following example is a CGI script that outputs to a Web page the Web links found in a given HTML file.

```python
import htmllib
import formatter, string, cgi

form = cgi.FieldStorage()

try:
    myfile = form["filename"].value
except:
    myfile = "index.html"

class ParserClass(htmllib.HTMLParser):
    def __init__(self, verbose=0):
        self.anchors = {}
        fmt = formatter.NullFormatter()
        htmllib.HTMLParser.__init__(self, fmt, verbose)
    def anchor_bgn(self, href, name, type):
        self.save_bgn()
        self.anchor = href
    def anchor_end(self):
        tagtext = string.strip(self.save_end())
        if self.anchor and tagtext:
            self.anchors[tagtext] = self.anchors.get(tagtext, []) + \
                                    [self.anchor]

filename = open(myfile)
htmldata = filename.read()
filename.close()
```

```
parserobj = ParserClass()
parserobj.feed(htmldata)
parserobj.close()

print "Content-type: text/html\n"

for key in p.anchors.keys():
    print key, p.anchors[key]
```

htmlentitydefs

The `htmlentitydefs` module contains a dictionary called `entitydefs` that contains all the definitions for the general entities defined by HTML 2.0, as demonstrated next:

```
import htmlentitydefs
htmlentitydef = htmlentitydefs.entitydefs.keys()
for key in htmlentitydef:
    print key, " = ", htmlentitydef[key]
```

formatter

The `formatter` module is used for generic output formatting by the `HTMLParser` class of the `htmllib` module. This module supports two interface definitions, each with multiple implementations: Formatter and Writer.

Formatter objects transform an abstract flow of formatting events into specific output events on writer objects. Formatters manage several stack structures to allow various properties of a writer object to be changed and restored; writers need not be able to handle relative changes nor any sort of "change back" operation. Specific writer properties which can be controlled via formatter objects are horizontal alignment, font, and left margin indentations. A mechanism is provided that supports providing arbitrary, non-exclusive style settings to a writer as well. Additional interfaces facilitate formatting events that are not reversible, such as paragraph separation. The *writer* interface is required by the formatter interface.

Writer objects encapsulate device interfaces. Abstract devices, such as file formats, are supported as well as physical devices. The provided implementations all work with abstract devices. The interface makes available mechanisms for setting the properties that formatter objects manage and inserting data into the output.

The Formatter Interface

Interfaces to create formatters are dependent on the specific formatter class being instantiated. The interfaces described as follows are the required interfaces, which all formatters must support once initialized.

One data element is defined at the module level: AS_IS. This value can be used in the font specification passed to the push_font() method described in the following, or as the new value to any other push_property() method. Pushing the AS_IS value allows the corresponding pop_property() method to be called without having to track whether the property was changed.

The following attributes are defined for formatter instance objects:

writer—Interacts with the formatter.

end_paragraph(*blanklines*)—Closes any open paragraphs and inserts at least blanklines before the next paragraph.

add_line_break()—Adds a hard line break if one does not already exist. This does not break the logical paragraph.

add_hor_rule(*args, **kw)—Inserts a horizontal rule in the output. A hard break is inserted if data is in the current paragraph, but the logical paragraph is not broken. The arguments and keywords are passed on to the writer's send_line_break() method.

add_flowing_data(*data*)—Provides data that should be formatted with collapsed whitespaces. Whitespace from preceeding and successive calls to add_flowing_data() is considered as well when the whitespace collapse is performed. The data that is passed to this method is expected to be word wrapped by the output device. Note that any word wrapping still must be performed by the writer object because of the need to rely on device and font information.

add_literal_data(*data*)—Provides data that should be passed to the writer unchanged. Whitespace, including newline and tab characters, is considered legal in the value of data.

add_label_data(*format, counter*)—Inserts a label that should be placed to the left of the current left margin. This should be used for constructing bulleted or numbered lists. If the format value is a string, it is interpreted as a format specification for counter, which should be an integer. The result of this formatting becomes the value of the label; if format is not a string, it is used as the label value directly. The label value is passed as the only argument to the writer's send_label_data() method. Interpretation of nonstring label values is dependent on the associated writer.

Format specifications are strings that, in combination with a counter value, are used to compute label values. Each character in the format string is copied to the label value, with some characters recognized to indicate a transformation on the counter value. Specifically, the character 1 represents the counter value formatter as an Arabic number, the characters A and a represent alphabetic representations of the counter value in upper- and lowercase, respectively, and I and i represent the counter value in Roman numerals, in upper- and lowercase. Note that the alphabetic and roman transformations require that the counter value be greater than zero.

flush_softspace()—Sends any pending whitespace buffered from a previous call to add_flowing_data() to the associated writer object. This should be called before any direct manipulation of the writer object.

push_alignment(align)—Pushes a new alignment setting onto the alignment stack. This might be AS_IS if no change is desired. If the alignment value is changed from the previous setting, the writer's new_alignment() method is called with the align value.

pop_alignment()—Restores the previous alignment.

push_font((size, italic, bold, teletype))—Changes some or all font properties of the writer object. Properties that are not set to AS_IS are set to the values passed in, whereas others are maintained at their current settings. The writer's new_font() method is called with the fully resolved font specification.

pop_font()—Restores the previous font.

push_margin(margin)—Increases the number of left margin indentations by one, associating the logical tag margin with the new indentation. The initial margin level is 0. Changed values of the logical tag must be true values; false values other than AS_IS are not sufficient to change the margin.

pop_margin()—Restores the previous margin.

push_style(*styles)—Pushes any number of arbitrary style specifications. All styles are pushed onto the styles stack in order. A tuple representing the entire stack, including AS_IS values, is passed to the writer's new_styles() method.

pop_style([n = 1])—Pops the last n style specifications passed to push_style(). A tuple representing the revised stack, including AS_IS values, is passed to the writer's new_styles() method.

set_spacing(spacing)—Sets the spacing style for the writer.

assert_line_data([flag = 1])—Informs the formatter that data has been added to the current paragraph out-of-band. This should be used when the writer has been manipulated directly. The optional flag argument can be set to false if the writer manipulations produced a hard line break at the end of the output.

Formatter Implementations

Two implementations of formatter objects are provided by this module. Most applications can use one of these classes without modification or subclassing.

NullFormatter([writer])—A formatter that does nothing. If writer is omitted, a NullWriter instance is created. No methods of the writer are called by NullFormatter instances. Implementations should inherit from this class if implementing a writer interface but don't need to inherit any implementation.

AbstractFormatter(writer)—The standard formatter. This implementation has demonstrated wide applicability to many writers, and can be used directly in most circumstances. It has been used to implement a full-featured WWW browser.

The Writer Interface

Interfaces to create writers are dependent on the specific writer class being instantiated. The interfaces described as follows are the required interfaces that all writers must support once initialized. Although most applications can use the AbstractFormatter class as a formatter, the writer must typically be provided by the application.

flush()—Flushes any buffered output or device control events.

new_alignment(align)—Sets the alignment style. The align value can be any object, but by convention is a string or None, where None indicates that the writer's preferred alignment should be used. Conventional align values are left, center, right, and justify.

new_font(font)—Sets the font style. The value of font will be None, indicating that the device's default font should be used, or a tuple of the form (size, italic, bold, teletype). Size will be a string indicating the size of font that should be used; specific strings and their interpretation must be defined by the application. The italic, bold, and teletype values are Boolean indicators specifying which of those font attributes should be used.

`new_margin(margin, level)`—Sets the margin level to the integer level and the logical tag to margin. Interpretation of the logical tag is at the writer's discretion; the only restriction on the value of the logical tag is that it not be a false value for non-zero values of level.

`new_spacing(spacing)`—Sets the spacing style to spacing.

`new_styles(styles)`—Sets additional styles. The styles value is a tuple of arbitrary values; the value `AS_IS` should be ignored. The styles tuple can be interpreted either as a set or as a stack depending on the requirements of the application and writer implementation.

`send_line_break()`—Breaks the current line.

`send_paragraph(number)`—Produces a paragraph separation of at least the given number of blank lines, or the equivalent. The blankline value will be an integer. Note that the implementation will receive a call to `send_line_break()` before this call if a line break is needed; this method should not include ending the last line of the paragraph. It is only responsible for vertical spacing between paragraphs.

`send_hor_rule(*args, **kw)`—Displays a horizontal rule on the output device. The arguments to this method are entirely application- and writer-specific, and should be interpreted with care. The method implementation can assume that a line break has already been issued via `send_line_break()`.

`send_flowing_data(data)`—Outputs character data that might be word wrapped and re-flowed as needed. Within any sequence of calls to this method, the writer can assume that spans of multiple whitespace characters have been collapsed to single space characters.

`send_literal_data(data)`—Outputs character data that has already been formatted for display. Generally, this should be interpreted to mean that line breaks indicated by newline characters should be preserved and no new line breaks should be introduced. The data can contain embedded newline and tab characters, unlike data provided to the `send_formatted_data()` interface.

`send_label_data(data)`—Sets data to the left of the current left margin, if possible. The value of data is not restricted; treatment of non-string values is entirely application- and writer-dependent. This method will only be called at the beginning of a line.

Writer Implementations

Three implementations of the writer object interface are provided as examples by this module. Most applications will need to derive new writer classes from the NullWriter class.

NullWriter()—A writer that only provides the interface definition; no actions are taken on any methods. This should be the base class for all writers that do not need to inherit any implementation methods.

AbstractWriter()—A writer that can be used in debugging formatters, but not much else. Each method simply announces itself by printing its name and arguments on standard output.

DumbWriter([*file*[, maxcol = 72]])—A simple writer class that writes output on the file object passed in as file or, if file is omitted, on standard output. The output is simply word wrapped to the number of columns specified by maxcol. This class is suitable for reflowing a sequence of paragraphs.

Using the Formatter Module

The following example removes all tags from an HTML file, leaving only the plain text left.

```
1: from htmllib import HTMLParser
2: from formatter import AbstractFormatter, DumbWriter
3: htmlfile = open("stuff.html")
4: parser = HTMLParser(AbstractFormatter(DumbWriter()))
5: parser.feed(htmlfile.read())
6: parser.close()
7: htmlfile.close()
```

The DumbWriter function is used here to dump all the non-tag contents of htmlfile to the standard output.

Note that the file opened by line 3 can also be a URL. You just need to import and use the urllib.urlopen function, like this:

```
from urllib import urlopen
htmlfile = urlopen('http://www.lessaworld.com/')
```

MIME Parsing and Manipulation

MIME (Multipurpose Internet Mail Extensions) is a standard for sending multipart multimedia data through Internet mail. This standard exposes mechanisms for specifying and describing the format of Internet message bodies.

A MIME-encoded message looks similar to the following:

```
Content-Type: multipart/mixed; boundary="====_238659232=="
Date: Mon, 03 Apr 2000 18:30:23  -0400
From: Andre Lessa <alessa@lessaworld.com>
To: Renata Lessa <rlessa@lessaworld.com>
Subject: Python Book


—====_238659232==
Content-Type: text/plain; charset="us-ascii"


Sorry Honey, I am late for dinner. I am still writing Chapter 13. Meanwhile,
take a look at the following Cooking material that you've asked me to find in
the Internet.


—====_238659232==
Content-Type: application/msword; name="cookmasters.doc"
Content-Transfer-Encoding: base64
Content-Disposition: attachment, filename=" cookmasters.doc"


GgjEPgkwIr4G29m1Lawr7GgjEPgkwIr4G29m14tifkAb3qPgGgjEPgkwIr4G29m1La29m14tifkAb
3qPgGgjEPgkwIr4G29m1Law29m14tifkAb3qPgGgjEPgkwIr4G29m1Lawr629m14tifkAb3qPgIr4
G29m1Lawr2GgjEPgkwIr4G29m1Lawr29m14tifkAb3qPg29m14tifkAb3qPgGgjEPgkwIr4G29m1L
awr8Ab3qPgGgjEPgkwIr4G29m1GgjEPgkwIr4G29m1Lawr7GgjEPgkwIr4G29m1Hawr0==
—====_238659232==—
```

Note that the message is broken into parts, and each part is delimited by a boundary. The boundary itself works like a separator, and its value is defined in the first line of the message, right next to the first content-type.

Every part starts with a boundary mark, and then it is followed by a set of RFC822 headers telling you what is the content-type and the encoding format of the data for that part, and next, separated by a blank line, we have the data itself.

Check out the last line of the message. Do you see the trailing — after the boundary? That's how the message identifies the final boundary.

The next couple of modules are tools for mail and news message processing that use MIME messages. For more information, check out

RFC 1521

```
http://info.internet.isi.edu/in-notes/rfc/files/rfc1521.txt
```

rfc822

The `rfc822` module parses mail headers that are defined by the Internet standard RFC 822. This standard specifies the syntax for text messages that are sent among computer users, within the framework of electronic mail. These headers are used in a number of contexts including mail handling and in the HTTP protocol. For more information, check out

Internet standards—Standard for ARPA Internet Text Messages

```
http://info.internet.isi.edu/in-notes/rfc/files/rfc822.txt
```

This module defines a class, `Message`, which represents a collection of email headers. It is used in various contexts, usually to read such headers from a file. This module also defines a helper class `AddressList` for parsing RFC822 addresses. A dictionary-like object represents the `Message` object, where the message headers are the dictionary keys.

mimetools

The `mimetools` module provides utility tools for parsing and manipulation of MIME multipart and encoded messages. This module contains a special dictionary-like object called `Message` that collects some information about MIME encoded messages. `mime-version`, `content-type`, `charset`, `to`, `date`, `from`, and `subject` are some examples of dictionary keys that the object possesses. This module also implements some utility functions. The `choose_boundary()` function creates a unique boundary string.

The next two functions encode and decode file objects based on the encoding format, which can be "quoted-printable", "base64", or "uuencode".

- `decode(inputfileobject, outputfileobject, encoding)`

- `encode(inputfileobject, outputfileobject, encoding)`

The functions `copyliteral(input, output)` and `copybinary(input, output)` read the input file (until EOF) and write them to the output file object. Note that the objects must be opened.

Take a look at the `message = mimetools.Message(fileobject)` function. This function returns a `Message` object derived from the `rfc822.Message` class. Therefore, it supports all the methods supported by `rfc822.Message`, plus the following ones:

`message.gettype()`—Returns the type/subtype from the content-type header. The default value is `text/plain`.

`message.getencoding()`—Returns the message encoding method. The default value is `7bit`.

`message.getplist()`—Returns the list of parameters from the content-type header.

`message.getmaintype()`—Returns the main type of the content-type header. The default value is `text`.

`message.getsubtype()`—Returns the subtype of the content-type header. The default value is `plain`.

`message.getparam(name)`—Returns the value of the first `name` parameter found in the content-type header.

MimeWriter

The `MimeWriter` module implements a generic file-writing class, also called `MimeWriter`, that is used to create MIME encoded multipart files (messages).

```
message = MimeWriter.MimeWriter(fileobject_forwriting)
```

The following function adds a header line (`"key: value"`) to the MIME message.

```
message.addheader(key, value [,prefix = 0])
```

If `prefix = 0`, the header line is appended to the end; if it is `1`, the line is inserted at the start.

Next, you have some methods that are exposed by the `message` object.

`message.flushheaders()`—Writes all headers to the file.

`message.startbody(ctype [,plist [,prefix = 1]])`—Specifies the content-type, and a list of additional parameters to be included in the message body. It returns a file-like object that must be used to write to the message body.

message.startmultipartbody(subtype [,boundary [,plist [,prefix = 1]]])—
Specifies the multipart subtype, a possible user-defined boundary, and a list of
additional parameters to be included in the multipart message subtype. It returns a
file-like object that must be used to write to the message body.

message.nextpart()—Creates a new part in a multipart message. The startbody
method must be called before calling this one.

message.lastpart()—Indicates the last part of a multipart message.

The next code introduces the basic usage of the MimeWriter module, along with
other supporting modules.

```
import MimeWriter
import quopri, base64

msgtext = "This message has 3 images as attachments."
files = ["sun.jpg", "rain.jpg", "beach.jpg"]
mimefile = "mymessage.msg"

mimemsg = MimeWriter.MimeWriter(sys.stdout)
mimemsg.addheader("Mime-Version","1.0")
mimemsg.startmultipartbody("mixed")

msgpart = mimemsg.nextpart()
msgpart.addheader("Content-Transfer-Encoding", "quoted-printable")
msgpart.startbody("text/plain")
quopri.encode(StringIO.StringIO(msgtext), mimefile, 0)

for file in files:
    msgpart = mimemsg.nextpart()
    msgpart.addheader("Content-Transfer-Encoding", "base64")
    msgpart.startbody("text/jpeg")
    base64.encode(open(file, "rb"), mimefile)

mimemsg.lastpart()
```

multifile

The multifile module enables you to treat distinct parts of a text file as file-like input
objects. Usually, it uses text files that are found in MIME encoded messages. This module

works by splitting a file into logical blocks that are delimited by a unique boundary string. Next, you will be exposed to the class implemented by this module: `MultiFile`.

`MultiFile (fp[, seekable])`
Create a multifile. You must instantiate this class with an input object argument for the `MultiFile` instance to get lines from, such as a file object returned by `open()`. `MultiFile` only looks at the input object's `readline()`,`seek()`, and `tell()` methods, and the latter two are only needed if you want random access to the individual MIME parts. To use `MultiFile` on a non-seekable stream object, set the optional seekable argument to false; this will prevent using the input object's `seek()` and `tell()` methods.

It will be useful to know that in `MultiFile`'s view of the world, text is composed of three kinds of lines: data, section-dividers, and end-markers. `MultiFile` is designed to support parsing of messages that might have multiple nested message parts, each with its own pattern for section-divider and end-marker lines.

A `MultiFile` instance has the following methods:

`push(str)`—Pushes a boundary string. When an appropriately decorated version of this boundary is found as an input line, it will be interpreted as a section-divider or end-marker. All subsequent reads will return the empty string to indicate end-of-file, until a call to `pop()` removes the boundary or a `next()` call re-enables it.

It is possible to push more than one boundary. Encountering the most-recently-pushed boundary will return EOF; encountering any other boundary will raise an error.

`readline(str)`—Reads a line. If the line is data (not a section-divider, end-marker, or real EOF), return it. If the line matches the most-recently-stacked boundary, return `''` and set `self.last` to `1` or `0` according to if the match is or is not an end-marker. If the line matches any other stacked boundary, raise an error. On encountering end-of-file on the underlying stream object, the method raises Error unless all boundaries have been popped.

`readlines(str)`—Returns all lines remaining in this part as a list of strings.

`read()`—Reads all lines, up to the next section. Returns them as a single (multiline) string. Note that this doesn't take a size argument.

`next()`—Skips lines to the next section (that is, reads lines until a section-divider or end-marker has been consumed). Returns true if there is such a section, false if an end-marker is seen. Re-enables the most-recently-pushed boundary.

`pop()`—Pops a section boundary. This boundary will no longer be interpreted as EOF.

`seek(pos[, whence])`—Seeks. Seek indices are relative to the start of the current section. The `pos` and `whence` arguments are interpreted as if for a file seek.

`tell()`—Returns the file position relative to the start of the current section.

`is_data(str)`—Returns true if `str` is data and false if it might be a section boundary. As written, it tests for a prefix other than - at the start of a line (which all MIME boundaries have), but it is declared so that it can be overridden in derived classes.

> **Note**
> Note that this test is intended as a fast guard for the real boundary tests; if it always returns false, it will merely slow processing, not cause it to fail.

`section_divider(str)`—Turns a boundary into a section-divider line. By default, this method prepends - (which MIME section boundaries have), but it is declared so that it can be overridden in derived classes. This method needs not append LF or CR-LF because a comparison with the result ignores trailing whitespace.

`end_marker(str)`—Turns a boundary string into an end-marker line. By default, this method prepends - and appends - (similar to a MIME-multipart end-of-message marker), but it is declared so that it can be overridden in derived classes. This method need not append LF or CR-LF, because a comparison with the result ignores trailing whitespace.

Finally, MultiFile instances have two public instance variables:

`level`—This is the nesting depth of the current part.

`last`—True if the last end-of-file was for an end-of-message marker.

The following code exemplifies the `multifile` module.

```
1: import multifile
2: import rfc822, cgi
3:
4: multipart = "multipart/"
5: filename=open("mymail.msg")
```

```
 6: msg = rfc822.Message(filename)
 7:
 8: msgtype, args = cgi.parse_header(msg["content-type"])
 9:
10: if msgtype[:10] == multipart:
11:     multifilehandle = multifile.MultiFile(filename)
12:     multifilehandle.push(args["boundary"])
13:     while multifilehandle.next():
14:         msg = rfc822.Message(multifilehandle)
15:         print msg.read()
16:     multifilehandle.pop()
17: else:
18:     print "This is not a multi-part message!"
19:     print "-------------------------------"
20:     print filename.read()
```

Line 6: msg is a dictionary-like object. You can apply dictionary methods to this object, such as msg.keys(), msg.values(), and msg.items().

Line 8: Parses the content-type header.

Lines 11-16: Handles the multipart message.

Line 15: Prints the multipart message.

Line 20: Prints the plain message, when necessary.

mailcap

The mailcap module is used to read mailcap files and to configure how MIME-aware applications react to files with different MIME types.

> **Note**
> Mailcap files are used to inform applications, including mail readers and Web browsers, how to process files with different MIME types. A small section of a mailcap file looks like this:
>
> *image/jpeg; imageviewer %s*
>
> *application/zip; gzip %s*

The next code demonstrates the usage of the mailcap module.

```
>>> import mailcap
>>> capsdict = mailcap.getcaps()
>>> command, rawentry = mailcap.findmatch(capsdict, "image/jpeg", \
                        filename="/usr/local/uid213")
>>> print command
```

```
imageviewer /usr/local/uid213
>>> print rawentry
image/jpeg; imageviewer %s
```

The `getcaps()` function reads the mailcap file and returns a dictionary mapping MIME types to mailcap entries; and the `findmatch()` function searches the dictionary for a specific MIME entry, returning a command line ready to be executed along with the raw mailcap entry.

mimetypes

The `mimetypes` module supports conversions between a filename or URL and the MIME type associated with the filename extension. Essentially, it is used to guess the MIME type associated with a file, based on its extension.

For example,

Filename extension	MIME type associated(Main type/Sub type)
.html	text/html
.gif	image/gif
.xml	application/xml

A complete list of extensions and their associated MIME types can be found by typing

```
import mimetypes
for EXTENSION in mimetypes.types_map.keys():
    print EXTENSION, " = ", mimetypes.types_map[EXTENSION]
```

Next, you have a list of functions exposed by the `mimetypes` module.

`mimetypes.guess_type(url_or_filename)`—Returns a tuple (type, encoding), such as (`'image/jpeg'`, None) and (`'application/zip'`, None).

`mimetypes.guess_extension(type)`—Tries to guess the file extension based on a MIME type.

`mimetypes.init([files])`—Initializes the module after reading a file stored in the following format:

```
  type/subtype:    extension1, extension2, ...
  ...
```

`mimetypes.read_mime_types(filename)`—Reads a file and returns a dictionary mapping MIME types and the filename extensions associated to that type.

The following dictionaries are also exposed by the `mimetypes` module.

`mimetypes.suffix_map`—Dictionary that maps suffixes to suffixes.

`mimetypes.encodings_map`—Dictionary that maps encoding types to filename extensions.

`mimetypes.types_map`—Dictionary that maps MIME types to filename extensions.

base64

The `base64` module performs `base64` encoding and decoding of arbitrary binary strings into text string that can be safely emailed or posted. This module is commonly used to encode binary data in mail attachments.

The arguments of the next functions can be either filenames or file objects. The first argument is open for reading:

```
base64.encode(messagefilehandle, outputfilehandle)
```

The second argument is open for writing:

```
base64.decode(encodedfilehandle, outputfilehandle)
```

This module also implements the functions *encodestring(stringtoencode)* and *decodestring(encodedstring)*, which are built on top of the `encode` and `decode` function. Both internally use the `StringIO` module in order to enable the use of the `base64` module to encode and decode strings. Note that the *decodestring()* function returns a string that contains the decoded binary data.

quopri

The `quopri` module performs quoted-printable transport encoding and decoding of MIME quoted-printable data, as defined in RFC 1521: "MIME (Multipurpose Internet Mail Extensions) Part One". The quoted-printable encoding is designed for data in which there are relatively few nonprintable characters; the base64 encoding scheme available via the base64 module is more compact if there are many such characters, as when sending a graphics file. This format is primarily used to encode text files.

`decode(input, output)` decodes the contents of the input file and writes the resulting decoded binary data to the output file. `input` and `output` must either be file objects or objects that mimic the file object interface. `input` will be read until `input.read()` returns an empty string.

`encode(input, output, quotetabs)` encodes the contents of the input file and writes the resulting quoted-printable data to the output file. `input` and `output` must either be file objects or objects that mimic the file object interface. `input` will be read until `input.read()` returns an empty string.

This module only supports file-to-file conversions. If you need to handle string objects, you need to convert them using the `StringIO` module.

```
import quopri
quopri.encode(infile, outfile, tabs=0)
quopri.decode(infile, outfile)
```

This module is purely based on plain U.S. ASCII text. Non-U.S. characters are mapped to an = followed by two hexadecimal digits. The = character resembles =3D, and whitespaces at the end of lines are represented by =20.

mailbox

The `mailbox` module implements classes that allow easy and uniform access to read various mailbox formats in a UNIX system.

```
import mailbox

mailboxname = "/tmp/mymailbox"
mbox = mailbox.UnixMailbox(open(mailboxname))

msgcounter = 0
while 1:
    mailmsg = mbox.next()
    if not mailmsg:
        break
    msgcounter = msgcounter + 1
    messagebody = mailmsg.fp.read()
    print messagebody
print
print "The message counter is %d" % (msgcounter)
```

mimify

The `mimify` module has functions to convert and process simple and multi-part mail messages to/from MIME format—messages are converted to plain text. This module can be used either as a command line tool, or as a regular Python module.

To encode, you need to type:

```
$mimify.py -e raw_message mime_message
```

or

```
import mimify, StringIO, sys
msgfilename = "msgfilename.msg"
filename = StringIO.StringIO()
mimify.unmimify(msgfilename, filename, 1)
file.seek(0)
mimify.mimify(filename, sys.stdout)
```

To decode, type

```
$mimify.py -f mime_message raw_message
```

or

```
import mimify, sys
mimify.unmimify(messagefilename, sys.stdout, 1)
```

Message(*file*[, *seekable*])

A `Message` instance is instantiated with an input object as parameter. `Message` relies only on the input object having a `readline()` method; in particular, ordinary file objects qualify. Instantiation reads headers from the input object up to a delimiter line (normally a blank line) and stores them in the instance.

This class can work with any input object that supports a `readline()` method. If the input object has seek and tell capability, the `rewindbody()` method will work; also, illegal lines will be pushed back onto the input stream. If the input object lacks seek and tell capability but has an `unread()` method that can push back a line of input, `Message` will use that to push back illegal lines. Thus, this class can be used to parse messages coming from a buffered stream.

The optional seekable argument is provided as a workaround for certain studio libraries in which `tell()` discards buffered data before discovering that the `lseek()` system call doesn't work. For maximum portability, you should set the seekable argument to zero to prevent that initial `tell()` when passing in an unseekable object such as a file object created from a socket object.

Input lines as read from the file might either be terminated by CR-LF or by a single linefeed; a terminating CR-LF is replaced by a single linefeed before the line is stored.

All header matching is done independent of upper- or lowercase; for example, `m['From']`, `m['from']`, and `m['FROM']` all yield the same result.

`AddressList(field)`—You can instantiate the `AddressList` helper class using a single string parameter, a comma-separated list of RFC 822 addresses to be parsed. (The parameter None yields an empty list.)

`parsedate(date)`—attempts to parse a date according to the rules in RFC 822. However, some mailers don't follow that format as specified, so `parsedate()` tries to guess correctly in such cases. `date` is a string containing an RFC 822 date, such as `'Mon, 20 Nov 1995 19:12:08 -0500'`. If it succeeds in parsing the date, `parsedate()` returns a 9-tuple that can be passed directly to `time.mktime()`; otherwise None will be returned.

`parsedate_tz(date)`—performs the same function as `parsedate()`, but returns either None or a 10-tuple; the first nine elements make up a tuple that can be passed directly to `time.mktime()`, and the tenth is the offset of the date's timezone from UTC (which is the official term for Greenwich Mean Time). (Note that the sign of the timezone offset is the opposite of the sign of the `time.timezone` variable for the same timezone; the latter variable follows the POSIX standard, whereas this module follows RFC 822.) If the input string has no timezone, the last element of the tuple returned is None.

`mktime_tz(tuple)`—Turn a 10-tuple as returned by `parsedate_tz()` into a UTC timestamp. It the timezone item in the tuple is None, assume local time. Minor deficiency: this first interprets the first eight elements as a local time and then compensates for the timezone difference; this might yield a slight error around daylight savings time switch dates. It is not enough to worry about for common use.

Message Objects

A message object behavior is very similar to a dictionary. A `Message` instance has also the following methods:

`rewindbody()`—Seeks to the start of the message body. This only works if the file object is seekable.

`isheader(line)`—Returns a line's canonicalized fieldname (the dictionary key that will be used to index it) if the line is a legal RFC822 header; otherwise returns None (implying that parsing should stop here and the line be pushed back on the input stream). It is sometimes useful to override this method in a subclass.

islast(*line*)—Returns true if the given line is a delimiter on which Message should stop. The delimiter line is consumed, and the file object's read location is positioned immediately after it. By default, this method just checks that the line is blank, but you can override it in a subclass.

iscomment(*line*)—Returns true if the given line should be ignored entirely, just skipped. By default, this is a stub that always returns false, but you can override it in a subclass.

getallmatchingheaders(*name*)—Returns a list of lines consisting of all headers matching name, if any. Each physical line, whether it is a continuation line or not, is a separate list item. Returns the empty list if no header matches name.

getfirstmatchingheader(*name*)—Returns a list of lines comprising the first header matching name, and its continuation line(s), if any. Returns None if no header matches name.

getrawheader(*name*)—Returns a single string consisting of the text after the colon in the first header matching name. This includes leading whitespace, the trailing linefeed, and internal linefeeds and whitespace if any continuation line(s) were present. Returns None if no header matches name.

getheader(*name*[, *default*])—Similar to getrawheader(name), but strips leading and trailing whitespace. Internal whitespace is not stripped. The optional default argument can be used to specify a different default to be returned when there is no header matching name.

get(*name*[, *default*])—An alias for getheader(), to make the interface more compatible with regular dictionaries.

getaddr(*name*)—Returns a pair (full name, email address) parsed from the string returned by getheader(name). If no header matching name exists, returns (None, None); otherwise both the full name and the address are (possibly empty) strings.

Example: If m's first From header contains the string 'alessa@lessaworld.com (Andre Lessa)', m.getaddr('From') will yield the pair ('Andre Lessa', 'alessa@lessaworld.com'). If the header contained 'Andre Lessa <alessa@lessaworld.com>' instead, it would yield the exact same result.

getaddrlist(*name*)—Similar to getaddr(list), but parses a header containing a list of email addresses (for example, a To header) and returns a list of (full name, email address) pairs (even if there was only one address in the header). If no header matches name, returns an empty list.

If multiple headers exist that match the named header (for example, if there are several CC headers), all are parsed for addresses. Any continuation lines that the named headers contain are also parsed.

Note that the current version of this function is not really correct. It yields bogus results if a full name contains a comma.

getdate(*name*)—Retrieves a header using getheader() and parses it into a 9-tuple compatible with time.mktime(). If no header matches name, or it is unparsable, returns None.

Date parsing appears to be a black art, and not all mailers adhere to the standard. Although it has been tested and found correct on a large collection of email from many sources, it is still possible that this function might occasionally yield an incorrect result.

getdate_tz(*name*)—Retrieves a header using getheader() and parses it into a 10-tuple; the first nine elements will make a tuple compatible with time.mktime(), and the 10th is a number giving the offset of the date's timezone from UTC. Similar to getdate(), if no header matches name, or it is unparsable, it returns None.

Message instances also support a read-only mapping interface. In particular: m[name] is similar to m.getheader(name), but raises KeyError if there is no matching header; and len(m), m.has_key(name), m.keys(), m.values(), and m.items() act as expected (and consistently).

Finally, Message instances have two public instance variables:

- headers—A list containing the entire set of header lines, in the order in which they were read (except that setitem calls can disturb this order). Each line contains a trailing newline. The blank line terminating the headers is not contained in the list.

- fp—The file object passed at instantiation time.

AddressList **Objects**

An AddressList instance has the following methods:

__len__(*name*)—Returns the number of addresses in the address list.

__str__(*name*)—Returns a string representation of the address list. Addresses are rendered in "name" <host@domain> form, comma separated.

__add__(*name*)—Returns an AddressList instance that contains all addresses in both AddressList operands, with duplicates removed (set union).

__sub__(*name*)—Returns an AddressList instance that contains every address in the left-hand AddressList operand that is not present in the right-hand address operand (set difference).

Finally, AddressList instances have one public instance variable: addresslist, which is a list of tuple string pairs, one per address. In each member, the first is the canonicalized name part of the address, the second is the route-address (@-separated host-domain pair).

The following example demonstrates the use of the rfc822 module:

```
import rfc822
mailbox_filename = "mymailbox.msg"

file_handle = open("mailbox_filename")
messagedic = rfc822.Message(file_handle)

content_type = messagedic["content-type"]
from_field = messagedic["From"]
to_field = messagedic.getaddr("To")
subject_field = messagedic["Subject"]

file_handle.close()
print content_type, from_field, to_field, subject_field
```

Generic Conversion Functions

The next couple of modules are used for general data conversions.

netrc

The netrc module parses, processes, and encapsulates the .netrc configuration file format used by UNIX FTP program and other FTP clients.

```
import netrc
netrc_filename = "/usr/local/myconfig.netrc"
netrccfg = netrc.netrc(netrc_filename)
```

```
l, a, p = netrccfg.authenticators("connection.msg")
print "My Login = %s" % (l)
print "My Password = %s" % (p)
print "My Account= %s" % (a)
```

mhlib

The `mhlib` module provides a Python interface to access MH folders/mailboxes and their contents. This module contains three basic classes:

`MH ([path[, profile]])`—Represents a particular collection of MH folders.

`Folder (mh, name)`—Represents a single folder and its messages.

`Message (folder, number[, name])`—Represents individual messages in a folder. The `Message` class is derived from `mimetools.Message`.

MH **Objects**

`MH` instances have the following methods:

`error(format[, ...])`—Prints an error message: can be overridden.

`getprofile(key)`—Returns a profile entry (`None` if not set).

`getpath()`—Returns the mailbox pathname.

`getcontext()`—Return the current folder name.

`setcontext(name)`—Sets the current folder name.

`listfolders()`—Returns a list of top-level folders.

`listallfolders()`—Returns a list of all folders.

`listsubfolders(name)`—Returns a list of direct subfolders of the given folder.

`listallsubfolders(name)`—Returns a list of all subfolders of the given folder.

`makefolder(name)`—Creates a new folder.

`deletefolder(name)`—Deletes a folder: must have no subfolders.

`openfolder(name)`—Returns a new open folder object.

Folder Objects

Folder instances represent open folders and have the following methods:

error(*format*[, ...])—Prints an error message; can be overridden.

getfullname()—Returns the folder's full pathname.

getsequencesfilename()—Returns the full pathname of the folder's sequences file.

getmessagefilename(*n*)—Returns the full pathname of message n of the folder.

listmessages()—Returns a list of messages in the folder (as numbers).

getcurrent()—Returns the current message number.

setcurrent(*n*)—Sets the current message number to n.

parsesequence(*seq*)—Parses msgs syntax into a list of messages.

getlast()—Gets last message, or 0 if no messages are in the folder.

setlast(*n*)—Sets last message (internal use only).

getsequences()—Returns dictionary of sequences in folder. The sequence names are used as keys, and the values are the lists of message numbers in the sequences.

putsequences(*dict*)—Returns dictionary of sequences in folder name: list.

removemessages(*list*)—Removes messages in list from folder.

refilemessages(*list*, *tofolder*)—Moves messages in list to other folder.

movemessage(*n*, *tofolder*, *ton*)—Moves one message to a given destination in another folder.

copymessage(*n*, *tofolder*, *ton*)—Copies one message to a given destination in another folder.

Message **Objects**

openmessage(*n*) returns a new open message object (costs a file descriptor).

binhex

The binhex module encodes and decodes files in binhex4 format. This format is commonly used to represent files on Macintosh systems.

```
import binhex, sys
infile = "filename.jpg"
binhex.binhex(infile, sys.stdout)
```

binhex(*inputfile*, *outputfile*) converts a binary file (*inputfile*) to a binhex file(*outputfile*).

hexbin(*inputfile* [, *outputfile*]) converts a binhex file (*inputfile*) back to a regular binary file (*outputfile*). When the output name is omitted, the interpreter uses the same one provided in the first argument.

uu

The uu module encodes and decodes files in uuencode format. This module does its job by transferring binary data over an ASCII-only connection. Wherever a file argument is expected, the methods accept a file-like object. For backwards compatibility, a string containing a pathname is also accepted, and the corresponding file will be opened for reading and writing; the pathname · is understood to mean the standard input or output. However, this interface is deprecated; it's better for the caller to open the file itself, and be sure that, when required, the mode is rb or wb on Windows or DOS.

The code of this module was contributed by Lance Ellinghouse and modified by Jack Jansen.

The uu module defines the following functions:

encode (*in_file*, *out_file*[, *name*[, *mode*]])—This function uuencodes file in_file into file out_file. The uuencoded file will have the header specifying name and mode as the defaults for the results of decoding the file. The default defaults are taken from in_file, or · and 0666, respectively.

decode (*in_file*[, *out_file*[, *mode*]])—This call decodes uuencoded file in_file placing the result on file out_file. If out_file is a pathname, the mode is also set. Defaults for out_file and mode are taken from the uuencode header.

Note that in the previous functions, both arguments can be either filenames or file objects.

This format used to be popular on the Usenet, but nowadays, it is being superceded by base64 encoding.

Each encoded data stream starts with a begin line, which also includes the file privileges, the filename, and ends with an end line, as you can see in the following example:

```
begin 755 executeprog.py
KF_EF_#JFJ! ...
end
```

`binascii`

The `binascii` module implements methods to convert data between binary and various `ASCII`-encoded binary representations, including `binhex`, `uu`, and `base64`. Note that normally, you would just use the `binhex`, `uu`, or `base64` modules rather than `binascii`.

This module implements two exceptions: `Error` (raised on errors), and `Incomplete` (raised on incomplete data). The following methods are implemented by this module:

`binascii.b2a_base64(`*binarydata*`)`—Converts a string of binary data to a string of base64-encoded characters.

`binascii.a2b_base64(`*string*`)`—Converts a string of base64-encoded data to binary.

`binascii.b2a_uu(`*binarydata*`)`—Converts a string of binary data to a string of uuencoded characters.

`binascii.a2b_uu(`*string*`)`—Converts a string of uuencoded data to binary.

`binascii.b2a_hqx(`*binarydata*`)`—Converts a string of binary data to a string of binhex4-encoded characters.

`binascii.a2b_hqx(`*string*`)`—Converts a string of binhex4-encoded data to binary.

`binascii.rledecode_hqx(`*binarydata*`)`—Decompresses the binary data using the *RLE (Run-Length Encoding)* method. If the binary data is incomplete, an Incomplete exception is raised.

`binascii.rleecode_hqx(`*binarydata*`)`—Compresses the binary data according to the RLE method.

`binascii.crc_hqx(`*binarydata*`, `*crc*`)`—Returns the checksum of a given binhex4-binary data. The argument `crc` indicates the checksum's starting value.

Note that starting with Python 2.0, there are two more functions to include in the list provided by the `binascii` module. They are called `b2a_hex` and `a2b_hex`. They are used to convert between binary data and its hexadecimal representation.

Summary

This chapter provides information concerning how to use Python for data parsing and manipulation. You learned how to interpret XML, SGML, and HTML documents and how to parse and manipulate email messages, among other things. As you might already know, Python can be used as a very effective and productive tool to parse and manipulate information from the Web.

Extensible Markup Language describes a class of data objects called XML documents and partially describes the behavior of computer programs that process them. For those who want to play around with XML in Python, there is a Python/XML package to serve several purposes at once. This package contains everything required for basic XML applications, along with documentation and sample code.

Besides that, the `xmllib` module serves as the basis for parsing text files formatted in XML. Note that `xmllib` is not XML 1.0 compliant, and it doesn't provide any Unicode support. It provides just simple XML support for ASCII only element and attribute names.

Many XML-based technologies are available for Python/XML development, such as

SAX—This is a common event-based interface for object-oriented XML parsers.

The Document Object Model (DOM)—This is a standard interface for manipulating XML and HTML documents developed by the World Wide Web Consortium. 4DOM is a Python library for XML and HTML processing and manipulation using the W3C's Document Object Model for interface.

4XSLT—This is an XML transformation processor based on the W3C's specification.

XML Bookmark Exchange Language (XBEL)—This is an Internet "bookmarks" interchange format.

SOAP—This is an XML/HTTP-based protocol for accessing services, objects, and servers in a platform-independent manner. Scarab is a minimal Python SOAP implementation.

PythonPoint—This has a simple XML markup language for doing presentation slides and converting them to PDF documents.

Pyxie—This is an Open Source XML processing library for Python.

XML-RPC—This is a specification and a set of implementations that allow software running on different operating systems and different environments to make procedure calls over the Internet. It is important to say that Python has its own implementation of XML-RPC.

XDR—This is a standard for data description and encoding. Protocols such as RPC and NFS use XDR to describe the format of their data.

But Python is not just XML. It also provides support for other markup languages.

The `sgmllib` module is an SGML (Standard Generalized Markup Language) parser subset. Although it has a simple implementation, it is powerful enough to build the HTML parser.

The `htmllib` module defines a parser class that can serve as a base for parsing text files formatted in HTML. Two helper modules are used by `htmllib`:

- The `htmlentitydefs` module is a dictionary that contains all the definitions for the general entities defined by HTML 2.0.

- The formatter module is used for generic output formatting by the `HTMLPARSER` class of the `htmllib` module.

Apart from markup languages, this chapter also covers mail messages manipulation.

MIME (Multipurpose Internet Mail Extensions) is a standard for sending multi-part multimedia data through Internet mail. This standard exposes mechanisms for specifying and describing the format of Internet message bodies. Python provides many modules to support MIME messages, including the following:

`mimetools`—Provides utility tools for parsing and manipulation of MIME multi-part and encoded messages.

`MimeWriter`—Implements a generic file-writing class that is used to create MIME encoded multi-part files (messages).

`multifile`—Enables you to treat distinct parts of a text file as file-like input objects.

`mailcap`—Reads mailcap files and configures how MIME-aware applications react to files with different MIME types.

`mimetypes`—Supports conversions between a filename or URL and the MIME type associated with the filename extension.

quopri—Performs quoted-printable transport encoding and decoding of MIME quoted-printable data.

mailbox—Implements classes that allow easy and uniform access to read various mailbox formats in a UNIX system.

mimify—Contains functions to convert and process simple and multi-part mail messages to/from MIME format.

rfc822—Parses mail headers that are defined by the Internet standard RFC 822.

Python uses the following modules for general data conversions:

netrc—Parses, processes, and encapsulates the .netrc configuration file format used by UNIX FTP program and other FTP clients.

mhlib—Provides a Python interface to access MH folders, mailboxes, and their contents.

base64—Performs base64 encoding and decoding of arbitrary binary strings into text string that can be safely emailed or posted.

binhex—Encodes and decodes files in binhex4 format. This format is commonly used to represent files on Macintosh systems.

uu—Encodes and decodes files in uuencode format.

binascii—Implements methods to convert data between binary and various ASCII-encoded binary representations, including binhex, uu, and base64.

PART IV
Graphical Interfaces

CHAPTER 14

Python and GUIs

My brain hurts

Those who are tired of text-based applications will find this chapter very helpful because it shows what the available GUI options are for designing Python graphic interfaces. After selecting your GUI toolkit of choice, you can come back to this chapter and check out the topic that shows how to design a good graphical interface.

Python GUI Toolkits

Choosing a toolkit for your *graphical user interface (GUI)* projects is not a simple thing. You need to research and compare what the features are that each option has to offer. When you decide to stick to one toolkit, you'd better be prepared to use it for some time. Toolkit implementations are so different that it becomes hard to change your code and your way of thinking from one toolkit to another whenever it comes time to move to a different implementation. Most of all, if you always jump from one OS to another, make sure that your GUI of choice is cross-platform, even though it is known how hard it is to implement a cross platform GUI these days (not just in Python). On the other hand, if you know that you will stay in a certain platform, such as Windows or Linux, for some time be sure that—depending on what platform you choose—there are a lot of options for you. Of course, by choosing a cross platform toolkit, you leave your options open (which is a good thing because you might change your mind in a few years).

Although you might decide to choose something different, the Python community has already chosen the standard choice for GUI development with Python—it is called Tkinter, and it's part of the standard Python distribution. For more information, see Chapter 15, "Tkinter."

Besides Tkinter, many other GUI solutions are supported by Python. This chapter exposes many of them.

STDWIN, which used to be the first word in GUI for Python, is now just an unsupported and obsolete platform-independent, low-level windowing interface.

Support for the wxWindows portable GUI class library is also available through the wxPython interface, which runs on multiple systems, such as GTK, Motif, MS Windows, and Mac. wxPython is a Python extension module that is quickly becoming acclaimed among Python developers by wrapping many of the wxWindows C++ classes.

Pythonwin is a Python GUI for Windows that includes an interface to the Microsoft Foundation Classes and a Python programming environment that uses this interface. By the way, this programming environment is also written in Python.

Other not-so-famous GUI options are also available:

- An object-oriented, cross-platform GUI based on the Microsoft Foundation Classes model called Wpy.

- Interfaces to WAFE, FOX, Motif, PLTK, and so forth.

- Bindings to Gnome, KDE, OPENGL, QT, and so on.

- For Mac systems, you can use its large set of modules that support the native Mac toolbox calls. Check out the documentation that comes with the Mac Python port for more information.

- As well as many others, as shown in this chapter.

As you can see, the number of options is large. The conclusion is that you need to think about today's reality and tomorrow's possibilities. Even though we know that Tkinter is doing a great job today, and it seems that it will for a long time, you should open your mind to other possibilities as well. Be sure that other nice tools out there exist. Tk is slower than most other toolkits (the one reason people find it acceptable is that it double buffers its widgets).

At this time, a couple of other bindings are becoming quite capable, such as the bindings for Gnome/GTK, QT, and KDE. These bindings fit nicer into their respective desktop environments.

The question that I left for you is, "What toolkit will be part of the next generation of standard GUIs for Python?" I see many alternatives: What about you? Most people will stick to Tkinter. That is for sure. And that's also the reason why the next chapter covers this fantastic toolkit implementation.

The Tkinter Module

Tkinter is Python's *de facto* standard GUI toolkit. It's the most cross-platform GUI. Many applications are written using Tkinter because it is a very powerful and flexible tool. Maybe the most notable features are its geometry management, which is much better than standard windows, and its efficient Text and Canvas widgets. Many toolkits support as good as or better geometry management (some of them are listed in this chapter).

Tkinter, which stands for *Tk interface*, is the standard Python interface to the Tk GUI toolkit from Ajuba (formerly Scriptics). Tkinter is a binding to Tcl/Tk that in former days was developed by Sun Labs. Actually it works on top of Tcl/Tk. To use Tkinter, you don't need to write Tcl code. Occasionally, you will need to consult the Tk documentation and the Tcl documentation because Tk's low-level event handling mechanism is considered part of Tcl.

Both Tk and Tkinter are available on most UNIX platforms, as well as on Windows and Macintosh systems. Some platforms come with Tcl/Tk as an optional part of the OS distribution or, in the case of Win32, as part of the Python install. Quite a lot of Linux distributions (and other free UNIX-like Operation Systems) install Tcl/Tk by default. Starting with the 8.0 release, Tk offers a native look and feel on all platforms.

If you ask yourself why you should use Tkinter, I would say that it is a mature and reliable solution for graphic applications, running on every platform where it is possible to run Tcl/Tk, which is basically every platform, but Macintosh. Tkinter and Macs are still negotiating a healthy version.

One of the most important reasons why Tkinter was chosen to be the official GUI option is because it seems to have a long life ahead of it. Many people are against this, but the fact is that Tkinter is available for Windows, UNIX, and Macintosh platforms, and being part of the Official Python distribution puts it in a position of constant upgrading.

Tkinter is probably the most documented Python GUI that you will find. As you can see in Chapter 15, there is a respectable knowledge base available for you, given its *de facto* standard status.

See the Tkinter documentation page on `http://www.python.org/` for more up-to-date information about this toolkit.

Overview of Other GUI Modules

Python's powerful object implementation and portability has encouraged the development of many other GUI toolkits. Consequently, you have a number of options to try before deciding which one is the best solution for your project.

Pythonwin/MFC

Pythonwin is a wrapper, written by Mark Hammond, to the *Microsoft Foundation Class Library (MFC)*. It is included within the Windows Python distribution.

Actually, Pythonwin is distributed as two key components—`Pythonwin.exe` and `win32ui.pyd`. The latter contains all the bindings to the MFC (tens of MFC objects are exposed, including Common Controls, Property Pages/Sheets, Toolbars, and so on), and the former is a simple wrapper that hosts `win32ui.pyd`, being just a sample program for the MFC user interface environment.

Pythonwin runs only on Windows, hence, if you need to have your program running on both Win32 and UNIX platforms, you can use the Tk libraries instead.

Using Pythonwin, you can design applications that are bound very tightly to Windows, using MFC in an interactive and interpreted environment to provide the features of the Windows user interface. The user interface environment provided by Pythonwin can be embedded in almost any other application—such as OLE clients/servers, Netscape plugins, and so on.

Inside the Pythonwin distribution, you will find a Help File (`Pythonwin.hlp`), which is a reference manual for all the objects exposed in Pythonwin. That is a great start for you.

Pythonwin's homepage provides resources documenting the Pythonwin GUI environment. There is also some general documentation on the MFC Architecture. After you install Pythonwin, you can find more details in the documentation that comes bundled in it. For more information, check out the Pythonwin home page at

`http://www.python.org/windows/pythonwin/`

This next document describes how to imbed the `win32ui` extension module in your own application:

```
http://www.python.org/windows/pythonwin/EmbeddingWin32ui.html
```

wxPython

wxPython is a GUI toolkit for the Python programming language that works like a wrapper to the wxWindows C++ library. It is written in Python and uses the LPGL license.

wxPython is a relatively fast cross-platform toolkit, and maybe it hasn't become the standard Python GUI yet because Tkinter is more portable. As a matter of fact, wxPython is the second most common GUI, coming just after Tkinter.

Currently only Win32 and UNIX-like systems with GTK are supported. There are plans to support wxPython on any platform running wxWindows.

wxWindows is a free, well-established, and well-documented set of libraries that allows C++ applications to compile and run on several different types of computers, with minimal source code changes.

The *wx* in the name wxWindows means w for Windows, and x for X system. It is supposed to be a way to say that it is a Windows system that supports both platforms.

Each supported GUI (such as GTK+, Windows, Motif, and Mac) has its own library provided by the wxWindows, which exposes natural API for all of them. The API is much simpler to use than other native GUI APIs. Note that you cannot use wxWindows as a GUI translator.

wxWindows provides a lot of extra built-in functionality for you as well, and you can decide whether you want to use it. Such extra features have the main goal of providing ways for you to develop user-friendly GUI applications. Included in this functionality are many useful dialogs, built-in HTML display and printing, support to virtual filesystems, OLE automation controller class, and Open GL support. It also offers access to common operating system operations, such as file copying and deletion, and network support for threads and sockets. wxWindows also supports basic data structures such as arrays, strings, linked lists, and hash tables. If you are coming from an MFC architecture, you can consider yourself lucky because both frameworks are very similar, which makes it easier to port applications from one to another. Python and wxWindows have a great thing in common, both had a object-oriented conception. That was one thing that made it possible to develop wxPython, a fully compatible interface to the libraries. Remember that it is very easy to translate C++ calls to Python calls.

wxPython is a very active Open Source project that makes its source code freely available for anyone who wants to use or modify it. If you want, you can also participate by contributing with new ideas and bug solutions for the project.

Using wxPython, it is easier to run the same program on multiple platforms without modification. Currently, wxPython supports Microsoft Windows and most UNIX-like systems.

This extension module allows programmers to use a strong, highly functional graphical user interface to easily write Python programs that can create instances of wxWindows 2.0 C++ classes, and invoke their methods.

wxPython classes are mirrored as closely as possible to the wxWindows class hierarchy. But, we need to consider the difference between Python and C++, and understand that we don't have a 100% match. However, these distinctions can be easily handled by Python. For example, some methods in the wxWindows library return multiple values by returning argument pointers; the equivalent Python method returns a tuple of values instead.

If you go to wxPython's Web site, you can get the latest version of wxPython, and optionally download a self-installer for Win32 systems. The distribution includes a pre-built extension module, documentation in HTML help format and a set of demos. You also have available, among other things, a Linux RPM, wxPython sources, and documentation in raw HTML.

If you will build wxPython from sources yourself, you will also need the wxWindows sources, available from `http://www.wxwindows.org/`.

wxPython has its own mailing list. It is not that difficult to find WxPython's creator, Robin Dunn, answering messages on the list. But as in any other list, always check the archives before posting a question.

A number of documentation resources are available for both wxPython and wxWindows. The wxPython interface is very close to the wxWindows implementation in C++, which makes most of the wxPython documentation be just simple notes attached to the C++ documents that describe the places where wxPython is different.

The Web site has a series of sample programs and documentation pages that can assist you in getting started with wxPython.

By downloading wxPython, you get two other documentation resources, on *Ogl* (for graphics) and an introduction to wxWindows, which has received additional wxPython material from Robin. This addendum demonstrates how all wxWindows classes are implemented in wxPython. Not all binaries contain this document, hence, you might need to get it directly from the Web site.

wxPython home page

```
http://wxpython.org/
```

wxPython Tutorial

```
http://wxpython.org/tutorial.html
```

STDWIN

STDWIN stands for *Standard Window Interface*. It is a platform-independent interface to C-based window systems. Currently, STDWIN is obsolete and unsupported, without any further development effort being made. The stdwin module has been removed for Python 2.0. The Python people say that if you want to use stdwin, you should grab an older Python release. There is not really any reason you would want to use this toolkit.

Python's stdwin module defines several new object types and functions that provide access to the functionality of the Standard Window Interface, STDWIN.

> **Tip**
> For a complete description of STDWIN, take a look at the documentation of STDWIN for C programmers (CWI report CR-R8817).

This module is available on systems to which STDWIN has been ported, including UNIX, Mac, and Windows. Initially, many Python developers had adopted this module, but later, most of them migrated to Tkinter mostly because of the limited functionality imposed by stdwin's design. However, if you install the latest available version available of this module, you can still use it as a solution for many types of applications. Of course, you probably wouldn't want to use stdwin ever.

The next example demonstrates a simple implementation of the stdwin module.

```
 1: import stdwin, stdwinevents
 2:
 3: def mainloop():
 4:     appwin = stdwin.open('Hello')
 5:     while 1:
 6:         (type, win, detail) = stdwin.getevent()
 7:         if type == stdwinevents.WE_DRAW:
 8:             draw = win.begindrawing()
 9:             draw.text((0, 0), 'Hello Python world')
10:             del draw
11:         elif type == stdwinevents.WE_CLOSE:
12:             break
```

```
13:
14: mainloop()
```

This small program works by creating a main loop, and checking the events that occur in the windowing environment. When the program starts, it creates and draws a window. Every time the window needs to be redrawn, a WE_DRAW event is caught by this program (line 7), triggering the line of code that draws a message in the window (line 9). This program only ends when the user closes the window, sending the WE_CLOSE event notification to the main loop (line 11).

The latest STDWIN distribution can be downloaded at

```
ftp://ftp.cwi.nl/pub/stdwin/index.html
```

PyQt

PyQt is a set of straightforward Python bindings for the Qt toolkit, which is written in C++. The bindings are implemented as a single Python module called *qt*, and this module exposes a very comprehensive collection of useful classes. The current version supports Qt versions 1.42 to 2.1.x. The main new feature is support for the new Qt v2.0.x widgets. PyQt will also compile with Qt v2.1.0-beta3, but the new Qt v2.1.x widgets are not yet supported.

> **Tip**
> QT is a cross-platform product between UNIX and Windows. The main difference is that you have to pay for using it on Windows platforms, whereas on UNIX, you just need to pay for proprietary usage. It is completely legal to use Qt commercially if you meet its license conditions.

PyQT's Web site is a good source of documentation about PyQT and QT itself. You can even learn how to migrate your QT calls from C++ to Python. But if you need more information about PyQT, you can use the PyQT mailing list.

PyQT: Development Tools for Qt Libraries

```
http://www.thekompany.com/projects/pykde
```

Check the following article, written by Boudewijn Rempt and Cameron Laird, about implementing QT bindings on the next release of Python:

```
http://www.sunworld.com/sunworldonline/swol-05-2000/swol-05-qt.html
```

PyKDE

PyKDE is a set of Python bindings, developed by Phil Thompson, for the KDE toolkit—the KDE classes. It is important to know that the Python bindings for the Qt toolkit (PyQt) must also be installed because it comes in a different package, and that KDE 2 is not yet supported. Just as KDE uses QT, PyKDE uses PyQT.

The bindings are implemented as a number of Python modules corresponding to the names of the separate KDE libraries; that is, `kdecore`, `kdeui`, `kfm`, `kfile`, `khtmlw`, and `kspell`. They support all KDE version 1 releases. Keep in mind that KDE is licensed under the LPGL.

You can find help and more information about PyKDE in the project mailing list, which is the same mailing list as for PyQT. Also, note that because PyKDE requires the KDE libraries, it runs only on the UNIX platform.

PyKDE: Development Tools for KDE Libraries

http://www.thekompany.com/projects/pykde

Python + KDE Tutorial and Examples, by Boudewijn Rempt

http://www.xs4all.nl/~bsarempt/python/tutorial.html

http://www.valdyas.org/python/tutorial.html

Wpy

Wpy is a class library system, based on the Microsoft Foundation Classes, that is used for writing GUI code easily in Python. Wpy is designed for simplicity and portability.

The Wpy Web site provides instructions about how to install the library and use it to run Python programs with windowing GUI capability on UNIX using Tk, Windows 3.1 (16-bit native), and Windows 95, 98, and NT (32-bit native). The source code and the main standard binary ports are available for download.

A Python/Wpy Netscape plug-in DLL is also provided. This plug-in enables you to write Wpy programs that access the Netscape plug-in API and run in the browser window.

Wpy Index

http://www.cwi.nl/ftp/python/wpy/

PyGTK

GTK+ is a Free Software GUI Toolkit that has a large number of widgets, primarily developed for use with the X Window System. Everything about GTK+ from the object-oriented design to the Free Software LGPL licensing allows you to code your project with the most freedom possible. GTK is similar to Qt, but the difference is that you can develop open software, free software, or even commercial non-free software without having to pay anything for licenses. GTK's license allows linking to proprietary applications although the library itself must remain free (in the sense of freedom). The upcoming GTK+ 2.0 includes multi-language support, and framebuffer, Mac, Windows, and BeOS ports are being worked on.

```
http://www.gtk.org/
```

PyGTK is a set of bindings developed by James Henstridge, for the GTK widget set and GNOME libraries that runs on any platform that supports GTK. It provides an object-oriented interface that is a slightly higher level than the C one. It automatically does all the type casting and reference counting that you would have to do normally with the C API. Talking about C, all the underlying C classes are documented on the GTK homepage.

Many simple examples come with PyGTK. They are a good start for your projects. Look in the pygtk/examples or pygnome/examples directory for details. The pygnome/examples directory is only part of the gnome-python package that is covered in the next section.

The following code, extracted from James Henstridge PyGTK's Web site, shows how simple it is to use the PyGTK module:

```python
from gtk import *

def hello_cb(button):
    print "Hello World"
    window.destroy()

window = GtkWindow(WINDOW_TOPLEVEL) # create a top level window
window.connect("destroy", mainquit) # quit the event loop on destruction
window.set_border_width(10)         # set padding round child widget

button = GtkButton("Hello World")
button.connect("clicked", hello_cb) # call hello_cb when clicked
window.add(button)                  # add button to window
button.show()                       # show button

window.show()
mainloop()                          # enter the main event loop
```

PyGTK is available for download at the following FTP sites:

```
ftp://ftp.gtk.org/pub/gtk/python/
```

```
ftp://ftp.python.org/pub/contrib/Graphics/
```

```
ftp://ftp.daa.com.au/pub/james/python/
```

More information about PyGTK can be found at James Henstridge's PyGTK home page:

```
http://www.daa.com.au/~james/pygtk/
```

pygtools, a Web site maintained by J.W. Bizzaro, is an excellent resource for PyGTK information. It contains the latest news about GNU development for Python, including GTK projects.

```
http://theopenlab.uml.edu/pygtools
```

If you need to implement GTK application on Windows, there are a couple of Python wrappers over GTK+ that you can use, such as

PyGTK on Win32, by Kevin J. Butler

```
http://theopenlab.uml.edu/pygtkwin/
```

PyGTK on Win32, by Hans Breuer

```
http://hans.breuer.org/ports/
```

Gnome-Python

The Gnome project has built a complete free and easy-to-use desktop environment for the user, as well as a powerful application framework for the software developer. For more information, check out

```
http://www.gnome.org/
```

The next Web address points you to a set of bindings for the Gnome libraries for use with python. Although `gnome-python` uses PyGTK, you don't need to have the PyGTK package compiled or individually installed before compiling `gnome-python`. This library runs on UNIX only, and it is licensed under the LGPL.

```
ftp://ftp.gnome.org/pub/GNOME/stable/sources/gnome-python/
```

Developing Gnome Applications with Gnome-Python is a very comprehensive article written by Daniel Solin that covers the main aspects of writing a program using Gnome-Python. It is located at

```
http://www.linuxdev.net/features/articles/05.24.2000/
```

PyOpenGL

OpenGL is the premier environment for developing portable, interactive 2D and 3D graphics applications from modeling to scientific to games. Since its introduction in 1992, OpenGL has become the industry's most widely used and supported 2D and 3D graphics *application programming interface (API)*, bringing thousands of applications to a wide variety of computer platforms. OpenGL fosters innovation and speeds application development by incorporating a broad set of rendering, texture mapping, special effects, and other powerful visualization functions. Developers can leverage the power of OpenGL across all popular desktop and workstation platforms, ensuring wide application deployment.

PyOpenGL (Python Tk-OpenGL Module) is the OpenGL-Widget for Python/Tk. Initially based on the Togl widget, this module was written by David Ascher, Mike Hartshorn, Jim Hugunin, and Tom Schwaller. PyOpenGL contains both a wrapper for the Togl Tk widget and bindings for OpenGL. The non-Tk portions of PyOpenGL can be used with other toolkits, such as PyGTK and others. For more information, see the following sites:

> History, installation, and tutorial for the Python Tk-OpenGL Module (with sample code).
>
> ```
> http://www.python.de/
> ```

wafepython

Wafe, which stands for *Widget Athena front end*, is a package that implements a symbolic, string-based interface based on Tcl to the X Toolkit, the Athena Widget Set, the OSF/Motif Widget Set (versions 1.1 to 2.0), and various complementary widget classes and extension packages. Using Wafe, one can develop applications with high-level graphical user interfaces in the scripting language Tcl, or one can use Wafe mostly as a graphical front end that provides an easy access to GUI programming for various programming languages.

Because Wafe can be easily linked with C programs, it can also be used to provide GUI functionality for other interpretative languages by extending these languages by a few commands. In the Wafe distribution are sample implementations for embedding Wafe in interpretative languages, including Python. These implementations provide a bidirectional interface from and to Wafe (for example, Wafe calls Python and Python calls Wafe).

> wafepython (a version of Python enhanced with Wafe commands)
>
> ```
> http://www.wu-wien.ac.at/wafe/wafe.html
> ```

pyFLTK

FLTK (Fast Light Tool Kit, pronounced "fulltick") is a C++ graphical user interface toolkit for X (UNIX), OpenGL, and WIN32 (Microsoft Windows NT 4.0, 95, or 98). It is also largely compatible with the XForms library. FLTK is currently maintained by a small group of developers across the world with a central repository in the United States, and it is distributed under the GNU Library GPL (LGPL).

FLTK was originally created to build in-house applications at Digital Domain for image processing and 3D graphics. The original author, Bill Spitzak, received permission from Digital Domain to release it to the public domain in the hopes that it could be used to make better, faster, and nicer-looking UNIX programs. Digital Domain has since withdrawn support for FLTK, but Bill is still able to work on it from time to time.

pyFLTK is the Python wrapper for the Fast Light Tool Kit graphical user interface library. The development team is using SWIG to create the wrapper.

Kevin Dalhausen and Bjorn Petterson, among others, are working on these bindings for Python. They conduct their work through a mailing list. The main goals of the Project are to develop usable Python and Perl wrappers for the FLTK library; to demonstrate the wrapper's functionality by converting the test programs supplied with FLTK to Python and Perl; and to allow the use of Fluid (FLTK User Interface Designer) to generate Python and Perl graphical user interfaces.

```
http://netpedia.net/hosting/fltk/
```

FXPy

FOX is a C++ based toolkit for developing GUIs easily and effectively. FOX runs on UNIX and Windows, and supports the LGPL kind of license. It offers a wide, and growing, collection of Controls and provides state of the art facilities such as drag and drop, selection, as well as OpenGL widgets for 3D graphical manipulation. FOX also implements icons, images, and user-convenience features such as status line help, and tooltips. Tooltips can even be used for 3D objects!

Considerable importance has been placed on making FOX one of the fastest toolkits around. To minimize memory use, FOX uses a number of techniques to speed up drawing and spatial layout of the GUI. Memory is conserved by allowing programmers to create and destroy GUI elements on-the-fly.

Even though FOX offers a large collection of Controls already, FOX leverages C++ to allow programmers to easily build additional Controls and GUI elements by taking existing controls and creating a derived class that simply adds or redefines the desired behavior.

One of the prime design goals of FOX is the ease of programming; thus, most controls can be created using a single line of C++ code; most parameters have sensible default values so that they may be omitted, and layout managers ensure that designers of GUIs do not have to worry about precise alignments.

Another nice feature of FOX that significantly reduces the number of lines of code which have to be written is FOX's ability to have widgets connect to each other, and pass certain commands between them. For example, a menu entry Hide Toolbar can be directly connected to the Toolbar, and cause it to hide.

Finally, FOX makes it easy to maintain the state of the GUI in an application by having the GUI elements automatically updating themselves by interrogating the application's state. This feature eliminates the large amount of effort that might go into sensitizing, graying out, checking/unchecking, and so on depending on the application state. For more information, check out

FOX

```
http://www.cfdrc.com/FOX/fox.html
```

FXPy is a Python extension module, written by Lyle Johnson, which provides an interface to the FOX GUI library. FXPy is a good Python extension, and up to this date, has a quite complete documentation.

FXPy

```
http://home.hiwaay.net/~johnson2/FXPy/
```

Motif

Fearing the success of Sun in creating a GUI standard, other UNIX vendors created a committee called the *Open Software Foundation (OSF)*. *Motif* is a widely-accepted set of user interface guidelines developed by this committee around 1989, to specify how an X Window System application should look and feel.

Motif is the market leader among UNIX GUI toolkits—the single most widely used toolkit in the UNIX world, and almost 10 years after its creation, it enjoys both the advantages and disadvantages of maturity. It has the most advanced support for text from languages other than English, a wealth of third-party tools support it, and hundreds of books and online documents explain it. The disadvantages are that it has regular performance, it is in decline, it is a lot more difficult to program than many other toolkits, and it is not suitable for the current object-oriented programming styles.

Motif is so ubiquitous that many UNIX users confuse it with GUI operations, window managers, or other pieces of technology, and some speak as if Motif is the only GUI foundation or toolkit.

Sjoerd Mullender bound Motif to Python in a package he calls the Python X Extension. Currently, this is a work in progress. For more information, check out

> Source of the Python X Extension
>
> `http://www.cwi.nl/ftp/sjoerd/index.html`

The following files are currently found in this site:

> X-extension.tar.gz—The complete source (including source of documentation).
>
> X-extension.ps.gz—The complete documentation in Postscript.
>
> X-extension.html.tar.gz—The complete documentation as a set of HTML files.
>
> vpApp.tar.gz—A GUI application framework for (X)Python.

PyAmulet

PyAmulet is another Python GUI. It wraps an underlying C library, called OpenAmulet. This GUI has been successfully tested on Windows platforms. For more information, check out

> PyAmulet home page
>
> `http://www.openip.org/html/pyamulet/`
>
> PyAmulet Documentation
>
> `http://www.openip.org/html/PyAmulet/`

DynWin

DynWin is a dynamic GUI class library for Windows (Win32) and Python. It looks similar to Java's Swing library. For more information, check out

> `http://www.nightmare.com/~rushing/dynwin/index.html`

JPI

The *Java Python Interface (JPI)* is an interface that allows Java and Python (*the C Implementation, not JPython*) to primitively work together. Therefore, you can use

Python as a scripting language for the Java language. Prototyping routines in Python, and later migrating them to Java is a simple and straightforward process because the similarity between both syntaxes is huge. This interface is a work in progress because it currently doesn't provide a total match between both languages.

This interface enables one to dynamically manipulate Java objects using a Python application, including GUI widget managers such as AWT, for example.

```
http://www.ndim.edrc.cmu.edu/dougc/jpi/Home.html
```

AWT

The *Abstract Windowing Toolkit (AWT)* is a user interface toolkit provided by the Java programming language class library.

AWT is very simple to use. Although the documentation that is currently provided in the Java distribution seems to scare AWT programmers away, the language is very strong and flexible. After you find the right direction, you will see yourself creating GUIs with your eyes closed.

As AWT is written in Java, you might want to use JPython in order to manipulate it because JPython gives convenient access to Java classes and packages. However, you can also try to use Python, also known as CPython, and JPI. Together, they can be used to prototype AWT objects and create bindings calling Python routines.

For more information about JPython and AWT, see Chapter 18, "JPython."

FORMS

FORMS is a module for the SGI IRIX platform that provides an interface to the FORMS Library developed by Mark Overmars.

Among other things that might interest you, you better pay attention to the terminology used by FORMS: The word *object* is used for buttons, sliders, and anything else that you can place in a form.

The Python interface to FORMS introduces two new Python object types: *form* objects (representing an entire form) and *FORMS* objects (representing one button, slider, and so on).

There are no "free objects" in the Python interface to FORMS, nor is there an easy way to add object classes written in Python. The FORMS interface to GL event handling is available, though, so you can mix FORMS with pure GL windows.

FORMS library interface for GUI applications

```
http://www.python.org/doc/current/lib/module-fl.html
```

Designing a Good Interface

The user interface is part of a program that interacts with the user of the program. User interfaces take many forms. These forms range in complexity from simple command-line interfaces to the point-and-click graphical user interfaces provided by many modern GUI applications.

A GUI is built of graphical elements generally called widgets. Typical widgets include such items as buttons, scrollbars, and text fields. Widgets allow the user to interact with the program and provide the user with visual feedback about the state of the program.

Widgets do not stand alone, but rather are found within windows. Windows contain and control the layout of widgets. Windows are themselves widgets, however, they are called *toplevel* widgets as they can't be placed inside other widgets.

A good interface makes it easy for users to tell the computer what they want to do, for the computer to request information from the users, and for the computer to present understandable information. Clear communication between the user and the computer is the working premise of a good user interface design. Some of the qualities that a good user interface must have are clear, consistent, simple, user-controlled, direct, forgiving, feedback provider, and aesthetic.

Following the next GUI design principles should help you create more effective, user-friendly interfaces while avoiding many design errors. Unfortunately, just following design principles cannot alone guarantee success because it is entirely possible to create completely unworkable interfaces while strictly adhering to the rules.

- Don't try to reinvent the wheel. The user must be able to anticipate the behavior of your program using knowledge gained from other programs.

- Provide adequate user feedback. Keep the user informed about his actions.

- Create a safe environment for exploration.

- Struggle to make your application self-evident, by making the actions easily recognizable for the components of your application.

- The user must be able to anticipate a widget's behavior from its visual properties.

- View every user warning and error dialog that your program generates as an opportunity to improve your interface.

- Do not abuse sound, color, animation, and multimedia clips. They are appropriate for education or entertainment, but effective use in other applications is difficult.

- You better try to avoid modal behaviors. Programs using modal behavior force the user to perform tasks in a specific order or otherwise modify the user's expected responses.

- Design your interface so that your users can accomplish their tasks while being minimally aware of the interface itself.

- And finally, help users customize and preserve their preferred work environment.

Summary

This chapter shows what the available GUI options are for designing Python graphic interfaces. Choosing a toolkit for your GUI projects is not a simple thing. Although you might decide to choose something different, the Python community has already chosen the standard choice for GUI development with Python—it is called *Tkinter*, and it's part of the standard Python distribution.

Besides *Tkinter*, many other GUI solutions are supported by Python. This chapter exposes many of them.

Pythonwin is a wrapper to the MFC. It is included within the Python distribution for Windows.

wxPython is a GUI toolkit for the Python programming language that works like a wrapper to the wxWindows C++ library.

STDWIN stands for *Standard Window Interface*. It is a platform-independent interface to C-based window systems. Currently, STDWIN is obsolete and unsupported, without any further development effort being made.

PyKDE is a set of Python bindings for the KDE toolkit—the KDE classes, which uses PyQt—a set of straightforward Python bindings for the Qt toolkit.

Wpy is a class library system, based on the Microsoft Foundation Classes, that is used for writing GUI code easily in Python.

PyGTK is a set of bindings for the GTK widget set and Gnome libraries that runs on any platform that supports GTK.

PyOpenGL (Python Tk-OpenGL Module) is the OpenGL-Widget for Python/Tk. *OpenGL* is the premier environment for developing portable, interactive 2D and 3D graphics applications.

Wafe, which stands for *Widget Athena front end*, is a package that implements a symbolic, string-based interface based on Tcl to the X Toolkit, the Athena Widget Set.

pyFLTK is the Python wrapper for the Fast Light Tool Kit graphical user interface library. FLTK is a C++ graphical user interface toolkit for X (UNIX), OpenGL, and WIN32 platforms—it is also largely compatible with the *XForms* library.

FXPy is a Python extension module, which provides an interface to the FOX GUI library. FOX is a C++ based toolkit for developing Graphical User Interfaces easily and effectively that runs on UNIX and Windows. It offers a wide collection of Controls, including support to drag and drop, selection, as well as OpenGL widgets for 3D graphical manipulation.

Motif is the market leader among UNIX GUI toolkits, and *Python X Extension* bounds it to Python.

PyAmulet is another Python GUI. It wraps an underlying C library, called *OpenAmulet*.

DynWin is a dynamic GUI class library for Win32 and Python.

The *Java Python Interface (JPI)* is an interface that allows Java and Python (the C Implementation, not JPython) to primitively work together.

The *Abstract Windowing Toolkit (AWT)* is a user interface toolkit provided by the Java programming language class library.

FORMS is a module for the *SGI IRIX* platform that provides an interface to the *FORMS* Library.

As you could see, the number of options is large. It is your choice to decide which one best fits your needs.

CHAPTER 15

Tkinter

Goodday, Bruce!

The focus here is to provide information about *Tkinter*, which has become the standard Python GUI. You will learn how it works and how you can create your first GUI-oriented applications.

Introduction to Tcl/Tk

Tk is a popular and endorsed toolkit developed by John Ousterhout that can handle windows, GUI events, and user interactions. This toolkit is provided as an extension for Tcl. That is why part of Tkinter is an interface to Tcl. Without these routines, the management of a GUI environment would require an application with many lines of code.

The toolkit was originally developed at the University of California, Berkeley, to be a supplement to Tcl (a language also developed by Ousterhout). After his transition to Sun Microsystems, he started a firm called Scriptics (currently known as Ajuba) just to take care of the Tk and Tcl development projects.

Nowadays, many languages use Tk, including Scheme, Perl, and Python. Tkinter is Python's interface to the Tk GUI toolkit. By the way, Tcl is the behind the scenes language that Tkinter uses to communicate with the Tk toolkit. Those who already know Tcl/Tk will have a nice time learning and using Python/Tkinter because both pairs have a bit of familiarity.

Both Tcl and Tk are open source products and their ongoing development is part of a collaboration effort between engineers at Scriptics and other users in the Tcl user community. Scriptics hosts the *CVS (Concurrent Versions System)* repository for the source code, and everyone else is welcome to submit source code changes and patches.

At this time, the latest stable version of Tcl/Tk is version 8.3. Among other things, this version is shipped with a Tcl/Tk Web browser plug-in that provides an alternative to Java programming for client-side Web applications. The plug-in provides a secure environment to run downloaded Tcl programs, in a way similar to Java applets.

If you are using a supported platform, the chances of easily finding a precompiled binary for your machine are extremely high. Tcl and Tk are highly portable, which allows them to run on many platforms, including Win32, Linux, IRIX, AIX, Solaris, BSD, Macintosh, and others. Therefore, it turns out to be very easy to implement Tkinter on all these platforms. For more information, check out

Tcl/Tk Documentation

```
http://dev.scriptics.com/doc/
```

Ajuba

```
http://www.ajubasolutions.com/
```

Tkinter

As you saw in the previous chapter, other options exist for GUI projects using Python. However, at this moment, Python has chosen to support Tkinter as its official GUI implementation.

Tkinter is a standard object-oriented interface to the Tk GUI API, which was originally written by Steen Lumholdt when he was in need for improving his GUI work with Python. In this chapter, you will see how easy it is to subclass Tk widgets using Python's facilities. Some say that it is even easier than when using Tcl's capabilities.

Don't worry. You don't need to know a thing about Tcl before start learning Tkinter— the only possible case is if you need to go through the Tcl/Tk documentation.

Tkinter is a mature cross-platform interface that provides a small set of basic widgets for your GUI applications. But this doesn't mean that you need to get stuck on that set. Tkinter is extensible, which means that you can use third-party widget packages as well. A *widget* is a user interface element, such as a *list box* or a *radio button*.

The only possible disadvantage of using Tkinter is the fact that it uses Tcl to make the calls to Tk. This middle step can slow down some programs.

The Tkinter toolkit is a powerful GUI framework that allows Python programs to work on Windows, UNIX, and Macintosh platforms. The main difference between Tkinter and other toolkits is the portability issue. Almost all other toolkits are good in some specific systems only. For example, KDE bindings (Linux), Pythonwin/MFC (Windows), and Mac toolbox bindings (Macs) are GUI implementations that provide support only for a specific platform. On the other hand, Tkinter allows you to write code that can run in many platforms without a single change.

Tkinter proves that the interface design of an application can be created separate from the application's business routines. When you choose Tkinter to be your GUI environment, you basically have to worry about where to put the right widgets and how to perfectly design your application. Another feature that it provides is a set of geometry management functions available to help you arrange the widgets all around the interface. After you finish with the visual design, you just need to bind the widget actions to the specific functions that you need to call, and *voilà*! Your graphical interface is ready.

Tkinter enables you to handle buttons and windows and define their properties in a glance. After designing and implementing your interface, it is possible to change the business functions of your application without changing one line of your GUI code. Isn't it great?

Some time ago, there wasn't almost any documentation available for Tkinter. However, since it became the standard Python GUI, a lot of material has been released about this toolkit. See the resources section at the end of this chapter for details.

Checking the Installation

Beginning with version 1.5.2, Tkinter has become part of the Windows binary distribution. Tkinter has been included with most UNIX distribution for a long time. The Tkinter package contains all necessary classes, constants, and functions that are required to wrap and use the Tk toolkit.

If you are running Microsoft Windows, the Python installer for Windows (version 1.5.2) comes with the version 8.0.5 of the Tcl/Tk installer. The same thing goes to Mac users.

If you are running any UNIX system, you must download, build, and install both Tcl and Tk from the source. You can download the files from `http://dev.scriptics.com/software/tcltk/8.0.html`. Follow the instructions contained in the README files, and the process should be very simple; that is, if you don't already have it installed (which most free UNIX-like systems do these days).

If for some reason, your need to download the latest version of Tcl/Tk, the files are available at `http://dev.scriptics.com/`. As I said before, depending on your platform, you can get binaries instead of downloading and compiling the source code.

Once you have Tkinter running in your system, you will find a low-level interface module called _tkinter that can be a DLL, a shared library, or statically linked to your interpreter; it all depends on your system. Note that _tkinter is mainly just a Python interface to the Tcl interpreter. On top of this low-level module, you have the `Tkinter` module, which is more readable, and is written in 100% pure Python. This module is the main module of the Tkinter package, and it imports a lot of other helper modules when it is imported, including `Tkconstants`.

Sometime ago, Windows users who had problems involving multiple copies of the Tcl/Tk DLLs floating around the system needed to have special attention when installing Tcl/Tk. Now, they can rest on *fixtk*, which is a utility that tries to locate the Tcl/Tk 8.0 DLLs on Windows systems.

Hello Python World

Now that you have your Tkinter installation ready to go, you just need to import the Tkinter module to start playing around with your system.

If you are using Windows, I suggest that you save files with the `.pyw` extension in order to have it executed by `pythonw.exe`, which doesn't open the interpreter console. On the other hand, if you decide to keep the `.py` extension, your GUI scripts will be executed by the command line interpreter (`python.exe`), which opens a DOS console.

The next program implements a simple Hello Python World example.

```
import Tkinter
import sys
win = Tkinter.Tk()
b = Tkinter.Button(win, text="Hello Python World!",command=sys.exit)
b.pack()
win.mainloop()
```

Note that we only use the `Tk()` method to create the main window for the application. To run this program, just call the script as you usually do with any other script. To quit the program, you just need to close the window. Figure 15.1 shows how this program looks in a Window system. Remember that other windows can be created as Toplevels.

Figure 15.1
This figure shows a Tkinter implementation of the standard Hello World example.

The next example uses a convenient way to load the Tkinter module (from Tkinter import *). Because this module only exposes names that are associated to GUI objects (such as button and Frame), you don't need to worry that much about namespace conflicts with your applications, and it becomes easier to read the code. Another feature shown in this example is that we can use a Toplevel instance instead of a Tk instance to store other widgets.

```
from Tkinter import *
root = Tk()
win = Toplevel(root)
win.pack()
Label(win, text= "Hello Python World" ).pack(side=TOP)
Button(win, text="Close", command=win.quit).pack(side=RIGHT)
win.mainloop()
```

You could have used win = Frame() instead of win.Toplevel(root). However, given that a frame acts differently depending on whether it has a parent or not (either a toplevel or just a widget to help with packing), this wouldn't be such a good idea.

Figure 15.2 shows how this code looks when it is executed.

Figure 15.2
This figure shows a small variation of the previous Hello World example.

OK, now let's see what is really happening in both examples. First, we have to import the Tkinter module. Then, we have to create a widget to hold the other objects. (In the first example we used a top-level window by calling the Tk() method and in the second one we used an instance of the Toplevel widget). Creating another Tk() instance is really starting up another instance of Tk—it is less expensive to create a Toplevel.

When we have a background, we can start adding widgets to it. In the first example, we added a single button, and in the second one, we added two widgets: a label and a button.

You don't necessarily associate a widget with its toplevel—you associate it with its parent widget (if you are adding a Button to a Frame that is a child of a Toplevel, you would pass the frame as the first argument). It is also necessary to pack the widgets in order to display them in the window. This last process is part of a concept called geometry management, which is used to manage the position and layout of widgets.

Both examples demonstrate how you can bind actions to the events that can occur in your widget. Here, we are using a specific attribute called *command* for this purpose. You can use keyword arguments to transport several attributes and their values to a widget, which is a simple way to handle multiple attributes.

The last thing that we need to do is to start an event loop. Note that the application only appears when you start the loop engine. Regular Python scripts are executed top to bottom, and when the last line of code is executed, the program quits. We don't want this kind of behavior in a GUI application. Therefore, we need to call the `mainloop()` method of the top-level window of our application. This method keeps the GUI indefinitely running until the window is closed. This loop is responsible for redrawing the window widgets whenever it becomes necessary, for handling events (such as key presses and mouse clicks), and for managing Tkinter operations, such as all the geometry management functions.

Note that the version of Tkinter shipped along with Python 2.0 also provides support for Unicode characters because Tkinter is now able to display Unicode string in Tk widgets. Talking about Python 2.0, Tkinter had some optimizations done in order to make some operations much faster. It is also good to mention that the support for Tcl/Tk 7.X versions has been dropped in this latest release.

Geometry Management

All Tkinter widgets have access to specific *geometry management* methods, which have the purpose of organizing widgets throughout the parent widget area. These methods are grouped in three distinct classes that provide a nice way to lay out child widgets in their parent widget. Tkinter exposes the following geometry manager classes: `pack`, `grid`, and `place`.

- `pack`—This geometry manager organizes widgets in blocks before placing them in the parent widget.

- `grid`—This geometry manager organizes widgets in a table-like structure in the parent widget.

- `place`—This geometry manager organizes widgets by placing them in a specific position in the parent widget.

Each one of these geometry managers has a specific purpose. The `pack` manager, for example, is convenient for application windows' design. On the other hand, the `grid` manager is perfect for designing dialogs because you can easily arrange the position of several widgets using an easy-to-figure-out table structure, behind the scenes. And last, but not least, we have the `place` manager. This manager is perfect for placing a widget in a specific position in a frame or window. However, it is not that useful to design complex structures because it requires a lot of specific information about the coordinates of the widget.

The usage of these methods is very simple. When you create a widget, such as

```
b = Button(root, text="Quit", padx=5, justify=CENTER)
```

You can apply the geometry method directly on the created object.

```
b.pack(side=RIGHT)
```

Or, if you do not want to create one more object instance, you can simply call the geometry method directly from the creation line:

```
Button(root, text="Quit", padx=5, justify=CENTER).pack(side=RIGHT)
```

pack()

The `pack` manager adds the widgets to the frame or the window based in the order that the widgets are packed. After creating a Frame widget, you can start adding widgets to it (the area where the Frame stores a widget is called a *parcel*). If you want to place a group of widgets next to each other, you can use the same *anchor* option for all of them. Therefore, they will be stored in the same parcel of the parent frame. If you don't specify any option, the widgets are added from top to bottom in the available spaces. Additionally, you can specify the frame *side* where you want to place the widget. The final widget position is based on the size of the parent frame as well as on the position of the other widgets already placed. Note that if you use Frames, you will spend much less time designing your interface.

The pack method provides the following options, which can be informed as direct assignments or as a dictionary variable:

expand—This option expands the widget to use all the remaining space after the other widgets have been informed. This is an important attribute to set so that the correct widgets use the extra space when the window is resized.

fill—This option defines how the widget should fill up the space provided by its parcel. Possible values: x, y, both, and none.

ipadx, ipady—These options are used along with the fill option to define the space, in pixels, around the widget.

padx, pady—These options define the space, in pixels, between widgets.

side—This option defines the side where we want to place the widget. Possible values: top, bottom, left, and right.

The following lines demonstrate how you can use these options when packing a widget:

```
topframe = Frame(root, relief=RAISED, borderwidth=2)
topframe.pack(side=TOP, fill=BOTH)
rightframe = Frame(root, relief=RAISED, borderwidth=2)
rightframe.pack(side=RIGHT, fill=BOTH, expand=1, padx=2, pady=2)
```

The default behavior is to measure the sizes in pixels, but if you prefer to use other measurement units, you just need to add a special suffix to each specific measured value. The possible values are c (for onscreen centimeters), m (for onscreen millimeters), i (for onscreen inches), and p (for printer's points—note that 1 printer point is equivalent to 1/72 inches). Check out the next line of code to understand how to use this feature. Note that the measurements are in centimeters.

```
rightframe.pack(side=RIGHT, fill=BOTH, expand=1, padx=4c, pady=3c)
```

grid()

The grid geometry manager is very flexible, which makes the task of designing dialogs very simple. It creates a grid pattern in the frame and allocates a space in each cell to hold a widget. To use it, you just need to inform the row and the column where you want to insert the widget. In order to use the pack method to collect results similar to the ones provided by this grid functionality, you would have to use a lot of frame widgets. Actually, it is quite often impossible to get the same configuration with pack() as you do with grid(). You won't necessarily get all the column/row boundaries to match with pack().

As an example of the grid method, consider the dialog at Figure 15.3.

Figure 15.3
Window organized with the grid method.

Now, check out the code that works behind the scenes to organize the widgets:

```
from Tkinter import *
root = Tk()

Label(root, text="Last Name:").grid(row=0, sticky=W)
Label(root, text="First Name:").grid(row=1, sticky=W)
Label(root, text="Phone #:").grid(row=2, sticky=W)
Label(root, text="email:").grid(row=3, sticky=W)
entry_ln = Entry(root)
entry_fn = Entry(root)
entry_ph = Entry(root)
entry_em = Entry(root)

entry_ln.grid(row=0, column=1)
entry_fn.grid(row=1, column=1)
entry_ph.grid(row=2, column=1)
entry_em.grid(row=3, column=1)
Label(root).grid(row=4, sticky=W)
Label(root, text="Skill set summary:").grid(row=5, sticky=W)
cb_gender = Checkbutton(root, text="Python")
cb_gender.grid(row=6, sticky=W)
cb_gender = Checkbutton(root, text="Perl")
cb_gender.grid(row=7, sticky=W)
b_apply = Button(root, text="Apply")
b_apply.grid(row=7, column = 1)
root.mainloop()
```

Note that we have to call the `grid` method for every single widget, always mentioning the row and the column where we want to place it. If for some reason, we don't use the `grid` method for a widget, which is placed just after a group of gridded widgets, this new widget is placed in the next available position beneath the gridded widgets.

For your information, the coordinate numbered (`0,0`) is given to the intersection of the first row on the top with the first column on the left side.

This method implements the following options:

`row`—The number of the row where we want to place the widget.

`column`—The number of the column where we want to place the widget.

`columnspan`—This option defines the number of columns that must be occupied by the widget.

`rowspan`—This option defines the number of rows that must be occupied by the widget.

place()

Similar to all the other managers, this one is available for all Tkinter standard widgets as well. The place geometry manager enables you to explicitly set the position and size of each widget, which can be either in terms of absolute or relative coordinates. You should only consider using this manager when you are in need of placing a widget in a specific position that is not possible to set automatically. The next code exemplifies the use of place:

```
lbl = Label(root, text="Name:")
lbl.place(relx=0.5, rely=2, anchor=LEFT)
```

The place geometry manager implements two methods: `place` and `place_configure`. Both of them can use the following as arguments:

`anchor`—Defines the part of widget that must be placed on the given coordinates. Possible values are N, NE, E, SE, SW, W, NW, and CENTER. The default value is NW, which is the top-left corner.

`bordermode`—Defines whether the given coordinates must consider the border size or not. The possible values are respectively OUTSIDE and INSIDE, which is the default value.

`height`, `width`—Define the widget's size in *pixels*.

in (in_)—Places the widget in a position relative to the given widget. Note that to use this option as a keyword option, you need to append an underscore to the option name.

relheight, relwidth—Define the relative size of the widget to the reference widget defined by the in_ option.

relx, rely—Define the relative position of the widget to the reference widget defined by the in_ option, or to the parent widget when the in_ option is not defined.

x, y—Define the absolute position of the widget, and the default value is 0 for each one of them.

Handling Tkinter Events

Usually, when you create a graphical interface for your application, you want to handle all the possible events that happen there, such as reading in each key in the keyboard (including the F1–F12 set, Ctrl, Alt, and Shift keys), tracking the actions upon the mouse button, or even controlling the window redraw events fired by the window manager. Tkinter handles that by allowing you to create bindings for every specific object. Actually, you can bind events to the widget instance itself, to the widget's Toplevel window, to the widget's class, and to your entire application (such as a global HELP functionality for the F1 function key).

After binding an event to a widget, you need to specify which function should be called at the time the event occurs. This function (or method) is called a *callback*. You can define callbacks for all kinds of windowing events, as you will see later. The following code demonstrates a simple callback functionality, which is associated to the command property from a specific widget.

```
from Tkinter import *
import sys
def close():
    sys.exit(0)

root = Tk()
button = Button(root)
button['text'] = "Close"
button['command'] = close
button.pack()
root.mainloop()
```

The next example binds the mouse-click event (`"<Button-1>"`) to a specific function in our program. Note that the event description is just a simple string. The mainloop keeps checking for this event, and when it catches the event, the function (event handler) is called. Note that an object is passed to the callback function carrying some information provided by the event.

```
from Tkinter import *
def ShowPosition(event):
    Top = Toplevel(root)
    xlabel = Label(Top)
    xlabel.pack()
    xlabel.config(text = "X = " + str(event.x))
    ylabel = Label(Top)
    ylabel.pack()
    ylabel.config(text = "Y = " + str(event.y))
    Top.mainloop()

root = Tk()
frame = Frame(root, width=200, height=200)
frame.bind("<Button-1>", ShowPosition)
frame.pack()
root.mainloop()
```

The next sections provided more events that you can use in your programs.

Mouse Events

When handling mouse event, use 1 for the left button, 2 for the middle button, and 3 for the right button. The following events are based on the left button, and you need to make the necessary changes in order to adapt them for usage with the other buttons. Before starting, you should know that the current position of the mouse pointer, the position relative to the widget, is provided in the x and y options of the event object passed to the callback.

If you bind to both a single click event and to a double click event, both bindings will be called whenever one of them is activated.

    `<Enter>`—The mouse pointer entered the widget.

    `<Leave>`—The mouse pointer left the widget.

    `<Button-1>`, `<ButtonPress-1>`, or `<1>`—A mouse button is pressed over the widget.

    `<B1-Motion>`—The mouse is moved, with mouse button 1 being held down.

<ButtonRelease-1>—Button 1 was released.

<Double-Button-1>—Button 1 was double-clicked.

Keyboard Events

The following events are exposed by the keyboard interface:

<Key>—The user has pressed any key. The instance object originated by the callback function carries an attribute called *char* that can be used to identify which key was pressed.

a—The user typed the letter a.

b—The user typed the letter b.

The same concept can be applied for all the other printable characters.

<Control-Up>—The user pressed the Control key, while pressing the Up arrow. This type of structure also allows you to use the keyword suffixes Up, Down, Left, and Right, and the keyword prefixes Control, Alt, and Shift.

<Return>—The user pressed the Enter key.

<Escape>—The user pressed the Esc key.

The same concept can also be applied for all the other special keys found in the keyboard, including: F1, F2, F3, F4, F5, F6, F7, F8, F9, F10, F11, F12, Num_Lock, Scroll_Lock, Caps_Lock, Print, Insert, Delete, Pause, Prior (*Page Up*), Next (*Page Down*), BackSpace, Tab, Cancel (*Break*), Control_L (any Control key), Alt_L (any Alt key), Shift_L (any Shift key), End, Home, Up, Down, Left, and Right.

Event Attributes

Next, I list all the attributes that are exposed by the instance objects originated by the callback functions:

char—Character code associated with a pressed key.

keycode—Key code associated with a pressed key.

keysym—Key symbol associated with a pressed key.

height, width—New size, in pixels, of a widget.

num—This attribute contains the mouse's button number associated with an event.

`widget`—Widget instance of the widget that has generated the event.

`x, y`—Current position, in pixels, of the mouse.

`x_root, y_root`—These attributes identify the current position of the mouse, in pixels, relative to the upper left corner of the screen.

`type`—Shows the event type.

Event Callbacks

The following methods are used to handle event callbacks by binding a Python function or method to an action that can be applied to a widget. You will also find some callback methods that handle alarm callbacks as well.

`after(milliseconds [, callback [, arguments]])`—Registers an alarm callback that accepts optional arguments. This callback is called after the given number of milliseconds. The returned value of this method is an identifier that can be used along with the `after_cancel` method in order to cancel the callback. If you call the `after` method using just the first argument, the application will block the event loop and wait for the given number of milliseconds.

`after_cancel(identifier)`—Cancels the alarm callback that possesses the given identifier.

`after_idle(callback, arguments)`—Registers a callback that is called whenever the system is idle, without anything going on in the mainloop.

`bindtags()`—Returns the binding search order used by the widget. The returned value is in a tuple format, and it lists the namespaces used to search for the bindings. You can modify this order by calling this method with the altered order as an argument.

`bind(event, callback)`—Defines the function or method (`callback`) that must be associated to the given event. Use the form `bind(event, callback, "+")` to handle multiple callbacks within the same binding.

`bind_all(event, callback)`—Defines the function or method (`callback`) that must be associated to the given event at the application level. Use the form `bind_all(event, callback, "+")` to handle multiple callbacks within the same binding. As an example, this can be used to set global accelerator/shortcut keys.

`bind_class(widgetclass, event, callback)`—Defines the function or method (`callback`) that must be associated to the given event at the given widget class.

Use the form `bind_class(widgetclass, event, callback, "+")` to handle multiple callbacks within the same binding.

`<Configure>`—Indicates that the widget was resized or moved to a new location. The instance object originated by the callback function carries two attributes that can be used to identify the new size of the widget: `height` and `width`. Note that the name comes from the fact that the `configure` event is emitted in X11 when a window is mapped or resized.

`unbind(event)`—Removes the bindings for the given event.

`unbind_all(event)`—Removes the bindings for the given event at the application level.

`unbind_class(class, event)`—Removes the bindings for the given event at the given widget class.

Protocols

The mechanism called *protocol handler* is responsible for the communication between the window manager and your application. Handling these protocols, you can intercept the messages provided by the system, and define exactly what you want to happen.

Usually, the protocols `WM_DELETE_WINDOW`, `WM_TAKE_FOCUS`, and `WM_SAVE_YOURSELF` are the ones mostly used. For details about the other supported protocols, see the *Inter-Client Communication Conventions Manual (ICCCM)* at

`http://tronche.com/gui/x/icccm/`

Although this convention was established for the X systems, the Tk library handles it on all platforms. These protocols are X specific. If you are running an X server on Windows or MacOS and have Tk compiled for X, it will do the same as on UNIX. That's because Tk ports map these calls to the equivalent actions on the other systems.

The necessary syntax to bind a handler to a protocol is

`widget.protocol(protocol, function_handler)`

Note that the widget must be a Toplevel widget. The following example demonstrates the use of the `WM_DELETE_WINDOW` protocol. The window manager generates this protocol when the user tries to close a window. Here, we are intercepting this protocol.

```
from Tkinter import *
import tkMessageBox
def protocolhandler():
    if tkMessageBox.askokcancel("Exit", "Wanna leave?"):
        if tkMessageBox.askokcancel("Exit", "Are you sure?"):
            if tkMessageBox.askokcancel("Exit", "Really?"):
                root.destroy()
root = Tk()
root.protocol("WM_DELETE_WINDOW", protocolhandler)
root.mainloop()
```

Just to let you know, the WM_SAVE_YOURSELF protocol is called by X window managers when the application should save a snapshot of its working set, and the WM_TAKE_FOCUS protocol is called by X window managers when the application gets the focus.

Tkinter Widgets

The typical Tkinter distribution contains a basic set of 15 widgets, and some extra classes.

The Tkinter reference that I present in this chapter only shows a small set of methods and attributes for each one of the available widgets. This list is provided just to give you some idea of what you can do with each one of the widgets, and it is doesn't have the intention to be a complete guide. If you need to go further in this topic, I suggest you look at the Tkinter resources pages that I list at the end of this chapter.

Widget Standard Options

Almost all widgets have access to a set of standard attributes that define special characteristics for each one of them, including color definitions and font types. The value for each one of these attributes can be determined at the creation time as

```
mylabel = Label(win, width=40)
```

Or, if you prefer, you can also define (or change) the values at the execution time using the configure method.

```
mylabel.configure(width=40)
```

The previous examples use *key/value* pairs to define the attribute values, but you can also use dictionaries to easily inform multiple attributes at once.

```
mysize = {"height"=2, "width"=40}
mylabel.configure(mysize)
```

Support for using dictionaries here is really for backward compatibility for programs written before Python 1.4 (which didn't support keyword arguments). It is not a good idea to use it with the latest versions of Python. The third way of changing properties is with

```
mylabel['height'] = 2
```

Next, I list common properties that are defined for all Tkinter widgets.

height
In buttons, labels, and text widgets, this attribute defines the height in number of characters. In all other widgets, it defines the height in pixels.

width
In buttons, labels, and text widgets, this attribute defines the width in number of characters. In all other widgets, it defines the width in pixels.

background(bg) **and** foreground(fg)
These attributes define the background and foreground (text) colors for a specific widget. It can be either a color name or a explicit hexadecimal notation RGB starting with #. It is usually used in one of the following formats: "#RRGGBB", "#RGB", and "#RRRRGGGGBBBB", depending on the number of colors allowed by your system.

If you are using either a Windows or a Macintosh system, the table that contains the available color names is already built into your system.

The following constants define the system colors that you can use within your Windows system.

```
SystemActiveBorder, SystemActiveCaption, SystemAppWorkspace,
SystemBackground, SystemButtonFace, SystemButtonHighlight,
SystemButtonShadow, SystemButtonText, SystemCaptionText, SystemDisabledText,
SystemHighlight, SystemHighlightText, SystemInactiveBorder,
SystemInactiveCaption, SystemInactiveCaptionText, SystemMenu, SystemMenuText,
SystemScrollbar, SystemWindow, SystemWindowFrame, SystemWindowText.
```

Note that you can change the colors at any time by editing the control panel settings.

The same concept goes for Mac systems. The available list of color names for the Macintosh platform is as follows:

SystemButtonFace	SystemMenuActive
SystemButtonFrame	SystemMenuActiveText
SystemButtonText	SystemMenuDisabled
SystemHighlight	SystemMenuText
SystemHighlightText	SystemWindowBody
SystemMenu	

On the other hand, if you are using a UNIX X windowing system, the table of color names is located in a file called `xrgb.txt`, which contains a list of color names and their corresponding RGB values, defined by the X Server.

relief

This attribute defines the style of a widget's border. All Tkinter widgets have a border, which might not be visible by default for some widgets. This attribute accepts the following values: SUNKEN, RIDGE, RAISED, or GROOVE for 3D appearance; and FLAT or SOLID for 2D appearance.

> **Tip**
> The border of a widget consists of a 3D relief and a focus highlight region (in most cases, this is a border outside the relief).

Highlight Settings

These attributes control the process of indicating whether a widget has the keyboard focus.

`highlightcolor` defines the color used to draw the highlight region when the widget has the keyboard focus.

`highlightbackground` defines the color used to draw the highlight region when the widget doesn't have the keyboard focus.

`highlightthickness` defines the width of the highlight region, in pixels.

borderwidth (bd)

This attribute defines the width of a widget relief border in number of pixels.

`text`
This attribute contains the widget caption text, using the `foreground` and `font` values to format it.

`justify`
This attribute defines how multiple lines of a text caption must line up. It can assume one of the following values: `LEFT`, `CENTER`, or `RIGHT`.

`font`
In certain widgets that support caption text, you can specify the font that you want to format the text with. The font specification must be in a valid tuple format that must contain the font family name, the font size, and a string listing the font styles that you want to apply (bold, italic, underline, and overstrike), as you can see in the following code example:

```
w1 = Tkinter.Label(root, text="Hello Python World", font=("Symbol", 8,
 "italic"))
w2 = Tkinter.Label(root, text="Hello Python World", font=("Times", 14,
 "bold italic"))
w3 = Tkinter.Label(root, text="Hello Python World", font=("Symbol", 8))
```

The next example shows how you can use the `Font` class provided by the `tkFont` module in order to create font instances. The great advantage of this style of programming is that in case you need to make changes to a given font format, the changes are replicated to every widget in which the font is mentioned.

```
import Tkinter, tkFont
root = Tkinter.Tk()
myfont = tkFont.Font(family="times", size=18, weight=tkFont.BOLD)
widget = Tkinter.Label(root, text="Hello Python World", font=myfont)
widget.pack()
Tkinter.mainloop()
```

We basically have three elements that we need to provide: The font family (name), the font size, and a list of the required style options. The font name follows the format used in Windows and X Systems, and we have at least the Times, Courier, and Helvetica families predefined. The font style options follow the specification detailed in Table 15.1.

PART IV   Graphical Interfaces

Table 15.1   *Available Options for Font Styles*

Font Style Option	Description
family	Font family
size	Font size in points
weight	Font thickness (NORMAL or BOLD)
slant	Font slant (NORMAL or ITALIC)
underline	Font underlining: (0) False, (1) True
overstrike	Font strikeout: (0) False, (1) True

The tkFont module also exposes the functions and methods listed in Tables 15.2 and 15.3, respectively.

Table 15.2   *Functions Provided by the* tkFont *Module*

Function	Description
families()	List available font families
names()	List names of user-defined fonts

Table 15.3   *Available Methods for a Font Class Instance*

Font Method	Description
actual(*options*)	Returns actual font attributes.
cget(*option*)	Gets configured font attribute.
config(), configure()	Gets a full set of configured fonts.
config(*options*), configure(options...)	Modifies one or more font attributes.
copy(*font object*)	Returns a copy of the font object.
measure(*text*)	Returns the width in integer format.
metrics(*options*)	Returns the font metrics.

You can customize your application to use platform dependent fonts, which are available on your system. For example, if you are running MS Windows, you can use Arial, Courier New, Fixedsys, MS Sans Serif, MS Serif, Symbol, System, Times New Roman, and others.

Some system fonts are also available for your usage (see Table 15.4), however, they don't allow you to change their style and size specifications. Be careful when porting applications that use system fonts because those fonts are tied to specific systems.

Table 15.4 *Examples of System Fonts*

Platform	System Font Examples
Windows	ansi, ansifixed, device, system, and systemfixed
Macintosh	application and system
UNIX	6x10 and fixed

command
This attribute associates a widget's activation with a Python function. Therefore, the function defined by this attribute is called when a specific action happens at the widget (like the click of a button).

variable
This attribute maps the widget value to a variable in such way that all changes made to the widget are reflected to this variable, and vice versa. This variable is an instance of one of the following classes: StringVar, IntVar, DoubleVar, or BooleanVar. These classes wrap a Tcl variable, which is required to use some of the Tk interfaces. All these instances implement at least two methods: get() and set(), which can be used to obtain and define a variable's value, respectively.

image, bitmap
These attributes define the image file or the bitmap file to be displayed within the widget.

anchor
This attribute defines either the location of a widget within a window, or the location of a text message within a widget. The possible values for this attribute are N, NE, E, SE, S, SW, W, NW, and CENTER.

padx, pady
Defines the padding between the widget's text or the widget's image and the widget border.

cursor
This attribute defines which mouse pointer (cursor) must be used when the mouse is moved over the widget. Some widgets (such as the Text widget) define this value by default. If you don't set this option, the parent widget's cursor is used by default. Some possible cursor values are crosshair, watch, xterm, fleur, and arrow. There are plenty of them for you to choose:

```
root.config(cursor="wait")      # Changes to the wait cursor
root.config(cursor="")          # Changes back to the normal cursor
```

Widgets Reference

Tkinter offers the following basic set of widgets. Note that these widgets are not defined or organized in any hierarchical way. Along with the set of methods that is defined by each widget, all widgets also support many general specific methods, such as the *geometry management methods*. This creates a wide coverage interface for each one of them.

Button—This widget defines a clickable button that can execute a specific operation when clicked.

Canvas—This widget is used to draw graphs, lines, polygons, and all other types of graphic elements. The main reason people use the canvas is because it takes care of all the items you add to it, and can take events on individual items in the canvas.

Checkbutton—This widget exposes a button that controls a variable that can have two distinct values. After clicking the button, the variable value toggles between the two possible values.

Entry—This widget implements a simple text entry field.

Frame—This widget works like a container for other widgets when creating a complex layout within a window. It helps you to organize the layout of the other widgets.

Label—This widget handles the exhibition of a text or an image.

Listbox—This widget displays a list of possible selections.

Menu—This widget is used to implement pull-down and pop-up menus.

Menubutton—This widget is used to implement pull-down menus and the toplevel menu bar.

Message—This widget displays a text message in a way similar to the label widget, but using powerful formatting capabilities.

Radiobutton—This widget is associated to a variable, and when clicked, the variable assumes its value. Usually many radiobuttons (each one carrying a different value) are associated to the same variable, and when one is clicked, it sets its value to the variable.

Scale—This widget provides a slider that helps you set the value of a numerical variable.

Scrollbar—This widget implements standard scrollbars that you can use along with other widgets, such as *listbox*, *canvas*, *entry*, and *text*.

Text—This widget display text that you can edit and format.

Toplevel—This widget is another container widget, just like the *frame* widget. However, it has its own toplevel window, which provides a window manager interface.

Button

The Button widget can implement a number of button types, which can display either text messages or images. See the previous `Hello World` code for an example of how to use the Button widget.

Some special methods implemented by the button widget are as follows:

flash()—Reverses and resets the foreground and background colors in order to cause a flashing effect.

invoke()—Executes the function defined in the `command` property.

The next properties are available for button widgets:

activebackground—The background color to use when the button is activated.

activeforeground—The foreground color to use when the button is activated.

bitmap—The bitmap to display in the button. This option is only used when the image option is omitted. The general available values for this option are gray12, gray25, gray50, gray75, hourglass, error, questhead, info, warning, and question. If you prefer, you can load the bitmap directly from an *XBM (X Bitmap)* file, just by prefixing the filename with an @ sign; for example, `bitmap=@hello.xbm`.

default—If set, identifies the default button.

disabledforeground—The foreground color that must be used when the button is disabled.

image—An image to display in the widget. If indicated, this option precedes both the `text` and `bitmap` options. Usually, before using this attribute, you need to create an image instance first, using the `image` subclasses, and then assign the instance to this attribute.

state—Defines the button state, which can be either NORMAL, ACTIVE, or DISABLED.

`takefocus`—Indicates whether the user can use the TAB key to change the focus to this button.

`text`—The text to display in the button. If the bitmap or image options are used, the text isn't displayed.

`underline`—Integer offset applied on the `text` value to identify which character must be underlined.

`wraplength`—Distance, in screen units, that determines when a button's text must be wrapped into multiple lines. The default configuration is to not accept wrapping.

Canvas

This widget is responsible for creating and displaying graphical items, such as arcs, bitmaps, images, lines, ovals, polygons, and rectangles, in a customized way. It works by providing a canvas into which you add the graphical items. The default behavior of this widget is to draw the graphic items on top of the other items added to the canvas first. When you have your canvas widget filled with the graphical items, you can manipulate them using a lot of methods provided by Tkinter. Note that you can create customized widgets this way by adding several layers of objects, and binding event callbacks to each one of these layers.

The Canvas widget supports the following standard items:

arc—Creates an arc item, which can be a chord, a pieslice, or a simple arc.

```
coord = 10, 50, 240, 210
widgetitem = canvas.create_arc(coord, start=0, extent=150, fill="blue")
```

bitmap—Creates a bitmap item, which can be a built-in bitmap, such as `"question"`, `"info"`, `"hourglass"`, `"warning"`, or one read from an XBM file.

```
widgetitem = canvas.create_bitmap(60, 30, bitmap="warning")
```

image—Creates an image item, which can be an instance of either the `BitmapImage` or the `PhotoImage` classes.

```
filename = PhotoImage(file="sunshine.gif")
widget = canvas.create_image(50, 50, anchor=NE, image=filename)
```

line—Creates a line item.

```
widgetitem = create_line(x0, y0, x1, y1, ..., xn, yn, options)
```

Some options are

width—Line's width. The default value is 1 pixel.

fill—Line's color. The default value is `black`.

oval—Creates a circle or an ellipse at the given coordinates. It takes two pairs of coordinates—the top left and bottom right corners of the bounding rectangle for the oval.

```
widgetitem = create_oval(x0, y0, x1, y1, options)
```

Some options are

fill—The color to use for the interior. If an empty string is given, the interior is not drawn. Default is empty (transparent).

outline—The color to use for the outline.

polygon—Creates a polygon item that must have at least three vertices.

```
widgetitem = create_polygon(x0, y0, x1, y1, x2, y2, ..., xn, yn, options)
```

Some options are

outline—Polygon outline's color. The default value is `black`.

splinesteps—Integer that defines the smoothness of the curves.

rectangle—Creates a rectangle item using the given coordinates.

```
widgetitem = create_rectangle(x0, y0, x1, y1, options)
```

Some options are

fill—The color to use for the rectangle interior. If an empty string is given, the interior is not drawn. The default is empty (transparent).

outline—The color to use for the outline. If an empty string is given, the outline is not drawn. The default is `black`.

text—Creates a text item at the given position, using the given options. Note that the text string itself is given by the text option.

```
widgetitem = create_text(x0, y0, options)
```

Some options are

anchor—Specifies the text position. The default value is `CENTER`.

fill—The color to use for the text. If an empty string is given, the text is not drawn. Default is empty (transparent).

window—Embeds a window at the given position based on the provided options.

```
widgetitem = create_window(x0, y0, options)
```

Some options are

window—The window widget to embed in the canvas.

anchor—Specifies the window position. The default value is `CENTER`.

Checkbutton

This widget implements a check box with two states: checked and unchecked; in other words, on and off or true and false.

The following attributes are available:

`onvalue`, `offvalue`—These attributes specify the values to store within the variable indicated by the `variable` property. If the button is not selected, the variable receives the `offvalue` value, receiving the `onvalue` value when the button is checked.

`indicatoron`—By setting this attribute to zero, you can make the whole widget to be the check box.

This widget exposes the following methods:

`select()`—Selects the check button and sets the value of the variable to `onvalue`.

`flash()`—Reverses and resets the foreground and background colors in order to cause a flashing effect.

`invoke()`—Executes the function defined in the `command` property.

`toggle()`—Reverses the state of the button. If it is on, it becomes off, and vice versa.

The following code demonstrates a call to the Checkbutton widget:

```
from Tkinter import *
win = Frame()
win.pack()
Checkbutton(win, text="Click here").pack(side=LEFT)
win.mainloop()
```

Figure 15.4 shows the output of this code.

Figure 15.4

The Checkbutton widget as it is displayed.

In case you are wondering how to use the variables listed previously, take a look at the following line, and check out how we would have to write the code to use them. var is the name of a variable of your program. When you say variable=<your variable>, you are asking the widget to assign to your variables the values of onvalue and offvalue whenever your button is checked or unchecked, respectively.

```
Checkbutton(master, variable=var, indicatoron=0).pack()
```

Entry

The Entry widget is implemented by users to enter a single line of text in a frame or in a window widget.

The following code exemplifies the use of this widget by creating a single line interface in which you can type expressions:

```
from Tkinter import *
from math import *
def calc():
    result = "= " + str(eval(expression.get()))
    label.config(text = result)

root = Tk()
frame = Frame(root)
label = Label(frame)
entry = Entry(frame)
expression = StringVar()
entry["textvariable"] = expression
button = Button(frame, text = "=", command = calc)
```

```
frame.pack()
entry.pack()
label.pack(side=LEFT)
button.pack(side=RIGHT)
frame.mainloop()
```

Figure 15.5 shows how the output of this code looks.

Figure 15.5
The Entry widget being used to implement an expression evaluator.

This widget provides the `textvariable` attribute, which contains the value either entered by the user or to be displayed. The `get()` method can be used to access this value, as well.

Frame

The Frame widget is very important for the process of grouping and organizing other widgets in a somehow friendly way. It works like a container, which is responsible for arranging the position of other widgets. It uses rectangular areas in the screen to organize the layout and to provide padding of these widgets. A frame can also be used as a foundation class to implement complex widgets.

In the next example, we create two frames responsible for aligning the colored buttons in two distinct rows:

```
from Tkinter import *
root = Tk()
frame = Frame(root)
frame.pack()
bottomframe = Frame(root)
bottomframe.pack(side=BOTTOM)

redbutton = Button(frame, text="Red", fg="red")
redbutton.pack(side=LEFT)
greenbutton = Button(frame, text="Brown", fg="brown")
greenbutton.pack(side=LEFT)
bluebutton = Button(frame, text="Blue", fg="blue")
bluebutton.pack(side=LEFT)
blackbutton = Button(bottomframe, text="Black", fg="black")
blackbutton.pack(side=BOTTOM)
root.mainloop()
```

You can check the output of this function by looking at Figure 15.6.

Figure 15.6
This window uses two frames to organize the buttons.

Label

This widget implements a display box where you can place text or images. The text displayed by this widget can be updated at any time you want. It is also possible to underline part of the text (like to identify a keyboard shortcut), and span the text across multiple lines.

```
label = Label(root, bg="white", relief =RAISED, borderwidth=3)
label.config(text="Whassup!")
```

If you want to easily manipulate the contents of a label widget when changing a single variable, use the `textvariable` option as demonstrated in the next example:

```
var = StringVar()
Label(root, textvariable=var).pack()
var.set("Hey!? How are you doing?")
```

Listbox

Using this widget, you create a list of text items that can be selected by the user. This list might contain several lines of information, and all lines must have the same properties. Depending on how the widget is configured (see the `selectmode` property in following list), the user is allowed to select multiple lines at the same time, which is very useful in many cases.

The Listbox widget implements the following properties:

`height`—Number of rows in the list. A value of 0 automatically resizes the widget to fit the largest option found. Setting the height to zero makes the listbox long enough to show all options at once.

`selectmode`—This option defines the type of list that you are creating. It can be either SINGLE, EXTENDED, MULTIPLE, or BROWSE.

`width`—Number of characters in each row. A value of 0 automatically resizes the widget to fit the largest option found.

The following methods are also provided:

`delete(row [,lastrow])`—Deletes the given `row`, or the rows between the given `row` and `lastrow`.

`get(row)`—Gets the string that starts at the given `row`.

`insert(row, string)`—Inserts the given `string` at the given `row`.

`see(row)`—Makes the given `row` visible for the user.

`select_clear()`—Clears the selection.

`select_set(startrow, endrow)`—Selects the rows starting at the `startrow` position and ending at the `endrow` position.

The following example demonstrates the use of a list box:

```
from Tkinter import *
root = Tk()
mylistbox = Listbox(root)
mylistbox.pack()
mylistbox.delete(0, END)
mylistbox.insert(END, "This is the row number 1")
for number in range(2,41):
    mylistbox.insert(END, "This is the row number " + str(number))
root.mainloop()
```

In order to see all the lines from the previous list, you are required to hold down the mouse button while dragging down the selection. This process can be largely simplified by using a Scrollbox widget along with the Listbox widget. Also check out the example found at the Scrollbox widget section.

Menu

The goal of this widget is to allow us to create all kinds of menus that can be used by our applications. The core functionality provides ways to create three menu types: pop-up, toplevel, and pull-down. It is also possible to use other extended widgets to implement new types of menus, such as the *OptionMenu* widget, which implements a special type that generates a pop-up list of items within a selection. You can't put arbitrary widgets in a menu. However, there are special menu item types such as radio menu items and check menu items that provide similar behavior to the widgets by the same name.

The menu widget exposes the following methods:

add_command(*options*)—Adds a menu item to the menu.

add_radiobutton(*options*)—Creates a radio button menu item.

add_checkbutton(*options*)—Creates a check button menu item.

add_cascade(*options*)—Creates a new hierarchical menu by associating a given menu to a parent menu.

add_separator()—Adds a separator line to the menu.

add(*type*, *options*)—Adds a specific type of menu item to the menu.

delete(**startindex** [,*endindex*])—Deletes the menu items ranging from startindex to endindex.

entryconfig(*index*, *options*)—Allows you to modify a menu item, which is identified by the index, and change its options.

index(*item*)—Returns the index number of the given menu item label.

The menu widget methods expose the following options:

accelerator—This is a keyboard alternative to the menu option that must be displayed as right justified next to the menu option. It's important to say here that this option doesn't automatically bind the given key to the option. You have to do it by yourself.

command—Name of the callback function that is called when the menu item is selected.

indicatorOn—Setting this option to true adds a switch next to the menu options. This small button allows an option to be toggled on and off.

label—This option defines the text of a menu item.

menu—This option is used by the add_cascade method to add a submenu (another Menu instance) to a menu.

selectColor—Switch's color. See the indicatorOn property.

state—Defines the menu item status. The possible values are normal, active, and disabled.

onvalue, offvalue—Values to be stored in the variable property. When the menu item is selected, the onvalue's value is copied to that property.

tearOff—By setting this option to `true`, a clickable separator is created in the top of the menu. Clicking on this separator, the menu item separates from the main menu, becoming part of a new window.

underline—Defines the index position of the character to be underlined.

value—The value of the attached radio button.

variable—The variable used to store a value.

Now, let's get back to practice and learn how to design menus. The basic rules are simple. First, you need to instantiate the menu class and anchor it to its parent widget. Then, you just need to use one of the add methods to include items to it.

The next example shows how to create a pop-up menu. Note that we have to bind a mouse action to a callback function that launches the menu (see Figure 15.7).

```
from Tkinter import *
def donothing():
    filewin = Toplevel(root)
    button = Button(filewin, text="Do nothing button")
    button.pack()


root = Tk()
menu = Menu(root, tearoff=0)
menu.add_command(label="Cut", command=donothing)
menu.add_command(label="Copy", command=donothing)
menu.add_command(label="Paste", command=donothing)
menu.add_command(label="Delete", command=donothing)
frame = Frame(root, width=100, height=100)
frame.pack()
def popupmenu(event):
    menu.post(event.x_root, event.y_root)
frame.bind("<Button-3>", popupmenu)
root.mainloop()
```

Figure 15.7

This pop-up menu is activated by right-clicking.

The next example demonstrates the creation and usage of a menu bar. This type of menu is placed on the top of toplevel windows (see Figure 15.8).

```
from Tkinter import *
def filemenu():
    filewin = Toplevel(root)
    fileclose = Button(filewin, text="Close Application")
    fileclose.config(command=root.quit)
    fileclose.pack()


root = Tk()
menubar = Menu(root)
menubar.add_command(label="File", command=filemenu)
menubar.add_command(label="Help")
root.config(menu=menubar)
root.mainloop()
```

Figure 15.8
The menu bar is placed on top of a toplevel window.

This last example demonstrates how to create pull-down menus, which is a type of menu that is bound to a parent menu (see Figure 15.9).

```
from Tkinter import *
def donothing():
    filewin = Toplevel(root)
    button = Button(filewin, text="Do nothing button")
    button.pack()


root = Tk()
menubar = Menu(root)
filemenu = Menu(menubar, tearoff=0)
filemenu.add_command(label="New", command=donothing)
filemenu.add_command(label="Open", command=donothing)
filemenu.add_command(label="Save", command=donothing)
filemenu.add_command(label="Save as...", command=donothing)
filemenu.add_command(label="Close", command=donothing)
filemenu.add_separator()
filemenu.add_command(label="Exit", command=root.quit)
menubar.add_cascade(label="File", menu=filemenu)
editmenu = Menu(menubar, tearoff=0)
```

```
editmenu.add_command(label="Undo", command=donothing)
editmenu.add_separator()
editmenu.add_command(label="Cut", command=donothing)
editmenu.add_command(label="Copy", command=donothing)
editmenu.add_command(label="Paste", command=donothing)
editmenu.add_command(label="Delete", command=donothing)
editmenu.add_command(label="Select All", command=donothing)
menubar.add_cascade(label="Edit", menu=editmenu)
helpmenu = Menu(menubar, tearoff=0)
helpmenu.add_command(label="Help Index", command=donothing)
helpmenu.add_command(label="About...", command=donothing)
menubar.add_cascade(label="Help", menu=helpmenu)
root.config(menu=menubar)
root.mainloop()
```

Figure 15.9
This pull-down menu is bound to a parent menu.

Menubutton
This widget was primarily used to display toplevel, pop-up, and pull-down menus. However, you can now use the menu widget to obtain the same functionality.

Message
This widget provides a multiline and noneditable object that displays texts, automatically breaking lines and justifying their contents. Its functionality is very similar to the one provided by the Label widget, except that it can also automatically wrap the text, maintaining a given width or aspect ratio. The following example creates a simple Message widget instance:

```
from Tkinter import *
txt = "This message demonstrates the usage of the Message Widget"

root = Tk()
msg = Message(root, text = txt)
msg.pack()
root.mainloop()
```

Figure 15.10 shows the output of this code.

Figure 15.10

A message displayed by the Message widget.

Radiobutton

This widget implements a multiple-choice button, which is a way to offer many possible selections to the user, and let her choose only one of them.

In order to implement this functionality, each group of radiobuttons must be associated to the same variable, and each one of the buttons must symbolize a single value. You can use the Tab key to switch from one radionbutton to another.

The following properties are made available by this widget:

command—Function to be called when the button is clicked.

variable—Variable to be updated when the button is clicked.

value—This attribute defines the value that must be stored in the variable when the button is clicked.

The following methods are also provided by this widget:

flash()—Reverses and resets the foreground and background colors in order to cause a flashing effect.

invoke()—Executes the function defined in the command property.

select()—Selects the radio button, setting the variable to value.

The following example creates three radiobuttons and displays the selected option on the label widget (see Figure 15.11):

```
from Tkinter import *
def sel():
    selection = "You selected the option " + str(var.get())
    label.config(text = selection)

root = Tk()
var = IntVar()
```

```
Radiobutton(root, text="Option 1", variable=var, value=1,
 command=sel).pack(anchor=W)
Radiobutton(root, text="Option 2", variable=var, value=2,
 command=sel).pack(anchor=W)
Radiobutton(root, text="Option 3", variable=var, value=3,
command=sel).pack(anchor=W)
label = Label(root)
label.pack()
root.mainloop()
```

Figure 15.11

This window exemplifies the use of radiobuttons.

Check out the next example. Just by setting the `indicatoron` attribute to `0`, we can change the visual design of our radio buttons (see Figure 15.12):

```
from Tkinter import *
def sel():
    selection = "You selected the option " + str(var.get())
    label.config(text = selection)

root = Tk()
var = IntVar()
r1 = Radiobutton(root, text="Option 1", variable=var, value=1, command=sel)
r2 = Radiobutton(root, text="Option 2", variable=var, value=2, command=sel)
r3 = Radiobutton(root, text="Option 3", variable=var, value=3, command=sel)

r1.config(indicatoron=0)
r2.config(indicatoron=0)
r3.config(indicatoron=0)

r1.pack(anchor=W)
r2.pack(anchor=W)
r3.pack(anchor=W)
label = Label(root)
label.pack()
root.mainloop()
```

Figure 15.12
An alternative way to use radiobuttons.

Scale

The Scale widget provides a graphical slider object that allows you to select values from a specific scale. In order to get and set values to or from the object, you need to use the following methods:

get()—This method gets the current scale value.

set(value)—This method sets the scale to a specific value.

The following example demonstrates the use of this widget (see Figure 15.13).

```
from Tkinter import *
def sel():
    selection = "Value = " + str(var.get())
    label.config(text = selection)

root = Tk()
var = DoubleVar()
scale = Scale(root, variable=var)
button = Button(root, text="Get Scale Value", command=sel)
label = Label(root)

scale.pack(anchor=CENTER)
button.pack(anchor=CENTER)
label.pack()
root.mainloop()
```

You could also implement the previous example using the Scale.get(), as demonstrated next.

```
from Tkinter import *

def sel():
    label.config(text = scale.get())
```

```
root = Tk()
var = DoubleVar()
scale = Scale(root)
button = Button(root, text="Get Scale Value", command=sel)
label = Label(root)

scale.pack(anchor=CENTER)
button.pack(anchor=CENTER)
label.pack()
root.mainloop()
```

Figure 15.13
Using a Scale widget to select values from a specific scale.

Scrollbar

This widget provides a slide controller that is used to implement vertical scrolled widgets, such as Listbox, Text, and Canvas. Note that you can also create horizontal scrollbars on Entry widgets.

This widget uses the `command` property to define the callback function that must be used to change the view in the widget.

Also, it implements the following two methods:

`set(first, last)`—Defines the fractions between 0 and 1 (representing the range 0%-100%) that delimits the current view.

`get()`—Returns the current scrollbar configuration settings.

The next example demonstrates how to link a vertical scrollbar to a Listbox widget. The steps are very simple. You first need to set the Listbox widget's `yscrollcommand` callback method to the `set` method of the scrollbar widget. Second, you need to set the scrollbar's command to the `yview` method of the Listbox widget. Every time the Listbox view is modified, the scrollbar's `set` method is called, and every time the scrollbar is changed, the Listbox's `yview` method is called, as well (see Figure 15.14).

```
from Tkinter import *
root = Tk()

scrollbar = Scrollbar(root)
scrollbar.pack(side=RIGHT, fill=Y)

mylist = Listbox(root, yscrollcommand=scrollbar.set)
for line in range(100):
    mylist.insert(END, "This is line number " + str(line))
mylist.pack(side=LEFT, fill=BOTH)

scrollbar.config(command=mylist.yview)
mainloop()
```

Figure 15.14
Here, the Scrollbar widget implements a vertical scrollbar for a Listbox widget.

If you need to use a horizontal scrollbar instead of a vertical scrollbar, the process is very simple. All you have to do is change the `orient` option in the Scrollbar initialization call, and replace the `yscrollcommand` and `yview` with `xscrollcommand` and `xview`. The following example implements these changes, as you can see in Figure 15.15.

```
from Tkinter import *
root = Tk()

scrollbar = Scrollbar(root, orient=HORIZONTAL)
scrollbar.pack(side=BOTTOM, fill=X)

mylist = Listbox(root, xscrollcommand=scrollbar.set)
for line in range(100):
    msg = "This is a very big line whose number is " + str(line)
    mylist.insert(END, msg)
mylist.pack(side=LEFT, fill=BOTH)

scrollbar.config(command=mylist.xview)
mainloop()
```

Figure 15.15
Here, the Scrollbar widget is used to implement a horizontal scrollbar for another Listbox widget.

Text

Text widgets provide advanced capabilities that allow you to edit a multiline text and format the way it has to be displayed, such as changing its color and font. You can also use elegant structures like tabs and marks to locate specific sections of the text, and apply changes to those areas. Moreover, you can embed windows and images in the text because this widget was designed to handle both plain and formatted text. if you need to split your text across multiple lines, you just have to insert \n (newline characters) at the position where you want to break the line.

> **Note**
> The main display area of the Grail Web browser used the Tk text widget.

The following attributes are exposed by Text widgets:

   state—This attribute has two possible values: normal and disabled. The former is used to define standard editable text boxes that accept inserts and deletes, and the latter is used for noneditable text boxes.

   tabs—This attribute provides a list of strings that identifies all the tab stops on the Text widget. Each list item is a concatenation of the index position of the tab stop and a justification sign (l, r, or c) that defines the justification of the tab (left, right, or center, respectively).

The following methods are exposed as well:

   delete(startindex [,endindex])—This method deletes a specific character or a range of text.

   get(startindex [,endindex])—This method returns a specific character or a range of text.

   index(index)—Returns the absolute value of an index based on the given index.

insert(index [,string]...)—This method inserts strings at the specified index location. If you need to insert elements other than strings, such as windows or images, use the window_create and image_create methods, respectively.

see(index)—This method returns true if the text located at the index position is visible.

Text widgets support three distinct helper structures: Marks, Tabs, and Indexes.

Marks are used to bookmark positions between two characters within a given text. Note that you cannot recognize the marked positions visually: You need to use the variables. The fact of being able to store positions without compromising the visual design allows you to use as many marks as you need without causing problems to the users. Tkinter offers two preconfigured marks for you: INSERT and CURRENT. The first one defines the cursor's insertion position, and the other one defines the closest position to the mouse pointer. We have the following methods available when handling marks:

index(mark)—Returns the line and column location of a specific mark.

mark_gravity(mark [,gravity])—Returns the gravity of the given mark. If the second argument is provided, the gravity is set for the given mark. This defines where new text must be inserted if someone tries to insert the text exactly on the mark position.

mark_names()—Returns all marks from the Text widget.

mark_set(mark, index)—Informs a new position to the given mark.

mark_unset(mark)—Removes the given mark from the Text widget.

Tags are used to associate names to regions of text, which makes easy the task of modifying the display settings of specific text areas. Tags are also used to bind event callbacks to specific ranges of text. Tkinter provides a preconfigured tag called SEL that matches the current selection. Next, are the available methods for handling tabs:

tag_add(tagname,startindex[,endindex] ...)—This method tags either the position defined by startindex, or a range delimited by the positions startindex and endindex.

tag_config—You can use this method to configure the tag properties, which include, justify (center, left, or right), tabs (this property has the same functionality of the Text widget tabs's property), and underline (used to underline the tagged text).

tag_delete(tagname)—This method is used to delete and remove a given tag.

tag_remove(tagname [,startindex[.endindex]] ...)—After applying this method, the given tag is removed from the provided area without deleting the actual tag definition.

The following example uses tags to format specific regions on the Text widget. Note that we use row/column pairs to define the ranges that we want to manipulate.

```
from Tkinter import *
def onclick():
    pass

root = Tk()
text = Text(root)
text.insert(INSERT, "Here, I start the text ...")
text.insert(END, "... and here, I finish it.")
text.pack()
text.tag_add("here", "1.0", "1.4")
text.tag_add("start", "1.8", "1.13")
text.tag_config("here", background="yellow", foreground="blue")
text.tag_config("start", background="black", foreground="green")
root.mainloop()
```

Indexes are used to point out the actual positions of characters, delimiting areas within a text.

The following index types are available: INSERT, CURRENT, END, line/column ("line.column"), line end ("line.end"), user-defined marks, user-defined tags ("tag.first", "tag.last"), selection (SEL_FIRST, SEL_LAST), window coordinate ("@x,y"), embedded object name (window, images), and expressions.

In order to demonstrate more uses of this widget, the next example inserts a Button widget right inside the text.

```
from Tkinter import *
def onclick():
    pass

root = Tk()
text = Text(root)
text.insert(INSERT, "Here, I start the text ...")
button = Button(text, text="I am a button", command=onclick)
```

```
text.window_create(INSERT, window=button)
text.insert(END, "... and here, I finish it.")
text.pack()
root.mainloop()
```

Toplevel

Toplevel widgets work as windows that are directly managed by the window manager. They do not necessarily have a parent widget on top of them. Toplevels do support geometry management, as you can control where children of a toplevel are placed, but you don't need to pack the toplevel itself. Their behavior is similar to Frame's. The difference is that Toplevel widgets are displayed in a top-level, separated window.

This widget supports all the methods mentioned next. Also note that these methods are also supported by the root window, which is originated by the Tk() call. Not necessarily all functions will work on your window manager because each one of the available window managers in the market has its own type of support definitions.

deiconify()—Displays the window, after using either the iconify or the withdraw methods.

frame()—Returns a system-specific window identifier.

group(*window*)—Adds the window to the window group administered by the given window.

iconify()—Turns the window into an icon, without destroying it.

protocol(*name, function*)—Registers a function as a callback which will be called for the given protocol. See the *Protocols* topic, which is located some pages ahead.

state()—Returns the current state of the window. Possible values are normal, iconic, withdrawn, and icon.

transient([*master*])—Turns the window into a temporary(transient) window for the given master, or to the window's parent, when no argument is given. These windows are automatically hidden when the master window is iconified or withdrawn.

withdraw()—Removes the window from the screen, without destroying it.

The following methods can be used either to set or to retrieve a specific information to or from the method call. If you call them without passing any arguments, they simply return their current value or state. On the other hand, if you inform the arguments, the expected action is executed.

`aspect(`*`minNumer`*`, `*`minDenom`*`, `*`maxNumer`*`, `*`maxDenom`*`)`—Controls the relation between window's width and height (aspect ratio). The aspect ratio is limited to lay between `minNumer`/`minDenom` and `maxNumer`/`maxDenom`. If you omit the arguments, this method returns the current constraints as a 4-tuple.

`client(`*`name`*`)`—Used under the X window system to define the `WM_CLIENT_MACHINE` property. It is the application that sets the `WM_*` properties. The window manager can make use of these properties when managing the windows.

`colormapwindows(`*`wlist...`*`)`—Used under the X window system to define the `WM_COLORMAP_WINDOWS` property.

`command(`*`value`*`)`—Used under the X window system to define the `WM_COMMAND` property.

`focusmodel(`*`model`*`)`—Sets the focus model.

`geometry(`*`geometry`*`)`—Changes the windows geometry by using the following argument format: `"widthxheight+xoffset+yoffset"`, showing the widget coordinates in pixels.

`iconbitmap(`*`bitmap`*`)`—Defines a monochrome icon bitmap to be used when the window gets iconified.

`iconmask(`*`bitmap`*`)`—Defines the icon bitmap mask to use when this window gets iconified.

`iconname(newName=`*`None`*`)`—Defines the icon name to be used when this window gets iconified.

`iconposition(`*`x`*`, `*`y`*`)`—Defines a suggestion for the icon position to be used when this window gets iconified.

`iconwindow(`*`window`*`)`—Defines the icon window that should be used as an icon when this window gets iconified.

`maxsize(`*`width`*`, `*`height`*`)`—Defines the maximum size for this window.

`minsize(`*`width`*`, `*`height`*`)`—Defines the minimum size for this window.

`overrideredirect(`*`flag`*`)`—Defines a flag different from 0 and tells the window manager to not add a title or borders to the window.

`positionfrom(`*`who`*`)`—Defines the position controller.

`resizable(`*width, height*`)`—Defines the resize flags, which control whether the window can be resized.

`sizefrom(`*who*`)`—Defines the size controller.

`title(`*string*`)`—Defines the window title.

Image

This class is used as a foundation to display graphic objects, including bitmaps and GIF images. Two subclasses are inherited from this class: `BitmapImage` and `PhotoImage`.

In order to using the following syntax:

`image = BitmapImage(`*options*`) or image = PhotoImage(`*options*`)`

The following functions can be used for image handling:

`image_names()`—Returns a list containing the names of all existing images.

`image_types()`—Returns a list containing all the existing types that were created.

After a image object is created, it provides the following methods: `image.type()`, `image.width()`, and `image.height()`, which return the type, actual width, and actual height of the image, respectively.

BitmapImage

This subclass is used to display bitmap images on widgets, including buttons, canvas, labels, and text. They really mean bitmap for *BitmapImage* (not a multicolor image, which most Windows users think of because of the `.BMP` format). A bitmap image represents a two color image (or 2 colors + transparency if a mask is used).

The following methods are exposed by this subclass. Table 15.5 shows the available options for these methods.

`cget(`*option*`)`—Returns the value of the given option.

`config(`*options*`)`, `configure(`*options*`)`—Changes the image options.

`height()`, `width()`—Returns the image dimension, in pixels.

`type()`—Returns the `"bitmap"` string.

Table 15.5   *Available Options for the BitmapImage Subclass*

BitmapImage Options	Description
background	Background color to be used.
data	String to be used instead of a file.
file	File to be read.
foreground	Foreground color to be used.
format	Specifies the file handler to be used.
maskdata	String that defines the contents of the mask in order to produce a 'shaped' bitmap.
maskfile	File that specifies the mask. If you specify both maskdata and maskfile, the former becomes used.
height, width	Requested dimensions for the image.

PhotoImage

This subclass is used to display full-color images on widgets, including buttons, canvas, labels, and text.

The following attributes are exposed by this subclass:

data—String to be used instead of a file.

file—File to be read.

height, width—Requested dimensions for the image.

This subclass offers native support to GIF and PPM files. In order to add an image to a widget, just implement the principle established by the following code:

```
from Tkinter import *
root = Tk()
frame = Frame(root)
myimage = PhotoImage(file="new.gif")
b = Button(root)
b.config(image= myimage)    # or  b.image = myimage
frame.pack()
b.pack()
root.mainloop()
```

General Widget Methods

Next, I list some of the methods inherited from the base Tk classes that are provided for all Tkinter widgets, which also includes the toplevel object that is generated by the Tk() method.

The following methods always apply to the widget object that makes the method call. To demonstrate it, the next code lines create a label widget, and use the `config` method to set the value of the `text` attribute for the label widget that we have just created.

```
lb = Label(root)
lb.config(text= "Hello Python World")
```

Now, let's see the available methods:

cget(*option*)—Returns a string that contains the current configuration value for the given option.

config(*options*), configure(*options*)—Sets the values for one or more options. When used without arguments, it returns a dictionary containing the current settings for all widget options.

destroy()—Destroys the widget, removing it from its namespace.

focus(), focus_set()—Sets the keyboard focus to the widget.

focus_displayof()—Returns the name of the window that contains the widget and has the focus.

focus_force()—Enforces the keyboard focus to the widget.

focus_get()—Returns the identity of the window with focus.

focus_lastfor()—Returns the identity of the most recent window to receive the input focus.

getvar(*variable*)—Returns the value of the provided Tkinter variable name.

grab_set()—Grabs all events for the current application to the widget.

grab_current()—Returns the identity of the widget that has set the grab functionality in the current application.

grab_release()—Releases the grab on the widget.

grab_set_global()—Grabs all events for the entire screen to the widget.

grab_status()—Returns None, local, or global, depending whether there is no grab set on window, a local grab is set, or a global grab is set, respectively.

keys()—Returns all the options available for this widget in a tuple format. In order to obtain the value of each one of these options, you can use the cget method.

lift([*object*]), tkraise([*object*])—Moves the widget to the top of the window stack, or if an object (a widget or a window) is provided, the widget is placed right above the informed object.

lower([*object*])—Moves the widget to the bottom of the window stack, or if an object (a widget or a window) is provided, the widget is placed right below the informed object.

mainloop()—Activates the main event loop.

quit()—Quits the main event loop.

setvar(variablename, value)—Sets a value to the given Tkinter variable name.

update()—Processes all pending tasks, such as geometry management and widgets redrawing. Be careful when using this method.

update_idletasks()—Processes all pending idle tasks.

tk_focusNext()—Returns the next widget that should have the keyboard focus.

tk_focusPrev()—Returns the previous widget that should have the keyboard focus.

wait_variable(*variable*)—Creates a local event that waits for the given Tkinter variable to change. This loop doesn't affect the application's mainloop.

wait_visibility(*widget*)—Creates a local event that waits for the given widget to become visible. This loop doesn't affect the application's mainloop.

wait_window(*widget*)—Creates a local event that waits for the given widget to be destroyed. This loop doesn't affect the application's mainloop.

winfo **(Widget Information) Methods**
This set of methods provides specific functionality for the windowing widgets.

winfo_cells()—Returns the number of cells in the widget's color map.

winfo_children()—Returns a list of widget instances for all the widget's children.

winfo_class()—Returns the Tkinter widget class name for the widget.

winfo_colormapfull()—Returns true if the widget's color map is full.

winfo_containing(*xcoord, ycoord*)—Returns the identity of the widget located at the given coordinate (relative to the upper left corner of the root window).

winfo_depth()—Returns the bit depth (8, 16, 24, or 32 bits per pixel) used to display the widget.

winfo_exists()—Returns true if a Tk window corresponds to the given widget.

winfo_fpixels(*number*)—Returns a floating point value, which is the result of the conversion of the given distance to the corresponding number of pixels.

winfo_geometry()—Returns a string in the format "widthxheight+xoffset+yoffset", showing the widget coordinates in pixels.

winfo_height(), winfo_width()—Return the widget's height and width, in pixels.

winfo_id()—Returns an integer that contains a platform-specific window identity corresponding to the given widget. On UNIX systems, this is the X window identifier; on Windows systems, this is the Window HWND; and on Macs, it is a non-useful value.

winfo_ismapped()—Returns true if the widget is currently mapped by the underlying window system.

winfo_manager()—Returns the name of the geometry manager that has been used to organize the widget.

winfo_name()—Returns the widget's name.

winfo_parent()—Returns the name of the widget's parent, or an empty string in case the widget doesn't have a parent widget/window.

winfo_pathname(*widget_id*)—Returns the pathname of the widget whose identity is given as the argument.

winfo_pixels(*number*)—Returns an integer value, which is the result of the conversion of the given distance to the corresponding number of pixels.

winfo_pointerx()—Returns the x coordinate of the mouse pointer (in pixels) when it is on the same screen of the widget.

winfo_pointerxy()—Returns a tuple of the x and y coordinates of the mouse pointer (in pixels) when it is on the same screen of the widget.

winfo_pointery()—Returns the y coordinate of the mouse pointer (in pixels) when it is on the same screen of the widget.

winfo_reqheight(), winfo_reqwidth()—Return the minimal height and width required by the widget in order to be entirely displayed.

winfo_rootx(), winfo_rooty()—Return the pixel coordinates (integer values) corresponding to the widget's upper left corner, relative to the upper left corner of root's window border.

winfo_screen()—Returns the screen name for the current window in the format display.screen. Note that it doesn't provide any useful information on non-X versions of Tk.

winfo_screencells()—Returns the number of cells in the default color map for widget's screen.

winfo_screendepth()—Returns the bit depth of the window widget.

winfo_screenheight(), winfo_screenwidth()—Returns the height and the width of the widget's screen, in pixels.

winfo_screenmmheight(), winfo_screenmmwidth()—Returns the height and the width of the widget's screen, in millimeters.

winfo_screenvisual()—Returns the default visual class used for widget's screen. Possible values include pseudocolor, directcolor, staticcolor, truecolor, grayscale, and staticgray.

winfo_toplevel()—Returns a widget instance of the top-level window containing the widget.

winfo_visual()—Returns the visual class used for the widget. Possible values include pseudocolor, directcolor, staticcolor, truecolor, grayscale, and staticgray.

winfo_x(), winfo_y()—Return the pixel coordinates (integer values) corresponding to the widget's upper left corner, relative to the upper left corner of its parent's window border.

Designing Applications

Up to this point, we've seen how to handle the properties and methods of Tkinter's widgets. Now, we will learn the basic steps to write real-world applications.

Tkinter is really powerful, and if you are not satisfied with the widgets that it offers, you can create your own set of widgets. A very interesting and customized widget that you should consider checking before learning how to create your own, is the TreeWidget, which is part of the latest idle distribution. This widget uses a Tk Canvas widget and some images to nicely simulate the TreeView Windows control.

The simplest windowing application that you can create consists of just one window, which is called the root window. The root window is created using the Tk() call.

```
from Tkinter import *
root = Tk()
root.mainloop()
```

If your application needs more than just one single window, you can use the Toplevel widget to create additional windows for you. This widget has a behavior very similar to the window generated by Tk(). This widget also dispenses the use of geometry management functions because the window manager displays this widget, immediately after you call it.

```
from Tkinter import *
def mywindow():
    top = Toplevel(root)

root = Tk()
b1 = Button(root, text="Create new window", command=mywindow)
b1.pack()
root.mainloop()
```

After adding a lot of windows to your application, maybe now you are wondering whether it would be OK to add a menu to your program. The following code does that for you.

```
from Tkinter import *
import sys
def newwindow():
    top = Toplevel(root)
def aboutwindow():
    who = Toplevel(root)
    Label(who, text="This is the about window").pack()

root = Tk()
menu = Menu(root)
root.config(menu=menu)

filemenu = Menu(menu)
menu.add_cascade(label="File", menu=filemenu)
filemenu.add_command(label="New", command=newwindow)
```

```
filemenu.add_separator()
filemenu.add_command(label="Exit", command=sys.exit)

helpmenu = Menu(menu)
menu.add_cascade(label="Help", menu=helpmenu)
helpmenu.add_command(label="About...", command=aboutwindow)

root.mainloop()
```

What's next? What about adding a toolbar to our little application? The simplest way to implement a toolbar is by taking a Frame widget and storing all the required buttons on it.

```
from Tkinter import *
import sys
def newwindow():
    top = Toplevel(root)
def aboutwindow():
    who = Toplevel(root)
    Label(who, text="This is the about window").pack()

root = Tk()
menu = Menu(root)
root.config(menu=menu)

filemenu = Menu(menu)
menu.add_cascade(label="File", menu=filemenu)
filemenu.add_command(label="New", command=newwindow)
filemenu.add_separator()
filemenu.add_command(label="Exit", command=sys.exit)

helpmenu = Menu(menu)
menu.add_cascade(label="Help", menu=helpmenu)
helpmenu.add_command(label="About...", command=aboutwindow)

toolbar = Frame(root)
newimage = PhotoImage(file="new.gif")
b1 = Button(toolbar, image=newimage, width=16, command=newwindow)
b1.pack(side=LEFT, padx=1, pady=1)
helpimage = PhotoImage(file="help.gif")
b2 = Button(toolbar, image=helpimage, width=16, command=aboutwindow)
b2.pack(side=LEFT, padx=1, pady=1)
toolbar.pack(side=TOP, fill=X)
root.mainloop()
```

As we want our toolbar to be on the highest area of our screen, we have to pack it on the top side of the Frame widget. The `fill` option being set to X in the toolbar widget enables the toolbar to extend itself, covering the entire extension of the parent frame size.

Note the usage of the PhotoImage class. This class is used to load the GIF files from disk and store them into variables. Then, these variables are passed to the Button options that handle images.

Let's move forward now. The next step is to create a status bar for our small application. We want this bar to be on the bottom side of the window.

```
from Tkinter import *
import sys
def newwindow():
    top = Toplevel(root)
    statusbar.config(text="This is a testing application.")

def aboutwindow():
    who = Toplevel(root)
    Label(who, text="This is the about window").pack()
    statusbar.config(text="Hi There!")

root = Tk()
menu = Menu(root)
root.config(menu=menu)

filemenu = Menu(menu)
menu.add_cascade(label="File", menu=filemenu)
filemenu.add_command(label="New", command=newwindow)
filemenu.add_separator()
filemenu.add_command(label="Exit", command=sys.exit)

helpmenu = Menu(menu)
menu.add_cascade(label="Help", menu=helpmenu)
helpmenu.add_command(label="About...", command=aboutwindow)

toolbar = Frame(root)
newimage = PhotoImage(file="new.gif")
b1 = Button(toolbar, image=newimage, width=16, command=newwindow)
b1.pack(side=LEFT, padx=1, pady=1)
helpimage = PhotoImage(file="help.gif")
b2 = Button(toolbar, image=helpimage, width=16, command=aboutwindow)
```

```
b2.pack(side=LEFT, padx=1, pady=1)
toolbar.pack(side=TOP, fill=X)

statusbar = Label(root, text="This is a testing application.", bd=1,
 relief=SUNKEN, anchor=W)
statusbar.pack(side=BOTTOM, fill=X)
```

As you could see, we used the Label widget to implement the statusbar in order to be able to change the text value later. Pretty nice, isn't it?

Now, have a look at the final shape of our interface (Figure 15.16).

Figure 15.16
This figure shows the complete example of designing the structure of an application using Tkinter.

In my opinion, one of the greatest things about designing GUI applications using Tkinter is the number of things that are already done and ready to be used by your applications. Some examples are the following modules, which are part of the Tkinter distribution, and implement common dialog boxes.

tkMessageBox—This module implements the classic Yes/No and Abort/Retry/Ignore dialog styles.

tkSimpleDialog—This module implements a base class that can be used to implement other modules.

tkFileDialog—This module implements a file dialog, which is very close to the file dialogs found in the Windows system.

tkColorChooser—This module implements a dialog that allows you to choose and pick a color.

The usage of these modules is very simple. The next example opens a file dialog box, which allows you to browse the files through your local directory, and returns the filename selected (see Figure 15.17).

```
from Tkinter import *
import tkFileDialog
def openwindows():
    statusbar.config(text = open.show())
```

```
root = Tk()
myfiletypes = [('Python files', '*.py'), ('All files', '*')]
open = tkFileDialog.Open(root, filetypes = myfiletypes)
Button(root, text="Open File Dialog", command=openwindows).pack()

statusbar = Label(root, text="", bd=1, relief=SUNKEN, anchor=W)
statusbar.pack(side=BOTTOM, fill=X)
root.mainloop()
```

As you could notice, this is a very simple example of the power of Tkinter, but the concept of creating a dialog is as simple as the concept of creating a window.

Figure 15.17
Note that the FileDialog returns the name of the selected file, and our application shows that name on the status bar.

After creating a Toplevel widget and making the call to open the dialog, the standard dialog only returns to the Toplevel widget when it is closed. When you start facing problems like this, you have several solution options, such as opening several dialogs and making them run in parallel. Or you can create the dialog and only return the control back to the Toplevel widget when the dialogs are closed by the user, creating a modal behavior. This solution is implemented using the wait_window method, which creates a local event loop, and only returns when the window informed as an argument is closed.

Although application modal dialogs are easier to program, most users find them much more annoying. If possible, only use modal dialogs where some action has to be performed before the application can continue.

That's it. Our overview about Tkinter ends here. Next you will see a toolkit that extends the set of available widgets you can use, and next you will find a list of useful resources for a more advanced approach on this topic.

PMW—Python Mega Widgets

PMW (Python Mega Widgets) is a toolkit for building high-level widgets in Python using the Tkinter module. This toolkit provides a framework that contains a variety of widgets richer than the one provided by Tkinter.

This package is 100% written in Python, which turns out to be a cross-platform widget library. Being highly configurable allows it to create additional widget collections by extending the basic Tkinter widget core set.

PMW provides many interesting and complex widgets, including: AboutDialog, Balloon, ButtonBox, ComboBox, ComboBoxDialog, Counter, CounterDialog, Dialog, EntryField, Group, LabeledWidget, MenuBar, MessageBar, MessageDialog, NoteBookR, NoteBookS, NoteBook, OptionMenu, PanedWidget, PromptDialog, RadioSelect, ScrolledCanvas, ScrolledField, ScrolledFrame, ScrolledListbox, ScrolledText, SelectionDialog, TextDialog, and TimeCounter.

This package is energetically maintained by its author, Greg McFarlane, and it has an extensive documentation. For more information about it, check out its Web site at

```
http://www.dscpl.com.au/pmw
```

Tkinter Resources

The following resources provide an excellent complement to the documentation offered by this chapter. They link to several Tk/Tkinter related sites.

Tkinter

```
http://www.python.org/topics/tkinter/
```

Matt Conway's Tkinter Life Preserver

```
http://www.python.org/doc/life-preserver/index.html
```

Tkinter Standard Dialogues

```
http://starship.python.net/crew/fredrik/py14/tkdialogs.htm
```

Tkinter: GUI programming with Python

```
http://www.nmt.edu/tcc/help/lang/python/tkinter.html
```

Python and Tkinter Programming, by John E. Grayson

```
http://www.manning.com/Grayson/Contents.html
```

An Introduction to Tkinter, by Fredrik Lundh

http://www.pythonware.com/library/tkinter/introduction/index.htm

Tkinter Class Reference Pages

http://www.pythonware.com/library/tkinter/tkclass/index.htm

Online Tcl/Tk Manual Pages—the official man pages at Scriptics

http://dev.scriptics.com/man/

Tk 8.0 man pages

http://dev.scriptics.com/man/tcl8.0/TkCmd/contents.htm

Ajuba (formerly Scriptics)—the company founded by Tcl/Tk's inventor, John
Ousterhout

http://www.ajubasolutions.com/

Vaults of Parnassus—User Interfaces and Widgets Section

http://www.vex.net/parnassus/

Summary

Tk is a popular and endorsed toolkit that can handle windows, GUI events, and user
interactions. Tkinter is Python's cross-platform interface to the Tk GUI toolkit that
enables you to handle buttons and windows, and define their properties at a glance.
The typical Tkinter distribution contains a basic set of 15 widgets, and some extra
classes that can be used by your GUI applications.

Button—This widget defines a clickable button that can execute a specific operation
when clicked.

Canvas—This widget is used to draw graphs, lines, polygons, and all other types of
graphic elements.

Checkbutton—This widget exposes a button that controls a variable that can have
two distinct values.

Entry—This widget implements a simple text entry field.

Frame—This widget works like a container for other widgets when creating a
complex layout within a window.

Label—This widget handles the exhibition of a text or an image.

Listbox—This widget displays a list of possible selections.

Menu—This widget is used to implement pull-down and pop-up menus.

Menubutton—This widget is used to implement pull-down menus.

Message—This widget displays a text message in a way similar to the label widget, but using powerful formatting capabilities.

Radiobutton—This widget is associated with a variable, and when clicked, the variable assumes its value.

Scale—This widget provides a slider that helps you set the value of a numerical variable.

Scrollbar—This widget implements standard scrollbars that you can use along with other widgets, such as listbox, canvas, entry, and text.

Text—This widget display text that you can edit and format.

Toplevel—This widget is another container widget, just like the frame widget.

Tkinter also provides the Image class. This class is used as a foundation to display graphic objects, including bitmaps and GIF images. Two subclasses are inherited from this class: BitmapImage and PhotoImage.

All these Tkinter widgets have access to specific geometry management methods, which have the purpose of organizing them throughout the parent widget area. These methods are grouped in three distinct classes that provide a nice way to lay out child widgets in their parent widget. Tkinter exposes the following geometry manager classes: pack, grid, and place.

Tkinter also allows you to create event bindings for every specific object, and after binding an event to a widget, you can specify which function should be called at the time the event occurs. This function (or method) is called callback.

To complement Tkinter, you can also use the Python Mega Widgets. PMW is a toolkit for building high-level widgets in Python using the Tkinter module that provides many interesting and complex widgets.

PART V
Developing with Python

CHAPTER 16

Development Environment

Always look on the bright side of life.

This chapter shows some performance and style suggestions for your code, now that you are probably writing your own programs. It also introduces you to the main GUI development environments that you can use to write Python applications.

Building Python Applications

Whenever you have to sit down in front of a computer to write a Python program, you should stick to a good coding style especially if you are working as part of a team. The clearer your code gets, the better it is to maintain it. The development process of writing Python application can be highly improved if you follow some basic guidelines.

I am sure that in most cases, after you have defined your project goal and gone through the development strategy stage, you will understand that Python might be a solution for your application problems.

Python is fairly easy to use, which requires less time to instruct developers. If, as part of the training, the style considerations are defined and taught, you can have a whole team of developers coding within the same pattern in a very short time. The maintenance time is also improved because Python is able to generate an extremely readable kind of code that allows developers to share their ideas without many problems.

Consequently, your development effort is reduced. As a matter of fact, the development time might be reduced as well. When comparing Python to other languages such as C or Java, an application written in one of these languages requires more lines of code—most of the time—than the same functionality written in Python.

Development Strategy

Writing a program is something very easy, but writing a good and optimized program requires some level of experience. A good way to start is to learn all the nuances of the language, which in our case involves learning Python. You should know a little bit of everything, and this book helps you learn most of them, including classes, modules, functions, exception handling, dynamic typing, GUI, operator overloading, indentation, and so forth.

Of course, you must know many other important items too.

Nowadays, the most important development efforts are focusing on the Internet. Python offers the basic necessary tools that you might need for your Web projects. Python can be used either for Web-based interface projects or to generate entire back-end frameworks, using tools such as Zope.

Note that by extending Grail, the Web browser written in Python, you can embed your Python application directly on it and distribute a browser to your clients that carries specific and customized interfaces.

Even if you don't use Grail, you can use any browser to provide GUI interfaces for your applications. Have you ever considered delivering information and products through the Web? If so, you can do it using Python.

Python is a perfect language for project prototyping. Python's design allows you to make changes very quickly. Later you can decide whether you will re-implement the code using a compiled language, or stick to Python and continue the development effort using the prototype as a startup. Remember that after spending some time creating a prototype, you probably have a huge amount of code that you do not want to throw away.

Prototyping with Python is very easy. You can, for example, wrap your code in a function inside a module and use a development environment, such as Pythonwin or IDLE, to run the script. To test this application, you just need to save it and execute it—very simple. No intermediate stages are necessary.

Python testing mechanisms also allow you to forge command-line arguments. You can test your command-line scripts by first setting their expected arguments to predefined values using the built-in variable sys.argv.

Along the development stage, you will soon see that Python can be easily used to code entire applications, without discarding the prototyped code.

If speed is a requirement, you can use a compiled language in the back-end side of your application to support the high-demand operations. Python, in this case, can be used as the front end of the application, leaving the hard work to the other language. This kind of implementation allows you to create black boxes of code, which get called by Python, and Python doesn't necessarily need to know what is happening behind the scenes because only the external interface of the compiled language needs to be exposed.

But whenever possible, select just Python. It is good to remember that supporting a scripting language is much easier than supporting a compiled language. The usage of a scripting language makes tasks such as debug the application, fix bugs, and add enhancements look very simple. Because we are not using a compiled language, we don't need to spend time compiling and linking the files. Updating client sites with the latest version of the application is also very easy because we just need to send the file that carries the changed Python module.

As you can see, a lot of thinking is involved in the process of preparing yourself to handle a Python development. Next, we will see some ideas about how to optimize your code, and how to write a program with style. Both are very important things that you must have in mind, not only when using Python, but also when writing in any other language.

Optimizing the Code

To prevent your program from running very slowly, you might consider following some basic Python optimization rules. By designing your application from the start with these guidelines in mind, you will certainly be satisfied with the final overall performance that you will get.

My goal in this section is to provide ways to generate acceptable performance in your Python routines. Note that I don't cover everything, but a good set of basic concepts is covered.

Many things can be done to reduce the processing time of your application. Remember that you have an interpreter being called every time you execute a Python script. Consequently, you need to work on your code in order to compensate that somehow. The fact that it is an interpreted language is a big concern, but by reducing the number of statements that get parsed, you can also reduce the interpreter overhead.

By the way, the Python interpreter has a command-line option (-O, which stands for *optimize*) that enables you to execute your code in such a way that some of the bytecode operations are not executed. Basically, it is used to remove the comments in the bytecode that give the line number where exceptions occur, and does not compile in the doc strings and a few other things. This flag does not give that much speed increase, and it makes things harder to debug.

Some useful optimization hints are as follows:

- Variables—Depending on how your variables are defined, the interpreter spends more or less time trying to figure out their values. Python deals with dynamic scope rules when trying to resolve variable names. After it finds a variable in the code, it first tries to discover if the variable is a local variable by looking at the local namespace dictionary. If it finds the variable, it grabs the variable's value. Otherwise, it searches in the global namespace dictionary, and if necessary, in the built-in namespace dictionary. As you can see, local variable lookups are pretty much faster than other types. Consequently, the access to their values is faster too. Also, local variable lookups are much faster because they correspond to indexing into an array, whereas global variable lookups correspond to hash table lookups. A good optimization hint might be that if you are using a global variable a lot in a function, assigning its value to a local variable can help a lot.

- Modules—Within a single script, you just need to import an external module once. Therefore, it is not necessary to have multiple `import` statements inside your code. Actually, you should avoid trying to re-import modules on your program. As a rule of thumb, put all the `import` statements in the very first part of your program header. However, calling `import` on a module multiple times is not really a problem because it is just a dictionary lookup.

  In cases where you have to do a lot of referencing to particular attributes of an external module, you should consider copying those elements to a single variable (when that's possible, of course) before starting to code—especially, if the references are made inside a loop.

  Whenever you import a module, the interpreter looks for a byte-compiled version of the module. In case it doesn't find any, it automatically bytecompiles the module and generates a .pyc file. So, the next time you try to import the module, the byte-compiled file will be there. As you can feel, .pyc files are executed much faster than regular .py files because they have already being interpreted by the interpreter prior to the execution. The suggestion here is to use byte-compiled modules the more you can. The Python code executes at the same speed no matter if there is a `.pyc` file or not. The only difference is that if there is a byte-compiled file, startup will be a bit quicker. The actual running speed of the code is no different.

- Strings—Use format strings whenever you need to concatenate strings with other variables. Check out the next concatenation forms.

```
name = "Andre"
print "Hello " + name
print "Hello %s" % (name)
```

Be sure that the second `print` statement is more optimized than the first one. The parentheses on the third line are not necessary. Another option would be

```
print "Hello", name
```

- Tkinter—Avoid creating unnecessary instances of widgets. If you are not planning to manipulate the attributes of a widget after it has been created, stick to direct calls to the class. In a GUI app, this won't affect the running speed that much—just the startup time.

  There is no reason to say

```
mybutton = Button(root, text="Close")
mybutton.pack(side=right)
```

  when you can simply use

```
mybutton = Button(root, text="Close").pack(side=right)
```

  Now, the interpreter has one less variable to handle.

  I open a parenthesis here to let you know that if you are testing a Tkinter application using IDLE, you need to comment your `mainloop()` command. That's because IDLE is already running inside a Tkinter mainloop, and calling another one might freeze your entire environment.

- Loops—You can optimize a lot of things in your loops in order to make them run smoothly. In a short list, I can tell you the following:

  - You should use built-in functions in your inner loop instead of using functions written in Python. By using built-in functions that support list manipulation (such as `map()`, `reduce()`, and `filter()`) instead of straight loops, you can move some of the loop overhead to the C code. Passing built-in functions to `map`, `reduce`, or `filter` gives even better performance.

- Whenever you have multiple levels of loop, it is worth it to optimize only the innermost one. When optimizing multiple-level loops, the idea is to reduce the number of memory allocations. Making the innermost loop to be the one with the fewer number of interactions should help your performance design.

- Working with local variables is a great thing that improves the processing time inside a loop. Whenever possible, copy all your global variables and attribute look-ups to local variables before entering a loop.

- If you use construction methods such as range(n) inside a nested loop, it is much faster to allocate the value range to a local variable outside the outmost loop, and use this variable in the loop definitions.

```
yRange = range(500)
for xItem in range(100000):
    for yItem in yRange:
        print xItem, yItem
```

- Another optimization here would be using xrange for the x for loop because a 100000 item list is a quite large list.

```
yRange = range(500)
for xItem in xrange(100000):
    for yItem in yRange:
        print xItem, yItem
```

- Functions—Python built-in functions are faster to execute than functions written in clean Python because the built-in functions are already written in C. map(),filter(), and reduce() are examples of built-in functions that can be used to beat the performance of functions written in Python. It is also good to know that Python handles function names as global constants. Having said that, the whole conception of namespace look-up that we saw previously also applies to functions as well. If you have the option to choose, use the map() function's implied loop than a for loop—it is much faster. The runtime of the loop functions that I mention here is highly dependent on what function you pass in. Passing a Python function will not be as fast as passing in a built-in function (such as the ones in the operator module).

In case you want to test the performance of your routines, you can use a simple concept, which is explained next. The idea is to measure the time spent between calling the routine and finishing its execution.

After you add these lines to your program, you can benchmark it and test new kinds of approach. Note that we have a little time overhead because we have to call the `time()` function.

First, you need to import the time module:

```
import time
```

Second, you just need to set a timer after executing and before starting your routine. This is done using the `time.clock()` function:

```
start_timer = time.clock()
call_your_routine()
end_timer = time.clock()
print end_timer-start_timer
```

Code optimization is a very complex science that is not restricted just to Python programs. Sometimes when you booster the performance in one place, it breaks something somewhere else. What I mean by that is that if the processing time of your application seems OK for you, don't touch it. I suggest that you to just try to optimize your code when a real performance problem is creating an unsupportable bottleneck in your application.

Chapter 17, "Development Tools," introduces the Python *Profiler* module to you. This tool can help you to identify the bottlenecks in your code.

The following links have some more additional thoughts about code optimization for Python applications:

Python Patterns—An Optimization Anecdote, essay by Guido Van Rossum

```
http://www.python.org/doc/essays/list2str.html
```

Python Performance Tips, by Skip Montanaro

```
http://www.musi-cal.com/~skip/python/fastpython.html
```

Style Guide

The following guidelines are directly based from some of the ideas of Guido van Rossum about how to write a Python program within style. The main quality that we need to acquire is the ability to decide exactly when we can apply these guidelines, and when it is better to be a little inconsistent and step out of these rules in order to have a more reliable implementation.

These are just suggestions. Feel free to write your code any way you want it. Nothing or no one will force you to follow these rules, but you will see by yourself how practical it is to have these guidelines in mind when coding a program.

Code Layout

Python's core definition says that we must delimit structures using indented blocks. A standard indentation consists of four spaces for each indentation level. Most of the time, you can alternatively use one tab instead of four spaces.

Try to write your code with lines containing less than 80 characters each. If it turns out to be necessary to break a line, use parentheses, brackets, and braces to continue the code on the next line, using a backslash only if that is not possible.

Blank lines are used to separate chunks of related code, such as top-level function and class definitions (two blank lines), class definition and the first method definition (one line), and methods definitions inside a class (one blank line). You can omit the blank lines in case your definitions have just one line each.

Handling whitespaces is another issue that you need to be aware of. The following are *bad* examples of whitespace usage:

```
lst = [ 3,4,5]          # After open parentheses, brackets or braces.
if var < 10 :           # Preceding a comma, semicolon, or colon.
xrange (7)              # Preceding the parenthesis of a function call.
car ["plate"]          # Preceding indexing or slicing brackets.
var      = 3           # Multiple whitespaces preceding an operator.
```

The next group of operators should always be preceded and followed by just one space on each side.

```
=, ==, <, >, !=, <>, <=, >=, in, not in, is, is not, and, or, not.
```

However, there is a special remark here for the = (equal) sign. Whenever it is used to indicate a keyword argument or a default parameter value, you should suppress the spaces that surround it.

```
def printvar(input=10):
    print input
printvar(input=20)
20
printvar()
10
```

Sometimes, arithmetic operators shouldn't be surrounded by spaces either. By avoiding whitespaces, you can make some expressions more readable, as you will see next.

```
var = (x+y * (w/z))
```

The previous expression resembles `((x+y) * (w/z))` when in fact it is
`(x+(y * (w/z)))`. A good way to write that would be

```
var = (x + y*(w/z))
```

Comments

If you decide to add comments to your code, you need to remember to keep them up-
to-date all the time. Otherwise, it can become more of a problem than being a helper
thing. Some of the basic rules for writing comments are listed next:

- Write your comments in plain English. For large projects with members of
  different nationalities, English is often the common language. Of course, if no
  developers know English, this rule is not a good idea.

- Capitalize the first word of sentences and phrases.

- Omit the period at the end of short comments.

- Never alter the case of identifiers. Remember that Python is case sensitive; thus,
  you should write your helper comments using the same notation used by the
  definition of the object that you are describing.

There are two kinds of comments: block comments and inline comments. The former
applies to the code that follows it, and the latter is put on the code's own line. Both
types require at least a single #, followed by a single space at the beginning of each
commented line. When writing block comments, insert a blank line above them, and
another one below each paragraph.

Be careful when using inline comments because it can cause over-pollution of text in
your code—comments are no substitute for readable code. Inline comments are best
used when preceded by at least two whitespace characters from the inline statement.

A *documentation string* is a special kind of comment that goes beyond the *remarking
concept* that we get when using the # literal. All objects that accept the usage of
documentation strings incorporate those strings to their structure, allowing you to
later query, read, and use their documentation strings (see Chapter 2, "Language
Review," for details).

Documentation strings are, by convention, surrounded by a triple quote structure on
each side. Do not use the documentation string to store a description. Instead, try to
be functional, showing the command's action. Things that you should try to register in
documentation strings include: the environment variables, files, routine objective, and

the syntax design of scripts, modules, functions, classes, and public methods exported by classes.

There are two types of documentation strings: the one-liners and the multi-line ones. The former must entirely fit in a single line, including the closing quotes, and you are not instructed to insert blank lines surrounding it. On the other hand, multi-line documentation strings are formed by a single line of documentation followed by a block that contains a complete description of the object. Note that we are instructed to insert a blank line between these two structures. Also, note that additional lines in a documentation string do not need to be indented following the pattern established by the first line (it does look nicer if they are though). Before typing the closing quotes, it is also advised that you enter a new paragraph in order to let the quotes stand in a line of their own.

Next, you will have some suggestions about what to include in the documentation string of modules, functions, methods, and classes.

Modules should document the objects they export, such as the classes, exceptions, and functions, with a one-line summary for each one of them.

Functions and methods should document their behavior, arguments (including optional arguments and keywords), return value(s), side effects, exceptions raised, and so forth. When documenting arguments, put each one of them in a single line and separate each name from its description using two dashes. Single blank lines separate lists of methods and functions from each other.

Classes should document their public methods and instance variable properties. If the class subclasses another class, you have to mention the superclasses as well, along with the differences between both implementations. As a suggestion, use the verbs override and extend to respectively indicate that a specific method entirely replaces, or acts in addition to the superclass's own method definition. It is also recommended that when creating the documentation string for a class, you should surround it using single blank lines.

Naming Styles and Conventions

When it comes time to name your objects and variables, you have a list of options to choose from. You just can't mix all styles throughout your code because it might cause a big mess. You need to be consistent, and I suggest that you stick to a pattern and use it in every part of your code. As I said before, many styles are available. You might already be a big fan of one of them without even knowing it. It is quite common to have different naming conventions for classes, functions, and variables (for instance, *CapWords* for classes, *lower_case_with_underscores* for functions). In order to give you an idea of what kind of different styles we have, the following case conventions are introduced to you:

x (single lowercase letter)

X (single uppercase letter)

lowercase

lower_case_with_underscores

UPPERCASE

UPPER_CASE_WITH_UNDERSCORES

CapitalizedWords (or CapWords)

mixedCase

Capitalized_Words_With_Underscores

The following leading/trailing underscore structures can be combined with any one of the previously listed naming styles. You can substitute the variable VAR for any other object name that you want (considering Python's rules for object naming seen in Chapter 2).

_VAR—Objects that have a single leading underscore indicate that the object can be used only on the local module namespace. The `from module import *` statement doesn't import objects that start with a single leading underscore. The main concern about writing global variables is that if you want to have the variable only visible by the module that defines it, you need to have an underscore preceding it.

VAR_—You need to append a trailing underscore to the end of the name in order to avoid naming conflicts whenever you want to use a Python keyword (such as print_) as your own variable. This is one just possible way of getting rid of a conflict with a Python keyword.

__VAR—The double leading underscore identifies class-private names.

__VAR__—When you have an object that has both leading and trailing underscores, you can consider yourself in front of an object that, in most cases, is defined by the Python interpreter. This definition applies to both objects and attributes that work under the user namespace, which includes the __init__ method. Try to avoid using this type of structure when naming your own objects because it might cause name conflicts in your application as future releases of Python arrive.

Although there is no current naming standard among the files that are part of the Python's Standard Library, I can list some guidelines that can make the task of naming new modules easier for you.

When creating modules, give them MixedCase or lowercase names. Use the first option whenever the module exports a single class or a bunch of related classes, and the second option when the module exports a group of functions. Also, note that module names are mapped to filenames in Python. Therefore, it is a good idea to pay special attention when giving a name to a module in order to avoid long names (module names can become truncated on some systems), and keep in mind that Python is case sensitive, which makes a module called `MyModule.py` different from a module called `mymodule.py`. If you have two modules where one is a low-level interface written in C/C++, and the other one is a high-level object-oriented interface written in Python, the almost common standard nowadays is to give the Python's module a CapWords name (it isn't quite as widely used). On the other hand, the C/C++ module should be written entirely using lowercase letters, and preceded by a leading underscore (this is pretty much standardized). A known example of this concept is the pair of modules `Tkinter` and `_tkinter`.

When writing class names, you can stick to the CapWords pattern. Although this is a convention used most of the time, you are encouraged to modify this rule when handling internal classes of modules that are not supposed to be exported. You have to precede these classes with leading underscores.

When working with exceptions, you have two options. Their names are usually written in lowercase letters when part of built-in modules, whereas the ones that are part of Python modules are usually written using CapitalizedWords. The main deciding factor for creating exception names is whether you expect people to normally use `from ... import *` or `import ...` in the module.

When naming functions, you are encouraged to use one from the next two style options: CapWords for functions that provide a large functionality (less used), and lowercase for functions that expose less useful classes.

When naming methods, you should stick to the CapWords style for methods that are published by an ILU interface. For all other cases, you should consider switching to lowercase. If you don't want a method to be visible by external methods or instances, you must put an underscore in front of it. As you can see in Chapter 5, "Object-Oriented Programming," the use of this same concept can be applied to certain attributes in order to make them available only to their classes. Note that this last feature can be easily manipulated using the `__dict__` attribute.

More details about these concepts can be found at

Python Style Guide, by Guido Van Rossum

`http://www.python.org/doc/essays/styleguide.html`

Integrated Development Environments

For years, many people have been writing and editing their Python programs using simple text editors, but now the scenario has changed because Python currently provides two efficient development environments for your usage. The first one is IDLE, a cross platform Integrated Development Environment for Python, and the other one is Pythonwin, a development environment specifically for the Windows platform.

IDLE

IDLE is written in Python and it uses Tkinter for the GUI interface. IDLE is portable and available for all Python platforms that support Tkinter, which includes UNIX, Windows, and Macintosh. Because it is written in Python, you can extend it in Python as well. Guido van Rossum, along with many others including Jeremy Hylton, Tim Peters, Moshe Zadka, and Mark Hammond are some of the people behind the development effort of the IDLE project. IDLE can be considered to be a fresh product because it was first released with version 1.5.2 of Python.

> **Tip**
> Some say that the name IDLE really comes from the surname of one of the actors who was part of the British troupe. Well, I don't know whether it is true or not.

The IDLE environment consists of several distinct modules, and each one of them is responsible for a very specific functionality within the whole environment. There are modules to handle the undo engine, the colorizer, the automatic indentation, the class browser, the debugger, and many other features.

The undo engine dynamically intercepts all buffer-changing operations, stacking the inverse of the commands. This engine also supports grouping options, which is used by some high-level commands in order to undo/redo multiple operations simultaneously. It also tracks changes made in open files in order to ask you to save them before effectively letting you close them.

The colorizer highlights Python syntax, and it works while IDLE is unoccupied. When you resume working, the colorizer stops.

IDLE implements a powerful editor window, which gets subclassed when an instance of the interactive shell window is created to provide you access to the Python interactive mode. This subclass is able to handle the execution of commands, including the command history management.

The editor window provides a set of functionality that allows you to create new files or browse through and edit existing Python scripts. Two other important browsing engines are also part of the IDLE environment: the Path Browser and the Class Browser. The former is used for searching modules through the directories listed in the sys.path variable, whereas the latter implements a simple Class Browser for finding the methods of classes.

IDLE also has a flexible search capability through its Find in Files dialog that lets you search through your files or the system files to find occurrences of identifiers or any other text fragments.

A debugging implementation, which can be configured using the Debug Control Panel, is also offered by IDLE. Keep in mind that this Debug is still in the process of development and tuning.

Among the features included in the latest release (version 0.5) of IDLE, I highlight the following ones:

- New functionality in the Shell window that displays *call tips* for functions that know the *documentation string*.

- New implementation for both the Path Browser and the Class Browser that is based on the tree widget navigation model. The Class and Path browsers now use a new version of the pyclbr.py module, which is used to parse a Python file to recognize class and method definitions and to find out the superclasses of a class.

- Better auto-indent capabilities. It is now possible to set the indent width and toggle between the use of tabs in the indentation. Now, the auto-indent functionality knows how to indent the blocks inside multiline statements.

- You can now import files as modules and run them as scripts from the File Editor.

- You can call IDLE with command-line arguments just as you normally do with the Python interpreter.

- A status bar was created to display the current line and column.

- The Comment out region feature now inserts two hashes (##) in order to be more distinguishing.

For more information, check out the following:

IDLE

`http://www.python.org/idle/`

IDLE-dev Mailing List

`http://www.python.org/mailman/listinfo/idle-dev`

Installing and Configuring IDLE

Previously, IDLE version 0.4 used to be automatically installed when you installed Python 1.5.2. The version 0.5, which is now available, can be downloaded from the IDLE page in the Python Web site. To install it, you just need to save the files in the `idle` subdirectory of your current Python installation. Note that you can still keep your prior version by renaming it to something like `idle4`.

In order to start IDLE on a Windows machine, you need to either access the IDLE icon on the Python Program's folder or double-click the file `idle.pyw`, which is located in the idle subdirectory of your installation. Note that you need to have Tkinter perfectly installed on your system in order to use IDLE, which means that in order to use IDLE you need to have one installation of Tcl/Tk running on your system. (Multiple Tcl/Tk installations might confuse Python.)

In order to run IDLE on a UNIX machine, first you need to obtain the source code, which usually is available along with the latest Python source code in the CVS tree—a *tarball* can also be downloaded from the IDLE homepage without any need to use CVS. Note that IDLE is part of most Python Distributions. Second, you just need to type `idle` to open IDLE's Python Shell Window. For more information, check out

Python CVS Page

`http://www.python.org/download/cvs.html`

Command Line Usage

The IDLE environment offers the following useful command-line arguments for your usage:

```
idle.py [-c command] [-d] [-e] [-s] [-t title] [args ...]
    -c command  run this command (see text below)
    -d          enable the debugger
    -e          edit mode (see text below)
    -s          run $IDLESTARTUP or $PYTHONSTARTUP first
```

```
-t title      defines the title of the shell window
args          arguments to be used
```

If `-e` is used, the arguments should be the files to be opened for editing. `sys.argv` receives the arguments passed to IDLE itself.

If `-c` is used, all arguments are placed in `sys.argv[1:...]`, with `sys.argv[0]` set to `'-c'`.

if neither `-e` nor `-c` is used, the first argument is a script that is executed with the remaining arguments in `sys.argv[1:...]` and `sys.argv[0]` set to the script name. If the script name is `'-'`, no script is executed, but an interactive Python session is started; the arguments are still available in `sys.argv`.

Python Shell

After calling the IDLE environment, the Python Shell Window pops up on the screen showing Python's interactive mode interface. As you can see, although you have the primary prompt >>>, no secondary prompt (...) is displayed. Sometimes, you might feel like, "Where is the prompt?" Or, the interpreter might appear to have stopped working in such a way that you cannot get a new prompt. The primary solution for these problems is to press CTRL+C in order to interrupt any running command, establish a keyboard interruption, and get back to the prompt. If you need to quickly get out of the interpreter environment and close the Pythonwin window, press CTRL+D at the primary prompt.

IDLE colorizes the shell elements according to their logical meanings and syntax definitions. Note that while you are typing the code, definitions become blue, strings become green, keywords become orange, comments become red, the interpreter's standard output becomes blue, and the standard input becomes black. When you execute the code, the console outputs are displayed in brown and the standard error messages are in dark green (see Figure 16.1. Observe that this figure, as all other figures shown in this book are not in color). This process happens in a background thread, and you can change the color scheme anytime you want just by editing the `ColorPrefs` class in `IdlePrefs.py` file.

IDLE provides automatic support for indentation, which is fired when you press the ENTER key after a block-opening statement. Pressing the BACKSPACE key moves you back to one level of the indentation structure. Note that this automatically happens when you insert a return, continue, break, pass, or raise statement.

Indentation options, including the indent level, can be fully configured, depending on your own choice. The default value of the indent level sets the tabulation to be equivalent to four spaces. An interesting feature is that it is possible to select a specific region and indent or dedent it (these options are available on the edit menu).

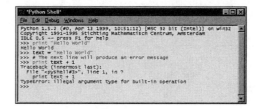

Figure 16.1
Note how IDLE uses colors to easily identify the various elements of the interface, such as the traceback messages.

Tip boxes are a new sensation in this latest version of IDLE. They are displayed when you type the opening parenthesis of functions (regular or built-in) and method calls (including class constructors) from the Python Standard Library. Their contents usually show a tip that lists the expected arguments. This feature is not limited to the functions defined by the Python environment. You can also use it while coding your own functions to automatically display their list of expected arguments. In addition to the list of arguments, you can also include an additional string to your tip box by adding a *documentation string* to your function/method definition. To close the tip window, you need to press ESC or click somewhere else in the window.

Another new feature introduced in this version is the word completion mechanism. Based on the list of the latest words introduced to the program, you can successively press ALT+/ to toggle between them in order to expand and complete the word that you have just started typing.

Something very interesting, but actually not new because it came from the previous version, is the command history mechanism. It works when you move the cursor to the end of a specific line, or block, and press ENTER. This action copies the whole line (or block) to the primary prompt. Alternatively, you can use the keys ALT+p and ALT+n to toggle between the latest commands matching what you have typed. When you find the one you want to use, press ENTER and the command is retrieved.

Note that you can freely edit the commands before really executing them (see Figure 16.2).

PART V   Developing with Python

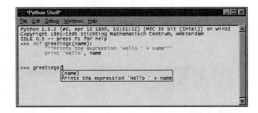

Figure 16.2
This example demonstrates how IDLE handles indentation, the word completion mechanism, and the call tips functionality.

In case you want to change the current font used on windows, you just need to open the `EditorWindow.py` file and define a new tuple value for the `font` entry in the `text` dictionary, such as

```
text['font'] = ("times", 12)
```

Keyboard Commands
Moving around in the IDLE buffer is fairly easy. For basic editing and navigation controls, you can use the following key bindings:

- Backspace deletes to the left of the cursor.

- DEL deletes to the right of the cursor.

- Arrow keys and Page Up/Down are used to move around the buffer.

- Home goes to the beginning of the line.

- End goes to the end of the line.

- CTRL+Home goes to the beginning of the file.

- CTRL+End goes to the end of the file.

IDLE offers you the chance to modify some of the keyboard binding settings. Check out the `Bindings.py` file for details.

File Menu
IDLE's File Editor allows you to create new scripts or browse and edit existing Python source files. The File Editor might also be brought up from the Path Browser or when you are using the Debugger. In all cases, a new File Editor window will be opened with the name of the file and the path to it as its title (or called Untitled if it is a new unsaved file).

> **Tip**
> A nice feature is almost hidden in the shell environment. If you click on the dotted line at the top of a menu, a new window is created containing the menu itself.

The following options are menu items located in the File menu:

New window—Creates and opens a new editing window for when you want to create a new Python source file.

Open...—Opens a dialog box that allows you to locate and open any Python source file on your local system.

Open module...—Asks you to enter the name of a module, and then it searches through all the directories listed in the sys.path. The module is opened after it has been found.

Class browser—Opens a small utility that shows the classes and methods stored in the current open file.

Path browser—Uses the sys.path variable as a startup helper for letting you browse directories, modules, classes, and methods.

Save—Saves the current window. If the title of the window is delimited by * literals, it indicates that the window has changed since the last time you saved it.

Save As...—Saves the current window using the given filename.

Save Copy As...—Saves the current window using the given filename. The difference when comparing this to the previous option, is that this one doesn't rename the current window as the name of the new file.

Close—Closes the current window.

Exit—Used to leave IDLE. It closes all windows and quits.

The following table lists some Emacs and Windows bindings for the previous set of Menu Options.

Table 16.1   *Keyboard Bindings for the File Menu*

Menu Option	Emacs Style Binding	Windows Binding
New	CTRL+x CTRL+n	CTRL+n
Open	CTRL+x CTRL+f	CTRL+o
Open Module	CTRL+x CTRL+m	CTRL+m

Table 16.1   *(continued)*

Menu Option	Emacs Style Binding	Windows Binding
Save	CTRL+x CTRL+s	CTRL+s
Save As	CTRL+x CTRL+w	ALT+s
Save Copy As	CTRL+x w	ALT+SHIFT+s

The Class and the Path Browsers

The Class Browser function is implemented in the `ClassBrowser.py` file. You can launch this browser by pressing ALT+C or by selecting the Class browser option of the File menu. Note that you need to have already opened a file in order to use this function (see Figure 16.3).

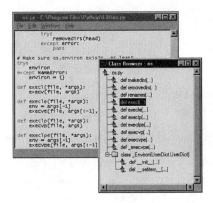

Figure 16.3
Class Browser.

The Path Browser is implemented in the `PathBrowser.py` file. This option creates a tree object that provides the following hierarchy structure:

```
Directory
    Python source file
        Class
            Class method
```

This structure is used to allow you to navigate through the directories listed in the Python `sys.path` variable. You just need to double-click on the upper level in order to expand all the sublevels. If you double-click on any of the sublevels of this tree, IDLE opens the associated object in a File Editor window for you. You can avoid that if you are just interested in browsing through the directories. Using the + and - marks on the left side of the tree allows you to expand and shrink the tree without opening the File Editor.

Because of some internal problems, this version of IDLE has a cosmetic error that lists some directories more than once in the tree (see Figure 16.4).

Figure 16.4
Path Browser.

Edit Menu

The following menu options are found in the Edit menu:

Undo—Used to undo the last change made to the current window. Note that IDLE supports up to 1000 changes to be undone.

Redo—Redoes last change.

Cut—Copies and deletes the current selection.

Copy—Copies selection.

Paste—Inserts the buffer value into the desired location.

Select All—Selects all contents of the edit buffer.

Find...—Allows you to search specific text patterns. You can even use regular expressions.

Find again—Finds previous search again.

Find selection—Searches for a given string within the selected area.

Find in Files—Allows you to search for a specific string inside files stored in your system.

Replace—Allows you to search and replace specific entries.

Go to line—Opens a dialog box where you have to type a line number. Then, it moves you to that line.

Indent region—Moves selected lines one tab (4 spaces) to the right.

Dedent region—Moves selected lines one tab (4 spaces) to the left.

Comment out region—Comments a block of lines by inserting ## in front of them.

Uncomment region—Gets rid of the leading # and ## from the selected region.

Tabify region—Converts leading spaces in a selection to tabs.

Untabify region—Converts all tabs in a selection to the correct number of spaces.

Toggle Tabs—Sets the type of the automatic indents. If you turn Tabs On, the indentation uses tabs and spaces. On the other hand, if you turn Tabs Off (default), the indentation uses only spaces.

New Indent width—Changes the width of the automatic indents.

Expand word—Expands the word you have entered to match another word that you have previously typed in the same buffer.

Format Paragraph—Formats the current selection as a paragraph.

Import module—Imports or reloads the module you are working on, adds the module name to the __main__ namespace, and opens the Shell window, if necessary.

Run script—Runs the script stored in the __main__ namespace, and adds the script name to the sys.argvp[] variable.

The following table lists some Emacs and Windows bindings for the previous set of Menu Options.

Table 16.2   *Keyboard Bindings for the Edit Menu*

Menu Options	Emacs Style Bindings	Windows Bindings
Cut	CTRL+w	CTRL+x
Paste	CTRL+y	CTRL+v
Copy	ALT+w, ESC+w	CTRL+c
Select All	ALT+a, ESC+a	ALT+a
Replace	CTRL+r	CTRL+h
Undo	CTRL+z	CTRL+z
Redo	ALT+z, ESC+z	CTRL+y
Find	CTRL+u CTRL+s	CTRL+f

Table 16.2   *(continued)*

Menu Options	Emacs Style Bindings	Windows Bindings
Find again	CTRL+u CTRL+s	CTRL+g, F3
Find selection	CTRL+s	CTRL+F3
Go to line	ALT+g, ESC+g	ALT+g
Indent Region	CTRL+]	CTRL+]
Dedent region	CTRL+[	CTRL+[
Comment out region	ALT+3	ALT+3
Uncomment region	ALT+4	ALT+4
Tabify region	ALT+5	ALT+5
Untabify region	ALT+6	ALT+6
Format Paragraph	ALT+q	ALT+q
Expand word	ALT+/	ALT+/
Toggle Tabs	ALT+t	ALT+t
New indent width	ALT+u	ALT+u
Import module	F5	F5
Run script	CTRL+F5	CTRL+F5

Windows Menu

This menu only provides the Zoom Height option, which is used to toggle the window between normal size (24x80) and the maximum allowed height.

The Windows menu is also used to list the name of all open windows. After you select a window from the list, the window pops up in the front of your screen (unless it is minimized and you have to click on the icon to maximize it).

Debug Menu

The debugging mechanism offers the following menu options.

Go to file/line

This option looks around the insert point for a filename and line number, opens the file, and shows the line. It is useful when you get a traceback message, and you want to go to the line that has caused the error. You just need to put the cursor somewhere in the line that displays the filename and the line number, and select the Go to File/Line option on the menu.

Stack Viewer

This option opens a tree widget that shows the stack traceback of the last exception. Note that it can be used separately from the debug mechanism.

Debugger

Opens the Debug Control Panel, which allows you to run commands in the shell under the debugger mechanism. In order to close the Panel, you can toggle the option off in the menu.

Auto-open Stack Viewer

Once set, this option automatically opens the stack viewer when a traceback message occurs.

The Debug mechanism that IDLE exposes allows you to

- Set breakpoints in a source code window.

- Execute a program and step through its statements.

- View the call stack. If necessary, you can right-click in the stack trace, and the debugger will move you to the corresponding section of the source code.

- Check the value of the local and global variables.

- Analyze the source code in the editor window as you step through the program.

The debugging process starts when you open a File Editor Window, and creates or imports a module. After you have the code available, you can double-click the lines that you want, and select the Set Breakpoint Here option, which highlights the line. Now, you need to select the Debug Control Panel option on the menu. Notice that although the Panel pops up on the screen, the message [DEBUG ON] is printed on the Shell Window. After clicking the Go button on the Debug Control Panel, the execution will stop at every breakpoint that it finds.

You can also debug code that is typed directly into the Shell Window (see Figure 16.5).

The Debug Control Panel is made up of five regular control buttons and four checkbuttons (see Figure 16.6).

Go button—Continues the execution of the program starting from the current point until it reaches the end of the program, or finds a break point.

Step button—Steps into the execution of the next statement.

Figure 16.5

Debugging a user function typed in the Shell Window.

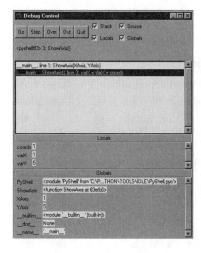

Figure 16.6

Using the Debug Control Panel to debug the function that we typed in Figure 16.5.

Over button—Fully executes the current statement without requiring you to step through its inner lines.

Out button—Resumes the execution of the program in order to leave (get out of) the current function.

Quit button—Quits the execution of the current program without leaving the debug mode. In order to leave the Debug Control Panel, you either need to toggle the menu option to OFF, or close the window Panel. Notice that when the Panel Window closes, the message [DEBUG OFF] is printed on the Shell Window.

Between the buttons and the stack area, you have the status area. This line lets you know where you are in the script. As you can see in Figure 16.6, we are in the line number 3 in a function called ShowAxis().

Next to the buttons are some checkbuttons responsible for setting the configuration of the Debug Control Panel area. They define what you want to see and trace.

Stack—Displays the call stack.

Source—Opens a File Editor Window for every file that is mentioned in the debugging process, highlighting the current line, which is being processed.

Locals—Displays the set of local variables (and their values) defined by the program for the current namespace.

Globals—Displays all the global variables (and their values), including the internal variables, defined by the program.

Writing an IDLE Extension

The way that IDLE has been set up allows you to write your own extensions and define new key bindings and menu entries for IDLE edit windows. There is a simple mechanism to load extensions when IDLE starts up and to attach them to each edit window.

For Guido's instructions on writing these extensions, take a look at the file `extend.txt`, which is located on your `idle` directory, or grab it online at

```
http://www.python.org/idle/idle-0.5/extend.txt
```

Python 2.0 and IDLE

Python 2.0 was released with IDLE 0.6, which includes some additional features and enhancements.

The main new features are

- You can install IDLE as a package now.

- Three new keystroke commands were added: Check module (Alt+F5), Import module (F5), and Run script (Ctrl+F5).

- A bar showing the line and column of the cursor was included at the bottom of the editor window.

- A command line was added to IDLE. This command line is very similar to the Python interpreter shell.

- You can now use IDLE to call several brands of browsers and triggering documents to open inside the browsers.

As for the enhancements, we can list improvements and optimizations to the following main areas:

- User interface.

- Syntax highlighting and auto-indentation.

- Class browser, which is now showing more information.

- Ability to set the *Tab width* as part of the user configuration set of option, which means that IDLE is now able to display the tabulation of a given file according to the user configuration settings.

- Call tips—they are now available in many locations.

Pythonwin

Pythonwin is implemented as a wrapper for the Microsoft Foundation Class library. The interactive and interpreted environment is in fact just a fully functional program created by Mark Hammond to demonstrate the full power of the interface between MFC and Python. Besides the development environment, you can use Pythonwin to write your own application, based on a given set of MFC objects. As of now, Pythonwin supports more than 30 MFC objects that are exposed by the Windows environment, which includes Common Controls, Property Pages/Sheets, Toolbars, and so forth.

Pythonwin's latest version (at this moment) is the beta 3 of version 2. This beta comes as part of the most recent 1.5.2 build for Windows (`win32all-132.exe`). Note that this version might be different at the time of your reading.

This version provides a stabilization of many features, including the debugger and the general IDE interface, which had a great advance compared to the prior Pythonwin version. This version also includes a number of other enhancements and bug fixes, such as a number of changes/enhancements to *Scintilla*, COM fixes (mainly in obscure situations), and the new full support for COM User Defined Types (Records/Structs). Preliminary `ADSI` support has been added, as well.

> **Note**
> `Scintilla` is a free source code editing component, whose development started as an effort to improve Pythonwin.

In order to install Pythonwin, you can download the file from the following address:

`http://starship.python.net/crew/mhammond/win32/Downloads.html`

If you also want to have access to the top-level functions in both the PythonPath and Module browsers, you need to download the latest version of the module `pyclbr.py`. This module is a standard Python module that has been updated since Python 1.5.2. To download the module and for more information, check out the following:

`http://starship.python.net/crew/mhammond/downloads/pyclbr.py`

Mark Hammond's Python Extensions

`http://starship.python.net/crew/mhammond/`

Pythonwin Documentation Index

`http://www.python.org/windows/pythonwin/`

Python for Windows Repository

`http://www.python.org/windows/`

The Pythonwin Environment

Pythonwin simulates the built-in Python interpreter by using the Microsoft Foundation Classes to implement an Interactive Development Framework.

> **Tip**
> You can study Pythonwin's code by examining the files located in the directory `\Pythonwin\pywin\framework` of your local Pythonwin installation.

The shell provided by the Interactive Window implements many known features inherited from IDLE, such as the history mechanism. Depending on where you place the cursor when pressing ENTER, you can either execute a command located at the end of your screen buffer, or copy a block of code from somewhere else to the end of your buffer. Note that the end of the screen buffer is the place where you have an active primary prompt.

When the line that you are typing has to be continued in another line, the code doesn't get executed. At this time, Python starts a new line using the secondary prompt . . . . After you enter a complete Python statement, Pythonwin tries to execute it. If your execution generates an exception in a file, the file is displayed to you in a separate window, pointing to the line that has caused the exception. If a COM object generates the exception, and the exception contains a reference to a WinHelp file, the help topic is opened to you.

Pythonwin has available all the standard file operations that follow the MFC framework. If necessary, you can create Python programs to implement plug-in support for other file types that are not currently supported by Pythowin.

The Locate option defined in the menu is used to quickly locate a specific Python script. It searches for the file throughout all the directories listed in the sys.path variable. If you need to locate a module in a package, replace the dot between the package name and the module name with a backslash.

The Import option tries to import or reload a given script. Pythonwin is the one that decides if the script needs to be imported or reloaded. Pythonwin also handles modules that use the old and historic ni module. If you have a .py file opened, you can use this option to save and import the file. If a file cannot be located, a File dialog pops up asking you to locate the file.

The Run option runs a script, as if the file was passed on the command line. A dialog is opened, asking the script name and arguments. If you already have a script file open and just want to execute it, press CTRL+SHIFT+R.

This version of Pythonwin is heavily similar to the latest version of IDLE (in new functionality). As Mark says, "Many of the new Pythonwin features below have come about simply by stealing code from IDLE." Pythonwin demonstrates its high integration with IDLE extensions by incorporating the ExpandWord extension module and IDLE's history capability.

Among other new features, the latest version of Pythonwin brings the following main changes:

- Support for simple toggling and definition of fixed and propertional fonts.

- Improved call tips and attribute expansion.

- Key binding for toggling between the interactive window and the most recently used editor window.

- Far improved find facility, including the ability to search across all open files.

Pythonwin provides an easily configurable color scheme because you can see the standard "Hello World" example shown in Figure 16.7. Note that example was written directly in the Interactive Window.

The View/Options item in the Menu is useful to configure a lot of small details, such as the color scheme, and Tabs and Whitespace configuration (see Figure 16.8).

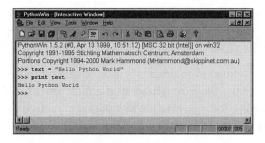

Figure 16.7

Interactive Window displaying Hello World.

Figure 16.8

The Tabs and Whitespace configuration tab on the Pythonwin Option dialog box.

Under the Tools menu, you have several routines that provide some special functionality. The first one called `Browser`, displays information about an object whose name you have to type in a dialog box.

The `Browse PythonPath` option splits the screen into two parts: the Python Path browser and the Interactive Window file editor. When you click on a program or program item (class, function, and so on) in the Path Browser, the right panel opens the given file and places you on the part of the code that defines the object you have just clicked (see Figure 16.9). Note that the interface looks much nicer when you use the latest version of the `pyclbr.py` module.

Another option provided is the ability to make changes on the Pythonwin Registry settings, as you can see in Figure 16.10. In order to open this window, you need to call the menu item named `Edit PythonPath`.

The next two options are used when you have to write COM interfaces using Python. The first option `COM Makepy utility` is mentioned in Chapter 7, "Objects Interfacing and Distribution." It lists all the available COM objects registered in the system and allows you to create a Python interface for them (see Figure 16.11). In this example, we are highlighting the Excel 8.0 Object Library in order to create a Python interface that will allow us to use Excel COM interface.

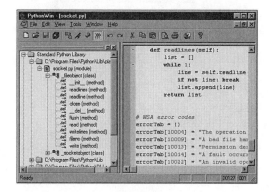

Figure 16.9
Python Projects: tree widget that displays Python directories and files.

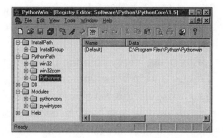

Figure 16.10
The Registry Editor allows you to make changes on the registry settings of Pythonwin.

Figure 16.11
A list of available COM libraries.

This next option COM Browser allows you to visualize all the properties of registered
COM objects (see Figure 16.12).

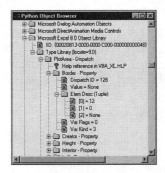

Figure 16.12
The Python Object Browser.

Pythonwin supports source code folding, which means that it has the capability to
collapse sections of source code into single lines, and later expand them back to the
original structure (see Figure 16.13). This folding featured was added to Pythonwin
thanks to Scintilla. You can fold and unfold any Python statement that introduces a
new block either by clicking on the indicator in the folding margin, by selecting one of
the folding keystrokes, or by using View, Folding menu. Note that the folding feature
must be enabled via the menu option View/Options/Editor dialog. You can also
change the configuration so that all files have only their top-levels folded when
opened. All editing functions work properly when code is folded. If necessary,
functions like find, replace, and goto are able to unfold the code before they start
performing their tasks. For more information, check out

Scintilla

```
http://www.scintilla.org
```

Pythonwin's debugger had a great improvement since the last version. To use the
Debug mechanism, you need to open a program and set the breakpoints on the code.
You can toggle the breakpoints by clicking on a specific line and using the F9 key
binding, as shown in Figure 16.13. You don't need to run the debugger just to set the
breakpoints; you can do that while the debugger is not running. While the debugger is
inactive, the breakpoints are shown without any coloring.

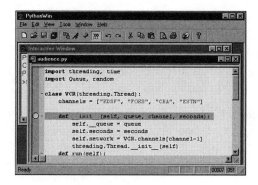

Figure 16.13

Opening a file and toggling the breakpoint.

You just can't let the breakpoints remain there and pray for something to happen. You need to activate the debugger by either using the Step in (F11) option, the Go (F5) option, or one of the shortcuts in the toolbar and in the menu. When you start the debugging process, all breakpoints become red (see Figure 16.14—note that as the figure isn't in color, it might feel that some colors are not easily identified in the book).

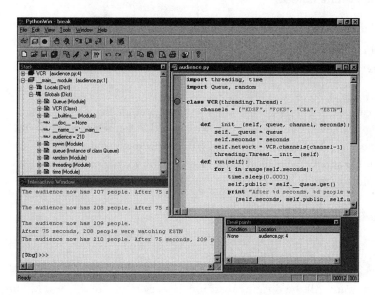

Figure 16.14

The Debug Framework.

In order to add watch variables and break-point conditions, you need to click on a specific part of the Debugging window. To add variables, you need to click on the Expression/Value text box and click on the <New item> text. The prompt will let you type the name of the variables that you want to watch. In case you want to delete something from there, you just need to press the Delete key.

If you close the Debugging toolbar, you can open it using the menu option View, Toolbars, Debugging. Note that this toolbar follows the standard found in other languages, as we can see in the Figure 16.14 (from left to right):

- Watch Window toggle option
- Stack Viewer Window toggle option
- Breakpoint List Window toggle option
- Option to toggle a breakpoint
- Option to clear all breakpoints
- Step into a statement
- Step over a function
- Step out of a structure
- Go
- Close the debugger

As you can see in Figure 16.14, when you select all debug windows to be open, you get a Debug Framework containing five windows. Let's go clockwise, starting from the top-left corner: We have the variable watch window, the stack viewer, the Python path browser, the interactive window that displays the source code, and a list of breakpoint conditions (on the bottom).

Keyboard Bindings

Pythonwin has a customizable keyboard binding mechanism that allows you to define your own custom events and keyboard bindings. All this information gets stored in a file called `default.cfg`, which is located in the `pywin` directory. You can freely edit this file if you want. All the documentation necessary to create the new bindings is kept in this file, including how to create your own configuration based on the default file. This last feature is a handful to incorporate into your system `default` file from new versions of Pythonwin without changing your code. This directory also contains a configuration file called IDLE.cfg that simulates the keyboard bindings of IDLE, providing a good customization example.

The bindings in Table 16.3 are part of Pythonwin's default configuration.

Table 16.3   *Pythonwin's Default Set of Bindings*

Keyboard Binding	Description
Alt+Q	Format the current paragraph
Alt+/	Apply the functionality that expands the word under the cursor
Alt+I	Show/hide the interactive window
Ctrl+W	View/hide whitespaces

Built-in Binding	Description
Ctrl+Z	Undo
Ctrl+Y	Redo
Ctrl+X	Cut
Ctrl+C	Copy
Ctrl+V	Paste
Ctrl+A	Select All
Ctrl+L	Cut the current line
Ctrl+Shift+L	Delete the current line
Ctrl+T	Swap the current line with the line above
Ctrl+U	Convert the selection to lowercase
Ctrl+Shift+U	Convert the selection to uppercase
Ctrl+Backspace	Delete the word to the left side of the cursor
BackSpace	Remove one indent to the left
Enter	Insert a newline and indent
Tab	Insert an indent, or perform a block indent in a given selection
Shift+Tab	Dedent the selected block
F2	Go to the next bookmark
Ctrl+F2	Add or remove a bookmark on the current line
Ctrl+G	Go to a specific line number
Alt+B	Add a simple comment banner at the current location
Alt+3	Block comment the selected region
Shift+Alt+3	Uncomment the selected region
Alt+4	Uncomment the selected region (IDLE's default binding)

Table 16.3   *(continued)*

Built-in Binding	Description
Alt+5	Tabify the selected region
Alt+6	Untabify the selected region
Ctrl+T	Toggle the use of tabs for the current file
Alt+U	Change the indent width for the current file
*Keypad*Plus	Expand a folded line, if it is located under the cursor
Alt+*Keypad*Plus	Expand all folds in the current file
*Keypad*Minus	Collapse a folded line, if it is located under the cursor
Alt+*Keypad*Minus	Collapse all folds in the current file
*Keypad*Multiply	Toggle between expanding and collapsing all top-level folds in the current file
Ctrl+*Keypad*Plus	Zoom-in for the current window
Ctrl+*Keypad*Minus	Zoom-out for the current window
Debugger Bindings	**Description**
F9	Toggle breakpoint on and off
F5	Activate the debugging process
Shift+F5	Stop the debugging process
F11	Single step into functions
F10	Step over functions
Shift+F11	Step out of the current function
Interactive Bindings	**Description**
Ctrl+Up	Show the previous command in the history list
Ctrl+Down	Show the next command in the history list

Command Line Arguments

Pythonwin accepts the following command line arguments. In case you need to make changes in any one of these commands, you just need to modify the `intpyapp.py` file.

```
/run scriptname arguments
```

This command runs the given script in the GUI environment and sends the output directly to Pythonwin's interactive window.

```
/runargs scriptname arguments
```

This command also runs the given script in the GUI enviroment. The difference between this and the previous command is that this one shows Pythonwin's "Run Script" dialog.

`/edit filename`

This command allows you to edit the given file. Currently, you can omit the `/edit` command because it is not strictly enforced.

`/app scriptname arguments`

This command runs an application script that is able to change the appearance of a Pythonwin program. For details, check the examples located in the Pythonwin application folder (`/Pythonwin/pywin/Demos/app`) of your Python installation.

Summary

This chapter shows some performance and style suggestions for your code now that you are probably writing your own programs. It also introduces you to the main GUI development environments that you can use to write Python applications.

Writing a program is very easy, but writing a good and optimized program requires some level of experience. A good way to start is to learn all the nuances of the language, which in our case involves learning Python.

Python is a perfect language for project prototyping. Python's design allows you to make changes very quickly. Along the development stage, you will soon see that Python can be easily used to code entire applications, without discarding the prototyped code.

Performing code optimization and writing a program with style are very important things that you must have in mind, not only when using Python, but also when writing in any other language.

For years, many people have been writing and editing their Python programs using simple text editors, but now the scenario has changed. Python currently provides two efficient development environments for your usage: IDLE, a cross platform Integrated Development Environment for Python, and Pythonwin, a development environment specifically for the Windows platform.

The next chapter introduces you to the Python-mode package for Emacs, which provides almost all the features in the IDLE and Pythonwin edit windows (and a few features they don't). This includes auto indentation, syntax highlighting, and so on. You can use Emacs on just about any UNIX-like system, and there is a Windows port as well.

CHAPTER 17

Development Tools

Wenn ist das Nunnstueck git und Slotermeyer?

Ja! Beierhund das oder die flipperwaldt gersput.

A handful of programming tools are introduced here. This chapter demonstrates how to go through all the development stages of creating a Python application. You will learn how to compile the Python interpreter, and how to debug, profile, and distribute Python programs.

The Development Process of Python Programs

At this point, it's presumed that you have already written many Python programs, and that you want more details and material covering development tools that can optimize the development stage of your applications. The next list of topics shows what is introduced in the chapter that can help you along the development process of your programs.

- How to compile the Python interpreter on Windows and UNIX platforms

- Available tools for code editing

- List of example scripts that come as part of the Python distribution

- How to generate executable Python bytecode files

- How to start the Python interpreter using different command line options
- How to debug and profile a Python program
- How to pack and distribute your Python application

Compiling Python

The Python source code distribution comes with complete instructions about how to compile the code for both Windows and UNIX platforms. The instructions about compiling for Windows are stored in the subdirectories /PCbuild and /PC—the UNIX instructions are separate. The /PC subdirectory contains complete project files to make several PC ports of Python.

If you want to compile Python on Windows, you need to start the Integrated Development Environment of your compiler and read in the native *project file* (or makefile) provided. This enables you to change any source files or build settings so you can make custom builds.

The following are important files that can help you configure the port of the source code to your favorite platform (in case it hasn't been ported yet).

config.h—An important configuration file specific to PCs. This is generated by the configure script on UNIX systems.

config.c—The list of C modules to include in the Python PC version. Manually edit this file to add or remove Python modules. This is auto-generated by the makesetup script on UNIX systems.

testpy.py—A Python test program. Run this to test your Python port. It should produce copious output, ending in a report on how many tests were OK, how many failed, and how many were skipped. Don't worry about skipped tests (these test unavailable optional features).

Windows

The Python distribution comes with instructions to compile the source code using many different tools, such as Microsoft Visual C++ Version 1.5 (16-bit Windows), Watcom C++ compiler, and IBM VisualAge C/C++ for OS/2. See the /PC/readme.txt file in the distribution tree for detailed instructions.

The instructions here cover the Microsoft Visual C++ Versions 5.0 and 6.0.

In order to build Python using this tool, the first thing you need to do is open the workspace `pcbuild.dsw` that is located under the `/PCbuild` directory. This directory also contains a `readme.txt` file with more instructions. Note that all files in this directory are used to build Python for Win32 platforms, which includes Windows 95, 98, and NT platforms.

Then, you just need to select the Debug or Release setting (using Set Active Configuration in the Build menu) and build the projects in the proper order, which is

1. python15 (this builds python15.dll and python15.lib)

2. python (this builds python.exe)

3. The other subprojects

If you select the Debug option, the files will be generated carrying a _d at the end of their name, such as `python15_d.dll`, `python_d.exe`, and `parser_d.pyd`.

We call subprojects—the other applications that don't come as part of the Python application—that include for example: Tcl/Tk, bsddb, and zlib. In order to build these projects, you might have to change some of the settings on your compiler, such as the include and library paths.

The following files and subdirectories of the distribution are useful and helpful when building Win32 versions of Python:

`python_nt.rc`—Resource compiler input for `python15.dll`.

`dl_nt.c, import_nt.c`—Additional sources used for 32-bit Windows features.

`getpathp.c`—Default `sys.path` calculations (for all PC platforms).

`dllbase_nt.txt`—A (manually maintained) list of base addresses for various DLLs, to avoid runtime relocation.

`example_nt`—This is a subdirectory that shows how to build an extension as a DLL.

UNIX

Binary distributions for the UNIX platforms are not made available by the Python Web site because the compilation process depends much on your system. In order to compile Python on a UNIX system, you first need to obtain the source code distribution. Note that the next guidelines are just a summary of the operations that you need to perform. This installation process, by default, installs Python under the `/usr/local` directory and presumes that you want to provide access to the `Tkinter` module too. If that's not the case, you can just skip the whole `Tcl/Tk/Tkinter` steps and install just the core Python environment. You can skip building Tcl and Tk if they are already installed on your system.

1. Create a root directory with three subdirectories underneath: Python, Tcl, and Tk.

2. Download the latest versions of these three programs, and save them on the respective subdirectories.

3. In each directory, you need to extract the files out of the package using a command such as this:

```
gunzip -c filename | tar xf -
```

4. Now, we need to configure and install Tcl and Tk. The actions below (steps 5, 6, and 7) need to be performed in both subdirectories, first for Tcl and later for Tk.

5. Go to the specific subdirectory.

6. Define the compiler and system options for the building process. You need to type the following command:

```
./configure
```

7. Run the utility commands that create and install the binary and library files.

```
make

make install
```

8. Now, we are ready to install Python. Go to the Python subdirectory.

9. Define the compiler and system options for the building process. You need to type the following command. Note that optionally, you can enable the threading option by passing the argument --with-thread to the configure command. Also, you might want to enable floating point exception support by passing the argument --enable-fpectl.

```
./configure
```

10. Copy the `Modules/Setup.in` file to the subdirectory `Modules/Setup`.

11. In order to enable the Tkinter module (because it is not enabled by default), you need to modify this file. This file is responsible for deciding the built-in modules that must be built along with Python. Modifying this file is not difficult, as you can see next. The following piece of file code shows where you need to change in order to enable Tkinter. This example shows what you might want to

uncomment because it can vary for different UNIX systems (what you see here should be fine for most systems though).

```
# The _tkinter module.
#
# The TKPATH variable is always enabled, to save you the effort.
TKPATH=:lib-tk


# The command for _tkinter is long and site specific.  Please
# uncomment and/or edit those parts as indicated.  If you don't have a
# specific extension (e.g. Tix or BLT), leave the corresponding line
# commented out.  (Leave the trailing backslashes in!  If you
# experience strange errors, you may want to join all uncommented
# lines and remove the backslashes -- the backslash interpretation is
# done by the shell's "read" command and it may not be implemented on
# every system.


#***Always uncomment this (leave the leading underscore in!):
_tkinter _tkinter.c tkappinit.c -DWITH_APPINIT \
#***Uncomment and edit to reflect where your Tcl/Tk headers are:
-I/usr/local/include \
#***Uncomment and edit to reflect where your X11 header files are:
-I/usr/X11R6/include \
#***Or uncomment this for Solaris:
#       -I/usr/openwin/include \
#***Uncomment and edit for Tix extension only:
#       -DWITH_TIX -ltix4.1.8.0 \
#***Uncomment and edit for BLT extension only:
#       -DWITH_BLT -I/usr/local/blt/blt8.0-unoff/include -lBLT8.0 \
#***Uncomment and edit for PIL (TkImaging) extension only:
#       -DWITH_PIL -I../Extensions/Imaging/libImaging  tkImaging.c \
#***Uncomment and edit for TOGL extension only:
#       -DWITH_TOGL togl.c \
#***Uncomment and edit to reflect where your Tcl/Tk libraries are:
-L/usr/local/lib \
#***Uncomment and edit to reflect your Tcl/Tk versions:
-ltk8.0 -ltcl8.0 \
#***Uncomment and edit to reflect where your X11 libraries are:
-L/usr/X11R6/lib \
#***Or uncomment this for Solaris:
#       -L/usr/openwin/lib \
#***Uncomment these for TOGL extension only:
#       -lGL -lGLU -lXext -lXmu \
#***Uncomment for AIX:
```

```
#      -lld \
#***Always uncomment this; X11 libraries to link with:
-lX11
```

12. Optionally, you can choose for building the modules as shared libraries. It is a good idea to build shared libraries because it will decrease the size of the Python binary, reduce the number of libraries it is linked to, and probably reduce its memory consumption. You need to look for the following lines in the Setup.in file, and make the small change that is indicated there.

```
# Uncommenting the following line tells makesetup that all following
# modules are to be built as shared libraries (see above for more
# detail; also note that *static* reverses this effect):
#*shared*
```

Note
Note that you can uncomment lines for other modules you want to build, as well.

13. Now, you just have to run the utility commands that creates and installs the Python executable and library files.

```
make
make install
```

14. Finally, sometimes you need to set up the environment variables: PATH, PYTHONPATH, TCL_LIBRARY, and TK_LIBRARY to the correct values. In most cases, this shouldn't be necessary because the programs are installed where they expect to be installed. Possibly having to add /usr/local/bin to PATH is probably all that is needed.

Editing Code

As you already know, Python provides two development environments that offer a lot of useful features which can help you while coding: Pythonwin and IDLE. However, for simple programs, or in case you don't have a graphical environment available, you can stick to simple text editors that can be used to handle the job very nicely.

On Windows systems, you can use editors such as Editpad and Notepad to write Python scripts; on DOS systems, EDIT, and on UNIX systems you have choices such as Pico, Vi, Emacs, and others.

Pico is a full screen editor that is reasonably intuitive. Pico's commands can be learned in just some minutes and Pico itself is good for editing small texts with just a few changes. However, you need commands that are more powerful when a text becomes bigger because Pico only has a limited number of commands. These commands are shown at the bottom of the editing screen. Also note that Pico makes limited use of mice. Pico is not 100% recommended for Python programming because it wasn't designed as a programmer's editor. It does things such as automatic word wrap, which might not be what you want.

Vi (visual editor) is another full screen editor that was seen as a big improvement over line editing. Vi is highly customizable, allows filtering, has number prefixes for commands, has an invocation of a shell, has better jump commands, can read in the result of external commands, save parts of text, substitute literal strings and regular expressions, and many other options. The vi clone *vim (vi improved)* can be scripted in Python among other languages.

JED is a freely available text editor for UNIX, VMS, MSDOS, OS/2, and MS Windows. This editor has many features, including drop-down menus, folding support, color syntax highlighting on color terminals, and emulation of Emacs, EDT, Wordstar, and Borland editors. It's said that the latest version of the JED editor has a Python mode, with many of the same features as the Emacs/XEmacs Python mode.

See its Web page for more information:

```
http://space.mit.edu/~davis/jed.html
```

Vi, Pico, and JED are certainly powerful editors. However, Emacs is quite a jump in feature variety. Emacs is a very extensible and customizable editor. The richness of Emacs makes it more difficult to learn, but it is worth the try. A version of Emacs called XEmacs (which is a very famous implementation) can also be used for writing Python programs.

Emacs

Emacs originally was an acronym for Editor MACroS. The heart of Emacs is an interpreter for *elisp (Emacs Lisp)*, which is a dialect of the Lisp programming language with extensions to support text editing. Currently, Emacs is much more than a text editor. Besides allowing you to edit several styles of source codes and other general-purpose files, it contains many extensions that provide support for features such as Web browsing and mail reading. Emacs is a GNU project, and it is maintained by the Free Software Foundation.

Some of the features of Emacs include

- Content sensitive major modes for a wide variety of file types, from plain text to source code to HTML files.

- Complete online documentation, including a tutorial for new users.

- Emacs is highly extensible through the Emacs Lisp language.

- Support for many human languages and their scripts.

- A large number of extensions which add other functionality (the GNU Emacs distribution includes many extensions).

Check out the GNU Emacs Web site for details:

```
http://www.gnu.org/software/emacs/
```

> **Note**
> XEmacs is a highly customizable open source text editor and application
> development system, which is based on GNU Emacs, and shares a lot of code with it.
> XEmacs is protected under the GNU Public License, and its emphasis is on modern
> graphical user interface support and an open software development model. XEmacs
> has an active development community and runs on Win32 and UNIX platforms. See
> `http://www.xemacs.org/` for details.

Emacs has its own section on the Python Web site, precisely at the following address:

```
http://www.python.org/emacs/
```

At that page, you can find a collection of links to several Emacs codes that might help with your Python programming. Most of the code works fine on top of the latest versions of both Emacs and XEmacs.

From that page, you can also get access to some Emacs modes that enable the coding of Python source code when using Emacs, such as the Python Mode, located at

```
http://www.python.org/emacs/python-mode/
```

You might want to byte-compile that python-mode file when installing it on your system, primarily for better performance. To do so, you need to open Emacs (or XEmacs) and execute the following commands. Note that you can safely ignore any byte compiler warnings.

```
C-x C-f /path/to/python-mode.el RET
M-x byte-compile-file RET
```

On the Web site, besides getting access to the latest release of the python-mode (the current version is 3.105), you can also obtain other useful stuff, which includes: a detailed list of changes since the last released version, installation notes, a FAQ, and a

Emacs/XEmacs compatibility details list, which brings special notes about Emacs/XEmacs versions and package interactions.

To install the python-mode package so that it can be used in Python, you would put it in the `site-lisp` directory, and edit your `site-start.el` to autoload `python-mode.el` and bind it to `.py` files.

The following links provide additional information related to the usage of Emacs/XEmacs along with Python.

The OO-Browser—This is a multi-windowed, interactive, object-oriented class browser that supports Python, and was designed for professional use under the Emacs editor. See the following Web site for details:

`http://www.beopen.com/manuals/alt-oobr-cover.html`

Introduction to Using OO-Browser with Python—This is a paper by Harri Pasanen, presented at the International Python Conference IV, June 1996.

`http://www.python.org/workshops/1996-06/papers/h.pasanen/`
`oobr_contents.html`

Python Library Reference Hot-Key Help System for XEmacs—This is Harri Pasanen's work. This program shows the Python Library Reference for the word under cursor every time you press the F1 key when in Python mode under the XEmacs.

`http://bigbear.pc.helsinki.fi/harri/`

Python Scripts

The Python distribution comes with lots of scripts that you can study and use. Those scripts are stored in two directories: `\Tools` and `\Demos`.

Table 17.1 lists programs that are stored in the `\Tools` directory.

Table 17.1 *Programs Stored in the Tools Directory*

Program	Description
bgen	Generates complete extension modules from a description (under development).
faqwiz	FAQ Wizard.
freeze	Creates a standalone executable from a Python program.

Table 17.1   *(continued)*

Program	Description
modulator	Interactively generates a boiler plate for an extension module. Works easiest if you have Tk.
Pynche	The PYthonically Natural Color and Hue Editor.
versioncheck	Checks whether you have the latest version of a specific package.
webchecker	Checks Web sites for bad links.

The `\Tools\Scripts` subdirectory contains a number of useful single-file programs. They are shown in Table 17.2.

Table 17.2   *Programs Stored in the Tools\Scripts Directory*

Program	Description
byteyears	Prints the product of a file's size and age
checkpyc	Checks presence and validity of `.pyc` files
classfix	Converts old class syntax to new
copytime	Copies one file's atime and mtime to another
crlf	Changes CRLF line endings to LF (Windows to UNIX)
cvsfiles	Prints a list of files that are under CVS
dutree	Formats du output as a tree sorted by size
eptags	Creates Emacs TAGS file for Python modules
findlinksto	Recursively finds symbolic links to a given path prefix
fixcid	Massive identifier substitution on C source files
fixheader	Adds some cpp magic to a C include file
fixnotice	Fixes the copyright notice in source files
fixps	Fixes Python scripts' first line (if #!)
ftpmirror	FTP mirror script
h2py	Translates `#defines` into Python assignments
ifdef	Removes `#if(n)def` groups from C sources
lfcr	Changes LF line endings to CRLF (UNIX to Windows)
linktree	Makes a copy of a tree with links to original files
lll	Finds and lists symbolic links in current directory
logmerge	Consolidates CVS/RCS logs read from stdin
mailerdaemon	Parses error messages from mailer daemons
methfix	Fixes old method syntax `def f(self, (a1, ..., aN)):`

Table 17.2   *(continued)*

Program	Description
mkreal	Turns a symbolic link into a real file or directory
ndiff	Intelligent diff between text files
nm2def	Creates a template for PC/python_nt.def
objgraph	Prints object graph from `nm` output on a library
pathfix	Changes `#!/usr/local/bin/python` into something else
pdeps	Prints dependencies between Python modules
pindent	Indents Python code, giving block-closing comments
ptags	Creates vi tags file for Python modules
rgrep	Reverses grep through a file
suff	Sorts a list of files by suffix
sum5	Prints md5 checksums of files
tabnanny	Checks inconsistent mixing of tabs and spaces
tabpolice	Checks for ambiguous indentation
texi2html	Converts GNU texinfo files into HTML
treesync	Synchronizes source trees
untabify	Replaces tabs with spaces in argument files
which	Finds a program in $PATH
xxci	Wrapper for rcsdiff and ci

The \Demo directory contains good examples of how to write Python code. The programs are described in Table 17.3.

Table 17.3   *Programs Stored in the Demo Directory*

Program	Description
classes	Some examples of how to use classes.
dns	Module that implements a DNS client.
embed	Example of embedding Python in another application (see also pysvr).
extend	Example of using the generic Makefile.pre.in from the Misc directory to build a statically linked or shared extension module.
ibrowse	Emacs info file browser (uses stdwin).
md5test	Test program for the optional md5 module.
metaclasses	Metaclasses examples.

Table 17.3   *(continued)*

Program	Description
pdist	Filesystem, RCS, and CVS client and server classes. This directory contains various modules and classes that support remote file system operations.
pysvr	Example of embedding Python in a threaded application.
rpc	Set of classes for building clients and servers for Sun RPC.
sockets	Examples for the new built-in module socket.
sgi	Demos that only run on Silicon Graphics machines.
stdwin	Demos that use the STDWIN library.
threads	Demos that use the thread module (for SGIs).
tkinter	Demos using the Tk interface.
zlib	zlib demo.

The directory /Demos/scripts contains a collection of useful executable Python scripts. They are presented in Table 17.4.

Table 17.4   *Programs Stored in the Demos/Scripts Directory*

Script	Description
fact	Factorizes numbers
from	Summarizes mailbox
ftpstats	Summarizes ftp daemon log file
lpwatch	Watches BSD line printer queues
markov	Markov chain simulation of words or characters
mboxconvvert	Converts MH or MMDF mailboxes to UNIX mailbox format
morse	Produces Morse code (audible or on AIFF file)
mpzpi	test mpz—prints digits of pi (compare pi.py)
pi	Prints all digits of pi—given enough time and memory
pp	Emulates some Perl command line options
primes	Prints prime numbers
script	Equivalent to BSD script
unbirthday	Prints unbirthday count
update	Updates a bunch of files according to a script

Generating an Executable Python Bytecode

When loading a module, the Python interpreter first tries to load a byte-compiled version of the module (a `.pyc` or `.pyo` bytecode file) from the system. If it doesn't find one, it automatically byte-compiles the module, and in case the permissions given to the user who is executing the command allow, a byte-compiled version of the module is saved in the disk for a later user. Note that it is a good idea to bytecompile all files before giving Python access to users who cannot save in that source directory. Otherwise, the interpreter has to byte-compile the module every time the module is loaded, which can slow down program startup considerably.

Even though a Python bytecode file can automatically be created when importing a module, you can manually create them whenever you need, as well. In order to explicitly byte-compile a source file (`.py`) to a `.pyc` (or `.pyo`) bytecode file, you just need to execute the following code:

```
import py_compile
pycompile.compile("anyfilename.py")
```

As you can see, the `py_compile` module provides a function called `compile()` that does all the jobs. The general syntax for this function is

```
compile(file [, cfile] [, dfile])
```

where,

`file`	source filename
`cfile`	target filename; defaults to source with c or o appended (c normally and o in optimizing mode, giving `.pyc` or `.pyo`)
`dfile`	filename to store error messages (defaults to source)

The `compileall` module can be used either as a script or as a module. It uses the `py_compile` module to byte-compile all installed files (or all files in selected directories).

The following example compiles all files from the current directory:

```
import compileall.py
compileall.compile_dir(".", force=1)
```

You can also use this module as a script, passing arguments to it. The syntax for usage as a script is as follows:

```
python compileall [-l] [-f] [-d destdir] [directory ...]
```

where,

-l	avoids recursing into directories
-f	forces rebuild even if timestamps are up-to-date
-d destdir	directory to store the error messages

The script reads the directories that are informed as arguments and compiles all the files that it finds there. If no directory arguments are given, the routine uses the sys.path variable.

Note that the current version doesn't recur down into subdirectories of a package. Another implementation detail is that it only recurs into the maximum number of 10 levels. (This number is hard coded in the module's code.) Also note that to generate both .pyc and .pyo files, you will need to run Python twice—once without the -O flag and once with it.

Interpreter

After installing Python, some special environment variables can be configured in order to guarantee the maximum usage of the Python environment. The following list shows some important environment variables recognized by the Python interpreter.

PYTHONPATH—This variable contains a list of directories used by the interpreter, as search path, when importing modules. The best installation strategy is to put extra Python modules in the /lib/python$(ver)/site-packages subdirectory under the root Python installation, so you can tell between standard Python packages and add-ons. Then you just need to set PYTHONPATH to your Python search path.

PYTHONSTARTUP—This variable contains the name of the directory that must have all its files automatically loaded at the time of starting the Python interpreter.

PATH(or path)—This is a system environment variable that contains the directory where the Python interpreter is located.

TCL_LIBRARY, TK_LIBRARY—These variables set the names of the directories where we can find the libraries for both the Tcl and Tk systems. You don't need to set these variables unless you move your Tcl or Tk files after building and installing them (the same as for Python).

Each system has a different way to set up these variables. For example, UNIX users running all *bourne* shell compatible shells, could type

```
PYTHONPATH=".:/usr/local/python/lib"
export PYTHONPATH
```

On the other hand, Windows and DOS users are familiar with the following syntax:

```
set PYTHONPATH=.;c:\python\lib
```

The Macintosh people must use the EditPythonPrefs program that comes along with their version of the Python distribution. Note that this application is also used to set up the values for the command line options that are passed to the interpreter.

When your system is able to locate the Python installation, you can call the interpreter by typing the command

```
python
```

invoking the interpreter without arguments, connecting the standard input to a tty device, executing commands interactively.

```
python filename
```

If you inform a filename, the interpreter tries to read and execute the contents of the file.

The next line shows the general syntax to start up the Python interpreter.

```
python [options] [-c cmd | filename | -] [file_arguments]
```

The command line options in Table 17.5 are available on Windows and UNIX systems.

Table 17.5 *Python Interpreter Command Line Options*

Option	Description
-d	Generates parser debugging information.
-i	Enters interactive mode after program execution.
-O	Sets optimized mode that optimizes bytecompiled files.
-OO	Acts like -O, but also strips *docstrings*.
-S	Prevents inclusion of the site initialization module.
-t	Reports warnings about inconsistent tab usage.

Table 17.5   *(continued)*

Option	Description
-u	Sets unbuffered binary stdout and stdin.
-v	Sets the verbose mode.
-x	Skips the first line of the source program.
-X	Disables class-based exceptions. Note that release 2.0 doesn't contain this option anymore—it has been removed. Standard exceptions cannot be strings anymore. They always have to be classes. Also note that since release 2.0 the exceptions module was converted from Python to a built-in C module.
-c cmd	Executes the provided Python command *cmd*. It's important to use double quotes here because the Python command can contain spaces.
-	using - as a filename makes the interpreter read from the standard input.

> **Note**
> Note that Python 2.0 brings the new -U command line option to you. This option tells the Python compiler to interpret all 8-bit string literals as Unicode string literals. You should hang on to this one as the support for 8-bit strings might be abandoned in future releases.

Whenever you inform the script's filename and additional arguments to the interpreter, that information gets stored in the sys.argv variable, which is a list of strings. To be part of this list, the arguments must appear after the filename or after the -.

When commands are read from a tty, the interpreter is said to be in interactive mode. In this mode, it prompts for the next command with the primary prompt, which is by default three greater than signs (>>>); for continuation lines, it prompts with the secondary prompt, which is by default three dots (...). Note that these prompts can be modified by changing the values of sys.ps1 and sys.ps2, respectively. Users might want to modify the default values of these variables by putting these definitions in a file that can be found in a directory in the $PYTHONSTARTUP directory.

When you start the interpreter, a welcome message is printed stating its version number and a copyright notice before printing the first prompt as follows:

```
Python 1.5.2 (#0, Apr 13 1999, 10:51:12) [MSC 32 bit (Intel)] on win32
Copyright 1991-1995 Stichting Mathematisch Centrum, Amsterdam
>>>
```

If you are using Python on a UNIX system, you can extend its line-editing features by using the GNU readline library. To check whether you have this library installed on your system, just press CONTROL+P on the primary prompt. If the letter P is echoed back to you, it means that you don't have access to the library. Otherwise, you can check the documentation and use all the editing and history features that are provided by the library.

To exit the interpreter, you can type an EOF character (Control+D on UNIX, Control+Z on DOS or Windows) at the primary prompt, import the sys module and call the sys.exit() function, or just raise the SystemExit exception.

In order to launch the Python applications, you have a different kind of approach, depending on your system. The UNIX people need to adjust the shebang in the first line of the Python program to point to the Python interpreter. On Windows, you can either click on the program icon or use batch files to transport arguments to the script (or to the interpreter). Note that you can also open your files without opening the interpreter; you just need to rename them to .pyw. This extension is associated with the pythonw.exe application, which is responsible for executing the script without opening a command window for the interpreter. If you are using a Macintosh system, you need to use some special programs that come as part of the Python distribution for Macintoshes. The first one is called BuildApplet. This program takes your program and generates a file that automatically starts up the interpreter and executes the code, when opened. The other program is called BuildApplication. This one takes your program and generates a standalone application that doesn't need a Python installation running behind the scenes. This application is useful for cases in which you want to distribute your Python application to other Macs that don't have Python installed.

Debugging the Application

Debugging a Python program is something that doesn't require too much work. The Standard Python Library comes with a debugger module called bdb that can be used by you to subclass your own debuggers. If you don't want to spend time writing your own debug, you can use the Python debugger (the pdb module), which is also part of the Python distribution. For those who need high-specialized debugging information, Python provides a disassembler module. And for those who only want to debug the value of variables, nothing works better than spreading a couple of print statements throughout your program.

If you decide to use the Python debugger, you will not regret it. This debugger allows you to set breakpoints, trace the values of local and global variables, step through the code, and many other attractive features.

Because it is written in Python, the debugger exemplifies a powerful feature of the Python language: the ability to create introspective applications, which means that we are able to write programs in Python that can handle and manipulate the execution of other programs.

The Base Debugger Module (bdb)

The bdb module exposes a framework for creating debuggers. This module provides a base class called bdb that allows you to create your own debuggers by subclassing the base class.

The following methods are available in this class. Note that derived classes should override the following four methods to gain control of the application.

user_call(frame, argument_list)—This method is called when there is the remote possibility that we ever need to stop in this function pass.

user_line(frame)—This method is called when we stop or break at this line pass.

user_return(frame, return_value)—This method is called when a return trap is set here.

user_exception(frame, (exc_type, exc_value, exc_traceback))—This method is called if an exception occurs, but only if we are to stop at or just below this level pass.

The following methods can be called by the derived classes and by the clients in order to affect the stepping state:

set_step()—Stops after one line of code

set_next(frame)—Stops on the next line in or below the given frame

set_return(frame)—Stops when returning from the given frame

set_trace()—Starts debugging from here

set_continue()—Doesn't stop except at breakpoints or when finished

set_quit()—Quits the debugging process

Derived classes and clients can call the following methods in order to manipulate breakpoints. These methods return an error message if something went wrong, and None if everything goes well.

`set_break(filename, lineno, temporary=0, cond = None)`—This method prints out the breakpoint line and filename:lineno.

`clear_break(filename, lineno)`—This method removes the breakpoint entry.

`clear_bpbynumber(arg)`—This method removes the breakpoint identified by the given number.

`clear_all_file_breaks(filename)`—This method removes all the breakpoints found in the given file.

`clear_all_breaks()`—This method removes all the active breakpoints from the current program.

`get_break(filename, lineno)`—This method returns true if the given file has a breakpoint in the given line number.

`get_breaks(filename, lineno)`—This method returns true if the given file has a breakpoint in the given line number.

`get_file_breaks(filename)`—This method returns a list of all breakpoints found in the given file.

`get_all_breaks()`—This method returns a list of all active breakpoints from the current program.

The following methods can be called by clients to use a debugger to debug a statement given as a string:

`run(command, globals=None, locals=None)`—Executes the string `command`, under the debugger control.

`runeval(expr, globals=None, locals=None)`—Evaluates the expression `expr` under the debugger control.

`runcall(func, *args)`—This method calls the single function `func` under the debugger control.

`set_trace()`—This method starts the debugger at the point at which this function is called. It is used to hard-code a debugger breakpoint into a specific code location.

The following example demonstrates how we can subclass the `bdb` class in order to design our own debug. This example is based on the testing routine included in the `bdb` module file.

```
import bdb
class Tdb(bdb.Bdb):
    def user_call(self, frame, args):
        name = frame.f_code.co_name
        if not name:
            name = '???'
        print '+++ call', name, args
    def user_line(self, frame):
        import linecache, string
        name = frame.f_code.co_name
        if not name:
            name = '???'
        fn = self.canonic(frame.f_code.co_filename)
        line = linecache.getline(fn, frame.f_lineno)
        print '+++', fn, frame.f_lineno, name, ':', string.strip(line)
    def user_return(self, frame, retval):
        print '+++ return', retval
    def user_exception(self, frame, exc_stuff):
        print '+++ exception', exc_stuff
        self.set_continue()

def factorials(n):
    for f in xrange(n, 0, -1):
        factorial = calc(f)
        print 'The factorial of %d is %d' % (f, factorial)

def calc(f):
    factorial = 1
    for n in xrange(f, 1, -1):
        factorial = factorial * n
    return factorial

def main():
    debug = Tdb()
    debug.run('factorials(3)')

main()
```

The Python Debugger (pdb)

The Python debugger is directly based on the bdb class, as you can see when examining its source code. To start the Python debugger, you need to import the pdb

module, and type one of the following commands: `run()`, `runeval()`, `runcall()`, or
`set_trace()`.

```
import pdb
def myprog(n):
    for l in xrange(n):
        print l
debub=pdb.Pdb()
debub.runcall(myprog,10)
```

The debugger will then pop up a prompt. The debugger's prompt is `'(Pdb) '`.

To use the debugger in its simplest form, type

```
import pdb
pdb.run('<a statement>')
```

This will stop in the first function call in `<a statement>`.

Alternatively, if a statement terminated with an unhandled exception, you can use pdb's
post-mortem facility to inspect the contents of the traceback:

```
>>> <a statement>
<exception traceback>
>>> import pdb
>>> pdb.pm()
```

The commands recognized by the debugger are listed in the next section. Note that
some commands have a short and a long form. The commands not recognized by the
debugger are assumed to be Python commands, and are executed in the context of the
program being debugged. Python statements can also be prefixed with an exclamation
point (!). This is a powerful way to inspect the program being debugged; it is even
possible to change variables. When an exception occurs in such a statement, the
exception name is printed, but the debugger's state is not changed.

The debugger supports aliases, which can save typing. And aliases can have parameters
(see the alias help entry) that allow one a certain level of adaptability to the context
under examination.

Multiple commands can be entered on a single line, separated by the pair ;;. No
intelligence is applied to separating the commands; the input is split at the first ;;,
even if it is in the middle of a quoted string.

If a file .pdbrc exists in the user's home directory or in the current directory, it is read
in and executed as if it had been typed at the debugger prompt. This is particularly
useful for aliases. If both files exist, the one in the home directory is read first and

aliases defined there can be overriden by the local file. Aside from aliases, the debugger is not directly programmable; but it is implemented as a class from which you can derive your own debugger class, which you can make as fancy as you like.

You can also invoke the Python debugger as a main program, on a script. Just use the following structure to start up the debugger.

```
import pdb
def main():
    # Add your code here
if __name__=='__main__':
    pdb.run('main()')
```

Debugger Commands

When you are at the debugger prompt, you can type any one of the following commands. Note that some of them have an abbreviated version. Next to each command, enclosed in brackets, you will find the command's optional arguments. Except for the `list` command, all commands can be repeated by entering a blank line at the prompt.

`h(elp)`—Prints the list of available commands.

`w(here)`—Prints a stack trace, with the most recent frame at the bottom. An arrow indicates the current frame, which determines the context of most commands.

`d(own)`—Moves the current frame one level down in the stack trace (to an older frame).

`u(p)`—Moves the current frame one level up in the stack trace (to a newer frame).

`b(reak) [ ([filename:]lineno | function) [, condition] ]`—With a `filename:line` number argument, set a break there. If filename is omitted, use the current file. With a function name, set a break at the first executable line of that function. Without an argument, list all breaks. Each breakpoint is assigned a number to which all the other breakpoint commands refer. The condition argument, if present, is a string that must evaluate to `true` in order for the breakpoint to be honored.

`tbreak [ ([filename:]lineno | function) [, condition] ]`—Temporary breakpoint, which is removed automatically when it is first hit. The arguments are the same as break.

`cl(ear) [bpnumber [bpnumber ...] ]`—With a space separated list of breakpoint numbers, clear those breakpoints. Without an argument, clear all breaks (but first ask confirmation).

`disable bpnumber [bpnumber ...]`—Disables the breakpoints given as a space separated list of breakpoint numbers. Disabling a breakpoint means that it cannot cause the program to stop execution. But unlike clearing a breakpoint, it remains in the list of breakpoints and can be (re-)enabled.

`enable bpnumber [bpnumber ...]`—Enables the breakpoints specified.

`ignore bpnumber count`—Sets the ignore count for the given breakpoint number. If the count is omitted, the ignore count is set to `0`. A breakpoint becomes active when the ignore count is zero. When non-zero, the count is decremented each time the breakpoint is reached and the breakpoint is not disabled and any associated condition evaluates to `true`.

`condition bpnumber condition`—Condition is an expression that must evaluate to `true` before the breakpoint is honored. If condition is absent, any existing condition is removed; that is, the breakpoint is made unconditional.

`s(tep)`—Executes the current line and stops at the first possible occasion (either in a called function or in the current function).

`n(ext)`—Continues execution until the next line in the current function is reached or it returns.

`r(eturn)`—Continues execution until the current function returns.

`c(ont(inue))`—Continues execution, only stops when a breakpoint is encountered.

`l(ist) [first [,last]]`—Lists source code for the current file. Without arguments, lists 11 lines around the current line or continues the previous listing. With one argument, lists 11 lines starting at that line. With two arguments, lists the given range; if the second argument is less than the first, it is a count.

`a(rgs)`—Prints the argument list of the current function.

`p expression`—Prints the value of the expression.

`(!) statement`—Executes the (one-line) statement in the context of the current stack frame. The exclamation point can be omitted unless the first word of the statement resembles a debugger command. To assign to a global variable, you must always prefix the command with a `global` command, for example

```
(Pdb) global list_options; list_options = ['-l']
(Pdb)
```

`whatis arg`—Prints the type of the argument.

`alias [name [command]]`—Creates an alias called `name` that executes `command`. The command must *not* be enclosed in quotes. Replaceable parameters can be indicated by %1, %2, and so on, whereas %* is replaced by all the parameters. If no command is given, the current alias for name is shown. If no name is given, all aliases are listed. Aliases might be nested and can contain anything that can be legally typed at the `pdb` prompt. Note that you *can* override internal pdb commands with aliases. Those internal commands are then hidden until the alias is removed. Aliasing is recursively applied to the first word of the command line; all other words in the line are left alone. As an example, here are two useful aliases (especially when placed in the `.pdbrc` file):

```
#Print instance variables (usage "pi classInst")
alias pi for k in %1.__dict__.keys(): print "%1.",k,"=",%1.__dict__[k]
#Print instance variables in self

alias ps pi self
```

`unalias name`—Deletes the specified alias.

`q(uit)`—Quit from the debugger. The program being executed is aborted.

Note
Some Python IDE's, such as Pythonwin, implement derived debuggers, and Emacs' Grand Unified Debugger can use pdb.

Disassembling Python Bytecodes

Python has a module called `dis`, which is used to disassemble Python bytecodes into mnemonics. This module exposes a function, which is also called `dis()` that is able to disassemble classes, methods, functions, or code. If you don't provide any argument to the function, it disassembles the last traceback.

```
>>> import dis
>>> def routine():
...     i = 5
...     for loop in xrange(i):
...         print 'Ni!'
>>>
>>> dis.dis(routine)
              0 SET_LINENO               1
```

```
            3 SET_LINENO          2
            6 LOAD_CONST          1 (5)
            9 STORE_FAST          0 (i)

           12 SET_LINENO          3
           15 SETUP_LOOP         33 (to 51)
           18 LOAD_GLOBAL         1 (xrange)
           21 LOAD_FAST           0 (i)
           24 CALL_FUNCTION       1
           27 LOAD_CONST          2 (0)

   >>      30 SET_LINENO          3
           33 FOR_LOOP           14 (to 50)
           36 STORE_FAST          1 (loop)

           39 SET_LINENO          4
           42 LOAD_CONST          3 ('Ni!')
           45 PRINT_ITEM
           46 PRINT_NEWLINE
           47 JUMP_ABSOLUTE      30
   >>      50 POP_BLOCK
   >>      51 LOAD_CONST          0 (None)
           54 RETURN_VALUE
```

Profiling Python

Profiling an application means to be able to sketch an image about what is going on behind the scenes when you execute a program.

The sys module is able to perform a very simple profiling task by telling you a little bit about what is going on after each function, method, or specific line gets executed.

sys.setprofiler(profiler_function)—This function implements a source code profiler, which identifies a function that must be executed whenever a function or method is called.

sys.settrace(tracer_function)—The functionality of this function is basically the same one of the setprofiler() function. However, this one is called whenever a new line is executed.

```
>>> import sys
>>> def profiler(frame, event, arguments):
...        print frame.f_code.co_name, frame.f_lineno, event, arguments
...
>>> sys.setprofile(profiler)
? 1 return None
>>> lst = ["Spam","Parrot","Knights"]
? 1 call None
? 1 return None
>>> def showlist(_lst):
...        for l in _lst:
...            print l
...        return _lst
...
? 1 call None
? 1 return None
>>> showlist(lst)
? 1 call None
showlist 1 call None
Spam
Parrot
Knights
showlist 4 return ['Spam', 'Parrot', 'Knights']
['Spam', 'Parrot', 'Knights']
? 1 return None
>>> sys.setprofile(None)
```

If you really want to perform a more complete and accurate study, you need to use the profiler module.

Python Profiler

The information provided here offers a brief overview about how to use the profile module to perform the analysis of the run time performance of a Python program. The original profile module was written by Sjoerd Mullender, and later Guido van Rossum applied some changes to it. All the original documentation is copyrighted by James Roskind (see copyright note in Appendix C, "Python Copyright Notices"), and reproduced here with slight modifications.

> **Note**
> Check out the module's original documentation for more information about its "deterministic profiling" implementation.

You have two possible ways to use the `profile` module. The first option is to import it, and make it call a function on your program that you want to analyze, such as

```
import profile
def main():
    for n in xrange(100):
        print n,
profile.run("main()")
```

The `run()` function generates a profiling report that can be manipulated using the `pstats` module (the report generating functions are in the `pstats` module).

The second option is to invoke the profiler as a main program and pass the script that needs to be profiled as an argument.

```
python profile.py scriptfile [arg...]
```

Next, you have the static member functions that are available for the profiler class. Note that an instance of `Profile()` is *not* needed to call them.

To profile an application with a main entry point of `foo()`, you would add the following to your module:

```
import profile
profile.run("foo()")
```

The previous action would cause `foo()` to be run, and a series of informative lines (the profile) to be printed. This approach is most useful when working with the interpreter. If you would like to save the results of a profile into a file for later examination, you can supply a filename as the second argument to the `run()` function:

```
import profile
profile.run("foo()", 'fooprof')
```

The primary entry point for the profiler is the global function `profile.run()`. It is typically used to create any profile information. The reports are formatted and printed using methods for the class `pstats.Stats`. The following is a description of all these standard entry points and functions. For a more in-depth view of some of the code, consider reading the later section on "Extensions: Deriving Better Profilers," which includes a discussion of how to derive better profilers from the classes presented, or reading the source code for these modules.

FUNCTION   profile.run(string, filename_opt)

This function takes a single argument that can be passed to the exec statement, and an optional filename. In all cases, this routine attempts to exec its first argument, and gathers profiling statistics from the execution. If no filename is present, this function automatically prints a simple profiling report, sorted by the standard name string (file/line/function-name) that is presented in each line. The following is a typical output from such a call:

```
main()
2706 function calls (2004 primitive calls) in 4.504 CPU seconds

Ordered by: standard name

ncalls   tottime  percall  cumtime  percall filename:lineno(function)
     2    0.006    0.003    0.953    0.477 pobject.py:75(save_objects)
   43/3    0.533    0.012    0.749    0.250 pobject.py:99(evaluate)
...
```

The first line indicates that this profile was generated by the call: profile.run('main()'), and hence the executed string is 'main()'. The second line indicates that 2706 calls were monitored. Of those calls, 2004 were *primitive*. We define primitive to mean that the call was not induced via recursion. The next line, Ordered by: standard name, indicates that the text string in the far right column was used to sort the output. The column headings include

ncalls stands for the number of calls.

tottime stands for the total time spent in the given function (and excluding time made in calls to sub-functions).

percall is the quotient of tottime divided by ncalls.

cumtime is the total time spent in this and all subfunctions (that is, from invocation till exit). This figure is accurate even for recursive functions.

percall is the quotient of cumtime divided by primitive calls.

filename:lineno(function) provides the respective data of each function.

When two numbers are in the first column (for instance, 43/3), the latter is the number of primitive calls, and the former is the actual number of calls. Note that when the function does not recurse, these two values are the same, and only the single figure is printed.

Analyzing Profiles with the `pstats` Module

The `pstats` module analyzes the data collected by the Python `profile` module. The following example demonstrates how we can use this module to manipulate the information generated by the `profile` module:

```
>>> import profile, pstats
>>> def main():
...       for n in xrange(3):
...           print n
...
>>> p = profile.Profile()
>>> p.run("main()")
0
1
2
<profile.Profile instance at 7c2c20>
>>> s = pstats.Stats(p)
>>> s.sort_stats("time", "name").print_stats()
3 function calls in 58.727 CPU seconds
   Ordered by: internal time, function name
   ncalls   tottime   percall   cumtime   percall filename:lineno(function)
        1    58.727    58.727    58.727    58.727 profile:0(main())
        1     0.000     0.000     0.000     0.000 <stdin>:1(main)
        1     0.000     0.000     0.000     0.000 <string>:1(?)
        0     0.000               0.000           profile:0(profiler)
<pstats.Stats instance at 7c2280>
>>>
```

This module exposes the `Stats(filename, ...)` class. This class is used for creating reports from data generated by the Profile class. It imports data either by direct access to members of Profile class, or by reading in a dictionary that was emitted (viamarshal) from the Profile class. When you want to review the profile, you should use the methods in the `pstats` module. Typically you would load the statistics data as follows:

```
import pstats
p = pstats.Stats('fooprof')
```

The class `Stats` (the previous code just created an instance of this class) has a variety of methods for manipulating and printing the data that was just read into "p". When you ran `profile.run()`, the result of three method calls was printed:

```
p.strip_dirs().sort_stats(-1).print_stats()
```

The first method removed the extraneous path from all the module names. The second method sorted all the entries according to the standard module/line/name string that is printed (this is to comply with the semantics of the old profiler). The third method printed out all the statistics. You might try the following sort calls:

```
p.sort_stats('name')
p.print_stats()
```

The first call will actually sort the list by function name, and the second call will print out the statistics. The following are some interesting calls to experiment with:

```
p.sort_stats('cumulative').print_stats(10)
```

This sorts the profile by cumulative time in a function, and then only prints the ten most significant lines. If you want to understand what algorithms are taking time, the previous line is what you would use.

If you were looking to see what functions were looping a lot, and taking a lot of time, you would do

```
p.sort_stats('time').print_stats(10)
```

This sorts according to time spent within each function, and then prints the statistics for the top ten functions.

You might also try

```
p.sort_stats('file').print_stats('__init__')
```

This will sort all the statistics by filename, and then print out statistics for only the class init methods (because they are spelled with __init__ in them). The sort_stats() method takes an arbitrary number of quoted strings to select the sort order. For example, sort_stats('time', 'name') sorts on the major key of "internal function time", and on the minor key of 'the name of the function'. As one final example, you could try:

```
p.sort_stats('time', 'cum').print_stats(.5, 'init')
```

This line sorts stats with a primary key of time and a secondary key of cumulative time, and then prints out some of the statistics. To be specific, the list is first culled down to 50% (.5) of its original size, and then only lines containing "init" are maintained, and that sub-sub-list is printed.

Note
All the print methods take an argument that indicates how many lines to print. If the arg is a floating point number between 0 and 1.0, it is taken as a decimal percentage of the available lines to be printed (for example, .1 means print 10% of all available lines). If it is an integer, it is taken to mean the number of lines of data that you want to have printed.

If you wondered what functions called the previous functions, you could now (p is still sorted according to the last criteria) do

```
p.print_callers(.5, 'init')
```

You would get a list of callers for each of the listed functions.

All methods from the Stats class return self, so you can string together commands such as

```
Stats('foo', 'goo').strip_dirs().sort_stats('calls').\
print_stats(5).print_callers(5)
```

This class constructor creates an instance of a statistics object from a filename (or set of filenames). Stats objects are manipulated by methods in order to print useful reports.

The file selected by the previous constructor must have been created by the corresponding version of profile. To be specific, there is *no* file compatibility guaranteed with future versions of this profiler, and there is no compatibility with files produced by other profilers (for example, the standard system profiler).

If several files are provided, all the statistics for identical functions will be coalesced so that an overall view of several processes can be considered in a single report. If additional files need to be combined with data in an existing Stats object, the add() method can be used. This can be used to average out the statistics for a short running program to increase the accuracy.

The following methods are exposed by the Stats class.

strip_dirs()—This method for the Stats class removes all leading path information from filenames. It is very useful in reducing the size of the printout to fit within (close to) 80 columns. This method modifies the object, and the striped information is lost. After performing a strip operation, the object is considered to have its entries in a random order, as it was just after object initialization and loading. If strip_dirs() causes two function names to be indistinguishable (that is, they are on the same line of the same filename, and have the same function name), the statistics for these two entries are accumulated into a single entry.

add(`filename`, ...)—This method of the `Stats` class accumulates additional profiling information into the current profiling object. Its arguments should refer to filenames created by the corresponding version of `profile.run()`. Statistics for identically named (file, line, name) functions are automatically accumulated into single function statistics.

sort_stats(`key`, ...)—This method modifies the `Stats` object by sorting it according to the supplied criteria. The argument is typically a string identifying the basis of a sort (for example: `"time"` or `"name"`).

When more than one key is provided, additional keys are used as secondary criteria when equality exists in all keys previously selected. For example, sort_stats(`'name'`, `'file'`) will sort all the entries according to their function name and resolve all ties (identical function names) by sorting by filename.

Abbreviations can be used for any key names as long as the abbreviation is unambiguous. The keys currently defined are shown in Table 17.6.

Table 17.6   *Abbreviations to Use as Sorting Keys*

Valid Argument	Meaning
`"calls"`	call count
`"cumulative"`	cumulative time
`"file"`	filename
`"module"`	filename
`"pcalls"`	primitive call count
`"line"`	line number
`"name"`	function name
`"nfl"`	name/file/line
`"stdname"`	standard name
`"time"`	internal time

Note that all sorts on statistics are in descending order (placing most time-consuming items first), whereas name, file, and line number searches are in ascending order (that is, alphabetical). The subtle distinction between `"nfl"` and `"stdname"` is that the standard name is a sort of the name as printed, which means that the embedded line numbers get compared in an odd way. For example, lines 3, 20, and 40 would (if the filenames were the same) appear in the string order `"20"`, `"3"`, and `"40"`. In contrast, "nfl" does a numeric compare of the line numbers. In fact, sort_stats("nfl") is the same as sort_stats("name", "file", "line").

> reverse_order()—This method for the Stats class reverses the ordering of the basic list within the object. This method is provided primarily for compatibility with the standard profiler. Its utility is questionable now that ascending versus descending order is properly selected based on the sort key of choice.

> print_stats(restriction, ...)—This method for the Stats class prints out a report as described in the profile.run() definition. The order of the printing is based on the last sort_stats() operation done on the object (subject to caveats in add() and strip_dirs()).

The arguments provided (if any) can be used to limit the list down to the significant entries. Initially, the list is taken to be the complete set of profiled functions. Each restriction is either an integer (to select a count of lines), or a decimal fraction between 0.0 and 1.0 inclusive (to select a percentage of lines), or a regular expression (to pattern match the standard name that is printed). If several restrictions are provided, they are applied sequentially. For example

```
print_stats(.1, "foo:")
```

would first limit the printing to the first 10% of list, and then only print functions that were part of filename ".*foo:". In contrast, the following command:

```
print_stats(".*foo:", .1)
```

would limit the list to all functions having filenames ".*foo:", and then proceed to only print the first 10% of them.

> print_callers(restrictions, ...)—This method for the Stats class prints a list of all functions that called each function in the profiled database. The ordering is identical to that provided by print_stats(), and the definition of the restricting argument is also identical. For convenience, a number is shown in parentheses after each caller to show how many times this specific call was made. A second non-parenthesized number is the cumulative time spent in the function at the right.

> print_callees(restrictions, ...)—This method for the Stats class prints a list of all functions that were called by the indicated function. Aside from this reversal of direction of calls (called versus was called by), the arguments and ordering are identical to the print_callers() method.

`ignore()`—This method of the `Stats` class is used to dispose of the value returned by earlier methods. All standard methods in this class return the instance that is being processed so that the commands can be strung together. For example

```
pstats.Stats('foofile').strip_dirs().sort_stats('cum').
print_stats().ignore()
```

would perform all the indicated functions, but it would not return the final reference to the `Stats` instance.

Limitations

There are two fundamental limitations on this profiler. The first is that it relies on the Python interpreter to dispatch `"call"`, `"return"`, and `"exception"` events. Compiled C code does not get interpreted, and hence is invisible to the profiler. All time spent in C code (including built-in functions) will be charged to the Python function that has invoked the C code. If the C code calls out to some native Python code, those calls will be profiled properly.

The second limitation has to do with accuracy of timing information. There is a fundamental problem with deterministic profilers involving accuracy. The most obvious restriction is that the underlying clock is only ticking at a rate (typically) of about .001 seconds. Hence no measurements will be more accurate than that underlying clock. If enough measurements are taken, the error will tend to average out. Unfortunately, removing this first error induces a second source of error.

The second problem is that it "takes a while" from when an event is dispatched until the profiler's call to get the time actually *gets* the state of the clock. Similarly, there is a certain amount of lag when exiting the profiler event handler from the time that the clock's value was obtained (and then squirreled away), until the user's code is once again executing. As a result, functions that are called many times, or call many functions, will typically accumulate this error.

The error that accumulates in this fashion is typically less than the accuracy of the clock (that is, less than one clock tick), but it *can* accumulate and become very significant. This profiler provides a means of calibrating itself for a given platform so that this error can be probabilistically (that is, on the average) removed. After the profiler is calibrated, it will be more accurate (in at least a square sense), but it will sometimes produce negative numbers (when call counts are exceptionally low, and the gods of probability work against you). Do *not* be alarmed by negative numbers in the profile.

They should *only* appear if you have calibrated your profiler, and the results are actually better than without calibration.

Calibration

The profiler class has a hard-coded constant added to each event handling time to compensate for the overhead of calling the time function, and storing away the results. The following procedure can be used to obtain this constant for a given platform.

```
import profile
pr = profile.Profile()
pr.calibrate(100)
pr.calibrate(100)
pr.calibrate(100)
```

The argument to `calibrate()` is the number of times to try to do the sample calls to get the CPU times. If your computer is *very* fast, you might have to do:

```
pr.calibrate(1000)
```

or even

```
pr.calibrate(10000)
```

The object of this exercise is to get a fairly consistent result. When you have a consistent answer, you are ready to use that number in the source code. For a Sun Sparcstation 1000 running Solaris 2.3, the magical number is about .00053. If you have a choice, you are better off with a smaller constant, and your results will *less often* show up as negative in profile statistics.

The following shows how the `trace_dispatch()` method in the `Profile` class should be modified to install the calibration constant on a Sun Sparcstation 1000:

```
def trace_dispatch(self, frame, event, arg):
    t = self.timer()
    t = t[0] + t[1] - self.t - .00053 # Calibration constant
    if self.dispatch[event](frame,t):
        t = self.timer()
        self.t = t[0] + t[1]
    else:
        r = self.timer()
        self.t = r[0] + r[1] - t # put back unrecorded delta
    return
```

Note that if there is no calibration constant, the line containing the calibration constant should simply say

```
t = t[0] + t[1] - self.t  # no calibration constant
```

You can also achieve the same results using a derived class (and the profiler will actually run equally fast), but the previous method is the simplest to use. If the profiler was made self calibrating, it would have made the initialization of the profiler class slower, and would have required some very fancy coding, or else the use of a variable where the constant .00053 was placed in the code shown. This is a *very* critical performance section, and there is no reason to use a variable lookup at this point when a constant can be used.

Extensions: Deriving Better Profilers

The `Profile` class of `profile` was written so that derived classes could be developed to extend the profiler. The following two examples of derived classes can be used to do profiling. If the reader is an avid Python programmer, it should be possible to use these as a model and create similar (and perchance better) profile classes.

If all you want to do is change how the timer is called, or which timer function is used, the basic class has an option for that in the constructor for the class. Consider passing the name of a function to call into the constructor:

```
pr = profile.Profile(your_time_func)
```

The resulting profiler will call your time function instead of `os.times()`. The function should return either a single number, or a list of numbers (similar to what `os.times()` returns). If the function returns a single time number or the list of returned numbers has length 2, you will get an especially fast version of the dispatch routine.

Be warned that you *should* calibrate the profiler class for the timer function that you choose. For most machines, a timer that returns a lone integer value will provide the best results in terms of low overhead during profiling. (`os.times` is pretty bad because it returns a tuple of floating point values, so all arithmetic is floating point in the profiler.) If you want to substitute a better timer in the cleanest fashion, you should derive a class, and simply put in the replacement dispatch method that better handles your timer call, along with the appropriate calibration constant.

Distributing Python Applications

You have more than one way to pack your Python files and distribute your application. It depends only on the kind of goal that you are trying to reach. Probably your greatest concern is about how to hide the source code of your application. Well... Some suggest the use of encryption algorithms, others the distribution of Python bytecode files. All these sound like good solutions, but they have their individual problems. If you are really worried about opening your code to the public, I suggest that you convert your Python application to C, and distribute a compiled executable. Ask yourself if it is really a benefit to hide the source to your program. It is just as bad to illegally distribute a program that comes with source, and could potentially increase the value to the client.

When creating your distribution package, it is important to keep in mind the directory location where you are saving your files. Python must know where to look. Python requires module files to be available in one or more directories listed in the sys.path. To see the current Python modules search path, start Python and type:

```
import sys
print sys.path
```

You can also allow your program to find a specific module placed somewhere else on the disk. For that, you just need to add one more entry in the sys.path list. In the next example, we intend to have a module called mymodule stored in a directory called /usr/users/andre, which is not part of the sys.path yet.

```
#!usr/local/bin/python
import sys
sys.path.insert(0,"/usr/users/andre")
import mymodule
mymodule.main()
```

If you are using Python on a Windows platform, you can try the following approach to pack all files on a single structure:

1. Create a root directory.

2. Put the following files on this directory: python.exe, pythonw.exe, _tkinter.pyd, python15.dll, tcl80.dll, tk80.dll, and any other specific libraries that your application might need.

3. Create three directories under the root: \LIB, \TCL, and \TK, and copy all the necessary files to these subdirectories.

4. Now, create a batch file where you set the value of the following variables: PYTHONPATH, TCL_LIBRARY, and TK_LIBRARY and create a call to your application in the file. Note that if you want to avoid opening the interpreter, you need to open your application using the pythonw application.

You can zip this entire structure and freely distribute it. The person who receives the package just has to execute the batch file to execute your application. If you want, you can change your program to use that previous technique of dynamically informing the path where your modules are located. Therefore, you don't need to configure the PYTHONPATH environment variable.

The Python distribution contains a tool that saves much time when you are dealing with distribution issues. This tool is called Freeze.

This tool is able to *freeze* a Python script into an executable in order to let you ship arbitrary Python programs to people who don't have Python. Note that in order to freeze programs that use Tkinter, Tcl/Tk must be installed on the target system.

Freeze works by converting all the Python code of your application to a stream of Python bytecodes that can be later executed by the Python interpreter. For each module that is opened, Freeze looks for other necessary modules too. After all modules are converted to bytecode format, Freeze glues them all, and creates a Makefile file that can be used by calling the make command. Note that the resulting executable contains all your code plus the Python interpreter and the necessary library modules. Therefore, you should expect a big file.

Freeze is a great option for the cases in which you don't want your users to see and copy your source code. Remember that the resulting file is an executable just like the ones created by regular compiled applications.

In order to use Freeze, you just need to perform a simple call, such as

```
python freeze.py hello.py
```

Freeze creates a number of files: frozen.c, config.c, and Makefile, plus one file for each Python module that gets included named M_<module>.c. To produce the frozen version of your program, you can simply type **"make"**. This should produce a binary file. If the filename argument to Freeze was hello.py, the binary will be called hello.

Details for usage under Win32 systems can be found on your own script at your local installation.

If you built Python with some required modules as shared libraries (DLLs), the frozen program will still require these extra files. If this is a problem (and it probably is if you are considering the freeze tool), you should recompile Python (using the previous instructions) with the required modules linked into the Python executable.

Note that you are not tied to the Freeze utility. There are a couple of other options available too. Check them out.

SqueezeTool

This is a program, written by Fredrik Lundh, that is able to squeeze a Python Application and all its support modules into a single, compressed package of bytecode files. Whenever it becomes necessary, a special script is used to open the package and run the bytecode files.

```
http://starship.python.net/crew/fredrik/ipa/squeeze.htm
```

Python2C—The Python to C Translator

Python2C is a Python to C translator, written by Bill Tutt and Greg Stein, that attempts to speed up Python code by removing a significant fraction of the Python interpreter overhead.

```
http://lima.mudlib.org/~rassilon/p2c/
```

Small Python

This tool was written by Greg Stein in order to create minimal Python distributions. Note that although it is built for Windows, the concept and source code can be useful for other Python platforms, as well.

```
http://www.lyra.org/greg/small/
```

Gordon McMillan's Installer

Gordon McMillan wrote this tool by taking Fredrik's Squeeze idea and Greg Stein's Small distribution, and combining them. The result is cross-platform, small (the python Standard Library fits in a 500K archive) and fast (much less I/O for an import) distribution installer for Python.

```
http://www.mcmillan-inc.com/install1.html
```

Distutils

Python 2.0 contains a brand-new distribution package as part of its Standard Library. This package is called `distutils`, and is totally documented in a new set of manuals that also join the official Python documentation. This package is able to create source and binary distributions.

The logic used by this package, automatically detects the platform, recognizes the compiler, compiles the C extension modules, and installs the distribution into the proper directory.

In order to install a script using this package, you need to run a `setup.py` script with the `install` command.

```
python setup.py install
```

Note that you need to write the `setup.py` script in order to execute the package. This file can be very simple when you are using only `.py` files, such as in the next example.

```
from distutils.core import setup
setup (name = "myapp", version = "1.0", py_modules = ["bikes",
  "cars"])
```

It is important to know that you are not tied to use only `.py` files; you can also use packages and C extensions. Check the official documentation for more details.

The `sdist` command, which can be passed to `python setup.py sdist`, builds a source distribution such as `myapp-1.0.tar.gz`.

You can also add you own commands—that isn't difficult at all. Bundled with the package, there are some contributed commands already written for you, such as `bdist_rpm` and `bdist_wininst`, which create an RPM distribution and a Windows installer, respectively.

Summary

This chapter demonstrates how to go through all the development stages of creating a Python application. You will learn how to compile the Python interpreter, and how to debug, profile, and distribute Python programs.

The Python source code distribution comes with complete instructions about how to compile the code for both Windows and UNIX platforms. These same instructions are given here in a general format overview.

Although there is a binary distribution for Windows systems, binary distributions for the UNIX platforms are not made available by the Python Web site because the compilation process depends much on your system.

As you already know, Python provides two development environments that offer a lot of useful features which can help you while coding: Pythonwin and IDLE. However, for simple programs, or in case you don't have a graphical environment available, you can stick to simple text editors that can be used to handle the job very nicely. On Windows systems, you can use editors such as Editpad and Notepad to write Python scripts; on DOS systems, EDIT, and on UNIX systems, you have choices like Pico, Vi, Emacs, and others. Note that Emacs lets you use a special Emacs mode, which is called Python Mode, to write Python programs.

The Python distribution comes with lots of scripts that you can study and use. Those scripts are stored in two directories: `\Tools` and `\Demos`.

Even though a Python bytecode file can automatically be created when importing a module, you can manually create them whenever you need. It is a good idea to bytecompile all files before giving Python access to users that cannot save in that source directory. Otherwise, the interpreter has to byte-compile the module every time the module is loaded, which can slow down program start-up considerably.

After installing Python, some special environment variables can be configured in order to guarantee the maximum usage of the Python environment.

Debugging a Python program is something that doesn't require too much work. The Standard Python Library comes with a debugger module called `bdb` that can be used by you to subclass your own debuggers. If you don't want to spend time writing your own debug, you can use the Python debugger (the `pdb` module), which is also part of the Python distribution. For those who need highly-specialized debugging information, Python provides a disassembler module called `dis`.

The information provided in this chapter also offers a brief overview about how to use the `profile` module to perform the analysis of the runtime performance of a Python program. Profiling an application means to be able to sketch an image about what is going on behind the scenes when you execute a program. In addition to that, it is also shown how to use the `pstats` module, which analyzes the data collected by the Python `profile` module.

When it comes time to distribute your application, you have more than one way to pack your Python files. It depends only on the kind of goal you are trying to reach. The Python distribution contains a tool that saves much time when you are dealing with distribution issues. This tool is called `Freeze`. You have other options too, such as `SqueezeTool` and Gordon McMillan's installer.

PART VI

Python and Java

CHAPTER

CHAPTER **18**

JPython

What a senseless waste of human life

This chapter shows you how easy it is to use all the power of Python within the elasticity of Java. JPython is the keyword for the secret of your success in the Java world.

Welcome to JPython

JPython is a Java implementation of the object-oriented scripting language called Python that has been certified as 100% pure Java. In other words, JPython does not use any of the C code of the original Python implementation. It is a version of Python that runs on top of the Java Virtual Machine. Thus, it allows you to run Python on any Java platform and enables your JPython applications to have access to any Java library that you might need.

JPython offers the same language as Python, but it has a different implementation. Python is a scripting language whose interpreter is written in C, which means that this implementation is called CPython. On the other hand, JPython re-implements the Python parser and interpreter in Java. Actually, the interpreter is available as a Java application, which allows Python programs to be created and seamlessly integrated with the Java platform. Note however that both types of implementation (Python and JPython) have their own pace.

Efforts are made to keep them in sync, but it is not guaranteed that this will always happen.

JPython carries a license that complies with the Open Source definition. It is freely available for both commercial and non-commercial use and is distributed with source code.

JPython was designed by Jim Hugunin, who is also the main author of the Numeric Python extensions. He has joined Guido at CNRI in 1998, leaving in mid-1999 to join the Xerox PARC team in California. When he left, Barry Warsaw took care of the JPython project, and he is the main person responsible for the project since then. Currently, JPython is maintained by Warsaw at BeOpen Python Labs.

At the Web site, you can always obtain the latest information about this implementation and download info. In case you are interested in downloading the source code, it is available via CVS. The latest version of JPython was released in January of 2000. Check out the JPython Official Web site at

```
http://www.jpython.org/
```

If you want to be in touch with other users, JPythoners have their own mailing list that you can use to discuss JPython, ask questions, and help other users as well. Check out the jpython-interest mailing list at

```
http://www.python.org/mailman/listinfo/jpython-interest
```

JPython Features

JPython's core is an interpreter engine, similar to CPython's, that provides support to the greater part of the Standard Python Library. JPython has a set of features that includes

- High-level built-in data types

- Dynamic typing

- Optional static compilation (which allows the creation of beans, applets, servlets, and so forth)

- Java classes and packages support

- A set of support libraries

- Interactive compilation direct to Java bytecodes (which enables JPython programs to run directly on a JVM, including running as applets in Web browser windows).

JPython uses the Java's introspection mechanism to understand the contents of the package, which means that when you want to import a Java library, say something such as

```
import java.awt
```

JPython first tries to find a Python package named `java`. And in case it doesn't find one, it uses the Java mechanism to search in the `CLASSPATH` system variable for a `.class` or `.jar` file that meets the requirement.

Another important aspect of JPython is that you can create JPython classes that subclass Java classes, extending JPython functionality without the need for using wrapper generators (such as SWIG—*Simplified Wrapper and Interface Generator*), provided the functionality is already implemented in Java code. Otherwise, you probably need to use the JNI interface to make the code available to JPython. This allows you to easily use the same set of classes that a regular Java application has access to. The opposite is also true. Java has total integration with JPython, and because JPython is 100% pure Java certified, you might embed JPython in your Java applications without any worries of compromising the portability of your application. If necessary, you can even pass JPython object instances back to Java (executing callbacks), and manipulate these instances in the Java application because any Java code that processes Java objects is also able to process JPython objects.

Sometimes, you might find JPython useful for testing your Java components. As JPython has total integration to the Java implementation, you can use it to call, test, and debug the functionality of Java functions through the interpreter. JPython is the perfect choice for controlling Java through an interactive language.

JPython also handles memory management with care in order to remove from you the responsibility of being worried about object circular references. To do so, it uses the power of the Java memory management mechanism, a mechanism that implements a garbage collector, which is executed at runtime.

JPython's performance is still not as good as the performance of CPython, but there is a lot of effort going on in order to make JVMs run faster.

CPython Versus Jpython

Both CPython and JPython are implementations of the same language: Python. Even though the development team tries to make both codes as compatible as possible, differences are inevitable. Each one of these languages is written using a different programming language: C and Java, respectively. This primary difference is more than enough to cause both codes to have many distinctive characteristics that are unlikely to disappear soon. The following is a short list of differences between both implementations:

- JPython uses a slightly modified interface to handle scientific notation. For example, if you type at the CPython interpreter the command `print 9E+54`, CPython will echo the number `9e+054`, whereas JPython will pop up `9.0E54`.

- JPython has everything implemented to be an instance of a class, which is opposite of CPython.

- JPython doesn't provide access to the `co_code` attribute of code objects because JPython code objects don't have access to any Python bytecodes as CPython code objects do. That's because the JVM hides their existence.

- JPython doesn't allow the use of Python extension modules written in C. If you want to use them, you need to rewrite them in Java, or use JNI to make the C code available to Java.

- JPython offers a Standard Python Library of modules slightly different than CPython does because the built-in modules, which are written in C, need to be ported to Java in order to be used by JPython. Some modules, such as `cPickle`, `cStringIO`, and `binascii`, have already been ported. Another possible option to access the built-in modules is by implementing a JNI bridge.

  By typing `import <modulename>`, and later `dir(<modulename>)`, you can check whether a module is available, and if so, what its interface looks like.

- JPython is able to catch the CTRL+C command when you want to leave the interpreter. However, CPython doesn't accept this shortcut to perform that same functionality.

- JPython implements the garbage collection mechanism native to Java, instead of the reference counting mechanism implemented by CPython.

- JPython doesn't provide any guarantees of telling you exactly when an object is about to be destroyed, as CPython does. Opposite to CPython, the `__del__()` method of the object is never called.

- JPython's interpreter has a set of command line options completely different from the ones recognized by the CPython interpreter.

The following Web page shows all known differences between the two implementations of the Python language, including the ones listed in this topic:

`http://www.jpython.org/docs/differences.html`

JPython Resource Links

A collection of Web links that provide useful information about JPython are as follows:

"Python and Java: The Best of Both Worlds," by Jim Hugunin

```
http://www.python.org/workshops/1997-10/proceedings/hugunin.html
```

"Python Programming in the JVM"

This is a very good and complete article about JPython, written by Rick Hightower.

```
http://www.sys-con.com/java/archives/0503/hightower/index.html
```

See also his other article in the Java Developer's Journal at

```
http://www.sys-con.com/java/archives/0502/hightower/index.html
```

Kirby Angell's article in Dr. Dobb's Journal

```
http://www.ddj.com/articles/1999/9904/9904toc.htm
```

Luke Andrew Cassady-Dorian's article in JavaPro magazine

```
http://www.devx.com/upload/free/features/javapro/1998/12dec98/ld1298/
ld1298.asp
```

"Java and Python: a Perfect Couple." This is an article at Developer.com by Guido van Rossum.

```
http://www.earthweb.com/dlink.resource-jhtml.72.1396.|repository||common|
content|article|19980817|gm_jpython|jpython~xml.0.jhtml?cda=true
```

Python Server Pages

PSP is a freely available server-side scripting engine. It is 100% written in Java, thus, it is portable to several platforms. PSP is mentioned here because it uses JPython as its scripting language. In order to use PSP, you need to have a Web Server that supports Java Servlets, or uses JRun from Live Software, which is a Java Servlet engine recommended for use with PSP.

```
http://www.ciobriefings.com/psp
```

Java Integration

If you want to use the Python language and Java integration, you can find in JPython a compatible and complementary couple for Java. Because JPython's interpreter is written in Java itself, you might think why you shouldn't go directly to the point, and use pure Java instead of using JPython. My advice is to go for JPython first because soon you will see how simple it is to do a lot of tasks using JPython's facilities (such as running a piece of Java code without the need for defining a single class). JPython has all the teaching principles on its background, which makes it a language of easy learning.

The full object-oriented programming model provided by the Python language (since its inception) brings power and clearness to the programmer world. This transparency when handling objects makes Python a natural choice for interoperating with Java's object-oriented design, and to be Java's scripting language. Other languages try, even though they were not created to be OO. Object-oriented programming became part of Perl programmer's life in version 5, and Tcl developers can only use OO through an extension called (itcl). It could be argued that Python evolved from the non-object oriented *ABC* the same way that Perl 5 evolved from Perl 4 and *incr tcl* from *tcl*, but Python had its evolutionary process carefully driven—almost a totally new development effort.

Of course, other scripting languages can be used along with Java and its JVM, but none of them beat JPython in portability and performance, mainly for two reasons: JPython's 100% Java certification, and JPython's capability to translate Python source code directly into optimized Java bytecodes, respectively.

Both Perl and Tcl offer scripting solutions, but none of the solutions offer a more significant value than the JPython solution.

- `Jacl` is a 100% Java re-design of the Tcl interpreter, which is considered to be much slower than JPython.

- `Tcl Blend` and `JPL` (for Perl) are other scripting solutions (not 100% Java) that expose some portability problems.

Of course, in both of these cases, it is probably easier to port the Tcl or Perl runtimes than to port the java virtual machine.

For more details about the Java language, you can check out `http://www.javasoft.com/`.

Java Certification

On July 13, 1998, it was announced that KeyLabs had completed testing JPython to certify that it is 100% pure Java.

> The 100% Pure Java Certification Program is part of Sun Microsystems initiative to promote the development of portable applications, applets, beans, class libraries, and servlets written using the Java Programming language. Certification consists of code analysis and testing by an independent test facility (in this case, KeyLabs) to identify compiled code that meets the 100% Pure Java Requirements. The 100% Pure Java certification standards and branding program is intended to give customers confidence in products that display the brand.

Even though JPython has got this certification, you cannot use the 100% Java brand for your own JPython programs. You need to make sure that your product passes the 100% Pure Java certification tests in order to have the rights to use the exclusive 100% Pure Java logo on your packing. For details about this process, read the Certification Guide located at

```
http://www.javasoft.com/100percent/
```

Java Links

If you want to use JPython, but you don't know Java yet, or need a quick review, check out the following Java Web sites:

The Java Community

At this Web site, you can join ongoing forums on a variety of Java topics, chat with Java experts, and access community resources, among other things.

```
http://developer.java.sun.com/developer/community
```

The Java Tutorial—a practical guide for programmers

```
http://java.sun.com/docs/books/tutorial
```

Downloading and Installing JPython

Next, you find the required steps that you need to perform in order to download and install JPython. Visit the following address, and download the latest version.

```
http://www.jpython.org/download.html
```

You have two choices for downloading JPython. You can either download the JPython version that contains the OROMatcher regular expression library, or the other version that doesn't contain it. Note that it's required that you decide between the two versions. Only if you decide to use the version that comes with the OROMatcher, will you have access to the re module. However, you will have to agree with a different kind of licensing.

Before spending time downloading the file, verify whether you have a working Java 1.1 or 1.2 compatible JVM installed. In case you don't have one, you will need to locate one on the Internet and install the right JVM for your system.

JPython is distributed as a self-extracting .class file created by InstallShield - Java Edition. To install JPython, you need to open the command line to the directory in which you have placed the JPython11.class file. Note that if you have downloaded the JPythonONLY11.class file, you must first rename it to JPython11.class.

```
ren JPythonONLY11.class JPython11.class
```

Then, type the following command to start the installation process.

```
<java interpreter> JPython11
```

Depending on your system, you have to type one of the following options. Note that you don't have to include the .class on the end of the filename.

```
java JPython11
jre JPython11
jview JPython11
```

In case you don't have a GUI, you need to add the following argument to the previous command: -o dir_to_install_to. JPython will install to the specified directory without activating the graphical installer.

After initiating the installation process, you will be prompted to accept the terms of the license (see Figure 18.1). Read it and say yes to continue with the process.

Remember to check the Installation Notes after completing the installation.

Now, you should be able to run JPython by typing the following command:

```
jpython
```

If you are using a Windows system, you can have access to JPython by double-clicking on its icon.

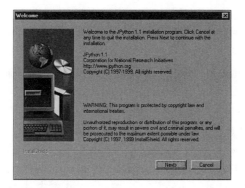

Figure 18.1
When you accept the terms of the license, JPython is installed on your system.

Downloading the CPython Library

As of now, JPython comes with support for only a small set of the standard Python modules. For those who will concentrate on development using Java packages, the modules provided by JPython should be fine, but note that CPython has a wide variety of useful modules.

If you already have CPython 1.5.1, 1.5.2, or a later version installed on your computer, you can use its library. If you don't have CPython installed, you can get its libraries from the JPython Web site. For example, the libraries for version 1.5.2 are stored in the following file:

```
http://www.jpython.org/pylib152e.jar
```

To install the standard Python libraries, use the following command:

```
jpython -jar pylib152e.jar
```

Besides the regular distribution download page, the latest snapshots of the JPython source code are always available via CVS too.

Licensing

Starting with version 1.1 beta 1, JPython has two separate distributions. This is because JPython uses a third-party library for handling regular expressions—the standard re module is implemented using OROMatcher, which is a regular expression library by ORO, Inc.

Because `OROMatcher` has a different kind of license, the JPython distribution that uses it requires a specific license as well because `OROMatcher` is not completely free software. (It doesn't allow you to have access to its source code.)

Currently, at the ORO Web site, you can find a note saying that the company plans to open source their software, releasing it under the Apache license, so the restrictions on using `OROMatcher` might be lifted. You should keep an eye on that.

However, JPython provides another distribution that comes without the library, which makes the regular expression capability not available. This distribution is a completely open source version of JPython. Note that if later you decide to use `OROMatcher`, you can accept its licensing agreement, and integrate it with the free distribution of JPython that you already have. Check out the OROMatcher site at

```
http://www.savarese.org/oro/
```

JVMs That Support JPython

As of now, JPython should run successfully on any bug-free fully 1.1 or 1.2 compliant Java Virtual Machine (JVM). Next, you have a list of Operating System specific JVMs. Even if your platform is not listed here, it doesn't mean that it doesn't have a JVM.

Linux

JDK 1.1.x and 1.2.x from blackdown.org—It is suggested that you use either the 1.1.7 JVM or 1.2 JVM.

```
http://www.blackdown.org/java-linux.html
```

IBM Developer Kit and Runtime Environment for Linux—This is IBM's new JVM for Linux.

```
http://www.ibm.com/java/jdk/118/linux/index.html
```

Sun's J2SE (1.2.2 JVM) for Linux—This is Sun's JVM ported to Linux. You need a free login to access the Sun Developer Connection.

```
http://developer.java.sun.com/
```

Win32 (Windows NT, 95, and 98)

JView from Microsoft—This JVM is installed when you install Microsoft Internet Explorer 4.0 or 5.0. Currently, this is the fastest JVM on which to run JPython.

```
http://www.microsoft.com/java/
```

Sun's JVM for Windows—Sun provides 1.2 (Java 2) and 1.1 Virtual Machines for the Windows platform. This is certainly the most compatible VM with the official Java specification.

```
http://www.javasoft.com/products/
```

Solaris

Although Solaris 2.6 comes with JDK 1.1.3, Solaris users will probably want to upgrade to either the JRE 1.1.7 or JRE 1.2.1 at least.

JRE 1.1.7 from Sun

```
http://www.javasoft.com/products/jdk/1.1/jre/index.html
```

JRE 1.2.1 from Sun

```
http://www.javasoft.com/products/jdk/1.2/
```

Irix

Here, you can get version 3.1 of the Java Development Environment from SGI, which is based on the 1.1.3 JVM.

```
http://www.sgi.com/developers/devtools/languages/java.html
```

Macintosh

Mizutori Tetsuya has made available an application called JPython Runner to make it easier to use JPython on Macintoshes.

```
http://www.bekkoame.ne.jp/~mizutori/java/index.html#jpythonrunner
```

See also the document "How to Run JPython on Macintosh."

```
http://www.bekkoame.ne.jp/~mizutori/java/index.html#howtojpython
```

The Interpreter

The JPython installation places several files on your system, including a set of modules, some sample programs, an application called jpythonc (which we will see later), and the JPython interpreter.

The JPython interpreter looks very similar to the CPython interpreter (see Figure 18.2). However, jpython is not a binary file, but a short script (or batch file, depending on your system) that invokes your local JVM, sets the Java property `install.path` to an appropriate value, and then runs the Java class file `org.python.util.jpython`.

Figure 18.2
If you glance at this screen, you might be confused whether JPython or CPython is running because both interpreters do look alike.

The following syntax shows the possible options that you can pass to JPython when invoking it from the shell. A list of options is shown in Table 18.1.

```
jpython [options] [-jar jar | -c cmd | file | -] [args]
```

Table 18.1   *List of the Interpreter Options and Arguments*

Option	Description
-i	Inspects interactively after running script and forces prompts, even if `stdin` does not appear to be a terminal.
-S	Doesn't imply import site on initialization.
-X	Disables class based standard exceptions.
-D*prop=value*	Sets the Java property `prop` to `value`.
-jar jar	Runs the program that is read from the `__run__`.py file in the specified `jar` file.
-c cmd	Runs the program passed in as the `cmd` string. This option terminates the options list.
file	Runs file as the program script.
-	Reads the program from standard input. This flag allows you to pipe a file into Jpython and have it treated correctly.
--help	Prints a usage message and exits.
--version	Prints JPython version number and exits.
args	Passes a list of arguments to the program in the `sys.argv[1:]` variable.

Because jpython is not a binary executable, but a simple script, you have to add the following line to the top of your JPython programs (only if you have a UNIX system), in order to make them executable.

```
#! /usr/bin/env jpython
```

Using something like #!/usr/bin/jpython/jpython will not work because this syntax requires jpython to be a binary executable (which is not the case).

You also need to make sure that jpython's directory is registered on your PATH variable.

Now let's take a look at the following code:

```
class jhello:
    def main(argv):
        print "Hello Python world!"


myapp=jhello()
myapp.main()
```

After saving this code in a file, called jhello.py, you can execute it by typing at your OS prompt:

```
jpython jhello.py
```

The JPython Registry

JPython, as Java, uses its own environment variable namespace. The reason for that is because there isn't a standard cross-platform way to handle environment variables, doing what the Windows Registry does for the Win32 platform, for example.

The required namespace can be obtained from the following sources:

1. The Java system properties, which are usually informed through the -D option on the command line prompt of the interpreter.

2. The JPython registry file, which contains prop=value pairs. The location of this file is identified according to the algorithm listed in the next subtopic.

3. The user's personal registry file, which contains correspondingly prop=value pairs of properties. This file is located at *user.home*"+"/.jpython.

The previous sources are listed in the same order in which they are invoked when trying to build the namespace. Note that if you have values provided for later options, they override the values defined by default for the prior options.

Registry Properties

Next is a list of the properties that are recognized by the JPython interpreter. You can easily study these and others, with more accuracy, by examining the JPython's registry file.

python.cachedir—Stores the name of the directory to use for caches. If no absolute path is informed, it is assumed that its location is relative to the sys.prefix variable.

python.jpythonc.classpath—Stores a list of extensions to the standard java.class.path property for use with jpythonc.

python.jpythonc.compiler—Contains the absolute (or relative) path of the Java compiler to use with jpythonc. If just the compiler name is provided, it is assumed that the executable can be located by looking at your system PATH variable.

python.jpythonc.compileropts—Keeps the list of options to pass to the Java compiler when using jpythonc.

python.path—Corresponds to CPython's PYTHONPATH environment variable.

python.security.respectJavaAccessibility—Setting this property to false (in case you have a Java 1.2 installation) provides you access to non-public members of classes, such as methods and constructors.

python.verbose—Setting this property to one of the following values:

"error", "warning", "message", "comment", "debug"

sets the verbosity level for varying degrees of informative messages. Note that these values are listed in order of increasing verbosity.

Finding the Registry File

The following steps are required to correctly identify the JPython registry file to use.

1. You need to create a root directory, which can be based either on the value of the property python.home, or the value of the property install.root, whichever is found first.

2. If none of them is found, JPython tries to locate a file called `jpython.jar` by looking at the system property `java.class.path`. Note that one of the paths listed in this property must explicitly include the `jpython.jar` file.

3. Now, that JPython has identified our root directory, it populates the values of both `sys.prefix` and `sys.exec_prefix` variables based on the root information.

4. The variable `sys.path` has an entry added to its list, `<rootdir>/Lib`, where `<rootdir>` is the root dir that we've found previously.

5. Our initial goal can be finally reached now because the registry file is stored at the `<rootdir>` directory, and to have permission to it, you just need to access the location `<rootdir>/registry`.

Creating Graphical Interfaces

Windowing applications are written in JPython using the same set of options that you have available for Java applications. Currently, the two names that you will hear most for this kind of implementation are `awt` and `swing`.

AWT stands for *Abstract Windowing Toolkit*, which is the official name for the Java GUI. Note that the syntax is very similar to Tkinter, thus it will not be a problem for you to understand and use it.

```
import java
frame = java.awt.Frame("Ni!", visible = 1)
labeltop = java.awt.Label("Hello Python World!")
frame.add(labeltop)
frame.pack()
```

JPython also contains a package called `pawt` (stands for Python AWT), which wrappes the access to `awt`, providing some additional functionality.

The successor of Java's windowing toolkit is provided as part of the Java Foundation Classes. This set of classes extends the original AWT by adding a comprehensive set of graphical user interface class libraries, commonly known as *JFC/Swing* GUI Components, or simply *Swing*. These components are simple to read and understand, and they are written in the Java programming language, without window-system–specific code. This causes less problems when distributing JPython applications because you do not rely on the code of a specific windowing system.

For details, see `http://java.sun.com/products/jfc/`.

At this page, you can download the latest version of the Java Foundation Classes (JFC)/Swing, which at this moment is in release 1.1.1. After downloading it, make sure that you have the following environment variables correctly defined: JAVA_HOME, SWING_HOME, CLASSPATH, and PATH.

Next, you have the section of the autoexec.bat of my Win98 machine that handles these definitions, for your information.

```
set JAVA_HOME=C:\JDK1.1.8
set SWING_HOME=C:\JDK1.1.8\swing-1.1.1
set PATH=%PATH%;%JAVA_HOME%\bin
set CLASSPATH=.;%JAVA_HOME%\lib\classes.zip
set CLASSPATH=%CLASSPATH%;%SWING_HOME%;%SWING_HOME%\swing.jar;
set CLASSPATH=%CLASSPATH%;%SWING_HOME%\windows.jar
```

The next code shows an example that uses the Python package pawt to access the swing components.

```
import java
import pawt
def exit(h):
    java.lang.System.exit(0)
frame = pawt.swing.JFrame('Ni! again!', visible=1)
display = pawt.swing.JTextField()
display.text = "Click on the button below to exit!"
frame.contentPane.add(display)
button = pawt.swing.JButton('Exit', actionPerformed=exit)
frame.contentPane.add(button)
frame.pack()
```

Embedding

As JPython and Java are extremely close to each other, it is not difficult to believe that you can embed JPython code inside a Java application, as well as embed Java code directly into your JPython applications. Both types of implementation are easily supported and coded. By extension, you could create new independent Python interpreters from jpython very easily, as well.

JPython in a Java Application

If you really need to embed JPython in a Java application, you have two main choices to choose from. The first option is to use the utility jpythonc to pick a JPython class and generate a Java .class file that can be called directly from inside your Java code, in a very straightforward away. See the next section of this chapter to learn how to use this utility.

The second option that you have is to import the PythonInterpreter object class into your Java code. This class allows you to have control of the Python interpreter from Java. The following example demonstrates how the code would be:

```
import org.python.util.PythonInterpreter;
import org.python.core.*;

public class GenNextYear {
    public static void main(String []args)
    throws PyException
    {
        PythonInterpreter interp = new PythonInterpreter();
        System.out.println("Hello Python World");
        interp.set("year", new PyInteger(2000));
        interp.exec("print 'This is year %d' % (age)");
        interp.exec("nextyear = year + 1");
        PyObject nyear = interp.get("nextyear");
        System.out.println("Next year is gonna be "+nyear);
    }
}
```

Note that we are able to set/access values to/from the interpreter besides executing commands at the interpreter prompt line.

Check the JavaDoc documentation located at the following address. It is all about org.python.util.PythonInterpreter.

http://www.jpython.org/docs/api/org.python.util.PythonInterpreter.html

Java in a JPython Application

Accessing Java from JPython is no big deal. You can normally work with Java libraries as if you were working with JPython libraries. The process is fully transparent to you. Remember that one of JPython's primary goals is to provide easy support to Java libraries.

JPython offers you access to all Java functionality available, which includes

- Support to JavaBean Properties. The use of JavaBeans is seen by JPython as a solution to simplify the task of talking to most other Java classes.

- If you need to handle Java Arrays in JPython, you need to use the `Jarray` object. Remember that some Java methods demand argument objects to be in Java array format.

Also good to remember is you can create Python classes that subclass Java classes. This is a helpful option when you need to pass information back and forth between both implementations (Python and Java). Note that you need to create a Python class with the same name of the module that carries class.

The following example shows how a user can instantiate a Java random number class and then interact with that instance:

```
C:\jpython>jpython
>>> from java.util import Random
>>> number = Random()
>>> number.nextInt()
-857296727
>>> print number.nextDouble()
0.5334538483666526
>>> number.nextInt()
-356857265
```

Note that we are establishing direct access to the Java library without using any kind of wrappers.

The following site is part of the original documentation showing how to use JPython along with Java:

```
http://www.jpython.com/docs/usejava.html
```

jpythonc

The JPython distribution provides a tool called `jpythonc` that works like a Python compiler for Java. This tool, which is actually just a JPython script, operates by taking a JPython source code (extension `.py`), and compiling it to real Java class bytecodes, which are executed by the *Java Runtime Environment (JRE)*. Therefore you can write your code in JPython, and later use `jpythonc` to generate a simple class, a JavaBean, a servlet, or an applet. Note that you need full access to a Java compiler in order to use `jpythonc`. Internally, the `jpythonc` tool creates a Java source file file, but it needs an external compiler to generate the compiled Java `.class` file.

Check the installation directory where you installed the JPython package. That's where the tool is located.

The `jpythonc` tool is very useful for embedding your JPython application in a Java application. After you generate the `.class` file, you are able to subclass Python classes in Java, and also to create JavaBeans, Servlets, and Applets from a Python class file.

The `jpythonc` script accepts several command line options, as listed next. The general format of the command's syntax is as follows:

```
jpythonc [options] [module]*
```

The available options are listed as follows. Note that the information provided between parenthesis shows a short way to say the same thing that the long name's option says.

`--package package`   (`-p package`)—Puts all compiled code into the named Java package.

`--jar jarfile`   (`-j jarfile`)—Specifies a `.jar` file to create and put the results of the freeze into. This option implies the `--deep` option.

`--deep`   (`-d`)—Compiles all Python dependencies of the module. This is used for creating applets.

`--core`   (`-c`)—Includes the core JPython libraries (about 130K). Needed for applets because Netscape doesn't yet support multiple archives. This option implies the `--deep` option.

`--all`   (`-a`)—Includes all the JPython libraries (everything in core + compiler and parser). This option implies the `--deep` option.

`--bean jarfile`   (`-b jarfile`)—Compiles into `jarfile`, including the correct manifest for the bean.

`--addpackages pkgs`   (`-A pkgs`)—Includes Java dependencies from this list of packages. Default is `org.python.modules` and `com.oroinc.text.regex`.

`--workdir directory`   (`-w directory`)—Specifies the working directory where the generated Java source code is placed. The default value is `./jpywork`.

`--skip modules`   (`-s modules`)—Doesn't include any of these modules in compilation. This is a comma-separated list of modules.

`--compiler path`   (`-C path`)—Uses a compiler different from `javac`. If this is set to `NONE`, compiles end with the generation of the Java source file. Alternatively, you can set the property `python.jpythonc.compiler` in the registry file.

`--compileropts options--`   (`-J options`)—Passes options directly to the Java compiler. Alternatively, you can set the property `python.jpythonc.compileropts` in the registry file.

`--falsenames names`   (`-f names`)—A comma-separated list of names that are always false. Can be used to short-circuit if clauses.

`--help`   (`-h`)—Prints a usage message and exits.

`[module]*`—A list of Python modules to freeze. Can be either module names that are located on the `python.path` or `.py` files.

In order to create an applet, the following syntax is suggested. Note that you need to use the `-core` option in order to include the JPython libraries as part of the applet.

```
jpythonc -core -deep -jar <appletapp.jar> *.py
```

In order to create a simple class, the following syntax is suggested:

```
jpythonc <yourapp.py>
```

Now, if you just need to create a bean, the following syntax should be used:

```
jpythonc -deep -bean <filename.jar> <beenname>
```

Running JPython Applets

Many people like Java because it makes easy the task of distributing interactive and dynamic pieces of code through the Web by using applets. An applet is a program written using the Java programming language, which can be included in an HTML page with the `<APPLET>` tag. This tag needs to reference a class file that is not part of the HTML page on which it is embedded. Applets do this with the CODE parameter, which tells the browser where to look for the compiled `.class` file. When your browser receives a request to load an applet from a site, it downloads the applet and uses your Java Virtual Machine to execute it.

Before you start testing your applets, make sure that you are using a browser that supports Java jdk1.1. The list of browsers that are currently jdk1.1-compliant include Microsoft's Internet Explorer 4.0 or later, and Netscape's Navigator 4.06 or later.

Okay. Now you also need to make sure that you don't have your class path variable pointing to any directories with JPython `.class` files. If you are running JVM on

UNIX, you need to check out your `CLASSPATH` environment variable. If you are running a Win32 virtual machine, you need to check out the registry entry `Classpath` under `LOCAL_MACHINE/Software/Microsoft/JavaVM/`.

The next JPython applet has the goal of displaying the message `"Hello Python World"`.

```
from java.applet import Applet
class HelloPythonWorld(Applet):
    def paint(self, gc):
        gc.drawString("Hello Python World", 12, 14)
```

If you want to test the applet to run it as a script too, add a few more lines to the end of the applet file. These lines will allow you to interactively test the applet functionality.

```
if __name__ == '__main__':
    import pawt
    pawt.test(HelloPythonWorld())
```

If you want to embed this applet in your Web page, you just need to inform the right values for the `applet` tag, such as

```
<applet code="HelloPythonWorld" archive="HelloPythonWorld.jar"
 width = 50 height = 100>
```

JPython applets need to carry the whole set of JPython libraries, which adds about 150KB to the final size of your applet. Another important consideration is that you can only use `eval` and `exec` commands in signed applets, which complies with the Java security definition.

The following Web link takes you to the official home of JPython, specifically to the applets page:

```
http://www.jpython.org/applets/
```

Summary

JPython is a Java implementation of the object-oriented scripting language Python that has been certified as 100% pure Java. Both CPython and JPython are implementations of the same language: Python. Even though the development team tries to make both codes as compatible as possible, differences are inevitable. Each one of these languages is written using a different programming language: C and Java, respectively. Note that JPython re-implements the CPython parser and interpreter in Java.

JPython has a set of features that include high-level built-in data types, dynamic typing, optional static compilation, Java classes and packages support, a set of support libraries, and interactive compilation direct to Java bytecodes.

JPython, as Java, uses its own environment variable namespace. The reason for that is because there isn't a standard cross-platform way to handle environment variables.

Windowing applications are written in JPython using the same set of options that you have available for Java applications. Currently, the two names that you will hear most for this kind of implementation are *awt* and *swing*.

As JPython and Java are extremely close to each other, it is not that difficult to believe that you can embed JPython code inside a Java application, as well as embed Java code directly into your JPython applications. Both types of implementation are easily supported and coded.

The JPython distribution provides a tool called `jpythonc` that works like a Python compiler for Java. Therefore you can write your code in JPython, and later use `jpythonc` to generate a simple class, a JavaBean, a servlet, or an applet.

PART VII

Appendixes

APPENDIX **A**

Python/C API

The intention of this appendix is to expose the C API that you need to use in order to create extension modules for your Python programs or to embed Python in your C/C++ applications. The information provided in this appendix is entirely extracted from the C/API reference manual, written by Guido van Rossum, which is part of the Python distribution (see copyright note in Appendix C, "Python Copyright Notices"). Note, however, that as you're reading, this document might be incomplete because new Python versions will be arriving soon. Check out the following address for the most up-to-date version of this work:

```
http://www.python.org/doc/api
```

For more information about how to use the API, check out Chapter 6, "Extending and Embedding Python," and the document *"Extending and Embedding the Python Interpreter,"* which also comes as part of the Python installation.

Python/C API

The Application Programmer's Interface to Python gives C and C++ programmers access to the Python interpreter at a variety of levels. The API is equally usable from C++, but for brevity it is generally referred to as the Python/C API. There are two fundamentally different reasons for using the Python/C API. The first reason is to write extension modules for specific purposes; these are C modules that extend the Python interpreter. This is probably the most common use. The second reason is to use Python as a component in a larger application; this technique is generally referred to as embedding Python in an application.

Writing an extension module is a relatively well-understood process in which a "cookbook" approach works well. Several tools automate the process to some extent. Although people have embedded Python in other applications since its early existence, the process of embedding Python is less straightforward than writing an extension.

Many API functions are useful independent of whether you're embedding or extending Python; moreover, most applications that embed Python will need to provide a custom extension as well, so it's probably a good idea to become familiar with writing an extension before attempting to embed Python in a real application.

Python 1.5 introduces a number of new API functions as well as some changes to the build process that make embedding much simpler. This book describes the 1.5.2 state of affairs.

Include Files

All function, type, and macro definitions needed to use the Python/C API are included in your code by the following line:

```
#include "Python.h"
```

This implies inclusion of the following standard headers: <stdio.h>, <string.h>, <errno.h>, and <stdlib.h> (if available).

All user visible names defined by Python.h (except those defined by the included standard headers) have one of the prefixes Py or _Py. Names beginning with _Py are for internal use by the Python implementation and should not be used by extension writers. Structure member names do not have a reserved prefix.

Important: User code should never define names that begin with Py or _Py. This confuses the reader and jeopardizes the portability of the user code to future Python versions, which might define additional names beginning with one of these prefixes.

The header files are typically installed with Python. On UNIX, these are located in the directories $prefix/include/pythonversion/ and $exec_prefix/include/pythonversion/, where $prefix and $exec_prefix are defined by the corresponding parameters to Python's configure script and the version is sys.version[:3]. On Windows, the headers are installed in $prefix/include, where $prefix is the installation directory specified to the installer.

To include the headers, place both directories (if different) on your compiler's search path for includes. Do not place the parent directories on the search path and then use `#include <python1.5/Python.h>`; this will break on multi-platform builds because the platform independent headers under `$prefix` include the platform specific headers from `$exec_prefix`.

Objects, Types, and Reference Counts

Most Python/C API functions have one or more arguments as well as a return value of type `PyObject*`. This type is a pointer to an opaque data type representing an arbitrary Python object. Because all Python object types are treated the same way by the Python language in most situations (for example, assignments, scope rules, and argument passing), it is only fitting that they should be represented by a single C type. Almost all Python objects live on the heap: You never declare an automatic or static variable of type PyObject; only pointer variables of type `PyObject*` can be declared. The sole exceptions are the type objects; because these must never be deallocated, they are typically static `PyTypeObject` objects.

All Python objects (even Python integers) have a type and a reference count. An object's type determines what kind of object it is (for example, an integer, a list, or a user-defined function; there are many more as explained in the Python Reference Manual). For each of the well-known types, there is a macro to check whether an object is of that type; for instance, `PyList_Check(a)` is true if (and only if) the object it points to is a Python list.

Reference Counts

The reference count is important because today's computers have a finite (and often severely limited) memory size; it counts how many different places there are that have a reference to an object. Such a place could be another object, a global (or static) C variable, or a local variable in some C function. When an object's reference count becomes zero, the object is deallocated. If it contains references to other objects, their reference count is decremented. Those other objects might be deallocated in turn, if this decrement makes their reference count become zero, and so on. (There's an obvious problem with objects that reference each other here; for now, the solution is don't do that.)

Reference counts are always manipulated explicitly. The normal way is to use the macro `Py_INCREF()` to increment an object's reference count by one, and `Py_DECREF()` to decrement it by one. The decref macro is considerably more complex than the incref one because it must check whether the reference count becomes zero, and then causes the object's deallocation by calling a function contained in the object's type structure. The type-specific deallocator takes care of decrementing the reference counts for other objects contained in the object, and so on, if this is a compound object type such as a list. There's no chance that the reference count can overflow; at least as many bits are used to hold the reference count as there are distinct memory locations in virtual memory (assuming `sizeof(long) >= sizeof(char *)`). Thus, the reference count increment is a simple operation. You should only pass a variable to `Py_DECREF` or `Py_XDECREF`. If you pass an expression, it will be evaluated multiple times (so don't use `Py_XDECREF(func(...))` to ignore the return value of a function).

It is not necessary to increment an object's reference count for every local variable that contains a pointer to an object. In theory, the object's reference count goes up by one when the variable is made to point to it, and it goes down by one when the variable goes out of scope. However, these two cancel each other out, so at the end, the reference count hasn't changed. The only real reason to use the reference count is to prevent the object from being deallocated as long as our variable is pointing to it. If we know that there is at least one other reference to the object that lives at least as long as our variable, there is no need to increment the reference count temporarily. An important situation in which this arises is in objects that are passed as arguments to C functions in an extension module that are called from Python; the call mechanism guarantees to hold a reference to every argument for the duration of the call.

However, a common pitfall is to extract an object from a list and hold on to it for a while without incrementing its reference count. Some other operation might conceivably remove the object from the list, decrementing its reference count, and possibly deallocating it. The real danger is that innocent-looking operations might invoke arbitrary Python code that could do this; there is a code path that allows control to flow back to the user from a `Py_DECREF()`, so almost any operation is potentially dangerous.

A safe approach is to always use the generic operations (functions whose name begins with `PyObject_`, `PyNumber_`, `PySequence_`, or `PyMapping_`). These operations always increment the reference count of the object they return. This leaves the caller with the responsibility to call `Py_DECREF()` when they are done with the result; this soon becomes second nature.

Reference Count Details

The reference count behavior of functions in the Python/C API is best explained in terms of ownership of references. Note that we talk of owning references, never of owning objects; objects are always shared. When a function owns a reference, it has to dispose of it properly—either by passing ownership on (usually to its caller) or by calling `Py_DECREF()` or `Py_XDECREF()`. When a function passes ownership of a reference on to its caller, the caller is said to receive a new reference. When no ownership is transferred, the caller is said to borrow the reference. Nothing needs to be done for a borrowed reference.

Conversely, when calling a function passes it a reference to an object, there are two possibilities: The function steals a reference to the object, or it does not. Few functions steal references; the two notable exceptions are PyList_SetItem() and PyTuple_SetItem(), which steal a reference to the item (but not to the tuple or list into which the item is put). These functions were designed to steal a reference because of a common idiom for populating a tuple or list with newly created objects; for example, the code to create the tuple (1, 2, "three") could look similar to this (forget about error handling for the moment):

```
PyObject *t;
t = PyTuple_New(3);
PyTuple_SetItem(t, 0, PyInt_FromLong(1L));
PyTuple_SetItem(t, 1, PyInt_FromLong(2L));
PyTuple_SetItem(t, 2, PyString_FromString("three"));
```

Incidentally, PyTuple_SetItem() is the only way to set tuple items; PySequence_SetItem() and PyObject_SetItem() refuse to do this because tuples are an immutable data type. You should only use PyTuple_SetItem() for tuples that you are creating yourself.

Equivalent code for populating a list can be written using PyList_New() and PyList_SetItem(). Such code can also use PySequence_SetItem(); this illustrates the difference between the two (the extra Py_DECREF() calls):

```
PyObject *l, *x;
l = PyList_New(3);
x = PyInt_FromLong(1L);
PySequence_SetItem(l, 0, x); Py_DECREF(x);
x = PyInt_FromLong(2L);
PySequence_SetItem(l, 1, x); Py_DECREF(x);
x = PyString_FromString("three");
PySequence_SetItem(l, 2, x); Py_DECREF(x);
```

You might find it strange that the recommended approach takes more code. However, in practice, you will rarely use these ways of creating and populating a tuple or list. There's a generic function, Py_BuildValue(), that can create most common objects from C values, directed by a format string. For example, the previous two blocks of code could be replaced by the following (which also takes care of the error checking):

```
PyObject *t, *l;
t = Py_BuildValue("(iis)", 1, 2, "three");
l = Py_BuildValue("[iis]", 1, 2, "three");
```

It is more common to use `PyObject_SetItem()` and become friends with items whose references you are only borrowing, like arguments that were passed in to the function you are writing. In that case, their behavior regarding reference counts is much saner because you don't have to increment a reference count so you can give a reference away (have it be stolen). For example, this function sets all items of a list (actually, any mutable sequence) to a given item:

```
int set_all(PyObject *target, PyObject *item)
{
    int i, n;
    n = PyObject_Length(target);
    if (n < 0)
        return -1;
    for (i = 0; i < n; i++) {
        if (PyObject_SetItem(target, i, item) < 0)
            return -1;
    }
    return 0;
}
```

The situation is slightly different for function return values. Although passing a reference to most functions does not change your ownership responsibilities for that reference, many functions that return a reference to an object give you ownership of the reference. The reason is simple: In many cases, the returned object is created on-the-fly, and the reference you get is the only reference to the object. Therefore, the generic functions that return object references, such as `PyObject_GetItem()` and `PySequence_GetItem()`, always return a new reference (that is, the caller becomes the owner of the reference).

It is important to realize that whether you own a reference returned by a function only depends on which function you call—the plumage (that is, the type of the object passed as an argument to the function) doesn't enter into it. Thus, if you extract an item from a list using `PyList_GetItem()`, you don't own the reference—but if you obtain the same item from the same list using `PySequence_GetItem()` (which happens to take exactly the same arguments), you do own a reference to the returned object.

Here is an example of how you could write a function that computes the sum of the items in a list of integers; once using `PyList_GetItem()`, once using `PySequence_GetItem()`:

```
long sum_list(PyObject *list)
{
    int i, n;
    long total = 0;
```

```
        PyObject *item;

        n = PyList_Size(list);
        if (n < 0)
            return -1; /* Not a list */
        for (i = 0; i < n; i++) {
            item = PyList_GetItem(list, i); /* Can't fail */
            if (!PyInt_Check(item)) continue; /* Skip non-integers */
            total += PyInt_AsLong(item);
        }
        return total;
}
long sum_sequence(PyObject *sequence)
{
        int i, n;
        long total = 0;
        PyObject *item;
        n = PyObject_Size(list);
        if (n < 0)
            return -1; /* Has no length */
        for (i = 0; i < n; i++) {
            item = PySequence_GetItem(list, i);
            if (item == NULL)
                return -1; /* Not a sequence, or other failure */
            if (PyInt_Check(item))
                total += PyInt_AsLong(item);
            Py_DECREF(item); /* Discard reference ownership */
        }
        return total;
}
```

Types

Few other data types play a significant role in the Python/C API; most are simple C types such as int, long, double, and char *. A few structure types are used to describe static tables used to list the functions exported by a module or the data attributes of a new object type. These will be discussed together with the functions that use them.

Exceptions

The Python programmer only needs to deal with exceptions if specific error handling is required; unhandled exceptions are automatically propagated to the caller, and then to the caller's caller, and so on, until they reach the top-level interpreter, where they are reported to the user accompanied by a stack traceback.

For C programmers, however, error checking always has to be explicit. All functions in the Python/C API can raise exceptions, unless an explicit claim is made otherwise in a function's documentation. In general, when a function encounters an error, it sets an exception, discards any object references that it owns, and returns an error indicator— usually NULL or -1. A few functions return a Boolean true/false result, with false indicating an error. Very few functions return no explicit error indicator or have an ambiguous return value and require explicit testing for errors with PyErr_Occurred()

Exception state is maintained in per-thread storage (this is equivalent to using global storage in an unthreaded application). A thread can be in one of two states: An exception has occurred, or it hasn't. The function PyErr_Occurred() can be used to check for this: It returns a borrowed reference to the exception type object when an exception has occurred, and NULL otherwise. There are a number of functions to set the exception state: PyErr_SetString() is the most common (though not the most general) function to set the exception state, and PyErr_Clear() clears the exception state.

The full exception state consists of three objects (all of which can be NULL): the exception type, the corresponding exception value, and the traceback. These have the same meanings as the Python object sys.exc_type, sys.exc_value, sys.exc_traceback; however, they are not the same: The Python objects represent the last exception being handled by a Python try ... except statement, whereas the C level exception state only exists while an exception is being passed on between C functions until it reaches the Python interpreter, which takes care of transferring it to sys.exc_type and friends.

Note that starting with Python 1.5, the preferred, thread-safe way to access the exception state from Python code is to call the function sys.exc_info(), which returns the per-thread exception state for Python code. Also, the semantics of both ways to access the exception state have changed so that a function which catches an exception will save and restore its thread exception state to preserve the exception state of its caller. This prevents common bugs in exception handling code caused by an innocent-looking function overwriting the exception being handled; it also reduces the often unwanted lifetime extension for objects that are referenced by the stack frames in the traceback.

As a general principle, a function that calls another function to perform some task should check whether the called function raised an exception, and if so, pass the exception state on to its caller. It should discard any object references that it owns, and returns an error indicator, but it should not set another exception—that would overwrite the exception just raised and lose important information about the exact cause of the error.

A simple example of detecting exceptions and passing them on is shown in the previous sum_sequence() example. It so happens that the example doesn't need to clean up any owned references when it detects an error. The following example function shows some error cleanup. First, to remind you why you like Python, we show the equivalent Python code:

```python
def incr_item(dict, key):
    try:
        item = dict[key]
    except KeyError:
        item = 0
    return item + 1
```

Here is the corresponding C code, in all its glory:

```c
int incr_item(PyObject *dict, PyObject *key)
{
    /* Objects all initialized to NULL for Py_XDECREF */
    PyObject *item = NULL, *const_one = NULL, *incremented_item = NULL;
    int rv = -1; /* Return value initialized to -1 (failure) */
    item = PyObject_GetItem(dict, key);
    if (item == NULL) {
        /* Handle KeyError only: */
        if (!PyErr_ExceptionMatches(PyExc_KeyError)) goto error;
        /* Clear the error and use zero: */
        PyErr_Clear();
        item = PyInt_FromLong(0L);
        if (item == NULL) goto error;
    }
    const_one = PyInt_FromLong(1L);
    if (const_one == NULL) goto error;
    incremented_item = PyNumber_Add(item, const_one);
    if (incremented_item == NULL) goto error;

    if (PyObject_SetItem(dict, key, incremented_item) < 0) goto error;
    rv = 0; /* Success */
    /* Continue with cleanup code */
 error:
    /* Cleanup code, shared by success and failure path */
    /* Use Py_XDECREF() to ignore NULL references */
    Py_XDECREF(item);
    Py_XDECREF(const_one);
    Py_XDECREF(incremented_item);
    return rv; /* -1 for error, 0 for success */
}
```

This example represents an endorsed use of the goto statement in C. It illustrates the use of `PyErr_ExceptionMatches()` and `PyErr_Clear()` to handle specific exceptions, and the use of `Py_XDECREF()` to dispose of owned references that might be NULL (note the X in the name; `Py_DECREF()` would crash when confronted with a NULL reference). It is important that the variables used to hold owned references are initialized to NULL for this to work; likewise, the proposed return value is initialized to -1 (failure) and only set to success after the final call made is successful.

Embedding Python

The one important task that only embedders (as opposed to extension writers) of the Python interpreter have to worry about is the initialization, and possibly the finalization, of the Python interpreter. Most functionality of the interpreter can only be used after the interpreter has been initialized.

The basic initialization function is `Py_Initialize()`. This initializes the table of loaded modules and creates the fundamental modules __builtin__, __main__, and sys. It also initializes the module search path (sys.path).

`Py_Initialize()` does not set the script argument list (sys.argv). If this variable is needed by Python code that will be executed later, it must be set explicitly with a call to `PySys_SetArgv(argc, argv)` subsequent to the call to `Py_Initialize()`.

On most systems (in particular, on UNIX and Windows, although the details are slightly different), `Py_Initialize()` calculates the module search path based on its best guess for the location of the standard Python interpreter executable, assuming that the Python library is found in a fixed location relative to the Python interpreter executable. In particular, it looks for a directory named lib/python1.5 (replacing 1.5 with the current interpreter version) relative to the parent directory where the executable named `"python"` is found on the shell command search path (the environment variable $PATH).

For instance, if the Python executable is found in /usr/local/bin/python, it will assume that the libraries are in /usr/local/lib/python1.5. (In fact, this particular path is also the *fallback* location, used when no executable file named `"python"` is found along $PATH, unless some other prefix is set when `configure` is called.) The user can override this behavior by setting the environment variable $PYTHONHOME, or insert additional directories in front of the standard path by setting $PYTHONPATH.

The embedding application can steer the search by calling `Py_SetProgramName(file)` before calling `Py_Initialize()`. Note that $PYTHONHOME still overrides this and $PYTHONPATH is still inserted in front of the standard path. An application that requires total control has to provide its own implementation of `Py_GetPath()`, `Py_GetPrefix()`,

Py_GetExecPrefix(), and Py_GetProgramFullPath() (all defined in Modules/
getpath.c).

Sometimes, it is desirable to uninitialize Python. For instance, the application might
want to start over (make another call to Py_Initialize()) or the application is simply
done with its use of Python and wants to free all memory allocated by Python. This
can be accomplished by calling Py_Finalize(). The function Py_IsInitialized()
returns true if Python is currently in the initialized state. More information about
these functions is given in a later section.

The Very High Level Layer

The functions in this section will let you execute Python source code given in a file or
a buffer, but they will not let you interact in a more detailed way with the interpreter.
Several of these functions accept a start symbol from the grammar as a parameter. The
available start symbols are Py_eval_input, Py_file_input, and Py_single_input.
These are described following the functions that accept them as parameters.

```
int PyRun_AnyFile(FILE *fp, char *filename)
```

If fp refers to a file associated with an interactive device (console or terminal input or
UNIX pseudo-terminal), returns the value of PyRun_InteractiveLoop(), otherwise
returns the result of PyRun_SimpleFile(). If filename is NULL, use "???" as the filename.

```
int PyRun_SimpleString(char *command)
```

Executes the Python source code from command in the __main__ module. If __main__
does not already exist, it is created. Returns 0 on success or -1 if an exception was
raised. If there was an error, it is not possible to get the exception information.

```
int PyRun_SimpleFile(FILE *fp, char *filename)
```

Similar to PyRun_SimpleString(), but the Python source code is read from fp instead
of an in-memory string. filename should be the name of the file.

```
int PyRun_InteractiveOne(FILE *fp, char *filename)
```

```
int PyRun_InteractiveLoop(FILE *fp, char *filename)
```

```
struct _node* PyParser_SimpleParseString(char *str, int start)
```

Parses Python source code from `str` using the start token start. The result can be used to create a code object that can be evaluated efficiently. This is useful if a code fragment must be evaluated many times.

```
struct _node* PyParser_SimpleParseFile(FILE *fp, char *filename,
int start)
```

Similar to `PyParser_SimpleParseString()`, but the Python source code is read from `fp` instead of an in-memory string. `filename` should be the name of the file.

```
PyObject* PyRun_String(char *str, int start, PyObject *globals,
PyObject *locals)
```

Executes Python source code from `str` in the context specified by the globals and locals dictionaries. The parameter start specifies the start token that should be used to parse the source code. Returns the result of executing the code as a Python object, or NULL if an exception was raised.

```
PyObject* PyRun_File(FILE *fp, char *filename, int start, PyObject
*globals, PyObject *locals)
```

Similar to `PyRun_String()`, but the Python source code is read from `fp` instead of an in-memory string. `filename` should be the name of the file.

```
PyObject* Py_CompileString(char *str, char *filename, int start)
```

Returns value: New reference. Parses and compiles the Python source code in `str`, returning the resulting code object. The start token is given by start; this can be used to constrain the code that can be compiled and should be `Py_eval_input`, `Py_file_input`, or `Py_single_input`. The filename specified by filename is used to construct the code object and can appear in tracebacks or SyntaxError exception messages. This returns NULL if the code cannot be parsed or compiled.

```
int Py_eval_input
```

The start symbol from the Python grammar for isolated expressions; for use with `Py_CompileString()`.

```
int Py_file_input
```

The start symbol from the Python grammar for sequences of statements as read from a file or other source; for use with `Py_CompileString()`. This is the symbol to use when compiling arbitrarily long Python source code.

```
int Py_single_input
```

The start symbol from the Python grammar for a single statement; for use with
`Py_CompileString()`. This is the symbol used for the interactive interpreter loop.

Reference Counting

The macros in this section are used for managing reference counts of Python objects.

`void Py_INCREF(PyObject *o)`

Increments the reference count for object o. The object must not be NULL; if you aren't
sure that it isn't NULL, use `Py_XINCREF()`.

`void Py_XINCREF(PyObject *o)`

Increments the reference count for object o. The object might be NULL, in which case
the macro has no effect.

`void Py_DECREF(PyObject *o)`

Decrements the reference count for object o. The object must not be NULL; if you
aren't sure that it isn't NULL, use `Py_XDECREF()`. If the reference count reaches zero, the
object's type's deallocation function (which must not be NULL) is invoked.

> **Caution**
> The deallocation function can cause arbitrary Python code to be invoked (for exam-
> ple, when a class instance with a __del__() method is deallocated). Although excep-
> tions in such code are not propagated, the executed code has free access to all
> Python global variables. This means that any object reachable from a global variable
> should be in a consistent state before `Py_DECREF()` is invoked. For example, code to
> delete an object from a list should copy a reference to the deleted object in a tempo-
> rary variable, update the list data structure, and then call `Py_DECREF()` for the tempo-
> rary variable.

`void Py_XDECREF(PyObject *o)`

Decrements the reference count for object o. The object might be NULL, in which case
the macro has no effect; otherwise the effect is the same as for `Py_DECREF()`, and the
same caution applies.

The following functions or macros are only for use within the interpreter core:
`_Py_Dealloc()`, `_Py_ForgetReference()`, `_Py_NewReference()`, as well as the global
variable `_Py_RefTotal`.

Exception Handling

The functions described in this section will let you handle and raise Python exceptions. It is important to understand some of the basics of Python exception handling. It works somewhat like the UNIX `errno` variable: There is a global indicator (per thread) of the last error that occurred. Most functions don't clear this on success, but will set it to indicate the cause of the error on failure. Most functions also return an error indicator, usually `NULL` if they are supposed to return a pointer, or `-1` if they return an integer (exception: the `PyArg_Parse*()` functions returns 1 for success and 0 for failure). When a function must fail because some function it called failed, it generally doesn't set the error indicator; the function it called already set it.

The error indicator consists of three Python objects corresponding to the Python variables: `sys.exc_type`, `sys.exc_value`, and `sys.exc_traceback`. API functions exist to interact with the error indicator in various ways. There is a separate error indicator for each thread.

```
void PyErr_Print()
```

Prints a standard traceback to `sys.stderr` and clears the error indicator. Call this function only when the error indicator is set. (Otherwise it will cause a fatal error.)

```
PyObject* PyErr_Occurred()
```

Return value: Borrowed reference. Tests whether the error indicator is set. If set, returns the exception type (the first argument to the last call to one of the `PyErr_Set*()` functions or to `PyErr_Restore()`). If not set, returns `NULL`. You do not own a reference to the return value, so you do not need to `Py_DECREF()` it.

> **Note**
> Do not compare the return value to a specific exception; use
> `PyErr_ExceptionMatches()` instead, shown as follows. (The comparison could easily fail because the exception might be an instance instead of a class, in the case of a class exception, or it might the subclass of the expected exception.)

```
int PyErr_ExceptionMatches(PyObject *exc)
```

Equivalent to `PyErr_GivenExceptionMatches(PyErr_Occurred(), exc)`. This should only be called when an exception is actually set; a memory access violation will occur if no exception has been raised.

```
int PyErr_GivenExceptionMatches(PyObject *given, PyObject *exc)
```

Return `true` if the given exception matches the exception in `exc`. If `exc` is a class object, this also returns `true` when given as an instance of a subclass. If `exc` is a tuple, all exceptions in the tuple (and recursively in subtuples) are searched for a match. If given is `NULL`, a memory access violation will occur.

```
void PyErr_NormalizeException(PyObject**exc, PyObject**val, PyObject**tb)
```

Under certain circumstances, the values returned by `PyErr_Fetch()` as follows can be *unnormalized*, meaning that `*exc` is a class object but `*val` is not an instance of the same class. This function can be used to instantiate the class in that case. If the values are already normalized, nothing happens. The delayed normalization is implemented to improve performance.

```
void PyErr_Clear()
```

Clears the error indicator. If the error indicator is not set, there is no effect.

```
void PyErr_Fetch(PyObject **ptype, PyObject **pvalue, PyObject **ptraceback)
```

Retrieves the error indicator into three variables whose addresses are passed. If the error indicator is not set, sets all three variables to `NULL`. If it is set, it will be cleared and you own a reference to each object retrieved. The value and traceback object might be `NULL` even when the type object is not.

> **Note**
> This function is normally only used by code that needs to handle exceptions or by code that needs to save and restore the error indicator temporarily.

```
void PyErr_Restore(PyObject *type, PyObject *value, PyObject *traceback)
```

Sets the error indicator from the three objects. If the error indicator is already set, it is cleared first. If the objects are `NULL`, the error indicator is cleared. Do not pass a `NULL` type and non-`NULL` value or traceback. The exception type should be a string or class; if it is a class, the value should be an instance of that class. Do not pass an invalid exception type or value. (Violating these rules will cause subtle problems later.) This call takes away a reference to each object; that is, you must own a reference to each object before the call and after the call you no longer own these references. (Warning: If you don't understand this, don't use this function.)

> **Note**
> This function is normally only used by code that needs to save and restore the error indicator temporarily.

```
void PyErr_SetString(PyObject *type, char *message)
```

This is the most common way to set the error indicator. The first argument specifies the exception type; it is normally one of the standard exceptions, for example, `PyExc_RuntimeError`. You need not increment its reference count. The second argument is an error message; it is converted to a string object.

```
void PyErr_SetObject(PyObject *type, PyObject *value)
```

This function is similar to `PyErr_SetString()` but lets you specify an arbitrary Python object for the value of the exception. You need not increment its reference count.

```
void PyErr_SetNone(PyObject *type)
```

This is a shorthand for `PyErr_SetObject(type, Py_None)`.

```
int PyErr_BadArgument()
```

This is a shorthand for `PyErr_SetString(PyExc_TypeError, message)`, where message indicates that a built-in operation was invoked with an illegal argument. It is mostly for internal use.

```
PyObject* PyErr_NoMemory()
```

Return value: Borrowed reference. This is a shorthand for `PyErr_SetNone(PyExc_MemoryError)`; it returns `NULL` so that an object allocation function can write `return PyErr_NoMemory();` when it runs out of memory.

```
PyObject* PyErr_SetFromErrno(PyObject *type)
```

This is a convenience function to raise an exception when a C library function has returned an error and set the C variable errno. It constructs a tuple object whose first item is the integer errno value and whose second item is the corresponding error message (gotten from `strerror()`), and then calls `PyErr_SetObject(type, object)`. On UNIX, when the errno value is `EINTR`, indicating an interrupted system call, this calls `PyErr_CheckSignals()`, and if that sets the error indicator, it is left set to that. The function always returns `NULL`, so a wrapper function around a system call can write `return PyErr_SetFromErrno();` when the system call returns an error.

```
void PyErr_BadInternalCall()
```

This is a shorthand for `PyErr_SetString(PyExc_TypeError, message)`, where a message indicates that an internal operation (for example, a Python/C API function) was invoked with an illegal argument. It is mostly for internal use.

```
int PyErr_CheckSignals()
```

This function interacts with Python's signal handling. It checks whether a signal has been sent to the processes and if so, invokes the corresponding signal handler. If the signal module is supported, this can invoke a signal handler written in Python. In all cases, the default effect for SIGINT is to raise the KeyboardInterrupt exception. If an exception is raised, the error indicator is set and the function returns 1; otherwise the function returns 0. The error indicator might or might not be cleared if it was previously set.

```
void PyErr_SetInterrupt()
```

This function is obsolete. It simulates the effect of a SIGINT signal arriving—the next time PyErr_CheckSignals() is called, KeyboardInterrupt will be raised. It can be called without holding the interpreter lock.

```
PyObject* PyErr_NewException(char *name, PyObject *base, PyObject *dict)
```

Return value: New reference. This utility function creates and returns a new exception object. The name argument must be the name of the new exception, a C string of the form module.class. The base and dict arguments are normally NULL. Normally, this creates a class object derived from the root for all exceptions, the built-in name Exception (accessible in C as PyExc_Exception). In this case the __module__ attribute of the new class is set to the first part (up to the last dot) of the name argument, and the class name is set to the last part (after the last dot). When the user has specified the -X command line option to use string exceptions, for backward compatibility, or when the base argument is not a class object (and not NULL), a string object created from the entire name argument is returned. The base argument can be used to specify an alternate base class. The dict argument can be used to specify a dictionary of class variables and methods.

Standard Exceptions

All standard Python exceptions are available as global variables whose names are PyExc_ followed by the Python exception name. These have the type PyObject*; they are all either class objects or string objects, depending on the use of the -X option to the interpreter. For completeness, all the variables are in Table A.1.

Table A.1 *C Variables for the Standard Python Exceptions*

C Name	Python Name	See Note below
PyExc_Exception	Exception	*
PyExc_StandardError	StandardError	*
PyExc_ArithmeticError	ArithmeticError	*
PyExc_LookupError	LookupError	*
PyExc_AssertionError	AssertionError	
PyExc_AttributeError	AttributeError	
PyExc_EOFError	EOFError	
PyExc_EnvironmentError	EnvironmentError	*
PyExc_FloatingPointError	FloatingPointError	
PyExc_IOError	IOError	
PyExc_ImportError	ImportError	
PyExc_IndexError	IndexError	
PyExc_KeyError	KeyError	
PyExc_KeyboardInterrupt	KeyboardInterrupt	
PyExc_MemoryError	MemoryError	
PyExc_NameError	NameError	
PyExc_NotImplementedError	NotImplementedError	
PyExc_OSError	OSError	
PyExc_OverflowError	OverflowError	
PyExc_RuntimeError	RuntimeError	
PyExc_SyntaxError	SyntaxError	
PyExc_SystemError	SystemError	
PyExc_SystemExit	SystemExit	
PyExc_TypeError	TypeError	
PyExc_ValueError	ValueError	
PyExc_ZeroDivisionError	ZeroDivisionError	

* This is a base class for other standard exceptions. If the -X interpreter command option is used, these will be tuples containing the string exceptions that would have otherwise been subclasses.

Deprecation of String Exceptions

The -X command-line option will be removed in Python 1.6/2.0. All exceptions built into Python or provided in the standard library will be classes derived from Exception.

String exceptions will still be supported in the interpreter to allow existing code to run unmodified, but this will also change in a future release.

Utilities

The functions in this section perform various utility tasks, such as parsing function arguments and constructing Python values from C values.

OS Utilities

```
int Py_FdIsInteractive(FILE *fp, char *filename)
```

Returns true (nonzero) if the standard I/O file fp with name filename is deemed inter-active. This is the case for files for which `isatty(fileno(fp))` is true. If the global flag `Py_InteractiveFlag` is true, this function also returns true if the name pointer is NULL or if the name is equal to one of the strings `"<stdin>"` or `"???"`.

```
long PyOS_GetLastModificationTime(char *filename)
```

Returns the time of last modification of the file `filename`. The result is encoded in the same way as the timestamp returned by the standard C library function `time()`.

Process Control

```
void Py_FatalError(char *message)
```

Prints a fatal error message and kills the process. No cleanup is performed. This func-tion should only be invoked when a condition is detected that would make it danger-ous to continue using the Python interpreter; for instance, when the object administration appears to be corrupted. On UNIX, the standard C library function `abort()` is called, which will attempt to produce a core file.

```
void Py_Exit(int status)
```

Exits the current process. This calls `Py_Finalize()` and then calls the standard C library function exit(status).

```
int Py_AtExit(void (*func) ())
```

Registers a cleanup function to be called by `Py_Finalize()`. The cleanup function will be called with no arguments and should return no value. At most, 32 cleanup functions can be registered. When the registration is successful, `Py_AtExit()` returns 0; on failure, it returns -1. The cleanup function registered last is called first. Each cleanup function will be called at most once. Because Python's internal finalization will have completed before the cleanup function, no Python APIs should be called by `func`.

Importing Modules

```
PyObject* PyImport_ImportModule(char *name)
```

Return value: New reference. This is a simplified interface to `PyImport_ImportModuleEx()` that follows, leaving the globals and locals arguments set to NULL. When the name argument contains a dot (in other words, when it specifies a submodule of a package), the fromlist argument is set to the list `['*']` so that the return value is the named module rather than the top-level package containing it as would otherwise be the case. (Unfortunately, this has an additional side effect when name in fact specifies a subpackage instead of a submodule: the submodules specified in the package's __all__ variable are loaded.) Returns a new reference to the imported module, or NULL with an exception set on failure (the module can still be created in this case—examine `sys.modules` to find out).

> **Note**
> This interface bypasses any import hooks installed with the `ihooks` module.

```
PyObject* PyImport_ImportModuleEx(char *name, PyObject *globals,
PyObject *locals, PyObject *fromlist)
```

Return value: New reference. Imports a module. This is best described by referring to the built-in Python function __import__() because the standard __import__() function calls this function directly.

The return value is a new reference to the imported module or top-level package, or NULL with an exception set on failure (the module might still be created in this case). As for __import__(), the return value when a submodule of a package was requested is normally the top-level package, unless a non-empty fromlist was given.

```
PyObject* PyImport_Import(PyObject *name)
```

Return value: New reference. This is a higher-level interface that calls the current "import hook function". It invokes the __import__() function from the __builtins__ of the current globals. This means that the import is done using whatever import hooks are installed in the current environment, for instance, by rexec or ihooks.

```
PyObject* PyImport_ReloadModule(PyObject *m)
```

Return value: New reference. Reloads a module. This is best described by referring to the built-in Python function `reload()` because the standard `reload()` function calls this function directly. Returns a new reference to the reloaded module, or NULL with an exception set on failure (the module still exists in this case).

```
PyObject* PyImport_AddModule(char *name)
```

Return value: Borrowed reference. Returns the module object corresponding to a module name. The name argument might be of the form `package.module`). First checks the modules dictionary if there's one there, and if not, creates a new one and inserts in in the modules dictionary. Warning: This function does not load or import the module; if the module wasn't already loaded, you will get an empty module object. Use `PyImport_ImportModule()` or one of its variants to import a module. Returns NULL with an exception set on failure.

```
PyObject* PyImport_ExecCodeModule(char *name, PyObject *co)
```

Return value: New reference. Given a module name (possibly of the form package.module) and a code object read from a Python bytecode file or obtained from the built-in function compile(), loads the module. Returns a new reference to the module object, or NULL with an exception set if an error occurred (the module can still be created in this case). This function would reload the module if it was already imported.

```
long PyImport_GetMagicNumber()
```

Returns the magic number for Python bytecode files (also known as `.pyc` and `.pyo` files). The magic number should be present in the first four bytes of the bytecode file, in little-endian byte order.

```
PyObject* PyImport_GetModuleDict()
```

Return value: Borrowed reference. Returns the dictionary used for the module administration (also known as `sys.modules`). Note that this is a per-interpreter variable.

```
void _PyImport_Init()
```

Initializes the import mechanism. For internal use only.

```
void PyImport_Cleanup()
```

Empties the module table. For internal use only.

```
void _PyImport_Fini()
```

Finalizes the import mechanism. For internal use only.

```
PyObject* _PyImport_FindExtension(char *, char *)
```

Return value: Borrowed reference. For internal use only.

```
PyObject* _PyImport_FixupExtension(char *, char *)
```

For internal use only.

```
int PyImport_ImportFrozenModule(char *)
```

Loads a frozen module. Returns 1 for success, 0 if the module is not found, and -1 with an exception set if the initialization failed. To access the imported module on a successful load, uses `PyImport_ImportModule()`. (Note the misnomer—this function would reload the module if it was already imported.)

```
struct _frozen
```

This is the structure type definition for frozen module descriptors, as generated by the freeze utility (see Tools/freeze/ in the Python source distribution). Its definition is

```
struct _frozen {
    char *name;
    unsigned char *code;
    int size;
};
```

```
struct _frozen* PyImport_FrozenModules
```

This pointer is initialized to point to an array of `struct _frozen` records, terminated by one whose members are all NULL or zero. When a frozen module is imported, it is searched in this table. Third-party code could play tricks with this to provide a dynamically created collection of frozen modules.

Abstract Objects Layer

The functions in this section interact with Python objects regardless of their type, or with wide classes of object types (for example, all numerical types, or all sequence types). When used on object types for which they do not apply, they will raise a Python exception.

Object Protocol

```
int PyObject_Print(PyObject *o, FILE *fp, int flags)
```

Prints an object o, on file fp. Returns -1 on error. The flags argument is used to enable certain printing options. The only option currently supported is Py_PRINT_RAW; if given, the str() of the object is written instead of the repr().

```
int PyObject_HasAttrString(PyObject *o, char *attr_name)
```

Returns 1 if o has the attribute attr_name, and 0 otherwise. This is equivalent to the Python expression "hasattr(o, attr_name)". This function always succeeds.

```
PyObject* PyObject_GetAttrString(PyObject *o, char *attr_name)
```

Return value: New reference. Retrieves an attribute named attr_name from object o. Returns the attribute value on success, or NULL on failure. This is the equivalent of the Python expression "o.attr_name".

```
int PyObject_HasAttr(PyObject *o, PyObject *attr_name)
```

Returns 1 if o has the attribute attr_name, and 0 otherwise. This is equivalent to the Python expression "hasattr(o, attr_name)". This function always succeeds.

```
PyObject* PyObject_GetAttr(PyObject *o, PyObject *attr_name)
```

Return value: New reference. Retrieves an attribute named attr_name from object o. Returns the attribute value on success, or NULL on failure. This is the equivalent of the Python expression "o.attr_name".

```
int PyObject_SetAttrString(PyObject *o, char *attr_name, PyObject *v)
```

Sets the value of the attribute named attr_name, for object o, to the value v. Returns -1 on failure. This is the equivalent of the Python statement "o.attr_name = v".

```
int PyObject_SetAttr(PyObject *o, PyObject *attr_name, PyObject *v)
```

Sets the value of the attribute named attr_name, for object o, to the value v. Returns -1 on failure. This is the equivalent of the Python statement "o.attr_name = v".

```
int PyObject_DelAttrString(PyObject *o, char *attr_name)
```

Deletes attribute named attr_name, for object o. Returns -1 on failure. This is the equivalent of the Python statement "del o.attr_name".

```
int PyObject_DelAttr(PyObject *o, PyObject *attr_name)
```

Deletes attribute named `attr_name`, for object o. Returns -1 on failure. This is the equivalent of the Python statement `"del o.attr_name"`.

```
int PyObject_Cmp(PyObject *o1, PyObject *o2, int *result)
```

Compares the values of o1 and o2 using a routine provided by o1, if one exists, otherwise with a routine provided by o2. The result of the comparison is returned in result. Returns -1 on failure. This is the equivalent of the Python statement `"result = cmp(o1, o2)"`.

```
int PyObject_Compare(PyObject *o1, PyObject *o2)
```

Compares the values of o1 and o2 using a routine provided by o1, if one exists, otherwise with a routine provided by o2. Returns the result of the comparison on success. On error, the value returned is undefined; uses `PyErr_Occurred()` to detect an error. This is equivalent to the Python expression `"cmp(o1, o2)"`.

```
PyObject* PyObject_Repr(PyObject *o)
```

Return value: New reference. Computes a string representation of object o. Returns the string representation on success, or NULL on failure. This is the equivalent of the Python expression `"repr(o)"`. Called by the `repr()` built-in function and by reverse quotes.

```
PyObject* PyObject_Str(PyObject *o)
```

Return value: New reference. Computes a string representation of object o. Returns the string representation on success, or NULL on failure. This is the equivalent of the Python expression `"str(o)"`. Called by the `str()` built-in function and by the print statement.

```
int PyCallable_Check(PyObject *o)
```

Determines if the object o is callable. Returns 1 if the object is callable and 0 otherwise. This function always succeeds.

```
PyObject* PyObject_CallObject(PyObject *callable_object, PyObject *args)
```

Return value: New reference. Calls a callable Python object `callable_object`, with arguments given by the tuple args. If no arguments are needed, args might be NULL. Returns the result of the call on success, or NULL on failure. This is the equivalent of the Python expression `"apply(o, args)"`.

```
PyObject* PyObject_CallFunction(PyObject *callable_object, char
*format,...)
```

Return value: New reference. Calls a callable Python object `callable_object`, with a variable number of C arguments. The C arguments are described using a `Py_BuildValue()` style format string. The format might be `NULL`, indicating that no arguments are provided. Returns the result of the call on success, or `NULL` on failure. This is the equivalent of the Python expression `"apply(o, args)"`.

```
PyObject* PyObject_CallMethod(PyObject *o, char *m, char *format, ...)
```

Return value: New reference. Calls the method named `m` of object `o` with a variable number of C arguments. The C arguments are described by a `Py_BuildValue()` format string. The format might be `NULL`, indicating that no arguments are provided. Returns the result of the call on success, or `NULL` on failure. This is the equivalent of the Python expression `"o.method(args)"`. Note that special method names, such as `__add__()`, `__getitem__()`, and so on are not supported. The specific abstract-object routines for these must be used.

```
int PyObject_Hash(PyObject *o)
```

Computes and returns the hash value of an object `o`. On failure, it returns `-1`. This is the equivalent of the Python expression `"hash(o)"`.

```
int PyObject_IsTrue(PyObject *o)
```

Returns `1` if the object `o` is considered to be `true`, and `0` otherwise. This is equivalent to the Python expression `"not not o"`. This function always succeeds.

```
PyObject* PyObject_Type(PyObject *o)
```

Return value: New reference. On success, returns a type object corresponding to the object type of object `o`. On failure, it returns `NULL`. This is equivalent to the Python expression `"type(o)"`.

```
int PyObject_Length(PyObject *o)
```

Returns the length of object `o`. If the object `o` provides both sequence and mapping protocols, the sequence length is returned. On error, `-1` is returned. This is the equivalent to the Python expression `"len(o)"`.

```
PyObject* PyObject_GetItem(PyObject *o, PyObject *key)
```

Return value: New reference. Returns the element of `o` corresponding to the object `key` or `NULL` on failure. This is the equivalent of the Python expression `"o[key]"`.

```
int PyObject_SetItem(PyObject *o, PyObject *key, PyObject *v)
```

Maps the object key to the value v. Returns -1 on failure. This is the equivalent of the Python statement "o[key] = v".

```
int PyObject_DelItem(PyObject *o, PyObject *key)
```

Deletes the mapping for key from o. Returns -1 on failure. This is the equivalent of the Python statement "del o[key]".

Number Protocol

```
int PyNumber_Check(PyObject *o)
```

Returns 1 if the object o provides numeric protocols, and false otherwise. This function always succeeds.

```
PyObject* PyNumber_Add(PyObject *o1, PyObject *o2)
```

Return value: New reference. Returns the result of adding o1 and o2, or NULL on failure. This is the equivalent of the Python expression "o1 + o2".

```
PyObject* PyNumber_Subtract(PyObject *o1, PyObject *o2)
```

Return value: New reference. Returns the result of subtracting o2 from o1, or NULL on failure. This is the equivalent of the Python expression "o1 - o2".

```
PyObject* PyNumber_Multiply(PyObject *o1, PyObject *o2)
```

Return value: New reference. Returns the result of multiplying o1 and o2, or NULL on failure. This is the equivalent of the Python expression "o1 * o2".

```
PyObject* PyNumber_Divide(PyObject *o1, PyObject *o2)
```

Return value: New reference. Returns the result of dividing o1 by o2, or NULL on failure. This is the equivalent of the Python expression "o1 / o2".

```
PyObject* PyNumber_Remainder(PyObject *o1, PyObject *o2)
```

Return value: New reference. Returns the remainder of dividing o1 by o2, or NULL on failure. This is the equivalent of the Python expression "o1 % o2".

```
PyObject* PyNumber_Divmod(PyObject *o1, PyObject *o2)
```

Return value: New reference. See the built-in function divmod(). Returns NULL on failure. This is the equivalent of the Python expression "divmod(o1, o2)".

```
PyObject* PyNumber_Power(PyObject *o1, PyObject *o2, PyObject *o3)
```

Return value: New reference. See the built-in function pow(). Returns NULL on failure. This is the equivalent of the Python expression "pow(o1, o2, o3)", where o3 is optional. If o3 is to be ignored, pass Py_None in its place (passing NULL for o3 would cause an illegal memory access).

```
PyObject* PyNumber_Negative(PyObject *o)
```

Return value: New reference. Returns the negation of o on success, or NULL on failure. This is the equivalent of the Python expression "-o"

```
PyObject* PyNumber_Positive(PyObject *o)
```

Return value: New reference. Returns o on success, or NULL on failure. This is the equivalent of the Python expression "+o".

```
PyObject* PyNumber_Absolute(PyObject *o)
```

Return value: New reference. Returns the absolute value of o, or NULL on failure. This is the equivalent of the Python expression "abs(o)".

```
PyObject* PyNumber_Invert(PyObject *o)
```

Return value: New reference. Returns the bitwise negation of o on success, or NULL on failure. This is the equivalent of the Python expression "~o".

```
PyObject* PyNumber_Lshift(PyObject *o1, PyObject *o2)
```

Return value: New reference. Returns the result of left shifting o1 by o2 on success, or NULL on failure. This is the equivalent of the Python expression "o1 << o2".

```
PyObject* PyNumber_Rshift(PyObject *o1, PyObject *o2)
```

Return value: New reference. Returns the result of right shifting o1 by o2 on success, or NULL on failure. This is the equivalent of the Python expression "o1 >> o2".

```
PyObject* PyNumber_And(PyObject *o1, PyObject *o2)
```

Return value: New reference. Returns the result of "anding" o1 and o2 on success and NULL on failure. This is the equivalent of the Python expression "o1 and o2".

```
PyObject* PyNumber_Xor(PyObject *o1, PyObject *o2)
```

Return value: New reference. Returns the bitwise exclusive or of o1 by o2 on success, or NULL on failure. This is the equivalent of the Python expression "o1 ^ o2".

```
PyObject* PyNumber_Or(PyObject *o1, PyObject *o2)
```

Return value: New reference. Returns the result of o1 and o2 on success, or NULL on failure. This is the equivalent of the Python expression "o1 or o2".

```
PyObject* PyNumber_Coerce(PyObject **p1, PyObject **p2)
```

This function takes the addresses of two variables of type PyObject*. If the objects pointed to by *p1 and *p2 have the same type, increment their reference count and return 0 (success). If the objects can be converted to a common numeric type, replace *p1 and *p2 by their converted value (with *new* reference counts), and return 0. If no conversion is possible, or if some other error occurs, return -1 (failure) and don't increment the reference counts. The call PyNumber_Coerce(&o1, &o2) is equivalent to the Python statement "o1, o2 = coerce(o1, o2)".

```
PyObject* PyNumber_Int(PyObject *o)
```

Return value: New reference. Returns the o converted to an integer object on success, or NULL on failure. This is the equivalent of the Python expression "int(o)".

```
PyObject* PyNumber_Long(PyObject *o)
```

Return value: New reference. Returns the o converted to a long integer object on success, or NULL on failure. This is the equivalent of the Python expression "long(o)".

```
PyObject* PyNumber_Float(PyObject *o)
```

Return value: New reference. Returns the o converted to a float object on success, or NULL on failure. This is the equivalent of the Python expression "float(o)".

Sequence Protocol

```
int PySequence_Check(PyObject *o)
```

Returns 1 if the object provides sequence protocol, and 0 otherwise. This function always succeeds.

```
int PySequence_Length(PyObject *o)
```

Returns the number of objects in sequence; o on success, and -1 on failure. For objects that do not provide sequence protocol, this is equivalent to the Python expression "len(o)".

```
PyObject* PySequence_Concat(PyObject *o1, PyObject *o2)
```

Return value: New reference. Returns the concatenation of o1 and o2 on success, and NULL on failure. This is the equivalent of the Python expression "o1 + o2".

```
PyObject* PySequence_Repeat(PyObject *o, int count)
```

Return value: New reference. Returns the result of repeating sequence object o count times, or NULL on failure. This is the equivalent of the Python expression "o * count".

```
PyObject* PySequence_GetItem(PyObject *o, int i)
```

Return value: New reference. Returns the ith element of o, or NULL on failure. This is the equivalent of the Python expression "o[i]".

```
PyObject* PySequence_GetSlice(PyObject *o, int i1, int i2)
```

Return value: New reference. Returns the slice of sequence object o between i1 and i2, or NULL on failure. This is the equivalent of the Python expression "o[i1:i2]".

```
int PySequence_SetItem(PyObject *o, int i, PyObject *v)
```

Assigns object v to the ith element of o. Returns -1 on failure. This is the equivalent of the Python statement "o[i] = v".

```
int PySequence_DelItem(PyObject *o, int i)
```

Deletes the ith element of object v. Returns -1 on failure. This is the equivalent of the Python statement "del o[i]".

```
int PySequence_SetSlice(PyObject *o, int i1, int i2, PyObject *v)
```

Assigns the sequence object v to the slice in sequence object o from i1 to i2. This is the equivalent of the Python statement "o[i1:i2] = v".

```
int PySequence_DelSlice(PyObject *o, int i1, int i2)
```

Deletes the slice in sequence object o from i1 to i2. Returns -1 on failure. This is the equivalent of the Python statement "del o[i1:i2]".

```
PyObject* PySequence_Tuple(PyObject *o)
```

Return value: New reference. Returns the o as a tuple on success, and NULL on failure. This is equivalent to the Python expression "tuple(o)".

```
int PySequence_Count(PyObject *o, PyObject *value)
```

Returns the number of occurrences of value in o; that is, returns the number of keys for which o[key] == value. On failure, returns -1. This is equivalent to the Python expression "o.count(value)".

```
int PySequence_Contains(PyObject *o, PyObject *value)
```

Determines if o contains value. If an item in o is equal to value, returns 1, otherwise returns 0. On error, returns -1. This is equivalent to the Python expression "value in o".

```
int PySequence_Index(PyObject *o, PyObject *value)
```

Returns the first index i for which o[i] == value. On error, returns -1. This is equivalent to the Python expression "o.index(value)".

Mapping Protocol

```
int PyMapping_Check(PyObject *o)
```

Returns 1 if the object provides mapping protocol, and 0 otherwise. This function always succeeds.

```
int PyMapping_Length(PyObject *o)
```

Returns the number of keys in object o on success, and -1 on failure. For objects that do not provide mapping protocol, this is equivalent to the Python expression "len(o)".

```
int PyMapping_DelItemString(PyObject *o, char *key)
```

Removes the mapping for object key from the object o. Returns -1 on failure. This is equivalent to the Python statement "del o[key]".

```
int PyMapping_DelItem(PyObject *o, PyObject *key)
```

Removes the mapping for object key from the object o. Returns -1 on failure. This is equivalent to the Python statement "del o[key]".

```
int PyMapping_HasKeyString(PyObject *o, char *key)
```

On success, returns 1 if the mapping object has the key identified by the key pointer, and 0 otherwise. This is equivalent to the Python expression "o.has_key(key)". This function always succeeds.

```
int PyMapping_HasKey(PyObject *o, PyObject *key)
```

Returns 1 if the mapping object has the key identified by the key pointer and 0 otherwise. This is equivalent to the Python expression "o.has_key(key)". This function always succeeds.

```
PyObject* PyMapping_Keys(PyObject *o)
```

Return value: New reference. On success, returns a list of the keys in object o. On failure, returns NULL. This is equivalent to the Python expression "o.keys()".

```
PyObject* PyMapping_Values(PyObject *o)
```

Return value: New reference. On success, returns a list of the values in object o. On failure, returns NULL. This is equivalent to the Python expression "o.values()".

```
PyObject* PyMapping_Items(PyObject *o)
```

Return value: New reference. On success, returns a list of the items in object o, where each item is a tuple containing a key-value pair. On failure, returns NULL. This is equivalent to the Python expression "o.items()".

```
PyObject* PyMapping_GetItemString(PyObject *o, char *key)
```

Return value: New reference. Returns element of o corresponding to the object key or NULL on failure. This is the equivalent of the Python expression "o[key]".

```
int PyMapping_SetItemString(PyObject *o, char *key, PyObject *v)
```

Maps the object key to the value v in object o. Returns -1 on failure. This is the equivalent of the Python statement "o[key] = v".

Concrete Objects Layer

The functions in this section are specific to certain Python object types. Passing them an object of the wrong type is not a good idea; if you receive an object from a Python program and you are not sure that it has the right type, you must perform a type check first; for example: to check that an object is a dictionary, use PyDict_Check(). This section is structured similar to the "family tree" of Python object types.

Fundamental Objects

This section describes Python type objects and the singleton object None.

Type Objects

PyTypeObject

The C structure of the objects used to describe built-in types.

PyObject* PyType_Type

This is the type object for type objects; it is the same object as types.TypeType in the Python layer.

int PyType_Check(PyObject *o)

Returns true if the object o is a type object.

int PyType_HasFeature(PyObject *o, int feature)

Returns true if the type object o sets the feature identified by the feature argument. Type features are denoted by single bit flags. The only defined feature flag is Py_TPFLAGS_HAVE_GETCHARBUFFER, which is described in a later section.

The None Object

Note that the PyTypeObject for None is not directly exposed in the Python/C API. Because None is a singleton, testing for object identity (using == in C) is sufficient. There is no PyNone_Check() function for the same reason.

PyObject* Py_None

The Python None object denotes lack of value. This object has no methods.

Sequence Objects

Generic operations on sequence objects were discussed in the previous subsection; this subsection deals with the specific kinds of sequence objects that are intrinsic to the Python language.

String Objects

PyStringObject

This subtype of PyObject represents a Python string object.

PyTypeObject PyString_Type

This instance of PyTypeObject represents the Python string type; it is the same object as types.TypeType in the Python layer.

```
int PyString_Check(PyObject *o)
```

Returns true if the object o is a string object.

```
PyObject* PyString_FromString(const char *v)
```

Return value: New reference. Returns a new string object with the value v on success, and NULL on failure.

```
PyObject* PyString_FromStringAndSize(const char *v, int len)
```

Return value: New reference. Returns a new string object with the value v and length len on success, and NULL on failure. If v is NULL, the contents of the string are uninitialized.

```
int PyString_Size(PyObject *string)
```

Returns the length of the string object identified by the given pointer.

```
int PyString_GET_SIZE(PyObject *string)
```

Macro form of PyString_GetSize() but without error checking.

```
char* PyString_AsString(PyObject *string)
```

Returns a null-terminated representation of the contents of string. The pointer refers to the internal buffer of string, not a copy. The data must not be modified in any way. It must not be de-allocated.

```
char* PyString_AS_STRING(PyObject *string)
```

Macro form of PyString_AsString() but without error checking.

```
void PyString_Concat(PyObject **string, PyObject *newpart)
```

Creates a new string object in *string containing the contents of newpart appended to string. The old value of string has its reference count decremented. If the new string cannot be created, the old reference to string will still be discarded and the value of *string will be set to NULL; the appropriate exception will be set.

```
void PyString_ConcatAndDel(PyObject **string, PyObject *newpart)
```

Creates a new string object in *string containing the contents of newpart appended to string. This version decrements the reference count of newpart.

```
int _PyString_Resize(PyObject **string, int newsize)
```

A way to resize a string object even though it is "immutable". Only use this to build up a brand new string object; don't use this if the string might already be known in other parts of the code.

```
PyObject* PyString_Format(PyObject *format, PyObject *args)
```

Return value: New reference. Returns a new string object from format and args. Analogous to format % args. The args argument must be a tuple.

```
void PyString_InternInPlace(PyObject **string)
```

Interns the argument *string in place. The argument must be the address of a pointer variable pointing to a Python string object. If there is an existing interned string that is the same as *string, it sets *string to it (decrementing the reference count of the old string object and incrementing the reference count of the interned string object), otherwise it leaves *string alone and interns it (incrementing its reference count). (Clarification: even though there is a lot of talk about reference counts, think of this function as reference-count–neutral; you own the object after the call if and only if you owned it before the call.)

```
PyObject* PyString_InternFromString(const char *v)
```

Return value: New reference. A combination of PyString_FromString() and PyString_InternInPlace(), returning either a new string object that has been interned, or a new ("owned") reference to an earlier interned string object with the same value.

Buffer Objects

Python objects implemented in C can export a group of functions called the *buffer interface*. These functions can be used by an object to expose its data in a raw, byte-oriented format. Clients of the object can use the buffer interface to access the object data directly, without needing to copy it first.

Two examples of objects that support the buffer interface are strings and arrays. The string object exposes the character contents in the buffer interface's byte-oriented form. An array can also expose its contents, but it should be noted that array elements can be multi-byte values.

An example user of the buffer interface is the file object's write() method. Any object that can export a series of bytes through the buffer interface can be written to a file. There are a number of format codes to PyArgs_ParseTuple() that operate against an object's buffer interface, returning data from the target object.

More information on the buffer interface is provided in the section "Buffer Object Structures," under the description for `PyBufferProcs`.

A buffer object is defined in the bufferobject.h header (included by Python.h). These objects look very similar to string objects at the Python programming level: They support slicing, indexing, concatenation, and some other standard string operations. However, their data can come from one of two sources: from a block of memory, or from another object that exports the buffer interface.

Buffer objects are useful as a way to expose the data from another object's buffer interface to the Python programmer. They can also be used as a zero-copy slicing mechanism. Using their ability to reference a block of memory, it is possible to expose any data to the Python programmer quite easily. The memory could be a large, constant array in a C extension, it could be a raw block of memory for manipulation before passing to an operating system library, or it could be used to pass around structured data in its native, in-memory format.

`PyBufferObject`

This subtype of PyObject represents a buffer object.

`PyTypeObject PyBuffer_Type`

The instance of PyTypeObject that represents the Python buffer type; it is the same object as `types.BufferType` in the Python layer.

`int Py_END_OF_BUFFER`

This constant can be passed as the size parameter to `PyBuffer_FromObject()` or `PyBuffer_FromReadWriteObject()`. It indicates that the new PyBufferObject should refer to the base object from the specified offset to the end of its exported buffer. Using this enables the caller to avoid querying the base object for its length.

`int PyBuffer_Check(PyObject *p)`

Returns `true` if the argument has type `PyBuffer_Type`.

`PyObject* PyBuffer_FromObject(PyObject *base, int offset, int size)`

Return value: New reference. Returns a new read-only buffer object. This raises TypeError if `base` doesn't support the read-only buffer protocol or doesn't provide exactly one buffer segment. It raises ValueError if `offset` is less than zero. The buffer will hold a reference to the `base` object, and the buffer's contents will refer to the `base` object's buffer interface, starting as position `offset` and extending for `size` bytes. If `size` is `Py_END_OF_BUFFER`, the new buffer's contents extend to the length of the base object's exported buffer data.

```
PyObject* PyBuffer_FromReadWriteObject(PyObject *base, int offset,
int size)
```

Return value: New reference. Returns a new writable buffer object. Parameters and exceptions are similar to those for `PyBuffer_FromObject()`. If the base object does not export the writable buffer protocol, TypeError is raised.

```
PyObject* PyBuffer_FromMemory(void *ptr, int size)
```

Return value: New reference. Returns a new read-only buffer object that reads from a specified location in memory, with a specified size. The caller is responsible for ensuring that the memory buffer, passed in as `ptr`, is not deallocated while the returned buffer object exists. Raises ValueError if `size` is less than zero. Note that `Py_END_OF_BUFFER` might not be passed for the size parameter; ValueError will be raised in that case.

```
PyObject* PyBuffer_FromReadWriteMemory(void *ptr, int size)
```

Return value: New reference. Similar to `PyBuffer_FromMemory()`, but the returned buffer is writable.

```
PyObject* PyBuffer_New(int size)
```

Return value: New reference. Returns a new writable buffer object that maintains its own memory buffer of size bytes. ValueError is returned if size is not zero or positive.

Tuple Objects

```
PyTupleObject
```

This subtype of PyObject represents a Python tuple object.

```
PyTypeObject PyTuple_Type
```

This instance of PyTypeObject represents the Python tuple type; it is the same object as `types.TupleType` in the Python layer.

```
int PyTuple_Check(PyObject *p)
```

Return `true` if the argument is a tuple object.

```
PyObject* PyTuple_New(int len)
```

Return value: New reference. Returns a new tuple object of size `len`, or NULL on failure.

```
int PyTuple_Size(PyTupleObject *p)
```

Takes a pointer to a tuple object, and returns the size of that tuple.

```
PyObject* PyTuple_GetItem(PyTupleObject *p, int pos)
```

Return value: Borrowed reference. Returns the object at position pos in the tuple pointed to by p. If pos is out of bounds, it returns NULL and sets an IndexError exception.

```
PyObject* PyTuple_GET_ITEM(PyTupleObject *p, int pos)
```

Return value: Borrowed reference. Does the same, but does no checking of its arguments.

```
PyObject* PyTuple_GetSlice(PyTupleObject *p, int low, int high)
```

Return value: New reference. Takes a slice of the tuple pointed to by p from low to high and returns it as a new tuple.

```
int PyTuple_SetItem(PyObject *p, int pos, PyObject *o)
```

Inserts a reference to object o at position pos of the tuple pointed to by p. It returns 0 on success.

> **Note**
> This function "steals" a reference to o.

```
void PyTuple_SET_ITEM(PyObject *p, int pos, PyObject *o)
```

Does the same, but does no error checking, and should only be used to fill in brand new tuples.

> **Note**
> This function "steals" a reference to o.

```
int _PyTuple_Resize(PyTupleObject *p, int newsize, int last_is_sticky)
```

Can be used to resize a tuple. newsize will be the new length of the tuple. Because tuples are supposed to be immutable, this should only be used if there is only one reference to the object. Do not use this if the tuple might already be known to some other part of the code. last_is_sticky is a flag—if true, the tuple will grow or shrink at the front, otherwise it will grow or shrink at the end. Think of this as destroying the old tuple and creating a new one, only more efficiently. Returns 0 on success and -1 on failure (in which case, a MemoryError or SystemError will be raised).

List Objects

`PyListObject`

This subtype of PyObject represents a Python list object.

`PyTypeObject PyList_Type`

This instance of PyTypeObject represents the Python list type. This is the same object as `types.ListType`.

`int PyList_Check(PyObject *p)`

Returns `true` if its argument is a PyListObject.

`PyObject* PyList_New(int len)`

Return value: New reference. Returns a new list of length `len` on success, or `NULL` on failure.

`int PyList_Size(PyObject *list)`

Returns the length of the list object in list; this is equivalent to `"len(list)"` on a list object.

`int PyList_GET_SIZE(PyObject *list)`

Macro form of `PyList_GetSize()` without error checking.

`PyObject* PyList_GetItem(PyObject *list, int index)`

Return value: Borrowed reference. Returns the object at position pos in the list pointed to by p. If pos is out of bounds, it returns `NULL` and sets an IndexError exception.

`PyObject* PyList_GET_ITEM(PyObject *list, int i)`

Return value: Borrowed reference. Macro form of `PyList_GetItem()` without error checking.

`int PyList_SetItem(PyObject *list, int index, PyObject *item)`

Sets the item at the position identified by the integer `index` in the given `list` to the value of the object identified by the pointer called `item`.

> **Note**
> This function "steals" a reference to item.

```
PyObject* PyList_SET_ITEM(PyObject *list, int i, PyObject *o)
```

Return value: Borrowed reference. Macro form of `PyList_SetItem()` without error checking.

> **Note**
> This function "steals" a reference to item.

```
int PyList_Insert(PyObject *list, int index, PyObject *item)
```

Inserts the item called `item` into the list called `list` in front of the index called `index`. Returns `0` if successful; returns `-1` and raises an exception if unsuccessful. Analogous to `list.insert(index, item)`.

```
int PyList_Append(PyObject *list, PyObject *item)
```

Appends the object item at the end of the list called `list`. Returns `0` if successful; returns `-1` and sets an exception if unsuccessful. Analogous to `list.append(item)`.

```
PyObject* PyList_GetSlice(PyObject *list, int low, int high)
```

Return value: New reference. Returns a list of the objects in list containing the objects between `low` and `high`. Returns `NULL` and sets an exception if unsuccessful. Analogous to `list[low:high]`.

```
int PyList_SetSlice(PyObject *list, int low, int high, PyObject
*itemlist)
```

Sets the slice of list between `low` and `high` to the contents of `itemlist`. Analogous to `list[low:high] = itemlist`. Returns `0` on success, `-1` on failure.

```
int PyList_Sort(PyObject *list)
```

Sorts the items of list in place. Returns `0` on success, `-1` on failure. This is equivalent to `"list.sort()"`.

```
int PyList_Reverse(PyObject *list)
```

Reverses the items of list in place. Returns `0` on success, `-1` on failure. This is the equivalent of `"list.reverse()"`.

```
PyObject* PyList_AsTuple(PyObject *list)
```

Return value: New reference. Returns a new tuple object containing the contents of list; equivalent to `"tuple(list)"`.

Mapping/Dictionary Objects

```
PyDictObject
```

This subtype of PyObject represents a Python dictionary object.

```
PyTypeObject PyDict_Type
```

This instance of PyTypeObject represents the Python dictionary type. This is exposed to Python programs as types.DictType and types.DictionaryType.

```
int PyDict_Check(PyObject *p)
```

Returns true if its argument is a PyDictObject.

```
PyObject* PyDict_New()
```

Return value: New reference. Returns a new empty dictionary, or NULL on failure.

```
void PyDict_Clear(PyObject *p)
```

Empties an existing dictionary of all key/value pairs.

```
int PyDict_SetItem(PyObject *p, PyObject *key, PyObject *val)
```

Inserts value into the dictionary with a key of key. key must be hashable; if it isn't, TypeError will be raised.

```
int PyDict_SetItemString(PyObject *p, char *key, PyObject *val)
```

Inserts value into the dictionary using key as a key. key should be a char*. The key object is created using PyString_FromString(key).

```
int PyDict_DelItem(PyObject *p, PyObject *key)
```

Removes the entry in dictionary p with key called key. key must be hashable; if it isn't, TypeError is raised.

```
int PyDict_DelItemString(PyObject *p, char *key)
```

Removes the entry in dictionary p which has a key specified by the string key.

```
PyObject* PyDict_GetItem(PyObject *p, PyObject *key)
```

Return value: Borrowed reference. Returns the object from dictionary p, which has a key called key. Returns NULL if the key called key is not present, but without setting an exception.

```
PyObject* PyDict_GetItemString(PyObject *p, char *key)
```

Return value: Borrowed reference. This is the same as `PyDict_GetItem()`, but key is specified as a `char*`, rather than a `PyObject*`.

```
PyObject* PyDict_Items(PyObject *p)
```

Return value: New reference. Returns a PyListObject containing all the items from the dictionary, as in the dictionary method `items()` (see Chapter 2, "Language Review").

```
PyObject* PyDict_Keys(PyObject *p)
```

Return value: New reference. Returns a PyListObject containing all the keys from the dictionary, as in the dictionary method `keys()` (see Chapter 2).

```
PyObject* PyDict_Values(PyObject *p)
```

Return value: New reference. Returns a PyListObject containing all the values from the dictionary p, as in the dictionary method `values()` (see Chapter 2).

```
int PyDict_Size(PyObject *p)
```

Returns the number of items in the dictionary. This is equivalent to `"len(p)"` on a dictionary.

Numeric Objects

Next, you have the API function for numerical objects, which are classified in: plain integer, long integer, floating point, and complex number objects.

Plain Integer Objects

```
PyIntObject
```

This subtype of PyObject represents a Python integer object.

```
PyTypeObject PyInt_Type
```

This instance of PyTypeObject represents the Python plain integer type. This is the same object as `types.IntType`.

```
int PyInt_Check(PyObject* o)
```

Return value: Borrowed reference. Returns `true` if o is of type `PyInt_Type`.

```
PyObject* PyInt_FromLong(long ival)
```

Return value: New reference. Creates a new integer object with a value of `ival`.

> **Tip**
> The current implementation keeps an array of integer objects for all integers
> between -1 and 100. When you create an int in that range, you actually just get back
> a reference to the existing object. So it should be possible to change the value of 1.
> It is suspected that the behavior of Python in this case is undefined.

```
long PyInt_AsLong(PyObject *io)
```

Will first attempt to cast the object to a PyIntObject, if it is not already one, and then return its value.

```
long PyInt_AS_LONG(PyObject *io)
```

Returns the value of the object io. No error checking is performed.

```
long PyInt_GetMax()
```

Returns the system's idea of the largest integer it can handle (`LONG_MAX`, as defined in the system header files).

Long Integer Objects

```
PyLongObject
```

This subtype of PyObject represents a Python long integer object.

```
PyTypeObject PyLong_Type
```

This instance of PyTypeObject represents the Python long integer type. This is the same object as `types.LongType`.

```
int PyLong_Check(PyObject *p)
```

Returns `true` if its argument is a PyLongObject.

```
PyObject* PyLong_FromLong(long v)
```

Return value: New reference. Returns a new PyLongObject object from v, or `NULL` on failure.

```
PyObject* PyLong_FromUnsignedLong(unsigned long v)
```

Return value: New reference. Returns a new PyLongObject object from a C unsigned long, or NULL on failure.

```
PyObject* PyLong_FromDouble(double v)
```

Return value: New reference. Returns a new PyLongObject object from the integer part of v, or NULL on failure.

```
long PyLong_AsLong(PyObject *pylong)
```

Returns a C long representation of the contents of pylong. If pylong is greater than LONG_MAX, an OverflowError is raised.OverflowError.

```
unsigned long PyLong_AsUnsignedLong(PyObject *pylong)
```

Returns a C unsigned long representation of the contents of pylong. If pylong is greater than ULONG_MAX, an OverflowError is raised.OverflowError.

```
double PyLong_AsDouble(PyObject *pylong)
```

Returns a C double representation of the contents of pylong.

```
PyObject* PyLong_FromString(char *str, char **pend, int base)
```

Return value: New reference. Returns a new PyLongObject based on the string value in str, which is interpreted according to the radix in base. If pend is non-NULL, *pend will point to the first character in str which follows the representation of the number. If base is 0, the radix will be determined based on the leading characters of str: if str starts with 0x or 0X, radix 16 will be used; if str starts with 0, radix 8 will be used; otherwise, radix 10 will be used. If base is not 0, it must be between 2 and 36, inclusive. Leading spaces are ignored. If there are no digits, ValueError will be raised.

Floating Point Objects

```
PyFloatObject
```

This subtype of PyObject represents a Python floating point object.

```
PyTypeObject PyFloat_Type
```

This instance of PyTypeObject represents the Python floating point type. This is the same object as types.FloatType.

```
int PyFloat_Check(PyObject *p)
```

Returns true if its argument is a PyFloatObject.

```
PyObject* PyFloat_FromDouble(double v)
```

Return value: New reference. Creates a PyFloatObject object from v, or NULL on failure.

```
double PyFloat_AsDouble(PyObject *pyfloat)
```

Returns a C double representation of the contents of pyfloat.

```
double PyFloat_AS_DOUBLE(PyObject *pyfloat)
```

Returns a C double representation of the contents of pyfloat, but without error checking.

Complex Number Objects

Python's complex number objects are implemented as two distinct types when viewed from the C API: one is the Python object exposed to Python programs, and the other is a C structure that represents the actual complex number value. The API provides functions for working with both.

Complex Numbers as C Structures

Note that the functions which accept these structures as parameters and return them as results do so by value rather than dereferencing them through pointers. This is consistent throughout the API.

```
Py_complex
```

This is the C structure that corresponds to the value portion of a Python complex number object. Most of the functions for dealing with complex number objects use structures of this type as input or output values, as appropriate. It is defined as

```
typedef struct {
    double real;
    double imag;
} Py_complex;

Py_complex _Py_c_sum(Py_complex left, Py_complex right)
```

Returns the sum of two complex numbers, using the C Py_complex representation.

```
Py_complex _Py_c_diff(Py_complex left, Py_complex right)
```

Returns the difference between two complex numbers, using the C `Py_complex` representation.

```
Py_complex _Py_c_neg(Py_complex complex)
```

Returns the negation of the complex number complex, using the C `Py_complex` representation.

```
Py_complex _Py_c_prod(Py_complex left, Py_complex right)
```

Returns the product of two complex numbers, using the C `Py_complex` representation.

```
Py_complex _Py_c_quot(Py_complex dividend, Py_complex divisor)
```

Returns the quotient of two complex numbers, using the C `Py_complex` representation.

```
Py_complex _Py_c_pow(Py_complex num, Py_complex exp)
```

Returns the exponentiation of `num` by `exp`, using the C `Py_complex` representation.

Complex Numbers as Python Objects
```
PyComplexObject
```

This subtype of PyObject represents a Python complex number object.

```
PyTypeObject PyComplex_Type
```

This instance of PyTypeObject represents the Python complex number type.

```
int PyComplex_Check(PyObject *p)
```

Returns `true` if its argument is a `PyComplexObject`.

```
PyObject* PyComplex_FromCComplex(Py_complex v)
```

Return value: New reference. Creates a new Python complex number object from a C `Py_complex` value.

```
PyObject* PyComplex_FromDoubles(double real, double imag)
```

Return value: New reference. Returns a new `PyComplexObject` object from `real` and `imag`.

```
double PyComplex_RealAsDouble(PyObject *op)
```

Returns the real part of op as a C double.

```
double PyComplex_ImagAsDouble(PyObject *op)
```

Returns the imaginary part of op as a C double.

```
Py_complex PyComplex_AsCComplex(PyObject *op)
```

Returns the Py_complex value of the complex number op.

Other Objects

Next, you have the list of API function for all the other objects, including File, Module, and C Objects.

File Objects

Python's built-in file objects are implemented entirely on the FILE* support from the C standard library. This is an implementation detail and might change in future releases of Python.

```
PyFileObject
```

This subtype of PyObject represents a Python file object.

```
PyTypeObject PyFile_Type
```

This instance of PyTypeObject represents the Python file type. This is exposed to Python programs as types.FileType.

```
int PyFile_Check(PyObject *p)
```

Returns true if its argument is a PyFileObject.

```
PyObject* PyFile_FromString(char *filename, char *mode)
```

Return value: New reference. On success, returns a new file object that is opened on the file given by filename, with a file mode given by mode, where mode has the same semantics as the standard C routine fopen(). On failure, returns NULL.

```
PyObject* PyFile_FromFile(FILE *fp, char *name, char *mode, int
(*close)(FILE*))
```

Return value: New reference. Creates a new PyFileObject from the already-open standard C file pointer, fp. The function close will be called when the file should be closed. Returns NULL on failure.

```
FILE* PyFile_AsFile(PyFileObject *p)
```

Returns the file object associated with p as a FILE*.

```
PyObject* PyFile_GetLine(PyObject *p, int n)
```

Return value: New reference. Equivalent to p.readline([n]), this function reads one line from the object p. p can be a file object or any object with a readline() method. If n is 0, exactly one line is read, regardless of the length of the line. If n is greater than 0, no more than n bytes will be read from the file; a partial line can be returned. In both cases, an empty string is returned if the end of the file is reached immediately. If n is less than 0, however, one line is read regardless of length, but EOFError is raised if the end of the file is reached immediately.

```
PyObject* PyFile_Name(PyObject *p)
```

Return value: Borrowed reference. Returns the name of the file specified by p as a string object.

```
void PyFile_SetBufSize(PyFileObject *p, int n)
```

Available on systems with setvbuf() only. This should only be called immediately after file object creation.

```
int PyFile_SoftSpace(PyObject *p, int newflag)
```

This function exists for internal use by the interpreter. Sets the softspace attribute of p to newflag and returns the previous value. p does not have to be a file object for this function to work properly; any object is supported (though it's only interesting if the softspace attribute can be set). This function clears any errors, and will return 0 as the previous value if the attribute either does not exist or if there were errors in retrieving it. There is no way to detect errors from this function, but doing so should not be needed.

```
int PyFile_WriteObject(PyObject *obj, PyFileObject *p, int flags)
```

Writes object obj to file object p. The only supported flag for flags is Py_PRINT_RAW; if given, the str() of the object is written instead of the repr(). Returns 0 on success or -1 on failure; the appropriate exception will be set.

```
int PyFile_WriteString(char *s, PyFileObject *p, int flags)
```

Writes string s to file object p. Returns 0 on success or -1 on failure; the appropriate exception will be set.

Module Objects

There are only a few functions special to module objects.

```
PyTypeObject PyModule_Type
```

This instance of PyTypeObject represents the Python module type. This is exposed to Python programs as `types.ModuleType`.

```
int PyModule_Check(PyObject *p)
```

Returns `true` if its argument is a module object.

```
PyObject* PyModule_New(char *name)
```

Return value: New reference. Returns a new module object with the __name__ attribute set to name. Only the module's __doc__ and __name__ attributes are filled in; the caller is responsible for providing a __file__ attribute.

```
PyObject* PyModule_GetDict(PyObject *module)
```

Return value: Borrowed reference. Returns the dictionary object that implements module's namespace; this object is the same as the __dict__ attribute of the module object. This function never fails.

```
char* PyModule_GetName(PyObject *module)
```

Returns module's __name__ value. If the module does not provide one, or if it is not a string, SystemError is raised and NULL is returned.

```
char* PyModule_GetFilename(PyObject *module)
```

Returns the name of the file from which module was loaded using module's __file__ attribute. If this is not defined, or if it is not a string, raises SystemError and returns NULL.

C Objects

Refer to the document "Extending and Embedding the Python Interpreter," section 1.12 ("*Providing a C API for an Extension Module*"), for more information on using these objects. This document is part of the Python distribution. Note that it is also available on-line at the `python.org`.

```
PyCObject
```

This subtype of PyObject represents an opaque value, useful for C extension modules that need to pass an opaque value (as a `void*` pointer) through Python code to other C code. It is often used to make a C function pointer defined in one module available to other modules, so the regular import mechanism can be used to access C APIs defined in dynamically loaded modules.

```
int PyCObject_Check(PyObject *p)
```

Returns `true` if its argument is a `PyCObject`.

```
PyObject* PyCObject_FromVoidPtr(void* cobj, void (*destr)(void *))
```

Return value: New reference. Creates a `PyCObject` from the `void *` `cobj`. The `destr` function will be called when the object is reclaimed, unless it is `NULL`.

```
PyObject* PyCObject_FromVoidPtrAndDesc(void* cobj, void* desc,
void (*destr)(void *, void *))
```

Return value: New reference. Creates a `PyCObject` from the `void *cobj`. The `destr` function will be called when the object is reclaimed. The `desc` argument can be used to pass extra callback data for the destructor function.

```
void* PyCObject_AsVoidPtr(PyObject* self)
```

Returns the object `void *` that the PyCObject self was created with.

```
void* PyCObject_GetDesc(PyObject* self)
```

Returns the description `void *` that the PyCObject self was created with.

Initialization, Finalization, and Threads

```
void Py_Initialize()
```

Initialize the Python interpreter. In an application embedding Python, this should be called before using any other Python/C API functions; with the exception of `Py_SetProgramName()`, `PyEval_InitThreads()`, `PyEval_ReleaseLock()`, and `PyEval_AcquireLock()`. This initializes the table of loaded modules (`sys.modules`), and creates the fundamental modules `__builtin__`, `__main__`, and `sys`. It also initializes the module search path (`sys.path`). It does not set `sys.argv`; it uses `PySys_SetArgv()` for that. This is a no-operation when called for a second time (without calling `Py_Finalize()` first). There is no return value; it is a fatal error if the initialization fails.

```
int Py_IsInitialized()
```

Returns `true` (nonzero) when the Python interpreter has been initialized, `false` (zero) if not. After `Py_Finalize()` is called, this returns `false` until `Py_Initialize()` is called again.

```
void Py_Finalize()
```

Undoes all initializations made by `Py_Initialize()` and subsequent uses of Python/C API functions, and destroys all sub-interpreters (see `Py_NewInterpreter()` in the following) that were created and not yet destroyed since the last call to `Py_Initialize()`. Ideally, this frees all memory allocated by the Python interpreter. This is a no-op when called for a second time (without calling `Py_Initialize()` again first). There is no return value; errors during finalization are ignored.

This function is provided for a number of reasons. An embedding application might want to restart Python without having to restart the application itself. An application that has loaded the Python interpreter from a dynamic link library (or DLL) might want to free all memory allocated by Python before unloading the DLL. During a hunt for memory leaks in an application, a developer might want to free all memory allocated by Python before exiting from the application.

Bugs and caveats include: The destruction of modules and objects in modules is done in random order; this can cause destructors (`__del__() methods`) to fail when they depend on other objects (even functions) or modules. Dynamically loaded extension modules loaded by Python are not unloaded. Small amounts of memory allocated by the Python interpreter might not be freed (if you find a leak, please report it to the development team). Memory tied up in circular references between objects is not freed. Some memory allocated by extension modules might not be freed. Some extension might not work properly if their initialization routine is called more than once; this can happen if an application calls `Py_Initialize()` and `Py_Finalize()` more than once.

```
PyThreadState* Py_NewInterpreter()
```

Creates a new sub-interpreter. This is an (almost) totally separate environment for the execution of Python code. In particular, the new interpreter has separate, independent versions of all imported modules, including the fundamental modules `__builtin__`, `__main__`, and `sys`. The table of loaded modules (`sys.modules`) and the module search path (`sys.path`) are also separate. The new environment has no `sys.argv` variable. It has new standard I/O stream file objects `sys.stdin`, `sys.stdout`, and `sys.stderr` (however, these refer to the same underlying FILE structures in the C library).

The return value points to the first thread state created in the new sub-interpreter. This thread state is made the current thread state. Note that no actual thread is created; see the discussion of thread states later. If the creation of the new interpreter is unsuccessful, NULL is returned; no exception is set because the exception state is stored in the current thread state and there might not be a current thread state. (Like all other Python/C API functions, the global interpreter lock must be held before calling this function and is still held when it returns; however, unlike most other Python/C API functions, there needn't be a current thread state on entry.)

Extension modules are shared between (sub-)interpreters as follows: the first time a particular extension is imported, it is initialized normally, and a (shallow) copy of its module's dictionary is squirreled away. When the same extension is imported by another (sub-)interpreter, a new module is initialized and filled with the contents of this copy; the extension's init function is not called. Note that this is different from what happens when an extension is imported after the interpreter has been completely re-initialized by calling Py_Finalize() and Py_Initialize(); in that case, the extension's initmodule function is called again.

Bugs and caveats include: Because sub-interpreters (and the main interpreter) are part of the same process, the insulation between them isn't perfect—for example, using low-level file operations like os.close(), they can (accidentally or maliciously) affect each other's open files. Because of the way extensions are shared between (sub-)interpreters, some extensions might not work properly; this is especially likely when the extension makes use of (static) global variables, or when the extension manipulates its module's dictionary after its initialization. It is possible to insert objects created in one sub-interpreter into a namespace of another sub-interpreter; this should be done with great care to avoid sharing user-defined functions, methods, instances or classes between sub-interpreters because import operations executed by such objects might affect the wrong (sub-)interpreter's dictionary of loaded modules.

Note
This is a hard-to-fix bug that will be addressed in a future release.

```
void Py_EndInterpreter(PyThreadState *tstate)
```

Destroys the (sub-)interpreter represented by the given thread state. The given thread state must be the current thread state. See the discussion of thread states later. When the call returns, the current thread state is NULL. All thread states associated with this interpreter are destroyed. (The global interpreter lock must be held before calling this function and is still held when it returns.) Py_Finalize() will destroy all sub-interpreters that haven't been explicitly destroyed at that point.

```
void Py_SetProgramName(char *name)
```

This function should be called before `Py_Initialize()` is called for the first time, if it is called at all. It tells the interpreter the value of the `argv[0]` argument to the `main()` function of the program. This is used by `Py_GetPath()` and some other following functions to find the Python runtime libraries relative to the interpreter executable. The default value is `python`. The argument should point to a zero-terminated character string in static storage whose contents will not change for the duration of the program's execution. No code in the Python interpreter will change the contents of this storage.

```
char* Py_GetProgramName()
```

Returns the program name set with `Py_SetProgramName()`, or the default. The returned string points into static storage; the caller should not modify its value.

```
char* Py_GetPrefix()
```

Returns the prefix for installed platform-independent files. This is derived through a number of complicated rules from the program name set with `Py_SetProgramName()` and some environment variables; for example, if the program name is `"/usr/local/bin/python"`, the prefix is `"/usr/local"`. The returned string points into static storage; the caller should not modify its value. This corresponds to the prefix variable in the top-level Makefile and the `--prefix` argument to the configure script at build time. The value is available to Python code as `sys.prefix`. It is only useful on UNIX. See also the next function.

```
char* Py_GetExecPrefix()
```

Returns the exec-prefix for installed platform-dependent files. This is derived through a number of complicated rules from the program name set with `Py_SetProgramName()` and some environment variables; for example, if the program name is `"/usr/local/bin/python"`, the exec-prefix is `"/usr/local"`. The returned string points into static storage; the caller should not modify its value. This corresponds to the `exec_prefix` variable in the top-level Makefile and the `--exec_prefix` argument to the configure script at build time. The value is available to Python code as `sys.exec_prefix`. It is only useful on UNIX.

The background is the exec-prefix differs from the prefix when platform dependent files (such as executables and shared libraries) are installed in a different directory tree. In a typical installation, platform dependent files can be installed in the `"/usr/local/plat"` subtree whereas platform independent files can be installed in `"/usr/local"`.

Generally speaking, a platform is a combination of hardware and software families, for example, Sparc machines running the Solaris 2.x operating system are considered the same platform, but Intel machines running Solaris 2.x are another platform, and Intel machines running Linux are yet another platform. Different major revisions of the same operating system generally also form different platforms. Non-UNIX operating systems are a different story; the installation strategies on those systems are so different that the prefix and exec-prefix are meaningless, and set to the empty string. Note that compiled Python bytecode files are platform independent (but not independent from the Python version by which they were compiled).

System administrators will know how to configure the mount or automount programs to share `"/usr/local"` between platforms while having `"/usr/local/plat"` be a different filesystem for each platform.

```
char* Py_GetProgramFullPath()
```

Returns the full program name of the Python executable; this is computed as a side-effect of deriving the default module search path from the program name (set by `Py_SetProgramName()` earlier). The returned string points into static storage; the caller should not modify its value. The value is available to Python code as `sys.executable`.

```
char* Py_GetPath()
```

Returns the default module search path; this is computed from the program name (set by `Py_SetProgramName()` earlier) and some environment variables. The returned string consists of a series of directory names separated by a platform dependent delimiter character. The delimiter character is : on UNIX, ; on DOS/Windows, and \n (the ASCII newline character) on Macintosh. The returned string points into static storage; the caller should not modify its value. The value is available to Python code as the list `sys.path`, which can be modified to change the future search path for loaded modules.

```
const char* Py_GetVersion()
```

Returns the version of this Python interpreter. This is a string that looks something like

```
"1.5 (#67, Dec 31 1997, 22:34:28) [GCC 2.7.2.2]"
```

The first word (up to the first space character) is the current Python version; the first three characters are the major and minor version separated by a period. The returned string points into static storage; the caller should not modify its value. The value is available to Python code as the list `sys.version`.

```
const char* Py_GetPlatform()
```

Returns the platform identifier for the current platform. On UNIX, this is formed from the official name of the operating system, converted to lowercase, followed by the major revision number; for example, for Solaris 2.x, which is also known as SunOS 5.x, the value is `sunos5`. On Macintosh, it is `mac`. On Windows, it is `win`. The returned string points into static storage; the caller should not modify its value. The value is available to Python code as `sys.platform`.

```
const char* Py_GetCopyright()
```

Returns the official copyright string for the current Python version; for example

```
"Copyright 1991-1995 Stichting Mathematisch Centrum, Amsterdam"
```

The returned string points into static storage; the caller should not modify its value. The value is available to Python code as the list `sys.copyright`.

```
const char* Py_GetCompiler()
```

Returns an indication of the compiler used to build the current Python version, in square brackets; for example

```
"[GCC 2.7.2.2]"
```

The returned string points into static storage; the caller should not modify its value. The value is available to Python code as part of the variable `sys.version`.

```
const char* Py_GetBuildInfo()
```

Return information about the sequence number and build date and time of the current Python interpreter instance; for example

```
"#67, Aug 1 1997, 22:34:28"
```

The returned string points into static storage; the caller should not modify its value. The value is available to Python code as part of the variable `sys.version`.

```
int PySys_SetArgv(int argc, char **argv)
```

Sets `sys.argv` based on `argc` and `argv`. These parameters are similar to those passed to the program's `main()` function with the difference that the first entry should refer to the script file to be executed rather than the executable hosting the Python interpreter. If there isn't a script that will be run, the first entry in `argv` can be an empty string. If this function fails to initialize `sys.argv`, a fatal condition is signaled using `Py_FatalError()`.

Initialization, Finalization, and Threads

Thread State and the Global Interpreter Lock

The Python interpreter is not fully thread safe. In order to support multithreaded Python programs, a global lock must be held by the current thread before it can safely access Python objects. Without the lock, even the simplest operations could cause problems in a multithreaded program: for example, when two threads simultaneously increment the reference count of the same object, the reference count could end up being incremented only once instead of twice.

Therefore, the rule exists that only the thread that has acquired the global interpreter lock can operate on Python objects or call Python/C API functions. In order to support multithreaded Python programs, the interpreter regularly releases and reacquires the lock—by default, every ten bytecode instructions (this can be changed with `sys.setcheckinterval()`). The lock is also released and reacquired around potentially blocking I/O operations such as reading or writing a file, so other threads can run while the thread that requests the I/O is waiting for the I/O operation to complete.

The Python interpreter needs to keep some bookkeeping information separate per thread—for this it uses a data structure called PyThreadState. This is new in Python 1.5; in earlier versions, such a state was stored in global variables, and switching threads could cause problems. In particular, exception handling is now thread safe when the application uses `sys.exc_info()` to access the exception last raised in the current thread.

There's one global variable left, however: the pointer to the current PyThreadState structure. Although most thread packages have a way to store per-thread global data, Python's internal platform independent thread abstraction doesn't support this yet. Therefore, the current thread state must be manipulated explicitly.

This is easy enough in most cases. Most code manipulating the global interpreter lock has the following simple structure:

```
Save the thread state in a local variable.
Release the interpreter lock.
...Do some blocking I/O operation...
Reacquire the interpreter lock.
Restore the thread state from the local variable.
```

This is so common that a pair of macros exists to simplify it:

```
Py_BEGIN_ALLOW_THREADS
...Do some blocking I/O operation...
Py_END_ALLOW_THREADS
```

The `Py_BEGIN_ALLOW_THREADS` macro opens a new block and declares a hidden local variable; the `Py_END_ALLOW_THREADS` macro closes the block. Another advantage of using these two macros is that when Python is compiled without thread support, they are defined empty, thus saving the thread state and lock manipulations.

When thread support is enabled, the previous block expands to the following code:

```
PyThreadState *_save;
_save = PyEval_SaveThread();
...Do some blocking I/O operation...
    PyEval_RestoreThread(_save);
```

Using even lower level primitives, we can get roughly the same effect as follows:

```
PyThreadState *_save;
_save = PyThreadState_Swap(NULL);
PyEval_ReleaseLock();
...Do some blocking I/O operation...
PyEval_AcquireLock();
PyThreadState_Swap(_save);
```

There are some subtle differences; in particular, `PyEval_RestoreThread()` saves and restores the value of the global variable `errno` because the lock manipulation does not guarantee that `errno` is left alone. Also, when thread support is disabled, `PyEval_SaveThread()` and `PyEval_RestoreThread()` don't manipulate the lock; in this case, `PyEval_ReleaseLock()` and `PyEval_AcquireLock()` are not available. This is done so that dynamically loaded extensions compiled with thread support enabled can be loaded by an interpreter that was compiled with disabled thread support.

The global interpreter lock is used to protect the pointer to the current thread state. When releasing the lock and saving the thread state, the current thread state pointer must be retrieved before the lock is released because another thread could immediately acquire the lock and store its own thread state in the global variable. Conversely, when acquiring the lock and restoring the thread state, the lock must be acquired before storing the thread state pointer.

Why so much detail about this? Because when threads are created from C, they don't have the global interpreter lock, nor is there a thread state data structure for them. Such threads must bootstrap themselves into existence, by first creating a thread state data structure, acquiring the lock, and finally storing their thread state pointer, before they can start using the Python/C API. When they are done, they should reset the thread state pointer, release the lock, and finally free their thread state data structure.

When creating a thread data structure, you need to provide an interpreter state data structure. The interpreter state data structure holds global data that is shared by all threads in an interpreter, for example the module administration (`sys.modules`). Depending on your needs, you can either create a new interpreter state data structure,

Initialization, Finalization, and Threads

or share the interpreter state data structure used by the Python main thread (to access the latter, you must obtain the thread state and access its interp member; this must be done by a thread that is created by Python or by the main thread after Python is initialized).

`PyInterpreterState`

This data structure represents the state shared by a number of cooperating threads. Threads belonging to the same interpreter share their module administration and a few other internal items. There are no public members in this structure.

Threads belonging to different interpreters initially share nothing, except process state like available memory, open file descriptors and such. The global interpreter lock is also shared by all threads, regardless of to which interpreter they belong.

`PyThreadState`

This data structure represents the state of a single thread. The only public data member is PyInterpreterState *interp, which points to this thread's interpreter state.

`void PyEval_InitThreads()`

Initialize and acquire the global interpreter lock. It should be called in the main thread before creating a second thread or engaging in any other thread operations such as `PyEval_ReleaseLock()` or `PyEval_ReleaseThread(tstate)`. It is not needed before calling `PyEval_SaveThread()` or `PyEval_RestoreThread()`.

This is a no-op when called for a second time. It is safe to call this function before calling `Py_Initialize()`.

When only the main thread exists, no lock operations are needed. This is a common situation (most Python programs do not use threads), and the lock operations slow the interpreter down a bit. Therefore, the lock is not created initially. This situation is equivalent to having acquired the lock: When there is only a single thread, all object accesses are safe. Therefore, when this function initializes the lock, it also acquires it. Before the Python thread module creates a new thread, knowing that either it has the lock or the lock hasn't been created yet, it calls `PyEval_InitThreads()`. When this call returns, it is guaranteed that the lock has been created and that it has acquired it.

It is not safe to call this function when it is unknown which thread (if any) currently has the global interpreter lock.

This function is not available when thread support is disabled at compile time.

```
void PyEval_AcquireLock()
```

Acquires the global interpreter lock. The lock must have been created earlier. If this thread already has the lock, a deadlock ensues. This function is not available when thread support is disabled at compile time.

```
void PyEval_ReleaseLock()
```

Releases the global interpreter lock. The lock must have been created earlier. This function is not available when thread support is disabled at compile time.

```
void PyEval_AcquireThread(PyThreadState *tstate)
```

Acquires the global interpreter lock and then sets the current thread state to `tstate`, which should not be `NULL`. The lock must have been created earlier. If this thread already has the lock, deadlock ensues. This function is not available when thread support is disabled at compile time.

```
void PyEval_ReleaseThread(PyThreadState *tstate)
```

Resets the current thread state to `NULL` and releases the global interpreter lock. The lock must have been created earlier and must be held by the current thread. The `tstate` argument, which must not be `NULL`, is only used to check that it represents the current thread state—if it isn't, a fatal error is reported. This function is not available when thread support is disabled at compile time.

```
PyThreadState* PyEval_SaveThread()
```

Releases the interpreter lock (if it has been created and thread support is enabled) and resets the thread state to `NULL`, returning the previous thread state (which is not `NULL`). If the lock has been created, the current thread must have acquired it. (This function is available even when thread support is disabled at compile time.)

```
void PyEval_RestoreThread(PyThreadState *tstate)
```

Acquires the interpreter lock (if it has been created and thread support is enabled) and sets the thread state to `tstate`, which must not be `NULL`. If the lock has been created, the current thread must not have acquired it, otherwise deadlock ensues. (This function is available even when thread support is disabled at compile time.)

The following macros are normally used without a trailing semicolon; look for example usage in the Python source distribution.

Initialization, Finalization, and Threads

`Py_BEGIN_ALLOW_THREADS`

This macro expands to `"{ PyThreadState *_save; _save = PyEval_SaveThread();"`.
Note that it contains an opening brace; it must be matched with the following
`Py_END_ALLOW_THREADS` macro. It is a no-op when thread support is disabled at compile
time.

`Py_END_ALLOW_THREADS`

This macro expands to `"PyEval_RestoreThread(_save); }"`. Note that it contains a
closing brace; it must be matched with an earlier `Py_BEGIN_ALLOW_THREADS` macro. See
earlier section for further discussion of this macro. It is a no-op when thread support is
disabled at compile time.

`Py_BEGIN_BLOCK_THREADS`

This macro expands to `"PyEval_RestoreThread(_save);"` that is, it is equivalent to
`Py_END_ALLOW_THREADS` without the closing brace. It is a no-op when thread support is
disabled at compile time.

`Py_BEGIN_UNBLOCK_THREADS`

This macro expands to `"_save = PyEval_SaveThread();"` that is, it is equivalent to
`Py_BEGIN_ALLOW_THREADS` without the opening brace and variable declaration. It is a
no-op when thread support is disabled at compile time.

All the following functions are only available when thread support is enabled at compile time, and must be called only when the interpreter lock has been created.

`PyInterpreterState* PyInterpreterState_New()`

Creates a new interpreter state object. The interpreter lock need not be held, but can
be held if it is necessary to serialize calls to this function.

   void `PyInterpreterState_Clear(PyInterpreterState *interp)`—Resets all information in an interpreter state object. The interpreter lock must be held.

   void `PyInterpreterState_Delete(PyInterpreterState *interp)`—Destroys an
   interpreter state object. The interpreter lock need not be held. The interpreter state
   must have been reset with a previous call to `PyInterpreterState_Clear()`.

   `PyThreadState* PyThreadState_New(PyInterpreterState *interp)`—Creates a
   new thread state object belonging to the given interpreter object. The interpreter
   lock need not be held, but might be held if it is necessary to serialize calls to this
   function.

void `PyThreadState_Clear(PyThreadState *tstate)`—Resets all information in a thread state object. The interpreter lock must be held.

void `PyThreadState_Delete(PyThreadState *tstate)`—Destroys a thread state object. The interpreter lock need not be held. The thread state must have been reset with a previous call to `PyThreadState_Clear()`.

`PyThreadState* PyThreadState_Get()`—Returns the current thread state. The interpreter lock must be held. When the current thread state is `NULL`, this issues a fatal error (so that the caller needn't check for `NULL`).

`PyThreadState* PyThreadState_Swap(PyThreadState *tstate)`—Swaps the current thread state with the thread state given by the argument `tstate`, which might be `NULL`. The interpreter lock must be held.

Memory Management

Memory management in Python involves a private heap containing all Python objects and data structures. The management of this private heap is ensured internally by the Python memory manager. The Python memory manager has different components that deal with various dynamic storage management aspects, such as sharing, segmentation, preallocation, or caching.

At the lowest level, a raw memory allocator ensures that there is enough room in the private heap for storing all Python-related data by interacting with the memory manager of the operating system. On top of the raw memory allocator, several object-specific allocators operate on the same heap and implement distinct memory management policies adapted to the peculiarities of every object type. For example, integer objects are managed within the heap different from strings, tuples, or dictionaries because integers imply different storage requirements and speed/space tradeoffs. The Python memory manager thus delegates some of the work to the object-specific allocators, but ensures that the latter operate within the bounds of the private heap.

It is important to understand that the management of the Python heap is performed by the interpreter itself and that the user has no control over it, even if she regularly manipulates object pointers to memory blocks inside that heap. The allocation of heap space for Python objects and other internal buffers is performed on demand by the Python memory manager through the Python/C API functions listed in this document.

To avoid memory corruption, extension writers should never try to operate on Python objects with the functions exported by the C library: `malloc()`, `calloc()`, `realloc()`, and `free()`. This will result in mixed calls between the C allocator and the Python

memory manager with fatal consequences because they implement different algorithms and operate on different heaps. However, one can safely allocate and release
memory blocks with the C library allocator for individual purposes, as shown in the
following example:

```
PyObject *res;
char *buf = (char *) malloc(BUFSIZ); /* for I/O */
if (buf == NULL)
    return PyErr_NoMemory();
...Do some I/O operation involving buf...
res = PyString_FromString(buf);
free(buf); /* malloc'ed */
return res;
```

In this example, the memory request for the I/O buffer is handled by the C library
allocator. The Python memory manager is involved only in the allocation of the string
object returned as a result.

In most situations, however, it is recommended to allocate memory from the Python
heap specifically because the latter is under control of the Python memory manager.
For example, this is required when the interpreter is extended with new object types
written in C. Another reason for using the Python heap is the desire to inform the
Python memory manager about the memory needs of the extension module. Even
when the requested memory is used exclusively for internal, highly-specific purposes,
delegating all memory requests to the Python memory manager causes the interpreter
to have a more accurate image of its memory footprint as a whole. Consequently,
under certain circumstances, the Python memory manager might or might not trigger
appropriate actions, such as garbage collection, memory compaction, or other preven-
tive procedures. Note that by using the C library allocator as shown in the previous
example, the allocated memory for the I/O buffer escapes completely the Python
memory manager.

Memory Interface

The following function sets, modeled after the ANSI C standard, are available for allo-
cating and releasing memory from the Python heap:

ANY*—Used to represent arbitrary blocks of memory. Values of this type should be
cast to the specific type that is needed.

ANY* PyMem_Malloc(size_t n)—Allocates n bytes and returns a pointer of type
ANY* to the allocated memory, or NULL if the request fails. Requesting zero bytes
returns a non-NULL pointer.

`ANY* PyMem_Realloc(ANY *p, size_t n)`—Resizes the memory block pointed to by p to n bytes. The contents will be unchanged to the minimum of the old and the new sizes. If p is NULL, the call is equivalent to `PyMem_Malloc(n)`; if n is equal to zero, the memory block is resized but is not freed, and the returned pointer is non-NULL. Unless p is NULL, it must have been returned by a previous call to `PyMem_Malloc()` or `PyMem_Realloc()`.

`void PyMem_Free(ANY *p)`—Frees the memory block pointed to by p, which must have been returned by a previous call to `PyMem_Malloc()` or `PyMem_Realloc()`. Otherwise, or if `PyMem_Free(p)` has been called before, undefined behavior occurs. If p is NULL, no operation is performed.

`ANY* Py_Malloc(size_t n)`—Same as `PyMem_Malloc()`, but calls `PyErr_NoMemory()` on failure.

`ANY* Py_Realloc(ANY *p, size_t n)`—Same as `PyMem_Realloc()`, but calls `PyErr_NoMemory()` on failure.

`void Py_Free(ANY *p)`—Same as `PyMem_Free()`.

The following type-oriented macros are provided for convenience. Note that TYPE refers to any C type.

`TYPE* PyMem_NEW(TYPE, size_t n)`—Same as `PyMem_Malloc()`, but allocates (n * sizeof(TYPE)) bytes of memory. Returns a pointer cast to TYPE*.

`TYPE* PyMem_RESIZE(ANY *p, TYPE, size_t n)`—Same as `PyMem_Realloc()`, but the memory block is resized to (n * sizeof(TYPE)) bytes. Returns a pointer cast to TYPE*.

`void PyMem_DEL(ANY *p)`—Same as `PyMem_Free()`.

Examples

Here is one example from the previous section, rewritten so that the I/O buffer is allocated from the Python heap by using the first function set:

```
PyObject *res;
char *buf = (char *) PyMem_Malloc(BUFSIZ); /* for I/O */
if (buf == NULL)
    return PyErr_NoMemory();
/* ...Do some I/O operation involving buf... */
res = PyString_FromString(buf);
PyMem_Free(buf); /* allocated with PyMem_Malloc */
return res;
```

With the second function set, the need to call `PyErr_NoMemory()` is obviated:

```
PyObject *res;
char *buf = (char *) Py_Malloc(BUFSIZ); /* for I/O */
if (buf == NULL)
    return NULL;
/* ...Do some I/O operation involving buf... */
res = PyString_FromString(buf);
Py_Free(buf); /* allocated with Py_Malloc */
return res;
```

Here's the same code using the macro set:

```
PyObject *res;
char *buf = PyMem_NEW(char, BUFSIZ); /* for I/O */
if (buf == NULL)
    return PyErr_NoMemory();
/* ...Do some I/O operation involving buf... */
res = PyString_FromString(buf);
PyMem_DEL(buf); /* allocated with PyMem_NEW */
return res;
```

Note that in the three previous examples, the buffer is always manipulated via functions/macros belonging to the same set. Indeed, it is required to use the same memory API family for a given memory block so that the risk of mixing different allocators is reduced to a minimum. The following code sequence contains two errors, one of which is labeled as fatal because it mixes two different allocators operating on different heaps.

```
char *buf1 = PyMem_NEW(char, BUFSIZ);
char *buf2 = (char *) malloc(BUFSIZ);
char *buf3 = (char *) PyMem_Malloc(BUFSIZ);
...
PyMem_DEL(buf3);  /* Wrong -- should be PyMem_Free() */
free(buf2);       /* Right -- allocated via malloc() */
free(buf1);       /* Fatal -- should be PyMem_DEL()  */
```

In addition to the functions aimed at handling raw memory blocks from the Python heap, objects in Python are allocated and released with `_PyObject_New()` and `_PyObject_NewVar()`, or with their corresponding macros `PyObject_NEW()` and `PyObject_NEW_VAR()`.

Defining New Object Types

```
PyObject* _PyObject_New(PyTypeObject *type)
```

Return value: New reference.

```
PyObject* _PyObject_NewVar(PyTypeObject *type, int size)
```

Return value: New reference.

Common Object Structures

Next, you have a list of object structures commonly used in type and method definitions.

PyObject	PyVarObject	
PyObject_HEAD	PyObject_HEAD_INIT	PyObject_VAR_HEAD
unaryfunc	binaryfunc	ternaryfunc
inquiry	coercion	intargfunc
intintargfunc	intobjargproc	intintobjargproc
objobjargproc	destructor	printfunc
getattrfunc	getattrofunc	setattrfunc
setattrofunc	cmpfunc	reprfunc
hashfunc		

The document *How to Write a Python Extension*, by Michael Reilly lists and explains the prototypes of these structures. It also demonstrates how to create new Python types.

```
http://starship.python.net/crew/arcege/extwriting/pyext.html
```

Mapping Object Structures

```
PyMappingMethods
```

Structure used to hold pointers to the functions used to implement the mapping protocol for an extension type.

Number Object Structures

PyNumberMethods

Structure used to hold pointers to the functions, which an extension type uses to implement the number protocol.

Sequence Object Structures

PySequenceMethods

Structure used to hold pointers to the functions which an object uses to implement the sequence protocol.

Buffer Object Structures

The buffer interface exports a model where an object can expose its internal data as a set of chunks of data, where each chunk is specified as a pointer/length pair. These chunks are called segments and are presumed to be non-contiguous in memory.

If an object does not export the buffer interface, its tp_as_buffer member in the PyTypeObject structure should be NULL. Otherwise, the tp_as_buffer will point to a PyBufferProcs structure.

> **Note**
> It is very important that your PyTypeObject structure uses Py_TPFLAGS_DEFAULT for the value of the tp_flags member rather than 0. This tells the Python runtime that your PyBufferProcs structure contains the bf_getcharbuffer slot. Older versions of Python did not have this member, so a new Python interpreter using an old extension needs to be able to test for its presence before using it.

PyBufferProcs

Structure used to hold the function pointers that define an implementation of the buffer protocol.

The first slot is bf_getreadbuffer, of type getreadbufferproc. If this slot is NULL, the object does not support reading from the internal data. This is nonsensical, so implementers should fill this in, but callers should test that the slot contains a non-NULL value.

The next slot is bf_getwritebuffer having type getwritebufferproc. This slot can be NULL if the object does not allow writing into its returned buffers.

The third slot is bf_getsegcount, with type getsegcountproc. This slot must not be NULL and is used to inform the caller of how many segments the object contains. Simple objects such as PyString_Type and PyBuffer_Type contain a single segment.

The last slot is `bf_getcharbuffer`, of type `getcharbufferproc`. This slot will only be present if the `Py_TPFLAGS_HAVE_GETCHARBUFFER` flag is present in the `tp_flags` field of the object's `PyTypeObject`. Before using this slot, the caller should test whether it is present by using the `PyType_HasFeature()` function. If present, it might be `NULL`, indicating that the object's contents cannot be used as 8-bit characters. The slot function can also raise an error if the object's contents cannot be interpreted as 8-bit characters. For example, if the object is an array that is configured to hold floating point values, an exception might be raised if a caller attempts to use `bf_getcharbuffer` to fetch a sequence of 8-bit characters. This notion of exporting the internal buffers as text is used to distinguish between objects that are binary in nature, and those which have character-based content.

> **Note**
> The current policy seems to state that these characters might be multibyte characters. This implies that a buffer size of N does not mean that there are N characters present.

`Py_TPFLAGS_HAVE_GETCHARBUFFER`

Flag bit set in the type structure to indicate that the `bf_getcharbuffer` slot is known. This being set does not indicate that the object supports the buffer interface or that the `bf_getcharbuffer` slot is non-`NULL`.

`int (*getreadbufferproc) (PyObject *self, int segment, void **ptrptr)`

Returns a pointer to a readable segment of the buffer. This function is allowed to raise an exception, in which case it must return -1. The segment that is passed must be zero or positive, and strictly less than the number of segments returned by the `bf_getsegcount` slot function. On success, returns 0 and sets *ptrptr to a pointer to the buffer memory.

`int (*getwritebufferproc) (PyObject *self, int segment, void **ptrptr)`

Returns a pointer to a writable memory buffer in *ptrptr; the memory buffer must correspond to buffer segment called segment. Must return -1 and set an exception on error. TypeError should be raised if the object only supports read-only buffers, and SystemError should be raised when segment specifies a segment that doesn't exist.

`int (*getsegcountproc) (PyObject *self, int *lenp)`

Returns the number of memory segments that comprise the buffer. If lenp is not NULL, the implementation must report the sum of the sizes (in bytes) of all segments in *lenp. The function cannot fail.

DEVELOPER'S HANDBOOK

APPENDIX B

Running Python on Specific Platforms

This appendix exposes particular details about using Python on specific platforms.

Python on Win32 Systems

As you might know at this point, Python has an official distribution for Win32 systems (Windows 95, Windows 98, Windows 2000, and Windows NT), called Pythonwin. In order to extend this distribution to its full power, you must get an installation package that contains Python Win32 Extensions. This set of extensions for Python exposes a good part of the Win32 API, along with other Win32 extensions. These extensions are part of the win32all installation package, which is available for download (including the source code) at

http://www.python.org/windows/win32/

You can obtain more detailed and up-to-date information at Mark Hammond starship's page. He is the creator and maintainer of these extensions.

http://starship.python.net/crew/mhammond/

After you download the latest win32all package, you will have access to the Microsoft Foundation Classes, the ODBC interface, the Microsoft Common Object Model (COM), and to several Windows NT services.

For details about the COM interface, see Chapters 7, "Objects Interfacing and Distribution," and 8, "Working with Databases," of this book. More information about using COM in a Python environment can be obtained at a COM Tutorial presented by Greg Stein and Mark Hammond, on a presentation given at IPC-6.

```
http://www.python.org/windows/win32com/COMTutorial/ppframe.htm
```

The following list shows the most important modules that are provided as part of the win32all package.

pythoncom—This module exposes a low-level mechanism that is used by Python to access the COM interface. See Chapter 7 for details.

win32api—This module offers a variety of functions that access the Win32 API. Those functions are capable of performing general tasks such as rebooting the machine and returning the computer and domain name of the local machine.

win32event—This module provides access to the synchronization functions available in the Win32 SDK.

win32evtlog—This module exposes functions that provide access to the Windows NT Event Log.

win32evtlogutil—This module provides additional control for the win32evtlog module.

win32file—This module provides natural file manipulation for reading and writing operations by using native Win32 API I/O functions.

win32net—This module is responsible for automating the administration of a Windows NT Network. Among other things, it controls users, user groups, the resources that are shared by multiple users, and the access to the security database.

win32pdh—This module exposes functions that provide access to the Windows NT Performance Monitor.

win32pdhutil—This module provides additional control for the win32pdh module.

win32pipe—This module works like a pipe between processes, allowing them to communicate with each other. The information that is sent to the pipe by one process can be read by another.

win32process—This module provides access to Win32 API functions that are related to thread and process management.

win32service—This module is responsible for managing services dependency, defining how services should start, and for actually initializing and stopping the services. Everything is done by accessing the Windows NT Service Control Manager.

win32serviceutil—This module provides additional control for the win32service module.

The next couple of paragraphs expose you to third-party programs created to handle specific Windows tasks. Note that many of these tasks can be replicated by writing programs that access the Win32 API.

The first thing I will discuss is about how to load and use DLL files from Python running under MS Windows. My suggestion for you is to use Sam Rushing's `calldll` extension, which allows you to call functions in any DLL. This extension is part of the dynawin package, a completely developed Win32 GUI development environment.

Also provided, there is a *callback* generator that lets external functions call back into Python as if it were C, and an ODBC module implemented using `calldll` (additional code for managing data sources, installing ODBC itself, and creating and maintaining Jet (Microsoft Access) databases is supplied, as well). For more information, check out

`http://www.nightmare.com/~rushing/dynwin/`

By looking at `http://www.nightmare.com/software.html`, you can download a good number of Win32-specific software that was also created by Rushing.

At Ken Seehof's Python Page, you can find several programs for the Windows platform, such as the Neural Integrator—a visual programming environment for prototyping neural networks and other directed graph-based programming models that can bring AI capabilities to your program. Once there, you can also obtain Wizard applications for the Pythonwin IDE, which can simplify many of your tasks, including the creation of extension modules. Be sure to have Visual C++ and Pythonwin, before trying to use the Wizards. Check out the following site:

`http://starship.python.net/crew/seehof/`

Windows programmers sometimes have the requirement to make changes on the Windows Registry. The win32all package contains a very interesting script, which is installed at the subdirectory `win32/scripts/regsetup.py` that enables you to edit the Windows Registry.

Another thing that we are always in need of is printing. It is your choice whether you use the Win32 API to handle that, or use a third-party module. The one that I mention here is a class developed by Bill Mailloux to print text to Windows printers. You can download the class at the following address:

http://musingattheruins.homepage.com/printer.html

The next example gives you a quick demonstration of how simple it is to use this module.

```
import printer
driver = printer.Printer()
driver.open()
driver.write("This sentence is going to be printed.")
driver.close()
del driver
```

If you want to install Python 2.0 on a Windows NT or Windows 2000 machine, you don't necessarily need to have administrator priviledges. If you have them, great! Python will write its registry info under the key HKEY_LOCAL_MACHINE. However, if you don't have *admin* rights, Python will write its registry info under the key HKEY_CURRENT_USER. The only difference between both kinds of installations is that the latter option blocks some specific functionalities, such as running Python scripts as NT services. Note that all the core functionality remains available for you in both installations.

Python on MacOS Systems

It is no big surprise that Python has a standard port for Macintoshes because Python itself was created on a Macintosh. This port is called MacPython and is maintained by Jack Jansen. MacPython applies to MacOS up to version 9. Installing Python on MacOS X (10) systems will be much more like a standard UNIX installation.

Python runs great on Apple Macintoshes, iMacs, iBooks, and so forth. Note that you can decide whether you want to install Python under the MacOS (using the MacPython distribution), under a Linux installation (in case you are using a distribution such as the Yellow Dog), or even under Java (using JPython, the Python interpreter written in Java). If you have Linux installed on your Mac, it is best for you to look at the UNIX section.

At this moment, the current stable distribution is 1.5.2. For this release, the installer is available in two forms: MacBinary format and BinHex format. It is suggested that the latter option should be used in case your browser mistreats MacBinary files. The installer can also install some optional extensions for you, including Tkinter, the Numerical, and Imaging modules.

Also included in the distribution (and optionally installed by the installer) is an integrated development environment written by Just van Rossum (Guido's brother), which includes an editor, debugger, and class browser.

The MacPython distribution contains the same set of extension modules that is available for almost every platform (sys, string, time, and so on). Besides that, it contains a set of modules that provide interfaces to specific MacOS services, including access to QuickTime and QuickDraw.

In order to download Python for Macintosh, the source code, and all the available documentation, check out Jack Jansen's MacPython Web page at

http://www.cwi.nl/~jack/macpython.html

The most noticeable differences between MacPython and the UNIX/Windows distributions are the following:

- It doesn't provide access to the standard POSIX features (pipes, forking, access to command-line interfaces, and so on). In particular, looking at the Mac module, you'll see what functions you can expect in the os module. If you compare this to the posix or winnt module, you'll see what is missing: Options like posix.fork are not available on the Mac.

- The threading mechanism is just starting to show up now (with Python 2.0), as the most recent versions of the GUSI development environment for MacOS support POSIX threads. Note that threading support using the user-space GNU pth library was also added to the language in the release 2.0. Consequently, now you have the option to run programs on Macintosh that are able to use Python's POSIX threading support.

- Tkinter works, but not as smoothly as it could. It is expected that when 1.6 binaries come out, things should be much better.

- Support for C extension modules is based on patches because most of them are written for UNIX or Windows.

- Porting a Python application from other systems to MacPython works fine, assuming it has been written in a cross-platform way.

Precise details on the differences in the standard distribution can be found in the Python Documentation—if a module or feature is not compatible with the Mac distribution, it will say so there. For more technical details, you might want to join the PythonMac SIG, which has discussions on Macintosh-specific aspects of Python. Check out

http://www.python.org/sigs/pythonmac-sig/

The official documentation for the Macintosh specific modules available in the MacPython distribution is located at

`http://www.python.org/doc/current/mac/mac.html`

Next, I list the description of those modules.

mac—This module implements the operating system dependent functionality provided by the standard module os. Note that it is best used when accessed through the os module.

macpath—This module is the Macintosh implementation of the os.path module.

> **Caution**
> You shouldn't try to use the previous two modules directly. Instead, use the os module.

ctb—This module provides a partial interface to the Macintosh Communications Toolbox. Currently, only Connection Manager tools are supported. It might not be available in all MacPython versions.

macconsole—This module is available on the Macintosh, provided Python has been built using the Think C compiler. It provides an interface to the Think console package, with which basic text windows can be created.

macdnr—This module provides an interface to the Macintosh Domain Name Resolver. It is usually used in conjunction with the mactcp module, to map hostnames to IP addresses. It might not be available in all MacPython versions.

macfs—This module provides support for Macintosh FSSpec handling, the Alias Manager, finder aliases, and the Standard File package.

ic—This module provides access to Macintosh Internet Config package, which stores preferences for Internet programs such as mail address, default homepage, and so on. Also, Internet Config contains an elaborate set of mappings from Macintosh creator/type codes to foreign filename extensions plus information on how to transfer files (binary, ascii, and so on).

MacOS—This module provides access to MacOS specific interpreter features, such as how the interpreter eventloop functions and the like. It is suggested that you use this module with care.

macostools—This module contains some convenience routines for file manipulation on the Macintosh.

`findertools`—This module provides wrapper routines around the finder's Apple Events interface.

`mactcp`—This module provides an interface to the Macintosh TCP/IP driver (MacTCP). There is an accompanying module, `macdnr`, which provides an interface to the name server (allowing you to translate hostnames to IP addresses), and a module `MACTCPconst` that has symbolic names for constants used by `MacTCP`. Note that because the built-in module `socket` is also available on the Macintosh, it is usually easier to use sockets instead of the Macintosh-specific `MacTCP` API.

`macspeech`—This module provides an interface to the Macintosh Speech Manager, allowing you to let the Macintosh utter phrases. You need a version of the Speech Manager extension (version 1 and 2 have been tested) in your Extensions folder for this to work. The module does not provide full access to all features of the Speech Manager yet. It might not be available in all MacPython versions.

`EasyDialogs`—The `EasyDialogs` module contains some basic dialogs for the Macintosh, modeled after the `stdwin` dialogs with similar names.

`FrameWork`—The `FrameWork` module contains classes that together provide a framework for an interactive Macintosh application. The programmer builds an application by creating subclasses that override various methods of the bases classes, thereby implementing the functionality wanted. Overriding functionality can often be done on various different levels. For instance, to handle clicks in a single dialog window in a non-standard way, it is not necessary to override the complete event handling.

`MiniAEFrame`—The module `MiniAEFrame` provides a framework for an application that can function as an Open Scripting Architecture (OSA) server, that is receive and process AppleEvents. It can be used in conjunction with `FrameWork` or standalone. This module is temporary; it will eventually be replaced by a module that handles argument names better and possibly automates making your application scriptable.

This Open Directory page provides many links for materials about MacPython available on the Web:

`http://dmoz.org/Computers/Systems/Macintosh/Development/Languages/Python/`

Python on UNIX Systems

Probably, UNIX users are the largest slice of the Python community pie graph, which consequently turns this system into the one that has the most tested distribution. The only thing that can be considered a negative aspect is the fact that you have to compile and build the distribution yourself. But that's understandable because there are several different types of UNIX out there. However, to make things simple, nowadays most Linux distributions already come with Python installed for you. You just need to check whether it is the latest version available.

Sometimes, people build Python with some modules disabled (for instance, optional modules and modules that belong to specific Operating Systems). If that's your case, and you feel that you are missing something such as the `Tkinter` module, you can rebuild Python yourself.

> **Note**
> The Tk toolkit is portable to many UNIX platforms, which makes Tkinter a portable GUI option across different UNIX systems.

In order to enable the modules that are disabled on your system, you need to copy the file `/Modules/Setup.in` (located at the source distribution) to `Setup`, and edit that file. Note that each line in the file lists the module name, the source file, compiler options, and linked libraries. Take a look in the following line:

```
#readline readline.c -lreadline -ltermcap
```

In order to add the GNU readline program to your Python executable, you need to uncomment the line, and rebuild the interpreter by typing the following commands in the top-level directory of the source tree. See Chapter 17, "Development Tools," for more details.

```
make
make install
```

The standard Python distribution contains some extensions that are specifically for UNIX systems, such as `crypt`, `dbm`, `gdbm`, `grp`, `pwd`, `stat`, and `termios`. These modules aren't available for Windows or for Mac platforms.

SGI systems, on the other hand, also have their specific modules, which are

- `al` and `AL` for handling the `audio` library
- `cd` for operating the `CD` library

- `fl`, `flp`, and `FL` for accessing the `FORMS` library
- `fm`, the font manager

SunOS/Solaris systems have their specific module as well: `sunaudiodev`, which is used to access the audio device.

There are also some Linux specific modules, such as `linuxaudiodev`, included with Python.

Other Platforms

Besides Win32 systems, Macintoshes, and UNIX systems, Python is also available for a couple of other platforms. Next is a list of some of these other distributions. If you are reluctant about building Python from the start on your system, maybe it is a good idea to look around and see if someone else has already done that. Maybe the binaries are already out there, just waiting for you.

Python for OS/2

Jeff Rush provides a Web page where he offers the download of Python binaries for OS/2:

`http://warped.cswnet.com/~jrush/python_os2/index.html`

Python for Windows 3.1

In order to run Python on 16-bit versions of the Windows OS (Windows 3.1, Windows 3.11, and Windows for Workgroups), you can use either the DOS binary distribution or the WPY package, which is based on the MFC classes. The main page for all Windows ports is located at `http://www.python.org/windows`. There you can find more information and download info.

Python for DOS

Hans Nowak's Python-DX is a no-longer maintained version of Python for 32-bit DOS, equivalent to Python 1.5.2:

`http://www.hvision.nl/~ivnowa/newsite/Python/Python-DX/python-dx.html`

Python for BeOS

Chris Herborth maintains ports of Python 1.5.2 for BeOS systems, which can be found at `http://www.bebits.com/app/606/`

Python for VMS

Uwe Zessin has a port of Python 1.5.x to OpenVMS that includes interfaces to many OpenVMS RTL and system service routines:

```
http://decus.decus.de/~zessin/python/index.html
```

Python for Psion

Duncan Booth is porting Python 1.5 to the Psion Series 5. Check out his Web site for more details:

```
http://dales.rmplc.co.uk/Duncan/PyPsion.htm
```

Python for Windows CE

Once again, Mark Hammond brings a great contribution to the Python community with his port of Python to the Windows CE platform. The current release can be installed on any Windows CE 2.0 or later HPC, or PPC devices running MIPS or SH3 processors. Note that you can install and run it directly from a flash memory card. This distribution comes with the Python interpreter, a subset of the standard python library modules, and many extension modules that provide access to the Win32 API. For more information, check out

```
http://starship.python.net/crew/mhammond/ce/
```

In case you are really into using Python in this type of system, there is an earlier port written by Brian Lloyd, that can be accessed at

```
http://www.digicool.com/~brian/PythonCE/index.html
```

Python for Anything Else

If your Operating System is not listed here, don't worry because if your system has a C compiler, chances are huge that it can run Python. The first thing you need to do is get your hands on the Python Source distribution at

```
http://www.python.org/download/download_source.html
```

The source code that you can download from the Python Web site comes ready to be built on UNIX and Win32 systems. But note that this source code is the starting point for porting Python to all other platforms. Good luck!

APPENDIX C

Python Copyright Notices

The following copyright notices provide the necessary credits to some of the material contained in this book.

Python's Copyright Notices supports Python itself, and most of the modules that are part of the standard distribution. Exceptions exist, such as the `profile` and the `pstats` modules, which have their own copyright notice. In Chapter 17, "Development Tools," we have part of the documentation and user manual of those modules covered by their copyright notice, which is presented in this appendix.

The last two copyrights listed in this section cover the JPython distribution. Depending on your choice of using or not the `OROMatcher` library (see Chapter 18, "JPython"), you have a specific copyright notice to obey.

Next, you have all the current type of licenses that are available for Python. Note that the definitive license for each component is the one distributed with the software.

Python 2.0 License Information

HISTORY OF THE SOFTWARE

Python was created in the early 1990s by Guido van Rossum at Stichting Mathematisch Centrum (CWI) in the Netherlands as a successor to a language called ABC. Guido is Python's principal author, although it includes many contributions from others. The last version released from CWI was Python 1.2. In 1995, Guido continued his work on Python at the Corporation for National Research Initiatives (CNRI) in Reston, Virginia, where he released several versions of the software. Python 1.6 was the last of the versions released by CNRI. In 2000, Guido and the Python core development team moved to BeOpen.com to form the BeOpen PythonLabs team (`www.pythonlabs.com`). Python 2.0 is the first release from PythonLabs. Thanks to the many outside volunteers who have worked under Guido's direction to make this release possible.

BEOPEN.COM TERMS AND CONDITIONS FOR PYTHON 2.0

BeOpen Python Open Source License Agreement Version 1

1. This LICENSE AGREEMENT is between BeOpen.com ("BeOpen"), having an office at 160 Saratoga Avenue, Santa Clara, CA 95051, and the Individual or Organization ("Licensee") accessing and otherwise using this software in source or binary form and its associated documentation ("the Software").

2. Subject to the terms and conditions of this BeOpen Python License Agreement, BeOpen hereby grants Licensee a non-exclusive, royalty-free, world-wide license to reproduce, analyze, test, perform and/or display publicly, prepare derivative works, distribute, and otherwise use the Software alone or in any derivative version, provided, however, that the BeOpen Python License is retained in the Software, alone or in any derivative version prepared by Licensee.

3. BeOpen is making the Software available to Licensee on an "AS IS" basis. BEOPEN MAKES NO REPRESENTATIONS OR WARRANTIES, EXPRESS OR IMPLIED. BY WAY OF EXAMPLE, BUT NOT LIMITATION, BEOPEN MAKES NO AND DISCLAIMS ANY REPRESENTATION OR WARRANTY OF MERCHANTABILITY OR FITNESS FOR ANY PARTICULAR PURPOSE OR THAT THE USE OF THE SOFTWARE WILL NOT INFRINGE ANY THIRD PARTY RIGHTS.

4. BEOPEN SHALL NOT BE LIABLE TO LICENSEE OR ANY OTHER USERS OF THE SOFTWARE FOR ANY INCIDENTAL, SPECIAL, OR CONSEQUENTIAL DAMAGES OR LOSS AS A RESULT OF USING, MODIFYING OR DISTRIBUTING THE SOFTWARE, OR ANY DERIVATIVE THEREOF, EVEN IF ADVISED OF THE POSSIBILITY THEREOF.

5. This License Agreement will automatically terminate upon a material breach of its terms and conditions.

6. This License Agreement shall be governed by and interpreted in all respects by the law of the State of California, excluding conflict of law provisions. Nothing in this License Agreement shall be deemed to create any relationship of agency, partnership, or joint venture between BeOpen and Licensee. This License Agreement does not grant permission to use BeOpen trademarks or trade names in a trademark sense to endorse or promote products or services of Licensee, or any third party. As an exception, the "BeOpen Python" logos available at `http://www.pythonlabs.com/logos.html` may be used according to the permissions granted on that web page.

7. By copying, installing or otherwise using the software, Licensee agrees to be bound by the terms and conditions of this License Agreement.

Python's Copyright Notice (version 1.6)

CNRI OPEN SOURCE LICENSE AGREEMENT

Python 1.6 is made available subject to the terms and conditions in CNRI's License Agreement. This Agreement together with Python 1.6 may be located on the Internet using the following unique, persistent identifier (known as a handle): 1895.22/1012. This Agreement may also be obtained from a proxy server on the Internet using the following URL: `http://hdl.handle.net/1895.22/1012`.

Python 1.6

CNRI OPEN SOURCE LICENSE AGREEMENT

IMPORTANT: PLEASE READ THE FOLLOWING AGREEMENT CARE-FULLY. BY CLICKING ON "ACCEPT" WHERE INDICATED BELOW, OR BY COPYING, INSTALLING OR OTHERWISE USING PYTHON 1.6 SOFTWARE, YOU ARE DEEMED TO HAVE AGREED TO THE TERMS AND CONDITIONS OF THIS LICENSE AGREEMENT.

1. This LICENSE AGREEMENT is between the Corporation for National Research Initiatives, having an office at 1895 Preston White Drive, Reston, VA 20191 ("CNRI"), and the Individual or Organization ("Licensee") accessing and otherwise using Python 1.6 software in source or binary form and its associated documentation, as released at the `www.python.org` Internet site on September 5, 2000 ("Python 1.6").

2. Subject to the terms and conditions of this License Agreement, CNRI hereby grants Licensee a nonexclusive, royalty-free, world-wide license to reproduce, analyze, test, perform and/or display publicly, prepare derivative works, distribute, and otherwise use Python 1.6 alone or in any derivative version, provided, however, that CNRI's License Agreement and CNRI's notice of copyright, i.e., "Copyright 1995-2000 Corporation for National Research Initiatives; All Rights Reserved" are retained in Python 1.6 alone or in any derivative version prepared by Licensee. Alternately, in lieu of CNRI's License Agreement, Licensee may substitute the following text (omitting the quotes): "Python 1.6 is made available subject to the terms and conditions in CNRI's License Agreement. This Agreement together with Python 1.6 may be located on the Internet using the following unique, persistent identifier (known as a handle): 1895.22/1012. This Agreement may also be obtained from a proxy server on the Internet using the following URL: `http://hdl.handle.net/1895.22/1012`".

3. In the event Licensee prepares a derivative work that is based on or incorporates Python 1.6 or any part thereof, and wants to make the derivative work available to others as provided herein, then Licensee hereby agrees to include in any such work a brief summary of the changes made to Python 1.6.

4. CNRI is making Python 1.6 available to Licensee on an "AS IS" basis. CNRI MAKES NO REPRESENTATIONS OR WARRANTIES, EXPRESS OR IMPLIED. BY WAY OF EXAMPLE, BUT NOT LIMITATION, CNRI MAKES NO AND DISCLAIMS ANY REPRESENTATION OR WARRANTY OF MERCHANTABILITY OR FITNESS FOR ANY PARTICULAR PURPOSE OR THAT THE USE OF PYTHON 1.6 WILL NOT INFRINGE ANY THIRD PARTY RIGHTS.

5. CNRI SHALL NOT BE LIABLE TO LICENSEE OR ANY OTHER USERS OF PYTHON 1.6 FOR ANY INCIDENTAL, SPECIAL, OR CONSEQUENTIAL DAMAGES OR LOSS AS A RESULT OF MODIFYING, DISTRIBUTING, OR OTHERWISE USING PYTHON 1.6, OR ANY DERIVATIVE THEREOF, EVEN IF ADVISED OF THE POSSIBILITY THEREOF.

6. This License Agreement will automatically terminate upon a material breach of its terms and conditions.

7. This License Agreement shall be governed by and interpreted in all respects by the law of the State of Virginia, excluding conflict of law provisions. Nothing in this License Agreement shall be deemed to create any relationship of agency, partnership, or joint venture between CNRI and Licensee. This License

Agreement does not grant permission to use CNRI trademarks or trade name in a trademark sense to endorse or promote products or services of Licensee, or any third party.

8. By clicking on the "ACCEPT" button where indicated, or by copying, installing or otherwise using Python 1.6, Licensee agrees to be bound by the terms and conditions of this License Agreement.

ACCEPT

Python's Copyright Notice (until version 1.5.2)

Copyright Notice of the `profile` and `pstats` Modules

Copyright Notice of JPython with OROMatcher

Copyright Notice of JPython with OROMatcher

("CNRI"), and the Individual or Organization ("Licensee") accessing and using JPython version 1.1.x in source or binary form and its associated documentation as provided herein ("Software").

Subject to the terms and conditions of this License Agreement, CNRI hereby grants Licensee a non-exclusive, non-transferable, royalty-free, world-wide license to reproduce, analyze, test, perform and/or display publicly, prepare derivative works, distribute, and otherwise use the Software alone or in any derivative version, provided, however, that CNRI's License Agreement and CNRI's notice of copyright, i.e., "Copyright ©1996-1999 Corporation for National Research Initiatives; All Rights Reserved" are both retained in the Software, alone or in any derivative version prepared by Licensee.

Alternatively, in lieu of CNRI's License Agreement, Licensee may substitute the following text (omitting the quotes), provided, however, that such text is displayed prominently in the Software alone or in any derivative version prepared by Licensee: "JPython (Version 1.1.x) is made available subject to the terms and conditions in CNRI's License Agreement. This Agreement may be located on the Internet using the following unique, persistent identifier (known as a handle): 1895.22/1006. The License may also be obtained from a proxy server on the Web using the following URL: http://hdl.handle.net/1895.22/1006."

In the event Licensee prepares a derivative work that is based on or incorporates the Software or any part thereof, and wants to make the derivative work available to the public as provided herein, then Licensee hereby agrees to indicate in any such work, in a prominently visible way, the nature of the modifications made to CNRI's Software.

Licensee may not use CNRI trademarks or trade name, including JPython or CNRI, in a trademark sense to endorse or promote products or services of Licensee, or any third party. Licensee may use the mark JPython in connection with Licensee's derivative versions that are based on or incorporate the Software, but only in the form "JPython-based _____," or equivalent.

The Software contains OROMatcher regular expression software from ORO, Inc. Copyright 1997 by ORO, Inc. ("ORO software"). OROMatcher (TM) is a trademark of Original Reusable Objects, Inc. Except as permitted by applicable law and this Agreement, Licensee may not decompile, reverse engineer, disassemble, or modify the ORO software provided herein. Licensee acknowledges that redistribution of the ORO software separate from JPython or direct use of the ORO software interfaces requires a separate license from ORO, Inc. http://www.oroinc.com/

CNRI is making the Software available to Licensee on an "AS IS" basis. CNRI MAKES NO REPRESENTATIONS OR WARRANTIES, EXPRESS OR

IMPLIED. BY WAY OF EXAMPLE, BUT NOT LIMITATION, CNRI MAKES NO AND DISCLAIMS ANY REPRESENTATION OR WARRANTY OF MER-CHANTABILITY OR FITNESS FOR ANY PARTICULAR PURPOSE OR THAT THE USE OF THE SOFTWARE WILL NOT INFRINGE ANY THIRD PARTY RIGHTS.

CNRI SHALL NOT BE LIABLE TO LICENSEE OR OTHER USERS OF THE SOFTWARE FOR ANY INCIDENTAL, SPECIAL OR CONSEQUENTIAL DAMAGES OR LOSS AS A RESULT OF USING, MODIFYING OR DISTRIB-UTING THE SOFTWARE, OR ANY DERIVATIVE THEREOF, EVEN IF ADVISED OF THE POSSIBILITY THEREOF. SOME STATES DO NOT ALLOW THE LIMITATION OR EXCLUSION OF LIABILITY SO THE ABOVE DISCLAIMER MAY NOT APPLY TO LICENSEE.

This License Agreement may be terminated by CNRI (i) immediately upon written notice from CNRI of any material breach by the Licensee, if the nature of the breach is such that it cannot be promptly remedied; or (ii) sixty (60) days following notice from CNRI to Licensee of a material remediable breach, if Licensee has not remedied such breach within that sixty-day period.

This License Agreement shall be governed by and interpreted in all respects by the law of the State of Virginia, excluding conflict of law provisions. Nothing in this Agreement shall be deemed to create any relationship of agency, partnership, or joint venture between CNRI and Licensee.

By clicking on the "ACCEPT" button where indicated, or by installing, copying or otherwise using the Software, Licensee agrees to be bound by the terms and conditions of this License Agreement.

Copyright Notice of JPython without OROMatcher

IMPORTANT: PLEASE READ THE FOLLOWING AGREEMENT CARE-FULLY.

BY CLICKING ON THE "ACCEPT" BUTTON WHERE INDICATED, OR BY INSTALLING, COPYING OR OTHERWISE USING THE SOFTWARE, YOU ARE DEEMED TO HAVE AGREED TO THE TERMS AND CONDI-TIONS OF THIS AGREEMENT.

Copyright Notice of JPython without OROMatcher

JPython version 1.1.x

This LICENSE AGREEMENT is between the Corporation for National Research Initiatives, having an office at 1895 Preston White Drive, Reston, VA 20191 ("CNRI"), and the Individual or Organization ("Licensee") accessing and using JPython version 1.1.x in source or binary form and its associated documentation as provided herein ("Software")

Subject to the terms and conditions of this License Agreement, CNRI hereby grants Licensee a non-exclusive, non-transferable, royalty-free, world-wide license to reproduce, analyze, test, perform and/or display publicly, prepare derivative works, distribute, and otherwise use the Software alone or in any derivative version, provided, however, that CNRI's License Agreement and CNRI's notice of copyright, i.e., "Copyright ©1996-1999 Corporation for National Research Initiatives; All Rights Reserved" are both retained in the Software, alone or in any derivative version prepared by Licensee.

Alternatively, in lieu of CNRI's License Agreement, Licensee may substitute the following text (omitting the quotes), provided, however, that such text is displayed prominently in the Software alone or in any derivative version prepared by Licensee: "JPython (Version 1.1.x) is made available subject to the terms and conditions in CNRI's License Agreement. This Agreement may be located on the Internet using the following unique, persistent identifier (known as a handle): 1895.22/1005. The License may also be obtained from a proxy server on the Web using the following URL: http://hdl.handle.net/1895.22/1005."

In the event Licensee prepares a derivative work that is based on or incorporates the Software or any part thereof, and wants to make the derivative work available to the public as provided herein, then Licensee hereby agrees to indicate in any such work, in a prominently visible way, the nature of the modifications made to CNRI's Software.

Licensee may not use CNRI trademarks or trade name, including JPython or CNRI, in a trademark sense to endorse or promote products or services of Licensee, or any third party. Licensee may use the mark JPython in connection with Licensee's derivative versions that are based on or incorporate the Software, but only in the form "JPython-based _____," or equivalent.

CNRI is making the Software available to Licensee on an "AS IS" basis. CNRI MAKES NO REPRESENTATIONS OR WARRANTIES, EXPRESS OR IMPLIED. BY WAY OF EXAMPLE, BUT NOT LIMITATION, CNRI MAKES NO AND DISCLAIMS ANY REPRESENTATION OR WARRANTY OF MERCHANTABILITY OR FITNESS FOR ANY PARTICULAR PURPOSE OR THAT

THE USE OF THE SOFTWARE WILL NOT INFRINGE ANY THIRD PARTY RIGHTS.

CNRI SHALL NOT BE LIABLE TO LICENSEE OR OTHER USERS OF THE SOFTWARE FOR ANY INCIDENTAL, SPECIAL OR CONSEQUENTIAL DAMAGES OR LOSS AS A RESULT OF USING, MODIFYING OR DISTRIBUTING THE SOFTWARE, OR ANY DERIVATIVE THEREOF, EVEN IF ADVISED OF THE POSSIBILITY THEREOF. SOME STATES DO NOT ALLOW THE LIMITATION OR EXCLUSION OF LIABILITY SO THE ABOVE DISCLAIMER MAY NOT APPLY TO LICENSEE.

This License Agreement may be terminated by CNRI (i) immediately upon written notice from CNRI of any material breach by the Licensee, if the nature of the breach is such that it cannot be promptly remedied; or (ii) sixty (60) days following notice from CNRI to Licensee of a material remediable breach, if Licensee has not remedied such breach within that sixty-day period.

This License Agreement shall be governed by and interpreted in all respects by the law of the State of Virginia, excluding conflict of law provisions. Nothing in this Agreement shall be deemed to create any relationship of agency, partnership, or joint venture between CNRI and Licensee.

By clicking on the "ACCEPT" button where indicated, or by installing, copying or otherwise using the Software, Licensee agrees to be bound by the terms and conditions of this License Agreement.

APPENDIX D
Migrating to Python 2.0

This book was originally planned to cover Python 1.5.2 and its transition to version 1.6. However, as release 2.0 was about to be released when the book was ready to go to the printer, we decided to make the necessary changes throughout the book in order to cover the new features that are part of the 2.0 release.

This appendix gives you a general overview about what has changed. More detailed information can be found inside each chapter of this book.

The release 2.0, launched by BeOpen/PythonLabs, starts a new life for Python as important features were incorporated to the product; many bugs were fixed; the code has become better documented; and a couple of optimizations were made.

Kuchling and Moshe Zadka wrote a document titled "What's New in Python 2.0" that lists in detail every single aspect of this new release:

```
http://starship.python.net/crew/amk/python/writing/
new-python/
```

Python 1.6 or Python 2.0. Which One to Choose?

For those of you who wonder what was the reason to launch version 1.6 when the 2.0 was about to be released, I can explain:

When Guido and his team decided to leave CNRI, that institution asked for a 1.6 release to be created. That release would have to contain all the Python code that was designed while the team was still working at CNRI.

Although a lot of changes were incorporated to version 2.0, version 1.6 is forward-compatible with Python 2.0. Note that both releases, 1.6final and 2.0beta1, were released on the same day (September 5, 2000).

New Development Process

Some business processes have changed after the main development team has left *CNRI*. Currently, *SourceForge* is hosting the Python project page at `http://sourceforge.net/projects/python/`.

At that page, you can report bugs, visualize the Python CVS tree, submit patches, and use the patch manager and the bug tracking tools.

From now on, a new kind of document must be used in order to discuss new possible features and expose the Python community to information about features that have been implemented. This new document records all the discussion about the possibility to include a new idea in a future Python release. These documents are called *Python Enhancement Proposals (PEPs)*, modeled on the Internet RFC process. It is said that they must provide a concise technical specification of the feature and a reason for the feature. They have to be used to collect input from the community and to document the design decisions that were approved. Each proposal has its own author as the sole responsible for managing it. Any kind of enhancement to the language must be documented by a PEP before it can be accepted as valid. For more information, check out

`http://python.sourceforge.net/peps/`

Enhancements

Python 2.0 comes bundled with many new features, bug fixes, and optimizations. The next list provides an appetizer for the main changes that were made, and that are about to be shown.

- Python 2.0's source code was converted to ANSI C. That means that you need an ANSI C compiler in order to compile Python. Compilers that only support K&R C will not be able to compile version 2.0. Note that this isn't a big problem, as just about every C compiler these days is ANSI C compliant.

- For those of you who had problems with the size of your source code, Python 2.0 has increased the limit of expressions and files in Python source code. That limit is now *2**32*. If compared to the *2**16* that we previously had, it can be considered a good limit.

- This new release also starts the porting of Python to 64-bit platforms. Currently, both Linux and Win64 are able to take care of that. Some extra effort was made especially for Intel's Itanium processor.

- The support to XML was fully extended. The `xml` package includes a renewed DOM interface and a SAX2 interface.

- All the internals of the `re` module were changed. Now, the regular expression engine is located in a new module called `SRE` written by Fredrik Lundh of Secret Labs AB. This was to allow Unicode strings to be used in regular expressions too. Pay attention to the `re` module as it continues to be the front-end module, which internally calls the `SRE` module.

- Many new modules were added. (Check them out throughout the book!)

- Many enhancements were made to IDLE. Python 2.0 is distributed with IDLE 0.6, which also contains a number of new features.

- Some methods had their syntax changed for enhancement purposes, including `listobj.insert()`, `listobj.append()`, and the methods from the `socket` module.

- Python 2.0 introduces the possibility to rename a module when importing it, for example, `import Module as OtherName`. Note that this syntax can also be used when importing symbols from a module, for instance:

```
from module import sym1 as sym2
```

- Now, you can also redirect your print statements to a file-like object, for example, `print >> fileobj, "Hello Python World"`.

The following are considered to be the most important changes in this new release.

Unicode Support

This is a long awaited feature that was finally added to the language. Unicode strings are a new sort of data type, which can handle up to 65,536 distinct characters, instead of being limited to the 256 used by the ASCII format. Python now comes with a library of *codecs* for converting between Unicode and the various character *encodings* in use. This library can be extended very easily.

List Comprehension

Whenever you need to compute a list (or lists) of elements in order to generate a new list, you can use this new and more efficient mechanism. It is offered for lists in order to replace the not-that-efficient method of using a `for` loop with an `if` statement and a `list.append()` call, for example, `newlist = [y+3 for y in range(15)]`

Strings Manipulation

Prior to version 2.0, you had to rely on the `string` module to manipulate your string objects. With this new release, the methods were pushed to the string type. Besides the methods that were inherited from the `string` module, two new methods were also added. Note that old `string` module was not removed from the distribution because it is still necessary for backward compatibility.

Augmented Assignment

Python 2.0 implements a full set of augmented assignment operators. This includes: +=, -=, *=, /=, %=, **=, &=, |=, ^=, »=, and «=

For example, instead of saying x = x+1, you can choose to say x += 1

Note that you can also specify methods for classes (such as __iadd__) in order to handle these new operators.

Garbage Collection

The Python interpreter is now using a new mechanism to collect unused objects. From time to time, this mechanism performs a cycle detection algorithm that searches for inaccessible cycles and deletes the participating objects. This process has been named *Garbage Collection of Cycles*.

There are a couple of parameters of the garbage collection that you can manipulate. The module `gc` provides functions that help you out with that. Of course, you always have the option to disable this feature. To do so, simply specify the argument "`--without-cycle-gc`" when running the Python configure script.

Maximum Recursion

Prior to version 2.0, Python's maximum recursion depth used to be decided when you compiled Python. Now, the maximum number of recursive calls that can be made by Python code is easily interpreted and modified by Python programs just by using the functions `sys.getrecursionlimit` and `sys.setrecursionlimit`, respectively. Note that the default number of recursive calls is set to 1000, and you can use the script `Misc/find_recursionlimit.py` that comes as part of the 2.0 distribution to help you figure out what is the best number to use on your system. After running this program, you can add a `setrecursionlimit()` call to the end of `site.py` so that this limit is used by all Python programs on the system.

Taking good care of this limit can help you trap infinite recursions of filling the C stack and causing a core dump or GPF on your system.

Expected Code Breaking

There are a couple of changes in Python 2.0 that you should be aware of because they could cause your current Python code to break.

- It's not possible to have string exceptions anymore. All standard exceptions can only be classes from now on. The `-X` command line option has been removed.

- The `\x` escape that you normally use for string literals now accepts only 2 hexa-decimal digits, instead of reading everything that you inform and taking only the lowest 8-bit of the given value. Note that not many people knew about or used this fact, so it should not cause any significant breakage.

- Prior to 2.0, there were some methods that accepted multiple arguments, and internally converted them to a tuple, such as the `.append()` method of a list object. Consequently, you could type `lstobj.append(3,4,5)`. After release 2.0, you need to inform an additional pair of parenthesis in order to avoid raising a `TypeError` exception. Thus, the right syntax has become `lstobj.append((3,4,5))`. Note that there are a couple of methods that still work in both ways, such as the `socket.connect()`. Also note that the script `Tools/scripts/checkappend.py` can be used to catch most occurrences of this mistake.

- When dealing with long integers, the `str()` function doesn't include the 'L' character anymore at the end of the string. Although, the `repr()` function still does. Therefore, if you cut the last position of our string in order to get rid of the 'L', you will now get rid of the last digit. So, be careful!

- Talking about `str()` and `repr()`, they now use different formatting precision string. The former uses `%.12g`, and the latter uses `%.17g`. Consequently, `repr()` might sometimes return more decimal places.

And always remember that you can depend on the support of the Python community to help you out with problems that you can't easily solve. If you think your problem is a common or simple problem, try reading the list archives or asking questions in the mailing lists. If it seems to be a bug, look at the CVS tree to see whether it has been fixed. If not, you can report it.

Good luck in your Python Adventure!

Index

Symbols

H

N

U